Chopin and his Critics
An Anthology

Chopin and his Critics
An Anthology
(up to World War I)

edited by **Irena Poniatowska**

Magdalena Dziadek (Poland)

Irina Nikolskaya (Russia)

Joachim Draheim (Germany and Austria)

Marie-Paule Rambeau (France)

Rosalba Agresta (England)

THE FRYDERYK CHOPIN INSTITUTE

WARSAW 2011

Graphic and typographic design
Artur Frankowski, Magdalena Frankowska, Studio Fontarte

Russian to Polish translation
Jan Kazem-Bek

Polish to English translation
Piotr Szymczak

Supervision and revision of English text
Jim Samson, John Comber

Index of names
Ewa Sławińska-Dahlig, Anna Dębska

Index of Chopin's works
Wojciech Bońkowski, Ewa Sławińska-Dahlig

Proofreading and editing
John Comber, Wojciech Bońkowski, Jerzy Michniewicz

Project co-ordination
Małgorzata Schodowska

The Fryderyk Chopin Institute
43 Tamka Street
00-355 Warsaw, Poland
www.chopin.nifc.pl

ISBN 978-83-61142-31-7

Contents

Introduction

Irena Poniatowska

In 1983, Vladimir Jankélévitch produced a book called *La musique et l'ineffable,* and it strikes me that his title would make a fine motto for a music critic in general. After all, music resists any attempt at verbalisation, and always preserves an inner core that remains literally inexpressible. Acts of translation are mediated through the writer's own *mentalité* and particular use of language, but acts of understanding need not always be verbal. Just as words refuse to do justice to our experience of an artwork, so there can never really be a perfect correspondence between music and life. For instance, argues Jankélévitch, we might treat the sonata as a kind of shorthand for the adventure of human existence, a full portrayal of the drama that unfolds between the cradle and the grave (an interpretation that has been applied to Chopin's Sonata in B flat minor). But music is not quite like the adventure that is life – a point that goes beyond the varying meanings embodied in words like "to be" or "like".[1] Music has a multiplicity of meanings, and words are likewise far from unequivocal. As a convention, language precludes unanimity. The world of ideas, including critical judgments and descriptions, is not the same as music per se. Language (be it colloquial or scholarly and rigorous) is unable to move beyond the level of metaphorical description. The Romantic period was acutely aware of the metaphorical nature of language, especially in poetry. But we must not forget that words have a power of their own

---

1 Vladimir Jankélévitch, *La musique et l'ineffable,* Paris 1983, pp. 22-3.

– they can cause harm in a very real sense. For a time at least, criticism can force an artwork out of circulation or lift it out of oblivion.

Art criticism is part of the broader field of art reception. Benedetto Croce pinned down several ways of understanding the activity of criticism. For some, a critic is a despotic teacher who does not hesitate to dictate what direction art should or should not take; for others, he or she is a kind of judge or sovereign monarch. In that kind of approach, the job of a critic is seen broadly to consist in winnowing out the ugly from the beautiful. In the process of artistic creation, artists tend to be the harshest (and earliest) critics of their own work, and at a later stage the public identifies the work's strengths and weaknesses in a process that may be either instantaneous or extended over a long period of time. In this way of looking at criticism, a question arises: who was it that actually established Chopin as a major composer? Was it the critics, or perhaps the multitudes of listeners (with the critics and the musicologists left merely to rubberstamp the wave of popular approval and to furnish specialist arguments in support of it)?

For Croce, there is also a third way of looking at criticism, which equates the exercise with an act of interpretation and commentary. Here, the critic's job is to furnish readers with factual information about the work, and to present the piece under discussion in its historical, biographical and ideological context. In this approach, the critic is a humble guide to the work of art, which he or she enriches by pointing out relevant contexts, forming suggestive associations and providing an exegesis. However, Croce points out that criticism aspires to being regarded as something more – it wants to have a sovereign status in no way inferior to art itself (if not actually superior to it).[2] And indeed, given the enriching effects of criticism, the idea that there is an art to it seems to be more than mere presumption and shores up the dignity of the pursuit, even if we find it hard to imagine that criticism could somehow replace or supplant art.

For Croce, a proper and legitimate critical discourse must combine the elements of being "educational", evaluative and interpretative. Critics offer their best guesses at the direction any given artistic phenomenon may take; they downplay some artistic trends and prioritise others. They must have a highly developed artistic taste and sensibility to appreciate the style and originality of an artwork. But above all, a critic must be possessed of cultural and historical competence, a well-developed analyti-

---

2 See Benedetto Croce, "Krytyka sztuki a historia sztuki" [Art criticism and art history], in *Zarys estetyki* [Preliminary notes on aesthetics], tr. and ed. Stanisław Gniadek, introduction by Zygmunt Czerny, Warsaw 1962.

cal faculty, a feel for what reception aesthetics calls the "historical horizon" and the "actual horizon". Familiarity with the past combines with a knowledge of the present to allow an expectation of the new. In so far as is possible, a critic should be able to identify the innovative qualities of a work as well as its links with tradition and its unique qualities. Another person's ideas and forms of expression always resist accurate and precise description – and so do one's own ideas and thoughts, for that matter. For Croce, a critic who tackles this task is a *philosophus additus artifici*.[3]

In "Chopin Reception: Theory, History, Analysis",[4] Jim Samson presents four aspects of Chopin as seen by French critics, German publishers, Russian composers and British music lovers. In France, Chopin tended to be viewed in terms of feminine softness, sophistication and intimacy; in Germany, various aspects of publishing activity such as music editions, biographical projects and musicological analyses led to a re-evaluation of Chopin as one of the major classical figures in music. In Russia, Chopin was seen as a nationalist composer of Slavic provenance, who combined local folkloric elements "with the most advanced techniques of contemporary European art music", whereas in Britain he was a more homely figure, favoured by piano-playing young women. According to Samson, "women were the main consumers and practitioners of an art firmly centred on the piano – the 'household orchestra'."[5] Thus, before we even look at the Chopin presented in this anthology of criticism, we get a glimpse of the Chopin icons in four countries as viewed from four different vantage points: by critics, publishers, composers and music lovers. Even in one and the same country, it is important to bear in mind that those four perspectives may yield a different image of Chopin. According to Samson, reception expresses primarily "our concern not just to situate the musical work within a broad social and cultural setting [...] but to interpret its relationship to the social world. [...] There are three levels on which music's social content might be addressed [...] the social 'cause' of a musical work [...] the social 'trace' imprinted on its materials [...] and the social production of its meanings."[6] Criticism operates on that third level of social content. It is, if you like, an echo of the music, reverberated by individual experience, shaped by one's culture and society in an act of reception-conditioned perception. I have written a number of studies and articles on the social reception of Chopin's music, with topics ranging from Liszt's Chopin

---

3 Ibid., p. 111.
4 In *Musica Jagellonica* 1, Kraków 1995, pp. 91-112.
5 Ibid., pp. 102, 103.
6 Ibid., p. 91.

monograph through literary commentaries on Chopin's Preludes[7] to reception aesthetics. The truth of a work of art may be a somewhat open-ended, idealised notion, but it needs all the same to take a specific detailed shape for every historical moment. Chopin criticism is voluminous and varied. Some critics, although they were in awe of his compositional talent, failed to appreciate fully his artistic ideas and criticised his innovative harmonies and textures or his smooth and melancholy mode of expression. Many critical pronouncements were highly subjective, and occasionally quite biting. This was coupled with the notion, prevalent in the nineteenth century, that a composer who concentrated on piano music (in contrast to composers of operas, symphonies or other large forms) could not be deemed truly great. It is also important to bear in mind that some of Chopin's works, especially from the late period, were little known and rarely performed. For instance, the Preludes as a complete cycle were not performed until the time of Busoni and Koczalski, with the first recording dating from 1926 (Alfred Cortot, His Master's Voice). After Chopin's pieces became firmly established in the repertoire of great pianists, the critical focus shifted from the pieces themselves to aspects of performance and interpretation. As a result, this overview of nineteenth-century Chopin criticism becomes an important key to recovering the response to his music that prevailed at the time of its greatest popularity in various European countries, when Chopin's works were being published and performed, either publicly, in salons and concert halls, or informally, in private homes. Such criticism provides an insight into the changing outlook on Chopin's music in the nineteenth century.

What was Chopin's own attitude to his critics? As a young man he showed a lively interest in the newspaper reviews and critical reactions of experienced musicians and colleagues. The first news report about the precocious composer and performer appeared in the Warsaw press in 1818, when Chopin was at the tender age of eight. When he gave two performances as part of a series of evening concerts in Warsaw, a piano concerto by Ferdinand Ries (24 February 1823) followed by John Field's Piano Concerto No. 5 (3 March), the *Kurier dla Płci Pięknej* [Courier for the fair sex]

---

7 Irena Poniatowska, "L'analyse métaphorique des œuvres de Chopin dans le livre de Liszt", in Artur Szklener, ed. *Analytical Perspectives on the Music of Chopin*, Warsaw 2003, pp. 241-53; "The Polish Reception of Chopin's Biography by Franz Liszt", in Halina Goldberg, ed., *The Age of Chopin. Interdisciplinary Inquiries*, Bloomington, Indiana 2004, pp. 259-77; "Sur les interprétations polysémiques des Préludes opus 28 de F. Chopin", in I. Poniatowska et al., eds. *Chopin and his Work in the Context of Culture*, 2 vols., Kraków 2003, ii, pp. 204-19; "Chopin – czwarty wieszcz" [Chopin – the fourth bard], in Wojciech Nowik, ed. *Topos narodowy w muzyce polskiej pierwszej połowy XIX wieku* [The national topos in the Polish music of the first half of the 19th century], Warsaw 2006, pp. 257-71.

ran two rave reviews on 26 February and 22 March, comparing Chopin favourably to the young Liszt, then enjoying early success in Vienna. Such opinions boosted Chopin's self-confidence and motivated him to work hard on his musical education. More pieces followed about Chopin's concerts in 1825, 1826 and 1829, the year he performed in Vienna. The *Allgemeine Theaterzeitung und Originalblatt für Kunst, Literatur und Geselliges Leben*[8] carried a piece by Joseph L. Blahetka which drew attention to the artistry of the young virtuoso who composed Variations on a theme from Mozart's *Don Giovanni* (first public performance) and identified Chopin as an artist of great promise. In a letter to his family dated 12 August,[9] the young composer expressed his relief at the lack of negative reactions, and he described how each of his variations was applauded one by one and how his friends, scattered around the concert hall in various strategic locations, reported no disgruntled rumblings in the audience. He was likewise pleased with the good reviews coming out after his second concert, which he dutifully related to Tytus Woyciechowski (notably the comment that his "need to make music" held the upper hand over his "desire to please"),[10] and he took to heart the observation that he needed to develop a more forceful touch, a comment that was soon brought up again after his public concerts in Warsaw in 1830 (M. Mochnacki). Another spate of reviews followed his two concerts in March, which featured his Concerto in F minor, the *Fantasy on Polish Airs* and the *Rondo à la krakowiak*. In them, Chopin was hailed as a "Paganini of the piano", and comparisons were made between his talent and national importance, on one hand, and Mozart's stature in the German-speaking world, on the other. The quality of Chopin's performance and composition was pronounced superior to Hummel's (especially on the strength of his Adagio and Rondo[11]), and it was prophesied that he would become one of Europe's greatest pianists and composers. Critics of a more conservative bent chimed in to caution against placing the youngster on a par with such grand masters of composition as Mozart, Beethoven and Rossini, and chided the composer for the excessive audacity of some of his harmonic ideas. Chopin was nettled by the criti-

---

8 *Allgemeine Theaterzeitung*, 100 (20 August 1829), pp. 408-9.

9 *Korespondencja Fryderyka Chopina tom 1, 1816-1831* [Correspondence of Fryderyk Chopin, vol. 1, 1816-1831], ed. Zofia Helman, Zbigniew Skowron and Hanna Wróblewska-Straus, Warsaw 2009, pp. 274-5.

10 *Allgemeine Theaterzeitung*, 105 (1 September 1829), pp.428-29. This opinion was mistranslated in *Gazeta Warszawska* (245 (14 September 1829), p. 2324) as "his palpable desire to please gets the better of the desire to make music", a comment that Chopin resented.

11 See *Kurier Warszawski*, 62 (5 March 1830), p. 309, *Dziennik Powszechny Krajowy*, 83 (25 March 1830), p. 414, *Gazeta Korespondenta Warszawskiego i Zagranicznego*, 66 (19 March 1830), pp. 537-8.

cism. While it was quite clear to him that the comparisons with Mozart were "patent nonsense" (letter to Tytus Woyciechowski, 10 April 1830), he considered some of the adverse criticism unfounded, and he bridled at the suggestion that he should study Rossini "without straightforwardly copying him". Nonetheless (or perhaps as a result of this), Chopin came up with the idea for a new concert, and got down to work. He played his Concerto in E minor at a farewell concert on 11 October 1830, and then again in Vienna on 11 June 1831. In a letter to Woyciechowski dated 12 December 1831, he made fun of a review of his Variations on a theme from *Don Giovanni* ("Là ci darem la mano"), which juxtaposed the individual variations with specific scenes from the opera. "That German's imagination could make one die of laughter", he wrote.[12]

Chopin gave his first Paris concert at the Salle Pleyel on 25 February 1832. Fétis attended, and despite minor quibbles (such as what he took to be Chopin's excessive liberties in phrasing or his unnecessarily opulent modulations) he recognised the originality of Chopin's musical concepts and the elegance and luminous grace of his performance.[13] By the mid 1830s Chopin was giving concerts with other artists. On 3 September 1833 he performed two movements of the Concerto in E minor, the "Là ci darem la mano" Variations and a *Duo concertant* with Franchomme, in Tours.[14] He wanted to make a name for himself in Paris, and any press references to his unique playing and composing style would have been a welcome boost to his reputation. However, following two orchestral performances in Paris at the Italian Theatre (5 April 1835) and the Conservatory (26 April 1835), as well as a joint concert given with Hiller on two pianos (22 February), there was renewed criticism about the excessive softness of his touch, and Chopin realised that his preferred setting should be solo salon performances given for small groups of listeners as part of a mixed programme alongside other artists. He gave another performance with orchestra in Rouen (at a benefit concert organised for Antoni Orłowski in 1838), but after that his concert days were over, save for a few isolated events in 1841, 1842 and 1848 in Paris, and again in 1848 in Britain. He might have had a complex about the softness of his touch, but rave reviews from experts extolling his "pianistic poetry" must have gone a long way towards compensating for this. We know that he resented

---

12 *Korespondencja Fryderyka Chopina*, ed. Bronisław E. Sydow, 2 vols., Warszawa 1955, i, p. 201 (hereafter *KFC*).

13 *Revue musicale*, 3 March 1832, pp. 38-39.

14 Jean Jude, *Pleyel 1757-1857. La Passion d'un siècle*, self-published, printed in Fondettes 2008, p. 134.

Liszt's review of the concert he gave on 26 April 1841.[15] Liszt opened his review with a description of the elite audience made up of aristocrats, plutocrats and talented artists, and went on to argue that Chopin's means of expression were too limited, and his instrument too imperfect, to convey fully his ideas. Chopin complained about this to his father, the tactful and subtle Mikołaj Chopin, who wrote back to point out that they "had been friends once, and it is a fine thing to outdo each other in good grace [delicacy]".[16] Despite this high-minded advice, Chopin, who valued friendship greatly, tended to harbour resentment for slights suffered at friendly hands. He had a famously sensitive personality, which prompted George Sand to comment in her *Histoire de ma vie* how his psyche seemed like "something skinned alive", and how he was "cut to the quick by the touch of a rose petal, the shadow of a fly".

With time, Chopin increasingly lost interest in the outside world, including critical writing. He was turning inwards, increasingly lost in his own world of composition, and brooding on the misery of a life lived under the burden of a wasting disease. With his health in steep decline, he was still able to muster an occasional witty comment or repartee, as he did in England to deny the rumours of an impending marriage. Even in the year of his death he was excitedly planning renovations to his Paris apartment – hope lingered on…

This anthology for international readers is a selection of Chopin criticism written before World War I in Poland, Russia, Germany and Austria, France, and Great Britain. It is a pioneering effort. No other anthologies of this kind are available, not even for individual nations.[17]

To facilitate the use of the material for scholarly purposes in the international context, sections in their original German-, French- and English-language versions are supplemented with an English translation of the Polish and Russian materials. We have plans for a separate translation project to make the Western-language materials available in Polish.

---

15   F. Liszt, "Concert de Chopin", *Revue et Gazette musicale de Paris*, 2 May 1841, pp. 245-6. Jean-Jacques Eigeldinger writes of that review in "Liszt rend compte du concert de Chopin [1841]: coup de force et enterrement de première classe. Documents", in I. Poniatowska and D. Pistone, eds., *Chopin parmi ses amis*, v: *Les pianistes-virtuoses à Paris autour de Chopin* (a Polish-French volume), Warsaw 1999, pp. 54-79; also in *L'univers musical de Chopin*, Paris 2000, pp. 251-63.

16   Letter from Mikołaj Chopin to Fryderyk Chopin, 16 October 1842, *KFC*, ii, p. 70.

17   There exists one Polish anthology of Polish music criticism pre-1939 (Stefan Jarociński, ed., *Antologia polskiej krytyki muzycznej XIX i XX wieku*, 1955), but it does not contain much critical material on Chopin.

The anthology comprises a series of studies by individual authors. Each is an attempt to present a synthetic country-by-country portrayal of Chopin criticism alongside a chronologically arranged compilation of excerpts from reviews and contemporary accounts of Chopin and his music written before 1914 (the Russian section is an exception in that the cut-off date has been moved forward to 1922 in order to include the first scholarly study of Chopin's life and music in Russian by Boris Asafyev). Each synthesis aims to illustrate the specific tone of Chopin criticism in the local context, and to demonstrate the evolution of the composer's reputation as exemplified by the primary material drawn from reviews and scholarly studies.

The wide-ranging material mainly comprises work by critics, but the selection also contains some commentaries by other composers, writers and popularisers. As a result, each section is unique in its choice of content, methodology and ideology. One section (Joachim Draheim's) examines reviews from two German-speaking countries (Germany and Austria), to include the local reviews of Chopin's concerts in Vienna.

Magdalena Dziadek's Polish section provides an insight into the formation of Chopin's image in Polish criticism, a surprisingly meandering process both in the composer's lifetime and after his death. In the context of Poland's struggle to regain national independence, Polish critics were at pains to emphasise Chopin's Polishness as the defining characteristic of his music, in order to claim the composer as a symbol of "the Polish cause" (with Stanisław Moniuszko emerging in the latter half of the nineteenth century as the second "singer of Polishness".) Dziadek demonstrates some of the limitations identified in contemporary critical understandings of Chopin's music. She registers the dissatisfaction with his choice of a single instrument (a criticism that would recur in other countries), and she describes a whole series of objections raised against his music, including the rather interesting notion that Chopin was incapable of producing extended forms or that he struggled with deficiencies in harmony and instrumentation, or that he was excessively "feminine" (this latter misunderstanding also emerges in a study by Zofia Chechlińska, which looks mainly at the writings of Jan Kleczyński on Chopin's music in performance and at Marceli Szulc's first monograph on Chopin, from 1873, rather than at popular journalism, but arrives at similar conclusions). It appears that Chopin's early works (including the dances) were valued more highly than the later ones, and the sonatas were deemed only partially successful (cf. Szulc and Schumann).[18] But for all their

---

18 Zofia Chechlińska, "Chopin Reception in nineteenth-century Poland", in Jim Samson, ed. *The Cambridge Companion to Chopin*, Cambridge 1992, pp. 214-5.

reservations, critics were unable to shake off their intuitive sense of Chopin's greatness. Writers and critics alike drew comparisons between the composer and the three greatest Polish Romantic poets, Mickiewicz, Słowacki and Krasiński, such that the composer came to be dubbed Poland's "fourth bard". The positivist period in Polish criticism saw attempts to arrive at a more objective analysis of Chopin's music, while the rising modernist currents at the turn of the twentieth century introduced the theme of Chopin's psychological dualism ("split personality"). Chopin's strong ties with Poland were regarded as a symptom of an ideological utopian tendency, and he was recognised as a major innovator who introduced new perspectives to European music.

This general outline of Chopin's image as it evolved over the course of changing periods and ideologies is corroborated by a carefully considered selection of critical writings ranging from the 1830s to the turn of the twentieth century (Stanisław Przybyszewski, Antoni Sygietyński, Stanisław Niewiadomski). The selection brings to light some interesting and novel interpretations, which have so far been overlooked in Polish criticism. In terms of Chopin's nineteenth-century reception in Poland, I would identify three main paradigms: 1. Chopin as a folk-inspired artist (especially present in the poetry written to Chopin's mazurkas and other pieces), 2. Chopin as a national hero (present in all nineteenth-century writing), and 3. Chopin as a subject for deconstruction or debunking (present in attempts at objective positivist analysis beginning in the 1870s and continuing through the emergence of the modernist wave).[19]

In her synthesis of Russian criticism, Irina Nikolskaya summarises the views of Russian critics, pianist-pedagogues (Anton Rubinstein), semi-amateur popularisers, composers belonging to The Five, and Scriabin. In terms of existing treatments of the subject, Nikolskaya gave a paper on Anton Rubinstein's interpretations of Chopin as a pianist and a critic at the Second International Chopin Congress in Warsaw (1999),[20] and some reference to Russian criticism has also been made by Grzegorz Wiśniewski in his *Chopin w kulturze rosyjskiej. Antologia* [Chopin in Russian culture: an anthology][21] but neither treatment comprised a substantial selection of Russian critical texts. Wiśniewski's book, whose focus extends all the way into the 1990s,

---

19 Irena Poniatowska, "Trois paradigmes de l'interprétation de Chopin en Pologne au XIXème siècle", *Ostinato rigore, Revue Internationale d'études musicales*, 15, Paris 2000, pp. 19-31.

20 Irina Nikolskaya, "Anton Rubinstein Interpreting Frédéric Chopin", in I. Poniatowska et al., eds., *Chopin and his Work in the Context of Culture*, 2 vols., Kraków 2003, ii, pp. 143-58.

21 Grzegorz Wiśniewski, *Chopin w kulturze rosyjskiej: Antologia* [Chopin in Russian culture: an anthology], Warsaw 2000. He edited an enlarged anthology *Fryderyk Chopin w oczach Rosjan* [F. Chopin in the eyes of the Russians], Warszawa 2010.

draws attention to Leo Tolstoy, who had a high regard for Chopin as a major artist in the "pantheon of Slavic art" (*What Is Art*? 1898), and to Anatoly Lunacharsky, a Marxist critic who recognised Chopin as a supra-historical representative of world culture in his essay on the cultural significance of Chopin's music (1910). For Lunacharsky, Chopin's polonaises invited comparison with the greatest "unfathomable" masterpieces of collaborative creative effort such as the Bible, Homer's epic poems, the *Kalevala* or Aeschylus' tragedies.[22] Thus, in order to tackle the problem of Russian critical responses to Chopin, it is necessary to move beyond the narrow confines of music criticism and to take into account the overall body of nineteenth-century Russian writing, editions and artistic interpretations relating to the composer. Based on Chopin's influence on Balakirev and his circle of composers, Jim Samson argues that Chopin was regarded in Russia as a recognised Slavic composer owing to his use of folkloric material (Nikolskaya illustrates this point by pointing to the comparisons Russian critics tended to draw between Chopin and Glinka). The overall tone of the Russian reviews is palpably deferential to Chopin's genius, though not free from the familiar objection that he cramped his talent with a self-imposed limitation to the piano. Russian critics noted Chopin's original harmony, his innovative textures and the remarkably aphoristic quality of his Preludes. The selection traces the interesting evolution of Scriabin's views on Chopin, as well as offering us Asafyev's mature and comprehensive portrayal. Some of the nineteenth-century accounts are gleaned from citations in post-war publications, but it seems that we are dealing with authentic and well-documented sources.

Joachim Draheim modestly refers to his synthesis as a compilation of critical writings with commentary. He notes the importance to Chopin studies of the relationship between Chopin and German musical culture in the composer's lifetime and later. This is an under-researched area. Schumann's unfinished variations on Chopin's Nocturne, Op. 15 No. 3 were not published until 1992, when Draheim himself shepherded the edition into print at B&H. We should also recognise that Chopin largely owed his own rapid rise in European music to the work of German publishers (Kistner, followed later by B&H), to well-informed and balanced writings by German critics (notably Schumann), and to his contacts with major German musicians. In 1833, Chopin dedicated the Nocturnes, Op. 15 to Hiller, and Adolf Gutmann, his loyal pupil, was the dedicatee of the Scherzo in C sharp minor, Op. 39. The anthology also contains critical writings sparked off by Chopin's Vienna concerts in 1829 and

---

22 Ibid. (*Chopin w kulturze rosyjskiej*), pp. 15-17.

1831. The most notable reviewers and critical works are identified and discussed, and a representative selection is carefully compiled. Finally, Draheim appends a richly researched bibliography of selected works relating directly or indirectly to such areas of interest as "Chopin in Germany", "Chopin's relationship with German music and musicians", "Chopin in the opinions and memoirs of the German press, musicians and writers".

Marie-Paule Rambeau takes a slightly different approach, as she arranges her selections of French Chopin criticism into a series of different themes. Part One, "In Chopin's Day", focuses on the following areas: A. "The artist's situation" (1. "But who is 'Mr. Chopin' from Warsaw?", 2. "Sketch of a composer who cannot be pigeonholed", 3. "On the value scale of the 'princes of the piano'", 4. "In the Romantic movement"); B. "The composer" (1. "Polishness: the native accent and writing in exile", 2. "An innovative language", 3. "Technical and formal solutions bold and disconcerting", 4. "His soul at his fingertips"); C. "The pianist" (1. "The improviser", 2. "Inspiration and work: a dialectical problem", 3. "A universe of predilection: the salons", 4. "The three concerts at Pleyel's: exceptional events"). Part Two, "After Chopin", comprises three main subjects: A. "Posthumous celebrations" (1. "Obituary chronicle", 2. "The perspective of posterity"); B. "The Chopin myth" (1. "The growing legend", 2. "Myths rejected", 3. "Notes of discord"); C. "Historical reception" (1. "The first standard monographs", 2. "Encyclopaedias", 3. "Chopin in literature", 4. "Reception by composers around the turn of the twentieth century"). The sections are arranged chronologically, with an overall architecture structured into thematic groupings of critical writings and excerpts. This structure allows us to tackle the problem of Chopin reception in France within the context of aesthetic currents, the specificity of French taste (*le goût français*), the editions of Chopin's works, and the composer's evolving reputation. Although this structure departs from the chronological arrangement used in the remaining sections of this anthology, we felt that its unique approach to the individual studies was worth preserving. The synthesis presented by M.-P. Rambeau positions Chopin within the context of French culture in the period of the July Monarchy, with its bourgeois rule and economic euphoria. A unique and original presence, Chopin proved difficult to classify for critics in his own day. After a concert Chopin gave in Rouen in 1838, Ernest Legouvé tellingly quipped that given a choice between Liszt and Thalberg, Chopin was the greatest of the two – in other words, *tertium datur*. Some critics were dissatisfied with his soft touch, while others found that his *toucher* was like "an angel's wing brushing along the keyboard". Not all of Chopin's genres were readily understood. Even Liszt, in his monograph on Chopin (Paris 1852), did not fully understand the concepts underlying the concertos ("we may discern in them more effort than inspiration") or indeed the late works, especially the Polonaise-Fantasy, which he said "giddied the brain" like a draught of Cyprian wine.[23] In a later letter to Princess Caroline Wittgenstein dated 1 January 1876, Liszt acknowledged his failure to understand Chopin's late works, and concluded that Chopin "shines alone in art's firmament".[24] As in other countries, some French critics were also unfairly critical of the composer. As Hans Heinrich Eggebrecht writes, not every documented interpretation should be taken as proof of understanding – both artistic interpretations by the great musicians as well critical opinions made by the great critics can be misguided.[25]

Rosalba Agresta's impeccable study of British criticism builds on her doctoral research on Chopin's British reception and editions. British critical reception is notable for its absence of concert reviews. Partly this was for the obvious reason that Chopin did not perform in England until 1848, so the British critics tended to focus instead on the editions by Chopin's indefatigable propagator, Wessel (whose proclivity for adding programmatic titles to Chopin's works was heartily resented by the composer). Still, the absence of reviews is something of an anomaly, since Chopin never played in Russia or Germany either (he visited Germany several times, but his performances there took place in salons, e.g. Wodziński's salon in Dresden, or in joint sessions with Schumann and Mendelssohn, a concert only once in Munich, August 1831), and yet his editions and performances by various musicians were discussed there. In Britain, Chopin was treated in his lifetime exclusively as a salon composer. The criticism was a mix of dilettantism and misunderstanding, creating an inescapable impression that Chopin's music was somehow incompatible with the tastes and sensibilities of British music lovers. Chopin himself noted in his letters the purely utilitarian approach to music in general that prevailed in the British Isles. The negative comments were in part also influenced by the reviewer's vested interests, ably revealed and analysed by Agresta.

In Britain, negative criticism mainly focused on Chopin's perceived eccentricities of harmony, texture and fingering. The innovative elements in his music were overlooked, and he was dismissed as an "artistic non-entity". This state of affairs

23   F. [Ferenc] Liszt, *F. Chopin*, Paris 1852, pp. 10, 45.

24   La Mara, *Franz Liszts Briefe*, 8 vols., Leipzig 1893-1905, vii, pp. 122-3

25   Hans Heinrich Eggebrecht, "Zur Wirkungsgeschichte der Musik Beethovens. Theorie der ästhetischen Identifikation", in Harry Goldschmidt, Karl-Heinz Köhler and Konrad Niemann, eds., *Bericht über den Internationalen Beethoven-Kongress*, Berlin 1977, p. 474.

did not change much after Chopin's death. An English translation of Liszt's *Life of Chopin* (Philadelphia, 1863) reinforced the perception entertained by British critics that Chopin was deficient in terms of orchestration and did not possess the ability to compose in the major genres (an opinion Liszt forcefully put forward in 1852 and later retracted). It seemed logical to British critics that, as a poet, Chopin could only express his individuality and nationality in small forms, and some critics speculated that this fact might have been the source of his melancholy. A handful of others, including Rev. Hugh Reginald Haweis, Joseph Bennett and A. Redgrave Cripps, tried to mount a defence of Chopin's musical vision, and the selection of excerpts anthologised by Agresta offers a glimpse of the various viewpoints.

We feel that closing the anthology with the British section makes for an intriguing dessert, not unlike a serving of English ginger chocolate, except that British Chopin criticism seems to contain more ginger than chocolate. It is not clear to what extent Chopin was aware of the tenor of British criticism on his music before his trip to England and Scotland in 1848.

This anthology offers a much-needed insight into a neglected area. Comparative analyses between the critics of various countries may serve a useful purpose in uncovering fundamental categories of Chopin reception, which were conditioned by the different cultural factors at play. It is hoped that the anthology will modify the stereotypes on the processes of Chopin reception in the nineteenth century, as our very notion of what music history is broadens out from a history of musical styles or evolving creative approaches to include the history of reception and criticism.

Fryderyk Chopin at the piano.
Eliza Radziwiłł, pencil drawing inscribed "Frédéric Chopin 1826" [1829?],
Collection: Muzeum Fryderyka Chopina, Warsaw [M/230].

Chopin in Polish music criticism before the First World War

Magdalena Dziadek

The Warsaw press followed Chopin's career quite closely ever since the early childhood performances that helped to propel him to *Wunderkind* status. In his later years, reports appeared on his progress as a pianist and composer. In the 1820s, most reviews were written in a tone of patriotic pride, with some of the praise rubbing off on the Main School of Music he attended. There was hardly a review of Chopin's concerts in Warsaw published at the time that failed to register the achievements of Elsner's class in the Main School of Music.

The younger generation of critics, who made their mark in the early 1830s writing for journals that subscribed to a Romantic ideology, were quick to claim Chopin as a representative of the Romantic school. In his in-depth analysis of Chopin's works, Maurycy Mochnacki (1803-1834) argued that the composer's artistic interests were in alignment with the aims of Romantic poetry and music, as a result of a shared fascination with Polish folk culture. In this context, popular culture was seen as a precious cultural legacy that shaped the distinctive character of a national culture. "Those unique qualities inherent in the melodies of different nations are now studied by composers of genius, who consider it as the most honourable of occupations to tend to and nourish those traditions that have not succumbed to the passage of centuries", Mochnacki wrote in 1830.[26] The tone of his comment was clearly indebted to the ideas of Johann Gottfried Herder (1744-1803), who was then perceived in Warsaw as a supreme authority on all matters musical and literary.[27] Mochnacki also singled out the Romantic qualities of originality and "feeling", which he felt were apparent in the way Chopin had assimilated "that beautiful simplicity of Polish song" [Mochnacki, 1830].*

---

26 In *Kurier Polski*, 92 (1830).

27 Kazimierz Brodziński was one of those influenced by Herder's ideas. Chopin attended Brodziński's lectures in his student days at the Main School of Music.

* notes in square brackets are references to material contained in this anthology, e.g. Mochnacki, 1830.

After Chopin left Poland (which was partitioned at the time by Russia, Austria and Prussia), Polish readers were able to follow his career closely through international press reports on his new works, with good reviews from foreign critics, considered a measure of the overwhelmingly positive response to his music, frequently published in the national press. In 1836, Józef Cichocki, publisher and editor of *Pamiętnik Muzyczny*, published Franz David Stoepel's appraisal of the Variations, Op. 2 and the Concerto in E minor, Op. 11, a review which had previously appeared in the *Gazette musicale de Paris* (1836/2-3). In the same year, the Poznań-based *Przyjaciel ludu* carried a feature on Chopin by Antoni Woykowski, who cited passages from Schumann's review of the Variations, Op. 2 and Gottfried Fink's review of the Etudes, Op. 10. Writing in 1845 for Eleonora Ziemięcka's journal *Pielgrzym*, Józef Brzowski included in his article "Słówko o smaku w muzyce" ['A word on musical taste'] a review from the *Gazette musicale* of a Paris concert Chopin gave in 1841. In later years, the writings of Schumann, Liszt and Heine were frequently mined for evidence of Chopin's European recognition as an artist of formidable stature.

Throughout the partitioned country, Polish journalists wrote about Chopin in a spirit of palpable concern for his health and well-being. A note in *Tygodnik Polski* published in Lwów in 1847[28] affords a glimpse of the close emotional ties that journalism was helping to foster between the expatriate composer and his fellow Poles: "We are receiving reports from Paris that the health of our compatriot, Chopin, is becoming increasingly frail; he no longer performs in public, and only gives rare concerts in private homes. On such occasions, the maestro's elegiac music, his pallid countenance and his dwindling vital powers make a painful impression."[29]

There had been earlier references to Chopin's "pallid countenance" from Antoni Woykowski, the first Polish author to come up with an original study of Chopin's music and one that attempts to place the composer within European music. Published in 1836 in *Przyjaciel Ludu* (Poznań), Woykowski's piece (like Mochnacki's before it) portrayed Chopin as a Romantic. In line with most nineteenth-century Polish commentary on Chopin, the study was underpinned by an intensely patriotic attitude. Woykowski described Chopin as a consummate master of piano music and drew bold comparisons with Beethoven's symphonic works, which were considered at the time as the pinnacle of musical achievement. He described Chopin's music as a product of "genius" in the Romantic sense of the word, which is to say that

---

28 The weekly was a mutation of *Dziennik Mód Paryskich*, one of Poland's first modern magazines, published in Lwów.

29 *Tygodnik Polski* 1847/8.

he equated genius with the audacity to compose new music fuelled by imagination and unfettered by rules. According to Woykowski, Chopin's music was "magical" in its metaphysical ability to penetrate the listener's very soul: it communicated emotions (as he put it, "the music cannot be understood by an unfeeling heart"), and had a novel and unique character of its own. Woykowski described that unique quality as "sorrowfulness" (*smętność*), and he believed that it derived as a quality from Polish popular folk songs. (For Woykowski, Chopin's music was "nationalistic", i.e. inspired by Polish folklore, "down to the very last note" [Woykowski, 1836].)

Another writer to theorize on the "national" character of Chopin's music was Marceli Antoni Szulc, who would later write the first Polish biography of Chopin (published in Poznań in 1873). Writing in 1842, Szulc formulated an important and enduringly influential idea of a continuity existing between Chopin's music and Polish Romantic poetry, the latter being epitomised by Adam Mickiewicz (1798-1855). For Szulc, the overlap between Romantic poetry and Chopin's music consisted in the Romantic aura of Slavic legend and fairy-tale. Symbolically, he referred to the legendary Ruthenian *guslar* (singer of folk epics) named Boyan to emphasize the fact that Poland's cultural identity was part of a wider Slavic heritage. Szulc juxtaposed the "unaffected" Romanticism of Chopin with the eccentricities of the Western European Romantics, and he was led to conclude that Chopin was superior to his Western rivals for being a Romantic "without a pose".

Both Woykowski and Szulc were highly attentive to German critical reactions to Chopin. Notably, Woykowski made an attempt to examine objectively the reasons why German critics such as Rellstab tended to dismiss Chopin's music (he put this down to the misunderstandings of an alien culture). Unlike Woykowski, who was so blinkered by his love of Chopin's music that he could find no fault with it, Szulc wrote from a more supposedly objective, pseudo-Classical perspective, and as such he was able to offer solemn pronouncements on the relative merits and demerits of Chopin's music, even if his language, drawing on Catholic traditions, often idealized or even sacralized the composer.

Chopin's death inaugurated a new phase of his critical reception in Poland, with one publication in particular having a major significance. Józef Sikorski's sizeable study, which appeared in 1849 in the Warsaw monthly *Biblioteka Warszawska*, was a bold and original synthesis that competently reviewed the current state of knowledge on Chopin within the context of music history, and did so from a specific and consistent philosophical vantage point (Sikorski was an adherent of Hegel). In his study, Sikorski tried to place Chopin's music within a contemporary context and he diagnosed it (correctly) as marking the transition from Classicism to Romanticism. For Sikorski, this period-straddling character of Chopin's music "made it a thing apart", and he attributed the music's uniqueness to aspects of Chopin's personality. Like most of his contemporaries, Sikorski considered Chopin's personality to have been dualistic, in the sense that it spanned the extremes of alienated despair and amused ironic detachment. Sikorski made a perceptive distinction between the "nationalistic" and the "cosmopolitan" elements in Chopin's music, and offered some highly pertinent comments on the composer's innovatory musical language in terms of melody, harmony, texture and rhythm [Sikorski, 1849].

In the event, Polish readers failed to do justice to the depth and complexity of Sikorski's synthesis, which they took by and large to be little more than a deferential homage paid to the deceased composer. The writer Zofia Klimańska objected to his gushing tone and soberly suggested that the talents of Stanisław Moniuszko would amply compensate the nation for the loss of Chopin. Published in 1850 in a Vilnius-based journal, *Pamiętnik Naukowy i Literacki*, Klimańska's comments launched a debate on the comparative merits of music by Chopin and Moniuszko, as well as on their respective positions in Polish and European culture – a debate that was destined to rumble on for decades, well into the 1920s. Although the debate was fraught with serious methodological problems (with merely a handful of the participants realizing that it was not possible meaningfully to compare operas or songs to piano pieces within the theoretical framework of nineteenth-century genre theory), it nonetheless formed a characteristic component of nineteenth-century Polish Chopin criticism.

Zofia Klimańska's appraisal was resolutely rebutted in *Gazeta Warszawska*, where an anonymous writer made it clear that having Moniuszko around was cold comfort for the loss of Chopin. Moniuszko felt personally injured by the comparison. In a letter to Józef Sikorski (who was a personal friend), he drew a distinction between Chopin, "a legitimate European great", and himself, a composer of "pieces for household use" – an area which he felt offered little room for soaring artistry.[30]

The debate on the comparative significance and value of the two composers entered a new phase following Moniuszko's death, in 1872. The demand for a posthumous appraisal of Moniuszko's achievements prompted Władysław Wiślicki to make some conciliatory comments. Writing in the weekly literary magazine *Kłosy*,

---

30 A letter of Stanisław Moniuszko to Józef Sikorski dated "Wilno, 11/23 December 1850". Quoted in Stanisław Moniuszko, *Listy zebrane* [Collected letters], ed. Witold Rudziński and Magdalena Stokowska, Kraków 1969, p. 161.

Wiślicki submitted that Chopin and Moniuszko were equally legitimate singers of the nation's muse [Wiślicki, 1872]. Several years later, the notable poet and literary critic Jan Karłowicz (1860-1926) took up Wiślicki's idea, arguing that it was time to lay the sterile debate to rest by recognising the major status of both composers, and to examine instead their respective unique qualities as national composers [Karłowicz, 1885].

The nineteenth-century penchant for comparisons of all sorts (comparison being a basic technique in music criticism) had spawned a large number of texts expounding on Chopin's position in contemporary music relative to other composers. Analogies with Schumann, Liszt and composer-pianists like Field, Hummel or Thalberg were standard fare. In a volume of his Paris reminiscences, Józef Brzowski (1805?-1888) placed Chopin alongside Liszt as a great pianistic innovator [Brzowski, 1845]. Brzowski's distinction between Liszt as a master of timbre and spectacular effect and Chopin as a singer of emotion became canonical in Polish music criticism. The distinction was usually attributed to the differences in temperament between the two composers. In Adam Münchheimer's phrase, "Liszt is a fire that burns; Chopin too is a fire, but he gives off blissful warmth instead".[31]

In 1884, Jan Kleczyński published a comparative study of Chopin and Schumann.[32] In it, he offered what turned out to be an enduringly influential diagnosis that contrasted Schumann's eccentricity with Chopin's "classical balance". Kleczyński's commentary served to characterise Chopin as a fully original and independent artist. This was a pointed polemical barb, presumably intended to counter the pejorative view taken of Chopin by foreign, mostly German, critics [Kleczyński, 1884].

As already pointed out, nineteenth-century Polish critics writing on Chopin made extensive use of foreign criticism, which they mined for support or challenged where it disagreed with their views. Among other things, Polish music criticism had assimilated the German view of Chopin as narrow and one-sided (limited, as it was, almost exclusively to minor piano genres), along with related arguments about his supposed inability to compose large forms and his deficiencies in the areas of harmony and orchestration.

---

31 Adam Münchheimer, "Chopin a Liszt" [Chopin and Liszt], *Echo Muzyczne, Teatralne i Artystyczne*, 41 (1899), p. 483.

32 Schuman's opinions about Chopin's music had been discussed by "U. U.", the author of the anonymous pamphlet *Robert Schumann o Fryderyku Chopinie. Studium spisane dla własnego pouczenia się przez* […] [Robert Schumann on Fryderyk Chopin. A study written for the self-education of…], Lwów, Gubrynowicz & Schmidt, 1876.

Józef Sikorski was the first Polish critic to address the issue of Chopin being attached exclusively to the piano [Sikorski, 1859]. His explanation was favourable to Chopin, as he argued that the composer's predilection for the piano stemmed from the very nature of his talent. Writing a decade later, Jan Kleczyński was less charitable in addressing the preponderance of piano pieces. Taking his cue from foreign writers, including Berlioz, Kleczyński wrote about Chopin's inability to compose extended forms, his shortcomings in the area of orchestration, and his predilection for salon genres. Kleczyński included a full list of such opinions in his short synthetic study entitled *Fryderyk Szopen* [Kleczyński, 1870], which was intended to fill a publishing gap by supplying a Polish monograph on Chopin. In his foreword, Kleczyński described his project as the fruit of "a decision taken long ago by the publishers" (the publishers were *Tygodnik Ilustrowany,* a leading nineteenth-century Warsaw weekly on literature and social commentary). Kleczyński was notable as an early debunker of the Chopin myth. Based in Paris during the period 1859-1866, he was able to include in his study a considerable trove of new information gleaned from Chopin's surviving friends and associates. His characterisation of the composer and of his music provided a counterbalance to Józef Sikorski's more panegyrical *Wspomnienie* [*In memoriam*] (1849). Kleczyński's particular debunking was rooted in the ideology of *pozytywizm,* a specifically Polish adaptation of the positivist philosophy of Auguste Comte, which was making itself felt in Warsaw's intellectual circles at the time. Two aspects of the debunking project were apparent. First, Kleczyński took a clear-eyed approach to Chopin's biography, with many an unsparing reference to the composer's professional setbacks as a pianist and to the low-ebb period in Chopin's private life and composing career in the wake of his entry into the salon scene. Secondly, he made some controversial claims about Chopin's decline late in life, the signs of which he identified in the composer's allegedly dwindling inspiration and in the "morbid manner" that supposedly characterised his late pieces.

Kleczyński's dogmatic assertions exerted a major influence on contemporary critics (he enjoyed considerable authority as a Chopin expert, and considered himself "practically a pupil" of the composer). It is a measure of his impact (and an interesting historical footnote) that his pronouncements later found their way into the first Polish textbooks on music history by Bolesław Wilczyński [Wilczyński, 1894] and Aleksander Poliński [Poliński, 1907], where they were cited as objectively and incontrovertibly true.

Thanks to its original aspects, Kleczyński's piece is notable for being more than just a reiteration of contemporary European opinions about Chopin's music. He tried to identify the links existing between Chopin's music and nineteenth-century Polish culture, with his analysis basically following the standard line of thinking which viewed Chopin as a product of Polish Romanticism. Kleczyński portrayed Chopin's music as existing "in parallel" with the great tradition of Polish Romantic poetry, which it supposedly complemented in an integral way. Two motives for such an approach are discernible. In addition to the obvious need of every biographer to map Chopin's music onto a specific historical context, his approach was also characteristic of the typically Romantic belief that music was somehow dignified and uplifted by being compared to poetry. The reason was obviously that poetry was seen at the time as the highest of art forms, but there was also the specifically Polish notion that Polish Romantic poetry was the purest emanation of the national "spirit" in the absence of an independent Polish state. Kleczyński's approach was not unique in this respect. In fact, most Polish critics of the day subscribed to the fashionable methods of heteronomous analysis, where music was studied in terms of its supposed programmatic or emotional "content". As a result, it was a popular exercise in the second half of the nineteenth century to interpret Chopin's music in the light of its presumed poetic qualities.

To Woykowski, Szulc and Sikorski it was already clear that Chopin had belonged to the Romantic generation, both as a Polish artist whose music formed a certain "parallel" with the poetry of Mickiewicz, and as a European figure who had helped to forge the new Romantic school. Particular credit must be given to the critical faculties of Sikorski, the first critic to offer a comprehensive analytical study of Chopin's complete œuvre, for his ability to appreciate the dynamic and evolving nature of Chopin's music which crossed period barriers in search of the supreme Romantic ideal of individual artistic fulfilment. Sikorski, whose appreciation for Chopin's music (including the late pieces) was complete and unqualified, believed that Chopin had earned a secure position among the world's greatest Romantic composers and justified the heterogeneous qualities of the late pieces on the basis of psychological factors. He believed that the late pieces owed their distinctive character to an admixture of "anguish", a quality he argued was fundamental to Chopin's personality [Sikorski, 1865]. In his conclusions, he added – correctly – that these "anguished" pieces would struggle to find appreciative listeners.

Kleczyński's was a second attempt at finding the supposed connections between Chopin's music on one hand, and the ideology and spirit of Polish Romantic literature on the other. Hamstrung by not having a methodology capable of articulating the interconnection, he had to content himself with barely hinting at the connections supposedly existing between Chopin's music and the poems of Adam Mickiewicz and Juliusz Słowacki. In the event, he tried to identify the alleged kinship indirectly, partly by resorting to a smokescreen of rhetorical questions aimed at forging a connection outside the realm of cold rationality, and partly by precariously positing some kind of essential identity of musical and literary content. For instance, Kleczyński drew parallels between Chopin's polonaises and the chivalric romance or between his ballades and the ballads of Mickiewicz and Bürger, and he wrapped things up by speculating (quite implausibly) on the supposed Italian literary connections of Chopin's nocturnes. Kleczyński's programmatic readings of Chopin's music show him to have been very much a man of his time, as do his interpretations of the "national" aspects of the music. Kleczyński saw in the uniquely Polish elements of Chopin's music a link to Polish Romantic ideology, associated with the wave of enthusiasm for folk culture which saw Chopin's contemporaries disperse into the countryside to collect and popularize Polish folklore. Kleczyński did not hesitate to argue that the mazurkas (Kleczyński's main area of focus in the piece) could not be appreciated by "foreigners" because they drew on the treasures of Polish national culture. This idea, which was underpinned by the Romantic concept of a unique "national understanding" based on shared biological origins, became canonical in nineteenth-century Polish thinking about Chopin.

Kleczyński concluded his work with a tirade that contrasted the "softness" and "femininity" of Chopin's music with the "daring masterpieces of the masters" (presumably meaning Beethoven). This was again grounded in the artistic discussions then taking place in the salons of Warsaw. An easy parallel can be found in the views of Jadwiga Łuszczewska (1834-1908), a famous woman author better known under her nom de plume Deotyma, who demonstratively preferred Beethoven (presumably for being more in keeping with the heroic tone of her own writing) over the "plaintive" music of Chopin. This attitude was not without its impassioned critics, including Józef Kenig, who complained about the shallowness of Polish Chopin criticism in an article published in 1856. He was pessimistic about the prospects for a prompt reversal of the trend, pointing out that there was no valuable Polish school of Chopin criticism capable of appreciating the composer's spiritual authenticity [Kenig, 1856]. Another critic, Eugeniusz Skrodzki ("Wielisław"), complained that Chopin's reputation was being jeopardised by amateurish performers, and that this threatened to undermine the composer's international stature [Skrodzki, 1882].

Kleczyński's comments about the "femininity" of Chopin's music were part of a wider critical debate about the composer's personality. The earliest psychological analyses of Chopin, some of them taking into account the influence of his friends and associates, appeared after the composer's death, but they were undoubtedly based on the orally transmitted memories of Józef Brzowski, Aleksander Jełowicki, Antoni Wodziński, Eugeniusz Skrodzki, Eleonora Ziemięcka and Zofia Zaleska. Such memories often painted an idealized picture. Based on the early biographies of Chopin and coloured with Romantic phraseology, they portrayed an artist extraordinaire, a poet and a mystic [Jełowicki, 1839; Kleczyński, 1879] endowed with a whole range of creative gifts, such as drawing, acting and improvising, and even literary talents [Karasowski, 1862; Skrodzki, 1882]; Chopin was pictured as a man of elegance and refined tastes [Kleczyński, 1870; Skrodzki, 1882; Sygietyński, 1899b; Kleczyński, 1892a; Hoesick, 1904], but also as a person with an atypical, "irregular" personality. The biographers pointed to such qualities as his unusually heightened sensitivity, his amorous disposition (Wodziński, 1870; Hoesick, 1904), his spirituality [Ziemięcka, 1862], a frequent tendency to lose himself in a state of ecstasy or dreaming forgetfulness [Jełowicki, 1839; Brzowski, 1871; Zaleska, 1843], his extreme mood swings [Karasowski, 1862; Sikorski, 1865; Wodziński, 1870], his romantic irony [Lisicka, 1894], his introverted personality [Ziemięcka, 1862] and his individualism [Przybyszewski, 1899b]. Based on this extensive list, Józef Sikorski created the first comprehensive psychological portrait of the composer [Sikorski, 1849]. Polish positivist critics relied on the stereotypical psychological portrait of Chopin pieced together from the early biographies of the composer and memoirs written by his friends and associates. Jan Kleczyński compiled the typical components in the abstract of a paper given at the Warszawskie Towarzystwo Muzyczne (Warsaw Music Society) in 1873. Under the heading of "Characteristic Traits" he listed "longing – empty levity – warm-heartedness towards trusted friends – refinement and dignity – simplicity".[33]

Another characteristic element appearing in the analyses of Chopin's personality in the second half of the nineteenth century was the emphasis afforded to the Christian underpinnings of his spirituality, which were supposed to have translated into an impeccably moral life. The reconstructors of Chopin's "soul" wanted to see the composer as an ethical ideal [Ziemięcka, 1862; Żeleński, 1899], and associated his supposedly unshakeable uprightness with the traditional upbringing he had received at home [Ziemięcka, 1862; Skrodzki, 1882; Hoesick, 1904]. This was a con-

---

33 Jan Kleczyński, "Fryderyk Szopen (odczyt wypowiedziany w Warszawskim Towarzystwie Muzycznym, w wigilię 64-tej rocznicy urodzin mistrza)" [Fryderyk Szopen, a lecture given at the Warsaw Music Society on the eve of the 64th anniversary of the maestro's birth], *Bluszcz*, 10 (1873), p. 73.

viction that needed some ingenious justification, given the well-known irregularities in Chopin's attitude towards matrimony or the church [Jełowicki, 1886]. The need to portray Chopin as a deeply religious person was perhaps the most typically Polish aspect of the biographical projects appearing at the time, as was the general conviction that Chopin had maintained strong emotional ties to his family (the latter belief being based on third-party reports of Chopin's behaviour when seeing family members and, in later years, on his available correspondence) [Karasowski, 1862; Ziemięcka, 1862; Skrodzki, 1882; Hoesick, 1904]. The writers who had compiled the accounts dating back to Chopin's period in exile made a connection between the supposed strong family ties and the "yearning" quality that characterized his music. When Fr. Aleksander Jełowicki wrote about Chopin's nostalgia for Poland he diagnosed it as really boiling down to the composer's longing for his mother and his family home [Jełowicki, 1839]. Chopin's widely perceived exile syndrome was almost invariably thought of in terms of the mismatch between his idyllic memories of home or native country on the one hand, and of the soullessness of the big city that was Paris on the other.

From the early 1880s onwards there emerged a renewed critical tendency to idealize the composer. This was caused by the emergence and development of a patriotically inspired cult of Chopin, itself a reprise of the familiar bardolatry previously restricted to the canonical trio of Polish Romantic poets (Adam Mickiewicz, Juliusz Słowacki and Zygmunt Krasiński). In his 1883 study entitled *Chopin i Grottger. Dwa szkice* (Chopin and Grottger: two sketches),[34] Stanisław Tarnowski explicitly referred to Chopin as the "fourth bard". Several authors were prompted by this tendency to remould Chopin's music and personality the better to fit the bardic mould (a bard being understood in Poland at the time to be a supernaturally inspired national leader). This entailed a categorical dismissal of any notions of Chopin's supposed weakness or "softness". Any feminine or childish characteristics had to be edited out, along with the composer's tendencies to fall into depression, or even into despair. When writing about the composer, the propagators of the Chopin cult began to replace such downbeat words as "despair" or "anguish" with the newly fashionable concepts of "pessimism" or "Weltschmerz". Both concepts duly made an appearance in Jan Kleczyński's article *O wykonywaniu dzieł Chopina* (On performing Chopin's works), published in 1879. Kleczyński, who had been issuing the standard pronouncements about Chopin's labile psyche shortly before,

---

34 First published in *Przegląd Polski*, 4 (1883), then as a separate publication in 1892 [editor's note].

now came up with a new interpretation, reinventing the composer as a nourisher of "the nation's vital forces", a wholesome influence befitting a national bard. In the same work, Kleczyński retracted his earlier "allegations" of the nervous distraction and un-Christian pessimism supposedly present in the late pieces,[35] which he now saw as indicative not so much of dwindling inspiration as of a process of internal transformation. This was not unlike the changes of heart experienced by the famous dramatic characters of Mickiewicz and Słowacki, which led to a triumphant heightening of their powers. Inevitably, Kleczyński's attempt to challenge the established perception of Chopin as a decadent (a notion whose emergence he predictably blamed on foreign critics), and thus to present the composer as a robust and forceful figure, sounded less than fully convincing. Realising this, Kleczyński offered a compromise. While allowing that Chopin's music had displayed certain negative qualities (which he continued to ascribe to the composer's fragile nerves and his "feminine" personality), he now highlighted its positive values, such as optimism and vitality, arguing that it was those positive qualities that should be foregrounded in performance. In scholarly terms, the most interesting aspect of Kleczyński's text was his attempt to connect Chopin's "longing" quality to his Slavic origins. In this, Kleczyński was inspired by Johann Schucht's concepts of the "Slavic character" of Chopin's music as contained in a 1878 study which Kleczyński had analysed and critiqued closely [Kleczyński, 1878].

Quite independently of this process of claiming Chopin as part of the national heritage, it is interesting to consider the origins of the persistent misconception that "foreigners" had purposely misunderstood or belittled Chopin's music, a notion that was underpinned by a set of specific political views. In the second half of the nineteenth century, music criticism in all three provinces of partitioned Poland was openly politicized. The increasingly frosty relations between the partitioning powers of Russia, Austria and Prussia (which grew steadily worse after 1870) contributed to the politicisation of the discourse. Thanks to the relatively liberal regulation of the press, most journals were able to reach readers freely across partition borders, which made it easy to circumvent the limitations imposed by state censorship in any one partition. As a result, anti-German allusions were rife in journals published in Warsaw (located in the Russian sector) although they were of most interest to the readers in Poznań, and the anti-Russian sentiment targeted at Warsaw readers ran

---

35 In a different text, entitled *Ostatnie chwile Chopina* (Chopin's final moments), published in 1880, Kleczyński joined the group of biographers who upheld a belief in the Christian background of Chopin's spirituality.

particularly high in the journals published in the Austrian-controlled province of Galicia. Published in the Russian-controlled Warsaw, Władysław Górski's anti-German article [Górski, 1883] was one such example of the journalistic game of political hide-and-seek. Górski's article formulated a plea for restoring Chopin and Polish culture in general to their rightful place in German thinking.[36] In Kleczyński's critical writings, the insensitive or ill-meaning "foreigners", when described in more detail, likewise tended to be identifiable as German. The obvious question arises as to why the Russians were spared the criticism. It is difficult to offer a conclusive answer in the absence of systematic research into the music culture of nineteenth-century Warsaw, including its assimilation into a broader Russian culture (a scholarly project which is currently in its early stages). Still, one could tentatively point to the fact that the Russian pianists who performed Chopin in nineteenth-century Warsaw (Anton Rubinstein, Mily Balakirev) were greatly esteemed in the city, and made contributions to Polish cultural projects (Rubinstein donated to the cause of erecting a monument to Moniuszko, and Balakirev played a part in the decision to erect a Chopin memorial at Żelazowa Wola).

Given the generally sober and constructive character of Polish "positivist" ideology,[37] it is paradoxical that Chopin critics in that period by and large produced a tide of "dumbed-down" interpretations. Heavily daubed with patriotic and sentimental overtones, such criticism relied for its insights either on the notion of Chopin's supposed "sorrowfulness" or on the imagined extra-musical content of his works, notably drawing on descriptions of Polish landscapes, rustic scenes and the traditional values of the landed gentry (there was also a parallel critical trend that focused on identifying "military" passages in Chopin's music, such as the trio in the Polonaise in A flat major, Op. 53, and then mapping them onto various glorious events in Poland's military history). Still, several important texts stand out that demonstrated an ongoing process of the assimilation of key positivist notions. Notable among those notions was the "naturalistic" idea of societies as biological constructs, a concept that was deemed useful in explaining the national character of Chopin's

---

36 Górski's text was published at a time when the Polish press was mounting a spirited campaign against the activity of the German Eastern Marches Society, a German nationalist and xenophobic organization promoting the Germanization of Poles living in the Prussian partition.

37 The positivist ideology was a specifically Polish adaptation of the philosophy of Auguste Comte. Taking shape in reaction to the collapse of the January Uprising against Russia (1863-4) and the wave of anti-Polish political and economic reprisals that followed, Polish positivist thought was based on a resolute rejection of Romantic sabre-rattling and mystical leanings in favour of constructive social and economic reforms [translator's note].

music. Stanisław Przybyszewski made use of the theory in his attempt to explain the connections existing between Chopin's music, the Polish peasantry and Poland in general. He deployed the psychological concept of "the emotional tone" of sensations, a term he borrowed from Théodule Ribot to corroborate his own theory that Chopin's music was derived from popular origins through a process of "psychological mimicry" purportedly shared by representatives of a single "race"[38] [Przybyszewski, 1899]. Przybyszewski went on to argue that Chopin's music and popular folk music were essentially identical, since they were both "primitive" forms of musical expression (i.e. both had retained the elemental "expressive" function over the symbolic one). In this sense, Przybyszewski believed that Chopin's music was in fact what he called "metamusic". Przybyszewski's ideas were countered quite effectively by Antoni Sygietyński, a heavyweight in late nineteenth-century Polish literary and music criticism, who objected to what he saw as Przybyszewski's incorrect judgments about the collective psyche of the Polish people [Sygietyński, 1899b].

Late nineteenth-century Chopin criticism in Poland was also influenced by the ripple effect of the contemporary Western debate on the crisis in European society and on the decadent character of Western culture. The text of Władysław Bogusławski [Bogusławski, 1888] contains a full list of arguments connected with the fin-de-siècle "theory of nervousness". Bogusławski portrays the audiences in the salons of Vienna and Paris as undiscerning and philistine in their cosmopolitan, consumerist attitudes. As such, Bogusławski argued, Chopin's blasé salon audiences were unable to appreciate the true, wholesome values of his music, which they misdiagnosed as being "morbid".

Zygmunt Noskowski took the same line of argument in an 1899 paper commenting on the putative essence of Chopin's music [Noskowski, 1902]. Noskowski used the metaphor of a hothouse to explain the West's lukewarm reactions to Chopin. This metaphor, which was already quite hackneyed in Noskowski's own day, argued that the philistine Western salon audiences were like hothouse plants – deracinated, superficial, sterile and empty. City-grown art, argued Noskowski, was bustling and greedy, it craved nothing besides fame, and as such it was merely an inferior substitute for authentic art, which should properly be rooted in the biological connection that linked the artist with nature (a belief that echoed the theories of Hippolyte Taine, a major influence on the Polish positivists). This marriage between the artist and nature fostered true poetry, argued Noskowski, and Chopin's music was saturated with

---

38 The term "race" being interpreted at the time as ethnic milieu [editor's note].

that quality. Noskowski compared Chopin's music to violets and lilies of the valley, common flowers growing abundantly in Polish fields and forests. Given the philistine fondness for hothouse blossoms arranged into fashionable but ultimately banal floral compositions, he says, Chopin was bound to be misunderstood when he entered the salon context with his unassuming musical poetry, and the true cognoscenti in their turn were disorientated by Chopin's originality. Chopin's original, poetry-filled music refused to bow down to fashion, opined Noskowski. It was ahead of its time, he said, and he concluded that one day its universality would be recognized, and it would claim back its rightful place in the European artistic pantheon.

Antoni Sygietyński (1850-1923), a leading exponent of Polish positivism, also worked hard to come up with a universalist interpretation of Chopin's music, and to establish it firmly in the European cultural consciousness. As already noted, Sygietyński opposed Przybyszewski's notions of Chopin's supposed biological affinity to Polish peasantry. For Sygietyński, this was an error of judgment on Przybyszewski's part, a critical misconception he attributed to the specific cultural fashion sweeping Poland at the time, and known as *chłopomania*, i.e. an idealisation of peasant culture, which was regarded in the second half of the nineteenth century as a healthy repository of creative energy and artistic inspiration. Instead, Sygietyński tried to revive the traditional notion of Chopin as a refined composer who sublimated popular inspirations, a consummate master focused on compositional technique and gifted with an exquisite awareness of his artistic autonomy. According to Sygietyński, the mystery of Chopin's individuality lay not so much in some kind of "essentialist" link between the composer and his native land and its people, but in the unique and spontaneous nature of his talent, with its internally driven creative energy. A typical latter-day positivist, Sygietyński also appealed for the revival of a traditional respect for such tools of critical inquiry as observation, study of origins and formal analysis [Sygietyński, 1899b]. He showcased the effectiveness of these approaches in his own anniversary sketch on Chopin [Sygietyński, 1899c], a virtuoso application of Taine's principle of three-pronged contextual criticism predicated on the aspects of *race, milieu, et moment.* In this sketch he revisited his earlier debate with Przybyszewski to offer his own analysis of the nature of Polish influences on Chopin's music. For Sygietyński, they included the heritage of the nation's "eternal soul", but also the "contexts and events" of Chopin's own life, including his "conditions of birth, upbringing and creative work". Sygietyński pointedly blue-pencilled Przybyszewski's geographical assumptions: apparently, Przybyszewski had misattributed to the composer his own native landscape of Kuyavia (Kujawy),[39] whereas Chopin's actual childhood landscapes were those of Mazovia (Mazowsze). More importantly, he countered Przybyszewski's conjecture that Chopin's education in popular music took place in country inns. He wrote about the country manor at Służewo,[40] where Chopin was able to immerse himself in the high culture of the Polish landed gentry.[41] Although Sygietyński endorsed the idea that popular music was a crucial inspiration on Chopin, he relegated it to the role of an initial impulse, which was subsequently filtered and refined by the composer's creative individuality, sophisticated tastes and technical perfectionism.

The turn of the nineteenth century witnessed a steep rise in the number and quality of Polish studies of Chopin. This upsurge of interest was partly motivated by a "succession of anniversaries"[42] (with the fiftieth anniversary of Chopin's death in 1899 followed by the centenary of his birth in 1910), but also by the revisionist attitude in music criticism that was triggered by the advent of modernism, associated with the circle known as "Young Poland". The most notable Chopin publications at that time included the first four monographs on the composer written by Polish authors: new editions of Marceli Antoni Szulc (*Fryderyk Chopin i utwory jego muzyczne*, Poznań 1873) and Maurycy Karasowski (*Friedrich Chopin. Sein Leben, seine Werke und Briefe*, Dresden 1877), as well as new studies by Ferdynand Hoesick (volume 1 of *Chopin. Życie i twórczość*, Warsaw 1904) and Henryk Opieński (*Chopin*, Lwów 1909). The first two studies were Romantic, in the sense that the biographers were primarily interested in portraying Chopin in a positive light, even if they did undertake the task of systematically collecting available facts about Chopin's biography, including source material not known to earlier biographers (for instance, Karasowski largely based his work on Chopin's correspondence, and subsequently published a separate major edition of the composer's letters, in 1882).

---

39 This topographical misunderstanding arose because Przybyszewski's description contained a verbatim passage from another of his works entitled *Vigilien*. The text cited here is a compilation of *Vigilien* and several earlier works by Przybyszewski, including his sketch *Z dziejów indywidualności twórczej: Chopin i Nietzsche* [From the history of artistic individuality: Chopin and Nietzsche] published in 1892.

40 A country estate belonging to the Wodziński family.

41 The issue of Chopin's relations with the nobility and its culture was widely discussed, and it formed a link with the Polish modernist cult of peasant culture (*chłopomania*). The rejection of *chłopomania* entailed a categorical dismissal of peasant elements for their primitivity, and a tendency to glorify the nobility as a constructive driving force in Polish history.

42 Cf. Mieczysław Tomaszewski, "Przypływy i odpływy fascynacji […]. W rytmie rocznic" [The ebbs and flows of fascination… To the rhythm of anniversaries], in *Chopin. Człowiek, dzieło, rezonans* [Chopin: the man, his work and its resonance], Poznań 1989, p. 745 ff.

By comparison, Hoesick's 1904 study[43] belonged to a different world. It was a valuable modern biography inspired by the ideas of positivist historiography, and involving a painstaking reconstruction not just of the composer's life but also of the artistic, historical, cultural and social aspects of his milieu. An able historian and documentarist, Hoesick nonetheless recognized his limited ability to appraise Chopin's music independently, and, like his predecessors, he relied heavily in his account of Chopin's music on the authority of foreign writers, mainly Niecks and Huneker.

In contrast, Henryk Opieński's 1909 study did include a synthetic appraisal of Chopin's works. The critical methodology and the characterization of the composer were very much of their time. The Young Poland period had introduced a range of new ideas and interpretations guided by modernist ideology, and new ways of understanding Chopin's music and its place in the history of music and culture were accompanied by fresh reflection on the riddle of Chopin's personality and the social aspects of his biography.

Polish modernist analyses of Chopin's personality continued to be guided by the nineteenth-century conjecture about his "psychological split". In Opieński's words: "On the face of it, Chopin went through life with the eyes of an amused, happy and occasionally peevish child, but there was in the eyes of his soul a deep and sad inward look."[44] Traits such as "loneliness" and "otherness" became stock epithets attached to Chopin by modernist critics taking their cues from Stanisław Przybyszewski's influential interpretation, where Chopin was presented as a decadent figure marked by a "morbid" excess of refinement [Przybyszewski, 1899].

Other influences that shaped the modernist image of Chopin included Nietzschean anthropology (which saw in Chopin's music the "eternal postulate of humanity" – Jachimecki 1910b), and, to a lesser degree, the theories of Sigmund Freud, which prompted Zdzisław Jachimecki to undertake a reappraisal of the culturally constructed sexual nature of Chopin's music (Jachimecki concluded that Chopin's music was "androgynous" – Jachimecki, 1910b).

After 1900, the two preponderant contexts of Chopin's biography (namely his Polishness and his expatriate existence) continued to loom large. Characteristically, the expatriate context gradually ceased to be seen as a corrosive influence on Chopin's personality and artistic development. The belief that Paris was a hostile environment or a trivial and stifling hothouse was no longer being aired in studies

---

43 *Chopin: życie i twórczość* [Chopin. His life and work], i: 1810-1830 [editor's note].
44 Henryk Opieński, *Chopin,* Lwów 1909, p. 44.

written between 1899 and 1910. In his anniversary paper (1899), Władysław Żeleński emphasised the fact that Chopin was able to develop as an artist thanks to his contacts with the cultural elites of Paris [Żeleński, 1899]. In the inter-war period, this new way of looking at Chopin's émigré experience engendered a fresh debate leading to a reversal of the traditional juxtaposition of influences (with the French connection now being seen as beneficial). This reversal, prompted by the works of such critics as Stanisław Niewiadomski, also downplayed Chopin's spiritual bond with Poland, once a mainstay of Polish Chopin criticism, treating it as little more than a mythical display of starry-eyed utopianism on Chopin's part.[45]

This realization of Chopin's connectedness with the cultural and intellectual elites of Paris was a facet in Chopin's broader reinvention as a "citizen of Europe". Coined by the Polish poet Cyprian Kamil Norwid (1821-1883), the phrase typified a series of influential commentaries that led to a reappraisal of Chopin's position in European culture. Chopin ceased to be regarded as a Polish immigrant in Paris, peddling his mazurkas and polonaises like so many exotic wares; he was now seen as a legitimate partner of other Romantic artists, a master who opened up new paths in European music, a figure on a par with Liszt or Wagner, who were both idolised in the modernist period [Chybiński, 1908; Jachimecki, 1910].

This reinvention of Chopin as a precursor of modernism was preceded by a re-interpretation of his connections with Romanticism. Writing with the benefit of hindsight, modernist critics were able to survey the Romantic period as a historical phenomenon, which made their syntheses more convincing and comprehensive. The point of departure for their reappraisal involved positing a connection between Chopin and the French Romantic poets, in order to reveal a supposed generational affinity in terms of mood and outlook. Alfred de Musset came in particularly handy with his description of the sensibilities of the age in *La Confession d'un enfant du siècle* (1836). The book was duly cited by Stanisław Tarnowski and Anna Maria Lisicka, and the latter came up with a convincing portrayal of Chopin's connections with his period along Mussetean lines, though Lisicka eventually fell short of diagnosing Chopin with Romantic "madness" (rather, she firmly insisted that the composer

---

45 In a short text written on the 100th anniversary of Chopin's departure from Warsaw, Niewiadomski wrote: "He spent the second [half of his life] in Paris, but it actually resulted in a heightened sense of love, nostalgia and duty for the country. In his mind, the distant suffering land from which he was forever cut off had attained vast and ideal proportions. He would have certainly loved it less had he stayed in the country and experienced at first hand all the inconveniences and humiliations borne by the subjugated Poles at the hands of their Russian oppressors" ("Fryderyk Szopen", *Orkiestra*, 1932/4).

represented "none of the negative or reprehensible aspects of Romanticism" [Lisicka, 1896]). Stanisław Tarnowski, who was also a literary critic, narrowed his field down to the connections between Chopin and the Polish Romantic poets, provoking a series of speculations as to whether Chopin could be considered as Poland's "fourth bard" [Tarnowski, 1892]. For Tarnowski, Chopin's works were the pinnacle of Polish musical art, and their non-verbal nature made it possible for them to transcend the linguistic limitations that prevented Polish Romantic literature from gaining wider recognition in Europe, on account of both the language barrier and the particularist perspective. In 1910, Stanisław Przybyszewski repeated this assertion [Przybyszewski, 1910]. Neither Tarnowski nor Przybyszewski bothered to present evidence for Chopin's elevated European stature, apparently taking the composer's recognition for granted.

This is in stark contrast to many other critics influenced by the modernist ideology of Young Poland, who expended much effort in analysing Chopin's impact on the West. They hailed the composer as one of the greatest innovators or "musical reformers", placing him on a par with Berlioz, Liszt and Wagner. The choice of names is significant, revealing that the Young Poland critics had successfully assimilated the ideas of modernist music criticism. According to Adolf Chybiński, Chopin, as an harmonic innovator, "had travelled along the same road" as Liszt and Wagner [Chybiński, 1908], and Zdzisław Jachimecki went so far as to suggest that Chopin "taught harmony to the nineteenth century" [Jachimecki, 1910b]. Both Chybiński and Jachimecki wrote about the impact of Chopin's music on the emergence of nationalistic currents in Russian, Czech and Scandinavian music. Jachimecki also noted Chopin's influence as a tone colourist, seeing the composer as a forerunner to the ideas of Richard Strauss and Claude Debussy. Typically, Chopin was often compared to Dante, Petrarch, Leonardo da Vinci or Michelangelo [Jachimecki, 1910b], a sign of Young Poland's upsurge of interest in Italian Renaissance culture. Similarly, the many analogies Jachimecki draws with the painting of various periods (from Watteau to Böcklin) betray the influence of modernist ideas about affinities between the different arts. Today, this kind of wide casting of critical nets seems like a cavalier approach to establishing the origins of Chopin's music, unabashed in its fanciful connections. Jachimecki is clearly a willing victim of this kind of overinterpretation, as he refuses to consider the historical context of Chopin's music so as better to uphold the unique nature of his genius [Jachimecki 1910b].

Those Young Poland critics who regarded Chopin as a singular phenomenon and a notable figure in European music inevitably placed the composer on a similar pedestal in the context of Polish music. The result was an unexpected re-emergence of the old problem of the comparative merits of Chopin and Moniuszko. For the impetuous Adolf Chybiński, Moniuszko symbolised all the backwardness and parochialism of Polish music, starved as it apparently was of good models and unable to make use of Chopin's achievements [Chybiński, 1908]. This mode of thinking was intended to throw into sharp relief the distance separating the nineteenth-century "Polish school" (eclectic, lacking in enterprise and ambition) and the efforts of such emerging composers as Szymanowski, Różycki and Karłowicz. In diagnosing the supposed divide, Zdzisław Jachimecki made the controversial claim that nineteenth-century Polish composers and teachers had betrayed the legacy of Chopin. Rather astoundingly, Jachimecki argued that Chopin's less gifted successors had relegated the composer to the category of foreign, non-Polish art, on account of its artistic superiority [Jachimecki, 1910a]. Jachimecki toned down his aggressive comments in a study entitled "Fryderyk Chopin" published in the same year in *Biblioteka Warszawska*, but he held fast to his allegation that teachers of composition in Polish conservatories were lecturing in an "anti-Chopinesque" vein.[46] According to Jachimecki, the works of the emerging composers (including Young Poland adherents) belonged to a "new era, with Chopin's spirit as the leader", and he explained the nature of that leadership (rather unhelpfully) as an adherence to the composer's "guiding ideals". In the context of Jachimecki's other writings, we may assume that the "guiding ideals" meant a reformist approach and an "aspiration to soar" towards superior spiritual and artistic qualities.

By around 1910, Polish criticism had come to regard Chopin's position as a reformer and lawgiver of new European music as a given, mainly based on the tone of international Chopin criticism. The new standards set by the harmony textbook of Louis and Thuille or the studies by Schreyer and Riemann [see Jachimecki, 1910b] led Polish critics to conclude that a more rigorous, "scholarly" approach was called for in Polish Chopin studies. This belief was shared not only by Young Poland reformers [Chybiński, 1908; Jachimecki, 1910b], but also by musical conservatives like Stanisław Niewiadomski, author of the important study *Chopin w nauce harmonii* [Niewiadomski, 1912]. Of course, there were crucial differences in their respective

---

46 His reference was to Zygmunt Noskowski (based at the Warszawski Instytut Muzyczny), Władysław Żeleński (based in Kraków) and Mieczysław Sołtys (who was affiliated with the conservatory of music of the Galicyjskie Towarzystwo [Society] Muzyczne in Lwów). The polemic was mainly aimed at Noskowski, whose reviews in *Kurier Poranny* and other Warsaw journals were very hostile to modernism in music.

approaches. Whereas the younger critics saw in Chopin the teacher, or at least co-author, of modern harmony, Niewiadomski portrayed him as a "neo-academician" who differed from traditional adherents of academic art insomuch that he made new rules instead of obeying existing ones [Niewiadomski, 1912], an idea that was indebted to Kleczyński's explanation of Chopin's classicism [Kleczyński, 1878]. Ultimately, both Niewiadomski and the younger critics had arrived at a convergent conclusion: instead of treating it as the subject of a cult, new composers should treat the inheritance of Chopin's music as a source of artistic ideas capable of injecting modernity and high artistic quality into Polish music. Niewiadomski believed that such a project could successfully compete with the new European music by continuing the nationalistic current in music initiated by Chopin, and other conservative critics such as Zygmunt Noskowski or Aleksander Poliński gave approving nods to the idea. The young "progressives" believed it was essential to continue the tradition of Chopin's universalism, but were remarkably vague about the specifics. In a way, the problem was of their own making. Once they had replaced traditional methods of analysis (the study of origins, style and compositional technique) with lofty pronouncements on the "Sphinx-like" nature of Chopin's music, any definition of "universality" was bound to prove elusive beyond such nebulous notions as the alleged perfection of Chopin's music (which was taken to mean an ideal marriage of form and content) or his ability to make full use of all available means of expression [Jachimecki, 1910b]. Young Poland critics believed that the essence of Chopin's music was encapsulated in its content and expression. Content was defined as an expression of feelings, an approach informed by psychologically inspired theories of art, notably the theory of Zygmunt Hausegger. Jachimecki also represented a departure from the tradition of banal programmatic readings in that he emphasised the "abstract nature" of the "emotional underpinning" of Chopin's music [Jachimecki, 1910b]. His was a radical position, and he stood practically alone; until 1914, the most popular form of Chopin criticism involved a reliance on literary descriptions based on such traditional topoi as Polish history or Polish landscape. Other critical approaches were rare, and they reflected the typical interests of Polish modernist literature, mainly the interest in legendary and fairy-tale material, such as the ancient mythical Slavic figures popularised by Young Poland writers, poets and painters [Poliński, 1907; Paderewski, 1911].

The traditional methods of interpreting Chopin's music as "national" (after 1900 we also see the emergence of other epithets, such as "of our race" or "of our tribe") remained the favoured tool of "committed" Chopin critics, whose interests in the scholarly debate were openly political. Critics like Tarnowski, Przybyszewski and Paderewski, who sympathised with the National Democratic party (the biggest political force in Poland before 1914), emphasised the importance of Chopin's music as a precious national heritage that gave a voice to the "soul of the nation", making it heard in Poland and abroad. To Przybyszewski, for instance, Europe was supposedly lying prostrate before Chopin, who was accordingly viewed as a new Messiah suffering for mankind, the colourful phrasing a clear attempt at reviving the Romantic myth of Polish messianism [Przybyszewski, 1910].

This kind of criticism, which was mostly occasioned by the centenary of Chopin's birth, in 1910, brought with it a deluge of rambling disquisitions that relied on comparisons between Chopin and the Polish Romantic bards (Mickiewicz, Słowacki, Krasiński), other famous Polish artists (Grottger, Matejko), or indeed figures such as Copernicus, Stańczyk (a celebrated wise fool who served several Polish kings in the sixteenth century) or Veit Stoss (a late medieval sculptor famous for a spectacular altarpiece in St. Mary's Church in Kraków). Most of the comparisons were indiscriminate and superficial, and Stanisław Niewiadomski may be taken as a good example of a critic prone to such facile analogy-drawing [Niewiadomski, 1910]. In this area of Chopin criticism, the most constructive speculations focused on the spiritual kinship between Chopin and the poet and playwright Juliusz Słowacki (1809-1849), a great favourite with Young Poland readers and critics. In his 1902 study "Słowacki i Chopin" (published in *Kurier Warszawski*, not anthologised here),[47] Ferdynand Hoesick, mentions the "peculiar" biographical similarities between the two artists and their shared role as "singers of the longing and the melancholy of the human soul in general, and of their own torn and bleeding hearts and souls in particular".[48]

The centenary celebrations in Lwów, a city where the popular (peasant) party enjoyed a strong following, gave rise to a by-product in the shape of an idea to bring Chopin's music "to the masses", i.e. making it accessible to peasants and workers. A big "people's concert of Chopin's music" aimed at the mass public took place in October 1910 (featuring choral arrangements of mazurkas produced by amateur choirs and the like), and the publicity materials for the concert were published in the Lwów-based *Słowo Polskie*. The idea was that Chopin's music, being popularly

---

47 This was one of several minor sketches written as an offshoot of his work on the monumental three-volume monograph *Chopin. Życie i twórczość* [Chopin. His life and works], published in 1911.

48 This pithy description of Hoesick's subject matter is taken from an overview published in *Kraj*, a journal published in St. Petersburg (supplement *Sztuka i Życie* 1903/2, p. 13, author: "B.").

inspired, would be immediately understandable to popular musicians and listeners [anonymous, 1910]. The idea of bringing Chopin's music to the people engendered a special type of writing. Journals targeted at peasant and working-class readers carried articles explaining Chopin's music and its role in Polish and international culture. The articles were written in a popular style, using popular imagery. Specifically, this involved the use of patriotic historical commentary, as well as poetry, descriptions of nature or scriptural passages which were meant to "illustrate" Chopin's music [Kalinowski, 1910].

The people who lay behind these efforts to bring Chopin to the masses were not alone in believing in his instinctive accessibility to Polish listeners. A similar sentiment was voiced by those interpreters who believed that Chopin's music was an expression of the collective "soul of the nation" [Przybyszewski, 1910; Paderewski, 1911]. The most common corollary to this idea was the notion that Chopin was incomprehensible to foreigners (meaning mostly Germans), and that only Poles could really understand his music. This opinion was mainly voiced in the provincial press, and it was challenged by professional critics who sought to promote Chopin as a European composer of universal significance. At the other extreme, Zdzisław Jachimecki was arguing that Chopin's music was intuitively accessible to musically illiterate lay audiences, or even to those who in other respects had no ear for music [Jachimecki, 1910b].

A separate area of Chopin criticism comprised comments on the performance and identity of his music. Already in Chopin's lifetime, Poles had claimed to hold the key to the proper, "authentic" interpretation of his music, of which they became the self-appointed custodians. In 1845, Józef Brzowski argued that a proper understanding of the composer's intentions was essential in performance [Brzowski, 1845], and Józef Kenig demanded that performers of Chopin's music should be suitably empathetic to its poetic content [Kenig, 1856]. First-hand accounts of Chopin's performances compiled from pupils and listeners were fashioned into a canon of orthodoxy invoked by Władysław Górski [Górski, 1880] and Wielisław [Skrodzki, 1882]. But there is a crucial difference. Whereas Wielisław had a Romantic way of thinking about Chopin's performances (enshrined in first-hand accounts, they offer a chance to communicate intangibly with the spirit of the composer), Górski is a typical positivist, to whom the value of first-hand accounts lies purely in the glimpse they offer of the original musical text, complete with the composer's performance markings. Górski insisted on painstaking loyalty in performance; his review of a concert by Aleksander Michałowski is generously interspersed with red flags, highlighting the pianist's departures from the Breitkopf & Härtel edition [Górski, 1885]. In so doing, Górski and other critics of his generation were not trying to shoehorn performers into a specific style of interpretation (the notion of a performance style was not even in use before the early 1900s), and they admitted the legitimacy of individualistic renditions [Górski, 1880], but they generally cautioned performers about going over the top. In other words, they believed that emotionality was legitimate as long as it did not degenerate into either mawkishness and sentimentality on the one hand, or cold and cerebral virtuosity on the other [Kenig, 1856; Sikorski, 1871; Kleczyński, 1875].

Jan Kleczyński was particularly voluble about Chopin's authorial interpretations, with which he could claim a second-hand familiarity based on the accounts of Princess Marcelina Czartoryska, a pupil of Chopin's. Kleczyński initially held a highly romanticised notion of the mechanism of that transfer, and actually believed that some of Chopin's female pupils benefited from a special spiritual kinship with the maestro (Kleczyński disregarded the male pupils completely on the strength of a private theory that women were intrinsically better placed to understand Chopin) [Kleczyński, 1894]. Kleczyński compiled a lot of specific information about what he believed was Chopin's own playing style. It was supposed to have been marked by a reluctance to engage in excessive virtuosity and a preference for *tempi rubati* and a toned-down, "colourless" sound [Kleczyński, 1879]. The stylistic boundaries of authentic Chopinesque style according to Kleczyński were informed by such concepts as simplicity, moderation, calmness, naturalness, poeticality and feeling. After a lifetime of studying Chopin's original performance style, Kleczyński later came to question the veracity of pupils' accounts, dismissing them as mythologized and subjective [Kleczyński, 1891]. Eventually, he came to reject the idea that Chopin's performances should be treated as exemplary models [Kleczyński, 1892a].

Some specific and important information on Chopin's performance style, also originating from Princess Marcelina Czartoryska, was related by Stanisław Tarnowski [Tarnowski, 1895], who restated the idea that a performer's foremost obligation consisted in grasping the authorial intention. In this sense, authorial intention was not understood in the mundane sense of a faithful reproduction of the musical text and its performance markings – the true challenge lay in being able to recognise and make apparent the unique style of a composer. It was this view that informed the formation of the critical canons of Chopin interpretation in the 1890s [Poliński, 1894; Bogusławski, 1899; Sygietyński, 1899a]. Sygietyński's comments, which were formulated from the "scientific" viewpoint, as befitted a positivist critic, characteristically relied for their reference point on the notion of an "ideal Chopin pianist". In the late

1890s, it was felt that the ideal had found its embodiment in the famous Polish pianists: Ignacy Jan Paderewski, Aleksander Michałowski and Józef Śliwiński. This kind of personified canon of interpretation was used as a universal comparative model for appraising other Chopin performances.

The problem of authenticity had also engendered a separate area of debate, which centred on the legitimacy or otherwise of transcribing or modifying the original pieces (e.g. by changing Chopin's orchestration in the concertos). Jan Kleczyński opposed any modifications that cheapened or trivialised the original pieces [Kleczyński, 1868], but he had no objection to enhancing the orchestral parts in the concertos, which he justified by invoking Chopin's limited skills in orchestration [Kleczyński, 1892b]. New works by Russian composers that drew heavily on Chopin's works, as well as Zygmunt Noskowski's orchestral transcripts of the *Marche funèbre*, the Prelude in C minor and the Etude in E major (Op. 10), all provoked a lively debate on whether there was any point to such orchestral arrangements of Chopin's pieces. The opinions in the debate ranged from a liberal approach [Kleczyński, 1892b; Poliński, 1892, 1904] to a rigorous condemnation of such arrangements as "sacrilegious" [Sygietyński, 1899d]. Of the Young Poland generation, Zdzisław Jachimecki was an important voice in favour of the practice, reflecting the characteristic modernist belief in the primary status of symphonic music. In the hands of an accomplished master of symphonic music, Jachimecki believed that Chopin's piano pieces had the potential to be creatively translated into orchestral terms [Jachimecki 1910b].

The early 1900s brought little change to the debate about performance.[49] Popular criticism, which as a rule continued to be highly politicised, reiterated the belief that Polish pianists held a privileged position as interpreters of Chopin's music, unlike foreign artists (mostly Germans), who supposedly struggled under a considerable handicap. The notion of an ideal Chopin performance came to be coloured by the actual performances of the great Polish pianists. One slightly farcical incident was symptomatic. In 1908, the Warsaw Philharmonic Hall announced plans to hold a "grand Chopin concert", intended to be a sort of competition between Polish and foreign artists. In the end, the event was aborted when most of the Polish greats

---

49   In 1910, Wanda Landowska published a study entitled "Interpretacja Chopina" [Interpreting Chopin], in *Literatura i Sztuka*, 5, a supplement to *Nowa Gazeta*, 82 (1910). This is an interesting attempt at identifying the structure of Chopin's individual style, but its viewpoint is that of a performer rather than a critic.

pulled out at the last moment;[50] apparently, the organisers saw little point in going ahead with the performances in the absence of their approximations to "the ideal". Early twentieth-century criticism successfully shaped the concept of a Chopin performance style, originating with Antoni Sygietyński's notion of "the character of the period" with regard to Chopin's music [Sygietyński, 1899a]. The ability of looking at Chopin's music in terms of "period" was a reflection of the modernist cult of history and old music – the idea of treating Chopin as a historical composer was already in the offing.

---

50 "Wiadomości bieżące" [Current news], *Kurier Warszawski*, 58 (27 February 1908).

Anthology

[Mochnacki, 1830] **Maurycy Mochnacki, [untitled], *Kurier Polski*, 103 (18 March 1830)**

[...] No one could accuse us of prejudice or patriotic swagger if we said that Chopin belonged to a small group of the foremost pianists; we shall leave it to the foreigners to declare how far ahead of the others he might be. The other day he played his pieces in a concert. It is difficult to tell which was greater, his composing talent or his masterly performance. The concert had originality, it had a beautiful singing tone, and it had some brilliant, challenging passages composed and played in perfect accord with the nature of the instrument. Everything was decked with feeling and fire, and blended harmoniously into a whole. The execution was agile, expressive and full of feeling, and Chopin cleared all technical problems seamlessly; given the beauty of the pieces, he could not but captivate the audience. The delight was universal, particularly when he played the Rondeau from his Concerto and a miscellany of Polish songs; in that felicitous rendition listeners were able to recognise a beautifully encased tune from his native village. It seems that there is nowhere on earth incapable of sustaining a genuine talent. Although Warsaw is hardly a city greatly enamoured of the fine arts, Chopin received all his musical education there, and he owes his origins and his development to the local teachers. Though he lived far from the more charismatic cultural centres, he was able to acquire and gather all that which enriches music and adorns the artist; he knew how to create his own compositions, and how to give them a course and a form all of their own. The land that stirred him to life with its song affected his musical temperament, and on occasion it is still discernible in his works: many a tone seems to be a felicitous reflection of our native harmonies. Under his touch, the simple mazurka gladly yields to transformations and modulations, retaining all the while its proper accent and expression. It takes a special kind of feeling to combine, as Chopin does, music of genius with a refined performance style and that beautiful simplicity of Polish song; for that, one has to know the echoes of our fields and forests – one has to be able to hear the song of the Polish peasant.

[Woykowski, 1836] **F. Antoni Woykowski, "Chopin",**
***Przyjaciel Ludu* [Poznań], 1836/28, pp. 223-224; 29, pp. 230-231; 30, p. 237.**

In recent years, Poland has given the musical world a genius without equal, and one who will probably remain unmatched for a long time to come. His name is Chopin. He deserves the appellation *maestro nonpareil,* both for his playing, which borders on the miraculous, and for his truly original, beautiful and complex pieces; the readers of *Przyjaciel Ludu* will be pleased to read this brief report on that musical Romantic – that Shakespeare, Byron and Mickiewicz of pianism.

[...] Early in the present century, Beethoven – that beautiful star shining on the musical horizon – followed in the footsteps of Haydn; in his Symphonies in D major, C minor, A major and F major, he was the first to call for "genius unfettered by rules". Even his compositions for the piano, not an instrument with which he was excessively familiar, show signs of his great genius that pointed a sure way to true beauty and perfection (e.g. in the Sonata in C sharp minor, Op. 27 No. 2 or his Sonata in D minor, Op. 32[51]). One might have expected other composers to follow in Beethoven's footsteps, but that did not happen. Almost all of his pupils were either content to imitate his works and ideas, or they took the old road of Mozart and Clementi, or else they started schools of their own in an attempt to please *everyone* with agreeable music. As a result, the quality of piano composition and performance began to plummet, with the effect that out of the millions of composers working between the time of Beethoven and that of Chopin there cannot have been more than two pianist-composers of any real note. Works by Kalkbrenner, Hummel, Cramer and innumerable others rely on the mere mechanical perfection of performance, and there is nothing in them to engage the listener's soul – no fire, no feeling, no song, no fancy. Ries, though in many ways better, cannot

---

51 Correctly: Op. 31 No. 2.

compare to Beethoven,[52] and it would likewise take Moscheles or Mendelssohn-Bartholdy very much time and effort indeed to come up with anything on a par with that great master's music[53]. And what shall we say about Herz, who was so fêted a few years ago? Or about Hünten, or Czerny? In their desire to win the crowd's applause they fell into step with those wretched standards, resulting in a further adulteration of good musical taste.

Those things being so, it was high time for a towering genius to step in and prevent a complete annihilation of good taste. Chopin has done that. He cared nothing for the applause of the populace, preferring the opinion of a *single truly knowledgeable musical expert* to the praise of *thousands* of less musically gifted persons. Trusting the force of that conviction, he boldly walked his path to achieve the highest degree of perfection. For him, music is a magical art that gives man a glimpse of his higher origins and lifts him from this vale of tears to the happier lands above.

Chopin's ascent to European fame began with a musical journey he undertook in 1829. Vienna in particular fêted him with great enthusiasm. Everywhere he played, the critics lauded him for his wonderful performances. No less admired were his improvised fantasias, which gave a freer rein to his bounteous, lofty and creative imagination than formal compositions ever could, with an almost miraculous effect. On such occasions, gone was his pallid complexion; the dark eyes were lambent with a superhuman fire, and an almost feverish blush arose on his mournful countenance. When the concluding chords floated through the hall, soft and plaintive like all of his improvised fantasias, a peal of applause mounted. A slight smile fleeted across his beautiful face, and pallidity returned to his cheeks, a sight that must have made him seem all the more appealing in the eyes of the ladies. In the same year of 1829 he visited Poznań, but did not perform, finding that there were no music-loving audiences in the city.[54] Alas! When will they be born? We are in the nineteenth century – it is about time we finally started to cultivate a generous love for the arts and the sciences!

---

52 Please note that I refer to Beethoven's piano compositions; as a composer of symphonies and the author of *Fidelio,* Beethoven's passing excellence may never find an equal [original footnote].

53 In their most recent compositions Moscheles and Mendelssohn-Bartholdy come very close to the Romantic school [original footnote].

54 This fact was also demonstrated on St. John's Day 1834, when Europe's foremost violinist, and a Pole at that, could not even recoup the cost of his concert [original footnote referring to concerts given by Henryk Wieniawski].

After visiting several other towns in his native Poland, Chopin returned briefly to Warsaw, and in 1830 he left for England, Germany and France.

Chopin's fame in Germany, England and France started with the publication of *Là ci darem la mano, Varié par Fr. Chopin,* Œuvre 2, which won extraordinary popularity and acclaim in Europe. Even the most loyal adherents of the old school admitted that Chopin was superior to all. Music journals were filled with reviews. The best were probably those by Wieck and the enthusiastic reports by Schumann, a talented composer and excellent pianist from Leipzig. [...] I shall quote an excerpt from Schumann's article to give an indication of the enthusiasm that greeted our compatriot, and to provide an insight into the pieces in question. [...][55]

It is easy to imagine the eagerness with which the world looked forward to new compositions by Chopin. The following pieces were published in 1833:

1. Polonaise for the piano and cello, Op. 3.
2. Mazurkas, Parts 1 and 2, Op. 6 and 7 (later followed by Part 3, Op. 17).
3. Trio, Op. 8.
4. Nocturnes, Op. 9 (later followed by Part 2, Op. 15).

These works, particularly the mazurkas and the Trio, exceeded all expectations. Northern Germany was the only place where the mazurkas were disliked. They were practically worshipped in southern Germany, France and England. Fétis in the *Revue musicale,* Fink in the *Allgemeine Musikalische Zeitung,* Schumann in the *Neue Zeitschrift für Musik,* the editors of the *Gazette musicale* – all of them could not praise enough the originality or the beauty of the works; the only dissenting voice was that of Rellstab, writing in his Berlin music journal *Iris im Gebiete der Tonkunst.* Without so much as the slightest idea about the songs and dances of our people, and completely ignorant of the spirit of Polish music, he dared not only to criticise but actually to deride the mazurkas. In particular, he complained about their plaintive tone! As if it were not that very plaintiveness, which waxes so generously in Chopin's mazurkas and other pieces, that gives them their charm and their unique expression. Constraints of space preclude a detailed analysis here, but each of those mazurkas holds enough beauty, poetry and grace to fill entire pages.

The mazurkas were followed by a Piano Trio dedicated to Prince Antoni Radziwiłł. This piece brims with new figures and conceits of remarkable beauty; it has

---

55 The lengthy quotation from Schumann's well-known review in *Allegemeine Musikalische Zeitung* which follows in the original is not included in this edition.

a potency that sweeps all before it, coupled with sadness and on occasion a more masculine despair; the individual sections are subject to much transformation and reordering, and are marked by curious rhythmic and harmonic complexities. A characteristically lyrical quality runs through the piece, coupled with a sense of order and symmetry. In a word, this is a work worthy of Chopin's talents; and the same applies to the nocturnes that followed it shortly afterwards.

As everyone knows, Field has heretofore been considered as the foremost composer of nocturnes. Chopin wanted to win the palm in this area of composition, and has naturally outstripped Field, whose nocturnes seem dry and dull in comparison with Chopin's wonderful works. His are unique in their songlike nature, their soaring ideas, rich harmonies and that highly distinctive, plaintive quality. Truly, Chopin's nocturnes are dreams of a tender, pure soul, violently moved by emotion on a silent night. They cannot be understood by an unfeeling heart.

It is enough to know those first nine works by our compatriot to concede that he has outstripped all pianists in winning undying fame; but this is nothing compared to his later works: his etudes, his divine Concerto, his wonderful Fantasia, his Polish songs, his Krakowiak, as beautiful as it is difficult, and his mournful Scherzo. The perfection and beauty of these works are beyond words. We can openly contend that no other nation can boast as great and truly national a composer. Chopin's works are Polish down to the very last note; every note is beautiful – truly beautiful – every note is divine, lofty and blessed!

"Chopin's studies (Etudes, Op. 10) are dedicated to Liszt, Europe's finest pianist save Chopin himself: an eloquent indication of the kind of pianist for whom Chopin has intended his studies. Probably they cannot be performed well by anyone except Chopin and Liszt. Mediocre pianists (such as those who believe that they can perform, perfectly and at a moment's notice, the most difficult works of the older composers, like Kalkbrenner, Ries, Hummel or Herz) will count themselves lucky if they can give a barely adequate rendition of one or two etudes after several months of solid practice; the more difficult ones, like the 2nd, 4th or 11th, remain completely out of their reach. [...]"[56]

Thus writes Fink, an adherent of the old school of composing, one who is probably unhappy to see the new school emerge victorious, and one who still finds an occasional word of praise for the works of Hummel, Kalkbrenner and many others. The etudes are a key to Chopin's subsequent works, such as his Concerto, Op. 11,

---

56 In the original, this passage is followed by excerpts from Gottfried Fink's reviews in *Allgemeine Musikalische Zeitung* published in 1834.

Fantasia on Polish Airs, Op. 13, Krakowiak, Op. 14, Rondeau in E flat major, Op. 16, and Scherzo, Op. 20.

The greatest of critics have already praised those works to the hilt, and it would be risible of me to seek new words of praise. It suffices to say that works of greater perfection and beauty are difficult to come by.

Mr. Chopin mostly resides in Paris. He plays many concerts, and they draw formidable crowds. The French pay solid gold for his lessons (apparently, 2 Louis d'or for one hour).[57] He has been remarkably successful. Nearly all the great composers have followed his example and joined the Romantic school. Suffice it to mention the famous Liszt (also in Paris), Hiller, Berlini,[58] Schumann, the beautiful and talented Clara Wieck, Pixis and Chaulieu, who joined the Romantics after composing 110 works.

Erstwhile composers like Herz, Hünten, Czerny and thousands more have practically fallen into oblivion. Once a man has tasted these heavenly tones, more mundane music holds no attraction for him. The former composers could be compared to the stars. They shone in the darkness, but what star can shine when the sun has risen? [...]

[Brzowski, 1837] **Józef Brzowski, "Wyjątki z podróży artystycznej do Niemiec i Francji odbytej w 1837 roku przez [...]" [Excerpts from an artistic journey made in 1837 to Germany and France by...],** *Kronika Rodzinna,* **1871/19, pp. 294-5.**

[...] There is a very clean and stately townhouse at 38 rue de la Chaussée d'Autin (rue Mont-Blanc), where our eminent composer and true artist, the Copernicus of the piano and the singer of feelings, was living at the time [...] The virtuoso was in a good mood, and he gladly sat down at the piano [...] He was particularly well-disposed that day, and played for us continuously all kinds of mazurkas, ballades, scherzos and nocturnes [...]

It is difficult to express just how striking was the bardic inspiration on his countenance. His face was pale, his eyes were sparkling, and there was an inwardness about him which made one think that he was in a state of hypnotic trance. it was obvious that he was hard at work, but the work was all spiritual. The physical mechanism was a mere means to make that work apparent. His performance and his expression were

---

57 According to recent reports, Mr. Chopin left Paris in November [original footnote].
58 The reference is to Vincenzo Bellini.

remarkably penetrating [...] He knew that his playing had made an impression – he could tell that from the listener's quickened pulse, stray tear and silent handshake. He asked for nothing more. [...]

[Jełowicki, 1839] **Rev. Aleksander Jełowicki, "Moje wspomnienia [1839]"**
[My memoirs], cited from the Instytut Wydawniczy PAX edition,
Warsaw 1970, p. 358.

[...] Another music-winged soul of the same sort[59] alighted with a gossamer touch on a human body; it is presently known as Szopen (Chopin). When I first met him in Warsaw, a mere child at the time, I foretold that he would have no equal in the world. My conjecture was correct; Chopin has since soared above everyone else. He had resolved to become a musician-poet, and now he is one; and there is no telling if what he composes is musical poetry or poetic music. And with all that, he has the natural touch of a fine Pole – a national feeling so ample that when he sits down at the piano, a Polish listener is guided back to Poland in his thoughts, he is led all around the country and into his family home, that very heart of Poland. Whenever I suffer from melancholy, I visit Chopin. I look at him, and it makes me feel better because we both miss our homeland and console each other in our shared longing. We reminisce about the old times, and when we get too lost in reverie he sits down at the piano while I snuff out the candle. The faint glow coming from the fireplace toys with Chopin's shadow, just as the light of memory toys with the shadows of the past; the din of a distant street occasionally swells up like the howling of a storm or the roar of a waterfall while Chopin weaves a magic spell on his piano, craming it full with sounds and voices, and making it sing his poetry. I know not how long he sings, for I always forget time entirely; he sings of our future happiness and our present misery, of nostalgia for one's mother and of longing for one's future, of the fears of this world and the joys of heaven; I sigh, and sigh again, and many a tear wells up in my eye; now my soul is agitated, and now it is peaceful again; his graceful music heals the heart's wounds like the whisperings of a magic healer; my soul feels bliss, and that momentary serenity accompanies me on my way home, it is present in my prayers and watches over my sleep. Then I dream of home, and wake up dreaming – but the birdsong turns into stallholders' cries, the babbling of the river is really the noise of the street, and dew is mud. [...]

---

59 The first was the famous singer Giovanni Battista Rubini.

[Szulc, 1842] **Marceli Antoni Szulc, "Przegląd ostatnich dzieł Chopina przez [...]" [An overview of Chopin's latest works by...],**
Tygodnik Literacki **[Poznań], 1842/10, pp. 76-79; 11, pp. 82-83.**

1) Allegro de concert op. 46, 2) Troisième Ballade op. 47, 3) Deux Nocturnes op. 48, 4) Fantaisie op. 49, 5) Polonaise op. 44, 6) Mazourka, 7) Tarantelle op. 48.

When writing not long ago about Chopin's newly published works,[60] we decided to print occasional reports about our Polish musician, given the scarcity of reliable news and the shortage of comprehensive reports. We have at present an excellent opportunity to follow through on our plans, as Mr. Chopin has generously bestowed on his expectant compatriots as many as seven works within the space of two months. It is those works that we presently intend to consider at some length.

First of all, we wish to tender our most heartfelt thanks to our precious bard for acquiescing to the request that we Poles have made on several occasions, pleading with him to augment our musical literature. Given our present situation, Mr. Chopin stands practically alone in his laudable course of action. Boyan, that leader of our ancient Slavic bards, has shattered his fiddle and will not be stirred from his silence.[61] Mr. Chopin is an heir to Boyan's powers; he keeps alive in our hearts the sacred torch of the nation. He is the most eloquent interpreter of national thought; his works are a holy temple; they are, in Mickiewicz's phrase, an ark containing the treasure of our nation's music;[62] they hold all that is noble, beautiful and exalted in a Polish breast; they are the threads of which the people's ideas are spun, a legacy of centuries, a laudable sign of the poetic aspirations of the Polish people. All this is evidenced in the composer's works outlined above. Now let us expound on each in more detail.

1) *Allegro de concert* (A major, 4/4). The general layout and plan of this piece makes it very clear that it was originally written with an orchestral accompaniment, so much so that it is possible to mark precisely the tutti passages, which are as follows: pages 4-8, pages 16-17, and page 23. The work is striking not so much for its melody, ideas or deep feeling as for its refinement, the fullness of its harmonies, the skilful use

---

60 See *Orędownik*, 1841/26 and 27 [original footnote].

61 Boyan was a legendary Ruthenian *guslar*, one of the heroes of *The Tale of Igor's Campaign*, an epic poem written in the Old Eastern Slavic language. Although the poem's authenticity is sometimes disputed by modern critics, it was much admired in Szulc's own day as a monument of ancient Slavic history. Cyprian Godebski was the first person to translate parts of the poem into Polish, in 1806.

62 An allusion to the apostrophe in Adam Mickiewicz's poem *Konrad Wallenrod*, where traditional folk poetry is referred to as "an ark of covenant between the days of old and now".

of various pianistic effects, the impressive passages, the strikingly bold transitions; in a word, the overall ornamentation of the piece. The second theme forms a less happy contrast [...] there is something old-fashioned and inept about it, with a mockingly repetitive pattern of octaves. This work appeals to the ear rather than to the heart, and it would not be unreasonable to believe that it was dashed off in a hurry – a piece of little worth in Mr. Chopin's own eyes.

Were this a work by anyone other than Chopin, we freely confess that we would have hailed it as an excellent achievement; but we are wont to measure Mr. Chopin against perfection. However, the genius of a true bard will not be concealed, as evidenced amply by the passages of great beauty scattered on page 8 (bars 2-4).

2) The third Ballade (A flat major, 6/8). We have read somewhere that many of Mr. Chopin's most momentous pieces have their origins in poetry, namely in the ballades and songs of Mickiewicz. If credible, this detail would eloquently demonstrate the spiritual affinity existing between the two bards, and it would cast new light on Mr. Chopin's artistic development. This ballade is so fresh, so redolent, so charming, airy and gracious, that one cannot but think that this is one of Mickiewicz's wonderful works captured by Mr. Chopin in a net of harmonious sound. In particular, the stanza (p. 6, bars 1-2), which repeats itself several times, is reminiscent of those strangely wondrous stories told by a nanny to lull an agitated child to sleep. The charming power of those magic circles wraps itself around us and takes us to unknown lands, into a realm of dreams and illusions. Then, a sudden note of anguish erupts, gradually swelling in a whirl of mad, fantastical processions that build up to an outburst of formidable violence. Still, the stanza knows how to weave a calming spell, and all is calm except the bass voice, which roams in chromatic passages looking for its metre. Finally, the bass too is calm, and the first theme returns in harmonic triumph, to conclude this exquisite poem that brims with life and truth.

3) *Deux Nocturnes.* No. 13 (G minor, 3/4). This nocturne is notable for its powerful, energetic bass, which adds a sense of virile resolution to the melody's sad mood. The melody clings to the bass voice as a fragile ivy frond climbs a mighty oak. The intermezzo (Poco più lento) is completely unique: gracious, generous and noble, it is like a man of adamant resolution, undaunted as he faces any peril or setback. A host of devils assaults him, and the jaws of a thousand monsters gape before him. Yet he stands tall, unwavering and immaculate. Such was the image fancifully engraved in my mind when I first played that exquisite notturno. No. 14 in F sharp minor, 4/4. The tune is plaintive, elegiac, nostalgic, like a memory of happiness past; it leaves a lasting impression of sadness, which even the intermezzo (D flat major, 2/4), though more

cheerful, cannot quite erase. But let us not dwell on this piece, since it has a similar background and mood to several other pieces by Chopin.

4) The Fantasia (F minor, 4/4) had been announced well in advance, and we do not know what has caused this delay in publication. The themes are Polish, full of sweetness and song, notably the melody on page 10 (3/4, B major, Lento sostenuto), which alone makes an impression when reprised towards the end of the work, fleetingly and, one might say, almost inadvertently. But it is invidious to point to specific examples of beauty in a work that is so beautiful as a whole. Although this genre is nominally free from formal constraints, our composer has not treated this liberty as a licence to indulge in the excesses of genius or the pleasures of chaos, or to come up with a mere workmanlike combination of several themes (à la Thalberg) with perfunctory ornamentation thrown in; rather, the connections are as profound as they are skilfully concealed from a casual glance. Each theme appears in its proper character, and taken together they form a distinctive and well-rounded shape. In the above-mentioned theme (B major, 3/4) there was but one infectious progression of chords that struck a strident note with us, not so much for violating the sacrosanct rules of music theory as because it seemed to be at complete odds with the angelic gentleness and sweetness of the melody. Still, only a modicum of harmonic knowledge is needed to allay this tartness with some slight changes.

5) The Polonaise (F minor, 3/4). It is an amusing sight indeed to observe the many imitators of Chopin who have found a taste for what they see as Chopin's wildness and eccentricity; to see them rage romantically against the world, scrambling and struggling as if they meant to shatter and annihilate it completely in their noble passion. One could compare them to those beggars who pretend to be disabled and cry out loudly to trick passers-by into a compassionate frame of mind. It is not so with Mr. Chopin. His sorrow is heartfelt, truthful, lofty and authentic. On occasion he grazes one's heart painfully, but he can also heal the wounds he has inflicted. His is the anguish of a noble soul, a soul who knows how to express his sufferings in an orderly fashion, for he is vigorous and resolute amid misfortune. Such is the idea that engenders this piece. At first, one is touched to the quick by a keen sense of anguish, which swells to enormous proportions, trying as it were to incinerate the heart and tear the breast open; then a mazurka emerges (A major, 3/4): a piece of strange beauty, redolent of angelic sweetness, agreeable and pleasing, so Polish in character that the ear cannot but succumb to its charms and alluring tones. Description is futile; one needs to play it, one must hear the astonishing contrast of expression, that unprepossessing link to the opening of the work, which first speaks coyly in the bass

register, then soars upwards in wild passages to introduce a polonaise tune marked by almost terrifying progressions and harmonies. At the end, the lugubrious tone prevails, swooning and expiring in elegiac tones.

6) The Mazurka (A minor, 3/4) is the second in a collection of pieces by various composers which the publishers entitled *Notre Temps*.[63] It is mysterious, inward-looking, contemplative. We shall not describe it at length, since Mr. Chopin's mazurkas are more or less familiar to everyone.

7) The Tarantella (A flat, 6/8). The tarantella is a kind of dance reportedly danced in the southern countries as a cure for people stung by scorpions. We have Rossini's exquisite tarantella in his *Soirées musicales,* which Liszt plays with incomparable expression. Our Tarantella likewise has the whirling, captivating and violent quality typical of the genre.

[...] [Chopin] belongs exclusively to our nation, and the nation ought to know about him. Just as a certain foreigner was once told that every single Pole knows several historical songs by heart,[64] so a time will come when Chopin's works will become widely known, because they are home-grown, perfect and purely Polish. The experience of emigration cannot erase this background or mark of Polishness; that cannot be done, whether by the German composers, with their unfathomable profundities, or by their French counterparts, with their enticing lightness of touch. [...]

[Zaleska, 1843] **Zofia Rosengardt Zaleska, *Pamiętnik* [Diary] [1843-1847]**
Cited in Władysław Hordyński, *Zofia Rosengardt Zaleska, uczennica Chopina i jej pamiętnik* [Zofia Rosengardt Zaleska, a pupil of Chopin, and her diary],
Roczniki Biblioteczne, **1961/4, p. 148.**

[Paris, 8 November 1843]:

[...] I found him by the fireplace, talking to some German. He looked changed, more so than on the previous occasion. Moral suffering leaves deep marks; but I cannot see them in his face – what one sees is rather a struggle of the imagination in a state of constant desire and striving. There are no signs of melancholy or resignation. He has an inward look, and seems to be examining life and the past. Then, when he is playing, I cannot look at him for fear of being blinded by the brilliance of his genius. His move-

---

63 The reference is to a collection of works by famous pianists published in Mainz by Schott's Söhne.

64 An allusion to a collection of songs by various composers entitled *Śpiewy historyczne* [Historical songs] published in 1816 with texts by Julian Ursyn Niemcewicz.

ments become convulsed, his breathing grows slower and heavier, his countenance even more pallid. He turns into a penitent sinner – a ray of divine grace descends, and his light-filled soul soars to his Creator in a prayer of contrition and thanksgiving. [...]

[Brzowski, 1845] **Józef Brzowski "Słówko o smaku w muzyce. Przez [...]"** **[A word on taste in music. By...],** *Pielgrzym,* **4, 1845, pp. 97-98.**

[...] Chopin [...] and Liszt can be justly deemed reformers of their instrument. The former is filled to the brim with an abundance of creative art and lofty poetry; he is able to draw every last good quality from his piano to render the depth of his feeling and thought. The latter challenges the piano, with its vast range of orchestral harmonies, to reflect the monumental scale of his passions [...] To understand those two pianists, as different from each other as Racine was different from Corneille, is to admit that the finest technique cannot produce music of such quality unless one is able to soar beyond mere workmanlike competence.

The conclusion is that musical performance is less straightforward or commonplace than it might appear; there are musicians and singers everywhere, and yet there are few performers whose performance is absolute and marked by true and sacred expression, and by an understanding of the composer. The performer is the second maker of a work, and it is a heavy responsibility indeed to be acting in the composer's place without tarnishing his work.

[Jełowicki, 1849] **List Fr. Aleksandra Jełowickiego do Ksawery Grocholskiej, 21 październik 1849 [Letter of Fr. Aleksander Jełowicki to Xawera Grocholska, 21 October 1849], cited in "Ostatnie chwile Szopena przez ks. A[Aleksandra] Jełowickiego opisane" [Chopin's dying moments as described by Rev. A.[leksander] Jełowicki],** *Kronika Rodzinna,* **1886, p. 588.**[65]

[...] He was always courteous, full of feeling and wit; he lived a life that seemed to be detached from the surrounding world, and yet he did not think of Heaven... Chopin did not have many good friends; instead, he knew many people of this world who were indifferent if not hostile to matters of faith; preoccupied with his fame and triumphs in the musical world, Chopin silenced his spiritual stirrings and forwent

---

65 An expanded version of this letter appeared after its first publication in *Tygodnik Ilustrowany* (1896/9, p. 162). The addressee was Countess Xawera Grocholska née Brzozowska, a patriotic activist from the region of Podolia and a memoirist (died 1872).

the spiritual exercises recommended by his mother, a true Polish woman; for him, religious practice was a mere memory of his childhood past...

Especially in his final years, the scepticism of his friends and companions struck deep roots in the soul of that great artist, and doubt weighed heavily on his heart. And yet he was never heard railing about the saints or other matters divine in the vein of common non-believers who disguise the triviality of their ideas under the pretence of bookish learning. From that he was protected by his innate nobility of feeling and delicacy of taste, which made itself felt in his art as well as in his deportment. [...]

[Sikorski, 1849] **Józef Sikorski "Wspomnienie Szopena przez..."**
[Chopin: *in memoriam*, by...], *Biblioteka Warszawska,* **vol. 4, 1849, pp. 510-551.**

It was a blessed generation that nurtured Chopin in its womb; a blessed land that rocked him to sleep with its songs, sustained him with its bread, and finally sent him out as one of its many costly gifts to the world! Rich are the lands lying along the river Vistula to have yielded such a crop; the nation is brimming with life, and its prophets of the high science of the future are far superior to those of other nations. This is the best kind of wealth! It can be used by everyone, and it multiplies miraculously like the wine in Cana of Galilee or the five loaves in the desert. It is not the first miracle of Polish abundance since the Piast times[66] and, God willing, not the last! [...]

[Chopin] had all the [qualities] necessary to be loved of men: he was generously charitable, frequently to the point of exposing himself to want; he was unstinting in his assistance to those who sought his advice or guarantee; he was highly intelligent and dignified in his demeanour; and many students of his works will be surprised to learn that he had a mercurial wit bordering on frivolity, and a Garrickean knack for impersonation that made it possible for him to imitate people's manner of speech, movement or facial expression in a way that showed a penetrating insight. [p. 523]

[...] Both as a composer and as a virtuoso, Chopin devoted himself almost exclusively to the piano, which was held at the time to be an instrument incapable of speaking directly to the soul. Chopin consigned that opinion to oblivion by demonstrating to almost miraculous effect the full use that could be made of that instrument. [p. 526]

---

66 The Piast dynasty was the first dynasty of Polish kings, who ruled the country from its inception until 1370 [translator's note].

[...] Chopin captured [...] Beethoven's thinking, and translated it into his own times; the closer he approached Beethoven, the more faithfully he reflected the image of his own time (though he was more singular than Beethoven, who had originally remained under the marked influence of Haydn and Mozart); the further away he moved from Beethoven, the more distinctive yet accurate that image became, with such qualities as peace (though inwardly troubled by storms), audacious ideas, and finally the ultimate bringing down of the floodgates separating humanity from the great ocean beyond. [...]

It is interesting to observe how his spirit gradually weaned itself off the influence of the composition schools of his formative years. Far from becoming enslaved to any one of the hallowed musical figures of the day, he drew on them freely while looking for ideas worthy of emulation. This is apparent in his early pieces, both in their overall form and structure, and in the texture of their musical ideas [...] At the same time, Chopin's ideas have a palpable audacity and freshness, an independence of course and a quality of invention that placed him above the rest of the composers [...] His was a unique talent, in which youthful elegance blended with tenderness, energy with caresses and soaring hope with sorrow, the lavishness of the music suggesting that his inexhaustible stores had hardly been tapped at all. Reportedly, his thought was so immeasurably abundant that no idea has ever appeared twice in his many compositions, excepting several passages of his own devising – and even those were modified and contained but few repetitions [...]. Doubtless, the early pieces were to an extent a product of the general musical aspirations of the time; he used familiar and much-admired forms to unlock the gates of the temple, and to join the magi of the piano within; and he used the general licence such forms afforded in order to introduce new ideas to the world. Having accomplished that, Chopin soon freed himself from such formal conventions and devised new genres to be filled with new content. This is not to say that his genres were completely original, for that would have been an impossibility; genres develop from one another, and can be ultimately traced to their shared, flexible and all-sufficient origin in aesthetics. Suffice it to say here that Chopin's expansive fancy extended further and deeper than that of those formulaic composers with their cramped and trammelled imaginations. Chopin did not shatter the constraints simply because [...] he wished to appear original or unique; it was the original and unique nature of his ideas that forced him to shatter the constraints.

The first works by Chopin are charmingly pure in their outlook on God's world, but even they contain glimpses of the spirit of despair emerging in places in a sorrowful tone; later, his spirit sinks ever deeper, experiencing every shade and hue of anguish: from quiet sorrowfulness to the kind of despair that abandons itself in the ascetic transports of a penitent soul. Perhaps it was his life's experience, or the separation from his family, or his solitude in the midst of noise and din, or the ailments of a frame wasted by disease, or perhaps it was it all those things taken together; suffice it to say that Chopin's works underwent a gradual closing-off from the world and became increasingly inward-looking. [...] At an early age, Chopin had developed a meditative attitude that prompted him to lose himself in the personal, intimate world of the piano. The seeds of that divorce of thought and deed that became so pronounced in later years were already guiding his actions early on, and it was this discontinuity that prevented him from composing vocal pieces.

The joyful elements in his works constitute a song that soars above the stars, a hopeful mother's thought as she leans in prayer over her infant's cradle; this song is a triumph born of suffering; sometimes it is a melancholy smile [...]. But humour, that trait of the perceptive spirit which was so abundant in Chopin, never veers into the overwrought extremes of satire, irony or sarcasm. In that man, who voluntarily resigned himself to acute suffering, the discrepancy between his high hopes and his unhappy reality was never translated into derision at, or defiance against, this pain-ridden world [...]

Chopin's depth, the formidable range of his ideas, so bold as to spill over conventional formal constraints in waves of infinity, make him practically the only true piano composer among the thousand musicians today whose names [...] will not survive except in booksellers' catalogues. His music frustrates the imitators; their arms sink resignedly after the first attempt, and they have to be contented with cranking out their mechanical wares [...]

Polishness [...] may not be the only notable quality about Chopin's melodies, but it is the most common and preeminent. Still, it would be a mistake to believe that Chopin's melody, or Chopin's music as such, is always Polish. In his vision, Chopin was too much a citizen of the world to remain exclusively bound by the Polish influence on his outlook, if not on his spirit [...] But there is folk music present in his work, and not merely in his mazurkas, krakowiaks or polonaises [...] Polish song is there to be found even if it is concealed and intertwined with passages of a more universal tone [...] How can it be identified? Well, who can define the smell of a violet? One recognises the scent even though one cannot define it. When Chopin arrived among the foreign nations and played our native music to them, the peoples of this world asked in wonderment: "What is that charming song, one so strong, so simple, so noble and new?" And they learned that it was Polish song [...].

Chopin's harmonies share the fate of his melodies [...] His eagerness to sustain a tune with an harmonic depth that is at the same time allied to a natural simplicity [...] is almost as important as the tune itself [...] With the exception of Beethoven, Chopin's harmonies are as noble, robust, deep, active and daring as those of no other composer since the times of the great Bach. [...] Bach was the only composer whose works lay on Chopin's piano long before his death [...] He made obvious use of Bach's works in his music, even if his approach was different [...], for instead of developing the individual voices, he traced paths for whole groups of them [...]. Thus, Bach's apparent complexity was elucidated by the intertwined filaments of clearly worked-out voices: in Chopin's music, the rising chords have an apparent cheerfulness, like layers of clouds rising from a precipice, with the spirit of harmony ascending a mountain slope to tackle the melody in a titanic clash [...] Chromaticism [...] spreads with a formidable opulence in Chopin's works. Perpetually challenging the diatonic scales, his chromatic notes disturb the serenity of melodies strung out on those scales [...] Diminished and augmented, his intervals [...] violently pound the heart, mercilessly inflicting many a painful wound. Add the frequent and tentative changes between major and minor keys, and an image emerges of an incessant wrestling match, so that Chopin's later works can be succinctly characterised by the metaphor of struggle. And if those mighty elemental forces were not enough, there is finally Chopin's rhythm, which is in no way weaker or poorer than the other two. [...]

[Klimańska, 1850] **Zofia K[limańska] z Brzozówki,**[67] **"List [...] do Wydawcy Pamiętnika" [Letter to the Publisher of the *Pamiętnik*], *Pamiętnik Literacko-Naukowy* [Vilnius] vol. II, 1850, pp. 120-121.**

I am a subscriber to *Biblioteka Warszawska* [...] There is a charming flower among its pages in the form of an article devoted to the memory of the late Chopin; his obituarist has all but merged his soul with that of our deceased compatriot, and the prophetic song of that Polish swan resounds in every particle of his soul, a soul that

---

67 Zofia Klimańska, née Chłopicka (1812-1870) – a writer, journalist and social activist who was also a competent pianist and composer. She was the initiator and de facto head of the *Pamiętnik Literacko-Naukowy*, a periodical edited by Romuald Podbereski published in Vilnius in the period 1849-1850 (see Władysław Korotyński, "Zofia Klimańska (Zofia z Brzozówki)", *Tygodnik Ilustrowany,* 1870/158).

has shed so many tears on the dead man's grave; and we would all be shedding those tears still, like a spring of perpetual sorrow, were it not for the fact that Moniuszko's song assuages our pain. All hail the heartfelt feeling inspired by the musician-bard, and all hail the native spark that inspires the journal.

[anonym, 1850] **"O ruchu literackim"** [**On the literary movement**], *Gazeta Warszawska*, 276, 19 October 1850, pp. 3-4.

The lady finds little that pleases her about *Biblioteka Warszawska* and seems to begrudge the bitter tears shed for Chopin by the author of the text; after the loss of the greatest of Polish composers she seems to find solace in Moniuszko's song. We do not wish to strip Mr. Moniuszko of his right to enjoy the warm feelings of his fellow Poles or the fame that his talent has won him – but Mrs. Zofia K. of Brzozówka must allow that no such easy consolation can be had after the loss of Chopin. We are of the opinion, and I believe that it is an opinion to which few will readily object, that even a Meyerbeer could not quite compensate us for the loss of a talent as great as Chopin's. It may appear impudent of us to consider Chopin's talents as superior to those of Moniuszko, but it is nothing but the truth. Chopin may well stand alone as a composer of comparable profundity, thoughtfulness, opulence and originality.

[...] Compared to Meyerbeer, [...] what can one say about Moniuszko? Presumably, musicians will not hold it against us that we compare concertos and salon pieces with dramatic musical works; therefore, I wish to remind you that our comparisons relate to the respective creative talents of the composers, and not to the pieces themselves.

[Kenig, 1856] **Józef Kenig, "Z powodu wydania pośmiertnych dzieł Chopina"** [**On the occasion of the publication of Chopin's posthumous works**], *Gazeta Warszawska*, 1856/121 (28 April / 10 May), p. 1.

[...] For us, Chopin's is still a music of the future rather than of the present, even though his tones – sorrowful, often despairing, always imaginative – strike such a resonant chord with the spirit; even his joy can be so painful as to make one's heart break at the memory of the green and merry years, a memory that returns in these black times, when all hope has been forsaken forever. Such is, for instance, that delightful mazurka trio in the Polonaise (Op. 44); the final chords of that passage of wild power are almost a relief. From whence did he learn that way of addressing us?

What spirit communicated those whispered words to him? It must have been a spirit of grief and longing that makes him so accessible to us; like us, he experiences paroxysms of great enthusiasm and noble vigour, of wondrous dreams of the poetic sun, but they leave behind little more than a fruitless weariness, a dispirited lack of the will to live, a wish for the grave. A musician poet is an Aeolian harp, made to chime in a nation's breath, expressing all its sorrows and delights; sometimes, it is only a providential instrument to vent our sighs and moans.

Chopin is an artist of the future, but not merely because of his influence; much time must pass before it will become clear just how much he is loved. As it is, the love is well-intentioned, but it lacks the foundation of solid knowledge. There is hardly a young lady in the country who does not play Chopin, and so do many grown women if they have not forgotten the music lessons of their youth. All play his music, venerate it and bow down to it. [...] Chopin was the most original of pianists, which means that a unique touch is an absolute prerequisite for any performer of his music. Technical skill and beauty, good touch and brilliance – those qualities, which unlock all of today's music pieces so successfully, often prove insufficient here. [...] What the performer needs is feeling, he must be a poet as much as a pianist. [...]

[Sikorski, 1859] **Józef Sikorski, "Fryderyka Chopina zbiór śpiewów polskich z towarzyszeniem fortepianu, ułożony z rękopismów oryginalnych i wydany przez J. Fontanę" [A collection of Fryderyk Chopin's Polish songs with piano accompaniment, edited and published from original manuscripts by J. Fontana],** *Ruch Muzyczny,* **40 (23 September (5 October) 1859), p. 345.**

[...] Chopin's proclivity for dreaminess, the mysterious depths of feeling that he plumbed ever more often, and the independence of his concepts all led him to translate his ideas into a mysterious and indefinite instrumental expression able to convey all those things that cannot be expressed with ordinary speech; in other words, to express the ineffable. In a way, the poet's words impinge on the composer's freedom. The musician will prove unfaithful when he fails to express as much; or even if he expresses as much, but does so in purely musical terms – though in the latter case this infidelity may simply demonstrate the musician's superiority and deeper insight. Still, in a case like that, the musician follows the lead of another, superficially at any rate, and essentially surrenders part of his sovereignty. A man of pronounced artistic independence, Chopin was clearly loath to be guided by other people's ideas.

Fontana states this unambiguously in the preface to this collection of songs: "Language imposes on music a certain ordering of ideas, a subservience of style and character to which Chopin was never willing to submit." It is also possible that the human voice, even though it is the most beautiful of the sounds found in music, held less allure for Chopin than his favourite instrument, the piano [...] Which composer has not felt that his germinating ideas sought a specific medium for their interpretation? Who would deny that Chopin would have been a different composer if the piano had not existed? Or, conversely, that the piano would have been a different instrument, were it not for Chopin's formative influence? [...]

[Karasowski, 1862] **Maurycy Karasowski, "Młodość Fryderyka Chopina" [The youth of Fryderyk Chopin],** *Biblioteka Warszawska,* **4/1 (1862) pp. 7-9.**

[...] If Chopin had focused his genius on a non-musical field such as literature, his creative gifts would certainly have soared to the heights of a profound poetic and original inspiration, similar to that which the world rightly admires in his musical work. On occasion, he performed in various theatricals and comedies. Whenever he forgot his lines and the prompt for some reason failed to cue him, the undeterred Fryderyk would launch into an improvisation, ad-libbing with such gusto – so aptly and perfectly – that nobody in the audience was able to spot the dilemma. We all know the fame and renown that this improvisatory knack would win him in his later years. [...]

Thus, when he was in the right mood his mightily creative spirit made improvisation seem facile; yet at the same time, he worked conscientiously and painstakingly on those works which were meant for publication. Preoccupied with a specific idea, he would sometimes fall silent and sit gloomily in a corner, shunning conversation; it is usual for highly-strung and sensitive souls to swing from lively merriment to numb and gloomy sadness. At times like those, he would become completely engrossed in the internal work that continued into the night. [...]

He studied folk music at its very source, and became so taken up with it – he had drawn so much of it into his soul – that it lasted him for a lifetime, and everything he composed reflected that music most faithfully, like a looking-glass held up to its spirit, that is to say its melodies, and to its body, that is to say its rhythms. [...]

[Ziemięcka, 1862] **Eleonora Ziemięcka, "Wspomnienie przez [...]" [*In memoriam, by...*], *Noworocznik (Kalendarz) Ilustrowany dla Polek na rok 1862* [Illustrated calendar for Polish women for the year 1862], Warsaw, A. Dzwonkowski, 1862, pp. 2-3.**

[...] I had the opportunity to meet that chosen soul, that musical genius who outstripped all the modern artists in profundity and artistic idealism. Indeed, Chopin himself was an ideal, he was himself the most wonderful instance of spiritual beauty. His frail frame, as yet untouched by illness[68] but strangely delicate, was like a light veil barely concealing his mighty spirit; perhaps no other man's immortal side had ever been more visible; one felt as if his soul alone was living, his bodily form a mere illusion. The revelation appeared inadvertent, for Chopin belonged to that kind of people who prefer concealment to ostentation. Indeed, so strong was his desire to remain concealed that it was in constant conflict with the ineluctably transparent nature of his mighty spirit, resulting in permanent play of irony; it was irony associated with genius, a strange quality that people who knew him well found painful and fascinating in equal measure.

I was fortunate to fully comprehend his disposition owing to a special relationship of trust [...] and friendship existing between his family and myself, which helped us to quickly form a frank and amicable relationship. We talked about our parents and sisters, about his venerable father, who had lived a teacher's dedicated and meritorious life that won him universal admiration; a spry old man at the time, his father continued to go about his duties with great diligence; we talked about his good mother, who was likewise admired by all for tending her children and assisting her husband in his laudable profession. We discussed Chopin's elder sister, the brilliant and angelical Ludwika, and Izabela, so full of feeling, dedication and noble aspirations, and the deceased Emily, who was a born poetess. [...] When we were discussing those things, which we did for hours and days on end, gone was the artistic genius, and a most loving son and devoted brother appeared in his place; the sense of inward struggle would lift, and he appeared perfectly comfortable, life blossoming on his pallid cheeks, the ironic outlook replaced by profound simplicity. Family affections were Chopin's second religion; with so much love and tenderness lavished on him in his cradle, those natural ties grew to unusual proportions. Oh, how his heart must have suffered when he was persuaded against his will to remain in a foreign country despite having so much love! [...]

---

68 i.e. in 1836 – the reference is to Ziemięcka's meeting with Chopin at Marienbad.

[Sikorski, 1865] **Józef Sikorski, "Przegląd muzyczny" [From the musical world],** *Tygodnik Ilustrowany,* **325 (1865), pp. 253-5.**

[...] Composers of genius are [...] like scientists of genius when they peer into a drop of water, an atom or a current of mysterious and invisible force in order to discover things unknown, to find new truths and explain the universal laws of nature – to harness new forces which, once tamed, can rock the world to its foundations. Like a scientist, an artist of this kind examines a trifling glint of light under his spiritual microscope to discover a mysterious world of profound ideas; in the secret corners of the soul he weaves a new light, a light that had remained hidden from his own sight until he wove it into existence [...]. His is no well-ordered weave; from beginning to end, it is based on the playful caprice of fancy. His logic [...] is the dream-like logic that combines the most daring and contradictory of visions, and yokes them together. To understand it, one must be dreaming oneself. Few succeed; the bizarre, dreamy details never reappear in the same constellation – nothing but the background stays the same. The mental background of a unique composer is different from that of other people, for the uniqueness of artists sets them apart from others, despite their shared humanity. It is a background formed by life's events, innumerable and impossible to know, which hold a much greater sway over the spirit's stirrings than we would be prepared to allow, given the spirit's might and independence. [...]

Why is Chopin so different from Beethoven in the way he dreams his dreams? Why is it that the former seems to focus on himself, whereas the latter launches into metaphysics? Is it a product of his personality, with all its attendant qualities, or is it a matter of fortuitous circumstance and the general spirit of their respective social worlds?

The background to Chopin's thought is twofold. On one hand, there is brightness, like the gaiety of vernal nature: all is pleasant, hopeful, smothered in caresses – now like a mood of joyful entertainment, now like excited expectation. [...] On the other hand, there is the dullness of an overcast sky, like a sweltering summer day pregnant with thunder, as when one longs for the storm to come and bring new freshness but fears its terrifying descent. This is like a tendril of pain trying to climb the tree of life after all the twigs of hope have been broken off. It is the mood that can be seen in a humorist's resigned attitude, a flagellant's whip, a desperate man's sarcasm. Here is the latter-day Job, deprived of health and spiritual possessions, who flaunts his misery and fulminates against his hostile fate. He cares nothing for the world, that mortuary of his ideals. He never smiles except when he thinks back to them.

Neither background reigns supreme over Chopin's ideas. The two are almost invariably mixed and blended to form an alternating, variegated hue. Very often one predominates over the other, giving rise to two separate worlds. [...]

[Kleczyński, 1868] **Jan Kleczyński, "Ze świata muzycznego" [From the music world],** *Tygodnik Ilustrowany,* **new series 20 (1868), p. 236.**

The [pianist's] worst fault[69] consisted in introducing what we believe were uncalled--for changes and embellishments in Chopin's well-known mazurka. On rare occasions, such ornaments in familiar pieces can be attractive, provided that the performer exercises great circumspection and adheres to the spirit of the original composition. So, for instance, Henselt introduced some new ornaments to Weber's *Invitation à la danse* which are quite felicitous, though it would not be unjustified to object even to those. However, Mr. Chodecki's changes rob Chopin's mazurka completely of its simplicity, and confer on it instead an air of virtuosity that appears quite strained and unnatural. Such liberties would be quite inexcusable with any master; they are all the more so in the case of Chopin, a consummate master of the secrets of the piano, who has so expertly attuned his pieces to the nature of his instrument.

[Kleczyński, 1870] **Jan Kleczyński, "Fryderyk Szopen" [Chopin],** *Tygodnik Ilustrowany,* **new series 106 (1870), pp. 13-14; 107, pp. 32-34; 108, pp. 42-43.**

It has long been a tradition for biographers to delve with curiosity into the private secrets of their subject, sometimes in a spirit of reverence, sometimes of tactlessness. Undeniably, the knowledge of what I might call a man's personal history may cast an important light on his works. This particularly applies to those master wordsmiths who recast the painful or merry chronicle of their feelings into inspired texts. But when an artist expresses himself in music, perhaps it is less important to know the circumstances that triggered a specific inspiration. The language of music is so mysterious as to frustrate the efforts of even the most proficient analysts. In the case of Chopin, his death happened so recently, with so many surviving friends and acquaintances, that the whole truth is perhaps impossible to know or, if known, to be made known to the public. For the moment at least, certain gaps must remain in the story of his life. However, we do not believe that such gaps are an obstacle to our

---

69 The pianist was Aleksander Chodecki.

knowledge and appreciation of his music. He has bequeathed his immortal works to us like a unique seal of individuality; they contain what we feel is the complex but lucid mystery of his spirit.

Chopin's works had the power to make sing the gold-stringed harp of Lilla of the Veneti,[70] and its sounds, once awakened, will continue to reverberate and spread ever further. He struck that mysterious tuning fork, and a mighty echo replied to his magic touch. Other masters in his time touched the same harp, but none was able to express the spirit of the time with comparable excellence. The so-called Romantic period was nothing but an anti-Hellenic or anti-Classical Renaissance; anything that smacked of convention was discarded, and the bards tapped the pristine spring of folk inspiration as a source of new strength, and of new life. We must not deny Chopin this substantive priority; indeed, we must treat it as paramount, the purest pearl in his crown; but our maestro also deserves credit for other illustrious contributions to artistic form; he found the true pulse of homely life and expressed it with perfect and ideal beauty. His highly noble and aesthetic nature did not merely produce wonderful ideas, but also endowed them with uncommon refinement. Later, we shall expound on this judgement and justify it with analyses of some of his works.

Drawing comparisons between geniuses is a dangerous exercise that easily leads to paradox, but we have often compared the ideas of Chopin with those of [Juliusz Słowacki], author of *Lilla Weneda*. The two were born in the same year, and the paths of their lives converged in that they both loved the same woman, though not at the same time; they even died within a short time of each other. And are there not affinities to be found between Chopin's caressing nocturnes and Słowacki's poem "W Szwajcarii" [In Switzerland]?

In his article "The Youth of Fryderyk Chopin", Mr. Maurycy Karasowski felt it necessary to defend our maestro from allegations of "effeminacy". Granted, it is a harsh word, and perhaps it was used unadvisedly; however, there is no denying that, despite the great energy of some of his works, the quality of "feminine softness" does indeed predominate in his music, and the life Chopin lived abroad may indeed have been conducive to a heightened state of nervous excitement. For all the respect and reverence I have for Chopin as a great genius and the composer of many master-

---

70 A literary reference to the 1840 play *Lilla Weneda* [Lilla of the Veneti] by Juliusz Słowacki, in which the Veneti (an ancient people inhabiting today's Poland) are routed by invading Slavs. Only the sound of their royal harp can save the Veneti in their desperate predicament, but the magic instrument is captured by the invaders. The harp is generally interpreted as a symbol of inspirational patriotic poetry [translator's note].

pieces, I cannot deny that his mature years did not quite live up to the promise of his younger days. We must not forget that he had bidden farewell to Warsaw at the age of twenty by performing his two concertos in E minor and F minor, and had already composed a sonata (Op. 4), a *Krakowiak* (Op. 14), a *Fantasia* (Op. 13), his variations on a theme from *Don Giovanni* (Op. 2), his wonderful mazurkas, nocturnes and etudes; that some of those early pieces were in no way inferior to what would come later and can still be treated on a par with his very best works.

What numerous treasures his genius had yielded by that time! Granted, their form was conventional, in the mould of Hummel – but how rich and inexhaustible the store of his inspiration! The freshness and vivacity of that first solo in the concerto in F minor, a special favourite with the composer himself! His piano recitative – how strange and original the idea, and how perfect the execution!

True, the orchestration in both concertos is inadequate,[71] and the trio, for all its wonderful passages, seems to show little talent for instrumentation; but those were easily forgivable faults in a composer so young. Possibly, Chopin would have composed true masterpieces for the orchestra had he not neglected that medium so completely.

But let us now move on to details of a strictly biographical nature [...].

Although [...] the works of Hummel and Field exerted a certain influence on Chopin's early pieces, his artistic moves were too daring even then to remain unchallenged by the critical luminaries of the day. The decision to construct the second theme in his Concerto in the tonic major rather than the dominant already bordered on impudence; let alone his use of a krakowiak and a mazurka in the finales of the two concertos, which could not but cause offense to the snuff-taking classicist fogeys of the German school. Indeed, amidst the more general interest of inquiring minds in folk song as a source for the sterling gold of inspiration, that young and resolute genius used his unique intuition to guess that the often coarse rhythms of our folk dances contained some kind of ideal prototype which, if developed, would place those rhythms on a par with the most celebrated masterpieces of German music. Thoroughly engrossed in his mission, he came up with a new kind of miniature tone poem he called the mazurka. Those mazurkas were not intended as pieces for dancing, although they fully preserved the character and the rhythms of their original

---

71 The late Berlioz summed up the orchestration of Chopin's concertos thus: "In a *tutti* passage one cannot hear a thing, and would most like to shout to the orchestra: 'Just start playing, God damn it!' And when they are accompanying the pianist they do nothing but get in his way. One almost wishes to cry: 'Be silent, you blockheads, and stop getting in the way!'" [original footnote].

models. He composed his earliest ones even before he left Warsaw, and he later did the same to polonaises by enhancing their rhythmic aspects and embroidering on this rhythmic canvas the most wonderful musical poems. And though today we may be familiar with these delightful dance pieces, many must have found it offensive at the time that Chopin wrote dances that were plaintive, melancholy and not actually intended for dancing. [...]

But the great maestro had difficulty finding his stride in a foreign and unfamiliar place. Despite the assistance provided by Polish families, he found it difficult in his early years in Paris to stand out from the multitude of other virtuosi. [...]

Dispirited [...] by his lack of success, Chopin considered moving to America. Apparently, those virtuosi who had grown weary of being applauded or ignored in Europe were eyeing America as a land of Canaan filled with ripening, golden grapes of hope. In the event, the entreaties of his family luckily persuaded him to forsake the design, the consequences of which could have been quite pernicious for the development of his genius.

At this time, the artist's fortune changed; his fame became more firmly established; there came enthusiastic invitations to the best houses and requests for lessons, the publishers enquired after his works, and with the restoration of his good fortunes his good humour and cheerful disposition returned.

For Chopin, like all true artists, was full of verve and vitality, qualities which actually bordered on empty frivolity when he was giving a free rein to gaiety. He had a particular knack for imitating the facial expressions, indeed the very countenances, of the people he wished to impersonate. On occasion, when he had long held a circle of close friends in thrall, playing and improvising, suddenly he came up with some high jinks of his own devising, and the surprised audience watched him transform into a Jewish pedlar or a travelling Englishwoman. Sometimes he would sit down at the piano, ruffle his hair in the manner of Liszt and imitate Liszt's playing style; or else he would sit straight as a ramrod and play in the stiff manner of the starched Thalberg.

Encouraged by success, Chopin ventured [...] to give a concert. It was already the year 1834. He gave the concert in the Italian Theatre before an audience made up of experts and people of cultivated tastes; and with a first-rate orchestra led by the famous Habeneck. And yet, the Concerto in E minor failed to produce the favourable impression he had hoped for. What could have been the reason? I posed this question to many of Chopin's friends and admirers whom I met in Paris, and I received different answers. One answer struck me in particular: apparently, Chopin's free and independent playing style made it difficult for him to blend seamlessly with an orchestral accompaniment. It may be that his frequent *tempo rubato* deprived his performance of that firmness that any orchestral or collective (non-solo) piece requires.

In fact, Chopin seemed to find the very idea of a concert unpleasant, since it went against the grain of his poetic manner of playing. Accustomed to losing himself in reverie, he was petrified by the sight of so many unfamiliar faces studying him with bland curiosity; for that reason, he refused flatly to perform in public, with very few exceptions.

In his book on Chopin, which contains many beautiful and heartfelt passages, despite the overall declamatory form, F. Liszt offers quite a perceptive diagnosis of Chopin's character in this respect. Apparently, Chopin had a strong sense of his own superiority, and despite the success his delightful performances enjoyed in the salons, he must have hankered after the approbation of larger audiences so that his fame could spread to wider circles. Discouraged by his several early failures he resolved to spare himself the pain, and concealed his injured *amour propre* under the mask of jokes and gaiety. But he understood that his playing style was deficient in terms of that brilliance of tone that captures a crowd. As he put it in conversation with Liszt, "Even if you fail to charm your audiences you can still deafen them. But what can I do?"

Chopin's talent developed most freely in contexts where the public had no need for deafening noise and understood every flight of the maestro's fancy, instantly grasping every idea, no matter how ethereal. And since only women and poets know how to listen in that way, it was their company that our virtuoso preferred. Liszt, Mme Sand and Heine have all described those delightful moments spent in Chopin's dimly-lit living room, when the maestro, shrouded in fantastical shadows, would give free rein to his fantasias and improvisations, and every listener perceived his music differently. [...]

That was how most of his dreamy nocturnes were composed, offering perhaps the most faithful reflection of the master's poetic soul. Even though he had composed some of them before leaving Warsaw, they mostly have that refined character of salon pieces, though without sacrificing their lofty exaltation and indeed their sometimes terrifying drama. One of them, in G minor (Op. 37), sounds like nostalgia incarnate, a cry of longing for one's family. Another nocturne (in F minor) sheds real tears of pain and anguish in its first theme; the passionate and forceful middle section vainly seeks to stir the piece from its torpor, but the pain and anguish return with ghastly force, and the nocturne dissolves into tears and nostalgia. Perhaps the most poetic are those two nocturnes which Chopin dedicated to Countess d'Apponyi. With the first nocturne for an accompaniment, one might easily pen the most poetic of poems.

It makes you think of wandering around the deserted Piazza San Marco in Venice on a quiet, moonlit night; next to you, the sea waves swell and subside silently, and a light breeze carries some fantastical sounds from afar, like the echo of an otherworldly melody. Suddenly, the air is filled with tension – you hear a growing din of mad, wild voices; masked men burst onto the scene, fighting; after a short skirmish one of them falls to the ground with a muffled groan; his companions lift the dead body and toss it into the deep sea. Then everything disappears like a recollected nightmare, and one cannot be sure if those were living men or just apparitions; as before, the calm sea laps against the granite steps, and a melancholy love song can be heard in the distance.

I have always associated the second nocturne (in D flat major), with its rich plume of diamond cascades and transparent rainbows, with Słowacki's poem "W Szwajcarii". For all we know, those two works, which are connected by such a spiritual affinity, may have been inspired by the same emotion.[72]

Chopin's last two nocturnes (Op. 62) bear the mark of that forced and painful creative effort that characterises Chopin's late pieces. Chopin had always been a meticulous composer who paid a great deal of attention to details. Given his irritability and weariness late in life, the painstaking approach became almost pathological, as the unhappy artist would spend days on end working on a single passage; dissatisfied with every new idea, he would impatiently crumple and discard his quill; tired out, in the end he would often return to his original idea, as Mme Sand reported.

Pieces like the Berceuse pose a considerable difficulty to performers, and especially to those who want to adhere to the composer's original idea; in Chopin's own performance, the bass rhythm was often regular and steady, whereas the right hand took playful liberties with the pulse of the piece, now edging closer to the bass, now distancing itself. Chopin often marked this unique playing style as "tempo rubato", leaving the interpretation to the performer's own discernment, as Liszt tells us. This gave his playing style a dreamy and poetic quality, the contours blurring and disappearing in the kind of transparent mist one sometimes sees in paintings by Delacroix. As I listened to Chopin's pupils in Paris – Princess M.C.,[73] Mme Dubris,[74]

---

72 This comparison is adopted by Hoesick in his monograph about Chopin [editor's note].

73 Marcelina Czartoryska, née Radziwiłł. Kleczyński did not identify her by name, as the princess expressly disapproved of any references being made to her person in the press.

74 The person Kleczyński seems to have in mind is Mme Dubois, i.e. Camille O'Meara (Dubois).

the late Mrs. Bohdanowa Zaleska [75]– I admired those hesitant, poetic rhythms that cloaked the main lines of a piece like a light flowing robe. Sometimes, this kind of rhythm was even used to delightful effect in the mazurkas, as in the case of the Mazurka No. 4 in that set, which was dedicated to Mme Lina Freppa. [...]

One should also mention his larger works, which were becoming increasingly popular at the time.

The fire-laced, delightfully poetic first Scherzo (Op. 20, first published by Schlesinger in Paris). The first two chords sound like a crack of thunder tearing the skies apart before the piece erupts like volcanic lava and rages vehemently for a long time before it settles down in a dreamy reverie, where the melody seems to emerge from under the ground. Of Chopin's four scherzos, the first is the most beautiful, along with the third (B flat minor) [sic], his most perfectly consummate piece of music, to which I shall return. Why Chopin gave such an unassuming, almost frivolous title to those passionate and profound works I have never been able to establish.

A similar originality and independence of creative thought can be discerned in Chopin's ballades. The first, in G minor, may not be honed to the same standard of perfection in every movement, but as a whole it is an important and striking piece. The second (Op. 38) is dedicated to Schumann. In a letter to Heinrich Dorn dated 16 September 1836, Schuman wrote: "Chopin has dedicated his new ballade to me. I consider it one of his most brilliant works; I even told him it was my favourite. He thought for a long while and replied with some emphasis: 'I am very pleased to hear it, for I think so myself'."

If I may be excused for expressing a personal preference, I have always been particularly drawn to his third ballade, in A flat major. It is the most honed and polished of his ballades; it harmonises with its title like no other. The opening passages sound like the introduction to a story; one seems to hear someone say: "Listen to this curious and terrible story". And that alluring, weaving song – does it not sound like the words of the maiden in "Świteź": "Come hither, young lad"?[76] The ending, with waves and currents whispering in the bass register as if narrating the terrible secret they have engulfed; does that not sound like the ballads of Mickiewicz? Is not Chopin's third ballade a sister to such ballads as "Świteź", "Świtezianka", "Rybka" and "Lenore"?[77]

---

75 Zofia Rosengardt-Zaleska, wife of Chopin's friend Bohdan Zaleski [editor's note].

76 Kleczyński's quotation is misattributed: the words are an inaccurate quotation from Adam Mickiewicz's ballad "Świtezianka", whereas the rest of his description refers to another ballad by Mickiewicz, "Świteź".

77 The titles of three ballads by Adam Mickiewicz and one ("Lenore") by Gottfried August Bürger.

I do not like the fourth ballade quite as much. It was probably composed in a period when Chopin found composition difficult, and consequently simplicity gives way to elaborate combinations.

Dating from the same period is the first *Grande Polonaise* for the piano and orchestra (Op. 22). This was not actually Chopin's first polonaise per se; in addition to the lesser pieces included in the posthumous edition, Chopin had composed a polonaise for the piano and cello in Vienna, which he dedicated to [Joseph] Merk.

The *Grande Polonaise* is excellent, a concert piece of incomparable elegance. However, his later polonaises would draw on the national spirit to a much greater extent. They alternated between such qualities as mournfulness, energy, passion and tender reverie, with the polonaise rhythms faithfully sustained throughout. The polonaise in A is the most brisk, almost dance-like; reportedly, Liszt often performed it in his concerts. [...]

Among Chopin's beautiful polonaises, none is as beautiful as his celebrated Polonaise in A flat major, which is as vast and majestic as it is thrilling. When played in its appropriate slow tempo, the trio, with the persistently recurring octave phrase (which is so often abused by the local virtuosi, who exploit it for false effects), represents the image of a knightly cavalcade approaching in solemn procession. What is the meaning of the ensuing wistful idyll? How can one explain those caressing passages that seem like so many dreamy echoes reverberating among trees? We might say that the knights have momentarily abandoned their military *hauteur* and are now listening to the soft babbling of the streams and to sweet words whispered more softly still between the rows of garden trees before they return to the stately rooms amid the sound of trumpets.

The last polonaise, which bears the title of a fantasia, bears the mark of morbidity in its compositional style. Some persons privy to the details of Chopin's life have told us about the mystical or allegorical meaning of its various passages; the interpretation commands respect for the beauty and nobility of the concept, but I must confess that I remain unconvinced that the piece is lucid or indeed intelligible overall. [...]

Let me now return [...] yet again to a comment I made in the beginning concerning Chopin's characteristic softness. Softness does not always preclude energy or passion, but the maestro had a way of smoothing out the sharper edges, as it were. The naturalists tell us that all of God's works have that blunted, smooth quality about them. Apparently, our Chopin had intuited that law of nature and applied it in the field of art. There are no rough contours to his music, even where it represents the savage and frenzied transports of the soul in his most impassioned works, such as the

Scherzo in B flat minor. Grace and pleasing softness reign supreme amid the throes of passion.

This dignified manner and aristocratic grace, which was so apparent in Chopin's personality, taste and general disposition, was the guide that protected him even at the time of greatest abandon from overstepping that line that "separates beauty from triviality". We believe that this characteristic, which was quite unique to Chopin among composers (not excepting even Schumann), should be emphasised in music history as a fact of major significance. Chopin never lost the angelic, Raphael-like purity of design, for everything about him was design and melody. Although he was proficient in the rules of the basso continuo, one cannot say that he ever used them voluntarily; indeed, on occasion he broke those rules with supreme freedom (viz. the succession of fifths in the Mazurka in C sharp minor, Op. 30), and obeyed only the song of inspiration that rang in his soul. None of his most beautiful or rare harmonic combinations showed any sign that they were heeding a set of rules: everything was the fruit of inspiration. [...]

We would wish for our readers to examine our argument impartially. At the beginning we said that Chopin's genius did not live up to its early promise. This is not meant to diminish the actual merit of the maestro, but it seems to us that had it not been for his bland existence in the salons, Chopin would not have developed that excessive nervous excitation; had it not been for the excited state of his nerves, perhaps he would have given us more works – strong, robust and generously designed – and perhaps his final works would not have succumbed to that somewhat diseased and morbid manner. [...]

We should supplement our cursory discussion of his works with the comment that where Chopin's genius engaged in formal play, he was more successful in those pieces containing a romantic content. The outcome was less felicitous in the classical forms, such as his three sonatas, the piano trio and the sonata for cello and piano. For all their delightful ideas, the execution of those pieces is at times excessively cumbersome and convoluted. [...]

[Wodziński, 1870] [**Antoni**] **Wodziński, "Kilka drobnych szczegółów z życia Fryderyka Chopina" (Some minor details from Fryderyk Chopin's life),** *Kłosy,* **249 (1870), p. 214.**

[...] There were in Chopin two conflicting dispositions – one of sadness, and one of gaiety; at times, the gaiety was so frivolous and infantile that anyone who later saw him in another of his fits of apathetic sorrow would have found it difficult to believe that two such contradictory currents could have converged in such a lovable and worthy human being.

His heart was tender like wax, one goddess or another always dwelling therein. [...]

[Józef Sikorski (?), 1871] **"Wiadomości literackie, artystyczne i naukowe"** [**News literary, artistic and scientific**], *Gazeta Polska,* **3 January 1871.**

Intelligence is not the sole factor [...] in the processes of artistic creation and performance; feeling is at least as important. Performers sometimes disregard this and abandon feeling for fear of appearing mawkish. We are of the opinion that we witnessed this situation at work in yesterday's performance of Chopin's nocturne. Is it possible that positivism has infiltrated piano music?[78]

[Wiślicki, 1872] **Władysław Wiślicki, "Stanisław Moniuszko", *Kłosy,* 364 (1872), p. 414.**

Many have composed dumkas, mazurkas, krakowiaks and polonaises; yet for all their talent, their pieces never ventured beyond the generic conventions and remained mere dumkas, mazurkas or polonaises. With works by Chopin or Moniuszko we cannot but feel that these two are national Slavic composers regardless of the genre in question, be it a concerto, a nocturne, a song, an opera or a sacred piece.

[Kleczyński, 1875] **Jan Kleczyński, "Ze świata muzycznego" [From the musical world], *Tygodnik Ilustrowany,* second series 378 (1875), p. 202.**

For his debut performance, P. Jelonkowski chose Chopin's Sonata in B flat minor, which is a thankless piece though not without some good qualities. In the first allegro, his adroit nuances and noble composure commanded considerable interest; the first theme of the scherzo was played somewhat too fast. One had the impression that the famous funeral march was too frigid; this piece must be played with a tearful soul. As everyone knows, the march is followed by a bizarre finale, an etude of sorts that Chopin flatly refused to change despite his friends' earnest entreaties.

---

78 From a review of a concert given by Aleksander Zarzycki.

That almost colourless passage continues to be an insoluble riddle to this day, unless one accepts Chopin's jocular explanation that it represents bored mourners hurrying back home.

[Kleczyński, 1878] **Jan Kleczyński, "Fryderyk Szopen i nowsza krytyka niemiecka" [Fryderyk Chopin and recent German criticism], *Bluszcz*, 1878/5, pp. 33-34.**

"His life was all suffering, and suffering was all his life". This is how a German musician, I. Schucht, concludes his study on Chopin's works (see *Neue Zeitschrift für Musik*, nos. 33, 34, 35, 36, 49, 50, 51, 52). At long last, we find in that interesting and well-written study a glimpse of that fairness towards our maestro that is newly stirring to life in Germany. In the wake of the detestable entry regrettably included in Mendel's new encyclopaedic dictionary,[79] the voice of Schucht brings true solace. In our brief discussion of the different phases of foreign Chopin criticism we must admit that Schucht's article, though not as eloquent as the biography of Chopin written by Liszt, is nonetheless important: it is a poised but heated rebuttal of detracting voices, and it places Chopin firmly among the Classics.

[...] the famous succession of fifths and sevenths in Chopin's Mazurka, Op. 30 No. 4 deserves to go down in music history, despite the loud dissenting voices of some (including even Messrs. Schucht and Schumann).

"His life was all suffering, and suffering was all his life". To many, these words encapsulate everything about Chopin and hold the key both to the allure of his works and to the certain negative quality that they possess, which could be indentified as their excessively monotonous, elegiac mood. Given the [Slavic] predilection for a somewhat sorrowful outlook, predating the Christian era, we must hold such a maestro dearest in our esteem, for his songs are like echoes of our souls, echoes that may occasionally reverberate with the sound of the trumpets of war, but more often carry the broad tones of idyllic songs, some serene and some sorrowful. As one of our philosophers has put it, "Every great idea has something wistful about it". If I am not mistaken, the words are [Karol] Libelt's. Applied to our native disposition at least, they are not at all paradoxical.

---

79 *Eine Encyklopädie der gesammten musikalischen Wissenschaften für Gebildete aller Stände*, ed. Hermann Mendel, Berlin, Mendel, 1870-1879.

The charge of excessive Polishness, of being "zu polnisch", which Schumann occasionally levelled against Chopin's works, has now reappeared in Herr Schucht's report.[80] In his analysis of Chopin's early works he notes the symptoms of their "supremely Slavic type", [...] that is to say "a fearful, trembling (Hangen und Bangen) and desperate clinging to a certain main idea, an inability to break free from a favourite image or concept, a kind of gyration within the narrow confines of the magic circle of one's dreams". Hence the difficulty inherent in performing those passages in Chopin's music where a single unchanged idea is repeated several times, argues Schucht (we mostly see such repetition in the mazurkas (e.g. Op. 30 No. 2, Op. 33 No. 2), and it is indeed a quality that characterises our people, with our tendency to ruminate on a single idea, even amid dancing and merriment).

[Kleczyński, 1879] **Jan Kleczyński, *O wykonywaniu dzieł Szopena. Trzy odczyty wypowiedziane w Resursie Obywatelskiej w Warszawie w d. 11, 15 i 17 marca 1879 r.* [On performing Chopin's works. Three talks given at the Citizens' Club in Warsaw on the 11th, 15th and 17th of March, 1879], Warsaw, J. Sikorski, 1879.**[81]

[...] As we have pointed out, those two elements – Slavic plaintiveness and French vivacity – converged to forge Chopin's spiritual essence. In his youth, in particular the vivacity presumably prevailed over the sorrow. The ease with which he was able to compose must have given him great satisfaction and joy, of the kind we usually see in young composers blessed with copious ideas. [...]

If a minor genre, such as the nocturne, could contain the purest pearls of poetry, then the larger and more finished ballades must surely be considered Chopin's most valuable music. Completely original and daring, their form follows no model; the maestro follows the dictates of his inspiration freely, repeating and reworking themes at will, and interweaving them with delightful passages with an impeccable logic and a respect for the connotations of the title "ballade". Chopin based the idea and the character of the pieces on the ballads by Mickiewicz. They are in fact dramatic

---

80 Kleczyński refers here to Johann Schucht's monograph *Friedrich Chopin und seine Werke*, Leipzig 1879 [editor's note].

81 Jan Kleczyński, *O wykonywaniu dzieł Chopina*, Warsaw 1879; Eng. tr. as Jean Kleczynski, *How to play Chopin. The works of Frederic Chopin and their proper interpretation*, tr. Alfred Whittingham, London, Reeves, 1896 [editor's note].

narratives full of variety and with a Romantic character. What matters most to us is that the ballades, especially the first three, contain music that is remarkably *healthy* and *robust*. The overall design is bold and lucid, the execution remarkably forceful. Some of the images they present may be dark, but they are *objective*, like those presented in plays or novels; in other words, the despair and sorrow fill the souls of the *characters* without penetrating the author's spirit. It must have been at a time when Chopin was composing such robust pieces that a friend of his [Antoni Orłowski] wrote (in 1834): "Chopin is hale and hearty; he turns French women's heads, and makes French men jealous. He is fashionable now, and the world will presently see gloves à la Chopin". I have expanded somewhat on this more robust aspect of Chopin's music mainly because it seems to have been somewhat overlooked by scholars (excepting Karasowski). His frail and ethereal frame, the grace and softness of his most popular works, finally his well-publicised illness and his anguish-filled final years have led many to believe that he had always been an irritable weakling; regrettably, many of his performers have consequently affected an air of languid listlessness and pretentious mannerism that goes against the spirit of his works. The wonderful poetry of his pieces, that melancholia that so touches our hearts, has proved detrimental to his reputation with indifferent listeners. And who is indifferent, if not his foreign audiences? Faced with so much nervous delicacy, they concluded that he was morbid (*un talent de chambre de malade*, as Field put it), and by placing undue emphasis on his weaker aspects or on those pieces which had been composed in exceptional states of mind they condemned his entire *oeuvre* as unsettling. Unfortunately, this opinion is shared even by some in Poland, and I am only debunking it here because I believe it leads to a morbid manner of performance. Many a boarding-school young lady playing Chopin with so-called *feeling* has no idea that his works might contain wholesome food for the spirit which ought not to be adulterated.[82] There are certain aspects of Chopin's music that might be considered negative were it not for the fact that to some degree they tend to contribute to the positive aspects. To an extent, Chopin frittered away some of his genius in the salons of Paris, and did not compose as many large pieces as one might have hoped on the basis of his early work, given the immeasurable riches of his nature [...].

---

82 Such false feeling has mostly the following characteristics: 1 – an excessive treatment of rubato passages that fails to observe the strictures of the stave; 2 – what I might call inverted expressiveness, i.e. emphasising those notes which ought to be weak and vice versa; 3 – a sentimental anticipation of the bass, which always precedes the upper part of the scale instead of being struck simultaneously, etc. [original footnote].

This is evident in the letter of Orłowski[83] quoted above: "He is mostly fine, the occasional pang of nostalgia for the home country excepted". There must have been other pangs of sorrow, too, such as the feeling of *Weltschmerz* that seems to afflict all deep souls regardless of historical period. It is at such times, when he reveals the suffering aspect of his nature and voices the soft plaints of an anguished spirit, that one finds him at his most engaging: those nocturnes in F minor, G minor, that etude in C sharp minor, the waltz in A minor have all won him much popularity among feeling hearts, particularly female ones. As someone has said, Chopin's music is "a complaint endowed with charm", *c'est une plainte qui a du charme.*

However, those who have been scouring Chopin's preludes for signs of alleged serious nervous distraction and loss of the will to live, which he supposedly experienced when composing them, have gone too far. We are faced here with a familiar phenomenon that can be observed in many other masters. Haydn knew little domestic happiness, and Beethoven was a misanthrope who shunned people; and yet all of Haydn's pieces strike a merry and frolicsome tone, and one would would look in vain among Beethoven's astonishingly serene and majestic works for those trivial nuisances of his troubled bachelor's life. Why? Because a man's daily goings-on are different from the times when he is touched by the ray of divine inspiration. Then, the joy that creative work brings makes him indifferent to this world and fills his soul with the blessings of immortality.

This is particularly applicable to Chopin, who was known for his reluctance to reveal his innermost feelings to the world. Similarly, his plaintive music rarely, if ever, actually demeans itself by laying bare the anguish of his soul.

Likewise, it is a rare prelude that contains that despairing aspect, and some of those that do date back to earlier periods. For instance, none of the preludes, except perhaps the Prelude in A minor (No. 2), palpably evinces any hint of nervous fragility, and yet Tarnowski gives a much earlier date of composition for that particular piece. For all the fanciful despair-laden interpretations one might indulge in, no other prelude actually shows signs of spiritual decline or loses its aesthetic beauty.

There is an account in Mme Sand's memoirs, one that has been recounted many times over, of how Chopin was composing one of his preludes during a long bout of rain, racked by anxiety for his dear ones far away, and fearing that they were dead. The first thing to say is that despite the widespread legend that the prelude in question was the Prelude in B minor (No. 6), the concept had not actually been developed

83 Antoni Orłowski, Chopin's colleague from the Main School of Music in Warsaw.

in its full magnificence until the Prelude in D flat major (No. 15), compared with which the Prelude in B minor is at best a preliminary sketch.

The background image in this piece is formed by the regular patter of raindrops, which lull the soul into a melancholy torpor; above the rainfall and the tearful natural world there floats a plaintive, sorrowful song; the middle section (in C sharp minor), which rises gradually from the mysterious, gloomy depths of the bass to mount a massive crescendo, paints a remarkably similar picture of a sense of inward terror provoked by black thoughts and agitated imagination. And yet, how beautiful is that piece, how complete, how rounded in artistic terms; in short, how very remote it seems from anything negative. Here, as in the other pieces, the aesthetic idea takes priority over the form to guide the spirit and prohibit any form of offensive expression.

And we have said nothing about the other preludes, some of them so free and light-humoured (E flat major No. 19, B major No. 21, F major No. 23, etc.); or about the last one, so potent, so strong and robust, ending in what seems like the firing of three cannons.

One piece that on the face of it lays bare an ocean of despair is the famous *Marche funèbre*. The unrelenting tolling of the bell strikes terror in the soul, and floating above it there is a melody so sad as to make the heart break – but who will dare to describe the piece as morbid? Anyone who has ever been in the situation so vividly represented by that music will surely understand how much grandeur and majesty is encompassed in that terrible, groaning pain. Besides, there is hope in the piece, too, as the middle section, with its cantilena in D flat major, makes abundantly clear.

Moving on to Chopin's most important pieces, the mazurkas, we hear again the charge that they are supposedly too doleful and melancholy. More arguments of the same kind can refute that charge.

In itself, a melancholy disposition is not a weakness, and neither is a delicate nature; a Slav and a Pole on his mother's side, Chopin had much of that native ache, and one can hardly consider it a fault that it mostly made itself felt in the mazurkas. Our people enjoy dancing to a mournful tune; the dancing may often be long and repetitive, but it is so beautiful and fitting, the melodies are redolent of so much tender kind-heartedness, they carry so much affection for people as brethren! It is a fault of ours that we love too much; and although it is a weakness, it encompasses an element that is highly ethical and Christian; we ought to bless those poets and maestros who have plucked it, as it were, from our very hearts, and revealed it to the world.

Finally, we could justifiably censure Chopin for being reprehensibly monotonous in his reliance on folk motifs if he had concentrated on nothing but the doleful tones, forgetting the brisk vigour (*dziarskość*) so characteristic of our nation. That quality, which has no equivalent descriptive term in other languages, is the most distinctive and elusive of our characteristics. The term combines life, strength and elegance with chivalric perseverance. Looking at that Polish alacrity, a foreigner would surely conclude that they must be a very kind-hearted people who dance like that; there is an exceptional abundance of *vigour* and *humour* to be found in many mazurkas [...].

Dogged by misfortune, Chopin did not lose heart. His *Allegro de concert,* Op. 46 is a late piece that was intended to become a fully-fledged concerto with several movements. A cheerful, unrestrained mood dominates the work, and in places it bears quite a distinct resemblance to passages from the introduction to the *Fantasia on Polish Airs,* Op. 13. [...] Also composed at that time was the Fantasia in F minor, one of his most beautiful works; and the celebrated "Heroic" Polonaise, Op. 53, was reportedly written while Chopin was sojourning in the country at Nohant; it is a piece that will stand out until the end of time as the most supreme embodiment of power and manly resolution [...]. Except that the creative effort was all the more difficult now, given the illness that was wrecking Chopin's frame, not to mention his delicate nervous constitution and all the other circumstances mentioned above. [...]

Indeed, those pieces which date from that period [of supposed decline] – not to mention others, such as the Berceuse, the Sonata in B minor and the Barcarolle – evince the familiar enlightened and self-assured genius. No decline of spirit is apparent (if we can speak of decline at all in the case of so fine a spirit) until possibly the period of the impending catastrophic break-up with Mme Sand and the ensuing short spell preceding his demise. In the last nocturnes and the cello sonata his thoughts do indeed take on an unwonted and excessive sense of confusion and heaviness; and his last mazurka, scrawled indistinctly by his weakened hand as he was lying on his sickbed, does indeed give the impression of utter weariness.

And yet even in that painful period, his spirit blossomed with hope and strength in a piece that may appear convoluted and deficient in grace, but which nonetheless contains a strikingly *mighty and triumphal idea*: the Polonaise-Fantasia, Op. 61. In that swansong of a great and suffering soul, we sense a spirited protest against the wasting illness, against death and decline; and we recognise the familiar Chopin, brimming with passion and faith. [...]

Perhaps music does not express negative states of the soul quite as clearly as poetry does, but are there not eloquent examples of negative influence that crushed or dimmed the ideal in the music of the other masters of our new age? Do we no longer notice in Schumann the excesses of excited imagination or the occasionally irritating phantasms?[84] And conversely, can we not discern in today's *realist* school[85] that their faith in the ideal has expired and is replaced by doubt and even sensuality? Confronted with such symptoms in Chopin, we would have to concede that his creative effort was hampered by negative influence; but having disproved it (several isolated instances are insufficient to mount a justified charge), the charge should collapse – and I believe it does. [...]

[Kleczyński, 1880] **Jan Kleczyński, "Ostatnie chwile Chopina" [Chopin's final moments],** *Echo Muzyczne,* **20 (1880), p. 158.**

[...] As a man, Chopin was the very model of nobility, poetry and grace. His deeply feeling heart needed much tenderness and care. When he failed to find that in people he looked to God, and that was the logical cause of his heartfelt religiosity; instilled into him in his childhood years, religion became a natural need, and although it occasionally waned over his lifetime, it came back when he was on his deathbed to wrap his final moments in true consolation. [...]

[Górski, 1880] **Władysław Górski, "Ze świata muzycznego" [From the musical world],** *Tygodnik Ilustrowany,* **third series 216 (1880), p. 102.**

[...] Rubinstein[86] made a colossal impression with Chopin's funeral march, though he has been accused of breaking from the tradition and disregarding the composer's original performance markings.

Well now, gentlemen! Not so long ago, Miss Krebs,[87] a fine artist though she is, gave an impeccably traditional performance, but her march was not merely funereal, it was lifeless. The very first requirement for a performer is to display true feeling,

---

84 Technically speaking, such symptoms are apparent in the excessive use of chromatic or enharmonic transitions and dissonances, and in the fact that the dissonances are often played *piano,* a practice which grates on the nerves and contravenes the established rules of performance [original footnote].

85 Kleczyński means Wagner and his imitators.

86 Anton Rubinstein.

87 Mary Krebs-Brenning.

and to breathe life into a piece. For that reason, absolute objectivity is only possible to a degree. Rubinstein could not but pour into that march his own emotions, which cannot be the same as Chopin's. There will be differences between two leaves growing on the same branch, let alone between two people's emotions. [...]

[Skrodzki, 1882] **Wielisław [Eugeniusz Skrodzki], "Kilka wspomnień o Szopenie" [Several memories of Chopin],** *Bluszcz,* **1882/32, p. 249; 1882/36, pp. 281-282.**

Every great man owes much of his greatness to his mother [...].[88]

Mrs. Chopin, who was loved and respected by all those who knew her, was the kind of industrious, provident and thrifty Polish lady who, by making small economies, lays the foundations for prosperity in old age but never succumbs to avarice or takes advantage of another [...]

Throughout his life, Chopin was [...] a man of a religious disposition. He may have owed this to his mother's devoutness; I remember how she would take him, meek and contrite, to confession; in the period when no obligatory masses were said at the Church of the Sisters of the Visitation[89] she would take him to the Carmelite church on Krakowskie Przedmieście Street, where he kneeled and prayed from a prayer book in front of her pew, from which she kept a watchful maternal eye on the boy. [...]

He was a remarkably kind and cultured man, with none of the idiosyncrasies so frequent in men of greatness. Quick-witted, lively and cheerful, he was always the soul of a party. He would play piano for four hands with my aunt[90] or improvise for hours; when she played, he turned the pages for her and readied her stool for the performance, whispering amused comments to her when she made a mistake. From the piano, he ran to albums lying on the table; he wrote, composed tolerable verse, and frequently drew or painted attractive miniatures. [...]

If they are to make a lasting impression on the listeners, Chopin's pieces have one major defect, which is that some of them, being entirely unique, all but demand

---

88 This sentence appears at a later point in the original text. I have taken the liberty of moving it to the foreground as a kind of motto.

89 Located next to the campus of Warsaw University, before the November Uprising it was the university church.

90 This was Ludwika Dupont, wife of Adolf Cichowski, who was the brother of Wielisław Skrodzki's mother. Ludwika Cichowska(Dupont) was friendly with Chopin's sisters [editor's note].

Chopin's spirit to sit at the piano during the performance. This is why we only appreciate the performances of his favourite female pupils who had managed to become immersed in the spirit of his performance, or at least had heard him play.

Badly performed, Chopin's works become burlesque pieces completely incomprehensible to cosmopolitan tastes. As a result, it is entirely possible that the Offenbachiads or the chaotic innovative pieces of Wagner will come to supplant Chopin's fame – why shouldn't they?

[Górski, 1883] **Władysław Górski, "Ze świata muzycznego"**
[From the musical world], *Tygodnik Ilustrowany*, **fourth series 6 (1883), p. 95.**

It is disagreeable to read what our Germanic neighbours have to say about our prehistory, about how we were apparently unable to build so much as a mud hut, or fashion a proper clay pot (see Klemm,[91] *Handbuch der germanischen Altertumskunde*, p. XIII ff.); and it is more disagreeable still to see that their views on art history mostly leave out any references to our undeniable achievements.

Recently, I have been reading one of their most recent music histories (*Geschichte der Musik*, Tübingen 1880[92]), whose author, Dr Köstlin, painstakingly covers every obscure German organist from the centuries past but never deigns to mention the names of such Polish composers as [Mikołaj] Gomółka, [Wacław] Szamotulski or [Grzegorz] Gorczycki.

Obviously, Köstlin could hardly have remained entirely silent about Chopin, whose pieces are played by practically every German woman these days; but he only mentions him as an epigone of the Schumann school. This is blatantly unfair, since Dr. Köstlin must be aware of the fact that Schumann himself had acknowledged the influence that the great works of Chopin exerted on his own pieces.

[Kleczyński, 1884] **Jan Kleczyński, "35-letnia [*sic*] rocznica śmierci Fryderyka Chopina" [The thirty-fifth anniversary of Chopin's death]**,
Echo Muzyczne, Teatralne i Artystyczne, **55 (1884), p. 557.**

[...] I venture to predict that to piano lovers (and possibly to others as well), Chopin's works will long remain the best, most concise and refined version of

---

91 Gustaw Friedrich Klemm.
92 Hans August Köstlin.

what music has to offer. Like Schumann, who created a new genre, the novelette, and made wonderful contributions in his Concerto, Quintet and symphonies, Chopin offers the same kind of wealth in the novel shape of his mazurkas, in the equally innovatory ballades and scherzos, or in the nocturnes, again a genre largely of Chopin's own devising. A moment's reflection on the two composers will reveal that although some of Schumann's individual ideas were superior in terms of originality, nonetheless he descended all too easily into eccentricity, and could not match the aesthetic restraint that gives so much vibrancy to Chopin's works.

The trajectory of contemporary opinion about Chopin's music is intriguing. Once I specifically browsed a number of large volumes of music journals from the 1830s. The things they wrote about Chopin! Epithets like *odd*, *ignorant* or *savage* assault the reader every step of the way. His technique appeared to pose utterly impossible difficulties; one reviewer argued that Chopin's Etudes (Op. 10), should they ever become popular, would vastly enrich those surgeons who specialised in the setting of broken hands and fingers... The Polish, Slavic nature of the pieces was criticised no less mordantly. Even Robert Schumann, Chopin's first noble "champion", was not beyond reproach in that he occasionally accused the composer of being "zu polnisch" and concluded that Chopin's Polish qualities were an example of an unfortunate artistic parochialism.

The French, who as a nation prize elegance, were quicker to adapt, possibly because they considered Chopin something of a compatriot, especially since he lived in Paris and could win popularity with his performances and his personal charm. To this day, the Germans have yet to accept him unreservedly in their conversation and criticism. Not long ago, Mendel's great dictionary[93] devoted as much space to Chopin's works in the music section as it did to the hot spice asafoetida in the culinary section![94] Perhaps Louis Ehlert was correct when he argued several years ago that the popularity of Chopin's works was only just beginning to develop, but that his pieces would stay uneclipsed for many decades, if not centuries![95]

In purely technical terms, Chopin's contribution to the piano remains unparalleled, even by Liszt. The elaboration of the accompaniment, the pedalling effects, the fingering, and the handling of his cantilenas; all are exemplary. For instance,

---

93 See above, n.79.

94 A resinous plant used as a condiment or a digestive aid, also known as "stinking gum" or "devil's dung".

95 A reference to *Aus der Tonwelt*, a collection of essays by Louis Ehlert (1877).

a piano tone, once struck, cannot swell in a crescendo – but this shortcoming is never apparent in Chopin's works! Many of Beethoven's phrases could benefit from being played on a violin or a clarinet, but this never happens with Chopin. On the contrary, transcribing them to another instrument is always detrimental to the overall effect, even where the transcriptions are as beautiful as those by Wilhelmj.[96] His decision not to tackle an opera was a conscious decision. "Leave me to my piano", he would say. "C'est mon affaire!" In formal terms, he is beyond reproach, except for his sonatas with their palpable sense of unease. His harmonies are a model example of opulence coupled with moderation – the kind of moderation that is so manifestly lacking in Liszt!

[Karłowicz, 1885] **Jan Karłowicz, "Rys żywota i twórczości Stanisława Moniuszki" [An outline of the life and works of Stanisław Moniuszko],** *Echo Muzyczne, Teatralne i Artystyczne,* **76 (2 (14) March 1885), pp. 103-104.**

Let us not ask [...] which one is higher or greater. Instead, let us consider where their greatness lies, which qualities bind them inseparably together, and which make them distinctive from each other.

Chopin is a sovereign master of the piano; Moniuszko, of song. With the odd exception or two, Chopin's songs are inferior to his piano pieces. Moniuszko's piano works, some of his polonaises excepted, are inferior to his vocal works. Both composers were nurtured and inspired by Polish folk songs and dances; both assimilated the most sophisticated forms of modern music; both originated new genres: polonaises and mazurkas for piano in the case of Chopin, vocal krakowiaks and mazurkas in the case of Moniuszko. Each is great in his own way. Genius knows no degree. [...]

Moniuszko is an unrecognised genius, Chopin is a recognised one. But his recognition occurred within my own memory [...]. It seems to me that a day of glory will rise for Moniuszko, as well. Our estimations of him are based on Western views, as was the case with Chopin. As soon as the Westerners have hailed Moniuszko as the king of song, we will promptly follow suit.

---

96 August Wilhelmj prepared numerous transcriptions of Chopin's works for piano and violin and for violin and orchestra [editor's note].

[Górski, 1885] **Władysław Górski, "Ze świata muzycznego" [From the musical world],** *Tygodnik Ilustrowany,* **fourth series 113 (1885), p. 140.**

Hans von Bülow played the pieces[97] in too realist a manner; it was a cool performance, a philosopher's performance, rather than a poet's. We could say off the cuff that we used to hear more accurate performances of Chopin's works coming from our own [Aleksander] Michałowski... I use the past tense advisedly, for Michałowski has recently been struggling to reproduce that effect. Today, there is in his playing a palpable inclination towards excessive sentimentality; at times, a listener might conclude that it is Prince Hamlet playing, not Michałowski; occasionally, he is somewhat too unceremonious about his Chopin. While performing the Scherzo in C sharp minor in one of his concerts at the Music Society, Mr. Michałowski often played *forte* where the composer had intended a *piano* passage and vice versa, and he changed the tempi and rhythms with the same unceremoniousness. In the middle section, which is in the key of D flat major (in the Breitkopf & Härtel edition, this is page 6, line 3, bars 3, 7 ff.), he accented some of the bass notes to produce a kind of trivial fanfare, an effect that was wholly unintended by the composer, as we can tell from the absence of accent marks in the original music. Chopin's emphasis was squarely on the melody played by the right hand, a feature that was rudely drowned out by Mr. Michałowski's fanfare.

[Bogusławski, 1888] **Władysław Bogusławski, "Szopen" [Chopin],** *Tygodnik Ilustrowany,* **fourth series 270 (1888), p. 130[98].**

Thirty-eight years have passed since Chopin died in Paris in the arms of his friends...

The death of that great artist has been described in music history as the passing of one of Romanticism's three resplendent stars, the man who used to shine alongside Mendelssohn and Schumann; it was a sad moment in the history of Polish art when that matchless national poet fell silent; and what has the present day to say?

---

97 The Warsaw press did not publish a full programme of von Bülow's recital, which was held at the Teatr Wielki and encompassed a mammoth programme ranging from Bach and Beethoven to Liszt, Brahms and Chopin. The only piece identified in a report published by *Kurier Warszawski* was Chopin's Nocturne [G major], Op. 37 No. 2 ("Wiadomości bieżące" [Current news], *Kurier Warszawski,* 41a, 29 January / 10 February 1885).

98 Reprinted from *Kurier Codzienny,* 17 October 1887.

In the present day, some have ventured to opine that Chopin's muse was in fact... diseased!

Perhaps we should disregard those foreign voices, seeing that they come from the same land where a cartoonish "Polish pianist", long-haired and pallid, has appeared in a book and on stage;[99] but we believe that this sign, though minor, is symptomatic.

Times have changed; forgotten are the moments when Chopin counted among his friends such giants of European literature and art as George Sand, Meyerbeer and Delacroix; today, the "Polish pianist" provokes guffaws among the populace, and Chopin's music is "morbid and nerve-fraying".

Such comments are never ventured with regard to Mendelssohn, who is presented as robustness, lucidity, serenity and tranquillity itself, or to Schumann, even though that great fantasist went mad, his late pieces a scholarly study in the kinship of genius and insanity.[100] No, only Chopin was a "diseased" poet...

Indeed, both Mendelssohn's health, calm serenity and satisfied smile on the one hand, and Schumann's feverish imagination, with its excited heights of mystical exaltation, on the other, have become canonical for cosmopolitan art and are deemed as rays of Europe's collective genius shining equally on every country and in every nation.

Not so with Chopin...

Chopin had bestowed much to Europe, but he has since been abandoned; he stands alone and isolated, carrying in him that something which now continues to "irritate and fray the nerves" more than it ever did.

Let us put ourselves in the position of that sensitive Europe.

She sits at the piano and has a mind to play one of Chopin's polonaises...

"Hum, a polonaise!... Dear me, how common! Every ball at court begins with one!"

"It is hardly conducive to a festive atmosphere, that music, is it?"

"You get the trumpets of war in one piece, the tolling of funeral bells in another, and in others still there is a calm and epic portrayal of grief, interrupted by a plaintive country idyll or a discordant cry of despair..."

"No, that is no good. Let us play a mazurka instead, shall we?... Mazurkas are so innocent and pure... The other day, Minister X and the wife of President Y danced such a lovely mazurka in traditional Polish costumes!..."

---

99 The reference is to George Sand's novel *Lucrezia Floriani*, whose male hero was modelled on Chopin.

100 In Bogusławski's times, such research was undertaken by Cesare Lombroso, author of *Genius and Madness* (1864).

"No, that is quite intolerable… what kind of mazurka is that? One cannot even dance to this music… If anything, it makes one want to cry… Why does he throw in those unsavoury admixtures! I've heard something like that on my way to a country house party; a shepherd was piping a melancholy tune, a Polish peasant was dancing in a country inn, tapping his feet in time to the music. I like those peasants, they come in really useful sometimes… But what business has Chopin got, dragging them all the way to Paris? Why all that drama?"

"Well, perhaps his waltzes will prove everything a waltz should be… I recall the dashing Ambassador Z… How blissfully we waltzed to the tune of 'On the Beautiful Blue Danube'…"

"He is an odd man, that Chopin, is he not?… In his hands, even a German piece simply will not be German… Who has ever heard a waltz like this? It is pure melancholy, a brooding sorrow from the banks of the Vistula… I really ought to drop a word in the right quarter. If that is not oppression perpetrated on the Germans, I do not know what is…"

And the exasperated Europe puts to one side the music sheets containing the dances, and reaches instead for what is nominally a more cosmopolitan type of music.

"Ah, nocturnes, those melodious sighs heard on a moonlit night… I used to have Field compose them for me. Mendelssohn brought them to perfection, they were like paintings of moonlit nights enlivened by mysterious elven dances."

"All I wish to ask is why couldn't Chopin have followed the example of Field or Mendelssohn?"

"In his nocturnes, the moon is overcast and one hears sobbing sighs; the elves look like Slavic *rusalkas*, and the maiden has such a stern and solemn countenance that I can hardly muster the courage to look into her eyes."

"Well, let us try and have a good laugh in Mr. Chopin's company. I am sure he can laugh; after all he has composed scherzos?…"

"What is that? All strident notes and no laughter? What are you doing, oh Poet? What storms are raging in your breast, what muffled groans escape your embittered heart? Whom are you mocking? Oh, the terrible, despairing irony! Stop that! I cannot stand that laughter!"

And Europe – that good old Europe who normally prefers the sound of crying to the sound of laughter – stops playing; she is agitated, so she takes a good sniff at her bottle of *sal volatile*, and soon returns to the piano.

It is time for the preludes. The artiste's countenance brightens.

"I truly hope Chopin will try to be a cosmopolitan poet in his preludes. Preludes… They are such good, blameless, innocuous pieces. They are little more than pretexts for improvisation."

She starts playing, and knits her brow.

Entire poems flutter from under her fingers, many distilled into a dozen bars or a few pages. Those are strange and mysterious pieces. Whether they encompass raging storms or serene smiles, each appears to presage some new and unknown thing to come.

"What could that be?" asks Europe worriedly. "What is it that these preludes are leading to?"

But she does not think long; we live hurried lives today, and we have no time to waste thinking about the things to come…

"I had better play a ballade. Ballades are a thing of the past. We have been thoroughly cured of Romanticism", remarks Europe with a degree of pride. "We no longer believe in ghosts and spectres."

She opens the pages of a ballade and starts playing.

The opening bars are calm, like a fairy-tale or a narrative of some legendary past. Then, a commotion erupts. Though peaceful at first, the stanza returns in a darkened form, sombre amid the sound of approaching thunder; rain descends noisily in heavy torrents; fantastical horror mounts, and a pealing tutti passage reveals a vision…

Europe is terrified; she is annoyed and distraught. She jumps to her feet, and firmly locks the lid of the piano.

The piano slams shut like a coffin lid and muffles the dying sounds of that last chord; but the great artist, who has organised and played in so many "concerts" cannot shake off the echoes of a simple ballade.

She concludes: "Chopin is morbid, this is nerve-fraying music."

She may well be right!

There are themes which, when repeated regularly in the Wagnerian, chaotic symphony of European life, jar on the civilised ears that would rather be deaf to the sound of great collective suffering; in sober minds purged of Romanticism, some ballades will smack of dated poetry… There are spirits that stubbornly linger in the daylight of positivist culture, with all its resolute disbelief in the afterlife.

They whisper that Chopin was a "diseased poet" and fondly imagine that the spirit can be kept under lock and key like the tones of a piano; they do not know that there are "diseases" that sustain whole societies, and a disease like Chopin's opens the minds of his compatriots to a poetry of pain that remains quite inaccessible to an amateurish performer like our Europe.

[Chlebowski, 1891] **Bronisław Chlebowski, "Fryderyk Chopin", *Ateneum,* 1891/3, p. 22.**

[...] In most of Chopin's pieces, the relationship between the emotion and the stimulus that triggered it evokes the pure femininity of his emotional life [...]. Feminine emotions are usually characterised either by the reverse proportion that exists between the objective value of an object and the subjective perception thereof, or else by a tendency to be equally delighted by the small everyday things and the most serious of matters. Knowing Chopin, we have every right to suppose that many of his works do indeed reflect such feminine emotions – those melancholy complaints about life's most trifling inconveniences, those fits of coquettish swooning, those eruptions of nervous exasperation. [...]

Both physically and psychologically, Chopin's emotional sensibility in his final years becomes morbidly oversensitive; as a result, among the quivering lines and waves of his emotion there appear feverish accelerations, sudden collapses and losses of consciousness that translate into formal obfuscation, vacillation and the bizarre. [...]

[Kleczyński, 1891] **Jan Kleczyński, "O Chopinie" [On Chopin], *Echo Muzyczne, Teatralne i Artystyczne,* 405 (1891), p. 350.**

While I was in Paris, I attempted to investigate [Chopin's playing style] in more detail, and I cannot describe my attempt as successful. The admiration was absolute and general to an extent that made any specific conclusions impossible. Unlike, say, people fondly remembering a revered teacher, those who remembered Chopin treated their memories like sacred shrine, to which the very idea of admitting a stranger seemed like sacrilege. "Divine, wonderful, unparalleled!" – no other kind of criticism was ever offered [...]. The specifics had been largely overlooked [...]. Chopin's personal mannerisms were presented as absolutes.

[Tarnowski, 1892] **Stanisław Tarnowski, "Fryderyk Chopin", in *Chopin i Grottger. Dwa szkice* [Chopin and Grottger. Two sketches], Kraków, Polska, 1892, pp. 7-8.**

[...] When thinking about nineteenth-century Polish poetry, Chopin involuntarily comes to mind; his polonaise conjures up in one's soul the final scenes of *Pan

Tadeusz;[101] the yearning, plaintive lines of Słowacki – who found it so hard "to be resigned to the kind of life he lived" and "to forget the guiding grace that used to lead his solitary youth to visit old graveyards"[102] – make one think of the scattered, mournful, nostalgic tones of Chopin's preludes and mazurkas, as if the music were simply a different way of expressing the selfsame ideas and feelings; when Krasiński's deep, despairing voice, like a latter-day Dante's, narrates the "purgatory of the present days" in his journey through Hell,[103] it seems that his grisly passage is accompanied by the hollow, terrifying chords that open Chopin's *Marche funèbre*. At a time when Poland's three bards were keeping watch over "the church of national remembrance" with "their seraphic wings and their angelic voices",[104] Chopin was the fourth bard, singing his mournful song like the nightingale in a poem, warbling over graves and smouldering ruins; and indeed, his song was more fortunate than theirs, because it alone "reached the general crowd". Whereas words, no matter how sublime or beautiful, are but dead letters to all except our compatriots, the non-specific language of tones is privileged in enabling us to "pour our soul into another's breast". Chopin's song of grief, which would have been inaccessible to others in the form of poetry, has spread around the world in the universal language of music to find comprehending admirers everywhere.

Indeed, only Chopin can give the foreign nations an intimation of that original, doleful and supremely Polish and patriotic inspiration that characterises our poetry. The very same inspiration breathed life into his music, complementing and translating the poetry, as it were [...]. There is a certain proximity between Chopin and the great poets of his time, with whom he shared certain qualities of emotion and inspiration; in some cases, the affinity extends even to traits of personality [...].

---

101 *Pan Tadeusz*, an epic poem by Adam Mickiewicz.

102 Two quotations from Juliusz Słowacki's digressive narrative poem *Beniowski* (Canto VIII).

103 The reference is to *Nie-boska komedia* [The un-divine comedy], a play by Zygmunt Krasiński (first edition 1835).

104 The canonical three bards were the Romantic poets Adam Mickiewicz, Juliusz Słowacki and Zygmunt Krasiński. The quotations in this passage are from Mickiewicz's poem *Konrad Wallenrod*.

[Kleczyński, 1892a] **Jan Kleczyński, "Koncert f-moll Chopina w interpretacji pani Essipow" [Chopin's Concerto in F minor as interpreted by Mme Essipov],** *Echo Muzyczne, Teatralne i Artystyczne,* **449 (1892), p. 220.**

[...] Her performance, so wondrously close to the Chopin tradition, has triggered a number of reflections which shall appear here in lieu of an ordinary review.

Chopin had a thoroughly aristocratic nature in the best sense of the word. It was not aristocratic in the sense of feeling privileged – he was aristocratic in his habits, likes and needs; he could not conceive of a life devoid of refinement, flowers or elegance. This refinement characterised *most* of Chopin's pieces and *all* of his performances.

The highlighted words in the previous sentence arguably point to the root cause of the difference existing between a Chopin *tradition*, which is kept alive by his pupils, and the independent interpretations of his music by some performers. Based on the model of the maestro's own wonderful and ideal performance style, his tradition has contributed to the forming of a unique interpretation of his works, which can probably be best described as aristocratic. It is of the type where the touch of the fingers must be soft, and musical phrases must radiate with the utmost simplicity, and even passion must take on a soft, velvety quality devoid of any disagreeable, jarring eruptions.

That highly aesthetic and aristocratic manner is not, I believe, *fully* in accord with the spirit of *all of his works*. Without a doubt, it is so in most cases; however, I do not believe that anyone could include in the same category such pieces as the boisterous preludes in G minor and D minor, or the development and ending of the Sonata in B flat minor or the Polonaise, Op. 53. Genius knows no limitations, and sometimes the power of inspiration may burst free from the constraints of the spirit. In those moments when his powers were at their height, I venture to argue that Chopin was able to transcend his own type of performance, a type that would have proved inadequate for such works. No matter how lovely Chopin's touch may have been, I believe that even his greatest admirers will admit that at times like those it was not powerful enough. [...]

[Kleczyński, 1892b] **Jan Kleczyński, "Nowa instrumentacja koncertu Chopin'a (e-moll) dokonana przez Adama Münchheimera" [Adam Münchheimer's new instrumentation of Chopin's Concerto in E minor],** *Echo Muzyczne, Teatralne i Artystyczne,* **456 (1892), p. 303.**

[...] In principle, one can hardly be expected to favour any modifications, adaptations, or – even worse – improvements when done to works composed by the great composers. They were usually masters of their craft, and most of their writings were aided by genuine inspiration. Any change to those fine works that faithfully reflect their times must border on sacrilege, and most will end in failure.

But there may be some exceptions even to that important rule, which, when impartially considered, will make certain kinds of compositional audacity appear less odious [...]. I believe that the instrumentation of Chopin's concertos is a case in point. Composed at a very early age, they show signs of diligent study in that area, but Chopin's genius was clearly so preoccupied with the piano that the orchestra took on a lesser importance. His instrumentation is often patchy and monotonous, relying as it does on the same tone for long stretches at a time. The orchestration is often quite distinct (at one point the orchestra even plays the theme with the piano in accompanimental role), which would suggest that the composer had intended a prominent role for it, except that in his inexperience he was unable to achieve the right combinations. Given this obvious authorial intention, is it actually impertinent to improve and supplement it? On the contrary, as long as the work is done with respect and painstaking care, the piece as a whole cannot but benefit from the effort. [...]

[Poliński, 1892] **Aleksander Poliński, "Przegląd muzyczny" [A musical survey],** *Tygodnik Ilustrowany,* **fifth series 115 (1892), p. 165.**

[...] Although he was a great musical poet, Chopin was by no means an all-round composer. Yet in his unique character he remains of greater interest than any other musical genius. He may have been inept at handling instrumentation or major genres, but as a composer of piano works he remains unparalleled to this day.

Hence the widespread belief that Chopin's works, which encompass "the heavenly echoes of all that he felt, loved, and suffered for", cannot be translated into the language of any other musical instrument, the piano being seen as an unmatched instrument for expressing the poetical ideas of his Romantic imagination.

Although this belief is widely shared and accepted, it cannot be considered as absolutely applicable. There are instances of orchestral rearrangements which are in no way inferior to Chopin's original efforts or at the very least do full justice to the beautiful qualities of his works. The trick is to know which of his works will lend themselves to an orchestral arrangement, and which will recoil in disgust from the exercise.

Noskowski has an uncommon talent in this respect, but even he is not always successful. In the gala evening performance celebrating the anniversary of Chopin's birth (1 March 1809), he included his orchestral arrangements of the Polonaise in A flat major and of two of the etudes, Op. 10 No. 3 (E major) and Op. 25 No. 12 (C minor), as well as two preludes rearranged for chorus and orchestra, in C minor and G major.

Although his orchestration of the polonaise could not be faulted, and although some of his tonal colouring was quite exquisite, the fine instrumental combinations were simply unable to live up to the piano's potential in the piece, and the original instrument was sorely missed. This is a fact for which Noskowski can hardly be held accountable, since it stems from the very nature of Chopin's music.

The same applies to the preludes in C minor and G major. Appended to the former was Noskowski's original poem entitled "Odlot ducha" [The spirit's soaring ascent], which he set to music in such a way that the prelude is first sung unvaried by the chorus with an orchestral accompaniment (Chopin's harmonies intact), before the orchestra goes on to intone the prelude (likewise unvaried) while the chorus sings in unison an exquisitely beautiful melody by Noskowski himself, designed to form a counterpoint to Chopin. The final effect is highly affecting in its beauty and skilful composition, but given the modifications it is no longer Chopin's exclusive property, a major part being unambiguously by Noskowski. The same reservation applies to the Prelude in G major, which has been turned into a choral piece entitled "Elfy" [Elves] (again with Noskowski's original poem).

The magnificent Etude in C minor benefited the least from an orchestral arrangement. This is hardy surprising, given that no instrument available in the orchestra could possibly replace the piano in those virtuosic passages which make such a striking impression in the original. The instrumentation of the Etude in E major was Noskowski's best effort, since that delightful piece lends itself well to orchestral arrangement and sounds just as beautiful when translated into wind instruments and strings. [...]

[Wilczyński, 1894] **Bolesław Wilczyński, *Historia muzyki w krótkim zarysie* [A concise history of music], Warsaw, Gebethner&Wolff, 1894, pp. 266-268.**

[...] All of Chopin's works bear the mark of a specifically Polish genius, namely a chivalric grandeur and an emotional idealism. This is true not only of his polonaises or mazurkas but also of his ballades and nocturnes, to say nothing of works that might at first appear to be totally divorced from any national source, such as the *Allegro de concert* or the Fantasia in F minor. Rather than try and carve out a virtuoso's fame for himself, Chopin preferred to remain within his circle of friends, and only to reveal the secrets of his genius to his chosen pupils. His artistic scope was limited; he lacked that masculine strength that makes an artist self-reliant and independent. For all his originality, Chopin preferred the restricted boundaries of his own life, drawing strength from that most subtle of social organisms, the salon, where he was surrounded by female adulation. He found the piano a sufficient instrument, and the minor genres were able to encompass all the content of his soul. That said, Chopin's greatness was apparent precisely in those minor genres. He breathed spirituality into the piano and turned the instrument into a living organism; his expression in performance came close to the very heights of emotional symbolism. The piano's dry staccato sounds soften and swell under the hands of that poet as he confers on them the fullness of the human voice. In the interests of expression, Chopin obliterates rhythmical regularity in his works; his melodies are propelled by a constantly changing motion – now slowing, now accelerating towards the resolution, sidestepping the beat with odd-numbered groups of notes as if he were struggling to break free from the bonds of the accompaniment. Always warm and triumphant, the melody clearly takes precedence over the harmony or the metre. And since his chords are often intended not so much to define the cadential structure of the music as to articulate his grandiose gestures, the maestro builds them up and extends them to unprecedented proportions, as the heavy and uniform matter of harmony undergoes transmutation into an ethereal ideal. This singing quality of Chopin's music is so pronounced that even his accompaniment weaves its own melodious charms; nay, more than that, it enters into an expressive dialogue with the main idea of the work. Chopin's style is distinctively chromatic, and he uses that chromatic character to express not merely gentle feelings but also the most soaring forms of lyricism. When the broad sweep of the melody progresses across far-ranging chromatic harmonic shifts and resolves itself in extraordinary drops, his singing technique is at its highest. The musical poet avoids common or trivial leaps and resolutions just as a bard avoids everyday phrases to condense a noble idea within the space of a few words. Chopin's poetry is a charming song whose echoes reverberate throughout the weave of a composition. It is unsurprising that such a lyrical poet was unable to expand his motifs on a large scale, or that he would become confused in his larger pieces, turning a classical sonata into a fantasia. Chopin did not compose programmatic music the way today's Romantics do. Still, his music is affecting enough, and its content is articulated with enough tone colour and expression to spur the creative impulse in the listener. In performance, Chopin's works (the polonaises, mazurkas and other characteristic pieces especially) present many difficulties which cannot be overcome by an ordinary technical virtuoso. The magnificent gestures of the Polonaise in A flat major have found a visual form in the watercolours of Kwiatkowski. The *Marche funèbre* and the Presto from the Sonata in B flat minor have inspired the poet Ujejski to compose vivid lyrical verse. [...]

[Poliński, 1894] **Aleksander Poliński, "Przegląd muzyczny"**
[A musical survey], *Tygodnik Ilustrowany,* **fifth series 252 (1894), p. 267.**

[...] What places him[105] in the most select group of original pianists is his unique way of realising other men's inspiration in performance, Chopin's in particular. His playing style is characterised by simplicity and a moderate use of tone colour. In his performances of the Ballade in F minor, the Nocturne in G major, the Polonaise in C minor or the Sonata in B flat minor, technical effects clearly play a subservient role; his aim is not so much to astonish with brilliant virtuosity or mere pianistic effects as to charm the listener with the poetry of the music, which he does by faithfully reproducing all the beauties of the original and expressing the ideas spoken in the mysterious language of the gods. Balakirev is more than a pianist: he is a poet. Whether one likes or dislikes his interpretations of Chopin, it must be admitted that he plays Chopin's works with painstaking, reverent care; he displays a consummate command of his favourite master's style and a thorough understanding of Chopin's authorial intentions. [...]

[Kleczyński, 1894] **Jan Kleczyński, "Śp. Marcellina [sic] z Radziwiłłów**
Czartoryska" [The late Marcelina Czartoryska, née Radziwiłł],
Tygodnik Ilustrowany, **, fifth series 233 (1894), p. 384.**

[...] The name of Princess Marcelina, one of the best pupils and interpreters of the immortal Chopin, is certainly familiar to anyone who has approached Chopin's immortal works with reverence, seeking models or examples with which to recreate their subtle and poetic nuances, but who never had a chance to hear the composer during his brief pilgrimage on this earth.

The Princess, a long-time resident of Paris, was Chopin's pupil for several years until she had assimilated his style perfectly. As we know, Chopin was an excitable and

---

105 Mily Balakirev.

independent artist endowed with an extraordinary charm; his taste was for refined elegance, in the form of both material objects and kindred souls nourished on ideals, who understand each other without speaking a word; hence the noble simplicity in the playing style of those performers who faithfully preserved his "tradition", where so many unspoken things were merely hinted at, but nonetheless appeared clear and distinct: refined in form, profound in content. Chopin did not relish the explicit, and he avoided gushing expressions of emotion. He was like a half-closed flower, whose subtle fragrance and beautiful shape were accessible to only a few select souls. Hence the spiritual touch, the delicate design and the muted tone colours, the rejection of public projection or virtuosic brilliance that we discern in his female pupils (for it was women, and notably Princess Marcelina, who were the main interpreters of Chopin's music in his lifetime).

[Tarnowski, 1895] **Stanisław Tarnowski, "Księżna Marcelina Czartoryska"** [**Princess Marcelina Czartoryska**], *Przegląd Polski*, 116 (1895), pp. 261, 291-2.

[...] Chopin has not died entirely, and never will, but while the Princess was with us we could hear him still from beyond his grave, her music a clear and persistent echo of his soul, his tones, and his poetry. [...]

Words cannot express Princess Marcelina's playing style! I for one should remain silent, since I am not a musician and needs must speak of those matters as a mere ignoramus. But to write about the Princess without mentioning her playing style would be like discussing the rainbow without once mentioning that it is airy and light, or omitting to mention that the colour blue was part of its spectrum; like discussing a flower without saying a word about its fragrance. Therefore I crave your indulgence for what must be an ignorant account of her music. If I appear like a blind man discussing colours, I hope my readers' imagination can mend my efforts.

My thoughts go back to an incident that took place in Podhajce[106] in the autumn of 1856. Ludwik Wodzicki asked the Princess what she believed was the most important precondition of a beautiful playing style. "Intelligence", she replied after a moment's thought. We were astonished. Intelligence? That lowly, cold and prosaic faculty? Smiling indulgently, the Princess [...] explained to us, the whippersnappers, that true intelligence involved feeling; indeed, it sometimes involved inspiration, just

---

106 A town in today's Ukraine; in the mid-nineteenth century the lands belonged to the Czartoryski family (translator's note).

as inspiration involved the intellect. Intellect was crucial for performance because the point of good performance is to give expression to the emotions or inspirations of the composer, not of the performer. A composer's piece should be played exactly in the way he intended it, and in keeping with his own understanding of it. A performance must be faithful; the performer must grasp the composer's ideas, his intentions and his feelings; these must be internalised and assimilated, and that cannot be done without intelligence. A performer should practice a denial of the self, and adapt the performance to the ideas, feelings and style of the composer in order to spell out every nuance of the composer's ideas, feelings or imagination, be it Haydn, or Mozart, or anyone else.

Either we are very much mistaken or the Princess was a fervent believer in that precept, which she observed in every particularity. When she sat at the piano, she put her individuality to one side; just as a good actor enters the character of Wallenstein or Prince Hamlet on stage and ceases to be himself, she would penetrate the composer's soul to render faithfully only those things that he himself had deposited in the piece. I am not competent to discuss her technique, though obviously such a fine, polished performance would not have been possible without considerable technical prowess. What was plain to the uninitiated eye, however, was the careful intelligence with which she adapted herself to the style of the composer and to the work at hand, coupled with moderation and an exceptionally refined taste. With Chopin in particular it would have been all too easy to cross the line into a mannered performance gushing with emotionality and nostalgic dreaminess, a universal affliction of Polish pianists of either sex who interpret Chopin's music these days; conversely, his German interpreters are too understated, fashioning an altogether too symmetrical and regular Chopin, with an outcome that is neither authentic nor beautiful. When playing Chopin, the Princess would reach the very outer limits of his Romantic character without straying into morbidity; now she hovered on the verge of madness in the twenty-fourth prelude, now she was petrified with despair in the second; in the seventh she rocked like an airy sylph reclining on a sunray, and the scope of her mazurkas ranged from coarse rustic robustness to the kind of doleful nostalgia one finds in the poems of Słowacki; her polonaise made one imagine the triumphal scenes of the victorious King John III Sobieski's return from Vienna;[107] in her *Marche funèbre*, the pealing of the ancient Sigismund Bell could be heard, along with the lamentations

---

107 An allusion to the relief of the siege of Vienna in 1683, a major battle in which Polish heavy cavalry played a notable role, and King John III Sobieski led a relief force to a decisive battle that crushed the Ottoman army [translator's note].

of a hundred thousand women and children – but for all that Romanticism and ethereal airiness she never once crossed that line that separates grace from exaggeration, honest feeling from pretence, or style and character from mannered affectation. She would come to the very brink – but never made that fatal final step. Perhaps that was her unique quality, that innate ability to bring out every last drop of light and grace in a piece of music, and to make even the most dull-witted of listeners understand it. She did that with powerful feeling, deep understanding and that aesthetic sense that overlooks nothing and lifts everything into a state that is enlightened, noble and full of life…

It is certain that every musician, every virtuoso will favour a certain kind of composition if it agrees best with his disposition and his playing style. Chopin was the Princess's speciality; it may be that no one has ever played him as well as she did, and probably no one ever will. [...]

[Lisicka, 1896] Anna Maria Lisicka, "Fryderyk Chopin" in *Ze świata muzyki* [From the world of music], Kraków, Polska, 1896, pp. 164-166.

[...] In order to accurately portray the personality of Chopin and the nature of his works one would have to dip one's quill in a colourful rainbow for an inkpot. For here one finds a fertile imagination with its fantastical leaping flames, an extraordinary emotional heat, the frenzied forces of momentary inspiration, and extremes of nervous excitability which seem to be almost feminine in that they could be triggered by the most unexpected and trifling of incidents. Granted, Chopin's era as a whole was basked in that rainbow hue. The warm breezes of Romanticism were blowing to all corners of the globe, sensations were more vivid, and emotions were more heated, though not necessarily more profound, than before. People fought passionately and cared about things that would in all probability be treated with perfect indifference today. Those were vivacious times, imbued with energy, when older people seemed altogether younger than the young generation of today. [...] Genius was easier to find than serenity. A diseased, nervous malaise raged indiscriminately like a kind of moral plague; the greater part of the people suffered from melancholy; others, especially the non-believers, propagated scepticism, an ideology whose ice-cold bitter drops continue to trickle to this day, but which was then blazing like a firebrand. The *best* of those lost souls succumbed to crazy mysticism and sank ever deeper when the firm soil of reality disappeared from under their feet. Those may have been abnormal deviations, but they were nonetheless heartfelt and spirited. Chopin's bodily and intellectual constitution was a perfect match for that electrically-charged period; he must be numbered among the Romantics, though we should always bear in mind that he was shielded from Romanticism's negative or reprehensible aspects by his deep-seated respect for tradition and his love of noble ideals [...]. He was a Romantic, but he was one of those few who embraced the positive and beautiful side of Romanticism, and turned away in disgust from its negative aspects. [...]

[Bogusławski, 1899], **Władysław Bogusławski, "Koncert Paderewskiego"** **[Paderewski's concert],** *Tygodnik Ilustrowany,* **1899/4, p. 76.**

[...] In his Chopin renditions, Paderewski took his listeners on a journey to their native world, where every feeling spoke [...] with a different and unique accent. There was great sadness in the first Allegro in the Concerto in F minor, but it was marked by solemnity and attentiveness. There was inexpressible sweetness in the Larghetto, interrupted by dramatic fits of agitation; his lyricism never dissolved into mawkishness, and the tragic tone of his recitatives never degenerated into empty dramatics. The Presto had the broad sweep of the mazurka, but the rhythm and the tempo were securely contained within those limits of artistic expression where a dance becomes elevated to the sphere of poetry. There was poetry in every note, flowing like a mighty current from the depths of each work, streaming through the performer's heart into the souls of his listeners.

[Sygietyński, 1899a] **Antoni Sygietyński, "Koncert z bajki" [A fairy-tale concert],** *Gazeta Polska,* **18 February / 2 March 1899, p. 1.**

[...] There has been recently much talk and writing in Poland about those performers of Chopin's music who are deemed exceptional, authentic and unique. To play Chopin in keeping with the character of the pieces and the nature of his historical period one must have at one's disposal a clear and impeccable technique, capable of expressing violent outbursts of emotion as well as sweet and tender feelings. One might add to that a moderate, balanced temperament and an artistic intelligence that ensures control over technical and tonal effects. Mr. Michałowski is one such pianist, and he produces an impressive Chopin: tempestuous without excess, broad, sonorous and thrilling. [...]

[Żeleński, 1899] **Władysław Żeleński, "Fryderyk Chopin w pięćdziesiątą rocznicę zgonu"** [Fryderyk Chopin on the fiftieth anniversary of his death], *Echo Muzyczne, Teatralne i Artystyczne*, 1899/41 (837), pp. 479, 482-3.

[...] In Poland, literary Romanticism begins with Mickiewicz, and musical Romanticism with Chopin. The latter must be regarded as the turning point of a new era [...]. Traditional Polish music, which exerted a lasting influence on [Chopin's music], weaves its own charm on the listeners. In his mazurkas, krakowiaks and polonaises, our charming, novel tunes captured the world with their imagination, grace, humour and excellence. They had about them a sense of nobility and serious purpose, a feeling of strength, and an inescapable tone of regret, yearning and sadness.

The rules and virtues practised in Chopin's formative environment in Warsaw were quite unlike those practiced by the bohemian circles of Paris. There were vexations and internal conflicts, all of which took a toll on Chopin's frail health. An exquisitely harmonious soul, he must have been particularly affected by life's dissonances. His nerves suffered, and so did his emotions. Chopin's correspondence, though very incomplete, bears a record of his warm affection for friends and family members, as well as his youthful passion for the first woman artist he had loved. When he lost her, he transferred his affections to a young woman whom he intended to marry [Maria Wodzińska], and who was also a choice of Juliusz Słowacki. But her family felt that the genius of neither the Poet nor the Musician was enough of a guarantee to secure their daughter's happiness, which they did not see as coming from an artistic union. Driven by his yearning for a loving and dedicated heart, Chopin went to an extreme, and developed a passionate love for George Sand. For the sake of his happiness and peace of mind, oh, that he had never met her!

Undeniably, the Parisian scene, with its teeming intellectual life, contributed a great deal to the development and growth of Chopin's talent. In Paris, he met some leading figures in art and European literature, people of talent and genius [...].

We can confidently boast one of the foremost musical figures, a man whose poetry, purity of heart and spiritual strength are in no way inferior to those of the world's greatest geniuses.

[Przybyszewski, 1899] **Stanisław Przybyszewski, "Ku czci mistrza" [In honour of the master],** *Życie* **[Kraków], 1899/19 and 20, pp. 351-6.**

I

[...] He who enjoys the inexhaustible charms of Chopin's music with his soul rather than his ears will be dazzled by an infinite procession of images and visions.

There is in his music the Polish peasant, with his fatalism and his humility as he leans in dull resignation over the coffin of his last child, spreading his arms helplessly: "The Lord gave and the Lord has taken away!" There is in it that same peasant, who will stoically brave the gravest of perils, and will dance until he drops in a country inn, spending all his hard-earned money on drink, foolhardy and indifferent to what the future might bring. Or when he flies into a rage at his lord's steward, pitchfork in hand; this is our peasant, with his primitive religious mysticism, who prostrates himself on the cold flagstones of a damp church to beg God's forgiveness or crawls on his knees through the mud on his way to some holy pilgrimage site.

An unending succession of images flows before our eyes, revealing the life of those people with their weddings and christenings, and their burials; the weeping sound of the fiddles, the booming sound of the bass, the regular piercing exclamations of dancers and the doleful wailing of mourners. Your eye surveys the long rows of dancers who dance with glasses on their heads without spilling a drop, all stamping, jumping and leaping to make the dirt floor shake.

Our native country with its peasant life is where Chopin's music found its most important root.

With its boundless nostalgia and sadness, that land drew the contours of his developing soul and carved out a valley for the mighty waves of his emotion. It was from the people that he learned the first forms – primitive but crucial – of that nostalgia and sad wistfulness which they had been cultivating for centuries.

The people use their music, which is based on mere a handful of tones, to express their primitive feelings of sadness and yearning (even the merriest of their songs swing constantly from cries of joy to wistfulness and grief), and it was that music – which seems to express the very natural world in the midst of which they grow up – that gave Chopin's music its distinctive character.

Chopin's music is a perfect embodiment of our country.

There is a kind of psychological mimicry in our souls. External mimicry is common in the animal kingdom: the pelts of desert animals resemble the colours of sand; butterflies that alight on certain trees will be shaped like the leaves of those trees, their wings a perfect image of the leaves' veins; the submarine fauna is crystal-shaped, and so on, endlessly.

The applicability of psychological mimicry to the soul.

Psychologically, we can only draw conclusions about external events by internalising them. To understand somebody else's fall, I need to picture myself falling, and to understand the speech of another, I need to repeat his words in my soul. Or, to be precise, I need to keep echoing them in my mind as they are being pronounced. As a result of that fundamental psychological mechanism, I end up reproducing in my soul everything that happens externally. [...]

What were Chopin's thoughts when he was taking a springtime walk among the rapeseed fields, as he looked at the ocean of tiny yellow flowers and listened to the buzzing swarms of bees alighting on the frail stalks? What can we know about the distant associations sparked off in his soul by the croaking of frogs on a quiet summer night? What generous impressions formed in his breast as he watched the long shadows of trees on a moonlit night in autumn? What was the swelling wave of his emotion every time he heard the weeping tone of the violin?

I said that Chopin must have borrowed the fundamental character and form of his music from the people, and so he did, for those impressions which the people perceived and transmuted into music must have provoked the same reaction in his soul.

But whereas a peasant's impressions were isolated and unconnected (except perhaps to similar earlier impressions of his own), in Chopin's soul each impression made a thousand connections with others, forming associations with the most distant and heterogeneous feelings, rippling out in the shape of an expanding circle to fill his entire soul.

Our land shaped Chopin's soul, fashioning it into a receptacle to hold all of his future impressions.

This is the root of the continuity and uniqueness of his works, the individuality and what I call the metamusical element of his music. [...]

Primitive man could not express his feelings in speech. Instead, he would sing them in long, drawn-out cries to express make his feelings and their continuity known. [...]

But after he had sung and spoken everything, he came to understand that there were feelings that could not be expressed in either language or song; emotions so strong that the range of the human voice could not encompass them, or so intangible that the quietest whisper, the softest weeping, could not express them directly.

Then, a miracle happened.

Man created one of the earliest artificial projections of a bodily organ: a musical instrument.

Strangely but undeniably, all the instruments we use are merely replications and expansions of our own organs; in other words, they are projections. [...]

A man whose art can imbue words or tones with emotion – someone who treats words not so much as mere signs or labels but as direct expressions of feeling, who knows that tones are not merely conventional forms of emotional expression but rather direct reproductions of the innermost wells of emotion – that man is an artist who writes meta-speech, i.e. poetry, and composes that which transcends music, i.e. meta-music.

We have had two mighty artists: Mickiewicz and Chopin.

An ordinary man vainly trying to express an elusive thought – one of those half-formed ideas that seem to express feelings rather than convey meanings – will scramble for uncommon words, he will try to forge new metaphors, modulate the voice and make expressive, rhythmical gestures with his hands; in a word, he is trying to restore the original value of words; he is singing his feelings, as it were.

To a remarkable degree, the same comments apply to Mickiewicz.

He was the first Polish poet to pinpoint the emotional quality of words by coining new concepts and establishing connections between the most widely disparate feelings in order to come up with a vivid and direct intimation of his meaning; his intuitive genius grouped words together in such a way as to turn them into music. [...]

For Chopin, expression was much easier.

Music has not yet been socialised, and as such it comes closest to the Absolute. Primal and quintessential, music is not contingent on the everyday. Music is the soul and intelligence of words, as beautifully expressed by Plato's symbolic metaphor of the days when humanity still reposed in the bosom of eternity. Like ourselves, the forms were all incorporeal song; as we began to hanker after shapes and desired to know ourselves in a bodily form, mankind fell to earth, and the forms fell to earth with us. Humankind took a bodily shape, and the lapsed forms were embodied in words. Only a few have retained a memory of their earlier life, and they keep singing.

Chopin was a man in whom all the forms and ideas were indeed still singing.

With nerves so extraordinarily sensitive that he reacted with volcanic eruptions to the most trifling of incidents – nerves like subtle tentacles that sensed the outer limits of human perception – Chopin could charm every unconscious feeling into music.

Every impalpable mood and every *je ne sais quoi* of feeling produced a distinct tone in his soul. Every shadowy event taking place in the soul, no matter how delicate or elusive, was transformed into an appropriate musical form. [...]

Unlike Wagner, whose music sought to portray the nature and feelings of his characters and was faithfully adapted to the action taking place on stage, Chopin was absolutely subjective, portraying nothing except the naked content of the soul in its outermost waves, for he encompassed the world with all its pain and suffering.

Thus, Chopin's music was a metamusical, absolute and exclusive expression of his emotions; indeed, his emotions were in themselves sounds a priori, unlike, say, Liszt, Rubinstein or Brahms, consummate workmen all, whose music nonetheless consisted of nothing but brilliant combinations of tones and phrases, and as such was devoid of true emotional power and unable to express moods except in the broadest of strokes.

II

As I have already pointed out,[108] our country shaped Chopin's soul and created in him a central nucleus around which all incoming impressions oscillated . Our land, with its melancholy and brooding sadness, deposited in him a thick sediment of nostalgia, which filtered and coloured each of his impressions. This longing was like the focal point of a process of suction that absorbed everything and infused it with its fire, disintegrating all other forms of feeling: in his soul, everything turned to nostalgia. [...]

There is a strange recurrent feeling which he frequently used in the endings of his compositions, particularly in the mazurkas.

It is a feeling of liberation similar to a deep breath drawn after a prolonged attack of asthma; it feels as if a gossamer membrane were being swept away from his soul, like autumnal mists lifting and melting over the fields when the bright sun rises, cold and majestic, over a steaming, frosty plain.

Also constantly recurring in his music is the memory of our country churches and evening devotions.

---

108 In this passage (up to and including the words "cold and majestic"), Przybyszewski recycles his earlier work *Zur Psychologie des Individuums. I. Chopin und Nietzsche*, Berlin, Fontane, 1892.

In my poem *Vigilien*,[109] I made an attempt at reproducing those noblest and most beautiful of Chopin's moods in words.

Dusky light in a country church. An expectant silence hides in the walls and ceilings; silence shrouded in the heady scent of incense; silence in the hollow, subterranean sound of the organ. A swelling sensation floats through the church like a distant tremor in the air, rising like a quiet whisper, flexing its muscles like a crouching tiger, and the silence ruptures; a pealing organ is heard, and a mighty, terrible song breaks free from the iron bands of expectant silence; the song presses against walls and bursts graves open – the song of pain and final judgment.

He was at his mightiest when death was spreading its terrible wings over his head.

Perhaps he could sense that disembodied spectre the presentiment of death running down his nerves, casting a shadow on his consciousness, unfolding the black drapes of his soul when the night fell, the tiny stars twinkling dully as the world appeared cramped and suffocating, the enormous masses of air compressing his lungs.

Suddenly, a terrible cry of fear and despair breaks out.

Do you recall the ending of the Sostenuto passage in his Scherzo in B minor?

Erupting amidst the unending and painful monotony of prayer and brooding grief there is that sudden chord, wild and violent.

That sudden bellowing of an animal pierced with a spear on a silent, sleepy steppe – that brutal cry of anguished agony, that chord like a wild, insane burst of laughter amid the mournful solemnity of an autumnal night – it is not music, it is a cry of the soul, naked and direct, overwrought and writhing in fear. This is more than music; it transcends music.

And when he realised that the end was coming, he rose to a giant stature, unique and extraordinary, as in his Polonaise in F sharp minor, his Sonata in B flat minor, and his Barcarolle. It was he – again I make bold to quote a paraphrase of my own poem, "Godzina cudu" [The miracle hour].[110] [...]

But what good are analyses or paraphrases, even if they are as brilliant and congenial as those of Kornel Ujejski?[111] Nothing can do justice to Chopin's power and charm, to his visions and dreams.

---

109 The passage that follows is taken from Przybyszewski's prose poem *Vigilien*, published in Germany in 1894 (excerpts of the poem were first published in Polish in 1898, in the periodical *Życie*).

110 Published in Kraków, in 1902.

111 Kornel Ujejski was a major Polish poet, whose works include *Tłómaczenia Szopena* [Translations of Chopin].

One would need to penetrate the very mystery of sounds, bearing in mind that each of his notes is not a discrete musical symbol but a naked beating heart, freshly torn out; the listener needs to be immersed in the pains and sufferings of that great master and penetrate his innermost depths, until the his soul has merged with that of the composer. In a word, one needs to sense the music that lies beyond music; one has to perceive it metamusically.

The itinerant virtuosi spawned in their thousands by Liszt, that brilliant master of musical histrionics, have killed our ability to intuit Chopin's soul.

That obnoxious bustle of trained fingers whizzing across the keyboard at breakneck pace can at most give us some idea of artistic workmanship and outward form, but it cannot begin to lift the veil of his grand mystery.

We have had some great geniuses who created metamusic: Beethoven, Schumann, Chopin…

Oh, could we but find people capable of reproducing their music…

This idea is the sole argument of my talk[112] – that Chopin's music is underpinned by the unparalleled riches and charms of our native country. That underneath his music there lies the vast ocean of the universal human soul, for Chopin alone in Polish music can say with our immortal bard:

"My name is Million!"[113]

[Sygietyński, 1899b] **Gosławiec [Antoni Sygietyński], "Porachunki" [Settling accounts]**, *Gazeta Polska*, **23 July / 3 August 1899, pp. 1-2.**

Zakopane, 24 July

Mundus vult decipi. – Metamusic. – Słowacki's letter.

So far, Mr. Przybyszewski's talk about Chopin's "metamusic" has been the spiritual high point of the season in Zakopane.[114]

"What do you mean, you are not coming to the talk?"… "They say all the tickets have sold out!" "What? I am simply determined to attend it, by hook or by crook!" "Is

---

112 Przybyszewski gave his talk at Zakopane in July 1899.

113 An allusion to the famous line "My name is Million, for I love and suffer for the millions", from Part III of Adam Mickiewicz's play *Dziady* [*Forefathers' Eve*].

114 This talk was published by the Kraków-based monthly *Życie* (1899/19–20); see also [Przybyszewski, 1899] in this anthology.

it really true that Mr. Przybyszewski will play the piano with one hand and discuss Chopin with the other?"… "Apparently, modest young ladies would be well advised to stay away from his talk. That naked soul of his… ahem…" "Last night I dreamed about Sabała.[115] His ghost was wandering about the Stara Polana playing a pipe while the parish housekeeper was scraping carrots and mocking his tunes on a fiddle made of spruce!"… "One night the dogs were howling despairingly, looking at the sky…" "For three days on end, all one could hear was their sound of 'Horla! Horla!'…"[116]

The *confisserie* "Pod Syreną", which offers a magnificent view of Giewont,[117] has been converted by the artists and the literati into a makeshift astrological station. The initiative could not have been more timely. For a week, a spectre kept appearing over Giewont after sunset; its mouth cast a gloomy nocturnal glow, its eyes were singing the joyous hymn of the chasms, its hands and feet were picturesquely weeping in time to the rhythm of isobaric lines,[118] and its flowing mane of purple hair emitted a despairing howl: *Horla! Horla!*…

"That *Horla* is Chopin's individuality", some said. "No, no: it is Nietzsche's naked soul", others countered. You are mistaken, gentlemen! That *Horla* is an incarnation of the spirits of Chopin *and* Nietzsche! It is the absolute twice over! […]

The public had turned up at seven sharp, and the room was barely able to hold the crowds. Among them was a large shaggy dog. Or was that a real dog? The highlander at the door spent a long time ineffectually trying to turn it out. When expelled through the front door, the dog would promptly return through the back door, and vice versa. In desperation, the intrepid gatekeeper finally tried to mount the hound, possibly hoping to ride on its back, and it was only then that the dog burst out of the vestibule, and both were suddenly lost in the infinite spaces outside. No mere dog, that. A devil, most probably, or at the very least an über-dog.

Mr. Przybyszewski "had no intention of expounding to the public the artistic qualities of Chopin's music". His business was not "life's fortuitous external lines", but the "essence" of Chopin's "soul". […]

Mr. Przybyszewski's language is rich in words that evoke concepts and aural moods; but his descriptions lack two fundamental qualities: vivid imagery and

---

115 The nickname of Jan Krzeptowski (1894), a folk singer and poet who epitomized the then newly fashionable culture of the Polish *górale* (highlanders) [translator's note].

116 The onomatopoeic sound of *Horla* is also the Polish title of Guy de Maupassant's short horror story ("Le Horla").

117 A famous mountain massif in the Tatra mountains which is visible from the fashionable resort of Zakopane [translator's note].

118 Isobars are contour lines of equal or constant pressure on a meteorological map.

balance. As a result, his seemingly picturesque description of Poland is in fact grey and dull like a wall covered in rough paper, on which a painter of great ambition but no skill – inspired, but technically inept and unskilled at using the instruments of his trade – has daubed a confusion of dramatic, convoluted lines, garish stains of colour and random blots to give vent to his passions, effusions, feelings and excesses of good and bad humour [...].

"But a man who *sees* the country and *feels* Chopin the way Mr. Przybyszewski does might argue that…" Not true. Mr. Przybyszewski has no argument to make: like his fellow decadents, he only has revealed visions – that Chopin "must have borrowed the fundamental character and form of his music from the people, and so he did", or that "in the expression of his feelings, as in the expression of the people's feelings, there is… metamusic."

Metamusic? Oh, most certainly. What throws into sharp relief Mr. Przybyszewski's ignorance of the musical craft (for I am speaking here of the simple rules of music and not of its essence, which is obscure to everyone except Mr. Przybyszewski and his fellow decadents) is his exclamation of wonder (or possibly delight) that Chopin "had allowed himself to be confined within the narrow confines of just two octaves, as practised by our people". *Just two*? In a million musicians, there is perhaps one who realises that the human voice, which is amply capable of expressing the entire range of emotions, spans two and a half octaves at the most. It is a pity that Mr. Przybyszewski is not that one man in a million who knows that singers term any composer a barbarian who makes use of that full scale, and throw even worse imprecations on those who go beyond this limit. [...]

[Sygietyński, 1899c] **Antoni Sygietyński, "Fryderyk Chopin (w 50 rocznicę zgonu)" [Fryderyk Chopin (on the 50th anniversary of his death)],** *Gazeta Polska,* **5/17 October 1899, pp. 1-2.**

"Upon one afternoon," Liszt writes, "when there were but three persons present, and Chopin had been playing for a long time, one of the most distinguished women in Paris remarked, that she felt always more and more filled with solemn meditation, such as might be awakened in presence of the grave-stones strewing those grounds in Turkey, whose shady recesses and bright beds of flowers promise only a gay garden to the startled traveller. She asked him what was the cause of the involuntary, yet sad veneration which subdued her heart while listening to these pieces, apparently presenting only sweet and graceful subjects: and by what name he called the strange emotion enclosed in his compositions, like ashes of the unknown dead in superbly sculptured urns of the purest alabaster...

Conquered by the appealing tears which moistened the beautiful eyes, with a candour rare indeed in this artist, so susceptible upon all that related to the secrets of the sacred relics buried in the gorgeous shrines of his music, he replied: 'that her heart had not deceived her in the gloom which she felt stealing upon her, for whatever might have been his transitory pleasures, he had never been free from a feeling which might almost be said to form the soil of his heart, and for which he could find no appropriate expression except in his own language, no other possessing a term equivalent to the Polish word: ŻAL!' As if his ear thirsted for the sound of this word, which expresses the whole range of emotions produced by an intense regret, through all the shades of feeling, from hatred to repentance, he repeated it again and again."[119]

He also said that although he was quite often merry, he was never free from that feeling which had been his innate companion from his birth.

The word *żal*[120] may be the key to a psychological riddle, but it does not in itself offer a comprehensive explanation of Chopin's music; within his narrow confines of piano music, Chopin was nonetheless broader, deeper and more versatile in terms of expression than many a genius able to draw on the full array of musical means. Chopin spoke for himself and for his background. Again, he was the most individual of poets, as well as the most national. [...]

According to Karasowski, Chopin would go to Służewo every summer, and whenever he heard an idyllic air or the sound of a fiddle floating from a house or an inn, he would approach the building and listen carefully, his soul submerged in the folk melody, imbibing its rhythms. At times like those, he could not be persuaded to leave. Lost in profound meditation, he listened until the air or the fiddle was silent. Then he would ask himself and those around him: "Who is the author of those beautiful melodies? The question is easy to answer: it was the immortal soul of the nation, which knows no beginning or end and finds a different embodiment in every individual to feel and express its diverse shapes and forms.

Its general outline and fundamental qualities are the work of centuries; individual artists have worked to refine its external forms and modes of expression.

---

119 Franz [Ferenz] Liszt, *Life of Chopin*, tr. Martha Walker Cook, 4th edn rev. (1880).
120 Wistful regret, sorrowfulness [translator's note]. See also footnote 122.

Chopin came into the world with that immortal soul in him. From his mother, Justyna Krzyżanowska, he inherited all his Polish qualities. His background and his life's events added the rest. [...]

But there is a melancholy teardrop at the bottom of every honest poet's soul that brings about a desirable artistic refraction of life's external images. Chopin is a case in point. His music is Polish to the core, but they are wrong who argue that it was also folk-inspired to the core. The immortal soul of the Polish people had to become immersed in Chopin's unique feeling and formal mastery in order to turn from a green shoot growing on fallow soil into a delightful blossom in the garden of the arts, and it was only as such that it took and grew in the soil of European culture. As one of his friends put it, Chopin was unique in having "a merry mind and a sorrowful heart". Of all the poets who have tried to interpret Chopin's music in verse, Włodzimierz Wolski perhaps comes closest to this truth in his "Tęsknica" [Yearning] (based on Mazurka, Op. 6 No. 4).

To study the unique qualities of Chopin's music, one would have to analyse each of his major works. With the single exception of sensual love, this music encompasses the entire scope of human emotions. It holds all that can be contained within the soul of a man of his background and artistic context.

As for matters of form and artistic technique, Chopin is a master nonpareil. He took his early lessons in fine style from Żywny and Elsner, and the internal structure of his works takes its cue from Bach and Cherubini. Perhaps here lie the origins of the delightful way in which he combined two or even three simultaneous melodic voices without resorting to strict counterpoint. Although he was a follower of Field and Hummel in terms of pianistic ideas, techniques and ornamentation, his inventiveness, refinement and noble effect far outstripped his models; to this day, he remains an unmatched piano virtuoso, unchallenged even by Liszt.

It is difficult to discuss his own playing style. There was a saying in Paris in 1830 that in the concert hall "Thalberg was a king, Liszt a prophet, Chopin a poet, Herz a barrister, Kalkbrenner a troubadour, Mrs. Pleyel a Sybill, and Döhler a fortepianist". What is certain is that his style was delicate and ductile (*plastyczny*). "His piano", wrote Moscheles, "was impressive in its subtlety without having to resort to strong *forte* passages. He captivated you like a singer who cares nothing for the accompaniment and obeys nothing but his own feeling". He was indeed an "Ariel of the piano", who prepared for concerts by playing Bach rather than his own pieces.

He lived an inner life. A reserved man, he had a distaste for performances or public displays of talent. In 1837, deeply hurt by the news that Maria Wodzińska, the would-be lady of the manor in Służewo, would not marry him, he left for London, where he spent several months without giving a single performance.

Passionately infatuated with Mme Sand (1837-1842), whom he had initially found loathsome, he lived a frenetic existence filled with feverish activity. Mme Sand provided an extremely interesting and valuable account of his work at the time.

"Chopin's creative activity", she wrote, "was astounding and sudden. Musical ideas would come to him unbidden, unpredicted and unforeseen. Sudden and unexpected, they arrived perfectly formed and brilliant. He found them when sitting at his piano or taking a walk. In the latter case, he would wait impatiently for the recreation to finish. Those flashes were followed by arduous moments of untiring work filled with hesitation and feverish, detailed revisions. When it was time to put to paper the perfect and complete works which he had first created in his mind, he analysed them endlessly, and when some stubborn detail remained intractable to his purposes he would fall into genuine despair. He locked himself in his study [at Nohant, Mme Sand's estate] and slaved away for days, crying, thrashing about wildly, snapping quills, often reworking a single bar a hundred times in succession."

Here is the solution to the riddle of that poet of incomparable feeling who was far above all his contemporaries in terms of his artistic ideas.

"Such was the extraordinary sensitivity of his mind", wrote Mme Sand, "that he could be injured to the quick by the shadow of a fly or a creased rose leaf". It is hardly surprising that Mme Sand, a woman of genius in her own right, who was "always prepared to smash an emptied bowl", was soon tired of that flower of nervous culture, one who could not love, dream or live outside of a hothouse. In the end, she rejected him "like a common invalid", and did not visit him until he was in his death throes (17 October 1849), when she was not allowed inside his apartment.

Chopin suffered greatly after their separation. One imagines that the words of Adam Mickewicz provide an apt reflection of the state of his soul at that time:

"My tears poured, copious and pure:
On my angelic childhood days,
And on my lofty, brooding youth,
On my disastrous manly years
My tears poured, copious and pure!"

The day before he died, he demanded that all his papers should be burned in his presence, along with any works he deemed inferior. "I owe this to the public and to myself that only my good works are published. It has been my lifelong rule, and I want to observe it now." This is the very model of an artist who loves his art above all else. Such an artist and such a man was Chopin, who believed that "from beyond, he would hear his friends playing in his memory". When Franchomme said that they would "play his sonata", he replied: "Oh, no. Play Mozart in memory of me" (this exchange took place in the presence of Princess Marcelina Czartoryska, Countess Delfina Potocka and Mrs. Jędrzejewicz).

He was a genius, and his unique moods and emotions inspired other artistic minds to broaden the scope of original art with new modes of expression. Humanity worships him, and yet he found faults with himself. Perhaps we should obey his wishes and commemorate anniversaries of his death with performances of Mozart's Requiem. He would listen "from beyond", and perhaps his *żal*, that wistful sorrow with which he came into this world, will be soothed by the sounds of music composed by that most serene and harmonious of geniuses.

[Sygietyński, 1899d] **Antoni Sygietyński, "Koncert chopinowski"**
[A Chopin concert], *Gazeta Polska,* **6/18 October 1899, p. 2.**

To celebrate the fiftieth anniversary of Chopin's death, yesterday the Music Society held a "special concert". The programme comprised some original pieces and adaptations, and the performers included Miss Maria Kamińska and Mr. Aleksander Michałowski, some choirs and an orchestra under the conductor Mr. Zygmunt Noskowski, and the "Lutnia" orchestra under its conductor, Mr. Piotr Maszyński. The dais was decorated with a marble bust of Chopin, the columns and walls were festooned with ivy and laurel, and listeners in festive attire filled the hall.

The programme featured two pieces by Chopin in Mr. Noskowski's arrangement (the Prelude in C minor and the *Marche funèbre*) .

Chopin was an inspired reformer of piano music. The nature of his music is so closely entwined with the character of his instrument that even choral or orchestral arrangements diminish the poetry and fullness of his sound instead of lending new strength and vibrancy to his works. At the very least, the fiftieth anniversary of the death of that master of unique and original music should not have been treated as an opportunity for supplementing his works with an alien verbal content, with new instrumentation or with additional harmonic figures. At the most, the organisers should have recreated the moment when Delfina Potocka, her voice half-choked with grief, sang to him Bellini's aria from *Beatrice di Tenda* on his deathbed, or perhaps "play something by Mozart in memory of him", to which the composer wished to listen "from beyond".

The Prelude in C minor is a plaintive elegy sung from the depths of the soul in a single breath. Mr. Noskowski's arrangement for mixed choir and orchestra turned it into a long-winded piece of melodrama, where the strident brass failed to coalesce with the hissing of the violins and the maudlin groans of the singers. The verses themselves are hardly a credit to Polish poetry. Anyone capable of inquiring of his own spirit: "Oh, whither doest thou soar? Art thou tired of living, or troubled by the world?" can hardly be considered an appropriate interpreter of the anguished emotion that vibrates in every note of the Prelude in C minor.

If anything, the arrangement of the *Marche funèbre* was even worse. The use of bassoons in the opening bars was a good choice, aptly reflecting the sombre mood of the piece, but after that the composition utterly fell to pieces. The differences in strength and sonority between the different instruments were simply too great, and the overall tone colour kept shifting from one moment to the next. It seemed for all the world like a drawing by Grottger copied onto a motley piece of cardboard. In the middle section, where Chopin combines a flowing melody in the Italian style with an intentionally modest accompaniment, Mr. Noskowski inserted elaborate harmonies of his own devising, robbing Chopin's piece of its distinctive beguiling simplicity. This goes beyond arranging the march for other instruments like, say, a military band. It is a perversion of Chopin's very spirit, amounting to a kind of sacrilege [...].

[Noskowski, 1902] **Zygmunt Noskowski, *Istota utworów Chopina***
[The quintessence of Chopin's works], Warsaw 1902,[121] **pp. 9-19.**

[...] Chopin was born at a time when Beethoven's artistic activity was at its height; his own art, for all its unique individuality, took a similar course [in keeping with the principle of "art for humanity"], as he followed in the German master's footsteps. Our musician became an interpreter of the mysteries of the human soul and human emotions; his own pain was submerged in the pain of humankind, such that his works later became common property all over the world. With his extraordinary sensitivity and physical delicacy, Chopin could soar freely to superterrestrial

---

121 Printed version of a talk given by Zygmunt Noskowski at a comemmorative event held on the 50th anniversary of Chopin's death by the Warszawskie Towarzystwo Muzyczne (Warsaw Music Society) in 1899. First published in *Wędrowiec*, 1900/27-31.

ideal spheres, where he seemed to communicate with spirits and gleaned unique ideas and inspirations. In all that, he never forgot that he was a child of the earth; he remembered the society he was born into, and sang its feelings with ease. It was part of his natural disposition, influenced by his childhood experiences, which he surveyed with the eye of a true poet. [...]

Opinions vary when it comes to identifying the main emotion that permeated the master's works. Some views are mutually contradictory or paradoxical. Some commentators identify it as sentimentality, others as melancholia, yet others as plaintiveness or an elegiac tone. We do know that Chopin proffered the aptest verdict where he described the key mood of his inspirations as *żałość* (grieving sorrow).[122] The word, which is so resistant to translation, was one that he very often repeated, as if wishing to embed within his very soul that emotion unknown to the foreign nations.

Żałość is not a form of yearning or anguish; it is neither meditative nor plaintive. It is wholly distinct from elegy or melancholy. This sense of grieving sorrow underpins nearly all Chopin's melodies, both in the major and the minor keys; it forms the main thrust of his ideas and makes them quite unique.

The grieving sorrow present in Chopin's works is far removed from gloom or pessimism. The maestro is nostalgic; he weeps and complains; when pain strikes, he succumbs to despair, which he portrays in extraordinary, strident chords. But even at times of greatest doubt he never scoffs or blasphemes. He never provokes those feelings in others that bring neither benefit nor credit to a man.

Granted, there is, on occasion, an excessive softness to his effusions of grief, which makes him sound more like a crying child than an injured man. But such was Chopin's natural disposition, an innate quality of his which was impossible either to change or to dislodge.

Our maestro was a man of subtle feeling and remarkable sensitivity. Both qualities were further heightened by physical and moral sufferings inevitably reflected in his works.

However we choose to describe that mood of Chopin's works – elegy, yearning, grief – it is important to point out that they are all predominated by the purest poetry that provokes indescribable emotions in the heart.

---

122 The word *żałość* was first used by Felicjan Faleński in his Polish translation of Liszt's *Life of Chopin* (Warsaw 1873), replacing Chopin's original (and similar) word *żal* [editor's note].

I do not use the term *purest poetry* unadvisedly, for it is that particular quality which I purpose to emphasise in his music.

Pure poetry resides in the natural world; it springs from nature's womb like a crystal-clear fountainhead that nourishes the arts, and artists. The artist who is the most sensitive to the wonders that surround him will also be the best prepared to take them into his very heart and soul by adding them to the treasure house of his imagination; the plainer his relationship with nature, the fresher and more innovative his inspirations will appear.

The freshness and purity of such artworks is apparent even to a layman's eye, and he will distinguish it easily from that rampant artificiality recently plaguing modern art. [...]

Music has been subject to that process ever since the emergence of so-called salon music. When was that kind of music born, by whom was it begotten? There is no satisfactory answer, just as no one can say when modern salon life first appeared, with all its suffocating qualities of excess and banality, like a deformed version of the salons of old that used to gather the most eminent artists and scholars. There was no room for good music when superficial chatter supplanted serious conversation, quotidian topics reigned supreme, and glib compliments drove out all appreciation of great art. Sonatas, quartets, classical arias or meaningful works that obeyed no formal constraints: such works could not be properly appreciated in that sterile environment and were duly replaced by musical confectionery with pretentious titles and ornamental covers. Suddenly, the salons were deluged with serenades, nocturnes, melancholies, *Pearl rains, Melodic posies,* and finally with waltzes and mazurkas (the latter bearing the comical appendage "de salon"). These were composed by musicians of various statures; some of them were quite talented, but they had all been raised on the cobbled streets of big cities and were starved of those sensations that only the experience of the natural world can bring. [...]

City life is usually philistine; it kills art and engenders artificiality. As products of city life, salon pieces can be compared to hothouse flowers, or to those fake roses, violets and lilies of the valley manufactured by our milliners.

The emergence of Chopin on that scene necessarily provoked contradictory and diverse opinions. Here was an artist who entered the stage with familiar salon genres like nocturnes, waltzes or mazurkas. The outcome was predictable. Those musicians who fancied themselves as authorities judged him by the titles of his works, without even bothering to take a look at his ideas. To them, Chopin was a mere salon composer. Those of a harsher disposition described his modulations as amateurish and concluded that he was unschooled in harmony. If anything, the misunderstanding in the salons was even greater. To the salon habitués he was a considerable disappointment, for here were nocturnes and mazurkas that disrupted peaceful digestion and brooked no bland indifference, unlike a Reverie or a Virgin's prayer.

Chopin entered the salons with a bunch of wild flowers in his hand, bringing a breath of fresh air into an atmosphere filled with exotic scents. The very novelty of his direction and ideas, the way he transcended everyday concerns [...] were a discouraging sign to the salon audiences. That is why his contemporaries were reluctant to include his pieces in their performances. [...]

Chopin did not compose for his contemporaries; he was a man ahead of his time, and his talent was only recognised and revered by posterity. In order for that to happen, the musical trends of his day had to decline and fall into oblivion, in order to make way for new, deeper currents.

Today, few voices would deny the existence of unique national schools in music, a fact that even great musicians were once reluctant to acknowledge. It is no longer controversial to argue that the unique character of a national music goes beyond mere dance rhythms and includes the general mood that reflects the spiritual qualities of a people. We owe this to the genius of Chopin, who gleaned his ideas and melodies among the Polish fields, meadows and forests. They sang their hymns to him and nourished his soul with poetic airs filled with simplicity and natural grace. Hence the quintessence of our master's works resides in the impressions of his childhood and early adolescence. Polish nature was Chopin's first teacher, dazzling him with its splendours and leaving an indelible trace which many years later was still visible in the great artist's spirit.

[Poliński, 1904] **Aleksander Poliński, "Chopin. Opera w 4-ch aktach osnuta na melodiach Fryderyka Chopina przez Joachima Oreficego [...]"** [*Chopin*: an opera in four acts based on the melodies of Fryderyk Chopin, by Giacomo Orefice...], *Kurier Warszawski*, 30 March 1904.

For a long time, no musician, whether Polish or foreign (but particularly Polish), was bold enough to transcribe Chopin's works for the orchestra. The seemingly insurmountable technical difficulties were part of the reason, but the main problem was the shrill objection posed by those tyros who, in order to conceal the fact that they have nothing to say, try to stand out from the grey crowd of nonentities by mounting the high horse of national sentiment to scream at the top of their lungs that transcribing melodies originally composed for the piano amounts to an act of sacrilege perpetrated against the musical pride of Poland.

At long last, sensible people have come to the conclusion that what sounds like angelic music when played on the piano must surely sound equally good when performed by an orchestra, whereas lacklustre music must remain lacklustre regardless of instrumentation. All it takes is a good selection of Chopin's pieces combined with a choice of fitting instruments. Some of Chopin's works do not lend themselves well to the exercise. Although some actually benefit from an orchestral arrangement, others lose their distinctive character and are only suitable for the piano. The famous funeral march is a case in point, since it is quite impossible to orchestrate it well (though obviously it has seen its share of bad orchestrations). [...]

[Hoesick, 1904] **Ferdynand Hoesick, *Chopin. Życie i twórczość* [Chopin. His life and works], vol. I (1810-1931), Warsaw 1904; edition cited: PWM, Kraków 1962, pp. 63-64, 103, 249.**

[...] The Chopins were a very loving family who lived a life of exemplary harmony: the children had a great affection for their parents, and the parents adored their children, who had as much reverence for their father as for their mother. It would be hard to imagine a household that was more harmonious, patriarchal or loving.

[...] [Chopin] was emotional by nature, and he had a heartfelt affection for his country. With his zealous heart and his aesthetic sensitivity, [Chopin] was extraordinarily sensitive to female charms from an early age, and he was justifiably described by some as amorous.

[...] Chopin was characterised by a remarkable degree of artistic invention of all kinds. Everything he touched turned out to be original and artistic. This applied to his writings and drawings, as well as his acting and miming skills, not to mention music. He even excelled at inventive parlour games, where he outstripped his peers and his elders alike with his wit and originality. For instance, he did extremely well at charades, both the Polish and the French variety, in which he would arrange other people into two or three different tableaux. In those, his exceptional taste was widely admired and thunderously applauded, as he aptly used ordinary household utensils to a very vivid effect.

[...] Given his boisterousness and his excitable nervous disposition [...] [Chopin] was often difficult for his companions, fretting and fuming for no good reason. After calming down, he would be sorry for his strops and scowls, and he was a dab hand at apologising to an offended party. But he was also capable of harbouring the most grotesque delusions and suspicions, and did not exactly make a docile slave in love. Spoiled and pampered, he had the capriciousness of a woman and the petulance of a child – his love was extraordinarily egotistical, his demands as unreasonable as they were ruthless. He did not always encounter meek submission, as he provoked in others a feeling of resistance and a desire to be freed from that despotic, torturing love.

[Poliński, 1907] **Aleksander Poliński, *Dzieje muzyki polskiej w zarysie***
[A brief history of Polish music], Lwów 1907, pp. 201-202.

[...] He must have been rocked in his cradle by the Polish maidens of old, who wove the magical strings of the Aeolian harp into his soul. The faintest breath of the familiar natural world would make him tremble; the softest whisper of a Polish field sparked off plaintive songs, strange legends, rhapsodies and rainbow-hued tales.

[...] Although Chopin was a great genius, he could hardly be described as a versatile composer [...]. His genius was confined to the single medium of piano music. But even if he did not match [Bach, Mozart, Beethoven] in this respect, he was in no way inferior to those artistic titans. First of all, in his own way he was more original than they were [...]. Thanks to his poetical expression, Romantic imagination and inexhaustible fancy, Chopin achieved quite unprecedented things in the area of piano music.

[...] His artistic and historical importance consists in having infused music with a number of fresh sensual elements. He found new ways to express emotion complete with subtle nuances and fine tremors of the heart. [...]

[Chybiński, 1908] **Adolf Chybiński, "Chopin – Moniuszko i ich stanowisko**
w muzyce polskiej" [Chopin and Moniuszko and their position in Polish music],
***Sfinks,* 1908/3, pp. 466-475.**

[...] When Moniuszko started composing, Chopin already had a number of published pieces to his name, which were not only among his finest works, but also among the most daringly modern Romantic compositions of the first half of the nineteenth century. In the company of Schuman, Liszt and Berlioz, Chopin was scaling new heights of musical achievement, conquering new worlds filled with immense riches.

Most of the harmonic innovations generally attributed to Wagner are already present in Chopin, and his influence on Liszt was also greater than is usually assumed

[...]. Both Liszt and Wagner borrowed heavily from Chopin. Their genius developed those ideas further, but Chopin can legitimately claim priority and deem those ideas his exclusive property for all time.

Wagner is as close to Chopin as he is to Berlioz. It would be a plain mistake to assume that Chopin was unrelated to Wagner; indeed, the similarities are surprisingly numerous. The harmonic material of both masters is in many respects identical, except that Wagner travelled further down that path, an opportunity denied to Chopin by his early demise. When writing about Wagner's harmony, future scholars will have no choice but to trace the causal continuities and origins of his harmonic concepts straight back to Chopin. One might say that Wagner was to Chopin in terms of harmony what he was to Berlioz in terms of orchestration. He is the corollary of both [...].

Chopin's fate was very much like that of Norwid or Słowacki. Those elements in Słowacki's œuvre that were marked by the greatest artistic tension and are now regarded as brilliant, noble and profound were for long years brutally ignored, forgotten and all but spat upon by venomous and backward ignoramuses; those great works of Chopin which best encapsulate his personality, grandeur and modernity had to wait just as long to attract the interest of the public and its "artists". Where are the new sonatas, etudes, scherzos, preludes, ballades, nocturnes and impromptus? Where is their distinctive progeny today, or even their imitations? Let us put to one side Polish music before Chopin's death in 1850, but how can we justify the attitude towards Chopin that prevailed in Polish music between 1850 and, say, 1880? Unlike other nations, which produced epigones of Mozart, Beethoven, Schumann or Mendelssohn, Poland has yielded no epigones of Chopin. There can be no better proof of the fact that Chopin was not understood, and no attempt had been made to grasp his epochal importance. We were unable to learn from his example.

He had imitators, it is true, but they chose the wrong path. Amid the deluge of dance pieces, we see the odd puny nocturne or etude, but their composers have made the mistake of assuming that Chopin's style consisted in simply combining the folk element with the refinement of a bourgeois living room. They had no need of Chopin as a model. Instead, they followed a different, *foreign* composer, a man of inferior genius and less individuality but altogether easier to comprehend and imitate. I mean Felix Mendelssohn-Bartholdy, of course, that polished and urbane composer who never taxed a listener or a musician with a demanding piece, a man who would not have looked amiss with a braided pigtail, generously powdered and tied with a ribbon. He it was who had the temerity to wrinkle his nose at the "excessive boldness" of Beethoven's Ninth Symphony or at Chopin's soaring music unconstrained by pseudo-

Classical convention. Instead of Chopin's sentiment, we have been overrun by Mendelssohn's ultra-Biedermeier sentimentality, with a further layer of marmalade from foreign opera, mostly Italian. A golden opportunity missed if ever there was one.

For all the commemorative fuss, the anniversary celebrations and the project to bring his heart home to Poland, we never paused to think about how we can feel and create together in unison with that great heart. We preferred to imitate foreign models [...]. Imitations of Mendelssohn's pseudo-Classicism can be seen as late as the works of Noskowski and Żeleński – and not in the oldest ones, either.

It was not so with our cousins, the Czechs and the Russians. The great composer of *The Bartered Bride*, an opera still performed in Germany but reprehensibly forgotten in Poland, was one of the first to draw on Chopin's music. Before 1860, he published piano pieces which were Chopinesque through and through, and he planned to make the same use of Czech polkas as Chopin had done of the mazurkas, an influence he expressly acknowledged. Published at the same time were the first piano pieces by Balakirev, which were so similar to Chopin's that they could be mistaken for some of his weaker works. At that time, Rossini, Gounod, Mendelssohn, the Italians and their imitators reigned supreme in Poland [...].

Just as Chopin's popular pieces stood in the way of a greater knowledge of his more significant works, there was another Polish composer characterised by a similar fondness for popular taste, who stood (perhaps inadvertently) arm in arm with Mendelssohn to obstruct Chopin's path to universal recognition, or at least to the emergence of a Chopin school in Poland.

That composer was Stanisław Moniuszko.

In fairness, Moniuszko cannot be described as a belated musical figure. The development of Polish opera from Elsner to Münchheimer reveals chronological strata made up of foreign influences. Elsner, who hesitated between Mozart and the Italians, was followed by Kurpiński, who was clearly of the Mozart school [...]. He was followed by Moniuszko, a highly eclectic talent who betrayed the influence of Mendelssohn, Spontini, Rossini and Weber, influences that can be seen clearly enough if we move beyond the entrenched, but false, belief that a composer's folk inspirations and national character are the only measure of his talent. After Moniuszko, who triggered the emergence of a "school" of his own, Polish music was subject to the influence of Meyerbeer and Verdi. [...]

The good honest composer of *Halka* was a far cry from Chopin's refinement, sophistication and *profundity of ideas*. Moniuszko was not exactly a man to set a river on fire – not that he ever made the attempt; beyond his adequate textures, which were unassuming but pure, Moniuszko gives us no remarkable offerings and exhibits no trace of unique genius or even technical dexterity. I do not wish to retrace the beaten path of those who have compared Moniuszko to Chopin; an immeasurable distance separates the two. Chopin is a genius – Moniuszko is not. Chopin resides in the Pantheon of the world's musical heroes – Moniuszko never ventured far out of Poland, and even in his lifetime he lagged behind the developments in Western music.

[Jachimecki, 1910a] **Zdzisław Jachimecki, "Wyraz i technika kompozytorska w muzyce polskiej" [Expression and compositional technique in Polish music],** *Przegląd Muzyczny,* **1910/20, p. 14.**

[...] The Polish public was familiar with the Italo-German 'Polishness' characteristic of Moniuszko's many works. His music constituted their musical education, representing a definition of musical 'Polishness' and a training in musical expression that inevitably removed real depth from emotion. This goes a long way towards explaining why the humble minor works of some older Polish composers meet with so much respect and popularity to this very day. Any daring spirit who wished to follow in Chopin's footsteps by soaring to the higher regions of art was condemned as un-Polish by his native mentors. Polish criticism became doctrinaire in the extreme, carping about any harmonic gesture that had the slightest grain of enterprise in it; any flight of inspiration, no matter how feeble compared to Chopin's ballades, was censured as an open renunciation of our native parochial ways and a treasonous homage to the Germans... We can tolerate perfectly well a Polish composer whose invention has been blunted by the dunderheaded ideas of Tosti; but that same composer would be guilty of an unforgivable crime if he were to take lessons in instrumentation from Wagner or Strauss, or if he rejected philistine habits in composition in order to follow Chopin's lead in original modulation or refined phrasing. We must recognise the fact that those technicalities of musical syntax (whether they be modelled on Chopin or on foreign composers) are just that – technicalities, technical solutions to express the feelings of a Polish heart; they form the technical component and not the essence of music. After all, Polish painters assimilated French impressionism and many other techniques to paint Polish landscapes, homes and faces. For all their foreign technique, their art is Polish. Polish poetry is another case in point.

In recent years, Polish music has entered a new path of development. It is to be hoped that those few young talents who have already given us many valuable and lasting works will benefit from an increased understanding of their aspirations.

We should be optimistic and seek a glorious future for Polish music; we should be warmly encouraging to our composers in their efforts, though we must sometimes be critical. We are convinced that our musical culture can only benefit from the rise of technical competence among musical practitioners, which serves as a solid frame for musical expression, helping us to find our way in the chaos of incongruent trends and endeavours. We should take our lessons from Chopin to reach the distant regions he was pointing towards. [...]

[Jachimecki, 1910b] Zdzisław Jachimecki, "Fryderyk Chopin", *Biblioteka Warszawska*, 1910/4, pp. 39-42, 44

Subtle poetic metaphors, rational explanations or detailed technical analyses are at best loosely connected to the art of Chopin that they are intended to elucidate. The link they form is feeble; it comes unstuck with the first heartbeat when a strain of Chopin's music enters the heart like a drop of one's own blood. Chopin's art is an aural version of the affects and ideas that weave through the soul but cannot be contained in verbal concepts; it uses the sense of hearing to communicate the ineffable to the self... His music was an eternal postulate of humanity, for Chopin stood outside the historical frame, alone and ill-prepared for his momentous mission; a unique man of genius, his way had not been announced by prophets or rehearsed by teachers. His spirit straddled the opposite ends of musical development; in many of his works the thread of his inspiration reaches all the way back to the dimly-lit temples of the ancient past, and yet he was an embodiment of modernity, a daring forerunner of future epochs. When the national sentiment moved him, he became our fourth bard, a historiographer of the nation's triumphs and disasters, a dramatist of epochal moments, a lyrical poet attuned to the landscape of Polish fields, woods and meadows, the epic singer of that hopeful part of our nation that continues to bear our "ark of the covenant".

The cult of Chopin is singularly motivated in Poland, but it would not have attained its present scale elsewhere if all his art had been specifically Polish. Chopin did not lose his universal human dimension in his polonaises or mazurkas, let alone in his other works. The artistry of his music deserves to be compared to the smile of the Mona Lisa. At the risk of stretching the simile to breaking point, his music and that painting are beautifully linked because his music depicts a mysterious and mournful smile just like that painted by Leonardo. This daring analogy was originally suggested by James Huneker in the specific context of his analysis of the Ballade in F minor, but

I want to extend its scope to include all of Chopin's music. In common with the art of Leonardo, there is a discernibly androgynous tendency to Chopin's music. In the face of St. John, as of the Mona Lisa, we see an amalgam of male and female qualities. In the visual arts, Leonardo's abstract ideas amounted to a reversal of natural models. In music, the same idea can be realised using analogous elements [...]. Chopin's music leads us towards a perfectly lyrical state not unlike Leonardo's poetic visual ideas. Utterly unprogrammatic, Chopin's music does not seek to impose on the listener any a priori non-musical elements; instead, his works form the seeds of a purely emotional programme, one that takes on different shapes depending on the interplay with the composer's creative idea. Chopin's works comprise a wide spectrum of diverse themes drawn from poetry and painting, ranging from Słowacki to Byron, Musset, Mickiewicz, Corot, Watteau, Turner and Segantini.

Although he was the subtlest of poets, Chopin was capable of staging moments of titanic power, tragic horror and majestic solemnity. Once we recognise the abundance of such moments in his works, it should be easier to dislodge the stubborn misconception that his music was composed for the female mind, a belief belied by Robert Schumann's description of his works as "cannons buried in flowers". In Chopin's music, those powerful explosions are not based on displays of raw kinetic power or muscular brutality; they are acts of tense volition, emanations of a creative spirit. Detached from their material context and conceived of as ideals, such passages in Chopin's works are characterised by supreme artistic dignity. They proudly trace rainbow-like arches, their thought soaring towards the world's zenith. The rainbow-hued bridge of chords suspended on the long pedal note in the Scherzo in C sharp minor is a case in point.

Similarly, we should seek to rectify some general misconceptions about Chopin's formal concepts. And we should engage in profound and rigorous study of the harmonic aspects of his work.

As is the case with every true genius, the spiritual nourishment provided by Chopin's art was not confined to a small band of fastidious gourmets and serious specialists; it remains accessible to all those who have a heart and know how to look into it.[123] His works provoke profound admiration among non-musical persons and those music lovers who have no grounding in the established criteria of musical artistry. A well-educated musician will find in Chopin's works a wealth of harmonic motifs

---

123 An allusion to a passage in "Oda do młodości" [An ode to youth], a well-known Romantic poem by Adam Mickiewicz: "Miej serce i patrzaj w serce" ("Have a heart, and look into it").

and expressive elements, and he will conclude that all of Chopin's art is one extended technical problem that merits exhaustive analysis. Chopin taught harmony to the whole of the nineteenth century. All progressive composers had no choice but to take their cue from his art, on which they were unable to improve within the same set of aesthetic ideas. Liszt and Wagner were both followers of Chopin's harmony. Both kept their tonality within the limits set down by Chopin and added little to his store of modulations and dissonances. Their musical expression did not go beyond Chopin's chromaticism, and the richness of their chords fell short of Chopin's. Suffice it to say that the harmony of *Tristan und Isolde*, the music drama that forms the climactic point in Wagner's career, mirrors that of Chopin's juvenile Sonata in C minor, Op. 4, an almost child-like piece that remained unpublished during the composer's lifetime because he did not deem it mature enough. In those passages where Wagner does not show us his German countenance, we find numerous reminiscences of Chopin, which bear witness to the similar means of expression employed by these two great composers. Although Wagner does not mention Chopin much in his writings, he knew his music well [...]. The sheet containing the cast of *Rienzi* bears the names of Berlioz, Liszt and Chopin written in Wagner's nervous handwriting. They were Wagner's artistic mentors, and indeed Liszt took him under his wing in daily life. It is difficult to understand why Wagner's art provoked so much fierce resistance in people who had assimilated Chopin and claimed him as part of their spiritual heritage. Why were they offended by Wagner's tonalities, which are so close to Chopin's? [...]

Although Chopin's music provided a direct source of instruction to the younger generation and remained unparalleled in music history in terms of its wealth of ideas, it took a long time before it could enter the harmony textbooks. Only recently have his works come to be treated as a source of theoretical knowledge and as perfect models. In his well-known book *Von Bach bis Wagner*, Johannes Schreyer devotes entire chapters to Chopin's harmony, complete with comprehensive analyses of his complex modulations. The excellent and practical harmony textbook by Louis and Thuille cites examples from Chopin's works at every stage of instruction and makes a particularly rational use of them in the concluding chapters. Dozens of harmonically interesting passages from Chopin's works have found their way into a study entitled *Neue musikalische Theorien und Phantasien* (whose author is only indentified as "an artist"[124]). There have also been some recent monographs which devote more

---

124 Heinrich Schenker, author of *Harmonielehre*, which was published in Berlin under the collective title stated above (1906).

attention to Chopin's harmony than the older studies. Foremost among these is Hugo Leichtentritt's monograph, a specialised but accessible study written with a great love for Chopin's music. At every opportunity Leichtentritt seeks to demonstrate the broad network of Chopin's influence, particularly on Wagner. In his *Geschichte der Musik seit Beethoven (1800-1900),* Hugo Riemann notes several brief passages demonstrating Chopin's extraordinary harmonic ideas. Niecks, as is well-known, neglected to include in his monograph a single musical example, which utterly compromised the scholarly credentials of his work. In his beautiful book on Chopin, Huneker by no means exhausted the subject of his harmony.

There are no Polish monographs on Chopin which present the composer with any degree of scholarly rigour, and such a study is quite essential given Chopin's steadily increasing influence. Grieg freely acknowledged that Chopin's influence taught him how to compose in the nationalist vein, Massenet and Saint-Saëns took cues from Chopin, and Russian composers such as Rimsky-Korsakov, Tchaikovsky, Arensky, Scriabin, Liadov and Rachmaninoff have all been young disciples of Chopin. George Sand's prophecy that a time would come when Chopin's works would be arranged for the orchestra is being repeatedly proven right in our own time, with the magically 'orchestral' tones of his piano music posing an irresistible challenge to those who aspire to bring out his vivid ideas in an orchestral form. Glazunov's suite, which was inspired by Chopin's art, as well as Orefice's famous opera seem to be works of genuine enthusiasm, and as such they deserve to be treated leniently.

At long last, the light of Chopin's genius has come to shine also in his native country, showing some promise for further growth and development. The generation which knew Chopin's music almost at first hand treated it with loving adulation but was reluctant to follow in his glorious footsteps in its own compositions. It is possible that our pseudo-Classicists and feeble Romantics simply lacked talent, and indeed they could hardly be blamed for their inability to scale comparable heights; but as music teachers and guides to new initiates they can be justly censured for failing to expose their students to Chopin's salutary influence. By pushing them instead into the ruts of academicism they have effectively applied a heavy brake to the sluggish wheels of Polish musical life.

This is not the right place to expound on Polishness in music, but our music lovers have long been grievously misguided about the issue. This has led to demands that new Polish music should bear the mark of national character. But such Polishness would be imaginary, its levels of artistic excellence quite primitive. The new epoch in Polish music history, guided by the spirit of Chopin, really begins with the piano compositions of Paderewski. Other members of the same Chopin-inspired movement include Melcer, partly Stojowski, the late Karłowicz, Różycki and Szymanowski. [...]

Chopin's sense of harmony ranged from the church modes to enharmony. By using enharmonic means, Chopin conjures up almost intangibly subtle differences in tone colour and melody, effects as subtle as have ever been produced by a piano. A typical example of Chopin's enharmony occurs in bar 9 of the Nocturne in B major (Op. 9 No. 3). Like a will-o'-the-wisp, the figure of fifths wanders across subtly devised intervals (d sharp – f – e – c sharp – d sharp; d – e – d sharp – c sharp – d). Chopin uses his enharmonic figures to profoundly change the tone colour of a piece and to achieve an oriental-sounding effect. We find passages in the Mazurka in A, No. 13 [i.e. Op. 17 No. 4] which all but justify the popular name of the piece.[125] [...]

No less than his preludes, nocturnes, ballades or scherzos, Chopin's etudes have inspired penetrating lyrical moods; major contrasts appear within their confines, with some containing crystalline reflections and cascading peals of laughter, while others groan in desperate anguish or emit the rolling thunder of rebellious might, and yet others (such as the Etude in E flat minor) seem to be whispering Michelangelo's wonderful words about the figure of the Night on Medici tombs:

Non veder, non sentir m'è gran ventura
Però non mi destar deh! Parla basso!

Oscar Wilde has remarked that many works of art in different genres were created for no better reason than because there was a genre in which to create them. Though seemingly paradoxical, the aphorism rings very true – but not when applied to Chopin. He composed few works in the classical genres such as sonata or rondo, and his sonatas were mostly criticised because they refused to yield to his unique individuality, which was unable to bow down to the formal demands based on the many works by Haydn, Mozart, Beethoven and their followers. Granted, the structure of the first movements in Chopin's sonatas may not conform to the classical scheme, but it is a surprising pronouncement that his sonatas should be described as "caprices" because Chopin had yoked under the same roof "four of his maddest children", to use Schumann's phrase. After all, a composer's task in the first movement of a sonata is to present a logical development of two thematic ideas, and to put their emotional and formal contrasts to the best possible use; within the scope of the

---

125 The piece was known as "the Little Jew".

four movements, his task is to develop some kind of poetic idea without necessarily presenting it in a shared theme. Today, we get a strong feeling that Chopin's sonatas are genuine dramatic poems; in the movements of the Sonatas in B flat minor and B minor there is a discernible continuity of thought, an abstract trajectory of emotional action with an iron consistency running through their component phases. [...]

Where Chopin introduced new genres, they often gave rise to entirely new directions in music, including symphonic music. Chopin's ballades, which spark veritably poetic programmes in the soul of a sensitive listener, formed one of the sources for the symphonic poems of Liszt. Chopin was too modest in calling them mere "ballades"; with all their Romantic content they fully deserved to be called "musical novels" – nowhere had the rhapsodic form been used to a more remarkable effect, and they are universally regarded as a pinnacle of piano music, and indeed of music in general. They are conspicuously laconic, especially given the abundance of meaningful content, a combination that only a small handful of the greatest composers can achieve. Although he had no background in psychology, Chopin was intimately familiar with human nature, and he realised that strong emotions are short-lived. It was his ambition to use brilliant but concise compositions in order to engage the listener's mind directly and immediately, and then steadily to raise the level of interest until it reached a climax, where the attentive listener becomes a partner in the act of artistic creation; in a word, his idea was to captivate the listener, and then to keep his appetite whetted, always looking forward to more. The Ballade in A flat major is an excellent example of this kind of expressive curve, both in terms of musical content and dynamics, where a long process of accumulation leads up to a sudden crisis, an elemental explosion. Even Beethoven, *mutatis mutandis,* was unable to achieve this kind of vertical climb or amplification within such a short space, as he often seems to finish a piece several times before it is actually over. [...]

Chopin marks the point in music history where the concept of tone colour attained a subtle, refined quality. In Classical works, the choice of key was a matter of perfect indifference. Tamino's aria in *The Magic Flute,* a passage from the "Oxford" Symphony or even pieces like the "Eroica" or the Kreuzer Sonata would sound no different if transposed by a given interval. In the case of Chopin, the choice of key is as important as the music itself. Each of his ideas took shape within a specific timbre, and like a brilliant painter Chopin was gifted with an incredibly accurate feel for the intensity of a given tone colour. In piano music, tone colour depends on the use of black and white keys, fingering differences resulting in differences of timbre. To realise the significance of Chopin's keys to the overall tone colour of his pieces, it is enough to transpose a brief snatch of his music by a semitone in either direction – several bars will suffice. The exercise makes it eminently obvious why we read so many painterly commentaries about Chopin's works, the nocturnes in particular. Their emotional background being saturated in colour, it can hardly be otherwise. Below are several excerpts from critics writing in poetic and painterly terms about Chopin's nocturnes. Writing about the Nocturne in F major, Op. 15, Ehlert comments that Chopin "interlaces the turbulent waves of his emotions with silver moon rays. Distant stars seem to glint in his nocturnes. His music owes a lot to those nebulous heavenly jewels. Chopin's nocturne is a dramatised ornament…" Huneker wrote about [...] [the nocturne-like Berceuse] that it modulated "from pigeon egg blue to Nile green, most misty and subtle", and a certain nocturne was to him "painted with Chopin's most ethereal brush". Leichtentritt believed that the Nocturne in C sharp minor, Op. 27 was "already devoid of light, almost a deep black". Unlike today's musical impressionists in France, who all but seek to portray atmospheric conditions and treat colour effects as a point of sole interest, Chopin was able, in a single nocturne (the one that reminded Kleczyński of a "quiet moonlit night" in Venice), to produce a "greater diversity of emotion and spiritual drama within the space of its four pages than many an opera does within four hundred", to quote Heinrich T. Finck's phrase. In terms of mood and artistic quality, Chopin's nocturnes could be compared to Watteau's *fêtes galantes* (Nocturne in G major, No. 12) or to Böcklin's *Sacred grove* (Nocturne in G minor, Op. 37).

Chopin's works offer a full display of the diversity and range of tone colour made available by the advent of modern instruments. Our maestro's piano compositions are mysterious reproductions of colourful musical pictures, their principal tone ideally reflecting all the hues, intensities and harmonies of his music. Playing Chopin is like playing a piano transcript of a Wagnerian opera, where the inner ear supplies from memory the missing orchestral timbre. Our soul sees the image of Chopin's inspiration, conjured up by the ecstasy produced by his music. [...]

Chopin never provided any theoretical underpinning for his ideas, and Delacroix once recorded him in his journal as arguing that Beethoven had actually disregarded certain perennial rules of music. Such facts might provoke some to question whether Chopin was even aware of the genius that resided in his own music. But that was not so. In a letter to Elsner from his first year in Paris, the brilliant young composer states clearly that he felt destined to complete a great and daring mission which he had set for himself, namely "to start a new era in art". This single sentence alone should dispel all doubts!

We sense clearly just how much Polish blood there is in Chopin's music: the world will not deny our claim to this most precious of our possessions. Camille Bellaigue wrote: "I do not know a more patriotic musician. Chopin is Polish to a greater degree than any Frenchman, Italian or German has ever felt part of his own nation. He is a Pole and nothing besides; his music emanates from that ravaged and battered country like its immortal soul." Heine saw Chopin's nature as a product of three nations and cultures: "Poland gave him the chivalry and the pain of history, France gave him the light touch and the grace, Germany the romantic pensiveness..." It should be noted that Germany also gave him the magnificent music of Bach: by studying *Das Wohltemperierte Klavier*, Chopin achieved "pure logic in music", as he put it himself in a conversation with Delacroix. The music of Chopin is like the obverse of the music of Bach, whose influence worked in terms of ideas rather than external formal similarities. Chopin's genius recast the influence into a new set of values, transforming the elements in the process. A paradoxical simile brings this process vividly to mind: he is like a brilliant sculptor inspired by the masterpieces of Velasquez to transform his paintings into sculptural form...

Such is Chopin's work: a sphinx, "a miracle apart". Chopin could speak of himself in lines borrowed from *Król Duch*:[126]

"Do they not know the tones, the deeds,

The torments dire I have explored

To find those spirits, millions strong?...

They've come from various parts, and suns diverse..."

Chopin's great art will be like the Soul of the nation:

"So let him sing a song for future tribes,

And steep our savage souls in ravish'd bliss!..."

[Niewiadomski, 1910] **Stanisław Niewiadomski, *O Fryderyku Szopenie* [On Fryderyk Chopin], Lwów, 1910, p. 3.**

[...] [Chopin's music] takes its rightful place alongside the works of Grottger and Matejko. It is as clear, simple and accessible as the ideas of our greatest poet; it reminds one of the warm, homely mood of *Pan Tadeusz*, or it swells with the power of *Dziady* [both by Adam Mickiewicz]. He shares an imaginative flair and a dazzling eloquence with the author of "Balladyna" [Juliusz Słowacki]. Chopin's power

---

126 Both quotations are from Juliusz Słowacki's poem *Król Duch* [The Spirit King].

to provoke tears, his purity of feeling, his uniqueness and brilliant concision all seem positively Grottgeresque: he had the same ability to capture drama on a single sheet of paper, and he used his piano much the same way Grottger used his pencil. The brilliant colours of our national past make one think of Matejko: Chopin's polonaises appear to be filled with glorious figures, and Stańczyk seems to have cast a wise and penetrating look into his scherzos… […]

[anonym, 1910] **"Wielki koncert ludowy Szopena"** [A great popular Chopin concert], *Słowo Polskie,* **491 (22 October 1910).**

The 100th anniversary of Chopin's birth has provided an opportunity for an unprecedented collective manifestation in honour of that immortal Maestro who was one of Poland's greatest geniuses. A few days from now, a multitude of artists and virtuosos will gather together to pay their homage […]. The whole intellectual and social elite will feast on the wonderful music of our magical bard.

But Chopin is more than an epitome of Polishness. He is also the quintessentially popular voice that expresses our collective soul. He took lessons from folk music, that disconsolate singer, lamenting over the nation's knightly graves, that Ark of the Covenant between the days of old and now. He sang the pain, the love and the longings of millions, and it is his right to reside forever in every Polish heart.

Sad and weary millions long for Chopin's music. Millions are weighed down by the heavy burden of life, including the workers and the peasants for whom music is the sole comfort and delight.

Chopin's music is intimately familiar in its Polishness. Quintessentially popular, it weaves its hidden charms in every Polish heart. It ought to govern souls and reign over millions. […]

[Kalinowski, 1910] **Kazimierz Kalinowski, "Fryderyk Szopen",** *Ziarno,* **1910/8, pp. 147-148.**

[…] Listen to Chopin's music with your hearts, and you shall hear all the echoes of the Polish countryside which the young maestro had assimilated into his dreamy, wistful soul. Afterwards, he nurtured those echoes in his breast, and made them sing every time his fingers touched the keys.

Chopin's music makes a vivid impression of charming Polish landscapes; white birches whisper in the wind and unbraid their green plaits; slender willow branches moan by streams and roadsides, and a rustling sound comes from the dry branches of a pear tree planted between two fields... There is the whistling wind in a pine wood that rings with the laughter of girls collecting mushrooms, and the rustling of a pristine forest with its hunting parties, and the mournful silence of trees standing motionless under their snow caps – and the barking of dogs in a distant village on a moonlit night, when wills-o'-the-wisp dance among the marshes and you hear the loud creaking of the old wooden crucifix with its rusty figure of Christ...

The ringing of sharpened scythe blades merges with the sound of sickles at work and the mewling of a shepherd's pipe. The neighing and lowing of livestock blends with the sound of willow pipes, the singing of the weary reapers on a sweltering morning, and the mysterious rustlings in gold and silver corn streaked with ribbons of poppies and cornflowers...

There is the splash of fish in a pond, and the pearly music of water cascading off mossy boulders when the rush of swollen streams drowns the groaning of spruce and fir trees growing by a rocky precipice... An owl cries out on the belfry and startles the long-eared bats that fly in circles over the porch of a traditional larchwood manor house...

Then you hear the buzzing swarms of bees along an ancient row of lime trees, and you smell the sweet honeyed fragrance of the old hives... A bargeman's song floats over the waves of the Vistula, and the wind carries the love plaint of a girl sitting in her garden, a stork nest gracing the roof of the cottage.[127] [...]

Ah, the amorous dramas we find in Chopin's minor masterpieces, decorated with all the ornaments of style... The outwardly cheerful rhythms of the mazurkas carry such a plaintive sense of yearning and despair, as in Kornel Ujejski's "terrible night", inspired by the second mazurka (Op. 6). [In his poem, Ujejski presents the image of a storm raging outside, with music playing in the inn but unable to penetrate the hearts. As the wind and the streaming rain buffet the window panes, there is such sadness in the heart, the rain falling on the soil like cleansing tears... And now a strapping lad suddenly springs up and wants to dance, he leads a vigorous mazurka like a military commander leading his troops into battle. The girls love him, they all flash smiles at him – except one, sitting gloomy in the corner and crying hot tears... translator's description]

---

127 The original goes on to quote a spurned girl's complaint about her faithless lover from Kornel Ujejski's *Tłómaczenia Szopena* [Translations of Chopin]. Similarly, the poetic image of a storm below, which is versified in the original, has been replaced by a prose paraphrase in the translation [translator's note].

In Chopin's music, we often hear that old Polish inn, which used to form the focal point of country life. We hear the dancing and the merrymaking of our lusty peasants, the booming sound of violin and bass alternating with snatches of song, as in that Mazurka No. 5 (Op. 7):

"the violins playing, a girl winking to two lads dancing a mazurka.

Let them sing, and let us see which one of them is best."

Time and time again the Maestro uses the most refined forms of salon music to reproduce faithfully those deceptively simple tunes of village musicians ringing in the stuffy interior of a roadside inn, with people singing and dancing. [...]

A moment later Chopin conjures up the soothing image of a silent country manor like the one in Sochaczew, which he remembered from his childhood. There is the mellow feeling that comes at dusk, when the flames crackle and hiss in the old-fashioned fireplace: the grandfather reminisces about his wartime experiences, the women burst into a merry song, the carved clock chimes its hourly tunes...

Some of his pieces are miniature dramas, tragic and heroic, like that "famous last stand" piece – the tender memory of Olszynka Grochowska[128] that sends a quivering tear down a veteran's silver moustache; sometimes you see the uniform facings of a white uhlan in a sea of amaranth and blue, and you hear the clang of swords and the roar of cannons in the Battle of Stoczek; an old soldier's tale conjures up a ghostly silhouette of General Pułaski[129] or of Prince Józef Poniatowski looming in the din of bloody battle, and you hear the pounding sound of hooves as the Polish light cavalry charges madly into the Somosierra pass at the orders of "the god of War..."[130]

At other times, the din of battle takes on a different quality: the piano sends forth the rustling sound of the winged hussars, the multitude of their pennants fluttering in the wind. It merges with the martial creaking of medieval knights and warriors. A vision of the future appears before tightly shut eyes, like a historical painting by Matejko... there are echoes of military triumphs on the eastern steppes, the victories of Chodkiewicz, Batory, Czarniecki, Żółkiewski, Sobieski... [...]

---

128 Fought on 25 February 1831, the Battle of Olszynka Grochowska was the largest battle in Poland's unsuccessful November Uprising against Russia. Though the Polish insurgents were nominally victorious, the clash was a pyrrhic victory that claimed several thousand lives on both sides of the conflict. The author goes on to make several references to nineteenth-century battles where Polish troops showed remarkable valour in combat [translator's note].

129 The original misspells the general's name as Puławski.

130 Kalinowski refers to the suicidal charge of the Polish *cheveaux-légers* at the Battle of Somosierra, which arguably handed Napoleon ("the god of War") a decisive victory in his Spanish campaign of 1808 [translator's note].

[Przybyszewski, 1910] **Stanisław Przybyszewski, *Szopen a naród* [Chopin and the nation], Kraków [1910], pp. 8-13; 17-18.**

[...] When it comes to the important issue of our nation's glory and historic stature within Europe, Chopin's contribution has no equal in Poland. Let us not delude ourselves: other than a handful of philologists, no one in Europe has ever heard of Mickiewicz; for Europeans, reading *Pan Tadeusz* is as much of a struggle as *The Mahabharata* or some other Hindu epic; Słowacki's works are immortal in Polish but all efforts to make them popular abroad have failed, and the dreary stage productions of his plays in France have caused nothing but embarrassment.

Chopin is our sole claim to fame in Europe. Indeed, there is not a corner in Europe but Chopin's praise is sung there in ringing dithyrambs. For the first time in ages, the proverbial *tout Europe* regards Poland with respect, and by bowing down to Chopin's genius pays homage to the Nation's soul instead of ignoring us or giving us the derisive look we have learned to expect.

For a stateless nation like ours, such historical events as the Relief of Vienna, the 3rd of May Constitution or even the Battle of Grunwald[131] are like relics displayed to contrite crowds, the modern equivalent of sackcloth and ashes as we do penance for the sins of our ancestors who brought our glorious royal past to ruin. It is right to parade them in Europe so that the old debts are not forgotten. But here, with the 100th anniversary of Chopin's birth, a Polish national holiday becomes a festivity for all of civilised mankind.

Our point is the NATIONAL character of Chopin's music. We tend to mention this quality with a strange trepidation, so it must be pointed out that Chopin was a national composer in just the same way that Bach was, or for that matter Beethoven, Schumann or Wagner.

To have added such immense riches to the spiritual treasure-house of humanity the way Chopin did, to have blazed new trails to infinity, is an achievement that goes well beyond the narrow scope of nationality.

And yet national ambition is understandable and justified. We understand all too well Chopin's continued significance for Europe. We realize that he is the envy of the nations.

---

131 The Relief of Vienna (1683) – see footnote 77; the Constitution of 3 May (1791) – designed to redress the political defects of the Polish-Lithuanian Commonwealth, it was Europe's first codified constitution; the Battle of Grunwald (1410) – a major military victory for Poland and Lithuania over the Order of Teutonic Knights [translator's note].

Consequently, although we are the most cultured nation in Europe (a fact I often emphasise), it is our duty to heroically and jealously defend every inch of that Mount Ararat on which the wandering Ark of Being came to rest, and to safeguard our glory from the rapacious claims of foreign occupying powers.

That Mount Ararat is the unflagging power of the Polish Soul, of which Chopin's music is arguably the most excellent embodiment.

In this respect, the foreign ring of Chopin's name seems like an unpleasant mishap, an irksome accident. Chopin's soul was Polish through and through, no less so than Matejko's or Grottger's... His soul was married to the soul of Poland by an inviolable sacred bond of sacramental vows.

Indeed, Poland could not have found a groom of more worth or dignity. [...]

With Chopin, we seem to be facing a baffling puzzle. According to Catholic hagiography, Providence afflicts certain individuals with horrible sufferings so that they atone for the sins of humanity. Thanks to their suffering, such martyrs of God's choosing bring about God's impenetrable designs. According to Huysmans, St. Lydwine [of Schiedam (1380-1433)] was one such individual. Before the higher power, all her sufferings and torments were as nothing compared to the atonement she had effected.

There was a similar quality to Chopin's life. All his external life is as nothing before his sacred mission, which was to bring forth from his breast the extraordinarily powerful genius of an entire nation. Properly, we should forget Chopin's existence and associate him only with that sacred manifestation of the nation's soul which he symbolises.

Let me repeat: Chopin was an emissary annointed by the Soul of the Nation to proclaim its grandeur, power and might. Hence, Chopin is an astonishing example of a great magnate of an artist who needed nothing other than generously to dispense the boundless treasures that the soul of the Nation had deposited in him over the centuries. His death was not late or premature; in that short life, the soul of the Nation had found its full expression. [...]

[Paderewski, 1911] **Ignacy Jan Paderewski, *O Szopenie* [On Chopin], Warsaw, 1911, pp. 10-21.**

[...] No nation can boast an abundance of mood and feeling comparable to ours. God's hand has strung our nation's harp with a multitude of chords, some soft and plaintive, others resonant and loud. We have the loving tenderness and the active resolution, we have the swollen lyricism and the chivalrous warlike strength; we have the maidenly yearning and the manly prudence, the tragic melancholy of age and the frivolous gaiety of youth. This may be the essence of our charm, or perhaps a serious flaw of our nation. The transitions are abrupt as we change from one moment to the next. In a blink, transports of joy give way to despairing sobs; noble enthusiasm is but a step away from dispirited dejection. Examples abound in every area of the nation's life: the political events and the social processes, the creative work and the daily toil, the social relations and the affairs of our daily lives – they are everywhere… Perhaps that is just the way we are, an innate quality. But when we compare ourselves to the contented and well-fed nations, it does begin to look like a flaw, a defect. If it is indeed a defect, we could describe it as a congenital national arythmia. It is presumably that arythmia of ours that causes our fickleness and lack of persistence; it is probably the source of our inability to act in a disciplined and collective fashion, a regrettably obvious affliction. Without doubt, this kind of arythmia finds its reflection in that wretchedly tragic course of our history.

[…] None of those great figures impelled by Providence to give the Polish soul a voice were able to give that arythmia as emphatic an expression as did Chopin. They were poets, constrained by verbal precision and clarity of concepts; a language, even one as strangely rich and beautiful as ours, cannot express everything. Chopin was a musician. And music alone was able to express that wavelike quality of our feelings with their infinite sweep and heroic resolve; those fits of rage that all but crush rocks, and that doubt-ridden powerlessness that darkens thought and stifles the will to act.

His music is tender and tempestuous, soft and passionate, plaintive and menacingly powerful. It gladly escapes the confines of metrical discipline, refuses to obey the rules of rhythm and loathes the metronome as if it were a despised government. Such music alone helps one hear, feel and know that all of Poland – the nation and its land – lives, feels and acts *in tempo rubato*.

How did Chopin come to give such ringing expression to the soul of his nation, why did his heart become the headwater that sent a crystalline stream from the Earth's unfathomed depths – mighty, life-giving and pure? This is a question we should pose to "the One who lays the womb of secrets bare…"[132] There is much that He has not divulged to us, and perhaps never will… […]

---

132 The reference is to God, as described by Juliusz Słowacki.

Chopin was born shortly after the triple murder perpetrated on our Fatherland. Napoleon was then a brightly shining star in the European firmament, and the luminous rays of hope he emitted would linger in Poland for many long years afterwards. Chopin's childhood days were spent in the relative liberty of the Kingdom of Poland,[133] which was like a heart carved out from the nation's living body. On the brink of the violent storm that engulfed all of former Poland,[134] Chopin left the country forever. With him, Chopin took what Mickiewicz had once described as the *genius loci,* which we prefer to call the *genius patriae* – the spirit of the native land, which remained with him until his dying day. We owe it to that spirit that foreign nations never succeeded in robbing us of Chopin; although it was certainly not for lack of trying on their part. Not even France, to which Chopin was bound with ties of blood on his father's side, dares usurp the rays of his glory. Unlike crowned heads – who are stripped of their original nationality upon ascending to the throne, their sceptred and crowned spirits being regarded as belonging to their subjects' race – Chopin's mysterious and profound emotionality, with its volcanic creative eruptions, could not be appropriated, for its does not have in it any French qualities. Its very form is characterised by aristocratic refinement rather than courtierly polish.

Even that strong and populous nation, landlocked for all its ambition to create a sea-like confluence of Slavic tributaries – the nation that has despoiled us so – has not dared to raise its hand against Chopin. Though he is a Slav, Chopin is nonetheless different. His beauty and charm, his abundance of colour, his dancing lights and shadows are far removed from the wise but grim and monotonous Russian muse, with its unsmiling countenance, that has apparently never been graced by a ray of happiness. A chasm yawns between Chopin's sad and tragic yearning, on the one hand, and the sense of despair that blows from those parts like a freezing wind from the bleak and boundless steppe, on the other.

Shortly after Chopin's departure, terrible oppression descended on his native country, notably in the neighbouring regions; it was a cruelty that cannot be explained except as blind and savage revenge inflicted on an innocent party for the long captivity its aggressors had experienced at the hands of nomadic peoples. Everything came to be banned: our language and religion, our history and traditional costume, our ways and folk songs, Słowacki, Krasiński, Mickiewicz... Chopin was the only

---

133 The Kingdom of Poland (1815-1915) was nominally a Polish state increasingly controlled by, and integrated with, the Russian Empire [translator's note].

134 A reference to the November Uprising of 1830 [translator's note].

thing they left us. And yet his music contained all those things we had been denied: the colourful *kontusz* garments, the gold-embroidered sashes, the fur-lined *czamaras* and the four-pointed peaked caps, the rattling of sabres and the light glinting in the upturned blades of the war scythes carried by our peasant troops, the moan escaping from a wounded breast and the mutiny of a subjugated spirit, the crosses on the graves and the small roadside churches in the country, the anxious prayers and the sufferings of occupation, the curses hurled at tyrants and the joyous songs of victory. Our secret thoughts went out to him during the long, anguished years of persecution and torture as our pained hearts sought comfort in his embrace. The hearts he comforted and helped, possibly converted… Chopin smuggled his contraband of Polishness in innocent-looking music sheets to his scattered compatriots; he was a priest who brought the holy sacrament of the Fatherland to our diaspora.

He now basks in earthly glory, shrouded in the rays of the undying gratitude of his fellow Poles, decorated with the fresh floral wreaths woven of our adulation and admiring love. But he does not stand alone. Even after his death, the *genius patriae*, the spirit of his native land, stands by his side…

A man, no matter how great, can neither stand above his nation nor step outside of it. He is a plant that has sprouted from his nation's seed, a blossom or an ear of corn – his greatness, beauty or strength a mere reflection of that nation's heart… It is possible that Chopin did not realize his own greatness. But we do know that his beauty was actually ours. He belongs to us, and we to him, for he is a perfect expression of our collective soul.

We should steel our hearts and persist; we should ready our minds for just, heroic deeds, we should nurture our faith to make it strong. With a soul as grand and immortal at this, our nation will not die…

[Niewiadomski, 1912] **Stanisław Niewiadomski, "Chopin w nauce harmonii" [Chopin in the teaching of harmony], in** *Obchód setnej rocznicy urodzin Fryderyka Chopina i Pierwszy Zjazd Muzyków Polskich we Lwowie.* *23 do 28 X 1910* **[Celebrations of the centenary of the birth of Fryderyk Chopin and the First Congress of Polish Musicians in Lviv. 23–28 October 1910], Lwów 1912, pp. 161-162.**

[...] Chopin and his music have been widely studied by biographers and theorists in works of varying length, purpose or scholarly rigour. But no one as yet has tackled the thematic and harmonic structure of his music or its contrapuntal aspects, with their scientific or technical elements. His music has been regarded as a Romantic product, its uniqueness, etherealness and general intangibility making it inadvisable to strip it of its fine diaphanous robes and to reveal the underlying skeleton for some positivist purpose. There was a fear that dry, indiscreet and heavy-handed analysis would ruin the music's charm, and so it was regarded purely as a beautiful phenomenon to the exclusion of its real substance. It seemed as if Chopin's music was based exclusively on feeling, caprice and fancy – so removed from precise rules or scientific pedantry that it would not have occurred to anyone to make it part of a curriculum. Rather than a musician in the strict professional sense, the composer was treated as an improvising dreamer, if not a brilliant amateur (as some did in Germany). In the past, lovers of Chopin's music were so respectful of the Classicist school and so trusting in the infallibility of its precepts that they hardly dared to take a closer look at their mischievous darling in case he somehow turned out to be inadequate. The parallel fifths in his mazurkas, though they seem hardly offensive, were not mentioned except in a shamefaced undertone.

Such an attitude was hardly conducive to hailing Chopin as an academic figure of great calibre. Unsurprisingly, his music continued to be ignored in scholarly work for quite some time after his death: musical citations from his works were nowhere to be found in scholarly books, and the theoretical school kept its distance, despite his enthusiastic reception by the performance school [...].

Gradually, Chopin's stature in music increased, particularly in Germany. It came to be noted that his music had proved more resistant to the passage of time than that of contemporaries like Mendelssohn and Schumann. Its affinities to modern music and its seminal qualities also became apparent: its freedom from rigid formal constraints was no longer criticised and its audacious harmonies ceased to offend, as did its chromaticism, modulations, transitions and chord substitutions. All these constituted a mine of inspiration that commanded scholarly esteem. Chopin showed a respect for the purity and rules of harmony, but he was also adept and original at exploring the scope such rules afforded. His liberty and invention led to a general expansion of musical expression. Things formerly regarded by scholars as exceptional or marginal came to the fore in Chopin's music, giving rise to new "rules", for it is not the rules that make a master. Rules are made by masters, especially by those who have assimilated the past and who look forward to the future, independent and strong... [...]

Portrait of Anton Rubinstein in the weekly magazine *Echo Muzyczne, Teatralne i Artystyczne*, 582 (1894), p. 562. Collection: Warszawskie Towarzystwo Muzyczne, Warsaw.

Fryderyk Chopin: nineteeth- and early twentieth-century Russian perspectives

Irina Nikolskaya

Fryderyk Chopin was a figure of interest to Russian pianists, composers and musicians almost from the very beginning of his career. In the 1820s and 1830s, works by Chopin were first heard in St. Petersburg in the salon of Maria Szymanowska, a well-known Polish pianist and composer. Then, in the 1830s, Chopin's music was performed by another notable pianist, Adolf von Henselt, the court pianist of the Empress of Russia. Other early performers included Chopin's Russian pupils, notably Maria Kalergis-Mukhanov.

The first press review in Russia related to an 1834 performance by Anton Gerke, and it included an appraisal of Chopin's music. Critical reactions in Russia were positive, for the most part. Some critics complained about the excessive complexity of his figurations, and about the technical problems his music posed for amateur performers, and others objected to the mannerist and feminine qualities of the music, but if there was a common thread running through the critical commentary it was one of respect for the originality of the Polish maestro and the "harmonic grace that imbued his works". In particular, Mikhail Ivanovich Glinka (1804-1857), often regarded as the father of the Russian school of composition, had a remarkably positive attitude to Chopin's music.

Chopin was written about on a regular basis, and enthusiastic commentaries were mixed with adverse criticism. Among the positive reactions was the comment that borrowings from Chopin's pianistic technique would "[lead] to the emergence of a so-called Romantic piano school of the highest standard". Another critic stated: "Chopin opens and, arguably, ends the modern era in piano performance. Metaphorically speaking, just as 'young Jupiter's forehead gave birth to [...] Minerva'", the goddess of arts and crafts as well as wisdom, so Chopin created a new pianistic style. Chopin's actual performing style was not familiar to many Russians at first hand, but among the notable exceptions were the young Anton Rubinstein, who visited Chopin in his Paris apartment in 1841, and Alexander Serov, a well-known critic and composer who attended one of Chopin's Paris concerts on 26 April 1841. Serov wrote: "I am referring to Franz Liszt, the most brilliant of pianists. [...] All piano virtuosos pale in comparison, with the sole exception of Chopin, that Raphael of the piano", a comment reminiscent of Heinrich Heine's earlier opinion that Chopin was a newcomer from the land of Mozart, Raphael and Goethe. Serov reiterated his opinion in 1843: "Chopin is a great composer who can be justifiably regarded as on a par with Mozart, Beethoven and Rossini".

On the other hand, critics drew attention to perceived shortcomings in Chopin's music, such as his penchant for minor genres (miniatures) and his inability to tackle orchestral forms. For instance, Vasily Botkin wrote an article in 1893 where rapturous comments about Chopin's pianistic technique and his "inconceivable melancholy and Romantic passion" were qualified by the following observation: "it is difficult to overlook the fact that this striving for exquisite originality pushes [Chopin] across the line of Romantic indefiniteness into the impenetrable darkness of desperate chaos. [...] [I]t should be noted that [this tendency] makes itself felt far less frequently in the minor pieces. This is perhaps to do with the very nature of Chopin's compositional talent, which displays ample artistic power and freedom in the small forms, but wilts and becomes tedious when called upon to produce things beyond its reach." Similar comments to the same effect seemed to indicate that not all critics of the day were able to recognize the originality and innovation of Chopin's musical language, which was quite ahead of its time. Such adversely critical comments may be contrasted with Liszt's spirited defence in *F. Chopin* (1852), where he defended Chopin's decision to remain within the scope of a single instrument and to compose mainly in the minor genres. According to Liszt, music was no different from poetry and painting, where minor works of art were not intrinsically inferior to longer plays or larger paintings.

Importantly, Chopin criticism in Russia recognized and highly appreciated the Polish elements in Chopin's works. The Polishness of his music was often discussed, and many critics drew comparisons with Russian music, notably with Mikhail Glinka. In 1857, Nikolai Khristianovich wrote: "Chopin was not a Polish national composer by dint of composing mazurkas or other Polish genres. The genre was not the point; what matters is the essence or spirit of his works. In the same way, Glinka was a Russian national composer in his incomparable opera [*Ivan Susanin*] and in his fantasia on a theme from the folk song 'Kamarinskaya'." Khristianovich also identified poetic and national elements in Chopin's nocturnes and ballades, and argued that Chopin represented an entire musical epoch in himself; he was an artist nonpareil, whose mazurkas were incomparably superior to even the most successful imitations.

"Perhaps a great talent will emerge one day to trace a similar course of development and outstrip his achievements; but the future appearance of a new Chopin is as difficult to imagine as the appearance of a new Byron, Molière or Pushkin…" In Serov's comment, "through Chopin's works, Europe became acquainted with peculiarly Slavic melodic shapes and modulations. Although his music was ridden with anguish and limited to the narrow confines of the piano, with many of his pieces composed in the minor genres, the 'Slavic' nature of his works gave them major artistic importance, on a par with such qualities as the genius of his inspiration, his profound honesty and his inner strength." For Russian musicians and critics, Chopin's form of expression and his melody were an embodiment of those Slavic qualities that were capable of rivalling Western music for distinctiveness.

One great admirer who made an enormous contribution to spreading the popularity of Chopin's music was Anton Rubinstein, an outspoken believer in the unsurpassed quality of Chopin's genius. "By nature, Chopin was hostile to all that is uncouth and common. He spent the latter half of his life in Paris, and it was probably to that influence that he owed the extraordinary elegance and supreme aristocratic grace of his music. I mean this in the best possible sense: his music was simple and natural, untainted by turgidity." On a different occasion, Rubinstein addressed the question of Chopin's preference for the piano largely to the exclusion of the orchestra or other instruments, an issue that puzzled many of his opponents and adherents alike; like Liszt before him, Rubinstein mounted a defence of Chopin's artistic freedom to choose one instrument. To Rubinstein, Chopin was the greatest composer since Beethoven, and he valued him above Schumann. Whereas in Schumann's music Rubinstein sensed an artificiality that extended even to expressions of noble, strong emotion, there was in his opinion a Slavic simplicity and honesty to Chopin's pieces. Rubinstein also noted that verbose expressions of feeling should not be mistaken for profundity; to him, excess was an enemy to forceful expression, and artistic forms tended to fare better for being compact and concise: "Chopin's briefest preludes produce a deeper impression and carry more artistic expression than many a fine symphony." According to Rubinstein, Chopin's preludes would have sufficed to immortalise the composer even if he had never written another note. To Rubinstein, Chopin's death actually marked the end of art, even if distinctive works did continue to be produced.

Rubinstein's interpretations of Chopin's works form a separate question, and it is one of fundamental importance. He was among the first in Russia to have recognized the remarkable, if often overlooked, psychological depth of Chopin's music.

Rubinstein essentially discovered the importance of the Sonata in B flat minor, and he communicated it to Europe, where the piece was not understood even by Liszt or Schumann, Chopin's most ardent adherents. In a break from an earlier tradition, Rubinstein was also the first pianist to perform the piece in its entirety. There is an account of an 1868 performance given in Paris to commemorate the painter Ary Scheffer, who painted one of Chopin's best-known portraits. In the artist's studio, Rubinstein played the *Marche funèbre* followed by the entire sonata.

Adelaida Hippius, Rubinstein's student at the music conservatory in St. Petersburg, recorded a comment by the famous cellist Karl Davydov (1838-1889): "Truly, after Rubinstein's performance no one else should presume to play [the Sonata in B flat minor]". In actual fact, the reverse happened, as many pianists were encouraged by Rubinstein's example to add the piece to their repertoires.

In Rubinstein's interpretation, the first movement combined tempestuousness with a sense of underlying anxiety, with the music dark and turbulent. Instead of playing the first theme as a succession of agitated individual phrases (the usual pianistic practice), he made an effort to make each motif distinct. The same vocal, expressive quality (modelled on agitated speech) was apparent in every element of performance. Listeners noted Rubinstein's ability to "make everything sing, even those things one would not have thought capable of song".

His interpretation of the *Marche funèbre*, already a fixture in all kinds of funereal celebrations, was characteristic. At the beginning and at the end, Rubinstein played four extra notes, as hollow and as soft as possible (B flat$_0$ and D flat$_1$). He played the opening bars *pianissimo* (the left hand in the opening bars playing an octave lower than the original), and gradually climbed to a *fortissimo* to evoke the image of an approaching cortège. In the final passage of the march (after the trio), he would unexpectedly launch into a *fortissimo* (instead of Chopin's original *piano*), and would gradually make it fade to nothing as if the cortège were receding in the distance.

For many years, Rubinstein remained silent about his interpretation of the finale, but in 1884 the young Ferruccio Busoni, writing for a Viennese journal, described how Rubinstein's excellent performance evoked the image of "autumnal wind blowing across an endless plain and whistling in tree crowns". Rubinstein played the last movement *prestissimo*, but despite the breakneck pace of his interpretation it was so expressive, logical and yielding that some of the notes disappeared altogether save where some scanty pedal work was used (he did not bring out the latent melodies). In his memoirs, Rachmaninoff remarked that Rubinstein's finale sounded like "reverberations in an enormous hall". Rubinstein played the concluding passage twice, the first time round replacing the chords in the final bar with a one-bar rest, the finale leaving a lingering sense of hollow hopelessness. Years later, Rubinstein described the last movement of the sonata as "a night gust of wind blowing over the graves", in what was not so much a philosophical reflection on life and death as a purely programmatic comment.

Throughout the 1880s and 1890s, lovers of piano music firmly associated the Sonata in B flat minor with Rubinstein. Josef Hofmann, Rubinstein's best student, learned about his master's death while he was on his way from London to Cheltenham; his concert programme that night included the famous sonata. When Hofmann played the first sounds of the *Marche funèbre*, all rose and listened to the entire movement standing, their heads hung low in memory of the deceased maestro.[1]

Rubinstein sought to heighten as much as possible the contrasts between the lyrical and the dramatic passages, and thus to achieve a bipolar opposition between two modes of expression, demonic passion and intimate confession. The sharp emotional contrasts often drew objections from those critics who preferred a more elegant and refined style. It was customary in that controversy to invoke the authority of Chopin's own performance style, which Rubinstein had had a chance to witness as a young man. Rubinstein roundly opposed the idea of there being some kind of mandatory style of performance in Chopin's music. He expressed his views in an article entitled "On music in Russia". "Chopin's particular playing style, with its soothing sounds, was something unique to the composer himself. It arose from the qualities of his character and as such it cannot under any circumstances be regarded as a hard and fast rule of Chopin performance. An amateur fascinated with Chopin will overlook this fact, and will treat Chopin's way of playing as a compulsory rule of performance" – an obvious mistake, argued Rubinstein, since even Chopin's famous *tempo rubato* was a product of "illness-induced exhaustion" and of the composer's intellectual and emotional agitation.[2] This was a far-fetched interpretation on Rubinstein's part, because Chopin's *tempi rubati* actually owed as much to folk performance practice (an early and lasting influence on Chopin) as to his own emotional state. Exhaustion and illness could hardly have been the reason for a performance style that Chopin had been using at different stages of his life, including periods of rejuvenation and vigour.

---

1 Josef Hofmann narrates the incident in a chapter on Rubinstein from his book *Piano Playing*, New York 1908.

2 Anton Rubinstein, "О музыке в России" [On music in Russia], *Век*, 1861/1, p. 36

Rubinstein started performing works by Chopin as a child in the 1840s, and by the 1870s and 1880s he was already familiar with the composer's entire œuvre. His contribution to international concert practice were the so-called "historical concerts", a grand series of seven concerts illustrating the development of piano music, where Chopin's music made up all of Concert 6 and half of Concert 7.

Rubinstein's interpretations of Chopin were unanimously perceived by his contemporaries as excessively focused on bringing out the dramatic and tragic elements even where other pianists tended to see no such emotions in the first place. Indeed, a certain penchant for dramatic excess is discernible in many of Rubinstein's statements and interpretations. For instance, his renditions of Chopin's etudes were perfectly furious affairs; Rubinstein was trying to capture what he believed was the composer's turbulent emotion, with the two last etudes in Op. 25 sounding in his interpretation like a mighty clash of primal elements. One concertgoer recorded an incident at one concert when the tense, fiery sound of the Etude in C sharp minor No. 12 reached such an extraordinary dramatic climax that the audience "got on their feet, such was the emotional tension. One lady shrieked: 'The artist is assuredly mad!'"[3]

With some exceptions, the composers known as The Five (and even more so their leading mentor, Vladimir Stasov) were enthusiastic about Chopin. César Cui wrote in his memoir: "We [i.e. Cui and Balakirev] were soon joined by Mussorgsky, Rimsky-Korsakov and Borodin (1855) to form a group of young composers; we had nowhere to learn (the conservatory did not yet exist), so we taught ourselves [...]. We played everything, and analysed every piece closely in terms of technique and artistry. [...] We were enthusiastic about Liszt and Berlioz, and we worshipped Chopin and Glinka."

The analogy Cui drew between Chopin and Glinka was indicative of Russian perceptions of Chopin. Russian critics were often particularly keen to foreground the Slavic elements in the music of these two composers. In a piece on Glinka's opera *Ivan Susanin*, Alexander Serov, a music critic of high reputation, argued that "the Russian peasant element needed balancing out with another Slavic element, a Polish one, drawn directly from Chopin's works". Obviously, similar parallels were drawn with the music of Alexander Dargomyzhsky (*Rusalka*), Anatoly Lyadov, César Cui and the early Scriabin, but the greatest affinity was perceived to have existed with Mikhail

---

3 Rubinstein, "Из короба мыслей" [From the treasure house of thought]. Quoted in Leo Barenboim, *Антон Григорьевич Рубинштейн* [Anton Grigorevich Rubinstein], ii (1867-1894), Leningrad 1962, p. 306.

Glinka. Chopin's Slavic elements and their connections with Russian folk music were mentioned by G. N. Timofeev in a pamphlet published on the fiftieth anniversary of Chopin's death: "Slavic elements dominate in his music. [...] In the melodies, be they Polish or not, we hear much of our native Russian element, which is present both in our folk songs and in the artistic music that developed so quickly following Glinka." On a side note, the book provoked a polemical article by one Ivanov, who questioned the value of Chopin's musical legacy and his pianistic talents. Ivanov's polemic met a passionate rebuttal of its own from Vladimir Stasov, the greatest authority on musical aesthetics at the time. Stasov likewise saw an analogy between Chopin and Glinka: "For Glinka, Chopin was the first harbinger of the possibility, indeed the necessity, of devising new forms to express those mysterious and passionate stirrings of the soul which are a unique quality of our century, and which have not been expressed (or possibly experienced) ever before. Chopin was Glinka's guide to new artistic forms, the equal to Beethoven in his capacity to express this newly opened world of the soul. [...] Chopin was the first composer to utilize the concept of folk melodies and folk genres. [...] He was the first composer to try and present folk melodies [...] in a true, unadulterated form, with their original colour and rhythm. He was the first to learn how to clothe them in appropriate harmonies, and the first to incorporate what the vulgar crowd believes are their 'rule violations' – he did not smooth them over, make them common or modern [...]. The ability to work with folkloric material had been first noted in our century among Slavic nations like the Russians and the Poles. The former saw the emergence of Glinka, the latter had Chopin." It is worth pointing out that Chopin did not in fact "present folk melodies [...] in a true, unadulterated form" (i.e. he never quoted extensively from actual folk melodies). What Stasov was actually referring to was what he perceived as the folk archetype underlying Chopin's artistic pieces, i.e. their emotional power and their ability to capture the essence of the folk spirit.

Other properties of Chopin's poetics were noted as well. Rimsky-Korsakov had interesting things to say about Chopin's harmonies: "[...] in his Etude in A flat major, where *harmony itself* seems to sing, we find sequences of chords that still remain unparalleled in modern music, including Wagner's. It will be years before people learn to appreciate them."

Obviously, there were also Russian composers who found Chopin's aesthetic alien. Pyotr Tchaikovsky, for one, was unimpressed by the Polish composer, despite the fact that he made use of Chopin's genres in his own music; his operas contain some mazurkas and a polonaise, and he wrote some piano mazurkas as well.

Alexander Scriabin went through a period of extreme Chopin fetishism in his childhood and adolescence, only to reject Chopin's aesthetic completely in later years, though there remain distinctly Chopinesque stylistic markers in much of his later work.

Musicological criticism in the last few decades of the nineteenth century and in the early 1900s examined a range of issues relating to Chopin's music. These included questions of biography and programmatic content in his music, as well as issues such as orchestral transcriptions, interpretations, Romantic pianism and Mily Balakirev's role in erecting a Chopin memorial in Żelazowa Wola.

The documents anthologized here include Stanislav Schlesinger's methodological study *Опыт дидактической систематики произведений Фр. Шопена* [The experience of a systematic study of Chopin's works for didactic purposes], which analyses the technical aspects of Chopin's music, including the interactivity of melody and harmony in the texture of the music, and in particular questions of rhythm and rubato. Schlesinger believed that "it is a piano teacher's task to assist every student [...] in achieving a level of technical and musical competence sufficient to commence the *study* of Chopin's works", and he gave a list of Chopin's works recommended for the purposes of study, arranged in ascending order of difficulty.

When Chopin's works became available in Russia, he immediately attained legendary status as a composer and was treated with veneration by both audiences and musicians – a situation that obtains to this very day.

Although *a terminus ante quem* of 1914 was adopted for the present anthology, I felt justified in ending it with fragments from Russia's first scholarly study of Chopin's music: the 1922 publication by Boris Asafyev (1884-1949).

Anthology

The earliest references to performances of Chopin's works in Russia date back to 1834, and they relate to **Anton Avgustovich Gerke**, the first real populariser of Chopin's music. The first performance of a work by Chopin in Russia took place on 11 April 1834 in St. Petersburg. Gerke played the Concerto in E minor and the Variations on "Là ci darem la mano" (Op. 2). The journal *Северная пчела* (**issue 80, 9 April 1834**) published a concert announcement by an unknown author: "The composer is already famous in Paris, but not yet in our parts [...]. Judging by the instrumental part (without the accompaniment), his works contain much that is new. They require extraordinary technique, as all the figurations seem quite extensive. If the orchestration lives up to the solo part, we must be dealing with a remarkable composer. Chopin is to his instrument what Lipiński is to the violin. Were it not for Gerke, we would have to wait a long time to hear this concerto, since it takes perfect technique and an extraordinary effort to perform."

Vasiliy Petrovich Botkin,[4] "Mr. Gerke's charity concert (11 April)", published in two journals, *Сын отечества* and *Северный архив*, 16 (1834), pp. 602-603.

[...] Although Chopin's works have been available in our music stores for three or four years, no one so far seems to have attempted to overcome the extraordinary difficulties those compositions bristle with. If Chopin ever decides to show in his compositions a greater charity for performers, and in any way take into account the physical capacity of pianists, he will doubtless take an important place among the

---

4 Botkin wrote under the pen-name Vasiliy Fortepianov

best known composers. His works are distinctly elegant. The cantabile sections are songlike, and his thematic ideas and figurations are highly original; his accompaniments are occasionally too complicated, but nonetheless they bear the unmistakeable mark of a true master's competent hand. The Concerto in E minor as performed by Mr. Gerke deserves to be included in the repertoire of the best pianists.

Anonymous, "Смесь. Музыкальные новости" [Pot-pourri. Musical news], *Библиотека для чтения* (1839), pp. 72-73.

[...] Gerke played Chopin's Concerto in E minor, a work that has changed the nature of piano playing. It poses a supremely difficult challenge to any performer, and none of our musicians besides Gerke are equal to the task. Fascinated amateurs and musicians had flocked to see the performer, and to hear the concerto for themselves. The great pianist Thalberg arrived at St. Petersburg on the same day, and he was in the audience. [...].

"Дневник В.Ф. Одоевского"[5] [Diary of V. F. Odoevsky], *Литературное наследство*, 22-24, pp. 250, 239. Entry for 4 January 1869:

[...] Klindworth played the concerto by Chopin. Naturally, I was surrounded on all sides by crowds asking my opinion. I resorted to a stratagem, replying: *Klindworth est fait pour la musique de Chopin* ('Klindworth is made for Chopin's music'). Mostly, I would leave it at that; but in a few cases I went on to add: *Il a dans son jeu tout le faux et la manière qui se trouvent dans la musique de Chopin et au bredouillage du compositeur il ajoute le sien avec une grace toute particulière* ('he encompasses in his performance all the falseness and mannerism that you find in Chopin's music, and augments the composer's stammering with his own, something he does with particular grace'). [...]

Modest Dmitrevich Rezvoy,[6] "Адольф Гензельт и нынешняя игра на фортепиано" [Adolf Henselt and modern pianism], *Северная пчела*, 107 (14 May 1838).

After receiving the basics of his musical education in Warsaw, in the absence of a first-class model Chopin polished the rare and original gem of his talent in seclu-

---

5 Vladimir Fyodorovich Odoevsky was one of the most eminent music critics in Russia.
6 A popular critic in the 1830s and 1840s.

sion. His performance style is reminiscent of Field's, but the speed of his hand movement, which has been brought to perfection, shows that we are dealing with a new and original system. His delicate, velvety performance perfectly matches the character of his pieces, which are imaginative yet nostalgic. He has created new modes of expression with the piano, and none of his predecessors could boast anything like the harmonic grace we can find in his music. Chopin's musical phrases are imbued with originality. He adorns his chords with countless ornaments and extra notes in order to bring out the beauty of his melodies and to pose technical challenges in his etudes. He has also promoted solo piano performances and minor character pieces rather than those extended forms of which the public had already grown weary. Chopin's remarkable talent was shaped during his youth, and his later music is unable to rival the early pieces. Still, he has given rise to countless imitators. At the very least, he has begun a new trend in piano performance, as we find other composers, including his seniors, borrowing from his methods. This has resulted in the emergence of a so-called Romantic piano school of the highest calibre. Chronologically speaking, should we perhaps also mention Liszt, whose remarkable technique transcends all limits? I hesitate to answer in the affirmative, since Liszt's performances break all the rules relating to musical form and proportion.

Chopin's compositional and performance styles are discernible in pieces by Hiller, Clara Wieck, Schumann and others. Even the restrained Thalberg, the modern representative of the Vienna school, is not wholly averse to using Chopin's methods in his performance. [...]

Probably by **Osip Ivanovich Senkovsky, in** *Библиотека для чтения*, **81 (1847), p. 51**.

[...] In his two collections of etudes, the Polish genius forged a new path, which is distinctive for its completely original treatment of melody. It would seem that melody disappears altogether, only to emerge unexpectedly out of complex figurations and broken chords. This entails a double effort on the part of the performer: firstly, complex passage-work must be played with fluent grace; secondly, the latent melody must be brought out through a differentiated touch and subtle, more or less continuous pedal work. Chopin has inaugurated and arguably ended the modern era in piano performance; like the brow of Jupiter, he gave birth to a Minerva so perfectly armed that it seems quite impossible to add anything to it. Understandably, a crowd of imitators appeared instantaneously, but they are left grasping at the bare skeleton of his music – no one but he is capable of grasping that music's essential soul and unique genius. Those so-called modern composers were quickly left floundering without the most important aspect of invention – melody. [...]

Vasiliy Petrovich Botkin, "Об эстетическом значении новой фортепианной школы" [On the aesthetic importance of the new pianistic school], in *Сочинения В.П. Боткина* [The works of V. P. Botkin], iii (Petersburg, 1892), pp. 71-72.

1850. [...] The profuse virtuosos who composed secular piano music saw their efforts come to an unhappy fruition in an interminable tinkling and chiming utterly devoid of feeling or spirit. Then, Chopin appeared; and the unfortunate instrument, which had degenerated under the prosaic touch of those jugglers almost to the role of a musical rattle, was instantaneously transformed by his artistic talent into a source of poetry and spirit.

Chopin's genius gave a wholly new character to piano music. The instrument spoke in the language of poetry and with a piercingly nostalgic Romanticism. Melancholy and nebulous, the composer's original melodies are wrapped in the permanent dusk of their noble harmonies. His miniatures, which consist of pure lyrical inspiration, are especially wonderful. He was the first to shake himself free from the conventions of contemporary piano music, as he rejected hackneyed passage-work and figuration and replaced them with exquisite new forms and successions. As the creator of poetic and spiritual melodies clad in intriguing and ingenious harmonic successions, Chopin reached the level of true genius. Unfortunately, it is difficult to overlook the fact that this striving for exquisite originality pushes the composer across the line of Romantic indefiniteness into the impenetrable darkness of desperate chaos. His odd proclivity for excessive chromaticism is the dark side of his brilliant talent, although it should be noted that it makes itself felt far less frequently in the minor pieces. This is perhaps to do with the very nature of Chopin's compositional talent, which displays ample artistic power and freedom in the small forms but wilts and becomes tedious when called upon to produce things beyond its reach.

Given that the charm of Chopin's music consists in its melancholy and its muted colours, it follows that it is only accessible to people with a well-developed sense of nuance and refined artistic sensibility. Owing to the nature of his talent, Chopin was unable to infuse a truly popular quality into his music, which is presumably a principal aim of piano music. Still, he was a major influence on other pianist composers. His etudes influenced the music of Liszt, Thalberg and Henselt, for example. The new school had to answer the question: is it possible to imbue piano music with a lyrical element without relapsing into the old flaws which so dogged the instrument first time round? [...]

Nikolay Khristyanovich,[7] "Шопен. Письма из провинции" [Chopin. Letters from the provinces], in *Письма о Шопене, Шуберте и Шумане* [Letters about Chopin, Schubert and Schumann (Moscow: P. I. Jurgenson, 1876).

[...] Chopin's brilliant preludes are twenty-four short words, but each made his heart boil, quiver and suffer in succession; in each his heart fills with anger, terror, yearning, tenderness or anguish; it cries and moans, then is caressed and given hope; there is delight, sadness and painful disappointment; the heart turns numb with terror, then freezes among the howling gusts of autumn wind; several bars later, it finds new faith that the sunshine will come back, and it blossoms with the pastoral sounds of spring. Every prelude is a separate whole, perfect and complete – a job wisely done and an obstacle successfully overcome.

Chopin was not a Polish national composer by dint of composing mazurkas or other Polish genres. The genre was not the point; what matters is the essence or spirit of his works. In the same way, Glinka was a Russian national composer in his incomparable opera [*Ivan Susanin*] and in his fantasia on a theme from the folk song 'Kamarinskaya', as well as in his song settings of Kukolnik. [...]

By analogy, Chopin is a national poet-composer in his nocturnes and ballades, whereas the mazurkas of his imitators, even the most successful ones, are ephemeral. In the works of his imitators, form is everything; in Chopin, form is the external symptom of an inner state.

That internal essence in his music conceals a special something that only Chopin knew. It was born with him, and he took it to his grave.

Chopin had done much for art, and he blazed new trails. Perhaps a great talent will emerge one day to trace a similar course of development and outstrip his achievements; but the future appearance of a new Chopin is as difficult to imagine as the appearance of a new Byron, Molière or Pushkin. [...]

---

7 Nikolay Filipovich Khristyanovich (1828–1890) was a lawyer by training and a musician by vocation.

Alexander Serov,[8] "О некоторый формах нынешней музыки" [On some forms of contemporary music] (1858), *Советская музыка*, 1949/5, p. 72.

[...] Chopin's originality and independence set him apart from other composers, and that means that his occasional formal shortcomings and his restriction to the piano as a medium take nothing away from his genius. Schumann made a fitting comment about his friend, whose spirit greatly influenced the mood and direction of his own brilliant music: "Obviously, he is endowed with a great originality; wherever it alights, there can be no mistaking the composer's name; he reveals an abundance of new forms, so subtle and daring as to command the highest respect. [...] As a composer he is, and will remain, the proudest and most audacious creative spirit of our times."

There are other important qualities in Chopin's character besides subtlety and audacity. One also finds in his music that straightforward tenderness and profundity he learnt from Bach and, to an even greater extent, from Beethoven…

After Beethoven's death, Chopin was the first of his successors to find a way into the most mysterious corners of the human soul; like no one else, Chopin could capture and express those mysterious passions in our spirit which may be the sole legacy of our century. [...] Through Chopin's works, Europe became well acquainted with peculiarly Slavic melodic shapes and modulations. Although his music was ridden with anguish and limited to the narrow confines of the piano, with many of his pieces composed in the minor genres, the 'Slavic' nature of his works gave them major artistic importance, on a par with such qualities as the genius of his inspiration, his profound honesty and his inner strength.

It is a testimony to the widespread popularity of Chopin's music among music lovers that F. Stellovsky, a music publisher from St. Petersburg, published his complete works in 1861. [...]

"Библиографическое известие" [Bibliographical news], *С-Петербургские ведомости*, 8 March 1861.

On the publication of the complete works for four hands by F. Chopin. The edition is dedicated *to the Poles*.

The whole educated world is familiar with Chopin's great and extraordinary talent; our society has consistently demonstrated an empathy with, indeed an en-

---

8 Alexander Nikolayevich Serov (1820–1871), an eminent Russian critic and composer.

thusiasm for, the great composer, whose works reflect the full and diverse range of human thought and emotion. Above all else, Chopin was an exponent of the Romantic spirit in music; he was unrivalled in that respect, and can be confidently described as the founder of the modern Romantic school. Invariably inspired and poetic, Chopin's works are astonishingly deep and emotionally powerful, with an elegant and graceful form. In his ballades – where he takes on the guise of an epic singer from his native country – and in his sonatas, nocturnes, etudes and scherzos, Chopin is a true poet, who provides models of ultimate artistry; Chopin's musical images reflect perfectly the local colour of Poland, its natural beauty and its passionate feeling. And this is no less the case in his Bolero, Tarantella and Barcarolle.

The fecundity of Chopin's creative invention is staggering: over a period of less than twenty years, he composed more than 200 works, each bearing the mark of genius and inspiration. Chopin belongs to all nations, but he is Polish first and foremost, in his delicate, enthralling motifs as well as in his irritability, impetuosity and vigour. Musically, his pieces have assimilated both a French character and that of German Romanticism; but in terms of the fundamental character of his works, Chopin belongs to Poland more than to any other nation on earth.

Despite his considerable and widespread fame, no European public has been able to see a complete edition of his works, because the publishing rights to his music are divided among a number of publishing houses all over Europe. This means that Russia is the only place where those works can be compiled and published in their entirety. Consequently, I have undertaken the major task of releasing a complete edition of Chopin's works in five volumes that comprise around 200 works on 1,200 large-sized pages, including a portrait and a biography of the composer.

Alexander Serov, "Русалка. Опера А.С. Даргомыжского" [*Rusalka*. An opera by A. S. Dargomyzhsky], in *Статьи о музыке* [On music] (Moscow 1986), pp. 71, 84.

[...] In the [Glinka] opera *Ivan Susanin (A Life for the Tsar),* the Slavic operatic style makes its first (and certainly *unintended*) appearance in all its magnificence.

Based on the life of the Russian peasantry, the patriotic storyline influenced the nature of the singing by rendering it as close as possible to our folk songs. The nationalistic direction of the music became a fact, but the Russian peasant element needed balancing out with another Slavic element, a Polish one, drawn directly from Chopin's works. [...]

[...] Those replies effect the transitions to the Allegro in A major.[9] Against this ferment, which precedes the launch of a new tempo, Natasha's part contains a highly original and elegant fioritura which sounds as though it were prompted by Chopin. [...]

Alexander Serov, "Нибелунгов перстень. Музыкально-драматическая поэма Рихарда Вагнера" [*The Ring of the Nibelung*, a music drama by Richard Wagner],[10] in *Статьи о музыке* [On music] (Moscow, 1986).

[...] Add to that the dreamy Chopin, who plumbed the innermost secrets of the psyche to emerge with an abundance of the subtlest of melodies and harmonies, unknown to Bach or Beethoven! [...]

The 1841 musical season

Paris, 20 April 1841

[...] I am referring to Franz Liszt, the most brilliant of pianists. That man of genius is with us again and giving us almost unimaginably enthralling concerts. [...] All piano virtuosos pale in comparison, with the sole exception of Chopin, that Raphael of the piano. [...]

The 1843 musical season

Letter 2

Paris, 26 March 1843

[...] There is only one pianist whom I value more highly than Thalberg. It is Chopin, and he is a composer far more than he is a virtuoso. With Chopin, I can overlook entirely the purely virtuosic element (which I loathe); rather I plummet into the depths of his music and am filled with the unforgettable anguish of those profound, emotion-saturated works. Chopin is a great composer, who can be justifiably regarded as on a par with Mozart, Beethoven and Rossini. [...]

César Cui (1835-1918) – composer and music critic, a member of The Five.

---

9 Now in reference to *Rusalka*.

10 An essay in which Serov; attacks the opponents of Wagner's music. Excerpts from pp. 41, 272 and 288 respectively.

César Cui, "Г-н [Карл] Гейман и г-жа [София] Ментер" [Mr. [Carl] Heymann and Mrs. [Sophie] Menter], *Голос,* **57 (3 March 1882).**

[...] It is difficult to justify a concert performance of Chopin's mazurkas in a virtuosic arrangement that is really quite different from the original version as intended by that great composer. Virtuosity ought not to cross certain lines for fear of degenerating into a tasteless attack on the very lifeblood of music. Such was Chopin's genius as a composer and pianist that his works cannot be amended or improved. If the point of the exercise was to demonstrate technical problems, then we can point out that there are many original works by Chopin, such as his etudes, where the technical problems are enough of a match for Mrs. Menter's colossal technique. [...]

"Первый концерт И[осифа] Гофмана" [Mr. J[osef] Hofmann's first concert], *Новости и биржевая газета,* **4 (4 January 1897).**

[...] Mr. Hofmann chose some of Chopin's rarely performed works for his programme. They included the Nocturne in B major (Op. 62 No. 1), with its recurrent theme, where every note is decorated with a trill. The nocturne is not universally agreed to be one of Chopin's most brilliant pieces. It bears the marks of weariness and ill health, but retains the sophisticated taste, the sense of beauty and the warmth that never left Chopin. The Mazurka in E minor (Op. 41 No. 2) is also one of Chopin's lesser-known mazurkas; its folk colour blends wondrously with a depth of feeling that is expressed with exquisite simplicity (the mazurka passed almost completely unnoticed in the performance).

The Polonaise in A flat major (Op. 53) is well known, and I only mention it in order to note the peculiarity of Mr. Hofmann's performance. He played the polonaise at a somewhat slower pace than is usual, and with less use of the sustaining pedal. As a result, the piece became more majestic and transparent. [...]

"Третий концерт И[осифа] Гофмана" [Mr. J[osef] Hofmann's third concert], *Новости и биржевая газета,* **5 (5 January 1897).**

[...] J. Hofmann played [...] Chopin, that embodiment of supreme elegance and feminine beauty, an inexhaustible and unmatched maker of melodies who communicated every stirring of his sensitive heart in a way that was honest, poetic and expressive. [...]

Mr. Hofmann was at his most impressive in the second part of the concert. This was hardly surprising, given that he performed Schumann (*Kreisleriana*) and Chopin (the Nocturne in C sharp minor, two preludes and the Sonata in B flat minor). The great composer and the great pianist merged into one to move the audience with irresistible power. Words fail us as we try to convey the expression, understanding and beauty present in Mr. Hofmann's articulation of the subtle nuances of *Kreisleriana*, or the depths he revealed in the nocturne, or the drama of the first movement of the sonata, or the crushing anguish of the funeral march (which was performed in Chopin's original version, rather than in Rubinstein's variant), or the epic scale and the poetry of the finale, which swept by like a gust of wind, now waxing strong, now fading and waning... [...]

César Cui, "Концерт Рубинштейна. Первый концерт Филармонического общества" [Rubinstein's concert. The first concert at the Philharmonic Society], *Санкт-Петербургские ведомости* , 54 (2 March 1865).

[...] Chopin was a different composer altogether. A true poet, he was filled with passion and true vitality. His anguished disposition and the musical limitations that dogged him throughout his musical career thwarted his efforts to compose large-scale works. He never once attempted to step beyond the narrow confines of piano music or to expand the formal aspects of his works, nor did he ever try to add further expression to his ideas by using a palette of orchestral colours. The sonatas exhibit the broadest sweep and range of all his works, but for all the occasional profundity and beauty of their materials, even they can be staggeringly infantile, misshapen and *haphazard* in their structure. Still, Chopin has an immense importance in music history owing to his influence on the public and on other composers [...].

The whole development of modern music could be summarized by way of the systematic reception of Beethoven, who transformed absolute music into a language of poetry and passion; through his influence on the poetic imagination, he portrayed ideas that were beyond *words*. But Beethoven's development was so rapid that only a handful of the most gifted individuals were able to keep up with him (viz. the nonsensical contemporary criticism of his late works)). To make music accessible to the masses, the elements of music needed to be exposed to a more modest degree of change. Chopin performed that task. His childlike, poetic and painfully tender sounds charmed all, especially in the composer's own exquisite performance;

idolized by the public, he constituted a more manageable step towards the understanding of modern music in its highest forms. In particular, we should not overlook the Polish and Ukrainian elements which are present in nearly all of his works, and which imbue them with a particular original grace. Nor should we forget the composer's influence on many works by Schumann, Glinka or Moniuszko. [...]

César Cui, "Русалка – опера А.С. Даргомыжского" [*Rusalka* – an opera by A. S. Dargomyzhsky], *Музыкальное обозрение* 20, 21, 22-23 (20 and 27 October 1888).

[...] There are composers whose every work is beautiful. A given piece may succeed or fail, but it will be beautiful in every case. This beauty is felt in the melody, the harmony, the accompaniment, the progressions – everywhere; every piece wears festive attire and seems to be basking in a magical light.

For an example of a composer who writes beautiful music, I would point to Chopin. This kind of ability to create alluring and compelling sound worlds – a feminine aspect of the composing talent – is necessary to portray fantastical things, yet Dargomyzhsky was almost completely devoid of it.[...]

Anton Rubinstein,[11] an article in *Неделя*, 20 (20 November 1894).

[...] Rubinstein popularized the works of Beethoven, Chopin and Schumann; he offered us concrete demonstrations of their genius, as it were, and placed them on the highest pedestal. [...]

Anton Rubinstein, "Фредерик Шопен" [Fryderyk Chopin], *Новости и биржевая газета*, 275 (6 October 1899).

Fifty years ago, on 17 October 1849 (5 October in the Julian calendar), Fryderyk Chopin, one of the greatest composers of all time, died in Paris.

An uninterested observer might conclude that Chopin's life was quiet and uneventful, unmarked by extraordinary events. But the composer's moral and spiritual life exerted a major influence on his art [...]; Chopin's double identity, and the fact

---

11 Anton Rubinstein (1829-1913), a world-famous Russian panist, conductor and entrepreneur.

that he had been shaped by two separate formative backgrounds, had a strong effect on his music, which combined French dynamism, grace, light and gaiety with Slavic solemnity and depth.

Chopin was a family man and a patriot. He was a devoted friend, brother and son, with a great affection for his sisters and his parents (he was unmarried), and he loved his native Poland and its landscapes, among which he had spent his younger years. I would like to recount a moving episode from the artist's life: when he was leaving Warsaw in 1830, the friends who were seeing him off gave him a silver goblet filled with Polish soil. He kept that handful of earth all his life, and requested that it be thrown on his coffin during his funeral; the wish was duly enacted. For political reasons, Chopin never returned to Poland, and he felt acutely the sufferings of his country. He missed his friends and loved ones, and poured all that heartfelt misery into his strange, poetic tones. To describe the doleful condition of his spirit, he used the Polish word *żal,* a term that combines the meaning of deep sadness and outraged grievance.

By nature, Chopin was hostile to all that is uncouth and common. He spent the latter half of his life in Paris, and it was probably to that influence that he owed the extraordinary elegance and supreme aristocratic grace of his music. I mean this in the best possible sense; his music was simple and natural, untainted by turgidity (Liszt is likewise a subtle and sophisticated aristocrat of the piano, but he is often superficial and conceited).

Those circumstances exerted a continuous influence on Chopin's music; but without his God-given talent or the inspiration provided by his genius, the circumstances alone would not have been sufficient to make him the great artist that he was.

Chopin's music has yet another notable quality: his œuvre is limited to solo piano music. There are only a few exceptions: two piano concertos (where the orchestra plays only a secondary role), a cello sonata and sixteen[12] Polish songs. In this respect, Chopin was unprecedented. Composers find it irresistibly tempting to try out the orchestral palette or to enjoy the sound of mass choirs, and the success of a dramatic piece is practically a guarantee of fame and wealth. Yet Chopin was content with the piano. There have been great composers, such as Brahms or Mendelssohn, who refrained from regular artistic production. But Chopin was alone in having composed no large-scale symphonic or vocal pieces such as masses, cantatas or oratorios. Nonetheless he was a versatile and gifted composer. What is the solution to that riddle? Perhaps his nervous disposition longed for instant expression, and preferred short, pithy pieces composed

---

12 Actually nineteen [editor's note].

on the spur of the moment, realizing how difficult it would have been to sustain the mood in a larger work over the span of a long creative process? Perhaps Chopin valued his deep, heartfelt feelings so highly that he was reluctant to entrust them to dozens of musicians and preferred the intimacy of small circles made up of kindly, empathetic individuals to the large crowds gathering in theatres and concert halls?

Does Chopin's decision to restrict himself to the piano detract from his fame and importance? It does no such thing. For me, Chopin is the greatest composer since Beethoven.

I value Chopin even more than I do Schumann. In Schumann's music, one sometimes hears a tone of artificial, unnatural German sentimentality, even as he is expressing strong and deep emotion; in Chopin's pieces, a Slavic quality of honest simplicity reigns supreme. As for the compact scale of his works, deep and strong feelings have no need of verbosity; on the contrary, verbosity makes them blunt and shallow. Thus, Chopin's briefest preludes produce a deeper impression and carry more artistic expression than many a fine symphony. The same principle applies in literature and in social communication. Concision, after all, tends to be one of the most highly valued qualities in both a writer and a conversationalist.

Chopin used a wide range of generic types. Almost all of them had existed before, but Chopin contributed greatly to the development of each, and transformed them beyond recognition.

There had been *waltzes* before Chopin, but they did not have the Chopinesque glow and elegance or that beautiful melody you find in the middle section of so many of his waltzes. Likewise, people had composed *polonaises* before (Ogiński, for example), and *mazurkas* can be found in many Polish folk songs, and yet Chopin expanded those dance pieces, infused them with a new spirit, and made them picturesque and expressive. There had also been *etudes* before, but they were dry pedagogical pieces intended for honing one's technique; Chopin's etudes are virtuosic, but they are also full of musical substance. There had been earlier *nocturnes* (Field), but they had none of that peculiar Chopinesque poetry. As for *ballades*, they had their prototype in pianistic battle pieces and similar story-telling works (Steibelt). But unlike those early onomatopoeic pieces, which were often unintentionally comical, Chopin's ballades are thrilling works that produce a powerful effect on the imagination. Unlike the others, the *preludes* are purely of Chopin's own making. They are fragments, sketches into which Chopin poured all of himself to express the diverse states of the soul with an extraordinary power. We might say that Chopin did for the piano prelude what Beethoven had done for the orchestral scherzo.

It is not my aim to appraise every single one of Chopin's works, nor to analyse his remarkable music in great detail. Let me just emphasize that he was unprecedented among composers in terms of the depth and power of his feelings; no one had been able to express their feelings in such a poetic, noble, tender, elegant and irresistible way. Some have described Chopin as a feminine artist or as a salon composer. They were mistaken; he encompassed the whole world, and it is to the whole world that he belongs. [...]

"Первые композиторские шаги Ц.А. Кюи" [César Cui's first steps as a composer][13].

[...] From my earliest childhood, I was fascinated by Chopin's music, and especially by his mazurkas. Cheap printed music was not available at the time, and my parents' means were very limited (my father taught French in a high school in Vilnius), so I copied Chopin's complete mazurkas by hand. I actually had no music paper, and had to draw the staves myself. [...] We [i.e. Cui and Balakirev] were soon joined by Mussorgsky, Rimsky-Korsakov and Borodin (1855) to form a group of young composers; we had nowhere to learn (the conservatory did not yet exist), so we taught ourselves [Cui is referring here to the emergence of The Five] We played everything, and analysed every piece closely in terms of technique and artistry. We were young, and our judgments were brusque. We scorned Mozart and Mendelssohn, and we contrasted the latter with Schumann, who was largely ignored at the time. We were enthusiastic about Liszt and Berlioz, and we worshipped Chopin and Glinka [...].

Anton Rubinstein, *Лекции по истории фортепианной литературы* [Lectures on the history of piano literature][14] (Moscow, 1974), pp. 74-83.

Chopin was an extraordinary personality on every count. He was a Pole, and although the music he wrote was subjective, its subject was the whole Polish nation. He was a man racked by illness, a frail, consumptive man with a fine poetic nature. He kept aloof from crowds and preferred to surround himself with his closest admirers,

---

13 Memoirs of César Cui written at the request of N. Drizen, editor of *Ежегодник императорских театров*, a yearly publication.

14 This text is based on a compilation of notes taken (mainly by César Cui) during Rubinstein's lectures, supplemented with the notes of Sophia Davos-Diekhterova and the Latvian critic Atis Kaulin. Rubinstein gave the lectures in 1888-89.

especially female ones. Everything he composed is recognizably unique, which is perhaps the most wonderful thing about his music. To this day, he has multitudes of imitators. After his death, all new etudes, ballades, nocturnes and mazurkas tended to be composed in the Chopinesque vein. "Let me play his works as often as possible, for he cannot be loved too much". Chopin had the rare quality of recognizing his own limitations and did not venture beyond piano music. All other composers wrote operas, symphonies, quartets, oratorios; only Chopin was content to stay within the confines of piano music. He made only a few exceptions to that rule: a cello sonata (dedicated to his friend Franchomme), a trio (a juvenile piece he did not think much of) and the sixteen Polish songs. Chopin was a genius of the piano, and we cherish his every note. His early works were poor and may seem uninteresting when compared to the harmonic and rhythmic complexities of Schumann, but they already afford glimpses of Chopin's future genius.

Op. 1, Rondo. This is a weak piece compared to Chopin's later works, but it already shows characteristic signs of original melody and pianistic technique. Other composers could tease interesting and dazzling effects from the piano too, but in Chopin's hands the instrument has a unique sound; one might say that Chopin is the soul of the piano.

Op. 2, Variations on "Là ci darem la mano". Rubinstein's audience being relatively unsophisticated, the pianist left this piece out of his programme. Whereas there are many Chopinesque qualities in the *Rondo à la mazur* (Op. 5), in this piece the composer seems to have been merely following the musical fashions of the day, and his passage-work has a disjointed quality that fails to cohere within the overall shape of the piece.

Chopin's artistic nature is on full display in his Nocturnes, Op. 9 (the first in a series of nocturnes dedicated to Mme Pleyel, who was regarded at the time as one of the finest women pianists alongside Clara Wieck). The second nocturne (in E flat major) has been performed and arranged for different instruments so often that it has lost all its freshness. Nine mazurkas from Op. 6 and 7 followed, but Rubinstein was only able to demonstrate interesting harmonic combinations in the middle section of the third mazurka [from Op. 6].

Etudes: 12 Etudes, Op. 10 and 12 Etudes, Op. 25. The composer is at his most "Chopinesque" in his etudes, though his ballades, mazurkas, nocturnes and other pieces are not far behind in this respect. Before Chopin, etudes were composed with a view to improving pianistic technique; Chopin infused them with noble and spiritual ideas. Chopin's etudes were widely imitated. Subsequently, programmatic etudes were often composed; for instance, Henselt composed etudes entitled "Orage, tu ne sauras m'abattre" [Oh tempest, thou canst not strike me down], "Si oiseau j'étais" [Were I a bird] and others. Chopin's etudes, on the other hand, are untitled. They are referred to as etudes because of their design and conception, but they carry no programmatic description. That is just as well; a musical mood can hardly be described as profound if it can be expressed in words; in the absence of a programme, music is enriched and is open to many more interpretations.

Mr. Rubinstein performed only the most characteristic of Chopin's etudes. Notable in the first is not only the remarkable technical demands but also the striking bass theme. In terms of technique, the passage-work alone furnishes enough fascinating material, particularly where played by both hands an octave apart. The Etude No. 3 in E major is one of the best known. It would take a very rich programme indeed to explicate this wondrous music! The Etude No. 5 in G flat major, which is known as the "Black Keys" Etude, because of their predominance in the piece, is a kind of magnificent joke. The same piece can be played equally well on the white keys in G major to make an excellent fingering exercise, and Rubinstein did just that. The Etude No. 6 in E flat minor defies interpretation, or indeed description. One is not sure whether to admire the beauty of the melody or perhaps the charm of the harmonic development. As Rubinstein points out, it is a piece that does not carry any title other than the word etude, and "in the absence of a programme, music is enriched, and is open to many more interpretations". If we can explain or narrate the storyline of a musical piece, in words, that music is "not lofty enough". The Etude No. 9 in F minor is a dramatic piece, and it too defies any attampt at description. The Etude No. 11 in E flat major, which is made up of brilliant passage-work, is exquisite music. The Etude No. 12 in C minor is a dramatic poem in its own right.

Of the other set of Etudes, Op. 25, Mr. Rubinstein played the Etude No. 1 in A flat major and the Etude No. 2 in F minor. Before performing the latter, he remarked that he would play it in Chopin's original version, which is different from the version usually heard in performance. The Etude was originally composed in a 3/4 metre, with the right hand playing triplet quavers to each crotchet beat. In each triplet, Mr. Rubinstein accented the first note slightly to retain the original rhythm of the etude. But the left hand part contains crotchet triplets, with the beginning of each triplet occurring at every half bar; this makes accurate performance quite difficult, since the hands must play independently of one another. To deal with this technical difficulty, pianists tend to shift the accents and place them in the middle of each bar, resulting in a change of metre from 3/4 to 6/4. This solution facilitates the performance considerably, but it does so at the expense of accuracy. The Etude No. 7 in C sharp minor is music of a truly rare character, unlike anything else, with the possible exception of Beethoven. As to the Etudes No. 10 in B minor, No. 11 in A minor and No. 12 in C minor: in Mr. Rubinstein's performance, the last two pieces sounded like a thunderstorm, a clash of mighty elements.

Op. 12, *Variations brillantes sur le rondeau favori "Je vends des scapulaires"* from the opera *Ludovic* by the then-fashionable composers Hérold and Halévy. These are agreeable variations, written in a manner somewhat against the grain of other works from that period; though more valuable than Chopin's first variations on "Là ci darem la mano", they are still little more than a nod to contemporary fashion. It is quite astonishing to consider that Chopin wrote those salon pieces in close proximity to such profound works at the etudes that preceded them or the nocturnes that followed. One might have thought it impossible to regress after composing such ambitious music; yet Chopin did return to writing salon pieces. Apparently, the fact that he was based in the metropolis that was Paris and craved outward glitter made its own claims on him.

Op. 15, three nocturnes. The first is remarkable compared with the flimsy variations that preceded it; the second, a highly popular piece, is well loved by the ladies; the third is astonishing and little else. Rubinstein described the three nocturnes as "dreamy", "nice and elegant", and "strange and quite unpopular", respectively.

Op. 17, four mazurkas. The last has a delightfully unusual ending. Although it is composed in the key of A minor, the mazurka ends in F major with a sixth chord in its first inversion.

Op. 18, Chopin's first waltz: very much a salon piece, and quite different from the composer's later waltzes.

Op. 20, the first scherzo. In formal terms, this piece can be described as a scherzo, in that it is a ternary structure with a trio, but in terms of content it is a highly dramatic piece. This brilliant work was again followed by an agreeable salon confection, *Grande polonaise brillante precedée d'un Andante spianato,* Op. 22, and that in turn was followed by another brilliant work, the first ballade (Op. 23). Chopin originated this genre; although many later composers would write ballades (including programmatic ones), those pieces were quite insubstantial. Chopin's works, despite their unassuming titles and lack of programme, are filled with musical activity.

Op. 24, four mazurkas. The second of these is composed in the ancient modes, and to do justice to the fourth would take an entire poem.

Op. 26, two polonaises. Each of these pieces makes it apparent that Chopin was becoming increasingly detached from popular taste and preferred to confine himself within a small group of close friends and kindred souls. A chasm separates the first polonaise (C sharp minor) from the *Grande polonaise brillante*, Op. 22 which had gone before. The earlier piece was composed in pursuit of fame and money, very much with the public in mind. The later one arises solely from a musical imperative. When it comes to the dramatic quality of the second polonaise (in E flat minor), words fail at its brilliance; in that piece, Chopin becomes the singer of his nation. [...]

Op. 27, two nocturnes which are similar in tone. The second is very agreeable, despite the fact that the emotional depth of the first nocturne makes it seem somewhat cloying in comparison.

Op. 28 comprises twenty-four preludes. Here are some absolutely unique works, which deserve to be every musician's Bible, on a par with Bach's *Das Wohltemperierte Klavier* and Beethoven's sonatas. The preludes are very brief pieces, and every single one of them is divine; in performance, each makes one forget the world. The infinite diversity, the grace of Nos. 3, 5 and 7, the drama and passion of Nos. 18 and 24, the shattering tragedy of No. 22! For all their sketchiness, these pieces are brimming with profound meanings. The Prelude No. 2 is a poem in its own right, No. 4 is a requiem, No. 20, a thirteen-bar funeral march. Consider the originality of the seventh or of the ending of No. 23! Prelude No. 15 is the best known, and its middle section has been variously interpreted; some, for instance, hear raindrops in its regular notes, but this is not the kind of explanation we should seek, for the prelude contains astoundingly beautiful music. The preludes would have sufficed to make Chopin's name immortal even if he had never written another note; but in fact he did go on to compose later works, some of which were just as immortal.

Op. 29, Impromptu, is a very agreeable piece, though it pales in comparison with the preludes.

Op. 30 comprises four mazurkas. The third of these has a very interesting ending, with intersecting major and minor modes. The ending of the fourth is notable for its series of "prohibited" parallel fifths. In Chopin's case, the succession cannot be described as unpleasant.

Op. 31 is the second Scherzo, an inordinately popular and spectacular piece whose novelty has worn off from being performed too often.

Op. 32, two nocturnes. As regards the first (in B major), the early editions contained some inaccuracies, which gave rise to some controversy over whether the ending should be in a major or a minor key. The minor key seems more likely; not only is it more in keeping with the dramatic character of the nocturne, but it also makes the piece more interesting, composed as it is in a major key itself.

Op. 33 contains four mazurkas. In his performance of the second, Tausig included elaborate but otiose ornamentation. The ending of the last mazurka contains two recurrent notes recorded in the treble clef but played by the left hand. In one edition the treble clef was mistakenly replaced by a bass clef. As a result, the two notes became transposed downwards by an octave and a sixth; the result sounded odd, but did not violate the logic of the piece.

Op. 34, *Trois valses brillantes*. The word *brillantes* in the title was possibly the publisher's marketing ploy, for the waltzes evoke a warm and tender mood quite out of keeping with the term.

Op. 35, the Sonata. The performance was given an uproarious ovation. The third movement was a supremely evocative portrayal of a cortège approaching and then receding in the distance, and the finale was a perfect illustration of a thunderstorm.

Op. 36, the second Impromptu. Mr. Rubinstein described the personal significance of the piece, which related to his memories. "In 1841, when I was eleven, I was taken to meet Chopin. The maestro played this Impromptu for me from a manuscript. Although I was a mere child, I found the meeting so impressive that I retain to this day the memory of all the furnishings in his ground floor rooms at 5 rue Tronchet, near St. Mary Magdalene's Church. I remember the Pleyel piano covered with green cloth standing in the middle of the room and bearing the legend, 'To Frédéric Chopin, a gift from Louis-Philippe'."

Op. 37, two nocturnes. The contrast between the two! The diversity and beauty of Chopin's music! He composed six volumes' worth of music, every single one of them fit for performance. This is not so with other composers, whose works one has to sift through in order to select the best pieces.

Op. 38, the second Ballade, a piece dedicated to Schumann. The music makes the dedicatee's identity abundantly clear. The staggering wealth of meaningful musical content... And all that despite the lack of a programme, the piece being unassumingly entitled "a ballade".

Op. 40, two polonaises. These two pieces illustrate Poland's past and future. ("The first brims with vigour, enthusiasm and fire; the second is a picture of despondency, sadness and yearning"). It is paradoxical, but the composer (as you could hear a moment ago) is not quite as odd as he may at first appear. Some people, like Hanslick, have argued that his music escapes characterisation; but I believe the meaning of these polonaises to be more obvious than any language. [Rubinstein was referring here to the then-fashionable book by Eduard Hanslick, *Vom Musikalisch-Schönen*, published in 1854 in Vienna and translated into a number of European languages, including Russian.]

Op. 41, four mazurkas. The third, in the key of B major, is a wonderful and original take on the *oberek* (a Polish folk dance).

Op. 42, a well-known waltz – "nice and charming".

Op. 43, the tarantella – "such an exceedingly agreeable and original piece, filled with beautiful harmonies undreamt of by the Italians!"

Op. 44, Polonaise. This polonaise could well be described as a fantasia, if only because of the mazurka included in the middle section of the piece.

Op. 45, a prelude; one of the most beautiful preludes, it is a wonderful poetic dream.

Op. 47, the third Ballade, we might call it the "Italian Ballade", on account of its Italian character.

Op. 48, two nocturnes. Mr. Rubinstein played them without commentary, noting only that both were very "important".

Op. 49, Fantasia. In the final stretch, Mr. Rubinstein made an addition of his own to Chopin's raging storm, perhaps on the spur of memories from the virtuosic days of his youth. A moment later, he said: "I caution you against playing the way I have done. I am old, and my career has run it course. You should play faithfully what is there in the music".

Op. 50, three mazurkas. The second has an exquisite melody, and the third – wonderful harmony and texture. This is an exceedingly beautiful work, with no mazurka elements remaining other than the metre and the rhythm. The ending contains some interesting harmonic successions, which are troubling, but beautiful.

Op. 51, the third Impromptu, Op. 52; the fourth Ballade, Op. 53; Polonaise; these works were performed without commentary.

Op. 55, two nocturnes. Oddly, the first nocturne (F minor) coincides with the point at which Chopin renounced the tone of anguish, drama or heroism in his music. His later pieces were marked by dreamy moods and an interest in complicated, original and innovative harmonies and modulations. The trend becomes apparent in the second nocturne in this opus and in the first mazurka of the subsequent Op. 56 (three mazurkas, the second a vigorous *oberek*).

Op. 57, the Berceuse (Lullaby). Many play it with too much feeling; it is a piece that contains nothing more than "an infant's featherlight thoughts".

Op. 58, the Sonata in B minor. The piece is well known, but little performed; for all its good qualities, it is inferior to the Sonata in B flat minor, especially in formal terms. The first movement does not have a reprise, and the musical development contains an abundance of modulations which are beautiful and interesting, and yet appear to be somehow morbid and diseased. The second theme, which is "worth all the gold in Peru", makes ample amends. The scherzo is laconic, with its two sections it palpably lacks a trio; it is more like an impromptu, pretty but not very serious. The largo comprises a series of unending modulations, and the finale is magnificent, though it seems strange that the first theme is followed by passage-work.

Op. 59, three mazurkas, composed for a new publishing house in Berlin. Mr. Rubinstein first heard these mazurkas in 1845 performed by Mendelssohn from a manuscript during one of the Sunday visits that he paid to Mendelssohn with his brother. Then, Mr. Rubinstein played the Barcarolle, Op. 60, two Nocturnes, Op. 62 (in the first, Chopin relishes the sound effects of the piano), three Mazurkas, Op. 63, three Waltzes, Op. 64 and the Fantasy-Impromptu, Op. 66. He performed only one of those pieces which were published posthumously, a polonaise which Chopin presumably composed in his youth.

Mr. Rubinstein ended his series of Chopin concerts with a performance of the wondrous etudes which Chopin contributed to Fétis and Moscheles's *Méthode des méthodes*, alongside other eminent composers of the day. Finally, Mr. Rubinstein said: "Music died along with Chopin. Many attractive works with a unique tone have been composed since, but in actual fact there is no art in them".

Anton Rubinstein, *Музыка и ее представители* [Music and its Representatives] (St. Petersburg, 2005), pp. 73-75.

[...] Great and famous pianists have always offered their loveliest and innermost gifts to the piano, but Chopin was the true singer, bard and soul of the instrument. I do not know whether the piano inspired Chopin's music or whether Chopin inspired the keys of the instrument. All I know is that such magnificent works could only be composed at the meeting point of those twin inspirations. Chopin's piano works contain tragic grandeur, romanticism, lyricism, heroism, drama, imagination, the hidden stirrings of the heart, dreams, splendours, majesty, simplicity and all other things besides, everything being expressed in the aptest way possible.

[...] His Preludes (which I consider to be the jewel in the crown of his œuvre), a majority of his etudes and nocturnes, the polonaises in E flat minor, C sharp minor, F sharp minor, A flat major and, in particular, in A major and in C minor, which seemed to me like (respectively) the picture of Poland's rise and flowering (A major) and her decline (C minor), the four ballades, the scherzos in B minor and in B flat minor, the sonatas in B minor and B flat minor, the latter of which is a complete drama in itself, whose final movement after that distinctive funeral march is what I like to call "a night gust of wind blowing over the graves", and finally, last but not least, his delightful mazurkas! Apart from in his polonaises and mazurkas, Chopin's music was not intended to be specifically Polish, but each of his works tells the story of Poland's past glory or laments her subsequent decline and fall, and all in the most exquisite music. In purely musical terms, his works are staggeringly beautiful. The form and technique are perfectly accomplished, the harmonies daring and innovative, and the overall effect often majestic.

Notably, if we discount a certain initial influence of Hummel on the composer, which was discernible in the penchant for passage-work in his early period, Chopin was one of few composers who appeared on the scene without any obvious predecessor.

[...] I believe that our music began with Palestrina, who to me marks the first period in our music, the period of the voice and the organ; Bach and Handel were its greatest and last representatives. The second period I call the instrumental period, a time which witnessed the development of the piano and the orchestra. That period stretched from [Carl] Philipp Emanuel Bach to Beethoven [...].

The third period, which I call the "lyrical-Romantic", began with Schubert and included Weber, Mendelssohn, Schumann and Chopin, who to me was the last representative of that period.

Grigori Timofeev,[15] *Фридерик Шопен. Очерк его жизни и музыкальной деятельности. По прежним и по новейшим (польским) источникам. К 50-летию со дня его смерти 5/17 октября 1849 года* [**Fryderyk Chopin, A brief outline of his life and music. Based on old and recent (Polish) sources. On the fiftieth anniversary of his death, 5 (17) October 1849] (St. Petersburg, 1899)**[16].

[...] Half a century has passed since the death of Chopin, the nineteenth-century's greatest lyricist, but his works – interesting, fresh, magnificently received by his contemporaries – are now gaining fresh attention and popularity. Chopin's genius is finding an ever growing number of enthusiasts. [...]

In Stuttgart, Chopin received the terrible news that Warsaw had been taken by the Russian troops on 8 September [1831]. He composed his famous Etude in C minor, which is known as the "Revolutionary" Etude. It begins with a dissonance in

---

15 Grigori Nikolayevich Timofeev (1866-1919). A former soldier, Timofeev studied music under St. Petersburg theorists. He was influenced by Vladimir Stasov, and he was a direct adherent of the Belaev Circle.

16 Excerpts from preface, pp. 18 and 46 respectively.

the right hand (a seventh chord in first inversion) followed by a violent rising passage in the left hand to convey the sense of despair and crushing loss. [...] Chopin's notes from the time provide a record of his despair. [...]

Slavic elements dominate in his music. This is why we Russians find Chopin's music so familiar. In the melodies, be they Polish or not, we hear much of our native Russian element, which is present both in our folk songs and in the artistic music that developed so quickly following Glinka. [...]

Vladimir Stasov,[17] "Непозволительная статья" [An unacceptable article],[18] *Новости*, 1899.

Several days ago, Mr. Ivanov – who is known for his numerous and invariably reprehensible previous articles – penned another one, a piece arousing particular abhorrence. What an odd man indeed! He simply cannot grasp the fact that he is mostly doing harm to himself. It takes an exceeding degree of circumspection for him to remain upright on that slippery path where he contradicts all received artistic opinion. To tread this path, he must be exercising all the care and precision his feeble mind and pathetic literary talents can muster to forestall his utter and damning exposure. [...]

This time, Mr. Ivanov's sortie is an attack on a recently published book by Mr. Timofeev, entitled *Fryderyk Chopin, A Short Outline of his Life and Music. On the 50th anniversary of his death*. Written with a generous and noble purpose in mind, the book is the product of diligent and painstaking work based on old and new materials. For all its modesty and unassuming air, it is a highly useful work. Similar examples of private initiative are not often seen in this country, regardless of the area of interest, and if for no other reason Mr. Timofeev's book deserves public gratitude as it revisits the great Slavic composer on the fiftieth anniversary of his death. Mr. Ivanov failed to comprehend this. Instead, he found it acceptable to cast aspersions on the author.

As luck would have it, the aspersions were wide of the mark and therefore ineffectual [...]. Please note his mode of attack.

---

17 Vladimir Vasileevich Stasov (1824-1906) – a leading Russian art critic. He was the guiding spirit and the inspiration behind the emergence of The Five.

18 The article takes issue with Mikhail Mikhailovich Ivanov's article published on 25 March 1899 in *Новое время* in St. Petersburg.

Mr. Ivanov writes: "Fifty years have passed since Chopin's death. Much has recently been said and written about this composer, which leads us to question the point of revisiting the topic". Is that not a fine argument? Mr. Ivanov deserves profuse thanks from those who have recently celebrated the memory of Pushkin and Mickiewicz so lavishly, organizing memorial events and publishing scores if not hundreds of anniversary monographs. Apparently, it was all pointless [...].

By Mr. Ivanov's generous leave, those who dare write about Chopin must do so on the basis of "the most recent material". The old materials are of no use; Mr. Ivanov is already familiar with them. Mr. Ivanov is dead right, there is no question about it. In his zeal, he accuses Timofeev of consistently overlooking the most recent findings (e.g. Ferdynand Hoesick's book published in 1899[19]) in favour of the old writers, "the youngest of whom wrote about Chopin twenty years ago, I mean people like Maurycy Karasowski, with his 1881[1882] biography of Chopin";[20] but for the most part Mr. Timofeev allegedly "relies on Liszt's 1852 book".[21] It is difficult to express our surprise, irritation and scorn for Mr. Ivanov. His charges are nothing less than a slanderous insult!

Of Karasowski's book, Mr. Timofeev made no use whatever, and his book contains only four quotations from Liszt's lengthy book. The entire pamphlet was based on other, most recent sources, including Niecks's well-known book (sadly, not available in Russian), published in English in 1888 and in German in 1890,[22] and secondly, the above-mentioned 1899 biography by Ferdynand Hoesick, which runs completely counter to Mr. Ivanov's accusations. Mr. Timofeev identifies Hoesick as his source of information in several places, only to be brazenly accused by Mr. Ivanov of ignoring it! Not that this blatant falsehood is in any way surprising in Mr. Ivanov, who naively admits in his article that he himself is not in any way familiar with Hoesick's book.

The monumental musical ignorance, the lack of education of that critic!

As a curiosity, one might add that those passages in Mr. Timofeev's study that relate to Chopin's parents, though ridiculed by Mr. Ivanov with a remarkable meas-

---

19 Ferdynand Hoesick, *Fryderyk Chopin. Zarys biograficzny* [A biographical sketch], St. Petersburg 1899 [1898, editor's note].

20 Polish edition, Warsaw 1882; German edition, Dresden 1877; English tr. Emily Hill, *Frédéric Chopin. His life and letters,* New York 1878, London 1879 [editor's note].

21 F. [Ferenc] Liszt, *F. Chopin,* Paris 1852[editor's note].

22 Frederick Niecks, *Frederick Chopin as a man and musician,* 2 vols., London 1888; Ger. tr. as *Friedrich Chopin als Mensch und als Musiker,* tr. Wilhelm Langhans, 2 vols., Leipzig 1890 [editor's note].

ure of stupidity, are based precisely on Hoesick's book, which Mr. Ivanov mindlessly advertises elsewhere in his attack.

But forget Hoesick. Mr. Ivanov is distinctly unimpressed even by such authorities as Liszt and Richard Wagner. He makes it known to the world that Liszt wrote "in a language that was completely incomprehensible and as opaque as that of Richard Wagner"; he suggests that "the literary works of both of those musical friends should be thoroughly looked over and examined", and that we cannot arrive at the actual meaning of their writings unless we discard the "garbage and cast-offs" that account for ninety-eight per cent of them, though in any case "Liszt's literary writings ought not to be taken too seriously". Obviously, I for one shall be waiting with bated breath for Mr. Ivanov to "look over and examine", in the light of his scanty knowledge, the writings of Liszt and Wagner (particularly the latter); doubtless, the outcome will be astonishing and edifying in equal measure. But before that happens, we shall continue to hold with the rest of Europe that Liszt and Wagner wrote highly interesting books which bore witness to their ample literary talents, with Liszt's book and some of his articles being quite simply works of genius. [...]

Mr. Ivanov's heroic exploits do not actually end there. To crown it all, he made it his aim to prove that Chopin had never been a pianist of note or talent. On the contrary, Mr. Ivanov argues craftily, Chopin was actually absolutely unremarkable as a pianist. And he concludes that Chopin's playing style was feminine. His grounds for this? Apparently, Chopin's playing style was neither forceful nor luminous. That Mr. Ivanov publishes such observations with twenty or thirty years' worth of concert-going to his name would suggest that he is labouring under the misconception that forceful or luminous expression are artistic goals per se, and that musicians may display no other valuable and magnificent qualities. True, it is a long-recognized fact that Chopin described himself to Liszt as not suited (unlike Liszt) for concert performances of the kind that sweep audiences off their feet. But there is a major difference between being unable to hold several thousand spectators in thrall, on the one hand, and "leaving people indifferent", on the other, as Mr. Ivanov argues was the case. Not only does Mr. Ivanov have some inaccurate notions about art; he is also trying to foist his way of thinking on others. He argues that Chopin "could not compete with the pianists active in Paris at the time (Moscheles and Kalkbrenner)" and that only "a few" of his "friends" appreciated him. Such a load of nonsense deserves nothing more than a hearty laugh; there is no point in becoming upset about such preposterous lies, or in repudiating them.

There are abundant printed sources in existence. Even if we put aside Liszt's brilliant and magnificent book with its page after page of earnest, fascinating accounts of Chopin as a performing pianist, or the soulful descriptions in Heine and George Sand, the numerous penetrating and empathetic opinions of Mendelssohn, Schumann, Meyerbeer, Fétis and so many others, there still remain the twelve pages in Niecks's book, crammed solid with countless reviews from newspapers, journals and books, as well as first-hand accounts of the profound impression that Chopin's performance, produced on listeners in concert halls and private salons. [...]

In order to weaken Liszt's testimony, it was Mr. Ivanov's pleasure to observe that the book on Chopin was largely written not by Liszt himself but rather by Princess Wittgenstein. Her ladyship's contribution to the writing of the book is widely known and indisputable; but Liszt did not need anyone, not even a princess, to feel and understand Chopin's music deeply, or to be overwhelmingly influenced by Chopin's playing style in the process of broadening and deepening his own. As regards his knowledge of ancient Poland, with its customs and historical figures, Liszt had acquired it from such talented and well-educated patriots as Mickiewicz, Słowacki and Niemcewicz a long time before he ever met the princess. In that respect, no princess would have been able to furnish him with new information.

Finally, Mr. Ivanov actually endeavours to persuade his readers that Chopin's biographers were mistaken in arguing that "Chopin was a great patriot who supposedly suffered greatly because of the unhappy fate of his native country; and accordingly they try to see in his works things that probably never even occurred to the composer. Chopin was in fact a highly pliable man and was easily reconciled to the realities at hand". No one with a modicum of knowledge about Chopin would waste his breath trying to dismiss such revelations.

You would do well, Mr. Ivanov, to get some learning and to read a little before you start writing about Chopin…

To cap it all, Mr. Ivanov had the insolence to entitle his article "How not to write". Never was an effort more soundly wasted: the gentleman's own example has long been demonstrating, clearly and successfully, "how not to write".

Vladimir Stasov, *Статьи о музыке* **[On music] (Moscow, 1974), p. 244
(written in 1857).**

[...] Plagal cadences have been used by Weber, Mendelssohn, Schumann and, above all, Chopin, in those of his piano pieces which evince a mood of sadness and loneliness reminiscent of Beethoven. But to Glinka this felt insufficient, after he had introduced some new forms in his opera *Ivan Susanin,* and after Chopin's own innovations in some of those contemplative and passionate flights of fancy which incorporate oriental scales and melodies and employ capricious, restive phrasing alongside ancient diatonic melodies and modulations. For Glinka, Chopin was the first harbinger of the possibility, if not the necessity, of devising new forms to express those mysterious and passionate stirrings of the soul which are a unique quality of our century, and have not been expressed (or possibly experienced) ever before. Chopin was Glinka's guide to new artistic forms, the equal to Beethoven in his capacity to express this newly opened world of the soul and to give it an artistic embodiment. Glinka's familiarity with Chopin's works in the period after he composed *A Life for the Tsar* was of crucial significance to his talent; but those works were only an indication of the possible new forms, an inspiration to blaze new trails, with Glinka unwittingly following his guide onto the path that Beethoven had trodden late in his life, a path that disappeared after Beethoven's death until Chopin rediscovered it and showed it to the world. [...]

Vladimir Stasov, *Статьи о музыке* **[On music] (Moscow, 1974), p. 376
(written in 1858).**

In our century, national banners were raised in the realm of science and the arts. Music followed suit, and after several early tentative attempts (including certain passages in Weber's *Oberon* and in Franz Schubert's Hungarian marches) Chopin was the first composer to adhere to the postulates of a national music that relied on local melodies and genres. [...] Chopin was the first composer to utilize the concept of folk melodies and folk genres (regardless of whether they were genuine articles or reworkings in the nationalistic vein). He was the first composer to try and present folk melodies [...] in a true, unadulterated form, with their original colour and rhythm. He was the first to learn how to clothe them in appropriate harmonies, and the first to incorporate what the vulgar crowd believes are their "rule violations" – he did not smooth them over, make them common or modern [...].

Vladimir Stasov. *Статьи о музыке* [On music] (Moscow, 1974), p. 75 (article first published in 1895).

In nationalist terms, the point is no longer to make an outward and superficial use of folk themes; even a talentless mediocrity can do that according to his personal preference. The point is truly to express the spirit of a nation, to sound its full depth and express its truth and beauty, to communicate true and original national characteristics. The ability to work with folkloric material had been first noted in our century among Slavic nations like the Russians and the Poles. The former saw the emergence of Glinka, the latter had Chopin.

Vladimir Stasov, "Музыка" [Music], in *Искусство XIX века* [Nineteenth-century art] (St. Petersburg, 1901), pp. 299-328.

[...] Berlioz had two artistic companions living in Paris: Chopin and Liszt. They were of different nationalities – a Frenchman, a Pole and a Hungarian. All three were young men of genius, ardently in love with their art, who converged in the fiery, vibrant and turbulent Romantic France of the 1830s. Although their characters were diametrically opposed, they did not realize it at the time and formed a powerful league to combat all that was outmoded, traditional and inherited. They were incredibly prolific and effective. It was not until the later years that their ways parted, as a result of their differences of character.

Berlioz and Chopin showed a certain affinity. Granted, nationalist ideals found no sympathy with Berlioz. Idealistic and cosmopolitan by nature, he never composed a single bar that could be described as characteristically French. Chopin, on the other hand, was a highly original and talented exponent of the nationalist element in music; indeed, to an unprecedented extent (with the possible exception of Weber). Although Chopin was only twenty years of age when he arrived in Paris, he was already fully-formed and self-aware, and no external influence could change his character significantly. The many years he spent in Paris proved beneficial to his development (unsurprisingly, given that he regularly brushed shoulders with the major literary, scholarly and artistic talents of the day), but took nothing away from his original talent. Chopin never wavered in his powerful sense of a Polish national tradition or in his attachment to his native country, and this conferred a sense of depth and splendour on his works. Berlioz, by contrast, had no hand in, nor interest in, the events taking place in France, and he felt equally at ease when praising Napoleon I and Napoleon III.

Berlioz had a consummate knowledge of all instruments and used them brilliantly in the way a great colourist uses all the different hues and shades of his palette. The one instrument he roundly ignored was the piano. He never composed any solo pieces for the piano and only used it as a member of the orchestra. Chopin, conversely, knew only one instrument – the piano – and ignored all the rest (even his favourite cello was relegated to the role of accompaniment in his duets or formed an orchestral part in his concerto). Berlioz favoured large-scale projects of broad sweep and boundless ambition; Chopin shunned them, apparently content with miniature, almost salon-like, forms. Berlioz composed symphonies, cantatas, oratorios, massive choruses, requiem masses and *Te Deums*; Chopin restricted himself to polonaises, mazurkas, waltzes, nocturnes, preludes, impromptus and sonatas, but never completed a single symphony. Chopin was a soloist and a virtuoso; Berlioz played no instrument other than the guitar and the Hungarian recorder. Chopin gave lessons all his life (mostly to aristocratic ladies); Berlioz never taught anything to anybody.

Those were the basic differences between Berlioz and Chopin, but there were similarities too. Both were reformers in their respective fields; both changed completely the nature and range of the instruments they used for expressing their moods, emotions and ideas. Berlioz effectively created a new type of orchestra, Chopin a new type of piano. Although the achievements of Hummel and Weber were probably pivotal for Chopin's pianistic technique, both were soon far outstripped by Chopin, who treated pianistic technique as the foundation for a new, vast and profound world that was unprecedented in music history. Chopin was a poet, an individualist, a lyricist. His internal world was rich in diversity; it abounded in events that were in their turn quiet, serene and weighty or turbulent, tragic and mighty. He clad all in delightfully poetic, charming and beautiful forms. In spite of their apparently small and limited scale, his preludes, nocturnes, etudes, mazurkas, polonaises and impromptus are filled with deep and profound meanings; with very few exceptions, his works are examples of programmatic music on a par with his exquisite ballades (which were explicitly identified as programmatic by the composer). Not even the staunchest critic of Chopin's Sonata No. 2 in B flat minor can doubt the programmatic nature of the piece. Its unique, world-famous funeral march is a vivid portrayal of a wretched nation filing past in a cortège to the sound of tolling bells; arguably, the finale of the same sonata is an even greater gift of genius and originality, interpreted by most listeners as inescapably evoking the forlorn whistling of wind over the dead man's grave. The music is no less programmatic than the chivalric or idyllic ballades. Likewise the second Scherzo in B flat minor is to many a portrayal of scenes involving Othello and Desdemona, while the Impromptu No. 3 in G flat major presents a delightful love scene between two lovers, and the *Grande Polonaise* in A flat major depicts cavalry in full gallop amid the warlike sounds of ringing bells and clashing swords;. The preludes 2 and 15, with their ringing of bells, portray a Spanish monastery, with its cloister garden and a procession of monks; and finally, the two mazurkas in C major (Op. 24 [nr 2] and Op. 56 [nr 2]) show graceful scenes from the idyllic lives of the Polish peasantry. The precise programme of many of his works may be difficult to identify (and in this they are no different from most works by Beethoven, Schumann, Liszt and other composers), but it seems incontrovertible that almost every single one of them has some kind of programmatic content. Chopin composed programmatic music like nearly all his fellow composers, but for unknown reasons he withheld the programmatic content of his pieces from the public. He went beyond merely combining sounds into intellectual systems, profound and elegant perhaps, but devoid of meaning. Instead, he wanted to give expression to the contents of his soul, to convey those inner feelings, images and events, and to show the internal life that remains invisible to a bystander. It was an overwhelmingly strong need and it was satisfied by the captivating, charming sounds and forms of his music. Profound meditation on the self and on the nation's moribund condition sits alongside narratives of his joys and sorrows; his dreams and enthusiasms are narrated together with moments of happiness and crushing anguish; sun-dappled love scenes are punctuated by quiet and serene images of nature. All this is Chopin's realm and mighty kingdom, where he holds those grand mysteries of his art known as sonatas, preludes, mazurkas, polonaises, scherzos, etudes and impromptus. To think that there have been connoisseurs who have tried to explicate those torrid currents of vigorous flame, like so many school principals standing by the blackboard with their rulers, to arrive at the triumphal conclusion that Chopin's sonatas were not so much genuine sonatas as assemblages of mad sounds, and that his scherzos (those deeply innovative and original works) were mere capricious play and not real music. Regrettably, even the great Schumann, a lifelong admirer and populariser of Chopin, failed to grasp his Sonata in B minor and concluded that it was the work of a madman. To think that this wise and talented man could be so mistaken about that efflorescence of such incredible originality! [...]

Русская музыкальная газета, 11 (1894)[23].

Two years ago, the famous Russian artist and Chopin enthusiast M. A. Balakirev came to Warsaw with a view to visiting Żelazowa Wola, the birthplace of the great Polish musician Fryderyk Chopin. As Balakirev was giving an account of his visit to the press, he noted the dilapidated condition of the house that once nurtured the musical genius. Encouraged by Balakirev's initiative, a committee formed by the Warsaw Music Society decided to abandon its impractical idea of building a Chopin museum in the remote village and resolved to erect a memorial instead.

For the unveiling ceremony, an upright piano was placed under the composer's favourite fir tree, and a beautiful improvised concert was held in memory of the composer. It comprised Chopin's music, with some of our own Chopin specialists par excellence among the performers, including [Aleksander] Michałowski, followed by [Jan] Kleczyński and finally Mily Balakirev. A number of preludes, nocturnes and mazurkas were heard. Imagine that delightful outdoor scene, with a crowd of people with bare heads listening intently to the immortal music of our beloved great composer...

The Chopin celebrations concluded with a grand concert held on Wednesday, 17 October [...] (the anniversary of the composer's death). It was organized by the Music Society in the Grand Theatre in Warsaw, and the proceeds went to setting up a Chopin scholarship. Balakirev took an active part in the celebrations by playing the Mazurka in A minor, the Nocturne in G major, the Polonaise in F minor and the Sonata in B flat minor.

It has been a long time since we heard such thunderous applause as that given to Mr. Balakirev. The packed house reacted enthusiastically to the Russian pianist, who played for an encore a newly discovered (unpublished) nocturne by Chopin.[24] On that memorable night, M. A. Balakirev was given a silver wreath bearing the legend: "To M. Balakirev, in memory of the unveiling of the Chopin memorial at Żelazowa Wola, 14 October 1894. The Warsaw Music Society.

---

23 An account of the unveiling of a Chopin memorial in Żelazowa Wola.

24 This was the so-called "Nocturne" in C sharp minor (*Lento con gran espressione*), written in 1830. Balakirev's copy, entitled *Reminiscences. Nocturne pour le piano,* is held at the Warsaw Music Society (WTM 24/Ch) [editor's note].

Boleslaus Grodsky,[25] *Русские музыканты и критики о Шопене* [Russian musicians and critics on Chopin], *Советская музыка*, 1949/5, p. 74.

[...] We know [...] about Balakirev's deep lifelong love for the music of that great Polish composer. Balakirev liked to play Chopin's music, he frequently expressed his admiration for the composer's genius, [...] and he wished to transcribe at least some of Chopin's works for orchestra. He was particularly successful in his last attempt, a transcription of four pieces arranged into a suite comprising an introduction, one of the slow etudes, a mazurka, a nocturne intermezzo and a scherzo finale. The orchestral version presented Chopin's pieces in brilliant kaleidoscopic colour; the orchestration is so successful and spectacular that one does not regret the change for one moment [...].

Letters of M. A. Balakirev on Chopin (ed. A. Lapunova), *Советская музыка*, 1949/10, pp. 63-64.

A letter from Balakirev to Louis-Albert Bourgault-Ducoudray[26] (undated [1894]).

Cher Monsieur et ami!

The fragmentary reports we occasionally read in our newspapers seem to suggest that the people of Paris have remembered their debt to Chopin, and will at last erect on Place Chopin a monument to that great composer who lived in Paris and treated France as his second motherland.

I would be very much obliged for some information on the state of the project. When can we expect to see the unveiling of the memorial? As a long-time admirer of Chopin's genius, I would very much wish to attend the ceremony. At one point, my admiration led to the erection of a Chopin memorial in Poland, something I had not actually intended, but which gave me great pleasure nonetheless. This is how it happened.

Tired with my official duties as the director of the Imperial Chapel, of which I was the Director until the death of Tsar Alexander III, I requested leave and went to Poland in the autumn of 1891 to find Chopin's birthplace in a little village. Upon

---

25 Grodsky was a biographer of Balakirev.

26 Louis-Albert Bourgault-Ducoudray (1840-1910), a major Breton conductor and composer with an interest in European folk music, especially that of Greece. In 1882, he presented Balakirev's poem *Tamara* in Paris [editor's note].

arriving at Warsaw, I contacted several individuals with serious musical interests and was finally able to locate the village of Żelazowa Wola, where I promptly went. As it turned out, the owner of the house had no idea that his estate had been Chopin's birthplace; indeed, he did not even know who Chopin was. The building that used to be the family home of the Chopins and the composer's actual birthplace was in a terrible condition, without so much as a floor in the best room. When I returned to Warsaw, several Polish journalists visited me. They were indignant to learn about the deplorable condition of the house and wrote a number of articles remonstrating about their compatriots' ingratitude. As a result, a Chopin memorial was erected and unveiled in Żelazowa Wola. As the project's inadvertent initiator, I was invited to the unveiling ceremony, held on 14 October 1894. Because of the thorny relations arising from the inexorable verdicts of history between our two related nations, no other Russian was honoured with an invitation, and since the Poles preferred private arrangements to a public collection of funds, the Chopin enthusiasts in Russia never got a chance to contribute a penny as a token of their love for the famous Polish genius.

I assume that your attitude will be different; although I would very much wish to assist your project in a material way, my musical scores being my sole capital, I must regretfully abstain from contributing. But if there is a French publisher willing to purchase my copyright to a French edition of my *Tamara* [Balakirev's symphonic poem with Georgian themes, 1882]. I should consider it my great honour and good fortune to donate the entire proceeds from my royalties to the Chopin memorial in Paris. [...]

Nikolay Rimsky-Korsakov,[27] *My Musical Life*, tr. Judah A. Joffe (New York, 1942), 397; Rus. orig. *Летопись моей жизни* [My life's chronicle], St. Petersburg 1909.

The thought of writing an opera on a Polish subject had long engrossed me. On the one hand, several Polish melodies, sung to me by my mother in my childhood, still haunted me, though I had already made use of them in composing a mazurka for the violin. On the other hand, Chopin's influence on me was indubitable, in the melodic turns of my music as well as in many of my harmonic devices; but this fact the gimlet-eyed critics had never observed, to be sure. The Polish national element

---

27 Nikolay Andreevich Rimsky-Korsakov (1844-1908) – Russian composer, conductor and music organiser.

in Chopin's compositions (which I worshipped) always aroused my delight. In any opera on a Polish subject I wished to pay homage to my rapture for this side of Chopin's music, and it seemed to me that I was capable of writing something Polish, national.

Rimsky-Korsakov, comment recounted by Vasiliy Vasilievich Yastrebtsev, author of *Римский-Корсаков Н.А. – Воспоминания* [N. A. Rimsky-Korsakov. *In memoriam*] (Petrograd 1917, new ed. Leningrad, 1960).

"It is difficult to comprehend how Chopin came to combine two such marvellous faculties, namely the talent of a great melodist and the gift of a most inspired and original harmonist. Unbelievably, in his Etude in A flat major, where *harmony itself* seems to sing, we find sequences of chords that still remain unparalleled in modern music, including Wagner's. It will be years before people learn to appreciate them. After listening to Chopin's incomparably poetic music, all other music sounds rough-hewn and heavy, not excepting such great composers as Beethoven or Schumann, not to mention Liszt; Wagner, whose music is too clever by half, I am beginning positively to despise. To me, the piano improvisations of Chopin seem like true music, in contrast to all that orchestral fretting which takes an army of trombones and kettledrums simply to perform".

Modest Tchaikovsky,[28] "Из семейных воспоминаний" [From family memories], in P. E. Vaydman, *П.И. Чайковский, Альманах, к 100-летию Государственного Дома-музея П.И. Чайковского в Клину* [P. I. Tchaikovsky, an almanac: on the 100th anniversary of the P. I. Tchaikovsky house and museum at Klin], 1995/1, p. 42.

From the memories of the governess Fanny Dürbach.
[...] "At Votkinsk we occasionally received visits from an exiled Pole, an army officer named Maszewski. A young man, he charmed the company. He was a fine amateur pianist, and was a dab hand at playing Chopin's mazurkas. Our little musician found each of Maszewski's visits a true festive occasion. At one point, our Pierre [Pyotr Tchaikovsky] learnt two mazurkas on his own, and played them so well that he was rewarded with a kiss from Maszewski. I had never seen Pierre so pleased or happy". [...]

---

28 Modest Ilyich Tchaikovsky (1850-1916) – the composer's younger brother and biographer.

Pyotr Tchaikovsky, "Второй концерт Русского музыкального общества – Русский концерт г. Славянского" [The second concert of the Russian Music Society – the Russian concert of Mr. Sławiański], in *Музыкально-критические статьи* [Articles in music criticism] (Moscow, 1953), p. 40.

[...] Mme Yesipova chose to play Chopin's first piano concerto, an exceedingly long and tiresome piece, mechanical and devoid of content, so I cannot approve of it. Obviously, it provided the pianist with ample opportunities for displaying her brilliant and impeccable technique, but in this case the end did not justify the means. [...] *Современная летопись*, 1871/46, pp. 12-13

Чайковский и Надежда Филаретовна фон-Мекк, Переписка [Tchaikovsky and Nadezhda von Meck:[29] correspondence], xi (1879-1881) (Moscow, 2004), pp. 1081-1082.
Yuly Engel,[30] "Шопен" [Chopin], *Русские ведомости*, 31 (9 February 1910).

[...] You will not believe [...] the wonderful sensations I get from immersing myself in [Mozart's] music! It is wholly different from that painful delight inflicted on me by Beethoven, Schumann, Chopin, and all post-Bach and post-Beethoven composers in general. Their music moves, frightens or delights, but it can never caress or lull one to sleep the way Mozart does [...]. The people of my generation have been immersed in modern music from childhood, so when we first found Mozart we were already familiar with Chopin's Byronic spirit of despair and disappointment. Personally, I was lucky enough to have been raised in a non-musical family, and consequently I had not been poisoned at an early age by the venom that permeates all music composed after Bach. [...]

Yuly Engel, *Шопен* [Chopin] – an article in *Русские ведомости*, 31 (9 February 1910).

A hundred years have passed since Chopin's birth, and sixty since his death. But can we really speak of his music as a thing of the past? Does not our heartbeat

---

29 Nadezhda von Meck was the widow of one of Russia's greatest railroad tycoons. She was a great admirer of Tchaikovsky's music and supported the composer for many years.
30 *Русские ведомости*

quicken in reaction to those dear immortal tones? Has Chopin ever been more popular or better loved?

And yet… A centenary is not a thing to be treated lightly. A lot has changed over the course of that century, and to us Chopin is no longer the same composer he was to his own generation or to his near-contemporaries. The evolution of our attitudes towards the composer is nothing new in the history of art; suffice it to point to the vivid example of Beethoven.

Beethoven, that great son of a great revolution, was the first to embody in his powerful music the subjective spiritual freedom of the *new* man; he was the first to make music a direct projection of the human soul, and he used familiar formal and harmonic means to stir the human spirit. And yet, as twentieth-century people brought up on his music, we tend to overlook that aspect of Beethoven's works in favour of their purely musical beauty and lithe grace; today, we are able to see well-controlled and beautiful temples where nothing but sprawling chaos could be seen a while ago; the Classicists are beginning to obscure the Romantics.

Chopin's case is somewhat similar. He was one of Beethoven's greatest successors, if not literally in formal terms, then at least in the similarity of the respective guiding spirits of their music. The unprecedented clarity of intimate feeling, the noble and graceful despair, the boundless freedom and novelty of musical expression: those are the qualities for which we prize Chopin today. But they are not the only or even the main reason we love him. For us, Chopin is not only the composer of nocturnes or the originator of the waltzes and mazurkas which made him famous in his lifetime, but also the creator of the ballades, the scherzos, the polonaises, the Sonata in B flat minor; he was a mighty artist, despite the fact that his art was contained within the narrow confines of piano music; he was a priest of musical beauty, and the most harrowing anguish was unable to disfigure his countenance; he was a painstaking master of form, who turned away from Field, Kalkbrenner and Hummel in favour of Bach, Mozart and Beethoven; in a word, Chopin was a genius who combined the unique and vivid qualities of Romantic individuality with the best and most timeless injunctions of the Classics. His genius opened wide the doors of the temple of the arts to the simple folk song, and he was the first to demonstrate to the world the unfathomable ocean of possibilities that sprang from merging the sophisticated art of the higher classes with the native, direct and simple inspiration of the lower.

The composer's artistic imagination first tapped Polish folk music for inspiration, then assimilated it and merged with it. The inexhaustible abundance of Chopin's melodies, his rhythmical and harmonic inspirations: all that was further boosted by a native Polish quality. I believe it was Schumann who described Chopin's music as "cannons buried in flowers". It is an apt idea, though imprecisely phrased. Chopin's remarkable power was psychological rather than physical. Irrespective of current politics, grateful humanity will nod appreciatively to hear the cry of "Poland has not died yet!"[31] for as long as his mazurkas and polonaises continue to be played. Each bar of Chopin's music, every rhythmical accent or turn of melodic phrase is characteristically Polish; his unfulfilled dream of a revived Polish state blended with the images of Poland's past greatness. And though Chopin was mostly a singer of sad and melancholy moods, his portrayals of Poland's past grandeur soar with dazzling splendour and might. Among the multitude of hearts moved by Chopin's music, Polish hearts will always beat the hardest.

But there is much more to the figure of Chopin than his Polishness. Like all truly great artists, he transcends the bounds of nationality or territory. His music turns the Polish term *żal*, or wistful sadness, into a universal emotion, a yearning for our "citizenship in heaven", a longing for the ideal world, that bright and inscrutable realm of the spirit that we persistently, painfully, hopelessly dream about.

Stanislav Schlesinger, *Опыт дидактической систематики произведений Фр. Шопена* [An experiment involving a systematic arrangement of F. Chopin's works for teaching purposes] (St. Petersburg, 1903).

"A brief outlook on Chopin as pianist and composer"
The young pianist became well known at an early age, mostly in aristocratic salons. He had a subdued but highly distinctive playing style, which he combined with a poetic charm to win over his listeners, mostly female. Prince Antoni Radziwiłł took an active interest in the career of the young composer and pianist, and introduced him into aristocratic circles.

That fortuitous act of princely mediation would have serious ramifications for Chopin's later career. At the time, his gift of improvisation was already winning him high praise. But the fact that he was performing for Polish aristocratic circles imposed certain limits on his genius. Shackled by aristocratic form and etiquette, his beloved art was unable to achieve the resolute and independent manliness he craved. Though highly original, our musical poet was confined within the narrow bounds

---

31 The opening words of the Polish national anthem [translator's note].

of aristocratic life and drew strength solely from society's most frail organisms, the salons, amid fantastical ovations and transports of delight. [...]

He found the piano sufficient for his purposes, and the miniatures he was composing were a full and accurate reflection of the contents of his sensitive soul. [...]

Given the unique combination of Polish and French elements that made up his character, Chopin became an original genius of leading aristocratic music salons. The elegiac tone of his creative ideas, shaped as they were out of the wretched fate of his people, was contained in folk dance forms, which offered fertile soil for the growth of original music forms. Quite independently, there was also Chopin's personality, which gave his bashful sensitivity a unique sensual expression.

L. Keller, *Преподавание фортепиано* [Piano education], (Moscow, P. Jurgenson, 1880), pp. 26-27.

Despite his narrow confinement within minor forms, Chopin excelled in small compositions. He breathed soul into the piano and gave it an organic life of its own, as he pushed piano performance to the very heights of expressive emotional power. In turns soft and powerful, in his hands the dry, brittle sound of the piano takes on the fullness, poetical quality and expressive potency of the human voice. Chopin relegates rhythmical regularity in the interest of distinctive expression; his melodies develop in an irregular fashion, alternately slowing down and speeding up on their way to closure; the accompaniment – now coming late, now prematurely – explores odd-numbered combinations of notes, as if to break free from the tyranny of pedantic regularity. His clear and triumphant melodies claim priority over the divisions imposed by chords and bars. Accordingly, chords in Chopin's works are not used just to define the phrases; instead, they either form magnificent sweeping gestures or become elaborated and extended on an immense scale to idealize the dense and complex harmonic material. The mellifluous melodic quality of his compositions often encompasses the accompaniment as well, as it occasionally enters into a dialogue with the main melodic idea. [...]

Chopin's complete works have been issued in six volumes [...] and every work is beautiful – steeped in deep feeling, extremely interesting and infinitely diverse. All his works – not just the mazurkas and polonaises, but also the ballades, scherzos and nocturnes, and even the *Allegro de concert* and Fantasia in F minor – are saturated by the Polish national genius, made abundantly clear by their tender idealism and chivalric splendour. Chopin's music is justifiably considered to be lyrical; everything about it is remarkably subjective, with hardly a single melody not inspired by a personal drama. [...]

[...] Chopin's extraordinarily remarkable and genial personality was endowed with an astounding, divine talent. A writer hoping to offer an accurate portrayal of Chopin's works ought to dip his quill in a rainbow in order to reflect the fantastical rays of his exuberant imagination, the extraordinary warmth of his feeling, the magnificent sweep of his inspiration or the highly developed, almost feminine sensitivity, which had a way of unpredictably manifesting itself on the spur of some trifling incident. [...]

[...] I have spent many years painstakingly studying Chopin's piano works, and have come to the conclusion that it is a piano teacher's task to assist every student [...] in achieving a level of technical and musical competence sufficient to commence the *study* of Chopin's works. I use the word study advisedly: these pieces should not be "done" in a casual, slipshod manner. Chopin is a great composer, who should command a much greater degree of respect and attention from piano teachers than is the case at present. In order to study anything, one needs a system where new things are introduced on the basis of earlier material.

Chopin's pieces reward study by revealing a sense of formal restraint combined with honest feeling, profound sensitivity and elevated, fascinating content; all his compositions are marked by a highly original and individualistic compositional style. From the elevated viewpoint of a teacher whose aim is to provide the pupil with moral, spiritual and aesthetic education, it is difficult to think of better teaching material than the works of that universally admired composer; Chopin's works should be regarded as the best and most beautiful teaching aids for achieving the highest goals of musical education and artistic development. Aimed directly at the loftiest spheres of the human spirit, his wondrous, delightful, idealistic works provide the best introduction to the Romantic school, which the pupils will undoubtedly find more accessible and comprehensible than the Classical school, with its sober realism and lucid, rational outlook on beauty – qualities which may fail to address the feelings and aesthetic needs of a pupil who finds Classicism wearisome because it fails to reflect the poetic world of life's real and colourful phenomena. [...]

Nikolai Kashkin,[32] **"Фредерик Шопен, 10-го (22-го) февраля 1810 – 9-го (22-го) февраля 1910"** [Fryderyk Chopin, 22 February 1810 – 22 February 1910], *Русское слово*, 31 (9 February 1910).

Today, we celebrate the centenary of Fryderyk Chopin's birth.

The nineteenth century abounded in musical talents of the highest calibre, and Fryderyk Chopin was among the foremost, despite the fact that he devoted his entire composing career to the narrow field of piano music; nonetheless, the strength and originality of his talent had a major impact on the course of music history, and it extended well beyond pianism, as he contributed to music new elements that reflected his unique artistic personality.

Rather than recount the familiar details of Chopin's biography, let us confine ourselves to an analysis of his music and artistic significance. [...]

Along with Mendelssohn and Schumann, Chopin formed a trio of leading Romantics in the first half of the nineteenth century. The originality of Chopin's talent meant that his place among contemporary composers was quite unique, partly on account of the distinctly Polish character permeating many of his pieces. Chopin was the first to import nationalistic folk elements into instrumental music, and in this respect his significance is comparable to that of Glinka, who at the same time introduced nationalistic elements into opera. There had been Polish artists and composers before Chopin, but in common with Glinka's predecessors they lacked originality in the European context. Chopin was not a musical innovator as a matter of principle; his tastes leaned towards past masters rather than contemporaries. He was on friendly terms with Mendelssohn and Schumann, but he had little esteem for their music; he disliked the works of Berlioz, his contemporary on the Paris scene, and found them completely incomprehensible. The music of his great personal friend, Liszt, likewise failed to win Chopin's respect. He valued Bach, Mozart and a handful of piano composers such as Field and Hummel. For Beethoven, he felt respect but little else.

Chopin was far less adept than Mendelssohn at composing classical instrumental forms, and the few he composed were largely free variations, although his Sonata in B flat minor, with its funeral march, is among the best examples of the sonata genre after Beethoven.

---

32 Nikolay Dimitrevich Kashkin (1839-1920) – Russian music critic and teacher, published on Russian music (Tchaikovsky, Rimsky-Korsakov, Taneev, N. G. Rubinstein).

Chopin was a great melodist. His beautiful melodies are broad and flexible, and though they might have betrayed some influence from Italian opera, which he had admired in his youth, they were nonetheless highly original, uniquely Chopinesque and, as often as not, distinctively Polish.

His music is at its most Polish in the mazurkas, those supremely refined versions of the Polish folk songs and dances of Chopin's youth; his polonaises are not far behind in this respect, as well as some of his 27 etudes and 25 preludes. Chopin combined a fine gift for melody with a remarkable mastery of harmony. In harmonic terms, miniatures such as the preludes in C minor and C sharp minor are quite simply works of genius; in the wholly unique finale of the Sonata in B flat minor, Chopin's harmonic genius is on display without actually using a single chord.

As a composer of nocturnes, Chopin continued the Field tradition, but his nocturnes are without equal. His larger piano works – such as the ballades, scherzos or his Fantasia in F minor – should be counted among the highest achievements of nineteenth-century piano music.

[...] he was one of the piano's greatest poets; his piano figuration and ornamentation constituted a unique pianistic style; temporarily overshadowed by the outward glitter of Liszt and his school, he is now regaining precedence. Chopin was imitated by many composers, some of them quite talented, but he remains unique and unmatched. As the entire civilized world is celebrating the memory of the great composer, the Slavic nations should unite their efforts to commemorate one of the most brilliant and perfect Slavic artists.

Nikolay Kashkin, "Музыка в XIX столетии, ч. II" [Music in the nineteenth century, part II], *Московские ведомости* 63 (5 March 1901).

[...] Because of his early formative environment, Chopin developed under the influence of German composers; his piano technique was originally influenced by the Viennese virtuoso school, then he came under the spell of the elegant and brilliant pianists flourishing in Paris in the 1830s and 1840s, and finally he was influenced by Liszt, who was also based in Paris at the time. Yet all that external influence only made itself felt early in the composer's career; by the age of thirty, Chopin was an independent and unique pianist and composer.

Chopin's two concertos were composed in his youth, before he moved to Paris, and as such they failed fully to express the composer's individuality; but the larger pieces composed in later years were veritable musical poems and inspired countless imitations. Chopin's Polish dances portray an idealized picture of his country's past and present. Some of his mazurkas depict peasant scenes described in the elegant idiom of the aristocratic salon. His miniatures – the preludes, the nocturnes, the impromptus and the poetic etudes – we should perhaps prize the most.

We have looked for connections between German Romantic poetry and music. But in the case of Chopin, it is clear that the French Romantics left no mark on him, though the figure of Alfred de Musset springs to mind, a writer and poet who showed an affinity with Chopin in terms of elegant expression and profound, heartfelt feeling. Although Chopin composed almost exclusively for the piano, an instrument with a limited palette of colours and expressive means, his melodic and harmonic genius place him on a par with the leading composers of the nineteenth century. The subjective lyricism of Schubert, Mendelssohn and Schumann found its highest and most perfect expression in Chopin. [...]

"А. Скрябин и И. Гофман о Шопене" [A. Scriabin and J. Hofmann on Chopin], *Русская музыкальная газета* 1910/13, p. 353.

On the centenary of Chopin's birth, our reporters speak to our young pianists about the brilliant composer. A correspondent of Утро России *in Moscow paid a visit to Mr. Scriabin, composer of the Poem of Ecstasy and a one-time self-described Chopin "worshipper", who made the following remarks.*

"It is true, I used to like Chopin. I worshipped him, actually", says Mr. Scriabin. "As a young boy I used to put Chopin's music under my pillow before going to bed. That fascination is over now. I have moved away from Chopin. In fact, I have moved so far away that today the sound of some naive nocturne of his makes me wonder why it used to make me cry... Now I prize Chopin only as a composer of exceptional musicality.

Chopin's musicality was remarkable, far outstripping his contemporaries in that respect. With that kind of talent he could have become the world's greatest composer; but alas, his musical gift did not go hand in hand with a comparable breadth of musical outlook.

His is not the only musical example of this kind of discrepancy. Berlioz, though a man of genius, was a poor musician. His insights were brilliant but he was unable to clothe them in a fitting musical form. Even Beethoven proved unable to live up to his own vision of the Ninth Symphony. Musically, the actual shape of the work falls short of the brilliance of the conception.

Also, Chopin's artistic personality was smothered under the weight of a nationalist ideology. He was unable to come up with a truly global or universal work: all of his music reflects the tragic experience of the Polish nation.

What is astounding about Chopin is that he did not evolve at all. He was a complete composer and a colourful personality beginning almost with his very first opus. He was a proud and highly moral man, and the two qualities are perfectly reflected in his music. In the absence of a biography, Chopin's life could be narrated based on his works alone".

Was he influenced by George Sand?

"Without a doubt. Sand had everything that Chopin lacked; she was broad-minded, and she had a deep and forceful personality. The volatile and wavering Chopin clung to her instinctively, and he was very much influenced by her as a man, though not as a composer, which is perhaps regrettable. His adherence to the nationalist ideology was so strong that even his estrangement from George Sand, a great personal misfortune to the composer, did not have a major influence on the character of his music. The separation sapped Chopin's dwindling vital powers, but it failed to contribute a single note to his late works. The suffering of the Polish nation continued to make up the entire content of his music".

Unlike the composer of the Poem of Ecstasy, who was quite casual in his dismissal of the "smothering" effects of Chopin's nationality, and indeed of Beethoven, Josef Hofmann expressed an enthusiasm for Chopin.

"I have loved Chopin since childhood, and his works make up the bulk of my concert repertoire these days. No other composer has been able to move me so profoundly. Chopin is a boundless ocean of imagination of the most poetic and diverse kind. There is not a single repetition in his works; every piece is a new world of poetic fancy. You sometimes get to see a similar creative imagination at work in our modernist composers, but they never stop repeating themselves. With Chopin, every piece is new. Another reason I perform Chopin's music is because he was probably the only composer to write exclusively for the piano. I also play quite a lot of Schumann, whose music easily yields to orchestral arrangement and can be played in a symphonic form. But Chopin's music does not yield itself to such a treatment. The whole orchestra is unable to communicate as much poetry and dreamy lyricism as Chopin's works do. The centenary of Chopin's birth has prompted the publication of numerous new publications about the composer. As a Pole and a musician, I am obviously pleased to see that his works are being performed increasingly often".

Yakov Milstein, "К. Н. Игумнов о Шопене" [K. N. Igumnov[33] on Chopin],
Советская музыка, **1949/10, pp. 52-53.**

[...] We often hear Chopin being described as a sentimental salon composer racked by a painful illness. This portrayal is profoundly mistaken. Although some isolated elements present in his music might seem to corroborate that opinion, Chopin was in actual fact an extraordinarily pithy and weighty composer.

Chopin knew how to merge personal experience with popular feeling and with the interests of his nation. Passionately patriotic to the last, he always had a great love and sympathy for other people. He was one of the most humane composers the world has ever seen.

Chopin was resolutely opposed to the kind of music that is devoid of emotional content: music that expresses no ideas, feelings or psychological states. In terms of mood, his extremely diverse music spanned the gamut of human feelings, ranging from the deeply personal and psychological experiences that he communicated in his nocturnes to the sweeping and brilliant polonaises that reflected the epic events of his nation's history. [...]

Chopin abhorred spuriousness and affectation. The most characteristic qualities of his creative personality were a majestic simplicity and a freedom from false pathos. Though privately he was a very reserved and undemonstrative person, as an artist he made truthfulness his aim, and his music is often painfully direct and honest. Only his music offers us a glimpse of the secrets of his soul [...].

Two approaches seem to me particularly ill-suited for performing Chopin's music. The first seeks to portray Chopin as a "suitable composer for young ladies", and it is marked by an excess of the emotionality and femininity that is so characteristic of the salons. Devoid of artistic value, this kind of performing manner could be roundly ignored were it not for its considerable popularity, even among professional pianists. The other mistaken type of performance is the "virtuoso" approach, which cannot be justified even by the obvious technical difficulty of the pieces and the opportunities they afford for the display of a pianist's prodigious technique. In this case, the term "prodigious" is actually a misnomer for a weak performance camouflaged by self-confidence and tinsel-like sparkle. Some of the "virtuosi" tend to approach Chopin in purely formal terms, others display excessive emotionality daubed with

---

33 Konstantin Nikolayevich Igumnov (1873-1948) – eminent Russian pianist and professor of music. His series of Chopin concerts (particularly in 1915-1916 and in the 1920s and 1930s) were a major event on Moscow's music scene.

spurious pathos and morbid passion, and yet others go to the opposite extreme to empty Chopin's music of all emotional content by shifting the emphasis to technical brilliance. For all their differences, such pianists display a common lack of understanding for Chopin's true artistic intentions and must be deemed equally unsatisfactory. [...]

Every work by Chopin follows a clear overall plan. Although there is no denying the importance of improvisation in his music, it should not be assumed that his music was composed in a single flash of inspiration. On the contrary, he worked painstakingly, revising the details and reworking the passages of every piece many times over; it took much toil and anguish before an early sketch had crystallized into its final shape. All this should be borne in mind when interpreting Chopin's music. To me, it seems unlikely that a vague and nebulous playing style with slow and hesitant tempi could reflect the essence of Chopin's artistic intentions. I fear that this kind of performance might easily prove to be a slippery slope leading to a narcissistic aesthetic and a subdued playing style better suited to the salons. [...]

In Liszt's beautiful phrase, "In his compositions, boldness is always justified; richness, even exuberance, never interferes with clarity; singularity never degenerates into uncouth fantasy; the sculpturing is never disorderly; the luxury of ornament never overloads the chaste eloquence of the principal lines".[34] Every performer of Chopin's music should bear those words in mind.

Whether interpreting Chopin or anyone else, a performer should always have a precise idea of the composer's intention; in other words, a perfect command of the actual text is a must.

Also of great importance in performing Chopin's music is a good feel for his rhythms. Interpreters of Chopin err mostly by falling into one of two extremes. Some plunge their interpretations arbitrarily into rhythmic anarchy and chaos. Such pianists should reflect on the enormous importance Chopin himself attached to rhythm. The composer famously said that the left hand should act as an orchestral conductor, imposing regularity on the performance. According to the account of [Karol] Mikuli, there was a metronome on Chopin's piano at every lesson he gave. However, the importance of rhythmical clarity should not choke the abundance of Chopin's rhythms with the clockwork monotony of the metronome. Those performers who are guilty on that count should bear in mind what Chopin himself termed *rubato*. We must not be confused by this apparent contradiction between the opposing requirements

---

34 Franz [Ferenc] Liszt, *Life of Chopin*, tr. Martha Walker Cook, 4th edn rev. (1880).

of rhythm and *rubato*. In Chopin's music, one cannot exist without the other. It is impossible to understand Chopin's *rubato* unless we are able to discern the line of overall rhythmical development in a composition.

For Chopin, the piano was not a colourless instrument. He cared greatly for tone colour and timbre. This is why a performer must have a perfect command of the different techniques of *toucher*. Chopin's cantilena, which is largely derived from the singing quality of the human voice, calls for sustained, songlike tones throughout the musical texture, and not merely in the dominant melodic voice. [...]

Cantilena performance calls for maximum proximity between the fingers and the keys. Inasmuch as is possible, the keys should be struck by the finger pads, i.e. the fleshy undersides of the fingertips. The aim is to achieve maximum contact, a natural merging of finger and key without any intervening barrier or separation... Regardless of the type of instrument, the fingers should feel the face of the keyboard, they should merge with it and produce liquid transitions from note to note in a soft pulse of the fingers. [...]

Boris Asafyev,[35] *Шопен (1810-1849)* [Chopin (1810-1849)] (excerpts).

Chopin was the kind of person whose biography boils down to a brief account, unless one decides to include either the nebulous halo of legend and worthless anecdote that surrounds every life, or the historical, social and private facts and events attendant on every great composer. Much has already been written of the sort, but one very important thing relating to Chopin's music is still missing: there is no reliable scholarship on the sources of his pianism, and there are no comprehensive studies of the means of expression (the musical idioms and ideas) that the composer used to formulate the subtle, crystalline song of his soul. In terms of purely biographical details, Vladimir Karenin's comprehensive study of George Sand remains an unsurpassed critical source.[36] Its second volume contains an intelligent account of Chopin's life, free from an admixture of legend (it covers in the main the most important period in Chopin's life after meeting George Sand). Karenin's material is superior to other biographies of Chopin in that it imposes a certain order on the troubled and

---

35 Boris Vladimirovich Asafyev (1884-1949) – Russian musicologist, music teacher and organizer writing under the nom de plume of Igor Glebov. A student of A. K. Ladov (composition class). This study was written in 1922.

36 Vladimir Karenin [pen-name of Varvara Dmitrievna Komarova-Stassova 1862-1942], *Жорж Санд, ее жизнь и произведения* [George Sand, her life and works], ii, St. Petersburg 1916; Fr. tr. as Wladimir Karénine, *George Sand, sa vie et ses œuvres* (1890) [editor's note].

psychologically complex story of the extremely retiring composer and the people he dealt with.

In purely musical terms, if we disregard Liszt's fascinating and poetic but ultimately shallow biography[37] or Paskhalov's short but significant book of musical ethnography,[38] there is no comparable study available to serve as a basis for examining Chopin against the background of contemporary music or for venturing speculation about his continued significance for (and possibly influence on) the composers of today. There are few matters of controversy when it comes to the structure and content of Chopin's most prevalent tonal schemes; but as we move on to examine the lines and colours of Chopin's music, or the most vital qualities of his melodic intonation,[39] or the tensions inherent in overcoming the conventional schemata of folk dances (and indeed the more general textural schemata contained in those works), all of which were open to the composer's musical imagination, we are faced with a series of unanswered questions. [...] Therefore, I shall make a tentative attempt at analysing that highly-strung, artistic and spiritual composer, whose refinement and aristocratic aloofness continue to hinder the understanding and popularity of his compositional achievement [...]. At first sight, Chopin's music appears to be *passé* and outmoded: a thing of justified but waning antiquarian interest. But that is mere appearance, and careful inspection will reveal that the issue is far from simple. To an extent, the popularity of Chopin's music today is a localised phenomenon. It is the same kind of popularity that he enjoyed in the exclusive salon circles of Paris in the 1830s and 1840s.[40] Given its intense impact over an extended period of time, the emotional palette of Chopin's music should be considered as forming a new system of musical expression. We can treat that implicit system as an unknown quantity, which, when understood, will offer a chance to develop Chopin's compositional methods and to assimilate them into modern piano music. The road to discovering the nature of his music leads through the study of the real nature of melodic development in Chopin's music.[41]

---

37 F.[erenc] Liszt, *F. Chopin*. It was available in the Russian translation of P. A. Zinovev (St. Petersburg 1887). Asafyev considered the book largely obsolete. Eng. tr. as *Life of Chopin*, tr. M. W. Cook.

38 Vyacheslav Paskhalov, *Шопен и польская народная музыка* [Chopin and Polish folk music], in *Музыкальный современник*, 1916, vols. 1 and 4; 1917, vols. 7-8.

39 Intonation (or intoning) was an aesthetic category introduced by Asafyev to denote melodic development in terms of pitch change and harmonics [editor's note].

40 It is an interesting fact that the great French painter Delacroix, a friend and admirer of Chopin, analysed his music closely to reinterpret it in visual terms. See *Journal d'Eugène Delacroix 1822-1863*, 3 vols., Paris 1893-1895; also George Sand, *Impressions et souvenirs*, Paris 1873 [original note].

41 A great admirer of Chopin, Scriabin tried to intuit the same path, but he only did so by model-

Although there are evident ties linking Chopin with his native country and its folk music (their influence on the composer's creative imagination is at its most palpable in his mazurkas), it would be factually incorrect to argue that all of Chopin's music shows a lasting and unquestionable connection with his country. This kind of ethnographical influence is much more pronounced in the case of Moniuszko, whose more direct and less processed music is to a far greater degree a natural product of the Polish soil. In contrast to Moniuszko, the shining force of Chopin's talent transports the Polish musical element far into the realm of sophisticated pianistic art, where it merges with complex non-Polish musical ingredients. In this sense, all of Chopin's music carries the mark of the unique ambition of an artist who was familiar with, and attracted to, contemporary culture's most subtle developments, but who was lucky enough not to have severed the ties with his native inheritance. Chopin became an educated representative of Polish upper-class culture, who propagated the views, thinking habits and values of his formative environment. In Paris, he became an emotional poet of Polish exile and a propagator of the Romantic ideals of the Polish aristocracy and intelligentsia. It is not possible to appraise adequately the emotional nature or the cultural influence of Chopin's music without realizing this fact.

In Russia, Chopin tends to be compared to Glinka, as a precursor of the nationalist school. Arguably, both have a shared point of departure in having appeared at a transitional phase in musical evolution, which preceded the emergence in both Poland and Russia of a purely bourgeois culture and ideology in music. For all their negative qualities, the gentry and the aristocrats had one advantage over the culture of the intelligentsia; they did not suffer from the effects of deracination and were free from bourgeois ideology, that specific urban ideology which inevitably infects the middle classes, whether we are talking of their leading representatives, who are entirely enmeshed in the spiritual culture of the city, or of those provincial elements permeated by the noxious influence of civilization that places a wedge between a man and his native land.[42] The clear and almost simultaneous awakening of musical consciousness in Poland and Russia as represented by Chopin and Glinka coincided propitiously with a period when the spiritual culture of the land-owning classes had not

---

ling his melodic intonation on Chopin's. In other words, we are dealing here with a kind of stylization. And to an extent, the same observation seems to apply to the modern French composer Ravel [original note].

42 In postulating a conflict between the city and the country, the land-owners and the bourgeoisie, I am making a transition from concepts connected with musical culture and ideology to the evolving consciousness and means of expression in music [original note].

yet lost its direct connection with the land. In spite of having assimilated the ideals of Western music, the best representatives of the land-owning class had inwardly maintained a communion with the folk music that had nurtured them. Familiar with the great achievements of foreign cultures, they nevertheless missed their native lands and returned to compose those wondrous songs in which fresh, colourful folk material was balanced by subtle taste and technical mastery over details.

The shared point of reference may explain the analogies existing between the music of Glinka and Chopin, but there are also far-reaching differences between the two. The contributing factors were many. The musical talents of the two composers sprang from different sources: Polish and Russian folk elements are quite dissimilar in their natural state. Polishness gravitates towards dance and instrumental music, while the Russian element inclines towards purely vocal music. The scale and impact of Western musical culture were likewise different in Poland and in Russia during the formative years of Chopin and Glinka, in the 1820s and 1830s. Also, given the different conditions of musical life in Warsaw and St. Petersburg, the two cultures were not infected to the same degree by the influence of bourgeois and "common" elements in music. Finally, where Chopin and Glinka ventured in search of inspiration beyond their respective local cultures, they each drew on a different influence. Glinka was primarily inspired by the Caucasus, with a secondary Italian influence. Chopin's formative influences included Berlin, Vienna and, enduringly and importantly, France. Their only shared characteristic was the fact that as musical reformers they both relied on the recent achievements of Western European musical individualism as well as that bedrock musical heritage represented by Mozart and other Classical composers, though even there they were not without their differences, with Chopin leaning towards Bach and Handel, and Glinka towards Gluck and early polyphony. When it came to piano composers, however, Glinka adored Hummel and Field, who belonged to the evolutionary line represented by Chopin.[43]

[...] For Chopin, chamber music was the most convenient and least demanding compositional style, given the composer's spiritual and physical disposition and the regular opportunities this medium afforded for presenting his music to true musical connoisseurs. Obviously, there was the inherent danger that Chopin would become

43 Obviously, Field's influence could be compared to a small tributary that flows into the mighty lake of Chopin's music: a rivulet rather than the main waterhead. It is precisely the presence of those subterranean sources, which remain almost completely obscure to critics, that makes it so complicated a process to analyse the essence of Chopin's music [original note].

a routine supplier of conventional salon pieces bedecked with ornamental passages, or else a polonaise specialist (a number of composers, notably Weber, had found the polonaise attractive, quite regardless of its Polish aspects).[44] Fortunately, the danger never materialised. [...]

Strength of character comes from overcoming one's limitations. In the case of Chopin, the problem of finding a unique artistic identity through internal struggle was not as pronounced as in the case of Beethoven [...]. Instead, what Chopin was facing was not so much a dubious middle way as a twofold temptation. On one hand, there was his penchant for a showy virtuoso style; on the other, a leaning towards opera. Chopin's friends were unsuccessful in trying to persuade him to yield to the latter; and he was less than entirely victorious where it came to the former. Many of his works bear witness to his virtuosic flair, e.g. his variations [Op. 2], the two concertos, the *Fantasia on Polish Airs, Rondo à la krakowiak* and *Andante spianato et Grande Polonaise brillante*. All those works are typical showpieces, and they make relatively skilful use of various contemporary pianistic devices; still, a powerful though inchoate will resides in those juvenile pieces and tries to gain expression by all means available, though it is obscured by alien influence. [...] In those works, despite some profound and valuable passages (such as the Larghetto in the second Concerto), the performer will find it hard to achieve a degree of tension comparable to that in the concertos of Beethoven or Liszt. [...] The problem, I believe, can be explained by pointing to the fundamental differences that separate the aforementioned variations by Chopin and Liszt's variations on a theme from the same opera, which were composed in the early 1840s (not to mention Liszt's concertos or his orchestral fantasias such as the paraphrase on *Dies irae*). Obviously, in using these examples, my intention is to illustrate the different approaches to the problem and the differences of age and temperament existing between the two composers. Chopin published his variations on a theme from *Don Giovanni* at the age of eighteen. Liszt, who was one year Chopin's junior, produced nothing of comparable stature at the time (i.e. in the late 1820s). Chopin's variations are primarily an exercise in showcasing superficial virtuosity and just a step beyond the Weberian scheme of passage-work and pedigreed harmonic devices (such as the overwhelming and overweening re-

---

44 Even in Poland, polonaises tended to express revolutionary tendencies rather than national identity. The nationalistic tendencies in Chopin's polonaises are very different from those of naive folk polonaises. It is like the difference between an unassuming walk by country lads and lasses, and a majestic procession of aristocrats. The polonaise is an element of the chivalric inheritance of the Polish landowning classes, the "rhythm of their life's march" [original note].

liance on the dominant seventh chord, wittily noted by the perceptive Glinka as a Weberian feature). Chopin affords greater importance to the diminished chord, making it less obtrusive and allowing it to supplement the harmonic structure. He extends figuration-based variation technique to the organic structure of the music by favouring thematic development over conventional ornamentation. Such qualities were highly distinctive among the blithe virtuoso productions of the day, and Chopin's variations were duly noted by such experts as Schumann, who kept a close eye on new composers. Still, those pieces were valuable for their ability to mesmerise audiences by accentuating the powerful creativity of the variations over the compact, constantly repeated theme (rather as Liszt's *Don Giovanni* paraphrase deepens Mozart's original concept and shows it in a new light). However, Chopin's music was too emotionally effusive and too closely focused on details to achieve on the concert stage the same level of tempestuous tension as Liszt's, and it fell to Liszt to inspire the subsequent course of nineteenth-century pianism. Liszt chose to focus on bravura, extravert projection, whereas Chopin preferred to confine himself to the inward-looking world of personal experience.

The struggle against the temptations of showy virtuosity inherent in stage performance helped Chopin to scale the most majestic heights of his talent. The piano pieces he composed in his early years in Paris (before meeting George Sand) are very different from the works composed in the immediately preceding period. Suffice it to mention the Ballade in G minor, the polonaises from Op. 26, the nocturnes from Op. 27, the mazurkas from Op. 24-33, the first two scherzos or the first volume of etudes. In those works, Chopin was already speaking a language of his own and had presumably realised his true strength, dictating the course of further artistic development capable of expressing his thoughts, dreams and yearnings. [...]

In Chopin's life, the conflicts that affected him were concentrated in the various stages of love's sorrows and, very strongly, in the outbursts of sadness connected with the fall of his native country. This outpouring of grief transformed the Polish patriot in voluntary exile pining for his country in nostalgic and grieving meditations, in turn dreaming and angry. These meditations, with their desire for revenge and their hallucinatory flashes of spiritual vision, were filled with rapturous delight as he transformed his dreams into those strangely-inspired harmonies.[45]

---

45 Based on the second volume of Karenin's, *Жорж Санд, ее жизнь и произведения* [George Sand, her life and works], which is devoted entirely to the relationship between Sand and Chopin [original note]. The original continues with an account of Chopin's relationship with George Sand [editor's note].

[...] During or just before his sojourn on Majorca, certainly during that fateful period when he realised he was going to lose Maria Wodzińska but before he became fully committed to a relationship with George Sand, Chopin composed his brilliant Preludes – twenty-four short works, each of which made his heart boil, quiver and suffer in succession; in each his heart fills with anger, terror, yearning, tenderness or anguish; it cries and moans, then is caressed and given hope; there is delight, sadness and painful disappointment; the heart turns numb with terror, and then freezes amid the howling gusts of autumn wind; several bars later it finds new faith that the sun will come out again, and it blossoms with the pastoral sounds of spring. Each prelude is a separate whole, perfect and complete – a job wisely done and an obstacle successfully taken – and that is just the stylistic aspect. When it comes to the emotional impact or the pathos of suffering and sympathy captured within the iron clutches of form and reinvented afresh in every prelude, we are dealing with one of the greatest wonders of creative imagination. Nocturnes can be sung throughout one's life, for there will always come states of lyrical serenity, contemplation and delight; the capricious rhythms of mazurkas can likewise be composed many times over in a single lifetime, for the spirit's *capriciousness* is more or less a permanent condition of subtle souls, particularly of those that react musically to external stimuli. We could also agree that the mind often finds itself immersed in the rocking and swirling tones of a waltz or the imperious rhythms of a heroic polonaise. But to compose a succession of musical moments wrought of pure suffering, and to modestly describe them as preludes, i.e. pieces which but precede greater things, that is the kind of test that comes only once in a lifetime. It is quite simple to find a way of communicating one's emotions by working within a musical blueprint without violating its rules. It is more difficult to use a blueprint with self-imposed limitations, and to tackle multiple problems in the way scientists or mathematicians do. But one way or the other, such difficulties can be overcome, because they have been set up by reason, and reason can master them.

But when we are faced in music with a phenomenon like Chopin's preludes, any discussion of difficulty or determination is beside the point. We are confronted with a seemingly simple phenomenon: here are several moments snatched from the entire range of psychological states, but each of them is perceived as a singular and discrete world delimited in its expression and organically connected with Chopin's music as a whole. By looking at those twenty-four moments as a whole in their rhythm of high and low tides, their juxtaposition of contrasts, and their inextricable unity of dynamics and emotional tension, our eyes survey a distinct gamut of psychological states: each moment appears in a new configuration of melodic gestures (intonations), and the lines of every musical phrase are inseparably connected with the supremely Chopinesque whole. [...]

It is an interesting fact that no blueprint has been theorised for Chopin's preludes. For some time, we have been witnessing a deluge of preludes (particularly in Russian music), which suggests that talentless individuals regard the prelude as a "free form"[46] to be filled with any musical content, no matter how preposterous – an exercise that cannot be done with impunity. The structure of a prelude tends to show immediately whether we are dealing with a composer capable of organic thought or with a trivial chatterer.

In his brilliant synthesis, Chopin discovered an organic system of melodic gestures (intonations) which are not confined within any default schemata or otherwise conditioned by the dynamics, tone progressions or malleability of a given piece. Chopin's achievements expand the limits of pianism and deepen our understanding of tonality; they introduce a whole new sphere of pianistic reflections and chiaroscuro effects, and as such they take on a heroic stature and should be considered as nothing short of extraordinary. [...]

As in the preludes, the form of the sonata [in B flat minor] arises not from any schematic rules but from an internal impulse combined with the dynamics of sound. As a whole, it produces a development of colourful, organically interconnected musical pictures: a masterly and precise system of melodic and harmonic gestures (intonations). It is worth noting how the sonata traces its course from a vibrant and emotional first movement to the cool, dispassionate streams of sound in the finale. This transition from personal experience to detachment gives the finale its staggering power, which goes far beyond the standard fare of rondos that usually wrap up a sonata.

Having established the supreme harmonic unity and finality of Chopin's climactic pieces, counterpointed by their dynamic and constant emotional flows, I ought to make a tentative attempt to touch on the problem of Chopin's aesthetic.

[...] The style of Chopin's music is characterised by sophisticated restraint; the tiniest details are carefully considered and balanced by an impeccably refined taste; it is a self-contained classical whole, where the stirrings of emotion are under control, the ideas are crystal-clear, and every melodic and harmonic gesture (intonation) is

---

46 The free form is nothing less than an exceptionally difficult undertaking: in each case, the composer attempts to solve a creative problem according to a unique concept (in keeping with the musical material and the artistic idea), rather than by mechanically filling out a ready-made formal template [original note].

an organic unit. In all of Chopin's output (his extended works and his miniatures alike), there is not a single melodic line that is in any way vague or un-Chopinesque. As I have said, the first struggle in Chopin's artistic development was with the showy virtuosic style; but there is also a second contradiction inherent in his art, one that plays out between *the emotional element* on the one hand, with its titanic striving for liberty, and *the artist's will* on the other, a *classical* influence that imposes order and discipline on the mental data and musical material. This contradiction must have formed a formidable obstacle in the painful process whereby his works matured, for although Chopin had an improvisational facility for arriving at the basic ideas of his works, such discoveries were followed by a long and arduous path towards the final version. The painter Delacroix made an interesting comment about that process in his diary: [...] "Chopin's improvisations were far more daring than his finished pieces. There is an analogy to be drawn with a sketch and a completed painting. Surely a painting is not the worse for being complete! Compared to the sketch, a finished painting may leave less scope for imagination. [...] When Correggio made the famous comment 'I too am a painter!' what he wanted to say was: 'Here is a beautiful work, and yet I could have invested the work with something that it is currently missing'. An artist does not ruin a work by finishing it; all he does is to delimit the scope of possible interpretations by presenting his own point of view; in the process, he displays the scale of his talent, but also lays bare its limitations".[47]

In the same diary, Delacroix also says: "On the sketch and the finished work (*sur le fini*). Chopin's improvisations were more daring than his finished works; bringing a work to completion does not ruin it, if a great artist does it".[48]

Chopin was nothing if not great. There are no unfinished moments in his works. Every part brings a new stage to completion. In the process of interpretation, the music's dynamic reveals the wider dynamic of emotions (a term that musicians will understand), involving a painful struggle with the musical material as new trails are blazed amid the chaos of sound and the surge of experience. In fact, there is an analogy to be drawn between Chopin's physical appearance – with his elegant clothes and fine furnishings, a man who despised all that was uncouth and common and kept aloof from the populace – and the elegant style of his works, where the economy of expression and the meticulous treatment of details serve the composer's vision perfectly. Chopin detested Berlioz's music for its expressive excess and felt

---

47 *Journal d'Eugène Delacroix*, ii (1850-1854), pp. 163-165.
48 Ibid., iii (1855-1863), p. 353.

that its internal logic failed to justify its stylistic extravagance; in a way, the sound process is crushed under its own weight, and to Chopin that was patent nonsense. Delacroix said: "My dear Chopin was superior to that school which combines the specific sound of each instrument with momentous musical impact. Undeniably, there are people, such as Berlioz, who think that way, and it seems to me that Chopin detested Berlioz and his music, which was nothing but an assemblage arising from a desire to contrast trombones with flutes and oboes".[49] Hence the appraisal of music from the viewpoint of Mozart's aesthetic, of which Chopin was an adherent, as indeed was Delacroix. Delacroix's diary contains this entry: "Mozart wrote in a letter somewhere that music was capable of expressing all passions, sorrows and sufferings. Nonetheless, he said, passions, violent or otherwise, should never be expressed to a degree that provokes disgust; similarly, music at its most terrible should not irritate (*affecter*) the ear, but blandish it and charm it. In other words, music should always remain music".[50] Add to this the interesting exchange between Chopin and Delacroix provoked by the painter's question about the nature and origin of music's logic, and we get a relatively clear idea of Chopin's aesthetic, which explains his composing method.

"He gave me to understand that harmony and counterpoint constituted logic; the fugue is pure logic embodied in music, and in order to become a master of the fugue one has to understand all that is rational and justifiable in music. I would be happy indeed, I thought, if I could learn all that affects *les musiciens vulgaires*. The feeling would give me some idea of the satisfaction that learned men worthy of the name derive from knowledge. True knowledge is not what we generally take it to be, i.e. a certain area of competence distinct from art; on the contrary, knowledge as understood by Chopin *was* art; and art – contrary to some philistine notions – was not a kind of vague inspiration that gropes its way in the dark and presents the visible (*pittoresque*) shape of things. Art is reason itself, decorated (*ornée*) by genius; it follows the path of destiny and is guided by the highest laws. This brings to my mind the difference between Mozart and Beethoven. Chopin told me that wherever Beethoven walked in the dark and suffered from a lack of unity, we should not put that down to some affected desire for originality; that quality of his merely means that he turns away from the immortal principles; Mozart, by contrast, never does that. In Mozart, every detail matters, and it functions in accord with the others; it forms a kind of song

---

49 Ibid., p. 399.
50 Ibid., p. 186.

(*forme un chant*) and develops in accordance with that principle; this is where the counterpoint makes itself visible. He also added that others were in the habit of learning chords before the rules of counterpoint, i.e. before the succession of melodic lines that lead to chords... Berlioz crams (*plaque*) chords in to fill up the intervals".[51] Still, Chopin's consistent adherence to Mozart's achievements or his admiration for Bach's *Wohltemperiertes Klavier*, or indeed his insistent castigation of Berlioz for abusing tonal colour (*timbre*) as an aim in itself are not sufficient for explaining the basic means of expression that Chopin was a master of: he was able to affect the listener through the emotional beauty and delicate shimmering of sound, i.e. through the boundless sphere of colour and glimmering reflections.

It must be stated with all firmness that the fine contours of Chopin's music, along with its chiaroscuro effects, its subtle nuances of reflected lunar light, its occasionally sharp and bizarre contrasts, its sometimes garish and sometimes dusky tones, the colourful beauty of its juxtaposed scales: all that is a realm of brilliant pianistic achievement in chamber music, a subtle blossom of French pianism. In Chopin's own time, it had been repeatedly foreshadowed with brilliant clarity. Field was the first to show a modest intimation of its future glories in his fine, sentimental nocturnes. Dances, which were once clearly demarcated by the formal ordering of dances in suites and related forms, came to find a lasting cohesion in Chopin's music in the form of tonal relationships, juxtapositions of registers, chord timbres, soft contours spilling subtle reflected light into the tonal space (particularly in the nocturnes). In Chopin's music, timbre plays a dominant role. This is the important aspect: a fine sense of colour and a specific timbre often impose on the pianist-composer the need for an involuntary departure from the abstract logical rules of musical development; the rules need to be replaced with a more colouristic approach, which makes use of the effects produced by successive timbres (splashes of sound, sometimes garish and colourful, sometimes gloomy), where the contours of melodic lines are subservient to colour.

We are not talking about timbre being superimposed on the musical contours, but rather about the dynamics of colour itself (though obviously this was circumscribed by the limited colour palette available to the piano). In Chopin's works, there are countless examples of this kind of painterly (colourist) treatment of voices or melodies! They are the major achievements of Chopin's piano music, and they obviously stem from his brilliant sense of colour rather than his love of Classical composers. In

---

51 Ibid., i (1823-50), p. 365.

this manner, Chopin's music corroborates the aforementioned phenomenon of the organic treatment of voices stemming from the composer's colouristic aims. Naturally, the way the pianist-composer realized those aims was no different from Berlioz's orchestral projects, and in implementing them Chopin shows an even greater affinity with the music of today. For all the charges Chopin levelled indiscriminately at Berlioz, his own aims were remarkably similar. Even Delacroix, when writing in his diaries about the problem of colour in painting, questioned Chopin's evidence and cited numerous instances where pianists had used painterly methods: "why use a succession of piano sounds, now dampened, now dazzling (*éclatants*), except to bring out the idea one is trying to express? We should judge the use of timbre interchangeably with the expression of ideas, and we have to grant that some timbres are palpably sensual and blissful quite independently of spiritual expression. I remember that the voice of a dispassionate and inexpressive singer was remarkably enthralling through the sheer quality of the sound. The same thing happens in painting..."[52] Obviously, in Chopin's music the sensual charm is always there to be sensed, in spite of it being emotionally distinctive and expressive.

The prioritising of colour in the organization of voices is no less important for realising the importance of Chopin's music today than my reflections on his melody and harmony (intonations), or on the organic structure of musical form in his works. That is why I would like to conclude my study with an anecdote recounted by George Sand, relating to the problem of colour in music, to vividly and comprehensively summarise Chopin's poetic music. Over a meal, Delacroix was talking about the theory of light reflections.[53] [...]

"A strange song was heard. The Maestro [Chopin] knew what he was doing. He was mocking those who try to force people and things to speak by imitating outward tones. [...] That is the greatness of [music] – it cannot talk in prose. When a nightingale sings on a starry night, a maestro does not demand that we learn or imitate the bird's song. A composer makes the human voice sing that special feeling we get from listening to a nightingale song; and even if the resulting music does not make one think of nightingales, nonetheless it delights one and makes one feel as if one were savouring the lulling tones of happy and contemplative nature on a wonderful night..."

---

52 Ibid., iii, p. 399.

53 The author recounts the scene on the basis of Karenin's *Жорж Санд, ее жизнь и произведения* [George Sand, her life and works] ii, p. 195. The original passage is published in this volume (p. 389) as part of the anthology of French criticism, edited by Marie-Paule Rambeau. It is an excerpt from George Sand's *Impressions et souvenirs*, pp. 85-87 [editor's note].

Nicolas-Eustache Maurin, *Quelques célèbres pianistes des années 1840*, 1842
Standing left to right: Jacob Rosenhain, Theodor Döhler, Fryderyk Chopin, Alexander
Dreyschock, Sigismond Thalberg; sitting: Edward Wolff, Adolf Henselt, Franz Liszt.
Litograph published in *Galerie de la Gazette Musicale*, 2 (1842); Collection: Muzeum Fryderyka
Chopina, Warsaw [M/2895].

Fryderyk Chopin im Urteil deutschsprachiger Autoren

Joachim Draheim

Das Verhältnis Chopins zum deutschen Musikleben seiner Zeit, zu deutscher Musik der Vergangenheit und Gegenwart, zu deutschen Musikverlagen und Musikern und sein Einfluss auf diese zu Lebzeiten und viel mehr noch nach seinem frühen Tode in der zweiten Hälfte des 19. Jahrhunderts war und ist eines der wichtigsten Themen der Chopin-Forschung, da es komplex und vielfältig und in mancher Hinsicht noch gar nicht ganz zu überschauen ist. So hat es z.B. viel zu lange gedauert, bis Robert Schumanns leider Fragment gebliebene Variationen über ein Nocturne von Chopin (op. 15, Nr. 3) für Klavier 1992 von Joachim Draheim bei Breitkopf & Härtel ediert und inzwischen auch mehrfach auf Tonträgern eingespielt wurden. Auf der anderen Seite ist es unstreitig, dass Chopin ohne seine deutschen Musikverleger, ohne die – lobenden wie tadelnden – Rezensionen in deutschen Musikfachzeitschriften, ohne seine mehr oder weniger intensiven Kontakte und Beziehungen zu deutschen Musikern wie Hummel, Moscheles, Pixis, August Alexander Klengel, Meyerbeer, Ferdinand Hiller, Schumann und Mendelssohn nicht so schnell in der Musikwelt anerkannt worden wäre, wie das zu Beginn der dreißiger Jahre des 19. Jahrhunderts geschah.

Chopin, der recht gut deutsch sprach und einmal sogar einen Brief in deutscher Sprache an die Mutter seines Freundes Ferdinand Hiller verfasste, das Deutsche aber nur selten benutzte, hat nur wenige Monate seines kurzen Lebens in einem deutschsprachigen Umfeld verbracht, die aber für seine Biographie und seine künstlerische Entwicklung zum Teil von großer Bedeutung waren. Bei der Kur in Bad Reinertz im Sommer 1825 gab der 15jährige zwei improvisierte Wohltätigkeitskonzerte, in Berlin im September 1825 hörte er Händels *Cäcilien-Ode* und Webers *Freischütz* und traf Alexander von Humboldt. Bei seinem ersten kurzen Aufenthalt in Wien 1829 knüpfte er Verbindungen zum Verlag Haslinger und wirkte mit Erfolg bei Konzerten mit. Sein zweiter Aufenthalt in der Musikmetropole dauerte acht Monate, vom November 1830 bis zum 20. Juli 1831 und brachte ihm wichtige und inspirierende musikalische und menschliche Eindrücke. Durch den Ausbruch des polnischen Aufstandes gegen die russische Okkupation im November 1830 wurde er von der geliebten Heimat abgeschnitten und kehrte nicht nach Warschau zurück, sondern siedelte im September 1831 nach Paris über, das ihm zum dauernden Exil werden sollte. Die beiden Aufenthalte in Leipzig am 27. September 1835 und 12. September 1836 waren kurz, aber von intensiven musikalischen Begegnungen mit Schumann, Mendelssohn, Clara und Friedrich Wieck und Vertretern des Verlags Breitkopf & Härtel erfüllt. Nicht vergessen sei auch das freundschaftliche Treffen mit Hiller und Mendelssohn während des Niederrheinischen Musikfestes in Aachen und in Düsseldorf im Mai 1834. In Dresden hielt Chopin am 9. September 1836 um die Hand der 17jährigen Maria Wodzińska an, zunächst mit Erfolg, aber – wie wir wissen – ohne „happy end".

Unter seinen engsten Freunden gibt es nur einen deutschen – Ferdinand Hiller – dem er 1833 die *Nocturnes* op. 15 widmete, unter seinen zahlreichen Schülern nur zwei deutsche von Bedeutung, zu denen man noch den Siebenbürger Sachsen Karl Filtsch rechnen kann: Friederike Streicher, der wir wertvolle Erinnerungen verdanken, und Adolf Gutmann, einer seiner Lieblingsschüler, der Widmungsträger des 3. *Scherzo* op. 39. Doch der Ruhm seiner Werke, um den sich vor allem Robert Schumann als unermüdlicher Propagandist verdient machte, verschaffte Chopin sehr bald Zugang zu deutschen Musikverlagen, vor allem jenen in Leipzig, dem Zentrum des europäischen Musikverlagswesens. Die von Chopin selbst veröffentlichten Opera 1–65 sind ausnahmslos auch oder zuerst bei deutschen Verlagen erschienen, und zwar die Opera 6–11, 13 und 14 bei Friedrich Kistner und die Opera 12, 15–18, 20–31, 33–42, 45–49, 52–58 und 60–65 bei Breitkopf & Härtel, dem renommiertesten Verlag dieser Zeit, der auch die marktbeherrschende „Allgemeine Musikalische Zeitung" in Leipzig herausgab. Dieser Verlag fühlte sich später wie selbstverständlich dafür verantwortlich, nicht nur die ersten Gesamtausgaben der Werke von Bach, Mozart, Schubert, Mendelssohn und Schumann, sondern auch von Chopin (1878–1880) zu organisieren – ein Unternehmen, bei dem man kaum Gewinn machen konnte. Dass man Chopin in Deutschland schon sehr früh gar nicht mehr als „ausländischen" Komponisten wahrnahm, zeigte am eindrucksvollsten der Jahrgang 1844 der „Allgemeinen Musikalischen Zeitung", dem ein Porträt des Komponisten mit der Unterschrift „Friedrich Chopin" vorangestellt war – die bis zum Ende des Jahrhunderts gebräuchliche Eindeutschung des Vornamens „Fryderyk" oder „Frédéric" in „Friedrich" darf nicht als Versuch einer anmaßenden Germanisierung des Komponisten, dessen nationales polnisches Profil man gerade in Deutschland anerkannte und besonders schätzte, sondern eher als eine „Ehreneinbürgerung" angesehen werden. Die Ehre eines Porträts in der „Allgemeinen Musikalischen Zeitung" war z.B. 1836 Meyerbeer, 1837 Mendelssohn, 1843 Liszt, 1845 Gade und 1847 Berlioz zuteil geworden – allesamt Musiker von europäischem Rang, die aber ein integraler Teil des deutschen Musiklebens geworden waren.

Welche Rolle bei dieser „Einbürgerung" Chopins die damals gerade aufblühende Musikkritik in Musikfachzeitschriften spielte, ist immer wieder betont, aber nicht eingehend untersucht worden. Neben den auch literarisch wertvollen Artikeln Robert Schumanns aus den Jahren 1831 bis 1843, die so berühmte Schlagworte wie „Hut ab, ihr Herren, ein Genie!" und „Chopins Werke sind unter Blumen eingesenkte Kanonen" enthielten, wurden nur noch die geifernde Ablehnung Ludwig Rellstabs und gelegentlich das etwas gequälte Lob Gottfried Wilhelm Finks wahrgenommen – Zwischentöne und Nebenstimmen, d.h. weitere und differenzierte Äußerungen zu Chopins ersten Werken von anderer Seite wurden dabei übersehen oder überhört.

Die vorliegende Anthologie will hier Abhilfe schaffen und die Diskussion über Chopin in der Sicht seiner deutschen Zeitgenossen sowie von wenigen prominenten Stimmen aus der zweiten Hälfte des 19. Jahrhunderts zunächst einmal auf ein sicheres Quellenfundament stellen, da viele dieser Texte nicht leicht zugänglich sind oder in dieser Zusammenstellung noch nie zu lesen waren. Bewusst verzichtet wurde deswegen auf einige in diesem Zusammenhang interessante Texte, die in der Chopin-Literatur bequem zugänglich sind, wie z.B. die Erinnerungen von Friederike Streicher, das ohnehin etwas aufgeblasene und nicht in jeder Hinsicht glaubhafte Buch von Wilhelm von Lenz sowie Chopins eigene Briefe aus Wien. Meine Sammlung enthält neben der vollständigen Dokumentation der Konzertkritiken aus Wien und München 1829 und 1831, deren wohlwollender Tenor sich allerdings kaum von den Beurteilungen anderer Musiker, die inzwischen restlos vergessen sind, unterscheidet, vor allem Rezensionen der Notenausgaben und zwei Lexikon-Artikel (Rudolf Hirsch, 1836, und Hugo Riemann, 1900), wie sie unterschiedlicher und aufschlussreicher nicht sein könnten, und somit fast alle Texte aus der Fachpresse, die zu Lebzeiten des Komponisten in deutscher Sprache erschienen sind. Durch die chronologische Anordnung wird nicht nur die Entwicklung und Differenzierung des Chopin-Bildes in Deutschland deutlich, sondern manche Andeutungen in den Rezensionen Schumanns, Finks und Rellstabs, die sich aufeinander beziehen, erst verständlich. Nicht zuletzt wird der bisher kaum thematisierte qualitative Abstand zwischen Schumanns geistvollen, prägnanten, von einer tiefen, aber nicht kritiklosen Bewunderung für Chopin getragenen poetischen Essays und den meist geschwätzigen, oft langweiligen und sich in haltlose theoretische Abhandlungen verlierenden Texten seiner Kollegen, an erster Stelle Gottfried Wilhelm Fink (1783–1846) und Ludwig Rellstab (1799–1860), schmerzlich erfahrbar.

Ludwig Rellstab, ein pensionierter Offizier, von dessen mäßigen Gedichten Franz Schubert (im *Schwanengesang*) einige vertonte und dem wir den Titel „Mondschein-Sonate" für Beethovens *Sonate cis-Moll* op. 27, Nr. 2 „verdanken", war offenbar der Prototyp des dilettantischen Musikkritikers schlechthin, der seine Ignoranz und sein reaktionäres Musikbild hinter einem Wust von schönen Worten, flachen Witzen und abstrusen Theorien zu verstecken suchte. Da er offenbar nicht richtig Klavier spielen konnte, beklagt er immer wieder die ungeheuren Schwierigkeiten von Chopins Klaviersatz, die für die meisten seiner Zeitgenossen, wenn sie denn wirkliche Musiker waren, keine unüberwindbaren Hindernisse darstellten. Der oberlehrerhafte Tonfall Rellstabs ist allerdings durchaus zeittypisch; er wird im Laufe der Jahre auch immer kleinlauter, je größer die Anerkennung Chopins in der Musikwelt wurde, und verstummt schließlich resigniert.

Der Theologe und Musikschriftsteller Gottfried Wilhelm Fink, ein umfassend gebildeter Musiker, wenn auch mit eher konservativen Ansichten, befand sich Chopins Werken gegenüber in einer Zwickmühle. Wie die ersten Texte zeigen, waren sie ihm nicht ganz geheuer und mit seinem noch ganz dem 18. Jahrhundert verhafteten Musikgeschmack nicht vereinbar, wenn auch eine so heftige Ablehnung wie die Rellstabs bei ihm niemals zu erkennen war. Da aber seit 1833 die Mehrzahl von Chopins Werken bei Breitkopf & Härtel in Leipzig erschien, dem Verlag, der auch die „Allgemeine Musikalische Zeitung" herausgab, deren Chefredakteur Fink von 1827 bis 1841 war, blieb ihm nichts anderes übrig, als relativ freundlich über Chopin zu schreiben, seine Bedeutung für die Musik hervorzuheben und das Publikum zu animieren, sich mit ihr auseinanderzusetzen. Der Verleger hätte sich Verrisse wie die Rellstabs in „Iris im Gebiete der Tonkunst" (die beim konkurrierenden Verlag Schott in Mainz erschien, mit dem Chopin nichts zu tun hatte) sicher verbeten. So wirkt das Lob Finks oft etwas mühsam und gedrechselt und von einer Fülle überflüssiger Gedankenspiele überlagert. Man bekommt aber den Eindruck, dass sich Fink redlich bemüht hat, Chopin zu verstehen, was ihm im Laufe der Jahre auch immer besser gelang, so dass wir seinen Kritiken doch viele interessante Beobachtungen entnehmen können.

Sein Nachfolger als Chopin-Rezensent in der „Allgemeinen Musikalischen Zeitung", der Philosophie-Professor August Kahlert aus und in Breslau (1807–1864), ein Bekannter Robert Schumanns, gehörte zu den Chopin-Enthusiasten der ersten Stunde, obwohl seine Zustimmung nicht ganz so flammend ist wie die Schumanns und auch kritische Töne enthält. Noch vor Chopins Tod, nach Schumann und neben Kahlert wandelt sich das Bild in der Presse, zu einer distanzierten Zustimmung, der

Anerkennung eines „Klassikers", in die sich erste Misstöne mischen, die in der Zeit nach 1850 immer lauter werden. Chopin wird mangelnder Formsinn, weichliche Sentimentalität und die Unfähigkeit, sich stilistisch weiter zu entwickeln, vorgeworfen, selbst von einem so klugen Kopf wie Eduard Hanslick (1825–1904), dem Freund von Brahms und geistvollen Widersacher Richard Wagners. Dass diese Vorwürfe eher auf die Unarten einer dilettantischen Interpretation der Werke Chopins als auf die Kompositionen selbst zielen, hat Louis Ehlert (1825–1884), Komponist und hervorragender Musikschriftsteller aus dem Dunstkreis Schumanns und Mendelssohns, schon 1859 hellsichtig erkannt. Die Urteile von Musikern und Musikschriftstellern werden durch zwei prominente Nicht-Musiker, Heinrich Heine und Friedrich Nietzsche (der freilich sein durchaus vorhandenes musikalisches Talent maßlos überschätzte) kontrapunktiert. Das letzte Wort hat der geniale Ferruccio Busoni (1866–1924), Komponist am Übergang von der Romantik zur Moderne, brillanter Musikschriftsteller (*Entwurf einer neuen Ästhetik der Tonkunst*) und – was im Falle Chopins das wichtigste ist – einer der größten Pianisten und Chopin-Interpreten aller Zeiten.

Die vorliegende Anthologie ist chronologisch angeordnet und bietet wohl erstmals eine zusammenhängende und vollständige Dokumentation der Konzertkritiken zu Chopins Konzerten in Wien und München 1829 und 1831, dazu alle Rezensionen Robert Schumanns in den Fassungen, wie sie in der „Allgemeinen Musikalischen Zeitung" und der „Neuen Zeitschrift für Musik" erschienen sind, nicht den behutsam redigierten Versionen in den *Gesammelten Schriften* (1854). Bei den Kritiken von Fink und Rellstab musste wegen ihrer Überlänge und phrasendreschenden Geschwätzigkeit eine repräsentative Auswahl getroffen werden; folgende Rezensionen wurden nicht aufgenommen, enthalten aber wenigstens z.T. interessante Aspekte, die bei einer näheren Untersuchung berücksichtigt werden müssten:

G. W. Fink: Rezension der *Etüden* op. 10, in: Allgemeine Musikalische Zeitung (= AMZ) 36/1834, Nr. 6 vom 5. Februar, Sp. 81–89

L. Rellstab: Rezension der 3 *Nocturnes* op. 15, in: Iris im Gebiete der Tonkunst (= Iris) 5/1834, Nr. 30 vom 25. Juli, S. 117/118

G. W. Fink: Rezension des *Klavierkonzerts e-Moll* op. 11, der *Variations brillantes* op. 12, der 3 *Nocturnes* op. 15 und des *Rondeau* op. 16, in: AMZ 36/1834, Nr. 33 vom 13. August, Sp. 537–543

L. Rellstab: Rezension des *Rondeau* op. 16, in: Iris 5/1834, Nr. 38 vom 19. September, S. 149/150

L. Rellstab: Rezension der *Grande Fantaisie sur des Airs polonais* für Klavier und Orchester op. 13, in: Iris 5/1834, Nr. 44 vom 31. Oktober, S. 174/175

G. W. Fink: Rezension des *Krakowiak* für Klavier und Orchester op. 14 und des *Grand Duo concertant* für Violoncello und Klavier von Chopin und Franchomme, in: AMZ 37/1835, Nr. 5 vom 4. Februar, Sp. 77/78

L. Rellstab: Rezension der *Grande Valse brillante* op. 18, in: Iris 6/1835, Nr. 26 vom 26. Juni, S. 102/103

G. W. Fink: Rezension der 4 *Mazurken* op. 24, in: AMZ 38/1836, Nr. 11 vom 16. März, Sp. 179

G. W. Fink: Rezension der *Grande Polonaise brillante précédee d'un Andante spianato* op. 22 und der 2 *Polonaisen* op. 26, in: AMZ 39/1837, Nr. 1 vom 4. Januar, Sp. 6–8

G. W. Fink: Rezension der 12 *Etüden* op. 25, in: AMZ 40/1838, Nr. 23 vom 6. Juni, Sp. 361–365

G. W. Fink: Rezension des *Impromptus As-Dur* op. 29, der 4 *Mazurken* op. 30 und des *Scherzo b-Moll* op. 31, in: AMZ 40/1838, Nr. 41 vom 10. Oktober, Sp. 665–668

L. Rellstab: Rezension des *Nocturne Es-Dur* op. 9, Nr. 2, in: Iris 10/1839, Nr. 27 vom 5. Juli, S. 105/106

G. W. Fink: Rezension der *Préludes* op. 28, der 4 *Mazurken* op. 33 und der 3 *Walzer* op. 34, in: AMZ 41/1839, Nr. 52 vom 25. Dezember, Sp. 1039–1041.

Hingewiesen sei hier auch noch auf die ausführliche Rezension eines anonymen Kritikers über Chopins „Nachgelassene Werke" in: „Neue Zeitschrift für Musik" 43/1855, Nr. 19 vom 2. November, S. 198–200. Für die Zeit nach Chopins Tod 1849, in der nach und nach biographische Darstellungen seines Lebens auch in deutscher Sprache erschienen, konnte angesichts des beschränkten Raumes nur eine kleine Auswahl prägnanter Essays und anderer Texte von z.T. prominenten Autoren geboten werden – für diese Zeit sei auf die ausführliche Bibliographie zum Thema „Chopin und Deutschland" verwiesen.

Für die Edition und Auswahl der Texte waren folgende Prinzipien maßgeblich:
1) Es sind – mit wenigen Ausnahmen – nur vollständige Texte aufgenommen, da aus dem Zusammenhang gerissene Zitate, wie bisher oft geschehen, hier nur ein verzerrtes Bild der Rezeption vermitteln können. Alle Auslassungen, die mit [...] gekennzeichnet sind, betreffen Passagen, die nichts oder nur wenig mit Chopin zu tun haben.

2) Die Orthographie der Texte ist strikt beibehalten, nur offensichtliche Schreib-fehler (Heine schreibt z.B. 1837 mit peinlicher Konsequenz „Choppin") sind still-schweigend verbessert. Ungewöhnliche Schreibweisen sind mit [sic!] gekennzeich-net. Die z.T. chaotische Zeichensetzung der Vorlagen wurde der besseren Lesbarkeit wegen behutsam modernisiert, vor allem überzählige Kommata getilgt.

3) Alle Ergänzungen des Herausgebers stehen in eckigen Klammern. Dies be-trifft z.B. Überschriften zu Texten, die keinen Titel haben, Opuszahlen von Chopins Werken, Erläuterungen zu unbekannten Namen, Werken und Begriffen, Einfügun-gen von Anmerkungen.

4) Die Anmerkungen des Herausgebers, mit 1, 2, 3 usw. gekennzeichnet, be-schränken sich auf wenige Angaben, die für das Verständnis der Texte notwendig sind; die Anmerkungen der Vorlagen sind, soweit für den Zusammenhang des Textes wichtig, unverändert übernommen.

Primär- und Sekundärliteratur zu den Themen:
„Chopin in Deutschland", „Chopins Beziehungen zu deutscher Musik
und deutschen Musikern", „Chopin im Urteil und in den Erinnerungen
von deutschen Musikern und Schriftstellern bzw. in der Presse" (Auswahl)

Ernst Burger, *Frédéric Chopin. Eine Lebenschronik in Bildern und Dokumenten*, München 1990 (abgekürzt: Burger)

Ferruccio Busoni, *Von der Einheit der Musik... Verstreute Aufzeichnungen*, Ber-lin 1922; Neuausgabe unter dem Titel *Wesen und Einheit der Musik*, revidiert und ergänzt von Joachim Herrmann, Berlin/Wunsiedel 1956

[Chopin, Briefe und Dokumente]:

Friedrich Chopins gesammelte Briefe. Zum erstenmal herausgegeben und getreu ins Deutsche übertragen von Bernhard Scharlitt, Leipzig 1911

Chopin. Gesammelte Briefe, übersetzt und herausgegeben von Dr. A. von Guttry, München 1928

Frédéric Chopin. Briefe und Dokumente, zusammengestellt und herausgegeben von Willi Reich, Zürich 1959

Fryderyk Chopin. Briefe. Herausgegeben mit einem Vorwort und Kommentaren von Krystyna Kobylańska. Aus dem Polnischen und Französischen übersetzt von Cae-sar Rymarowicz, Berlin 1983

Joachim Draheim, *Schumann und Chopin*, in: Schumann-Studien 3/4, hrsg. von Gerd Nauhaus, Köln 1994, S. 221–239

Joachim Draheim, *Robert Schumanns Variationen über ein Nocturne von Chopin*, in: *Chopin w kręgu przyjaciół, Chopin im Umkreis seiner Freunde III*, hrsg. von Irena Poniatowska, Warszawa 1997, S. 90–107 (Text in Polnisch und Deutsch)

Joachim Draheim, *Hommage à Frédéric Chopin*, in: *Chopin and his work in the context of culture. Studies edited by Irena Poniatowska*, Vol. 2, Kraków 2003, S. 241–248

Joachim Draheim, *Fryderyk Chopin in the eyes of Robert Schumann, Felix Mendelssohn Bartholdy and Heinrich Heine*, in: *Analytical Perspectives on the music of Chopin, edited by Artur Szklener*, Warszawa 2004, S. 255–274

Louis Ehlert, *Briefe über Musik an eine Freundin*, Berlin 1859, ²1868, ³1879

Louis Ehlert, *Frédéric Chopin*, in: *Aus der Tonwelt. Essays*, Berlin 1877, S. 283–309

Jean-Jacques Eigeldinger, *Chopin vu par ses élèves*, Neuchâtel 1970, ⁴2006

Imogen Fellinger, *Brahms zur Edition Chopinscher Klavierwerke*, in: *Musicae Scientiae Collectanea. Festschrift für Karl Gustav Fellerer zum 70. Geburtstag…*, hrsg. von Heinrich Hüschen, Köln 1973, S. 110–116

Eduard Hanslick, *Aus dem Tagebuch eines Musikers. (Der „Modernen Oper" VI. Theil.). Kritiken und Schilderungen*, Berlin 1892

Eduard Hanslick, *Chopin*, in: *Aus neuer und neuester Zeit. (Der modernen Oper IX. Teil.) Musikalische Kritiken und Schilderungen*, Berlin ²1900

Eduard Hanslick. Sämtliche Schriften – Historisch-kritische Ausgabe, Band I, 5: *Aufsätze und Rezensionen 1859–1861*, hrsg. und kommentiert von Dietmar Strauß, Wien/Köln/Weimar 2005

Heinrich Heine. Zeitungberichte über Musik und Malerei, hrsg. von Michael Mann, Frankfurt am Main 1964 (abgekürzt: Mann)

Michael Heinemann, *Bach – Beethoven und Chopin. Zu Fryderyk Chopins Sonate Nr. 1 c-Moll Op. 4*, in: *Chopin and his Work in the Context of Culture. Studies edited by Irena Poniatowska*, Vol. 1, Kraków 2003, S. 404–410

Ferdinand Hiller, *Felix Mendelssohn-Bartholdy. Briefe und Erinnerungen*, Köln 1874

Helena Hryszczyńska, *Schubert – Nourrit – Chopin*, in: *Chopin and his Work in the Context of Culture. Studies edited by Irena Poniatowska*, Vol. 1, Kraków 2003, S. 496–505

F. Gustav Jansen, *Die Davidsbündler. Aus Robert Schumann's Sturm- und Drangperiode*, Leipzig 1883, Reprint: Walluf bei Wiesbaden 1973 (zu Chopins Begegnung mit Henriette Voigt)

Ute Jung-Kaiser, *„Im Traumreich der Poesie beheimatet sein"... Chopins Klang-poesie im Spiegel der Literatur*, in: *Chopin, der Antistar*, hrsg. von Ute Jung-Kaiser und Matthias Kruse, Hildesheim/Zürich/New York 2010, S. 81–142

Jeffrey Kallberg, *Chopin, Rellstab, and the Immorality of Innovation*, in: *Chopin 1849/1999. Aspekte der Rezeptions- und Interpretationsgeschichte*, hrsg. von Andreas Ballstaedt, Schliengen 2003, S. 183–196

Moritz Karasowski, *Friedrich Chopin. Sein Leben und seine Briefe. Zweite, gänz-lich umgearbeitete und mit neuen Originalbriefen bereicherte Ausgabe*, Dresden 1878

Andrzej Koszewski, *Das Wienerische in Chopins Walzern*, in: Chopin-Jahrbuch 1963, hrsg. von Franz Zagiba, Wien 1963, S. 27–42

Joachim Krüger-Riebow, *Chopins Aufenthalte in Deutschland*, in: *Chopin-Alma-nach zur hundertsten Wiederkehr des Todesjahres von Fryderyk Chopin*. Hrsg. vom Chopin-Komitee in Deutschland, Potsdam 1949, S. 8–33

Hugo Leichtentritt, *Frédéric Chopin*, Berlin 1905, zweite, verbesserte Auflage 1920

Wilhelm von Lenz, *Die großen Pianoforte-Virtuosen unserer Zeit aus persönli-cher Bekanntschaft. Liszt – Chopin – Tausig – Henselt*, Berlin 1872, Reprint: Düssel-dorf 2000, [2]2006

Helmut Loos, *Werke Chopins im Konzertrepertoire Clara Schumanns*, in: *Chopin w kręgu przyjaciół, Chopin im Umkreis seiner Freunde III*, hrsg. von Irena Ponia-towska, Warszawa 1997, S. 54–89 (Text in Polnisch und Deutsch)

Helmut Loos, *Schumann und Chopin – rezeptionsgeschichtlich*, in: *Chopin and his Work in the Context of Culture. Studies edited by Irena Poniatowska*, Vol. 2, Kraków 2003, S. 195–203

Tomi Mäkelä, *„Dieser geniale, geschmackvolle, feinfühlende Componist und Vir-tuos möge Ihnen auch hier zum Muster dienen." Das Chopin-Bild von Friedrich Wieck*, in: *Chopin and his Work in the Context of Culture. Studies edited by Irena Poniatowska*, Vol. 2, Kraków 2003, S. 106–113

Aus Moscheles' Leben. Nach Briefen und Tagebüchern, hrsg. von seiner Frau, 2 Bände, Leipzig 1872/73

Erich Hermann Müller von Asow, *Fryderyk Chopin in Deutschland*, in: Chopin-Jahrbuch 1963, hrsg. von Franz Zagiba, Wien 1963, S. 161–215

W. Neumann, *Friedrich Franz Chopin*, Kassel 1855

Friedrich Niecks, *Friedrich Chopin als Mensch und Musiker. Vom Verfasser ver-mehrt und aus dem Englischen übertragen von Dr. W.[ilhelm] Langhans*, 2 Bände, Leipzig 1890

Klaus Wolfgang Niemöller, *Chopin im Davidsbund Robert Schumanns. Aspekte einer komplexen Beziehung,* in: *Chopin im Umkreis seiner Freunde III,* hrsg. von Irena Poniatowska, Warszawa 1997, S. 14–53 (Text in Polnisch und Deutsch)

Klaus Wolfgang Niemöller, *„Ich hatte mehrere Jahre in Paris … fast täglich mit Chopin verkehrt". Chopin und Ferdinand Hiller, eine Freundschaft,* in: *Chopin and his work in the context of culture. Studies edited by Irena Poniatowska,* Vol. 1, Kraków 2003, S. 160–170

Klaus Wolfgang Niemöller, *Das Nachwirken von Chopin im Klavierschaffen von Ferdinand Hiller,* in: *Chopin 1849/1999. Aspekte der Rezeptions- und Interpretationsgeschichte,* hrsg. von Andreas Ballstaedt, Schliengen 2003, S. 155–166

Friedrich Nietzsche. Werke in sechs Bänden, hrsg. von Karl Schlechta, zweiter Band: *Menschliches, Allzumenschliches u.a.,* München/Wien 1980

Arnold Niggli: *Friedrich Chopin's Leben und Werke. Vortrag gehalten in Aarau den 21. März 1878,* Leipzig 1879

Walter Pass / Gerda Leber-Hagenau / Alicja Kowalska u.a., *Chopin in Wien / Reisen nach Wien / Rezensionen über Chopin in Wien,* in: *Festschrift '99 anlässlich des 150. Todestages von Fryderyk Chopin,* hrsg. von Tadeusz Krzeszowik, Wien 1999, S. 21–27, 48–49, 63–65

Richard Prilisauer, *Fryderyk Chopin und Friedrich Nietzsche,* in: Chopin-Jahrbuch 1970, hrsg. von Franz Zagiba, Wien 1970, S. 197–207

Robert Schumann, *Gesammelte Schriften über Musik und Musiker,* 4 Bände, Leipzig 1854, Reprint: Wiesbaden 1985, in 2 Bänden, mit einem Nachwort von Gerd Nauhaus und einem Register von Ingeborg Singer

Robert Schumann. Gesammelte Schriften über Musik und Musiker. Fünfte Auflage, mit den durchgesehenen Nachträgen und Erläuterungen zur 4. Auflage und weiteren hrsg. von Martin Kreisig, 2 Bände, Leipzig 1914

Walther Siegmund-Schultze, *Chopin und Brahms,* in: *The Book of the First International Musicological Congress Devoted to the Works of Frederick Chopin. Warszawa 16th–22nd February 1960,* Warszawa 1963, S. 388–395

Mieczysław Tomaszewski, *Frédéric Chopin und seine Zeit,* Laaber 1999

Angelika Varga-Behrer, *„Hut ab, ihr Herren, ein Genie". Studien zur Chopin-Rezeption in der zeitgenössischen Musikpresse Deutschlands und Frankreichs,* Mainz u.a. 2010

Hans Volkmann, *Chopin in Dresden. Neue Daten zu seiner Lebens- und Liebesgeschichte,* Dresden 1933 (Sonderabdruck aus der Wissenschaftlichen Beilage des Dresdner Anzeigers vom 18. und 25. April und 9. Mai 1933)

Cosima Wagner. Die Tagebücher, 4 Bände (1869–1883). Ediert und kommentiert von Martin Gregor-Dellin und Dietrich Mack, München/Zürich ²1982 (mit zahlreichen aufschlussreichen Erwähnungen von Werken Chopins)

Franz Zagiba, *Chopin und Wien*, Wien 1951 (leider im Detail nicht zuverlässig)

Franz Zagiba, *Chopin als Mozartverehrer / Chopin und Tobias Haslinger*, in: Chopin-Jahrbuch 1956, hrsg. von Franz Zagiba, S. 177–215

Franz Zagiba, *Zur Errichtung einer Chopin-Gedächtnisstätte in Wien. Eine Gliederung der Forschungsergebnisse zum Thema „Chopin und Wien" in Form einer Ausstellung*, in: Chopin-Jahrbuch 1970, hrsg. von Franz Zagiba, S. 147–182

Maria Zduniak, *Die Korrespondenz von Breitkopf & Härtel über die erste kritische Gesamtausgabe der sämtlichen Werke von Fryderyk Chopin*, in: *Chopin and his work in the context of culture. Studies edited by Irena Poniatowska*, Vol. 2, Kraków 2003, S. 249–268

Tadeusz A. Zieliński, *Chopin. Sein Leben, sein Werk, seine Zeit*, aus dem Polnischen von Martina Homma und Monika Brockmann übersetzt, Mainz 2008

Elżbieta Zwolińska, *Aus dem Repertoire des jungen Chopin: Klavierkonzert cis-moll Op. 55 von Ferdinand Ries*, in: *Chopin and his work in the context of culture. Studies edited by Irena Poniatowska*, Vol. 1, Kraków 2003, S. 489–495

Anthologie (1829–1916)

Rezensionen von Chopins erstem Konzert in Wien am 11. August 1829 (*Variationen* op. 2, freie Phantasie)

Allgemeine Theaterzeitung und Originalblatt für Kunst, Literatur und geselliges Leben (Herausgeber und Redacteur: Adolf Bäuerle), Nr. 100 vom 20. August 1829 (unter „Neuigkeiten.")

Vor Kurzem ließ sich im k. k. Hofoperntheater nächst dem Kärnthnerthore ein junger Mann auf dem Pianoforte hören, dessen Name: Hr. C h o p i n , bisher in der musikalischen Welt gar nie ausgesprochen worden war. Desto mehr wurde man überrascht, da man nicht blos ein schönes, sondern wirklich ein sehr ausgezeichnetes Talent in ihm entdeckte, dem man wegen der Eigenthümlichkeit seines Spieles, als seiner Composition, fast schon ein wenig Genialität beylegen dürfte, wenigstens in dem Sinne abweichender Formen und hervorspringender Individualität.

Sein Spiel hat, wie seine Composition, von der man in dieser Produktion freylich nur Variationen hörte, einen gewissen Character von Bescheidenheit, vermög welcher dieser junge Mann es gar nicht darauf anzulegen scheint, brilliren zu wollen, obwohl sein Spiel Schwierigkeiten besiegte, deren Ueberwindung selbst hier, in der Heimath der Klavier-Virtuosität, auffallen mußte, sondern der mit fast ironischer Naivetät es sich einfallen läßt, ein größeres Publikum mit Musik als Musik unterhalten zu wollen. Und siehe da! es gelang ihm; das unbefangene Publikum lohnte mit reichem Beyfalle.

Sein Anschlag, obwohl nett und sicher, hat wenig von dem Glanze, durch den sich unsere Virtuosen sogleich mit den ersten Takten als solche ankündigen, er markirt nur schwach, wie ein Conversierender in einer Gesellschaft gescheidter Leute, nicht mit jenem rhetorischen à plomb, der bey den Virtuosen für unerläßlich gehalten wird. Er spielt ganz ruhig weg, ohne dem kühnen Aufschwung, der den Künstler sonst sogleich von dem Dilettanten unterscheidet, und dennoch erkannte unser zartfühlendes und feinsinniges Publikum in dem fremden, noch unberühmten Jünglinge sogleich den wahren Künstler, und dieser Abend gab dem unbefangenen Beobachter das angenehme Schauspiel eines Publikums, das als moralische Person betrachtet, sich als Virtuose im Auffassen und Würdigen einer keineswegs pomphaften und dennoch höchst edlen und erfreulichen Kunstleistung, sich als ein wahrer Kenner zeigte.

Der junge Mann hat in seinem Spiele Fehler bemerken lassen, und sogar bedeutende Fehler, worunter vielleicht vorzüglich die Nichtbeachtung der Ankündigung beginnender musikalischer Construktionen durch den Accent heraus zu heben wäre, und dennoch wurde er als ein Künstler erkannt, von dem man sich das Vorzüglichste versprechen kann, wenn er erst mehr und vielerley gehört haben wird. Er kommt von Warschau, und dieß ist sein erster Ausflug aus seiner Vaterstadt. Er kam nicht, um sich hören zu lassen, sondern wurde zur aufmunternden Darlegung seiner Tüchtigkeit zu seiner eigenen Ueberraschung dazu veranlaßt. So wie er im Spiele als ein frey dastehender, schöner, junger Baum voll duftiger Blüthen und reifender Früchte sich zeigte, so entwickelte er eben so viele würdige Eigenthümlichkeit in seiner Composition, in der neue Figuren, neue Passagen, neue Formen, in der Introduktion, in der ersten, zweyten und vierten Variation, und in der Gestaltung des M o z a r t ' schen Themas zur schließenden Polacca sich entwickelten. In seiner Unbefangenheit ließ der junge Virtuos es sich eingehen, zum Schlusse des Concertes mit einer freyen Phantasie vor unserem Publikum aufzutreten, vor dem, außer B e e t h o v e n und H u m m e l, noch wenig Improvisatoren Gnade gefunden haben. Wenn der junge Mann durch mehrfachen Wechsel der Themata es vorzüglich auf Amusement angelegt hatte, so war der ruhige Fluß der Gedanken, die sichere Verbindung derselben, und die reine Durchführung dennoch genügender Beweis von seiner Fähigkeit für diese seltene Gabe. Hr. C h o p i n machte heute einem kleinen Publikum so viel Vergnügen, daß man wirklich wünschen muß, er möchte vielleicht bey einem nochmahligen Auftreten vor einem größerem sich hören lassen. – In diesem Concerte zeichnete sich auch Dem. V e l t h e i m königl. sächsische Kammersängerinn, durch angenehme, weiche und gut gebildete Stimme und Bravour als tüchtige Künstlerinn im Vortrage einer Arie von V a c c a j und einer andern von R o s s i n i aus.

Wiener Zeitschrift für Kunst, Literatur, Theater und Mode vom 22. August 1829

[...] Ein Hr. Chopin trat als Clavierspieler auf und trug zuerst ein Rondeau[1], dann Variationen von seiner Composition vor. Er executirt die größten Schwierigkeiten mit Accuratesse und Präcision und führt alle Passagen mit Reinheit aus. Der Beyfall, den man diesem geschickten Künstler zollte, war sehr groß; besonders aber sprach das Concertstück mit Orchesterbegleitung an. Die zweite Nummer war ein Accumulat von Schwierigkeiten, in welchem er seine ganze Gewandtheit zeigte. Er erhielt viel Beyfall und ward hervorgerufen. [...]

Allgemeine Musikalische Zeitung [in Leipzig] vom 18. November 1829 (31/1829, Nr. 46, Sp. 757/58) unter „Nachrichten. Wien"

Am 11ten [August], ebendaselbst [Kärntnertortheater]: Concert der Dem. Veltheim: Arie von Rossini, und Rondo variato von Vaccaj. Mit dem Notenblatte in der Hand scheint dieser ehrenwerthe Gast in seinem individuellen Elemente zu seyn. Herr Chopin, Pianist aus Warschau, dem Vernehmen nach Würfel's Schüler, führte sich als Meister vom ersten Range ein. Die ausgezeichnete Zartheit seines Anschlags, eine unbeschreibliche mechanische Fertigkeit, sein vollendetes, der tiefsten Empfindung abgelauschtes Nuanciren, Tragen und Schwellen der Töne, des Vortrags so seltene Klarheit und seine durch hohe Genialität gestempelten Erzeugnisse – Bravour-Variationen, Rondeau, freye Phantasie, – geben den von der Natur so überaus freygebig bedachten, selbstkräftigen Virtuosen zu erkennen, der, ohne vorher gegangenes Ausposaunen, als eines der leuchtendsten Meteore am musikalischen Horizonte erscheint.[2]

---

1 Der *Krakowiak* (Rondo) op. 14 stand auf dem Programm vom 11. August, wurde aber aus probentechnischen Gründen abgesetzt und durch die freie Phantasie ersetzt. Das Stück wurde dann im zweiten Wiener Konzert am 18. August aufgeführt. Wahrscheinlich bezieht aber der Bericht auch das zweite Konzert mit ein, obwohl dies nicht ausdrücklich angegeben ist.

2 Der Bericht könnte, wie der von 1831, von Franz Sales Kandler sein. Chopin war wohl nur ganz kurz Schüler des böhmischen Komponisten, Dirigenten, Organisten und Pianisten Wilhelm Würfel (1791–1832).

Rezensionen von Chopins zweitem Konzert in Wien am 18. August 1829 (*Variationen* op. 2, *Krakowiak* op. 14, freie Phantasie)

Wiener Zeitschrift für Kunst, Literatur, Theater und Mode vom 29. August 1829

Dienstags, den 18. August spielte Hr. Friedrich Chopin abermals in diesem Theater und trug ein neues Rondeau [*Krakowiak* op. 14] für das Fortepiano mit Orchesterbegleitung von seiner Composition vor. Dies Tonstück ist durchaus in chromatischem Style gehalten und erhebt sich wenig zur Freundlichkeit, hat aber Momente, die sich durch Tiefe und gedankenvolle Verwebung auszeichnen. Im Ganzen scheint ihm etwas mehr Mannigfaltigkeit zu fehlen. Der Meister zeigte seine große Gewandtheit als Klavierspieler darin vollkommen und besiegte die größten Schwierigkeiten mit Glück. Eine längere Anwesenheit in Wien dürfte seinem Anschlage sowohl, als auch seinem Zusammenspielen mit dem Orchester von Nutzen seyn. Er erhielt reichlichen Beyfall und wurde wiederholt gerufen. [...]

Zum Schlusse spielte Hr. F. Chopin heute noch die Variationen über ein Thema Mozart's, welche er schon in seinem ersten Concerte mit so viel Bravour und Glück vorgetragen hatte. Die freundliche und doch gehaltvolle Mannigfaltigkeit dieses Tonstücks so wie das schöne, gelungene Spiel erwarben dem Klavierspieler auch heute wieder lauten, ausgezeichneten Beyfall. Kenner und Liebhaber gaben ihm ihre Anerkennung seines kunstfertigen Spiels froh und laut zu erkennen. Dieser junge Mann, der dem Vernehmen nach seine frühere Bildung dem Hrn. Würfel zu verdanken hat, zeigt ein ernstes Streben in seiner Composition, das Orchester durch interessante Verbindung mit dem Fortepiano zu verweben. [...]

Der Sammler – Ein Unterhaltungsblatt vom 29. August 1829 (unter „Notizen")

[...] An Hrn. Friederich Chopin lernten wir einen Clavierspieler der ausgezeichneten Art kennen. – Die Zartheit seines Anschlags, seine kaum gesehene Fertigkeit, sein meisterliches, der tiefsten Empfindung abgelauschtes Nüancieren und Tragen der Tempi, die Klarheit seines Vortrages und die Genialität seiner Composition geben den von der Natur reich bedachten, selbstkräftigen Virtuosen zu erkennen, um so mehr, da er außer dem frühen Unterricht des damals noch in Rußland wirkenden, hochverdienten Professors und Kapellmeisters Würfel, ohne fremdes Zuthun, durch seinen eigenen Genius, als einer der leuchtendsten Meteore hervorging. Wir werden nächstens Gelegenheit nehmen, uns hierüber deutlicher und weitläufiger vernehmen zu lassen [nicht erschienen]. [...]

Allgemeine Theaterzeitung und Originalblatt für Kunst, Literatur und geselliges Leben (Herausgeber und Redacteur: Adolf Bäuerle) Nr. 105 vom 1. September 1829 (unter „Neuigkeiten.")

Der Klavierspieler, Hr. C h o p i n aus Warschau, hat auch in einem zweiten Concerte so gespielt, daß das Urtheil, welches man über sein Spiel sowohl, als auch über seine Composition in diesen Blättern über sein erstes Concert fällte, in diesem abermahl gerechtfertigt wurde. Er ist ein junger Mann, der auf eigenthümlichen Weg geht, auf diesem Wege zu gefallen weiß, obwohl seine Art und Weise in Spiel wie in Schreibart von der gewöhnlichen Concertisten-Form bedeutend abweicht, und zwar zumahl hierin, daß das Streben: Musik zu machen, dem Streben: zu gefallen bey ihm auf eine merkliche Weise vorherrscht. Hr. C h o p i n gefiel auch heute allgemein [...]

Allgemeiner Musikalischer Anzeiger [Wien] vom 26. September 1829 (unter „Notizen")

[...] Eine neue, aber sehr interessante Erscheinung war dem musikalischen Wien Hr. Friedrich Chopin. Composition, Fertigkeit, Vortrag, alles kann vortrefflich genannt werden, und der allgemeinste Beyfall war der Lohn des Künstlers.[3]

Ludwig Rellstab: Rezension der *Variationen* op. 2, in: Iris im Gebiete der Tonkunst 1/1830, Nr. 37/38 vom 5. November, S. 5

Odeon, 27. Lieferung. „La ci darem la mano" varié pour le Pfte. av. Orch. par Frederic Chopin. Op. 2. Ebendas. [Wien, Tobias Haslinger] Pr. 4 Fl.

Das Werk gehört ganz in die Classe des obigen. Es scheint überdies die Bestimmung des Odeon zu seyn, nur Werke dieser Gattung aufzunehmen. Eine Introduction versucht sich den Schein zu geben, als ob das Thema ein wenig gearbeitet werden solle; es scheint auch fast so. Hierauf beginnt das Thema selbst mit den nachfolgenden Variationen. Wir wollten dem Componisten aus der schon oben gesche-

---

3 Diese Notiz bezieht sich mit Sicherheit auf beide Konzerte.

henen Erwägung alle seine Passagen, Rouladen, Doppeltriller, Doppelläufe u. dgl. sehr gern zu gute halten, obwohl er das Thema beinahe mit den Läufern überläuft, und in der Trillerkette es erdrosselnd aufhängt, allein eine Frage möchten wir ihm doch thun: Warum giebt er dem Thema einen Auftakt, den Mozart nicht dazu geschrieben hat? Aus diesem kleinen Zuge ergiebt sich das äußerst geringe Gefühl des Componisten für eine melodische Construction, für Schönheit im Rhythmus. Die überflüssige Auftaktsnote hängt so ungeschickt wie ein fünftes Rad, oder ein fünfter Fuß, oder ein Höcker auf der Brust, an dem schönen regelmäßig gebauten Thema. – – Herr Chopin ist muthmaßlich ein Pohle; wenigstens darf man es vermuthen, denn er hat sein Werk einem Pohlen [Tytus Woyciechowski] dedicirt, wenn man auch den Vandalismus, den er gegen die Mozartsche Melodie begangen hat, nicht zu den Kennzeichen rechnen wollte, daß das Werk aus einem rohen slavischen Völkerstamme hervorgewachsen ist. Deswegen aber vermuthlich hängt er am Schluß eine Polacca an, wobei mir heimlich statt der Worte, „Gieb mir die Hand, mein Leben" immer etwas anderes, als etwa „Ach schenke mir das Leben", oder sonst eine Phrase der Angst und Noth vor dem Ohr und auf der Zunge schwebte. – Indessen ist Hr. Chopin doch gewiß den Klavierspielerinnen und Spielern ein willkommener Mann, und sie werden ihm den Ehrenplatz im Odeon, den ihm seine Arbeit verschafft hat, gewiß von Herzen gönnen.

Rezensionen von Chopins drittem (4. April 1831, Konzert der Sängerin Garzia-Vestris) und viertem (11. Juni 1831, Wohltätigkeitskonzert für den Tänzer D. Mattis, *Konzert e-Moll* op. 11) Auftreten in Wien

Von den in Chopins Brief an seine Familie vom 16. [?] Juli 1831 und von Karasowski (a.a.O., S. 195) erwähnten lobenden Kritiken aus Wien sind nur zwei erhalten sowie eine Anzeige des Konzerts am 4. April 1831 in der Wiener „Allgemeinen Theaterzeitung" vom 2. April 1831 (Zagiba 1951 a.a.O., S. 59/60).

Friedrich August Kanne: Rezension von Chopins viertem Konzert in Wien am 11. Juni 1831, in: Allgemeine Theaterzeitung und Originalblatt für Kunst, Literatur, Mode und geselliges Leben (Herausgeber und Redacteur: Adolf Bäuerle) Nr. 73 vom 18. Juni 1831

In einer am 11. Juny stattgehabten Akademie, welche mit der Aufführung der Ouvertüre zu W e b e r s „Euryanthe" begann, hörten wir den ersten Satz eines neuen Konzertes für das Pianoforte, komponirt und vorgetragen von Hrn. Friedrich C h o p i n. Dieser junge Tonkünstler aus Warschau, welcher seit längerer Zeit zur Befriedigung seiner Liebe zur Tonkunst sich in Wien aufhält, gehört zu der Gattung von Künstlern, welche nicht etwa durch amusante musikalische Bagatellen im Modegeschmack sich eine ephemere Celebrität erkaufen, sondern ihren eigenen Weg wandeln, und ihre ganze künstlerische Tendenz auch in ihrem ersten Werke gleich unverholen aussprechen wollen. Sein ernster Styl wurde durch die E moll Tonart schon von selbst bedingt und von dem Kompositeur mit viel Erfindungsgeist und Kenntniß der harmonischen Kunst ausgeführt. In seinen Motiven findet man Originalität und Tiefe, seine Perioden sind meistens durch einen schönen Baß interessant, und seine Passagen durch neue Figuren im Klaviersatz ausgestattet. Bey diesen Vorzügen, von denen der letztere besonders selten ist, finden wir aber zu erwähnen, daß manche Passagen etwas zu sehr in die Länge ausgedehnt, und zuwenig durch Kraftmomente des Orchesters unterstützt sind. Sein Spiel zeigt die größte Fertigkeit bey einem sehr diskreten Anschlage, seine Figuren sind rein ausgearbeitet, nur verschiebt der junge Virtuos seinen Takt etwas zu willkührlich, und scheint keine Sorgfalt auf die Bereitung einer brillanten, die Zuhörer spannenden Cadenz wenden zu wollen. Dieß sind Nebensachen, welche bey so großen vorhandenen Vorzügen durch Uebung und Erfahrung schon von selbst verbessert werden. Der Spieler erhielt nach dem Ende des ersten Satzes vom Konzerte, das er in zwey Abtheilungen spielte, Beyfall und wurde gerufen. Die nähmliche Ehre wiederfuhr ihm, als er später das Adagio und Rondo vortrug, in welchem gesangreiche Stellen mit brillanten Figuren auf interessante Art abwechseln, und dem Spieler alle Gelegenheit darbiethen, seine Gewandtheit in Passagen sowohl, als in ausdrucksvollen Stellen zu zeigen. Er spielte ein wohlklingendes Fortepiano vom Hof-Instrumentenmacher Konrad G r a f. Wir hegen die Hoffnung den jungen Virtuosen bald einen bedeutenden Rang unter den besten Pianisten einnehmen zu sehen. Ein recht hübsches Vokal-Quartett wurde zwischen dem Clavier-Konzerte von den Herren S t a u d i g l, E m m i n g e r, R u p p r e c h t und R i- c h a t s c h e c k [recte: Tichatschek] (Mitglieder des Opernpersonals vom genannten Theater) mit Reinheit und Ausdruck vorgetragen und laut applaudirt.

F. A. Kanne.

**Franz Sales Kandler: Notiz über Chopins viertes Konzert in Wien am 11. Juni 1831,
in: Allgemeine Musikalische Zeitung [Leipzig] 33/1831, Nr. 38
vom 21. September, Sp. 624 unter „Nachrichten. Wien. Musikalische Chronik
des 2ten Quartals. (Beschluss.)"**

Hr. Chopin, gleichfalls aus der Sarmatischen Hauptstadt [Warschau, wie der
zuvor erwähnte Geiger Stanisław Serwaczyński]; der sich bereits während seiner vor-
jährigen Anwesenheit als Pianist vom ersten Range geltend machte. Die Ausführung
seines neuesten, ernst stylisirten Concertes in E minore [op. 11] gab keine Veranlassung, unser früheres Urtheil zu widerrufen. Wer es so redlich meint mit der wahren
Kunst, dem gebührt auch wahre Hochachtung. –

**Anonymus: Rezension von Chopins Konzert in München am 28. August 1831,
in: Flora. Ein Unterhaltungsblatt vom 30. August 1831 (*Klavierkonzert e-Moll*
op. 11, *Grande Fantaisie sur des Airs polonais* op. 13 für Klavier und Orchester)
[Burger a.a.O., S. 74]**

Conzert des Herrn Chopin aus Warschau.

Am 28. d. gab Hr. T. C h o p i n [sic!] aus Warschau ein Mittagsconzert im Saale
des philharmonischen Vereins, das von einer sehr gewählten Versammlung besucht
wurde. Hr. C h o p i n trug ein Conzert aus E-moll von seiner eigenen Composition auf dem Fortepiano vor und zeigte eine ausgezeichnete Virtuosität in der Behandlung seines Instrumentes; bei einer ausgebildeten Fertigkeit wurde besonders
eine liebliche Zartheit des Spiels und ein schöner und charakteristischer Vortrag der
Motive bemerkbar. Die Composition war im Ganzen brillant und gut gesetzt, ohne
gerade durch besondere Neuheit oder einen tieferen Charakter zu überraschen, mit
Ausnahme des Rondo's, dessen Hauptgedanke sowohl, als die figurirten Mittelsätze
durch eine eigenthümliche Verbindung eines melancholischen Zuges mit einem Ca-
priccio einen eigenen Reiz entwickelte, und deshalb auch besonders ansprach. Der
Conzertgeber trug zuletzt eine Phantasie über polnische Nationallieder vor. Es liegt
in den slavischen Volksliedern ein Etwas, das beinahe nie seine Wirkung verfehlt,
dessen Grund sich aber schwer nachweisen und erklären läßt, denn es ist nicht allein
der Rhythmus und der schnelle Uebergang von Moll in Dur, der diesen Reiz hervor-
bringt; Niemand hat es wohl besser verstanden, den nationellen Charakter solcher
Lieder mit einem brillanten Conzertspiel in Verbindung zu bringen als Bernhard

Romberg, der durch seine Compositionen dieser Art, durch sein Meisterspiel gehoben, einen eigenen Zauber zu verbreiten wußte. Ganz in dieser Art war die Phantasie
des Herrn C h o p i n, der sich allgemeinen Beifall erwarb. Hr. B a y e r[4] sang eine
Cavatine von Schubert mit Begleitung vom Pianoforte und Clarinette. Hr. B a y e r
trug diese seelenvolle, tief empfundenen Composition des verewigten Meisters mit
innigem, überströmenden Gefühle vor, und wurde von Hrn. B ä r m a n n[5] jun. mehr
als unterstützt, denn es war in der That ein Wettgesang; dieser junge Virtuos wird
auf seinem Instrumente gewiß noch die höchste Stufe erreichen, und wir können
ihm kein größeres Lob ertheilen, als wenn wir versichern, daß er jetzt schon seines
berühmten Namens würdig ist. Ein vom Hrn. Kapellmeister S t u n z[6] sehr schön
componirter vierstimmiger Gesang wurde vortrefflich ausgeführt von Mad. P e l l e-
g r i n i und den HH. B a y e r, L e n z[7] und H a r m.

Robert Schumann / Gottfried Wilhelm Fink: Rezensionen der *Variationen* op. 2 in: Allgemeine Musikalische Zeitung 33/1831, Nr. 49 vom 7. Dezember, Sp. 805–811

Vorbemerkung.

Wir geben hier einmal über Ein Werk zwey Beurtheilungen; die erste von einem
jungen Manne, einem Zöglinge der neusten Zeit, der sich genannt hat; die andere von
einem angesehenen und würdigen Repräsentanten der ältern Schule, der sich nicht
genannt hat: allein, wir versichern und haben es kaum nöthig, von einem durchaus
tüchtigen, vollgeübt und umsichtig kenntnissreichen.

Wir meinen, durch diese Zusammenstellung nicht nur unsere Aufmerksamkeit
auf den Verf. des zu besprechenden Werkes auf hier ungewöhnliche Weise an den
Tag zu legen, sondern auch zugleich, und ganz besonders, unseren geehrten Lesern
zu mancherley eigenen und höchst nützlichen Vergleichungen Veranlassung zu bieten, die mit ihrem grossen Nutzen eine Unterhaltung gewähren, die zu viel Anziehendes hat, als dass sie irgend einem denkenden Musikfreunde anders als höchst

---

4 Aloys Bayer (1802–1883), bekannter Tenor, 1823–1843 am Hoftheater in München.
5 Carl Baermann (1810–1885), Klarinettist und Komponist, Sohn des mit Weber, Meyerbeer und
Mendelssohn befreundeten Klarinettisten und Komponisten Heinrich Joseph Baermann (1784–1847),
beide als 1. Klarinettisten der Münchener Hofkapelle tätig.
6 Joseph Hartmann Stuntz (1793–1859), Schweizer Komponist und Dirigent, seit 1823 als Kapellmeister in München.
7 Leopold Lenz (1803–1862), Sänger (Bariton) und Komponist, seit 1826 in München.

willkommen seyn könnte. Mit dem Werke in der Hand wird es wohl am glücklichsten gelingen.

Die Redaction.

I. *Von K.* [sic!] *Schumann.*

Ein Opus II.

– – – Eusebius trat neulich leise zur Thüre herein. Du kennst das ironische Lächeln auf dem blassen Gesichte, mit dem er zu spannen sucht. Ich sass mit Florestan am Klavier. Florestan ist, wie Du weisst, einer von den seltenen Musikmenschen, die alles Zukünftige, Neue, Ausserordentliche schon wie lange vorher geahnt haben; das Seltsame ist ihnen im andern Augenblicke nicht seltsam mehr; das Ungewöhnliche wird im Moment ihr Eigenthum. Eusebius hingegen, so schwärmerisch als gelassen, zieht Blüthe nach Blüthe aus; er fasst schwerer, aber sicherer an, geniesst seltener, aber langsamer und länger; dann ist auch sein Studium strenger und sein Vortrag im Klavierspiele besonnener, aber auch zarter und mechanisch vollendeter als der Florestans. – Mit den Worten: „Hut ab, ihr Herren, ein Genie", legte Eusebius ein Musikstück auf, das wir leicht als einen Satz aus dem Haslinger'schen Odeon erkannten. Den Titel durften wir weiter nicht sehen. Ich blätterte gedankenlos im Buche; diess verhüllte Geniessen der Musik ohne Töne hat etwas Zauberisches. Ueberdiess scheint mir, hat jeder Componist seine eigenthümlichen Notengestaltungen für das Auge: Beethoven sieht anders auf dem Papier als Mozart, etwa wie Jean Paul'sche Prosa anders als Göthe'sche. Hier aber war mir's, als blickten mich lauter fremde Augen, Blumenaugen, Basiliskenaugen, Pfauenaugen, Mädchenaugen wundersam an: an manchen Stellen ward es lichter – ich glaubte Mozart's „Là ci darem la mano" durch hundert Accorde geschlungen zu sehen, Leporello schien mich ordentlich wie anzublinzeln und Don Juan flog im weissen Mantel vor mir vorüber. „Nun spiel's", meinte Florestan lachend zu Eusebius, „wir wollen Dir die Ohren und uns die Augen zuhalten." Eusebius gewährte; in eine Fensternische gedrückt hörten wir zu. Eusebius spielte wie begeistert und führte unzählige Gestalten des lebendigsten Lebens vorüber; es ist, als wenn der frische Geist des Augenblicks die Finger über ihre Mechanik hinaushebt. Freylich bestand Florestan's ganzer Beyfall, ein seliges Lächeln abgerechnet, in nichts als in den Worten: dass die Variationen etwa von Beethoven oder Franz Schubert seyn konnten, wären sie nämlich Klavier-Virtuosen gewesen – wie er aber nach dem Titelblatte fuhr, weiter nichts las, als:

Là ci darem la mano, varié pour le Pianoforte par Frédéric Chopin, Opus 2, und wie wir beyde verwundert ausriefen: ein Opus zwey und wie Eusebius hinzufügte: Wien, bey Haslinger und wie die Gesichter ziemlich glühten vom ungemeinen Erstaunen und ausser etlichen Ausrufen wenig zu unterscheiden war, als: „Ja, das ist wieder einmal etwas Vernünftiges – Chopin – ich habe den Namen nie gehört – wer mag er seyn – jedenfalls – ein Genie – lacht dort nicht Zerline oder gar Leporello" – – so entstand freylich eine Scene, die ich nicht beschreiben mag. Erhitzt vom Wein, Chopin und Hin- und Herreden, gingen wir fort zum Meister Raro, der viel lachte und wenig Neugier zeigte nach dem Opus zwey: „denn ich kenn' Euch schon und euren neumodischen Enthusiasmus von Herz und Hünten – nun bringt mir nun den Chopin einmal her." Wir versprachen's zum andern Tag. Eusebius nahm bald ruhig Gute Nacht: ich blieb eine Weile bey'm Meister Raro; Florestan, der seit einiger Zeit keine Wohnung hat, flog durch die mondhelle Gasse meinem Hause zu. Um Mitternacht fand ich ihn in meiner Stube auf dem Sopha liegend und die Augen geschlossen. Chopin's Variationen, begann er wie im Schlafe, gehen mir noch im Kopfe um: gewiss, fuhr er fort, ist das Ganze dramatisch und hinreichend Chopinisch, obgleich ich Paganini'-schen Vortrag und Field'schen Anschlag in Eusebius Spiel vermisst habe; die Einleitung, so abgeschlossen sie in sich ist – (kannst Du Dich auf Leporello's Terzensprünge besinnen? –) scheint mir am wenigsten in das Ganze einzuklappen; aber das Thema – (warum hat er's aber aus B geschrieben?) – die Variationen, der Schlusssatz und das Adagio, das ist freylich etwas und zu viel – da guckt der Genius aus jedem Tacte. Natürlich, lieber Julius, sind Don Juan, Zerline, Leporello und Masetto die redenden Charactere (die Tutti nicht mitgerechnet) – Zerlinen's Antwort im Thema ist verliebt genug bezeichnet, die erste Variation wäre vielleicht etwas vornehm und kokett zu nennen – der spanische Grande schäkert darin sehr liebenswürdig mit der Bauernjungfer. Das gibt sich jedoch von selbst in der zweyten, die schon viel vertrauter, komischer, zänkischer ist, ordentlich als wenn zwey Liebende sich haschen und mehr als gewöhnlich lachen. Wie ändert sich aber schon Alles in der dritten! Lauter Mondschein und Feenzauber ist darin, sag' ich Dir; Masetto steht zwar von fern und flucht ziemlich vernehmlich, obgleich Don Juan sich wenig stören lässt. – Nun aber die vierte, was hältst Du davon, Julius? – (Eusebius spielte sie ganz rein) – springt sie nicht keck und frech und geht an den Mann, obgleich das Adagio (es scheint mir natürlich, dass Chopin den ersten Theil wiederholen lässt) aus B moll spielt, was nicht besser passen kann, da es den Don Juan wie moralisch an sein Beginnen mahnt – schlimm ist's freylich und schön, dass Leporello hinter dem Gebückten lauscht, lacht und spottet und dass Oboen und Clarinetten zauberisch locken und herausquellen und dass das aufgeblühte B dur den ersten Kuss der Liebe recht bezeichnet. Das ist nun aber Alles nichts gegen den letzten Satz – hast Du noch Wein, Julius? – das ist das ganze Finale im Mozart – lauter springende Champagnerstöpsel (das Ganze geht aus Champagner), klirrende Flaschen – Leporello's Stimme dazwischen, dann die fassenden, haschenden Geister, der entrinnende Don Juan – und dann der kecke Schluss, der schön beruhigt und wirklich abschliesst. Er habe, so beschloss Florestan, in der Schweiz ein ähnliches Gefühl gehabt. Wenn nämlich an schönen Tagen die Abendsonne bis an die Gletscherspitzen roth und rosa hinaufklimme, dann zerflattere und zerfliege, so läge über alle Berge und Thäler ein leiser Duft, aber der Gletscher stände ruhig, kalt und fest, wie ein Titane da, w i e a u s T r ä u m e n e r w a c h t . – Nun erwache aber auch Du zu neuen Träumen, Julius, und schlafe! – Herzensflorestan, erwiederte ich, alle diese Privatgefühle sind vielleicht zu loben, da sie bunt sind; aber so subjectiv sie dennoch bleiben und so wenig Absicht Chopin seinem Genius abzulauschen braucht, so beug' ich doch mein Haupt seinem Genius, seinem festen Streben, seinem Fleisse und seiner Fantasie." Hierauf entschliefen wir.

„Là ci darem la mano" varié pour le Pianof. avec acc. d'Orchestre etc.
par Frédéric Chopin. Œuvre 2. Vienne, chez T. Haslinger. Prix 2 Thlr. 16 Gr.

'S ist ein wunderlich Ding, wenn die verehrte Redaction Tonwerke von Gehalt und Form des oben angeführten zur beurtheilenden Anzeige u n s e r e i n e m zusendet! – Wer ist der „unser einem?" höre ich die Leser der musikal. Zeitung fragen. – Antwort: diessmal ein Mann aus der wirklich guten alten Zeit; einer, der auch so ziemlich alles Gute und Tüchtige, das für das Pianoforte seit vierzig Jahren erschienen ist, zu kennen und selbst gespielt zu haben meint; der ferner seit seinen Jünglingsjahren redlich gestrebt hat, sich frey zu machen von Einseitigkeit und jetzt glaubt in der That so frey von dieser zu seyn, als uns schwachen Menschen das überhaupt irgend gelingen mag. – Mindestens ist es seit ein paar Decennien schon, dass Rec. sich bewusst ist, nach dem N a m e n eines Componisten wenig gefragt zu haben (oder doch gewiss nicht mehr, als verständige Kunstfreunde überhaupt nach N a m e n zu fragen pflegen) – wenn es galt, ein Urtheil zu fällen über dessen Werk. – Es thut daher bey Rec. dem Herrn Chopin nicht den mindesten Eintrag, dass dessen Name demselben unbekannt war, bis das oben angeführte Werk ihm vor die Augen kam. Aber nach Gehalt und Form fragt Rec. allerdings und er glaubt mit besonderm Rechte, selbst wenn es sich nur um einen Satz Variationen handelt, über ein Thema,

wie das wohl funfzigmal schon sonst variirte: Là ci darem la mano. – Denn eben in
s o l c h e n Fällen gilt es vorzugsweise auszumitteln, ob dem gewählten Thema w e -
s e n t l i c h neue Seiten abgewonnen wurden; nicht ob man einige neue Figuren- und
Passagenwerke ersann, an welchem, Gott sey's geklagt, die neuste Zeit so grossen
Ueberfluss hat, als an Schriften über die Cholera, deren C o n t a g i o s i t ä t mit
besserm Grunde in Zweifel zu ziehen ist, als die jenes leidigen, in allen musikalischen
Landen immer mehr und mehr aufflackernden leeren Passagenkrames.

Rec. hat die Gewohnheit, bevor er ein Urtheil zu fällen wagt, das zu beurthei-
lende Werk vor allen Dingen durchzulesen, und dann, so gut als das bey B r a v o u r -
s a c h e n möglich ist, im Z u s a m m e n h a n g e durchzuspielen. Ueber den auf
solche Weise empfangenen Eindruck bringt er schnell das Nöthigste zu Papier, lässt
dann das Ganze mehre Tage – manchmal wohl, wie die Redaction ihm bezeugen
wird – M o n a t e ruhen und nimmt dann das Werk wieder vor, um es zu s t u d i r e n,
d. h. um genau zu ergründen: was hat der Autor gewollt und wie und durch welche
Mittel ist ihm sein Kunstbestreben gelungen oder nicht. – Nur sehr selten ereignete
es sich, dass jenes s k i z z i r t e Urtheil durch das spätere S t u d i u m des Werkes
um seine Autorität kam. Meistens wurde es, im Wesentlichen wenigstens, durch dasselbe bestätigt. Es bedurfte nur noch einer sorgsamern Ausführung des Einzelnen.
Jener Entwurf aber blieb, vollständig gerechtfertigt vor dem Gewissen des Rec., die
Basis der Beurtheilung. Fiat applicatio in dem concreten Falle auf das oben benannte
Werk. Des Rec. s k i z z i r t e s Urtheil nach dem e r s t e n Eindrucke lautete:

„Eines der gewaltigsten Bravourstücke! Es erfordert ungeheuer grosse Hände.
Alles ist, für beyde Hände, übervoll gepackt. Nur g a n z tüchtige Spieler – so etwa
Paganini's auf dem Pianof. – werden es bezwingen und ausführen, wie sich's gehört.
Allenfalls k a n n man's, auch mit Händen, die nicht ganz so gross sind als ein paar
mässige Bratschen, einstudiren bis auf Var. 4 und insbesondere Var. 5, pag. 17, wo
unter anderm

(man merke wohl, dass der dissonirende Accord
nicht harpeggirt, sondern g e b u n d e n in
das Ges dur ü b e r s c h l e i c h e n soll) –
vorkommt. Aber man wird doch nur unverhältniss-
mässig gering belohnt. – N i c h t s als
Bravour- und Figurenwerk! – Uebrigens,
Härten abgerechnet, wie z. B. pag. 9.

dergl. u.

und pag. 12.

u. s. w.

die nun einmal in unserer Zeit – das grammatische Gewissen der Autoren nicht eben beschweren und von den Ohren der jetzigen Generation, wie es scheint, mit Leichtigkeit – sit venia verbo – verdaut werden, leidlich correct."

Rec. wüsste diesen Contouren, nach wiederholter mehrmaliger und gewissenhafter Durchsicht, keinen wesentlichen Strich hinzuzufügen oder an ihnen etwas auszulöschen. Allenfalls mag, für die Liebhaber solcher Compositionen, noch bemerkt seyn: das Orchester hat wenig mehr zu thun als ritornellmässig einzugreifen. Nach einer Einleitung, die in der Principalstimme fünf Folioseiten einnimmt (Largo, B dur, späterhin ein klein wenig bewegter) folgen: das Thema; diesem vier Variationen in raschem Zeitmaasse, eine Variation, Adagio B moll und endlich zum Schlusse ein à la polacca auf 8 Seiten in B dur.

In Bezug auf die ä u s s e r e Ausstattung dieses, die 27ste Lieferung des Odeon ausmachenden Paradewerks, braucht wohl etwas Lobendes nicht noch gesagt zu werden. Der Haslinger'sche Verlag zeichnet sich stets durch deutliche Schrift, guten Druck und schönes Papier aus. Auffallende Druckfehler, deren Verbesserung nicht sogleich in die Augen fallen, sind dem Rec. nicht vorgekommen. Doch kann er nicht für die Orchesterstimmen stehen, da er das Werkchen mit dem Orchester nicht gehört hat.

Nachbemerkung.

Später wurde uns noch eine dritte Beurtheilung dieses Werkes von Hrn. Friedrich Wieck, Lehrer des Pianofortespiels allhier, eingesendet, deren Aufnahme uns nur der Raum nicht erlaubt. Sie ist im Sinne des Hrn. Schumann verfasst, der ein Schüler des Hrn. Wieck ist.[8]

Die Redaction.

Friedrich Wieck: Rezension der *Variationen* op. 2, in: Caecilia 14/1832, S. 219–224

Herr *Chopin*, Pianist aus Warschau, welcher gegenwärtig in Paris als ein Stern erster Grösse glänzt, hat unter obigem bescheidenen Titel [„*Là ci darem la mano" varié pour le pianoforte, avec Accompagnement d'Orchestre*] ein g r o s s e s B r a v o u r - s t ü c k m i t O r c h e s t e r geliefert, das der Beachtung aller Virtuosen, denen die grossartige Field'sche Schule nicht unbekannt ist und die in der praktischen Darstellung etwas Höheres suchen als die Darlegung blos mechanischer Fertigkeit, um so mehr werth sein dürfte, als diese Composition zugleich dem Gebildeten verständlich und fasslich und in harmonischer Hinsicht bedeutend und höchst interessant genannt werden kann.

Ich weiss nicht, ob *Chopin* unmittelbarer Schüler von *Field* ist; aber aus der ganzen Anlage des Stückes, dessen schwärmerischer Charakter auf jeder Seite unsere Empfindung in Anspruch nimmt, aus der Art der Passagen, die oft überraschend und ganz neu, und dabei mit einer gewissen Solidität dargestellt, schon an sich selbst einen Kunstgenuss gewähren, aus seiner Applicatur, die er gewagten und ganz ungewöhnlichen Wendungen sehr zweckmässig beigefügt, – und aus seiner vortrefflichen meisterhaften Bezeichnung oder Andeutung des Vortrages, erhellt deutlich, dass er mit *Field's* seelenvoller musikalischen Sprache ganz vertraut sein [muss] und dessen Spielart sich praktisch angeeignet hat.

Hieraus möge aber das Publikum nicht folgern, als sei hier von einer Nachahmung *Field's* die Rede. Nein! das Werk steht in jeder Hinsicht ganz selbstständig da und verräth eben so sehr die genaueste Bekanntschaft mit der leichten, graziösen, aber rein mechanischen Wiener Spielart, mit welcher viele Virtuosen (in Ermangelung *Field'*scher Schüler, welche Russland meist für sich behalten zu haben scheint) bis in

---

8 Diese Rezension erschien in: Caecilia 14/1832, S. 219–224 (vgl. den folgenden Text) und in: Der Komet 3/1832, Nr. 7, S. 53–55, Nr. 8, S. 61–64.

die neuere Zeit so viele Namen erzeugten, als die Kenntniss der neuesten, pikanten, vielleicht frivolen, aber eleganten und sehr geschmackvollen französischen Schule, die *H. Herz* und andere mit so viel Glück ausgebildet hat und in der unter andern *Pixis* sein geistreiches und originelles Concert, Op. 100, und *Kalkbrenner* und *Moscheles* mehrere allgemein bekannte und beliebte Concert-Stücke geschrieben haben, ohne weiter bei denselben den Einfluss der *Field*'schen und Wiener Spielart verkennen zu wollen.

Herr *Chopin* hat das Duett aus *Don Juan* zum Thema gewählt, nicht blos um Variationen darüber zu schreiben; sondern er hat grade dieses Thema benutzt, um das ganze gewagte, wilde, verwegene und in Liebe schwelgende Leben und Treiben eines *Don Juan* anzudeuten. Er hat dies, nach meiner Meinung, in den genialsten und kühnsten Zügen gethan, und ich möchte in diesem, wie soll ich sagen, Phantasie-Bravourstück, auch nicht einen Takt entbehren, so charakteristisch scheint mir Alles hingestellt, vom ersten Takte der grossen und originellen Introduction an, bis zum letzten, der von Champagner-Rausch überströmenden Polonaise.

Tongemälde zu componiren ist eine gewagte Sache! – sie mit Worten beschreiben und der Composition, so zu sagen, einen Text unterzulegen, ist es in gewisser Hinsicht noch mehr. – Ich will es versuchsweise wagen.

I n t r o d u c t i o n (B-dur). Das Quartett berührt, in contrapunktischer Nachahmung, 8 Takte hindurch, den 1. Takt das Themas, und in Ges beginnt das Pianoforte edel und ernst das Solo. Bald wird es wärmer und feuriger, und bis zu dem „*Più mosso*" möchte ich die Liebeserklärung, welche dem *Zerlinchen* bevorsteht, zwar kühn, aber noch anständig nennen. In den ersten Takten des „*Più mosso*" tritt das Quartett warnend in b-moll auf, als plötzlich Don Juan, in gewagten Octaven, risoluto entgegen tritt. Das Quartett wiederholt obige Wendung in f-moll, und Don Juan widersetzt sich noch kühner und gewagter in schwer mit beiden Händen zu spielendem und nach dem Basse zustürzendem unisono. Das Orchester tritt wieder in der Dominante von b-moll auf, als, nach 2 Takten, das Solo ernst und kräftig beginnt und zu einem zärtlichen pp. übergeht, bis, nach sehr eleganten und höchst lebendigen Figuren in der rechten Hand, (die einen sehr delikaten Anschlag verlangen, alsdann aber auch selbst dem *Zerlinchen* wohlgefallen dürften), die Fermate eintritt, wo die linke Hand, mit ungewöhnlichen Vorschlägen den ersten Takt des Themas leise berührt, während die rechte, in Terzen und Sexten, eine unruhige Triolenbewegung ausführt. – Er nimmt einen kühnen und kräftigen Anlauf, *risoluto*, – zum

T h e m a , schön und höchst zierlich gesetzt und mit wenigen, aber anständigen Manieren geschmückt; (übrigens nicht leicht und mit grosser Aufmerksamkeit zu spielen und schon den grossen und sinnigen Pianoforte-Spieler verrathend.)

V a r. I. sehr schwer und kühn, herrlich gearbeitet, eine wahre *Don Juan's* – Variation und viel schwieriger gut zu spielen, als es dem Zuhörer scheint. *Don Juan* wagt Alles – aber dennoch mit Anstand und höchst interessant. Das Orchester begleitet Alles mit schöner Discretion. – Ein kräftiges Tutti, aus dem Thema genommen, schliesst.

V a r. II. ist doch gar zu schalkhaft! Läuft denn *Don Juan* unisono mit dem *Leporello*, in den geschwindesten, wunderlichsten und ängstlichsten Bewegungen herum, – um – das *Zerlinchen* zu suchen? – Das Orchester deutet, bescheiden und ruhig, das Thema dazu an. – Welcher saubere Anschlag und welch richtiges Aufheben der Finger wird hierzu verlangt, um es in dem Geiste des Komponisten zu spielen! –

V a r. III. Er hat sie gefunden; – wie fein galant, nie zärtlich koset der Weltmann mit ihr! – Aber – seht ihr den ängstlichen, eifersüchtigen *Masetto* in der linken Hand? – Er gebehrdet sich ja so wunderlich, so seltsam, – so ungewöhnlich; – aber *Don Juan* lässt sich einmal nicht stören! – Diese Variation (sie ist ohne Begleitung) schön vorzutragen, dürfte nur wahrer Virtuosität gelingen, und mögen nie ungeweihte Hände dies schöne lebendige Bild besudeln.

V a r. IV. ist wieder eine Bravour-Variation, die einen mehr als gewöhnlichen Bravour-Spieler verlangt; übrigens s e h r d a n k b a r genannt werden muss. *Don Juan* wagt hier Viel – der Spieler auch; er wage es mit Glück! der Erfolg wird erwünscht seyn.

Ein Tutti von 15 Takten, was unsere gereizte Empfindung wieder etwas herabstimmt, führt uns zu

V a r. V. (b-moll), ein kleines Adagio, aber voll von originellen und poetischen Zügen – grösser als manches l a n g e. – *Don Juan* stürzt sich wild ins Leben. – Grauet ihn wohl selbst? – (Im 4. Takte wollen wir ein ⌢ auf der Pause machen.) – Hört ihr da die Pauken solo aus der Ferne u n h e i m l i c h wirbeln? – *Don Juan* umfasst liebend (Alles schweigt) das *Zerlinchen* in Des-dur; – schön und einfach.

Doch schon sehe ich den *Leporello* ängstlich herbeieilen im 7. Takt und – *Don Juan* spottet seiner schon im 8.

Was wagt *Don Juan* im 2. Theile dieses schönen Adagio? – Wird er kühner, zudringlicher – unanständiger vielleicht? – Nein, seines Sieges gewiss, beschwört er die Geliebte nur mit süssen und feinen Zärtlichkeiten – mit einer und derselben Figur in der linken Hand. Das liebende und geliebte Wesen, wie ängstlich bewegt es sich in der rechten, bald in banger Verwirrung, bald in süsser Wonne. Was soll sie thun, gegenüber einem so gewandten, feinen und galanten Ritter? – Sie reicht ihm willig die Hand. – Und nun zu dem

F i n a l e. Welch schönes, lebendiges, galantes Polonaisen-Thema! – Die Fort-
führung wie reich an harmonischen Wendungen, wie neu! – Hat es der Komponist
bei schäumendem Champagner componirt? oder soll es der Virtuos n u r nach dem
Genusse des sprudelnden Weines spielen? oder der Zuhörer nur bei Champagner
geniessen? –

Könnte ich mit diesen schwachen Worten etwas dazu beitragen, dass dieses in
einem phantastischen, aber edlen Style geschriebene Bravourstück, ohne durch seine
Schwierigkeiten abgeschreckt zu werden – nicht unter vielen character- und phan-
tasieleeren Kompositionen begraben und vergessen werde; so haben diese kleinen
ästhetischen Rhapsodien ihren Zweck erreicht. Sollte aber dadurch der geistreiche
Komponist sich bewogen fühlen, den wahrhaft gebildeten Virtuosen seine meisterhaften Conzerte nicht länger mehr vorzuenthalten; so würde ich dadurch ermuthigt
werden, nächstens einige Bruchstücke aus meiner bald zu erscheinenden Methodik
über das jetzige Pianoforte-Spiel und über dessen höhere und höchste Ausbildung
durch die Vervollkommnung unsrer Pianoforte (ich meine einiger Meister von
Frankreich, England und Deutschland) herbeigeführt, den denkenden Virtuosen
und allseitig gebildeten Lehrern zur Prüfung vorzulegen.

Friedrich Wieck, *)
Lehrer des Pianoforte-Spiels in Leipzig.

Gottfried Wilhelm Fink: Rezension der 4 *Mazurken* op. 6, in: Allgemeine Musikalische Zeitung 35/1833, Nr. 12 vom 20. März, Sp. 200

Wer den reizenden Tanz der Polen, den vorzüglich in dieser Gattung unnach-
ahmlichen, näher kennt; wer es weiss, wie zierlich und sicher sich die tanzenden Paare
jedem veränderten Accente anzuschmiegen wissen, wird das Pikante des besondern
Rhythmus in den Masurken zu würdigen verstehen. Die hier gelieferten sind nun ganz
vorzüglich pikant, in des Verfassers Manier, auch im Harmonischen seltsam gehalten.
Es zieht sich mitten durch die oft wunderlich accentuirte Tanzlust ein eigener Geist
der Trauer, wie eine tief und heimlich seufzende Macht, die durch den grossen Cont-

---

*) Auch im hiesigen Hofconcerte [in Darmstadt am 5. Februar 1832] hat die vierzehnjährige Toch-
ter des H. Verfassers der vorstehenden Anzeige die angezeigte *Chopinsche* Composition mit allgemei-
nem Beifalle vorgetragen. Zwar sind, heut zu Tage, Wunderkinder kein rechtes Wunder mehr. „Was
macht man doch nicht Alles fürs Geld!" rief jener Bauer der in der Stadt zum Erstenmal einen Colibri
sah; – „Was macht man doch nicht Alles fürs Geld!" möchte ich eben so beim Anblick mancher fünf-
und sechsjährigen Virtuöschen ausrufen. – [...] [Notiz von Gottfried Weber]

rast nur noch unheimlicher waltet. Wir können nicht sagen, dass alle diese Tänze an Werth sich gleich wären: aber die meisten werden Alle, die sie zu spielen verstehen (sie sind, gut vorgetragen, nichts weniger als leicht) auf ganz eigenthümliche Weise anlocken. Man nehme sie nur vor und bewerbe sich selbst um die nähere Bekanntschaft derselben. Unterhaltung findet man sicher; ja wir vermuthen, dass sie dem Geschmacke der Meisten ganz besonders zusagen werden. Schöne Ausstattung brauchen wir bey hiesigen Verlagsartikeln kaum noch anzuzeigen: sie ist vortrefflich.

Gottfried Wilhelm Fink: Rezension des *Klaviertrios g-Moll* op. 8 und der 3 *Nocturnes* op. 9
in: Allgemeine Musikalische Zeitung 35/1833, Nr. 22 vom 29. Mai, Sp. 357–360

Dieser noch junge Componist, ein Pole, wird unseren geehrten Lesern schon bekannt seyn, namentlich durch seine Variationen über Mozart's Là ci darem la mano, die von Allen als gute, nicht wenig schwierige Veränderungen angesehen, von einem Theile neuer Pianofortespieler überaus hoch gehoben wurden. Dass dieser junge, talentvolle Mann, unter den Einflüssen eines Field und in anderer Hinsicht eines Beethoven lebend, von ihnen und ganz besonders von den Drängnissen einer gewaltig wirkenden Zeit innerlich gefördert, der neuen Romantik sich angeschlossen hat und in dieser, die den individuellen Gestaltungen grössere Freyheit gestattet als irgend eine andere, seine Eigenthümlichkeit mit einer Leidenschaft walten lässt, welche zur Beflügelung des neuromantischen Schwunges nothwendiges Erforderniss scheint, wird Niemand anders erwarten, dem das Wesen unserer Tage nicht völlig fremd geblieben ist. Wenn jedes Mal die neue Form dem jungen Leben die liebste ist, wenn sich die von und in ihrer Zeit genährten jugendlichen Geister am leichtesten und sichersten gerade in dieser das Meiste in der Gegenwart geltenden Form bewegen: so wüssten wir kaum, was man mit Recht dagegen einwenden könnte, selbst wenn man, von einer frühern Zeit gepflegt und für eine andere Form desshalb eingenommen, mit dem frischesten Leben älterer Erfahrung und Liebe vergangene Tage entschwundener Traulichkeit mit den Augen eines Bräutigams begrüssen sollte. – [...]

Es ist in dem Trio fast Alles neu : die Schule, sie ist die neuromantische; die Kunst des Pianofortespiels; das Individuelle, Eigenthümliche, oder auch Geniale, das in einer Leidenschaft, sich so seltsam treibend, mit jener liebenswürdigen Innigkeit zusammenhält, mischt, wechselt, dass ihr bewegliches Bild dem Zeichner kaum Zeit lässt, es sicher und treu zu fassen, wie er gern möchte; selbst die Stellung der Phrasen ist ungewöhnlich. – Das Alles aber wäre nur ein zweydeutiger Ruhm, wenn nicht der Geist, der gleich alte und gleich neue, die neue Form durchhauchte und sinnig machte.

Versuchen wir nun des Tongebildes seltsam eigenthümliche Art in Kürze zu schildern.

Der erste Satz, All. con fuoco, 4/4, G moll, tritt fest und stark auf, grossartig gedacht, die immer reissende Bewegung bändigend, nicht erstickend. Ueberall macht sie sich Luft in kühnen Eigenheiten vielfach theils harmonischer, theils rhythmischer Verschlingungen und seltsamer Stellungen, die sich nicht selten sogar in wunderlich eingemischten Durchgangstönen der gebrochenen Accorde offenbaren. Und bey allem ganz eigenen Wechsel der Glieder und der Gruppirungen derselben, bey allen durchaus neuen und starken Bravourfiguren und kühnen Gruppen derselben herrscht eine einigende Empfindung, ein sangbar charaktervoller Klang, eine Ordnung und Symmetrie durch das wundersam neu Bewegte, dass wir auch das Eigenste als am Orte und als schön empfinden. Es ist, als wenn ein blasser Mann einen hohen Grabhügel, unter dem seine Liebe schläft, geschäftig ebnete und in einen Blumengarten umwandelte; dann mit freundlichen Kindern spielt, in deren Spiel ein hohes Leichengesicht würdig lächelt, nach dem der blasse Mann sich sehnt. – Die Kinder, die mit ihm sind, sehen's nicht, ihr Spiel wird rühriger; das Scherzo, con moto, ma non troppo, 3/4, beginnt. Er scherzt mit ihnen, immer das in Thränen lächelnde Auge nach der Schattengestalt und in die Tiefe gerichtet, in die er zuweilen, das Spiel auf dem Hügel vergessend, sich schmerzlich versenkt. Also freylich ein eigenes Scherzo, aber schön, recht schön. Es ist Warschau's Kind, das hier in Tönen seines Lebens Lust den Lüften singt. – Und im Adagio sostenuto, 3/4, Es dur, weint sanfter bewegt die Klage endlich auf, ein wundersames Wehmuthslied, in dem sich Schmerz und Sehnsucht geschwisterlich umarmen. Im Geiste fest geschmiegt an die schlummernden Kinder der Liebe söhnt der Kummer sich aus mit dem widrigen Geschick.

Getheilt zwischen Leben und Tod, fühlt er das Recht des Lebens und die Pflicht des Wirkens, mischt sich unter die Züge der fremdfühlenden Menschen und will ihnen werden, was er vermag. Im Allegretto, 2/4 (Finale) schreitet er munter und freundlich mit den Wandelnden vorwärts und hat den Riss im Herzen, der nicht heilen will; schlägt alle Kraft empor, munter, rüstig, freundlich und doch zum Tode betrübt.

So etwa ist der Wehmuthsgesang, der in das Gewand der Freude sich verhüllt. – Das wieder zu geben, wird an und für sich nicht leicht seyn. Volles, starkes Gefühl im Kräftigsten, Grossen wie im Zarten spricht es wechselnd an. Dazu oft noch die ganz neuen, fremdartigen, keinesweges der Mode entnommenen Passagen, die nicht zu selten ermüdend sind; wo Sprünge und Rückungen nicht fehlen. Es verlangt demnach durchaus gewiegte Spieler und besonders viel Kraft und Fertigkeit in der linken Hand; es ist schwer, wenn es nicht blos den Noten nach, sondern mit Ausdruck und Leidenschaft, überhaupt geistvoll vorgetragen werden soll. Dann wird es tief eingehen und K e n n e r werden es äusserst brillant finden. Die Streichinstrumente sind nicht schwer, sie verlangen einen singenden, discreten, oft halb lauten Vortrag, damit sie das Rechte bringen. – Wer es einmal gut hörte oder spielte, hört und spielt es sicher öfter; es ist ein anziehendes Werk.

Gute Pianofortespieler mögen auch das folgende nicht übersehen:

Trois Nocturnes pour le Pianof. composées – par Fr. Chopin. Oeuv. 9. Ebendaselbst [wie op. 8 bei Fr. Kistner in Leipzig]. Pr. 14 Gr.

Dem Serenadenmässigen ist auch hier das Ernste, gefühlvoll Grosse zugesellt. Der Gesang hat etwas an Field's schöne Manier Erinnerndes, nur harmonisch wechselnder ist Alles. Man muss Sprünge und Bindungen gut verstehen, oder sich dafür besonders üben wollen, wenn diese schönen Nachtgesänge gebührend ausgeführt werden sollen. Wir rathen jedem Pianofortespieler von nicht zu geringer Bildung, beyde Werke genau kennen zu lernen.

Ludwig Rellstab: Rezension des *Klaviertrios g-Moll* op. 8, in: Iris im Gebiete der Tonkunst 4/1833, Nr. 26 vom 28. Juni, S. 101–102

Es ist nicht leicht über ein complicirtes Werk dieser Gattung zu urtheilen, wenn man nicht eine vollständige Ausführung derselben gehört hat. Denn nicht allein, daß man die Parthien der Violine und des Cello beim Durchspielen der Clavierparthie[9] zu ergänzen hat, daß man sich oft mühsam in den einzelnen Stimmen Raths darüber erholen muß, so erfordert es auch diese Art von Compositionen, daß man sie in einem Fluß und in einer gewissen Vollkommenheit vortragen hört. Das bloße Lesen der Noten kann zwar das trockene äußere Bild eines Werkes verschaffen, allein wenn schöner Vortrag mit zu den Bedingungen gehört, unter denen es erst einen wahren Genuß verschaffen kann, reicht man mit dem einen Ohr allein nicht aus. Denn wäre dies der Fall, so könnte man aller Virtuosität in der Welt entbehren, da es uns ja immer frei stände, die schwersten Concerte von Hummel, Moscheles und Kalkbrenner noch viel präciser, runder, feuriger u. s. w. im Lesen zu hören, als diese Meister sie ausführen. Ja,

---

9 Kammermusikwerke mit Klavier wurden damals noch nicht als Partitur, sondern nur in Stimmen, allenfalls mit Stichnoten in der Klavierstimme, gedruckt.

wir könnten Sonaten für zehn Hände, für zwanzig Fortepiano's spielen, die überhaupt gar nicht ausführbar wären, wohl aber in der Idee gehört werden könnten, wenn diese nämlich dazu ausreichte. Indessen dieses innere Hören erreicht einen gewissen Grad, und man mag es zu einer noch so großen Fertigkeit darin gebracht haben, so gehört zu gewissen Dingen durchaus die Wirklichkeit, die Substantiirung des Gedankens, um einen richtigen Standpunkt dafür zu gewinnen. Dies ist unter andern mit diesem auf einen sehr fertigen Clavierspieler berechneten Trio der Fall. Ein vollständiges Urtheil darüber dürfen wir uns daher nicht erlauben, einzelne Anmerkungen indessen lassen sich daran knüpfen, und werden uns der Wahrheit näher führen. Der Componist besitzt Feuer und geht wirklich auf Erfindung aus; es ist ihm nicht darum zu thun, allein für die Finger zu arbeiten. Er liebt stark markirte Rhythmen und kräftige Harmonik. Seine Melodien suchen eine edle Haltung anzunehmen; nur ist er uns zu sparsam damit, was jedoch auf einer Täuschung beruhen kann, da wir die Parthien der Violine und des ohne Zweifel (da das Werk dem verstorbenen Fürsten Radziwill gewidmet ist) sehr vortheilhaft behandelten Cello nur aus den einzelnen Stimmen und aus der Combination ergänzen können. Indessen haben wir doch in dem ganzen Trio kaum einige Takte gefunden, die ohne rasche Passagenbewegung wären, so daß man also selbst bei sehr melodischer Behandlung der Saiteninstrumente doch nicht recht zu einem eigentlichen Ruhepunkte kommen kann, wie dies in Beethoven's Arbeiten dieser Gattung oft mit so sehr wohlthätiger Wirkung der Fall ist. Im Ganzen strebt uns der Componist zu viel nach Eigenthümlichkeit (wir sollten sagen Besonderheit), statt sich des natürlichen Flusses zu befleißigen, der durch das allgemeine Kunstgesetz geregelten Schönheit vorzugsweise zu huldigen. Dies bemerken wir besonders in seinen Clavierpassagen, die stets eine unnatürliche, der Hand und dem Ohr widerstrebende Verbindung der Intervallen aufsuchen, oft wo gar nichts dadurch gewonnen wird als eine unnütz vergrößerte Schwierigkeit. Im Ganzen ist die Arbeit jedoch sehr ehrenwerth und schlägt trotz einiger nebenirrender Pfade eine bessere Richtung ein, als die gewöhnlichen Produkte neuerer Componisten. Wir machen daher das Publikum besonders auf diesen jungen Autor aufmerksam.

Ludwig Rellstab: Rezension der 4 *Mazurken* op. 7,
in: Iris im Gebiete der Tonkunst 4/1833, Nr. 28 vom 12. Juli, S. 110–112

Wir haben neulich ein Trio von demselben Componisten recht günstig beurtheilen dürfen. Beim Anblick dieser Mazurkas aber möchten wir alles Lob, welches wir damals gespendet haben, zurückziehen und dagegen die Tadelsandeutungen in wahre Anklagen verwandeln. Denn nur zu sehr rechtfertigt es sich hier, was wir damals vermuthend aussprachen, daß der Verfasser eine Neigung habe, gesucht und unnatürlich zu schreiben; wenigstens in den vorliegenden Tänzen sättigt er sich in dieser Leidenschaft bis zum cklcn Uebermaaß. In Aufsuchung ohrzerreißender Dissonanzen, gequälter Uebergänge, schneidender Modulationen, widerwärtiger Verrenkungen der Melodie und des Rhythmus, ist er ganz unermüdlich und wir möchten sagen unerschöpflich. Alles, worauf man nur verfallen kann, wird hervorgesucht, um den Effect bizarrer Originalität zu erzeugen, zumal aber die fremdartigsten Tonarten, die unnatürlichsten Lagen der Accorde, die widerhaarigsten Zusammenstellungen in Betreff der Fingersetzung. Weiß denn der Verfasser nicht, daß der Maaßstab der Armuth an Genie immer mit den Mitteln wächst, die man hervorsucht, um eine Wirkung zu erzeugen? Weiß er nicht, daß gerade die häßlichen Frauenzimmer sich am meisten mit Flören und Bändern und *Culs de Paris* behängen, ihre mageren Arme in die gepufftesten *Gigots* stecken und die fahle Haut mit her dichtesten Schminke übertünchen? Hat er denn jemals geglaubt, daß die geschmacklosen Muttergottesbilder in Kleidern von *Drap d'Or* und *Drap d'argent* mit Perlen und Brillanten beladen dadurch zu Kunstwerken würden? Sollte er nie gesehen haben, in wie einfache Gewande Raphael seine Gestalten hüllt, wie viel einfacher noch die Gewandung der Antike ist? Aber es verlohnt wahrlich nicht der Mühe, daß ich der verdrehten Masureks des Herrn Chopin wegen so lange Philippiken halte. Er ist aber auch nur das Vehikel meines Zorns, und ich donnere, blitze und wettere hier gegen die ganze Verirrung, gegen diesen abtrünnigen Götzendienst der Kunst los, wodurch die Heilige zur Buhlerin ober zur Fratze entwürdigt wird. – Nachdem wir unsern Zorn ausgetobt haben, wollen wir einige gelindere Worte der Ermahnung nachfließen lassen, wie Mütter nach einer Züchtigung pflegen. Wir geben zu, daß eine Seltsamkeit hie und da einen gewissen Reiz ausübt, und daß es bisweilen in der Laune eines Genies liegen kann barock zu sein. Daher vergeben wir auch Herrn Chopin seinen ersten Masurka [sic!], denn warum sollte er nicht einmal auf einen recht seltsamen Einfall gerathen sein und die Laune haben ihn auszuführen? Da aber der folgende noch ärger ist, der dritte sich wieder steigert und so fort, so läßt sich daraus ersehen, daß der Componist das Seltsame sucht, weil er nichts Natürliches zu geben vermag. Und sieht er denn nicht, wie sehr er sich über die Erfindung täuscht, wie oft alles nur in einzelnen Hülfsmitteln, durchaus nicht in der Sache selbst liegt? Er spiele einmal seinen Masurka No. 4 in *Es moll* in *E moll*, und er wird sehen, wie unbedeutend das ist, was er eigentlich erfunden zu haben glaubte. Aber woher kommt es, daß wir jetzt so häufig auf solche grobe Verirrungen stoßen? Antwort: Weil kein Schüler mehr unter der Aufsicht eines

Meisters reif wird, sondern Jeder seine Studien absolvirt glaubt, wenn er gelernt hat, daß man keine Quinten machen soll. Das höchste und schwierigste Studium, die eigentliche Bildung des Kunstsinns und Geschmacks halten die Herren für überflüssig, denn wie Schiller singt: „dem genialen Geschlecht wird Alles im Traum bescheert." Hätte Herr Chopin diese Composition einem Meister vorgelegt, so würde dieser sie ihm hoffentlich zerrissen vor die Füße geworfen haben, was wir hiermit symbolisch thun wollen.

Ludwig Rellstab: Rezension der 3 *Nocturnes* op. 9, in: Iris im Gebiete der Tonkunst 4/1833, Nr. 31 vom 2. August, S. 121–122

Vor nicht gar langer Zeit haben wir in einem Trio des Verfassers viel Gutes anerkennen, vor kürzerer dagegen, bei Gelegenheit einiger von ihm componirten Mazurka's, uns aufs Strengste gegen seine Geschmacklosigkeit und die gesuchte Originalität erklären müssen. Die vorliegenden Notturno's halten ungefähr die Mitte zwischen beiden Kompositionen. Auf der Bahn des guten Geschmacks wird der Komponist durch sein Vorbild, John Field, gehalten, dessen reizende kleine Musikstücke, die unter dem Namen Romanzen oder Notturno's bereits seit zwanzig Jahren ihren frischen Reiz bewahren (sie wurden vorzüglich durch Ludwig Berger, der sie selbst sehr meisterhaft spielte, in Deutschland bekannt gemacht) und zum Prototypus aller Versuche in dieser Gattung gedient haben. So hält sich denn auch Herr Chopin so genau an die von John Field eingeschlagene Bahn, daß er ihn in Melodie, in der Art des Accompagnements u. s. w. förmlich copirt, ohne ihm jedoch direkt etwas zu entlehnen. In sofern klängen also die Notturno's recht gut, allein viel Verdienst können wir Herrn Chopin dabei nicht zuschreiben. Jetzt kommt aber die Schattenseite derselben. Um nämlich doch auch etwas Originelles zu haben, hat Herr Chopin die Schönheit dadurch zu erhöhen geglaubt, daß er alle Mittel in einem verstärkten Grade anwendet; wo Field lächelt, macht Herr Chopin eine grinsende Grimasse, wo Field seufzt, stöhnt Herr Chopin, Field zuckt die Achseln, Herr Chopin macht einen Katzenbuckel, Field thut etwas Gewürz an seine Speise, Herr Chopin eine Hand voll Cayenne-Pfeffer. Wir wollen zwar dem Verfasser daraus keinen strengen Vorwurf machen, denn die übertriebenen Accentuirungen sind leider so in der Mode, daß man ihm Manches dabei zu Gute halten muß. Dazu kommt das Bedürfniß anders zu schreiben als Andere; da aber die natürlichen Wege gar zu betreten sind, so muß man dabei fast unwillkürlich unnatürliche einschlagen. Field z. B. hat ein leichtes guitarrenartiges Accompagnement, welches vortrefflich in der Hand liegt, zu seinen

Romanzen gesetzt; Herr Chopin ahmt dies nach, aber verrenkt die Lage so, daß man sich fast die Finger zerbrechen muß, um die Figuren zu spielen, und man glauben sollte, es habe sie jemand gesetzt, der des Instruments ganz unkundig wäre, und daher durch Ungeschicklichkeit alle diese unnützen Schwierigkeiten häufte. Ferner hat Herr Chopin wieder nicht versäumt, sich die fremdesten Tonarten zu wählen, B moll, H dur, und freilich auch Es dur, aber in dieser letztern Tonart denn auch so modulirt, daß man in einem wahren Irrgarten zu seyn glaubt. Kurz, wie gesagt, wenn man Fields reizende Romanzen vor einen verzerrenden Hohlspiegel hielte, so daß aus jedem feineren Ausdruck ein grob aufgetragener wird, so erhält man Chopins Arbeit. Aber so mächtig bleibt die Kraft eines schönen Vorbildes, daß es selbst in dieser Entstellung noch von einnehmender Wirkung sein kann, so, daß für Jemand, der Fields Arbeiten nicht kennte, Herr Chopin wohl gar als erfindungsreich und geschmackvoll gelten könnte, zumal wenn sich Jemand die Mühe gegeben hätte, die unbequemen, holprigen und dabei so sehr undankbaren Schwierigkeiten so zu überwinden, daß sie glatt und eben dahin flössen. Wir beschwören daher Herrn Chopin, der wahrlich nicht ohne Talent ist, zur Wahrheit und Natur zurückzukehren, und seine schönen Gaben nicht so muthwillig selbst zu zertreten und zu verzerren. Er folge doch ja der Bahn der Meister so lange er vermag, und suche nicht schon am Anfange seines Weges originell und selbstständig zu seyn. Die Eigenthümlichkeit bildet sich dann später wie als Gesinnung im Leben, so als Kraft in der Kunst von selbst heraus, und um so mehr, je mehr man allgemein gültigen Gesetzen, dort der Sittlichkeit, hier der Schönheit gefolgt ist.

Ludwig Rellstab: Rezension der 12 *Etüden* op. 10,
in: Iris im Gebiete der Tonkunst 5/1834, Nr. 5 vom 31. Januar, S. 18–20

Es ist nicht gar lange her, daß ich dem Leser der Iris versprach, ihn einen Blick in meine Briefsammlung thun zu lassen. Jetzt scheint mir der günstige Augenblick gekommen, da ich sonst nicht wohl weiß, wie ich eine Recension über die Chopinschen Etüden anfangen soll. Ich war nämlich so frei gewesen, die Werke des obigen Autors nicht sowohl unter die genialen, als unter die ganz verkehrten und verdrehten zu stellen, die gleich denen mancher neueren, weil sie auf natürlichem Wege nichts Eigenthümliches und zugleich Schönes mehr zu erzeugen wissen, auf die Idee gerathen, das Unnatürlichste und Verzerrteste müsse deshalb etwas werth seyn, weil es eben ungewöhnlich ist. Sie thun damit freilich nichts als was Horaz in der ars poetica als Beispiel des Wahnsinns aufstellt, d. h. „Humano capiti cervicem equinam jungunt et varias inducunt plumas, undique collatis membris ut turpiter"[10] – – etc. – Allein wie der Dichter rufen wir: Spectatum admissi, risum teneatis, amici?[11] Je nun, wir lachten dann auch bisweilen und suchten die Leser der Iris gleichfalls dazu zu bringen. Dies aber schnitt den genialen Schöpfern der neuen Wunder in die tiefste Seele, und eines Tages, – ich glaubte der Donner erschlüge mich, so gefesselt stand ich vor Entsetzen – erhielt ich folgenden Brief aus Leipzig durch Einschluß, den ich dem Leser hiermit vorlege, und ihn ernstlich um seine Ansicht darüber frage. Ich copire gewissenhaft wörtlich; es thut mir nur leid, daß ich kein fac simile geben kann, welches ebenfalls noch sein Interesse haben würde. Also gedachter Brief lautet*):

P. P.

Sie sind doch ein recht schlechter Mensch und nicht werth, dass Sie Gottes Erdboden k e n n e n (sic) noch trägt. Der König von Preussen hätte Sie sollen auf der Festung sitzen lassen[12]; er hätte dann der Welt einen Rebellen, einen Ruhestörer und einen schändlichen Menschenfeind entrückt, der wahrscheinlich noch einmal in seinem eigenen Blute ersticken wird. Eine Unzahl (oder Anzahl; das Manuscript ist undeutlich) Feinde nicht nur in Berlin, sondern in allen Städten, die ich auf meiner Kunstreise in verflossenem Sommer berührt habe, habe ich bemerkt, besonders recht viel hier in Leipzig, wo ich Ihnen dies zur Nachricht schreibe, damit Sie künftig Ihre Gesinnung ändern und nicht zu lieblos gegen andere Menschen handeln. Noch einmal ein schlechter, schlechter Streich, und es ist um Sie geschehn! Verstehen Sie mich, Sie kleiner Mensch, Sie liebloser und partheiischer Recensentenhund, Sie musikalischer Schnur[r]bart, Sie Berliner Witzemacher etc.

Allerunterthänigster *C h o p i n.*

---

10 Horaz, *Ars poetica*, V. 1–3 (Text verändert):
Wollte zum Kopf eines Menschen ein Maler den Hals eines Pferdes fügen und Gliedmaßen, von überallher zusammengelesen, mit buntem Gefieder bekleiden, so daß als Fisch von häßlicher Schwärze [endet das oben so reizende Weib.]

11 Horaz, *Ars poetica*, V. 5:
Könntet ihr da wohl, sobald man euch zur Besichtigung zuließ, euch das Lachen verbeißen, Freunde? (deutsche Übersetzung von Bernhard Kytzler)

*) Das Original steht Jedem zur Ansicht bei mir frei.

12 Rellstab war wegen einer Satire auf die berühmte Sängerin Henriette Sontag bzw. deren Anhänger und der Verspottung des englischen Gesandten in Berlin 1826 zu drei Monaten Festungshaft verurteilt worden.

Daß dich die Pest! Der Leser kann sich denken, wie ich erschreckt zusammenfuhr und neunmal die Stunde verfluchte, wo ich mir einen so furchtbaren Feind geweckt hatte, gegen den Herr Spontini zu Nichts verschwindet. Ob Herr Chopin den Brief selbst geschrieben? Ich weiß es nicht und werde es nicht behaupten, drucke das Aktenstück aber hier ab, damit er es anerkennen oder widerlegen kann. Inzwischen ist es doch gut, daß der Leser erfährt, was ich eigentlich für ein Giftgeschwür bin für die Menschheit, und gut, daß ich selbst erfahre, wie mir die nächste Recension über Herrn Chopin mindestens den Hals kostet, wenn nicht mehr, da er mir zuverlässig entweder durch besagten Componisten selbst oder seinen Pseudonymus gebrochen wird. Denn wie gesagt, ich glaube noch kaum, daß Herr Chopin den Brief geschrieben, und glaube es nicht zu seinem Besten, da er wahrlich dem Schreiber stärkeren Abzug vom guten Ruf thut als dem Empfänger, der ihn ohne Umstände bekannt macht. Was soll derselbe aber nun mit Hrn. Chopins Werken thun? Greift er sie an, so glaubt die Welt und Hr. Chopin, es sei Rache, und er verliert gegen beide den Vortheil, sie wahrhaft von der Verkehrtheit der *Opera Chopiniana* zu überzeugen; lobt er sie, so sieht Jedermann aber, daß es aus Todesangst geschieht, denn der Briefschreiber sagt, es sey um ihn, den Redakteur der Iris nämlich, geschehen, wenn er nicht von Stund an alles bewundere. Ein verfluchtes Dilemma, woraus sich der Henker helfe! Publikum, du siehst hier die Recensentenfreuden! Du siehst, was für Blumen uns armen Kritikern in der Stille blühen. – Doch kurz und gut. Wir sind entschlossen bei der Wahrheit zu bleiben. So wie Herr Chopin ein Wunderwerk, etwa einen neuen Don Juan oder Fidelio, oder Sinfonia eroica, oder eine Beethovensche Sonate in Cis moll liefert, so wollen wir ihn bewundern, daß uns die Sprache zum Ausdruck unserer Gefühle fehlt. So lange er aber solche Mißgeburten ausheckt wie obige Etüden, die ich allen meinen Freunden, und zumal den Klavierspielern, zur wahren Belustigung gezeigt, so lange wollen wir über diese eben so lachen wie über seinen Brief. Eine Special-Recension der 12 neuen Apostel, die Herr Chopin in obigen 12 Stücken in die Welt geschickt hat, erlasse man uns jedoch und begnüge sich mit der wohl nicht unnützen Bemerkung, daß, wer verrenkte Finger hat, sie an diesen Etüden vielleicht wieder ins Grade bringt, wer nicht, sich aber sehr davor hüten und sie nicht spielen muß, ohne Herrn v o n G r ä f e oder D i e f f e n b a c h[13] in der Nähe zu haben, die überhaupt, wenn diese Art Klavierspiel in die Mode kommt, als Assistenten berühmter Klavierlehrer vielleicht eine ganz neue Art der Praxis bekommen könnten.

---

13 Bekannte Berliner Ärzte.

Heinrich Panofka: Correspondenz aus Paris, März 1834, in: Neue Zeitschrift für Musik 1/1834, Nr. 1 vom 3. April, S. 4

Sie kennen Liszt und Chopin. Diese sind es vorzugsweise, welche, den Beifall des großen Haufens verschmähend, muthvoll, das glänzende Beispiel Paganini's im Auge, in der Darstellung dieselbe Bahn betreten, die der Genius Beethoven's in der Composition erschloß. Die Musik ist ihnen die Kunst, welche den Menschen sein höheres Princip ahnen läßt und ihn aus dem Treiben des gemeinen Lebens in den Isistempel führt, wo die Natur in heiligen, nie gehörten und doch verständlichen Lauten mit ihm spricht; daher ihr Vortrag ein großartiger, den Forderungen des gebildeten Gefühls und tiefern Gemüths entsprechender.

Chopin's Spiel ist so innig mit seinen Compositionen verschmolzen, daß Sie diese nur genau zu kennen brauchen, um einen deutlichen Begriff von seiner begeisterten, sinnig zarten Vortragsweise zu bekommen. [...]

Heinrich Panofka: Correspondenz aus Paris, April 1834, in: Neue Zeitschrift für Musik 1/1834, Nr. 4 vom 14. April, S. 16

[...] Von Chopin erscheint eben ein Concertrondo in Fdur [*Krakowiak F-Dur* op. 14 für Klavier und Orchester]. Viel Zartheit in der Instrumentation, das Passagenwerk, das er um seine Melodieen legt, neu und in seiner Art, die Themas nicht sehr bedeutend, zu nationell-polnisch. Ich fürchte, daß er sich, wie Spohr, mit dem er überhaupt manche Vorzüge wie Fehler teilt, in einen gewissen Stil festschreiben wird. Er sieht wohl v e r s c h i e d e n e Dinge, aber er sieht sie stets mit d e m s e l b e n Auge. Vielleicht wirft ihn einmal das Leben in eine andre Sphäre. –

Heinrich Panofka: Briefe aus Paris. (Schluß), in: Neue Zeitschrift für Musik 1/1834, Nr. 16 vom 26. Mai, S. 64

Die meisten der genannten Pianisten sind bei Ihnen gekannt, und es wird Ihnen daher vielleicht lieb sein, etwas über Chopin und Liszt zu hören. Zuerst von Chopin.

Er spielte seine Notturnos und einige der Etuden. So wie es ganz natürlich ist, daß man beim Anschauen dieser Compositionen leicht die Unausführlichkeit derselben vermuthen könnte, da man eine Masse der schwierigsten Figuren und Accordengriffe vor sich hat, so unbedingt muß man Chopin einen seltenen Meister nennen, da alles dies von ihm in einer Weise ausgeführt wird, die unsere ganze Bewunderung in Anspruch nimmt. Sein Spiel ist vollendet in allen Beziehungen. Da ist Ton, Kraft, unendliche Grazie, Leidenschaft, tiefes Gefühl, eine Sauberkeit und Leichtigkeit in der Ausführung, die nichts zu wünschen läßt, und was das Bedeutendste ist, Originalität im Vortrage seiner in vielfacher Hinsicht originellen Compositionen. Diese tragen alle das Gepräge jener jugendlichen Melancholie, die jedes gebildete Gemüth in der Entwickelungszeit empfindet. Wenn andere in der freien Natur, bei Berg und Bach, liebeseufzen, so componirt Chopin; wenn sie uns mit ihren Stoßseufzern zur Verzweiflung bringen, so erfreut er uns. Er ist mit Recht der beliebteste Clavierspieler. – Der Gegensatz zu Chopin ist Liszt, über den Sie in einem nächsten Bericht Näheres erfahren sollen. [...]

Ludwig Rellstab: Rezension des *Klavierkonzerts e-Moll* op. 11, in: Iris im Gebiete der Tonkunst 5/1834, Nr. 23 vom 6. Juni, S. 89/90

Auf dem Titel dieses Concertstücks steht gedruckt: Executé par l'Auteur dans ses Concerts à Paris. Es scheint, daß man das hinzusetzen mußte, um zu beweisen, daß es Jemand giebt, der sich so viel Mühe ohne Resultat geben kann. Das vorliegende Werk ist nämlich unbedingt das schwierigste, was wir jemals gesehn, so daß alle von Kalkbrenner, Moscheles, Hummel u. s. w. dagegen nur als ein Spielwerk erscheinen. Allein die Schwierigkeiten sind von der Art, daß sie nach unserer Einsicht weder das Instrument weiter fördern, noch dem Spieler größeren Dank bei den Hörern verschaffen, zwei Eigenschaften, die im Grunde genommen freilich dasselbe bedeuten. Man muß immer erst förmlich berechnen, ob eine Passage, wie Hr. Chopin sie schreibt, schwer ist oder nicht. Niemand kann mit dem Ohr in solcher Schnelligkeit combiniren, ob gewisse Tonverbindungen den Fingern große Hindernisse in den Weg legen oder nicht, ob man z. B. den vierten Finger über den kleinen setzen muß u. dergl. mehr. Fast alle Schwierigkeiten in dem vorliegenden Concert reduciren sich also auf eine höchst unbequeme Lage der Passagen in der Hand, und meist wäre mit sehr einfachen Mitteln die Sache nicht nur leichter, sondern sogar l e i c h t gemacht, ohne daß man der Wirkung etwas schadete. Daß man hier und da eine Kleinigkeit gewinnt, dadurch daß man die Schwierigkeiten von Hrn. Chopin buchstäblich nimmt, wollen wir nicht in Abrede seyn; allein es ist die Frage, ob die Ausbeute der Mühe lohnt. [...]

Wir sind fest überzeugt, daß Herr Chopin trotz aller Studien dieser Art, ein Concert von Beethoven oder Mozart, ja auch Dussek [?Dusík] und Hummel nicht schöner spielen wird als so mancher unserer vaterländischen Klavierspieler. Was ist also der Gewinnst dabei? Nur die Schwierigkeiten, die die Kunst des Virtuosen oder das musikalische Gebiet an sich wesentlich erweitern, heißen wir gut. Darum sind Paganini's vielstimmige Sätze vortrefflich und verdienen geübt zu werden, seine Flageolettstückchen dagegen meistentheils ganz unbrauchbar. – Was nun das Concert selbst als Composition anlangt, so müssen wir zugeben, daß es nicht ohne Sinn für edlere Gedanken und Auffassungen in der Musik geschrieben ist. Allein wie sich so oft aus den Ausschweifungen nach einer Seite die umgekehrten erzeugen, so scheint die triviale Weichlichkeit der italiänischen Musik den Componisten zu dem Gegensatz geführt zu haben, und er vertieft oder besser verirrt und verwickelt sich in ein Uebermaaß harmonischer Combinationen, daß einem ganz krank und weh dabei zu Muthe werden kann. Indessen sehen wir dergleichen Dinge doch mit einigem Trost an. Dem Menschen ist nämlich ein gewisses Maaß gegeben, über das er weder im Bösen noch im Guten, im Verkehrten noch im Wahrhaften hinaus kommen kann. Und wie kein Bildhauer den Phidias, kein Dichter den Sophokles an Adel zu überbieten vermag, so muß auch der Zeitpunkt solcher Verirrungen seinem Ende nahe seyn, wie die, welche wir vor uns haben. Schon hat sich in der theatralischen Kunst das Melodram am Gräßlichen und Widernatürlichen erschöpft, und muß zur Wahrheit und Natur zurückkehren, weil hier das Gebiet zu Ende ist; eben so hoffen wir, werde sich die Musik einerseits in Flachheit (Rossini, Mercadante u. s. w.), andererseits in der Ueberreizung (Chopin und seine Nachahmer) todt und stumpf gearbeitet haben. Auch Hr. Chopin fühlt dies vielleicht bald selbst und kehrt auf den Weg der Einfachheit und Wahrheit zurück.

Heinrich Panofka: Briefe aus Paris. (Schluß), IV., Anfang August 1834,
in: Neue Zeitschrift für Musik 1/1834, Nr. 41 vom 21. August, S. 163

Verwundert lesen wir hier in der Iris, die Hr. Rellstab redigirt, die heftigen Ausfälle gegen die Compositionen Chopin's.

Wenn schon gemeinhin in dem kritischen Treiben unserer Tage fast nichts mehr aufzufallen vermag, außer ruhiger Ernst, Parteilosigkeit, klares Wissen und gründliches Eindringen in den zu beurtheilenden Gegenstand – wenn schon wir gewiß sind, daß der sonst so geistreiche Rellstab nicht im Stande sein wird, die Chopin'schen Compositionen vollkommen zu beurtheilen, bevor er sie nicht von ihm selbst hörte, was gerade bei Chopin's Werken eine conditio sine qua non der Beurtheilung ist – so befremdet es uns dennoch, daß gerade Rellstab, der stets freimüthig und nachdrücklich dem Unfug des gewöhnlichen Treibens sich entgegenstellt, die wirklich poetische und ächt künstlerische Natur Chopin's mißkennt, während er nicht selten geringeren Talenten Gerechtigkeit widerfahren läßt.

Ein flüchtiges Ueberschauen Chopin'scher Compositionen genügt nicht, um eine Ahnung davon zu haben; von ihm gehört, sind sie klar und schön, originell und edel. Er ist ein fühlender Künstler, mit einer lebendigen Phantasie und wahrer Poesie begabt und ein ganz eigenthümlicher, außerordentlicher Clavierspieler, der, was wenige können, auf dem Piano vermag. – [...]

Ludwig Rellstab: Rezension der *Variations brillantes* op. 12, in: Iris im Gebiete der Tonkunst 5/1834, Nr. 35 vom 29. August, S. 138/139

Zwar ist dieses Werkchen keineswegs frei von den g e s u c h t e n Fehlern, über die wir schon so oft bei den Arbeiten des Componisten geeifert haben: jedennoch gefällt es uns sehr wohl. Wir erinnern uns noch der ersten Arbeit, die wir von Chopin sahen; es war ein Trio in Es-dur, in welchem wir ebenfalls sowohl die Hauptmotive als vieles andere loben durften. Dies führen wir aus dem Grunde an, damit man sehe, wie keineswegs ein blinder Parteigeist uns geleitet hat, sondern jedem unserer Urtheile eine genaue Durchsicht des Werkes und reifliche Ueberlegung vorangegangen ist. Eben diese bestimmt uns auch, die vorliegenden Variationen für eine sehr gelungene Arbeit zu erklären. Einmal ist das Thema glücklich gewählt, indem es sich mit seinen originellen und doch natürlichen Wendungen sehr zur Variirung eignet. Zweitens müssen wir aber auch die Variationen selbst loben, welche originell, sehr voneinander verschieden und doch (mit geringer Ausnahme einzelner Stellen) in natürlichem Fluß geschrieben sind. Gleich die erste Variation hat darin vollkommen unseren Beifall, noch mehr aber die zweite, welche zwar sehr schwer ist, aber auch schön gespielt, von reizender Wirkung seyn muß. Die letzte Variation ist die brillanteste, enthält aber auch am meisten von g e s u c h t e n Schwicrigkeiten, wiewohl im Ganzen, gegen Chopins übrige Werke gehalten, doch ein mildes Maaß derselben beobachtet ist.

Gottfried Wilhelm Fink: Rezension der *Grande Valse brillante* op. 18, in: Allgemeine Musikalische Zeitung 36/1834, Nr. 50 vom 10. Dezember, Sp. 844

Ein frischer, schöner, auf 8 Noten-Folioseiten durchgeführter grosser Walzer, wirklich glanzvoll und echt tanzlich, ohne dass Chopin's Art und Wesen bey aller

Anmuth des Gehaltes, die der Gegenstand fordert, vermisst würde. Man kaufe, spiele, siege und – werde besiegt zu Lust und Freude. Wir sind gewiss, dass gute Spieler sich höchlich daran ergötzen.

Ludwig Rellstab: Rezension des *Bolero* op. 19, in: Iris im Gebiete der Tonkunst 6/1835, Nr. 9 vom 27. Februar, S. 34/35

Erst vor kurzem hat der Redakteur der Iris die ungemein günstige Rezension seines Blattes in der Leipziger neuen Zeitschrift für Musik gelesen[14]; ein Urtheil, das ihm um so erfreulicher sein durfte, als es muthmaßlich von einem jungen geistreichen Musiker herrührt, dem der Redakteur hinsichtlich seiner Compositionen oft streng genug entgegengetreten ist.[15] Nur in einem Punkte wird derselbe unser Gegner, nämlich was unsere Meinung über Chopin anlangt. Aber so sehr wir den besten Willen hegen uns ihm anzuschließen, und so sehr wir die allgemeine Ansicht des Verfassers theilen, daß man nie auf einer bestimmten Stufe der Kunstbildung abgeschlossen stehen bleiben, sondern alle neuern Richtungen verfolgen müsse; so tief wir auch in den Verdacht gerathen, schon jetzt in rüstigster Kraft hinter der Zeit zurückzubleiben, so wenig können wir uns von seiner Ansicht über Chopin überzeugen. Wir müssen das ganze Streben dieses Componisten für eine Verirrung halten; für eine, die auf entschiedenem Talent beruht, aber dennoch eine bleibt. Daß Chopin einen Erfolg in der Welt erlangt, kann uns keinen Augenblick irre machen, denn er erweitert das Gebiet der Virtuosität und zeigt durch sein Beispiel, daß er hier nur Schwierigeres, nicht Unmögliches will. Die Virtuosität verhält sich aber zur Composition wie die Bekleidung zur Körperschönheit. Zu allen Zeiten hat die erstere auf Kosten der letzteren eitle verkehrte Siege erfochten und den falschen Schönheitssinn der flachen Menge in unermeßlicher Majorität für sich gehabt. Eine hübsche Frau, die eine neue Mode erfindet, wird schnell Nachahmerinnen finden, wenngleich sie mit der Tracht einen Schritt rückwärts im Gebiet der Schönheit thut. Was ist denn Rossini's Geheimniß, die Masse zu gewinnen, als die Kunst, dem eitlen Putz der Gesangsvirtuosität geschickt zu huldigen und ihm neue Bahnen zu brechen? So Chopin. Daß er abentheuerliche grotesk romantische Trachten wählt, wo Rossini Schminke und Flittergold gebraucht, macht in dem wesentlichen Verhältniß der Sache keinen

---

14 Vgl. S. 254-56.
15 Bezieht sich auf Rellstabs dümmliche und naseweise Rezensionen von Schumanns *Abegg-Variationen* op. 1 (in: Iris im Gebiete der Tonkunst 3/1832, Nr. 8 vom 24. Februar, S. 31 und 32) und *Papillons* op. 2 (in: Iris im Gebiete der Tonkunst 3/1832, Nr. 21 vom 25. Mai, S. 83).

Unterschied. In dem vorliegenden Bolero thut er dies, durch die charakteristischen Formen eines Nationaltanzes unterstützt, mit Geschick. Jedermann wird diese Composition gern hören, wenn sie gut vorgetragen wird; er wird einräumen, daß sie das Produkt eines edler strebenden Geistes ist, als z. B. Kalkbrenner, Moscheles, Herz u. A. entwickeln. Aber eben so wird jeder Unbefangene auch einsehen, daß das ganze Werk seine Basis völlig verliert, wenn es nicht mehr ein schwierig zu spielendes ist; daß die Erfindung sich darin nur auf ein erzwungenes Abweichen von dem Natürlichen erstreckt; daß zwar Vieles, ja wir möchten sagen Alles, ungewöhnlich ist, mit dieser negativen Eigenschaft aber auch seine ganze Bedeutung erschöpft. Wer uns in diesem Werk acht zusammenhängend schöne Takte, ja nur eine einzige s c h ö n e melodische Phrase, eine einzige harmonische Combination nachweisen könnte, die sich ohne stachlige Dissonanzen, ohne den eckigen Irrlichtgang unnatürlicher Fortschreitungen, einfach nach dem Kunstgesetz, welchem Gluck, Mozart, Haydn huldigten, gestaltete, der sollte uns ein magnus Apollo sein. Indessen ist dieses Werkchen doch, wenngleich es nach unserer Meinung nie einen Componisten bezeichnen kann, der Epoche in der Kunst zu machen berufen ist, eines, welches einen Virtuosen dieser Art, was wir Chopin nie absprechen wollen, charakterisirt, wiewohl wir selbst in der Virtuosität diese Richtung, die nur ein übertragener, nicht selbst geschaffener Paganinismus ist (man thäte daher besser, ihn Paganismus zu nennen), zwar toleriren, aber nie erfreulich finden konnten. Somit sei denn der Bolero von Chopin der Welt empfohlen; das andere will ich, mit Göthe zu reden, nicht wiederholen. Ich habe es leider nur schon zu oft wiederholen müssen.

Gottfried Wilhelm Fink: Rezension des *Scherzo h-Moll* op. 20, in: Allgemeine Musikalische Zeitung 37/1835, Nr. 21 vom 27. Mai, Sp. 337/338

Wieder ein Scherz von Chopin, ganz in seiner Weise, fast noch leidenschaftlicher als manches frühere, worüber wir ausführlich berichteten. Schmerzentbrannt braust es in H moll, 3/4, nach 2 langen, starken, aus vollschrillender Höhe des Sextenaccordes von E moll in die Tiefe des Quintsextenaccordes von Fis dur sich stürzenden Kraftschreien, presto con fuoco, seltsam bewegt und bewegend daher, bald zögernd und verweilend, wie im Sinnen verloren über das wirbelnde Weh, bald in einzelnen langen Tönen wie klagende Sehnsucht wehmüthig erschütternd, worauf es desto anhaltender, doch immer von Neuem wieder wie brütend düster versunken, aufgehalten oder verlangend, feurig treibend sich Luft macht, einerlei Wesen fort und fort umklammernd, das es selbst in dem langsamern, wie in fernsüssen Erinnerungen sich wiegenden Zwischensatze aus H dur nicht verlässt, wo es besonders im ungewissen Schwanken des schön verzögerten Uebergangs und ungewohnter Führungen sich kund thut, bis plötzlich nach leisem Cisdur ff der Schmerzensschrei des Sextenaccordes im E moll in hohen Tönen ergreifend und unerwartet durchbricht. Nur noch 3 Takte – und schmerzlich aus seiner schönen Schattenwelt herausgerissen, bricht das Toben des Wehs molto con fuoco in H moll und im ersten tempo, der ersten Empfindung völlig treu, wieder los, bis zu einem furchtbaren und langen Angstruf sich drängend, nach welchem es sich mit neuaufloderndem Feuer dem Ende entgegenstürzt. Das ist Chopin's Scherz, der mich manchmal schon in meinen 4 Wänden wunderlich ergriffen hat. Nur verlangt dieser Scherz noch etwas anders als Fertigkeit. Vor Einem nur ist mir bange; das ist das Heer der Nachahmer, vor dem uns der Himmel in dieser Art vorzüglich gütig bewahren wolle: sonst erhalten wir furchtbare Larven, greuliche Genialitäten, die nicht sterben, wenn man sie auch mit Füssen tritt.

Ludwig Rellstab: Rezension der 4 *Mazurken* op. 17,
in: Iris im Gebiete der Tonkunst 6/1835, Nr. 28 vom 10. Juli, S. 111

Der Componist scheint mit seinen fortrückenden Arbeiten einzusehen, daß Schwierigkeit nicht das Z i e l der wirklich musikalischen Compositionen sein soll; vielleicht kommt er nach und nach auf den letzten, richtigen Begriff davon, daß sie fast immer nur ein nothwendiges Uebel ist. Der Geschickteste ist gewiß der, der ohne neue combinirte Mittel zu gebrauchen, neu combinirte Gedanken hat. In gewissen Beziehungen kann man dies an den vorliegenden Masurka's rühmen; sie haben eine pikante Nationalität und, ohne ueberschwer zu sein, doch manche für das Instrument neue und in der Combination interessante Wendungen. Dahin rechnen wir einige harmonische Zusammenstellungen, obwohl sie mehr gesucht als gefunden sind; gewisse überraschende Wendungen im Rhythmus, namentlich bei den Uebergängen eines Mitteltheils in das Grundthema des ersten; endlich einige graziöse Verzierungen in der Melodie. Im zweiten Masurka ist der Satz: System 2, Takt 2 u. s. f.[16] bis zur Rückkehr des Thema's (eine harmonische Tendenz) sehr originell und schön in der Wirkung. Im letzten Masurka dagegen werden uns der harmonischen Verflechtungen und gesuchten Dissonanzen doch etwas zu viel. Dergleichen e i n m a l zu finden, unterhält; es zur Basis der Erfindung gemacht zu sehen, erzeugt Monotonie und somit Gleichgültigkeit.

---

16 Bezieht sich auf den deutschen Erstdruck, Leipzig 1834, Breitkopf & Härtel.

Robert Schumann: Rezensionen der *Konzerte e-Moll* op. 11 und *f-Moll* op. 21, in: Neue Zeitschrift für Musik 4/1836, Nr. 33 vom 22. April, S. 137–139 (unter „Pianoforte. Concerte. (Schluß.)")

1.

Sobald ihr überhaupt Widersacher findet, junge Künstler, so sehr wollet Euch dieses Zeichens Eurer Talentkraft freuen und diese für um so bedeutender halten, je widerhaariger jene. Immerhin bleibt es auffallend, daß in den sehr trocknen Jahren vor **1830**, wo man dem Himmel um jeden bessern Strohhalm hätte danken sollen, selbst die Kritik, die freilich immer hintennach kommen wird, wenn sie nicht von productiven Köpfen ausgeht, noch lange mit der Anerkennung Chopins achselzuckend anstand, ja daß einer sich zu sagen erkühnte, Chopins Compositionen wären nur zum Zerreissen oder Zerrissenwerden gut.[17] Genug davon. Auch der Herzog von Modena hat Louis Philipp noch nicht anerkannt, und steht der Barricadenthron auch nicht auf goldnen Füßen, so doch sicher nicht des Herzogs halber. Sollte ich vielleicht hier beiläufig einer berühmten Pantoffel-Zeitung [= Allgemeine Musikalische Zeitung] erwähnen, die uns zuweilen, wie wir hören (denn wir lesen sie nicht und schmeicheln uns hierin einige wenige Aehnlichkeit mit Beethoven zu besitzen [s. B's Studien, v. Seyfried herausgeg.]), die uns also zuweilen unter der Maske anlächeln soll mit sanftestem Dolchauge und nur deshalb, weil ich einmal zu einem ihrer Mitarbeiter, der etwas über Chopins Don-Juan-Variationen geschrieben, lachend gemeint: er, der Mitarbeiter, habe wie ein schlechter Vers, ein Paar Füße zu viel, die man ihm gelegentlich abzuschneiden beabsichtigte! – Sollte ich mich heute, wo ich eben vom Chopinschen F-Moll-Concerte komme, dessen erinnern? Bewahre. Milch gegen Gift, kühle blaue Milch! Denn was ist ein ganzer Jahrgang einer musikalischen Zeitung gegen ein Concert von Chopin? Was Magisterwahnsinn gegen dichterischen? Was zehn Redactionskronen gegen ein Adagio im zweiten Concert? Und wahrhaftig, Davidsbündler, keiner Anrede hielt ich Euch werth, getrautet Ihr Euch nicht solche Werke selbst zu machen, als über die Ihr schreibt, einige ausgenommen, wie eben dies zweite Concert, an das wir sämmtlich nicht hinankönnen, oder nur mit den Lippen, den Saum zu küssen. Fort mit den Musikzeitungen! Ja, Triumph und letzter Endzweck einer guten müßte sein (worauf auch schon viele hinarbeiten), wenn sie

---

17   Rezension der 4 *Mazurken* op. 7 von Ludwig Rellstab in: Iris im Gebiete der Tonkunst 4/1833, Nr. 28 vom 12. Juli, S. 112 (vgl. S. 247-249).

es so hoch brächte, daß sie Niemand mehr läse aus Ennui, daß die Welt vor lauter Productivität nichts mehr hören wollte vom Schreiber darüber; – aufrichtiger Kritiker höchstes Streben, sich (wie sich auch manche bemühen) gänzlich überflüssig zu machen; – beste Art, über Musik zu reden, die, zu schweigen. Lustige Gedanken sind das eines Zeitungsschreibers, die sich nicht einbilden sollten, daß sie die Herrgotts der Künstler, da diese sie doch verhungern lassen könnten. Fort mit den Zeitungen! Kömmt sie hoch, die Kritik, so ist sie immer erst ein leidlicher Dünger für zukünftige Werke; Gottes Sonne gebiert aber auch ohne dies genug. Noch einmal, warum über Chopin schreiben? Warum Leser zur Langeweile zwingen? Warum nicht aus erster Hand schöpfen, selbst spielen, selbst schreiben, selbst componiren? Zum letztenmal, fort mit den musikalischen Zeitungen, besonderen und sonstigen!

Florestan

2.

Ginge es dem Tollkopf, dem Florestan nach, so wäre er im Stande, Obiges eine Recension zu nennen, ja mit selbiger die ganze Zeitung zu schließen. Bedenke er aber, daß wir noch eine alte Pflicht gegen Chopin zu erfüllen haben, über den wir noch gar nichts in unsern Büchern aufgezeichnet und daß uns die Welt unsere Sprachlosigkeit aus Verehrung am Ende gar für etwas anderes auslegen möchte. Denn wenn eine Verherrlichung durch Worte (die schönste ist ihm schon in tausend Herzen zu Theil worden) bis jetzt ausgeblieben, so suche ich den Grund einestheils in der Aengstlichkeit, die Einem bei einem Gegenstande befällt, über den man am öftersten und liebsten mit seinem Sinnen verweilt, daß man nämlich der Würde des Vorwurfs nicht angemessen genug sprechen, ihn in seiner Tiefe und Höhe nicht allseitig ergreifen könnte, – anderntheils in den innern Kunstbeziehungen, in denen wir zu diesem Componisten zu stehen bekennen; endlich aber unterblieb sie auch, weil Chopin in seinen letzten Compositionen nicht einen andern, aber einen höhern Weg einzuschlagen scheint, über dessen Richtung und muthmaßliches Ziel wir erst noch klarer zu werden hofften, auswärtigen geliebten Verbündeten davon Rechenschaft abzulegen...

Das Genie schafft Reiche, dessen kleinere Staaten wiederum von höherer Hand unter die Talente vertheilt werden, damit diese, was dem ersteren in seiner tausendfach angesprochenen und ausströmenden Thätigkeit ohnmöglich, im einzelnen organisiren, zur Vollendung bringen. Wie vordem z. B. Hummel der Stimme Mozarts folgte, daß er die Gedanken des Meisters in eine glänzendere fliegende Umhüllung kleidete, so Chopin der Beethovens. Oder ohne Bild: wie Hummel den Styl Mozarts den Einzelnen, dem Virtuosen zum Genuß im besonderen Instrumente verarbeitete, so führte Chopin Beethovenschen Geist in den Concertsaal.

Chopin trat nicht mit einer Orchesterarmee auf, wie Großgenies thun; er besitzt nur eine kleine Cohorte, aber sie gehört ihm ganzeigen bis auf den letzten Helden.

Seinen Unterricht aber hatte er bei den Mächtigsten erhalten, bei Beethoven, Schubert, Field. Wollen wir annehmen, der erste bildete seinen Geist in Kühnheit, der andere sein Herz in Zartheit, der dritte seine Hand in Fertigkeit.

Also stand er ausgestattet mit tiefen Kenntnissen seiner Kunst, mit Einsicht in seine Kraft und demnach vollauf gerüstet mit Muth, als im Jahre **1830** die große Völkerstimme im Westen sich erhob. Hunderte von Jünglingen warteten des Augenblicks: aber Chopin war der Erste auf dem Wall oben, hinter dem eine feige Restauration, ein zwergiges Philisterium im Schlafe lag. Wie fielen da die Schläge rechts und links und die Dicken wachten erbost auf und schrieen: „Seht die Frechen"; Andere aber im Rücken der Angreifenden: „des herrlichen Muthes."

Dazu aber und zum günstigen Aufeinandertreffen der Zeit und der Verhältnisse that das Schicksal noch etwas, Chopin vor allen andern kenntlich und interessant zu machen, eine starke originelle Nationalität und zwar die polnische. Und wie diese jetzt in schwarzen Gewändern geht, so ergreift sie uns am sinnenden Künstler noch heftiger. Heil ihm, daß ihm das neutrale Deutschland nicht im ersten Augenblick zu beifällig zusprach und daß ihn sein Genius gleich nach einer der Welthauptstädte[18] entführte, wo er frei dichten und zürnen konnte. Denn wüßte der gewaltige selbstherrschende Monarch[19], wie in Chopins Werken, in den einfachen Weisen seiner Mazurkas, ihm ein gefährlicher Feind droht, er würde die Musik verbieten. Chopins Werke sind unter Blumen eingesenkte Kanonen.

In dieser seiner Herkunft, im Schicksale seines Landes, ruht so die Erklärung seiner Vorzüge, wie auch die seiner Fehler. Wenn von Schwärmerei, Grazie, Sinnesfeinheit, wenn von Geistesgegenwart, Gluth und Adel die Rede ist, wer dächte da nicht an ihn, aber wer auch nicht, wenn von Wunderlichkeit, kranker Excentricität, ja von Haß und Wildheit!

Solch Gepräge der schärfsten Nationalität tragen sämmtliche früheren Dichtungen Chopins.

Aber die Kunst verlangte mehr. Das kleine Interesse der Scholle, auf der er geboren, mußte sich dem großweltbürgerlichen zum Opfer bringen, und schon verliert

---

18 Paris.
19 Der russische Zar.

sich in seinen neueren Werken die zu specielle sarmatische Physiognomie, und ihr Ausdruck wird sich nach und nach zu jener allgemeinen idealen neigen, als deren Bildner uns seit lange die himmlischen Griechen gegolten, so daß wir auf einer andern Bahn am Ende uns wieder im Mozart begrüßen.

Ich sagte: „nach und nach"; denn gänzlich wird und soll er seine Abstammung nicht verläugnen. Aber um so mehr er sich von ihr entfernt, um so mehr seine Bedeutung für das Allgemeine der Kunst zunehmen wird. Sollten wir uns über die Bedeutung, die er zum Theil schon genommen, in schmalen Worten in etwas erklären, so müßten wir sagen, daß er zur Erkenntniß beitrage, deren Begründung immer dringlicher scheint: Ein Fortschritt unsrer Kunst erfolge erst mit einem Gewaltschritte der Künstler zu einer geistigen Aristokratie, nach deren Statuten die Kenntniß des niederen Handwerks nicht blos verlangt, sondern schon vorausgesetzt, und nach denen Niemand zugelassen würde, der nicht so viel Talent mitbrächte, das selbst zu leisten, was er von Andern fordert, also Phantasie, Gemüth und Geist – nach der ewigen Lehre: daß das Schönste unsrer Kunst nur der ersten entspringe, die es zum andern führe, über deren beider Vereinigung der Geist schwebe – und dies alles, um die höhere Epoche einer allgemeinen musikalischen Bildung herbeizuführen, wo über das Echte eben so wenig ein Zweifel herrsche wie über die zahllosen Gestalten, in denen es erscheinen könne, unter m u s i k a l i s c h aber jenes innere lebendige Mitsingen, jene thätigwerdende Mitleidenschaft, jene Fähigkeit des schnellen Aufnehmens und Wiedergebens zu verstehen sei, damit in der Vermählung des Componisten und Virtuosen zum Künstler, der Productivität und Reproductivität zur Künstlerschaft, dem Ziele der Kunst immer näher gekommen werde.

E u s e b i u s.

Robert Schumann: Rezension der *Nocturnes* op. 27, in: Neue Zeitschrift für Musik 4/1836, Nr. 40 vom 17. Mai, S. 168 (unter „Pianoforte. Kurze Stücke. (Fortsetzung)")

Da wir aber gerade bei den Notturnos stehen, so will ich gar nicht leugnen, wie mich während dieses Schreibens zwei neue von C h o p i n[20] in Cis-Moll und Des-Dur unaufhörlich beschäftigten, die ich, wie viele seiner früheren, (namentlich die in F-Dur und G-Moll) [op. 15, Nr. 1 und 3] neben denen von Field für Ideale dieser Gattung, ja für das Herzinnigste und Verklärteste halte, was nur in der Musik

---

20 2 Nocturnes. Oeuv. 27. (Breitkopf & Härtel)

erdacht werden könne. Lernen läßt es sich wohl nicht, wie man in so kleinem Raum so Unendliches sammeln könne: aber übe man sich in Bescheidenheit bei Betrachtung solch hoher dichterischen Vollendung; denn wie es hier vom Herzen quillt, u n - m i t t e l b a r , wie Goethe jenes Urausfließende nennt, übervoll, selig im Schmerz, unnachahmlich, laßt es uns bekennen und stolz sein auf den Mann unsrer Kunst.

Robert Schumann: Rezension des *Grand Duo concertant sur des thèmes de „Robert le diable"* für Klavier und Violoncello von Chopin und Auguste Franchomme, in: Neue Zeitschrift für Musik 4/1836, Nr. 46 vom 7. Juni, S. 191

Ein Stück für einen Salon, wo hinter gräflichen Schultern hin und wieder der Kopf eines berühmten Künstlers hervortaucht, also nicht für Theekränze, wo zur Conversation aufgespielt wird, sondern für gebildetste Cirkel, die dem Künstler die Achtung bezeigen, die sein Stand verdient. Es scheint mir durchaus von Chopin entworfen zu sein und Franchomme hatte zu Allem leicht ja zu sagen; denn was Chopin berührt, nimmt Gestalt und Geist an und auch in diesem kleinern Salonstyl drückt er sich mit einer Grazie und Vornehmheit aus, gegen die aller Anstand anderer brillant schreibender Componisten sammt ihrer ganzen Feinheit in der Luft zerfährt. –

Wäre der ganze Robert der Teufel voll solcher Gedanken, als Chopin aus ihm zu seinem Duo gewählt, so müßte man seinen Namen umtaufen. Jedenfalls zeigt sich auch hier der Finger Chopins, der sie so phantastisch ausgeführt, hier verhüllend, dort entschleiernd, daß sie einem noch lange im Ohr und Herzen fortklingen. Der Vorwurf der Länge, den ängstliche Virtuosen vielleicht dem Stücke machen, wäre nicht unrecht: auf der zwölften Seite erlahmt es sogar an Bewegung; ächt Chopin'sch aber reißt es dann auf der dreizehnten ungeduldig in die Saiten und nun geht es im Flug dem Ende mit seinen Wellenfiguren zu. Sollten wir noch hinzusetzen, daß wir das Duo bestens empfehlen?

Gottfried Wilhelm Fink: Rezension der 2 *Nocturnes* op. 27, in: Allgemeine Musikalische Zeitung 38/1836, Nr. 29 vom 20. Juli, Sp. 472/473

Wir haben von diesem bei einer grossen Anzahl tüchtiger Pianofortespieler u. Liebhaber des Instrumentes u. der neuen Dichtungsart für dasselbe sehr beliebten Componisten noch nichts gesehen u. gehört, was nicht durchaus in seiner ganz eigenthümlichen Weise erfunden u. durchgeführt worden wäre. Wir kennen aber fast Alles, nur sehr Weniges ausgenommen, z. B. das erste Werk [*Rondo* op. 1], was von ihm gedruckt erschienen ist. Das individuell Rallentirende, was der Componist selbst in seiner Spielweise mit eindringlich wirkender Freiheit ausüben soll, was auch selbst aus den Notenzeichen seiner Compositionen sich auffordernd herausstellt, so dass es oft nicht zu vermeiden ist; das Originelle seiner oft ganz fremdartigen, zuweilen schmerzlich aufreizenden Accordverbindungen; das tiefe Umschleiern der harmonischen Grundverhältnisse durch Vorausnahmen, Verzögerungen u. wunderlich trübende Durchgänge; das schnelle u. unerwartete Abbrechen in stechenden Dissonanzen; das überraschende Fortschreiten in treffend freundliche oder wehmüthige oder sanft schmelzende Melodieen u. Harmonieen, in denen er nie oder doch nur selten lange verweilt u. dergl. mehr – Alles dies, was diesem Componisten einen für sich u. in ganz eigener Weise stehenden Kunstcharakter gibt, der schlechterdings von Andern im Wesentlichen nicht nachgeahmt werden kann und, wo es äusserlich geschieht, nur zum grössten Nachtheil des Unüberlegten versucht wird, findet sich vereint in den beiden Sätzen dieses neuen Heftes im reichen Maasse u. doch so, dass es im Einzelnen neu ist, nur sich selbst im Hauptcharakter gleich, begünstigt noch vom Namen der Gebilde, Nocturnen, die in ihm keinen andern als einen schwärmerisch dunkeln Farbenton zulassen. Das Einzelne, nicht selten im Mantel der Nacht sich Bergende, kann u. soll nicht nach seiner Gestalt aus einander gelegt werden, da der ganze Zusammenhang der Dichtung mehr von der Ahnung gefühlt als vom Lichte des Tages verblendet sein will, das dem Schatten u. der Dämmerung nicht befreundet sein kann. Es ist der Traum, der seine Ringeltänze mit der Sehnsucht feiert, die sich den Schmerz erkohr, weil sie die Freude, die sie liebt, nicht wiederfinden konnte. Darum werden diese neuen Nocturnen wie die ältern, so verschieden sie auch von jenen sind, immer wieder vor allem weiblich gestimmten Herzen höchst anziehend sein. Es ist ein mährchenhafter Reiz darin, etwa wie wenn der Elfenkönig mit seinen Töchtern lockt. Es ist die Schwärmerei, die gern im Sternenschimmer durch die Haine spielt. Chopin's Freunde können sicher sein, dass sie ihn wiederfinden, wie sie ihn am Liebsten sehen.

Gottfried Wilhelm Fink: Rezension des *Klavierkonzerts f-Moll* op. 21, in: Allgemeine Musikalische Zeitung 38/1836, Nr. 33 vom 17. August, Sp. 537/542

Was das Eigenthümliche der Compositionsweise dieses Verfassers ausmacht, ist in frühern Beurtheilungen hinlänglich dargestellt worden, auch durch verbreiteten Gebrauch der Werke dieses Pianofortevirtuosen so allgemein bekannt, dass wir darüber nichts weiter hinzuzufügen haben. Wir geben also sogleich einen übersichtlichen

Umriss des Werkes nach der Originalpartitur.[21] Der erste Satz, Maestoso, 4/4, F moll, mit [Viertelnote] = 138 bezeichnet, beginnt in einer ziemlich ausgeführten Einleitung des vollen Orchesters mit folgendem Hauptgedanken: [Notenzitat Takte 1–11]

Im Quintsextaccorde pp. nur mit Streichinstrumenten schliessend, setzt das Soloinstrument in demselben Accorde ff ein, in die Hauptmelodie bald u. wirksam übergehend: [Notenzitat Takte 71–75]

An schicklichen Stellen wird natürlich die Melodie mit klaviermässigen Verzierungen in allerlei ungeraden oder nicht nach genauer Takteintheilung auszuführenden Olen [= Triolen, Quintolen usw.] geschmückt, das Melodische abermals angenehm lange genug gehalten, um die Hauptmelodie gehörig einzuprägen, ehe zu stärkern Bravouren fortgeschritten wird. Eine solche, zwar nicht ungewöhnliche, aber sachgemässe Behandlung hilft der Klarheit des Satzes bedeutend u. macht die folgenden Virtuosenpassagen desto erwünschter. Nachdem diese Bravourgänge in Chopin's Weise weder zu kurze noch zu lange Zeit in grössere Spannung versetzt haben, kehrt beim con anima ein neuer, aus dem ersten genommener, melodischer Satz in gutem Wechsel wieder, angenehm verziert, nur mehr als der erste mit den dem Verf. gewohnten Fortschritten etwas dunkler gefärbt, doch weniger als sonst. Diese dunkleren Schattirungen liegen in dieser Composition besonders weit mehr in Wechsel- u. Durchgangsnoten als in massenhaften Accordbewegungen, die hier durchaus nicht vorwalten; man könnte es im Accordenwechsel sogar einfach nennen; Nebentöne u. Figurenverschiedenheiten wirken das Hauptsächlichste. Die Instrumentalbegleitung des ersten Abschnittes, der in C moll schliesst, ist so einfach als möglich; nur Streichinstrumente geben die Accorde ohne allen Nebenschmuck, so dass der Solospieler gewisslich nicht bedeckt wird. Diese Einrichtung waltet im ganzen Concerte vor; nur selten u. dann vereinzelt lässt sich ausser dem Streichquartett noch ein Blasinstrument zum Solo des Pianoforte vernehmen, noch seltener treten einige, und dann nicht lange, zusammen. Am meisten noch mischen sich einige Blasinstrumente in der Weiterführung zum ersten Hauptabschnitt in C dur verschönernd ein, worauf das volle Orchester einen einleitenden Zwischensatz hören lässt, auf welchen das Soloinstrument seine erste Melodie in F moll einfach wieder zu Gehör bringt; es versteht sich, dass die Zwischenverzierungen nicht fehlen. As-dur herrscht bald mehr vor u. verliert sich im starken Wechsel u. vollen Bravouren in

---

21 Da eine gedruckte Partitur des Werkes erst 1865 erschien, muss Fink damals die Stichvorlage für Breitkopf & Härtel (Warschau, Nationalbibliothek, Mus. 215 Cim., Faksimile-Edition, hrsg. von Jan Ekier, Warschau, NIFC, 2005) in Leipzig eingesehen haben!

die Haupttonart, wo die Fortschreitung aus F moll nach G dur, durch die Septime auf C sogleich in F moll zurückgehend, zwar etwas Frappantes, aber natürlich nichts Unangenehmes hat, da es eben nur Durchgangsaccord ist. Im ersten Theile fand sich zwischen C moll u. D dur dasselbe. Die Wiederkehr gewinnt also noch das Symmetrische für sich, was in der Regel angenehm wirkt. Auch die Figuren stehen im Zusammenhange mit den frühern, so dass das Ganze für die Hörer nicht eben schwer aufzufassen ist.

Das Larghetto, 4/4, As dur, ♩ = 56, schliesst sich mit seiner 5taktigen Tutti-Einleitung genau an eine Idee des vorigen und beginnt sein Solo auf folgende einfach sangbare Weise: [Notenzitat Takte 6–17]

Nach einiger Triolen- u. Sextolen-Weiterspinnung erneut sich der Gesang mit Zwischenschmuck in 29, 27, 15, 14 auf den halben Takt u. ergeht sich in ähnlichen Wendungen, bis sich das Anfangsspiel der Instrumente kurz einwebt u. zum Tremolo derselben ein sehr verziertes Recit. appassionato einen wirksamen Zwischengesang im Unisono mit beiden Händen bildet, wozu die Blasinstrumente nur die recitativischen Zwischenschläge u. ein paar Füllungsaccorde zur Einleitung in die Cadenzen bringen, worauf das Thema noch einmal anklingt und in kurzer Haltung das sanft eingängliche Ganze, leise verschwimmend, beendet.

Der Schlusssatz, All. vivace, 3/4, F moll, ist in der Art eines Masurek mit folgendem Anfangsmotiv: [Notenzitat Takte 1–10]

Der 13 gedruckte Seiten lang durchgeführte Satz bewegt sich in seinen Bravouren grösstentheils in Triolen u. schliesst mit einem brillanten Solo in F dur gleichfalls in Triolen.

Es ist seinem Grundbaue nach offenbar einfacher angelegt u. für die Hörer übersichtlicher, fasslicher gehalten als das erste Concert. Eine Vergleichung beider in Hinsicht ihrer Schönheit würde vergeblich angestellt werden, weil man jetzt der Mehrzahl nach nicht nach dem Begriffe des Schönen, sondern nach willkürlichem Wohlgefallen zu urtheilen oder vielmehr zu schätzen beliebt, wobei freilich wenig oder nichts Begründetes gewonnen werden kann. Wir lassen uns daher auf eine solche Vergleichung auch nicht ein, meinen aber, es werde dieses zweite Concert um seiner leichtern Fasslichkeit willen höchst wahrscheinlich einen noch allgemeineren Eingang finden. Der Vortragende wird im Allgemeinen eben so viel zu thun haben als im ersten Concerte. Allerdings lässt sich das mehr oder minder Schwere, wie jedes Bezügliche, nicht so genau, wie mit Waage und Elle, messen; dem Einen fallen diese Art Bravourgänge schwerer, dem Andern jene: dennoch wird im Ganzen die Lösung dieser Aufgabe mit nicht geringern Schwierigkeiten zu ringen haben. Es empfiehlt sich also allen tüchtigen Pianofortespielern zur Erstärkung ihrer Fertigkeiten von selbst, so dass es Keiner unbeachtet lassen wird, der mit der Zeit fortgehen und sich von allen Seiten vervollkommnen will.

Robert Schumann: Rezension der *Variationen* op. 12,
in: Neue Zeitschrift für Musik 5/1836, Nr. 20 vom 6. September, S. 79

> Schwarze Röcke, seidne Strümpfe,
> Weiße, höfliche Manschetten,
> Sanfte Reden, Embrassiren –
> Ach! wenn sie nur Herzen hätten! –
>   H e i n e.[22]

Variationen für Pianoforte.
Dritter Gang.

G. M. O s b o r n e, Var. üb. e. Th. v. Donizetti. Op. 16. – 20 Gr. – Breitkopf u. Härtel. [… 6 weitere Variationswerke, u.a. von Friedrich Kalkbrenner, Charles Schuncke und Theodor Döhler], L u d w i g S c h u n c k e, Concertvar. üb. e. Th. v. Fr. Schubert. Op. 14. – Mit Orch. 2 Thlr. 12 Gr., Pfte all. 1 Thlr. – Breitkopf u. Härtel. Fr. C h o p i n, Var. üb. e. Th. aus Ludovic v. Herold u. Halevy. Op. 12. – 16 Gr. – Breitkopf u. H.

Die beste Recension über die meisten obiger Variationen las der Leser so eben im Motto. Sie gehören sämmtlich dem Salon oder dem Concertsaal an und halten sich, das letzte Heft ausgenommen, von aller poetischen Sphäre weit entfernt. Denn auch in diesem Genre muß C h o p i n der Preis zuerkannt werden. Jenem großen Schauspieler gleich, der auch als Lattenträger über das Theater gehend, vom Publicum jubelnd empfangen wurde, kann er seinen hohen Geist in keiner Lage verläugnen; was ihn umgibt, nimmt von ihm an und fügt sich, noch so spröde, seiner Meisterhand. Im Uebrigen versteht sich, daß die Variationen, zu seinen Originalwerken genommen, in keinen Anschlag gebracht werden können. [...]

---

22 Das Motto steht direkt unter der Titelei der ersten Seite dieser Nummer der Zeitschrift. Das Zitat stammt aus dem Prolog zu *Aus der Harzreise* (1824) aus Heinrich Heines *Buch der Lieder* (1. Ausgabe 1827).

Ludwig Rellstab: Rezension des *Klavierkonzerts f-Moll* op. 21,
in: Iris im Gebiete der Tonkunst 7/1836, Nr. 44 vom 28. Oktober, S. 174/175

Ein neues Concert von C h o p i n ist bei dem Ansehn und Einfluss, welchen sich dieser Componist jetzt im Gebiet des Klavierspiels erworben hat, eine w i c h t i g e Erscheinung, die auch der Redakteur der Iris mit Interesse betrachtet. In der Etude und im Concert sind die schwierigen Aufgaben an ihrer Stelle. Wir wollen damit nicht gesagt haben, daß jede Art der Schwierigkeit dort gut zu heißen sei. Das eine aber ist wenigstens der Ort, wo man das Schwere und durch das Schwere lernen soll, das andere der, wo man zeigen soll, daß man es erlernt und überwunden hat. Wenn daher der Componist dem Concertspieler solche Aufgaben stellt, so kann man ihn deshalb nicht tadeln. Das vorliegende Werk (Fmoll) ist, wie sich voraussehen läßt, s e h r schwierig; allein sei es, daß das Auge, welches sich so gut übt wie die Hand, sich nach und nach an das Lesen C h o p i nscher Aufgaben gewöhnt hat, oder daß sich auch hier die älteren Wendungen zu wiederholen anfangen, oder endlich, daß der Componist sich nicht mehr ganz so im Aufsuchen des Allerseltsamsten und Schwierigsten gefällt wie sonst – genug, wir lasen dieses Concert schon mit einer gewissen Behaglichkeit, und es erschien uns durchaus nicht so völlig unnatürlich wie manche früheren Arbeiten. Dessenungeachtet stellt Herr C h o p i n seinen Spielern, wie sich leicht denken läßt, immer noch außerordentlich schwierige und ungewöhnliche Preisfragen. Selten wird man eine Passage finden, wie andere sie zu setzen pflegen, selten eine reine Tonleiter, einen gewöhnlich gebrochenen Akkord; seine Vorliebe für sehr gesperrte Lagen und schwierige Griffe hat der Componist beibehalten. Doch das versteht sich bei einer Chopinschen Composition, die darauf berechnet ist, öffentlich damit zu glänzen, ja Erstaunen zu erregen, eigentlich ganz von selbst. Wir wollen also davon unsere Leser nicht weiter unterhalten, es sei denn, daß ein außerordentlicher Fall uns dazu veranlaßte. Betrachten wir daher die Composition als solche näher. Dies hat freilich einige Schwierigkeiten bei einem mit Orchester gedachten Werke, und einem Orchester, welches zuverlässig keine unbedeutende Rolle spielt. Doch ist die Klavierstimme, auch was die Orchesterparthie anlangt, sehr vollständig arrangirt, und die w e s e n t l i c h e n Eigenschaften der Composition lassen sich gewiß daraus erkennen. Zuerst müssen wir bekennen, daß uns die Tutti sämmtlich sehr wohl gefallen. Es herrscht durchweg ein edler Stil darin; die Harmonie ist zwar nicht ganz frei von dem, was man g e s u c h t nennt, allein sie bewegt sich dafür auch nie in trivialen Wendungen, sondern es spricht sich auch darin ein höheres Kunstgefühl aus. Die rhythmischen Effekte sind oft sehr schön. Nur wäre es uns lieb gewesen, hie und da wenigstens Spuren einer solideren

Arbeit zu entdecken; doch wie emsig der Componist auch für sein Solospiel den Gang der Stimmen herausrechnet, um schöne Effecte zu machen, für das Tutti ist er darin nicht so aufmerksam gewesen. Die Soli, die Hauptsache für ein Virtuosenconcert, tragen ebenfalls alle den Charakter eines edleren Geschmackes, wenngleich derselbe sich nicht ganz frei von Bizarrerien hält, nicht durch das Prinzip der E i n f a c h h e i t (man glaubt nicht, wie unendlich wichtig dies für die Kunst ist) geläutert erscheint. Doch ist hier ein schönes verschmolzenes Spiel durchaus nothwendig, um den rechten Gesichtspunkt für das Werk aufzufassen, seine Strahlen concentrirt in den Brennpunkt der Wirksamkeit fallen zu lassen. Wir finden einen Reichthum reiner Passagen, einzelne höchst geschmackvolle und pikante Verzierungen, fein und sinnig calculirte Combinationen in der Stimmenführung; besonders aber geht der Componist darauf aus, keinen Finger unbeschäftigt zu lassen, sondern jedem noch hie und da eine kleine Nebenarbeit zu der Hauptarbeit aufzulegen. Genug, das Concert interessirt sehr; schade nur, daß kein rechter Bau darin ist, daß es mehr eine Sammlung schwerer Details als ein überdachtes Ganze bildet. Selbst in kleinen Abschnitten merken wir diesen Mangel höherer Formenbildung, und sogar in den Passagen fehlt das, was man Periodenbau derselben nennt, und was z. B. Dusseck [sic!] so sehr schön hatte. – Wir hegen die Hoffnung, im Laufe des Winters das Concert einmal öffentlich zu hören, denn jetzt ist es ein Ehrenpunkt für jeden Klavierspieler, Chopin zu spielen.

Robert Schumann: Rezension des *Klaviertrios g-Moll* op. 8, in: Neue Zeitschrift für Musik 5/1836, Nr. 52 vom 27. Dezember, S. 207–208 (unter „Trio's. (Schluß.)")

Bei Besprechung der noch übrigen Trio's von M o s c h e l e s [op. 84], C h o p i n [op. 8] und S c h u b e r t [op. 99][23] kommt mir allerdings zu Statten, daß ich sie gehört und leidlich genug, das erstere nämlich einigemal vom Componisten selbst, das andere von Clara Wieck und den Gebrüdern Müller und das Schubert'sche von Mendelssohn und David.

Welche hohe Stellen diesen Componisten in unsern Blättern gesichert sind, braucht nicht wiederholt zu werden. Ueber Geist und Wesen ihrer Composition findet sich an verschiedenen Orten mit Wärme und Kenntniß Geschriebenes.

[...]

---

23 Titel und Opuszahlen der drei Trios als Anmerkung unten auf der Seite, bei Chopin: 1stes Trio f. Pf., Viol. u. Vcello. W. 8. – 1 Thlr. 20 Gr. Bei Kistner.

Vom Trio von C h o p i n setze ich voraus, daß es, schon vor einigen Jahren erschienen[24], den Meisten der Leser bekannt ist. Kann man es Florestan verdenken, wenn er sich etwas darauf einbildet, den wie aus einer unbekannten Welt kommenden Jüngling zuerst, leider an einem sehr einschläfernden Ort [1831 in der Allgemeinen Musikalischen Zeitung], in die Oeffentlichkeit eingeführt zu haben? Und wie hat Chopin die Prophezeiung wahr gemacht, wie ist er unbefleckt und hochadelig aus dem Kampf mit heimtückischen Pfaffen und Ignoranten vorgegangen, wie strebt er noch immer, und nur einfacher und künstlerischer! Denn auch das Trio gehört Chopins früherer Periode an, wo er dem Virtuosen noch etwas Vorrecht einräumte. Wer wollte aber der Entwickelung einer solchen abweichenden Eigenthümlichkeit künstlich vorgreifen, dazu einer solchen energischen Natur, die sich eher selbst aufriebe, als sich von Andern ein Gesetz geben zu lassen! So hat Chopin schon verschiedene Stadien zurückgelegt, immer vollständig, immer siegreich; das Schwierigste ist ihm jetzt zum Kinderspiel worden, daß er es wegwirft und als eine echte Künstlernatur das Einfachere vorzieht. – Was könnte ich über dieses Trio sagen, was sich nicht jeder gefühlvolle Mensch selbst darüber gesagt hätte! Ist es denn nicht so edel als möglich, so schwärmerisch, wie noch kein Dichter gesungen hat, vollkommen im Kleinsten wie im Ganzen, jede Note Musik und Leben? Armer Berliner Recensent, der du von all dieser Schönheit noch nichts geahnet, nie etwas ahnen wirst, armer Mann![25]

Rudolf Hirsch: Biographie Chopins,
in: *Gallerie Lebender Tondichter. Biographisch-kritischer Beitrag,* Wien 1836, S. 21–22

Chopin
– *Friedrich* –

C o m p o s i t e u r und C l a v i e r v i r t u o s e,

(Geboren um 1804.)

Friedrich C h o p i n, ein Schüler des Warschauer Conservatoriums, ein College des [Tomasz Napoleon] v. N i d e c k i, Capellmeisters bei dem Theater in der Leopoldstadt, von welchem sich in diesem Buche eine biographische Skizze befindet

---

24 Das *Trio* entstand 1828/29 und erschien 1833 bei Kistner in Leipzig.
25 Ludwig Rellstab.

[S. 99 ff.], ist um das Jahr 1804 geboren; er ist der Sohn eines Professors der französischen Sprache zu Warschau.

Vor einigen Jahren [1829 und 1831] hielt sich C h o p i n in Wien auf, gegenwärtig soll er an dem Conservatorium der Musik zu Paris Professor sein. Ch. ist als Claviervirtuose sehr schätzenswerth; als Componist für sein Instrument hat er eine unbestrittene Originalität und verdiente in seinen Werken weit mehr cultivirt zu werden, als es gegenwärtig bei uns geschieht.

Von dem Leben C h o p i n' s meldet kein Lexikon oder musikalisches Werk etwas; die wenigen Daten, welche ich hier mitgetheilt, verdanke ich einem entfernten Bekannten dieses geniereichen Mannes. – Ich kenne von den Compositionen Ch's. ein großes Concert [op. 11], Variationen über ein Thema aus dem „Don Juan" [op. 2] und zwei Hefte Mazurken [wahrscheinlich op. 6 und 7], die voll Originalität sind. Sein Satz ist sehr kunstreich, fordert die geübtesten, denkendsten Spieler. Ch. gefällt sich in einem Stile, der manchmal fast gar nicht ausführbar ist, da seine Accorde eine solche Spannung der Hände fordern, wie sie nicht der zehnte Spieler hat; man ahnet oft gar nicht die Schwierigkeiten seiner Passagen.

Im Auslande genießen seine Werke, deren zwar nicht über zwölf Nummern [recte: ca. 20] erschienen sind, eine ausgezeichnete Anerkennung; ein Beweis mehr, daß es nicht nöthig sei, viel zu schreiben, um aufzufallen und seine Anhänger zu finden.

Nach dem Conterfei dieses seltenen Talentes, das in Mainz erschien, zu urtheilen, ist C h o p i n ein ausgezeichnet schöner Mann, voll Ernst und Geist im Antlitz.

Mitten in Paris, in Frankreich so zu schreiben, wie C h o p i n – seine Arbeiten können mit den Producten eines H e r z, A d a m, K a l k b r e n n e r etc. etc. nicht verglichen werden – und nicht dem Zeitschwindel anheimfallen: fürwahr, dazu braucht es innere Kraft, ein wahres Erglühen für die Kunst und ihre Kinder.

[Die außerordentliche Fehlerhaftigkeit dieses Artikels ist zeittypisch und den damaligen beschränkten Kommunikationsmöglichkeiten geschuldet.]

Gottfried Wilhelm Fink: Rezension der *Ballade g-Moll* op. 23,
in: Allgemeine Musikalische Zeitung 39/1837, Nr. 2 vom 11. Januar, Sp. 25–26

Musikalisches Album.

Album Musical. Sammlung der neuesten Originalcompositionen für Piano und Gesang von *F. Chopin, F. Hünten, F. Liszt, C. Löwe, F. Mendelssohn, G. Meyerbeer,*

Panseron, L. Spohr, poetisch eröffnet von *Fr. Rückert*. Leipzig, bei Breitkopf u. Härtel. Pr. 4 Thlr. Prachtausgabe 6 Thlr.

[...]

Das erste musikalische Stück ist eine Ballade [op. 23] ohne Worte für's Pianof. von Chopin. Hat man Lieder ohne Worte, warum soll man nicht auch Balladen ohne Worte haben? Ueberhaupt liebt es die neuere Musik, Geschichten in Tönen zu dichten. Es würde zu weit führen und hier nicht am Orte sein, wollte ich mich auf die pedantische Frage einlassen, ob man in dieser Romantik zu weit gehe: angemessener wird es sein, von dem Eindrucke zu sprechen, den diese Ballade auf mich und mehrere Hörer der Töne dieses Sternbeschauers der Nacht hervorbrachte. Anfangs war es durchaus kein günstiger; zu schroff und seltsam trat mir Manches entgegen, und hätte ich nach dem ersten Anhören mein Urtheil abzugeben gehabt, hätte ich nur achselzuckend ehrlich herausgesagt: Mir ist diese Geschichte zu wunderlich! Das thue ich aber nie, halte es vielmehr für pflicht- und ehrvergessen, sobald von einem kritischen Urtheile die Rede ist. Ich habe nun diese Ballade 5mal gehört und sie hat mir immer besser gefallen. Vielleicht ergeht es Andern eben so. Sie ist zu eigenthümlich und will aufgefasst sein; selbst wenn sie gut vorgetragen wird, werden dennoch die Meisten wohlthun, wenn sie ihr Urtheil erst nach öfterm Hören abgeben. Der Vortrag derselben ist nicht leicht; sie verlangt Spieler, die mit Chopin's Compositionen vertraut sind, die ich öfter geschildert habe. Es bliebe nichts übrig, als eine dichterische Auslegung des Gedichts zu geben, die, nicht schwierig, Jeder sich selbst am Besten gibt. –

Robert Schumann: Rezension über den *Walzer* op. 18, den *Bolero* op. 19 und die 2 *Polonaisen* op. 26, in: Neue Zeitschrift für Musik 6/1837, Nr. 40 vom 19. Mai, S. 159/160

Bericht an Jeanquirit in Augsburg
über
den letzten kunsthistorischen Ball beim Redacteur *.*.

Lies und staune, Geliebter! Der Redacteur der „neu'sten mus. Zeitschrift" pflegt nämlich alljährlich wenigstens einmal eine Art kunsthistorischen Balles zu geben: die Geladenen denken ihretwegen; der Fuchs lächelt aber ganz heimlich dazu, da er sich dadurch nur des verdrüßlichen Durchgehens der Tanzliteratur überheben, vielleicht auch des Eindrucks der Musik auf das Publicum um so sicherer sein will – mit einem Worte, da er mit dem Feste Kritik, ja die lebendigste bezweckt. Du sollst den Patron noch kennen lernen. Zwar waren auch mir Gerüchte über die sonderbare wenig tanzliche Musik, die wir als seine Maschinen daselbst abschleifen müssen an den Füßen, zugekommen; indeß, wie dürfte ein junger Künstler solche Einladung ausschlagen? Wallfahrteten wir nicht im Gegentheil geschmückten Opferthieren gleich und schaarenweise in den Festsaal? Hat der Redacteur etwa keine Töchter, bei denen sich mit Vortheil zu insinuiren, – eine ungemein lang, die viel recensiren soll in der „Neusten", und dann eine jüngere, eigentlich Malerin, die Unschuld selbst, – Mädchen, Jeanquirit, die ein grenzenloses Unheil über mich gebracht! Ueberhaupt aber wünschte ich dich an jenem Abend mehr als je her. Auf- und abwandelnde Componisten, zusehende schöne Mütter von Dilettantinnen, der **sche Gesandte mit Schwester, Musikverleger in Röcken, ein Paar reiche Jüdinnen, an Säulen ange-lehnte Davidsbündler, – kurz nur mit Mühe konnte ich durch und zur Mitredactri-ce (A m b r o s i a heißt die Riesin), sie zur ersten Polonaise aufzuziehen. (Unten kannst du das Tanzprogramm lesen*). Viel sprachen wir zusammen, z. B. ich über das eigentliche Wesen der Polonaise, und wie wir uns auch darin als Deutsche zeig-ten, daß wir selbst im Tanz den verschiedenartigsten Völkern nachfußten, und daß Strauß in dieser Hinsicht (und vielleicht nur in dieser, schaltete Ambrosia ein) ein wahrer Heiland, und daß der letzte Tact der Polonaise mit seinem Schlußfall etwas Trauriges für mich habe u. dgl.. Seit der Eroberung von Warschau, bemerkte meine

---

*) Tanzordnung
Erste Abtheilung.
Große pathetische Polonaise v. J. N o w a k o w s k i. Op. 11 –
Walzer von F. C h o p i n. Op. 12 [recte: 18].
[… 3 weitere Werke von J. Brzowsky, C. H. Zöllner und F. Ries].

In der Pause: Boleros [sic!] von Chopin. Op. 19

Zweite Abtheilung.
[… 3 Werke von C. Krägen, Liszt und E. Wolff].
Zwei Polonaisen von C h o p i n. Op. 22 [recte: 26].

Anm.: Diese eher novellistische Rezension ist nur verständlich, wenn man weiß, dass sich hinter dem Pseudonym Jeanquirit der Pianist und Komponist Stephen Heller, damals in Augsburg tätig, verbirgt, der auch Mitarbeiter der Neuen Zeitschrift für Musik war. Hinter „Ambrosia" dürfte sich eine musikali-sche Freundin Schumanns (Henriette Voigt?), hinter „Beda" wahrscheinlich die seit September 1837 mit Schumann verlobte Clara Wieck verbergen. Der Liederkomponist Carl Banck, bis 1836 Mitarbeiter der Neuen Zeitschrift für Musik, hatte sich zum Gegner Schumanns gewandelt, zumal er sich Hoffnungen auf Clara Wieck machte. Schumann hatte sich zuvor über ihn lustig gemacht, was er auch später noch öfter tat.

Tänzerin, tanze auch ich diesen Tanz immer mit einer Furcht, es möchte etwa ein Kosak eintreten mit einem Verdict – die armen Polen! seufzte sie, – meine B e d a spielt Chopin nie ohne Thränen. . (I c h) Wie edel Sie fühlen, – und wie artig melodiös ist auch die Polonaise dieses neuen polnischen Componisten [Nowakowski], die wir soeben tanzen. (S i e) In der That, das Trio spricht mich sehr an, aber wie sehr à la Chopin! – So hatte sie denn die romantische Schule zum zweitenmal bei den Haaren hergezogen, mich über solche zu erforschen. Mit aller Liebenswürdigkeit und Schlauheit verfuhr ich, vortheilhaftesten Eindruck für mich und künftige Werke aus dem Gespräche zu ziehen; immer lästiger wurde mir's aber, je mehr sie mich mit ihren liebedurstigen Augen beschoß. Zum Glück endigte der Tanz. Kaum abgetreten rief sie mich zurück und flüsterte: „die letzte Polonaise von Chopin an so künstlerischer Hand zu feiern, würde mich" – mich glücklich machen, schloß ich mich verbeugend. Eine Schlacht war gewonnen, aber der Roman begann erst. Mein Nächstes war, B e d a, die jüngere Schwester, zum Chopin'schen Walzer [op. 18] aufzusuchen. Wunder nahm es mich, daß mir der Engelskopf, den ich heute zum erstenmal sah, zusagte, den Tanz nämlich und überhaupt, da mir E u s e b i u s einen Augenblick zuvor verstimmt genug gesagt, sie hätte ihm ihn hocherröthend verweigert. Kurz, mit mir tanzte sie. Schwebte und jubelte ich aber je, in diesen Augenblicken war's. Zwar konnte ich nur einige „Ja" aus ihr hervorlocken, aber diese sprach sie so seelenvoll, so fein nüancirt in ihren verschiedenen Beziehungen, daß ich immer lauter fortschmetterte als Nachtigall. Beda, glaub' ich, schwiege eher, als daß sie ein widersprechendes Nein über ihre Lippen bringen könnte: um so unbegreiflicher, Jeanquirit, war mir der Korb an Euseb. Als uns nun Chopin's Körper- und Geisterhebender Walzer immer tiefer einhüllte in seine dunklen Fluthen und Beda immer schwermüthiger in das Gedränge blickte, lenkte ich das Gespräch leise auf Chopin selbst. Kaum, daß sie den Namen gehört, als sie mich zum erstenmal ganz anblickte mit großen guten Augen. „Und Sie kennen ihn?" Ich gab zu. „Und haben ihn gehört?" Ihre Gestalt ward immer hehrer. „Und haben ihn sprechen gehört?" Und wie ich ihr jetzt erzählte, daß es schon ein unvergeßlich Bild gäbe, ihn wie einen träumenden Seher am Klavier sitzen zu sehen, und wie man sich bei seinem Spiele wie der von ihm erschaffene Traum vorkäme, und wie er die heillose Gewohnheit habe, nach dem Schlusse jedes Stückes mit einem Finger über die pfeifende Claviatur hinzufahren, sich gleichsam mit Gewalt von seinem Traum loszumachen, und wie er sein zartes Leben schonen müsse, – schmiegte sie sich immer ängstlich freudiger an mich an und wollte mehr und mehr über ihn wissen. Chopin, schöner Herzensräuber, niemals beneidete ich dich, aber in dieser Minute wahrhaftig stark. Im

Grunde aber, Jeanquirit, war ich dumm, und nichts als der Pinsel, der ihr das Bild ihres Heiligen erst recht kußnahe vor die Seele geführt, und wirklich dumm. „Bin ich kindisch", sagte sie am Schlußstretto, „wenn ich Ihnen gestehe, daß ich mir, ohne ihn je gesehen zu haben, sein Bild gemalt, – und holen will ich's Ihnen, und sagen Sie mir, ob ich recht getroffen, – und ja Niemandem etwas davon?" Bei den letzten Worten fühlte ich ihren Händedruck. Am Abschied bat ich sie noch um einen Tanz: „sie hätte keinen mehr, als die letzte Chopin'sche Polonaise, und mit Freuden tanze sie mit mir." Erlaß mir, Bester, dir von meiner Langweile während der folgenden Tänze zu erzählen. [...]

„aber Frl. Beda fängt so eben den Boleros [sic!, op. 19 von Chopin] an..". Grundes genug, ihm [Hrn. de Knapp = Carl Banck] den Rücken zu kehren. Du kennst diese zarte liebetrunkene Composition, dies Bild von südlicher Gluth und Schüchternheit, von Hingebung und Zurückhaltung – und nun Beda mit schwärmerischer Lieblichkeit am Clavier, das Bild ihres Geliebten in und vielleicht am Herzen, mir, m i r es zu zeigen.. Fort lief ich beim letzten Gedanken und hoffte nur noch von der letzten Polonaise. [...]

Robert Schumann: Rezension über das *Rondeau à la Mazur* op. 5,
in: Neue Zeitschrift für Musik 6/1837, Nr. 41 vom 23. Mai, S. 163, 165
(unter „Rondo's für Pianoforte.")

Das Rondeau von C h o p i n ist vielleicht schon im achtzehnten Jahre geschrieben [1826/27, erschienen 1828], aber erst vor kurzem erschienen. Die große Jugend des Componisten ließe sich höchstens an einigen verwickelten Stellen, aus denen er sich nicht so schnell herauszufinden weiß, errathen (so am Schluß der S. 6.), im übrigen ist das Rondo durch und durch Chopin'sch, mithin schön, schwärmerisch, voll Grazie. Wer ihn noch nicht kennt, wird am Besten mit diesem Stück den Anfang machen.

Heinrich Heine: [Über Chopin],
in: *Über die französische Bühne. Vertraute Briefe an August Lewald, 10. Brief,*
in: Allgemeine Theater-Revue 1837. Hrsg. von August Lewald. Dritter Jahrgang.
Für 1838, *10. Brief*, S. 235–248, dort S. 247 (auch: Burger, S. 159, Mann,
S. 104/105). Geschrieben im Mai 1837 in einem Dorf bei Paris.

Es wäre ungerecht, wenn ich bei dieser Gelegenheit nicht eines Pianisten erwähnen wollte, der neben Lißt [sic!] am meisten gefeiert wird. Es ist Chopin, und dieser kann zugleich als Beispiel dienen, wie es einem außerordentlichen Menschen nicht genügt, in der technischen Vollendung mit den Besten seines Faches rivalisiren zu können. Chopin ist nicht damit zufrieden, daß seine Hände, ob ihrer Fertigkeit, von anderen Händen beifällig beklatscht werden; er strebt nach einem besseren Lorbeer, seine Finger sind nur die Diener seiner Seele und diese wird applaudirt von Leuten, die nicht bloß mit den Ohren hören, sondern auch mit der Seele. Er ist daher der Liebling jener Elite, die in der Musik die höchsten Geistesgenüsse sucht, sein Ruhm ist aristokratischer Art, sein Ruhm ist parfümirt von den Lobsprüchen der guten Gesellschaft, er ist vornehm wie seine Person.

Chopin ist von französischen Eltern in Polen geboren und hat einen Theil seiner Erziehung in Deutschland genossen. Diese Einflüsse dreier Nationalitäten machen seine Persönlichkeit zu einer höchst merkwürdigen Erscheinung; er hat sich nämlich das Beste angeeignet, wodurch sich die drei Völker auszeichnen. Polen gab ihm seinen chevaleresken Sinn und seinen geschichtlichen Schmerz, Frankreich gab ihm seine leichte Anmuth, seine Grazie, Deutschland gab ihm den romantischen Tiefsinn... Die Natur aber gab ihm eine zierliche, schlanke, etwas schmächtige Gestalt, das edelste Herz und das Genie. Ja, dem Chopin muß man Genie zusprechen, in der vollen Bedeutung des Worts; er ist nicht bloß Virtuose, er ist auch Poet, er kann uns die Poesie, die in seiner Seele lebt, zur Anschauung bringen, er ist Tondichter, und nichts gleicht dem Genuß, den er uns verschafft, wenn er am Clavier sitzt und improvisirt. Er ist alsdann weder Pole, noch Franzose, noch Deutscher, er verräth dann einen weit höheren Ursprung, man merkt alsdann, er stammt aus dem Lande Mozarts, Raffaels, Goethes, sein wahres Vaterland ist das Traumreich der Poesie. Wenn er am Clavier sizt [sic!] und improvisirt, ist es mir, als besuche mich ein Landsmann aus der geliebten Heimath und erzähle mir die kuriosesten Dinge, die während meiner Abwesenheit dort passirt sind... Manchmal möchte' ich ihn mit Fragen unterbrechen: Und wie gehts der schönen Nixe, die ihren silbernen Schleier so kokett um die grünen Locken zu binden wußte? Verfolgt sie noch immer der weißbärtige Meergott mit seiner närrisch abgestandenen Liebe? Sind bei uns die Rosen noch immer so flammenstolz? Singen die Bäume noch immer so schön im Mondschein?...

Robert Schumann: Rezension der 12 *Etüden* op. 25,
in: Neue Zeitschrift für Musik 7/1837, Nr. 50 vom 22. Dezember, S. 199/200.

Museum.

5.

12 E t u d e n f ü r P i a n o f o r t e

von

Friedrich Chopin

* *
*

[op. 25. – Zwei Hefte. – Breitkopf & Härtel.]

Wie dürfte denn dieser in unserm Museum fehlen, auf den wir so oft schon
gedeutet, wie auf einen seltenen Stern in später Nachtstunde! Wohin seine Bahn
geht und führt, wie lange, wie glänzend noch, wer weiß es? So oft er sich aber zeigte, war's dasselbe tiefdunkele Glühen, derselbe Kern des Lichts, dieselbe Schärfe,
daß ihn hätte ein Kind herausfinden müssen. Bei diesen Etuden kömmt mir noch
zu Statten, daß ich sie meist von Chopin selbst gehört, und „sehr à la Chopin spielt
er selbige" flüsterte mir Florestan dabei in's Ohr. Denke man sich, eine Aeolsharfe
hätte alle Tonleitern und es würfe diese eine künstlerische Hand in allerhand phantastischen Verzierungen durcheinander, doch so, daß immer ein tieferer Grundton
und eine weich fortsingende höhere Stimme hörbar – und man hat ungefähr ein
Bild seines Spieles. Kein Wunder aber, daß uns gerade die Stücke die liebsten geworden, die wir von ihm gehört, und so sei denn vor Allem die erste in As-Dur
erwähnt, mehr ein Gedicht als eine Etude. Man irrt aber, wenn man meint, er
hätte da jede der kleinen Noten deutlich hören lassen; es war mehr ein Wogen des
As-Dur-Accordes, vom Pedal hier und da von Neuem in die Höhe gehoben; aber
durch die Harmonieen hindurch vernahm man in großen Tönen Melodie, eine
wundersame, und nur in der Mitte trat einmal neben jenem Hauptgesang auch
eine Tenorstimme aus den Accorden deutlicher hervor. Nach der Etude wird's Einem, wie nach einem sel'gen Bild, im Traum gesehen, das man, schon halbwach,
noch einmal erhaschen möchte; reden ließ sich wenig darüber und loben gar nicht.
Er kam alsbald zur andern in F-Moll, die zweite im Buch, ebenfalls eine, in der
sich einem seine Eigenthümlichkeit unvergeßlich einprägt, so reizend, träumerisch und leise, etwa wie das Singen eines Kindes im Schlafe. Wiederum schön,
aber wenig neu im Charakter als in der Figur folgte die in F-Dur; hier galt es mehr,
die Bravour zu zeigen, die liebenswürdigste, und wir mußten den Meister sehr

darum rühmen... Doch wozu der beschreibenden Worte! Sind sie doch sämmtlich Zeichen der kühnen, ihm innewohnenden Schöpferkraft, wahrhafte Dichtergebilde, im Einzelnen nicht ohne kleine Flecken, im Ganzen immerhin mächtig und ergreifend. Meine aufrichtigste Meinung indeß nicht zu verschweigen, so scheint mir allerdings das Totalgewicht der früheren großen Sammlung bedeutender. Es kann dies aber keinen Verdacht etwa auf eine Verringerung von Chopin's Kunstnatur oder auf ein Rückwärtsgekommensein abgeben, da diese jetzt erschienenen ziemlich alle mit jenen zugleich entstanden und nur einzelne, denen man auch ihre größere Meisterschaft ansieht, wie die erste in As und die letzte prachtvolle in C-Moll, erst vor Kurzem. Daß unser Freund überhaupt aber jetzt wenig schafft und Werke größeren Umfangs gar nicht, ist leider auch wahr, und daran mag wohl das spielende lockre Paris einige Schuld haben. Nehmen wir indeß lieber an, daß es nach so vielen Stürmen in einer Künstlerbrust allerdings einiger Ruhe bedarf, und daß er dann vielleicht, neu gestärkt, den ferneren Sonnen zueilen wird, deren uns der Genius immer neue enthüllt.

E u s e b i u s.

Robert Schumann: Rezension des *Impromptus As-Dur* op. 29,
der 4 *Mazurken* op. 30 und des *Scherzo b-Moll* op. 31,
in: Neue Zeitschrift für Musik 9/1838, Nr. 45 vom 4. Dezember, S. 179/180

Chopin kann schon gar nichts mehr schreiben, wo man nicht im 7ten, 8ten Tacte ausrufen müßte: „das ist von ihm!" Man hat das Manier genannt und gesagt, er schreite nicht vorwärts. Aber man sollte dankbarer sein. Ist es denn nicht dieselbe originelle Kraft, die euch schon aus seinen ersten Werken so wunderbar entgegenleuchtet, im ersten Augenblick euch verwirrt gemacht, später euch entzückt hat? und wenn er euch eine Reihe der seltensten Schöpfungen gegeben und ihr ihn leichter versteht, verlangt ihr ihn auf einmal anders? Das hieße einen Granatenbaum umhacken, weil er immer Granaten, euch jährlich dieselben Früchte wiederbringt. Es sind aber bei ihm nicht einmal dieselben, der Stamm wohl der nämliche, die Früchte aber in Geschmack und Wuchs die verschiedenartigsten. So wüßte ich obigem I m p r o m [p] t u , so wenig es im ganzen Umkreis seiner Werke zu bedeuten hat, kaum eine andere Chopin'sche Composition zu vergleichen; es ist wiederum so sein in der Form, eine Cantilene zu Anfang und Ende von reizendem Figurenwerk eingeschlossen, so ein eigentliches Improm[p]tu, nichts mehr und nichts weniger, daß ihm nichts anderes seiner Composition an die Seite zu stellen. Das S c h e r z o erinnert in seinem leidenschaftlichen Charakter schon mehr an seinen Vorgänger: immerhin bleibt es ein höchst fesselndes Stück, nicht uneben einem Lord Byron'schen Gedicht zu vergleichen, so zart, so keck, so liebe- wie verachtungsvoll. Für Alle paßt das freilich nicht. Die M a z u r e k hat Chopin gleichfalls zur kleinen Kunstform emporgehoben; so viele er geschrieben, so gleichen sich nur wenige. Irgend einen poetischen Zug, etwas neues in der Form oder im Ausdruck hat fast jede. So ist es in der zweiten der obengenannten das Streben der H-Moll-Tonart nach Fis-Moll, wie sie denn auch (man merkt es kaum) in Fis schließt; in der zweiten das Schwanken der Tonarten zwischen weicher und harter, bis endlich die große Terz gewinnt; so in der letzten, die jedoch eine matte Strophe (auf S. 13) hat, der plötzliche Schluß mit den Quinten, über die die deutschen Cantoren die Hände über die Köpfe zusammenschlagen werden. Eine Bemerkung beiläufig: die verschiedenen Zeitalter hören auch verschieden. In den besten Kirchenwerken der alten Italiener findet man Quintenfortschreitungen, sie müssen ihnen also nicht schlecht geklungen haben. Bei Bach und Händel kommen ebenfalls welche vor, doch in gebrochener Weise, und überhaupt selten; die große Kunst der Stimmenverflechtung mied alle Parallelgänge. In der Mozart'schen Periode verschwinden sie gänzlich. Nun trabten die großen Theoretiker hinterher und verboten bei Todesstrafe, bis wieder Beethoven auftrat und die schönsten Quinten einfließen ließ, namentlich in chromatischer Folge. Nun soll natürlich ein so chromatischer Quintengang, wird er etwa zwanzig Tacte lang fortgesetzt, nicht als etwas Treffliches, sondern als etwas äußerst Schlechtes ausgezeichnet werden, gleichfalls soll man dergleichen aber auch nicht einzeln aus dem Ganzen herausheben, sondern in Bezug zum Vorhergehenden, im Zusammenhang hören, und dann wüßte ich nicht, wer es uns verwehren könnte, nach einer Figur wie diese:

[Notenzitat *Mazurka cis-Moll* op. 30, Nr. 4, Takte 15–16]

gegen den Schluß hin so zu schreiben:

[Notenzitat *Mazurka cis-Moll* op. 30, Nr. 4, Takte 124–127]

und dann etwa zu schließen wie folgt:

[Notenzitat *Mazurka cis-Moll* op. 30, Nr. 4, Takte 129–139 (Schluss)]

Und so seid mir gegrüßt, liebe Quinten! Dem Schüler streichen wir weg, was schülerhaft; dem schwärmerischen Jüngling hören wir gern zu und vom Meister lassen wir uns gar Alles gefallen, was schön klingt und singt.

Robert Schumann: Rezension der 4 *Mazurken* op. 33, der 3 *Walzer* op. 34
und der *Préludes* op. 28,
in: Neue Zeitschrift für Musik 11/1839, Nr. 41 vom 19. November, S. 161–163
(unter „Phantasien, Capricen etc. für Pianoforte. (Schluß.)")

Von neuen Compositionen C h o p i n's haben wir, außer ein Heft Mazurken und drei Walzern, eine merkwürdige Sammlung von Präludien zu erwähnen. Er gestaltet sich immer lichter und leichter – oder ist's Gewöhnung an seine Weise? – So werden die Mazurken [op. 33] im Augenblick anmuthen und scheinen uns populärer als die frühern: vor allen müssen die drei Walzer [op. 34] gefallen, andern Schlages als die gewöhnlichen, und in der Art, wie sie nur einem Chopin beikommen können, wenn er in das Tanzgemenge, das er eben hebt durch sein Vorspielen, großkünstlerisch hineinsieht und andere Dinge denkend, als was da getanzt wird. Ein so fluthendes Leben bewegt sich darin, daß sie wirklich im Tanzsalon improvisirt zu sein scheinen. Die Präludien [op. 28] bezeichnete ich als merkwürdig. Gesteh', daß ich mir sie anders dachte und wie seine Etuden im größten Styl geführt. Beinahe das Gegenteil; es sind Skizzen, Etudenanfänge, oder will man, Ruinen, einzelne Adlerfittige, alles bunt und wild durcheinander. Aber mit feiner Perlenschrift steht in jedem der Stücke „Friedrich Chopin schrieb's"; man erkennt ihn in den Pausen am heftigen Athmen. Er ist und bleibt der kühnste und stolzeste Dichtergeist der Zeit. Auch Krankes, Fieberhaftes, Abstoßendes enthält das Heft; so suche jeder, was ihm frommt, und bleibe nur der Philister weg. Was ist ein Philister?

Ein hohler Darm

Von Furcht und Hoffnung ausgefüllt,

Daß Gott erbarm!

Schließen wir besänftigender mit dem schön Schiller'schen:

Jenes Gesetz, das mit ehernem Stab den Sträubenden lenket, Dir nicht gilt's. Was du thust, was dir gefällt, ist Gesetz.

R.S.

Gottfried Wilhelm Fink: Rezension der *Sonate b-Moll* op. 35,
des *Impromptu Fis-Dur* op. 36 und der 2 *Nocturnes* op. 37,
in: Allgemeine Musikalische Zeitung 42/1840, Nr. 28 vom 8. Juli, Sp. 569–573

Chopin ist in seiner Art eigenthümlich und hat sich in diese besondere Weise so eingelebt, dass er sie in keinem einzigen seiner Werke verleugnet, auch in den vorliegenden nicht. Stets sind seine Formen von einer Dämmerung umflossen, zu deren Nebelduft Schatten der Erinnerung bald leise sich erheben und mit der Sehnsucht spielen, bald im Sturme graus und schaurig vorüberjagen. In der Gruppirung lebt das Eigne seiner Erfindung; die Formen seiner Gestalten zeichnet er mit der Kraft des Rhythmus, des unzerstörbaren, wenn nicht widerliche Missgeburten in's Dasein gerufen werden sollen; die dämmernde Umhüllung dagegen dampft auf vom umgestürzten Throne der Harmonie, an deren Gesetzlichkeit vernichtende Gluth eines Erdbrandes zehrt, der, vom Gewitter der Zeit erregt, kaum eher gehemmt werden möchte, als bis das Entzündbare verborgenen Stoffes sich verkohlte. Aber von den aufgelösten Metallen jenes Thrones mischt sich im Kessel des Brandes ein eigenes Metall, gleich korinthischem Erz, aus dem sich viel Schönes wieder formen lassen wird, sobald es der abgekühlten Asche neu entnommen werden kann. Das Echte geht nimmer auf ewige Zeiten verloren; es reinigt sich vielmehr im Feuer, wovon das neues Leben Erzeugende unvergänglicher Elementarkraft gar nicht ergriffen werden kann. So ist es auch mit unserer Harmonie. Man stecke uns das Haus über den Köpfen an: retten wir die Köpfe, so steht ein neues und hoffentlich ein festeres und schöneres wieder da, ehe man es meinen sollte, dass sich die Freude verjüngt. So ist denn nichts verloren, wo nur die Thatkraft lebt. [...]

Auf diese Art bleibt die Musik auch ohne lichtvollen Zusammenhang der Harmonie nicht nur noch reizend genug, sondern sie wird für manche Gefühlsrichtungen sogar nicht selten doppelt reizend, eben wenn vorzugsweise bedeutsame Gestalten durch Rhythmus und Melodie hervorgehoben und in glückliche Gruppen gestellt worden sind. Der sternbesäete Nachtmantel der Harmonie, die doch nicht alles Lichtes entbehrt, gibt wohl noch dem Ganzen den Reiz des verstärkt Mystischen, was weiblich gestimmten Seelen oft so theuer ist, als die Erinnerung an ihre erste Liebe.

In diesen Mysterien dichtet Chopin, immer sich selbst treu, immer im Dämmerschein und oft glücklich genug in seiner eigenthümlichen Weise. In dieser Art ist er einzig, und alle Nachahmung, die sich Einige gelüsten lassen, muss zu Schanden werden, sobald sie ernst gemeint ist. Darum sind wir auch nicht gegen ihn, so wenig wir auch seine Behandlung des harmonischen Theiles der Kunst billigen. In jene Schatten der Dämmerung uns versetzend, vermögen wir an seinen gelungensten Gaben uns so zu erfreuen, als irgend ein Neuromantiker, so wenig wir auch zu ihnen gerechnet zu werden uns würdig genug fühlen. [...]

In der vorliegenden Sonate, die weder eine Hummelsche noch eine Beethovensche noch irgend eine andere als seine eigenthümliche Sonate ist, hat er in seiner Weise etwas so Schönes geliefert als in irgend einem seiner früheren Werke.

Es wogt etwas Karakteristisches, seltsam und doch abgeschlossen in sich, aus den vier Sätzen, die in der Regel, wechselnd mit drei Hauptsätzen, ein Tonbild ohne Worte vollkommen abzurunden vermögen. Die Sonatenform ist also die gewöhnliche; das rhythmische Gefüge, der gegliederte Tanz der Tonmassen ist geregelt, die Eintheilung der Touren in symmetrischer Wiederkehr nicht zu verschlungen, vielmehr leicht fasslich für den Hörer, sobald der Vortragende mit den Schwierigkeiten, die sich zuweilen bieten, zu spielen versteht. Hauptgestalt ist die Leidenschaft, die schmerzbewegt ihre Hand auf ein verwundetes Herz legt; vom Hall und Schall unheimlicher Akkordschläge und im Rausche der Tonfiguren, die wild sich brechen, flattern die Locken. An ihrer Seite steht die Wehmuth, die bald sanft melodisch klagt, bald freundlich tröstet, vertraut mit dem Kummer und ergeben dem Geschick. Ein Spuk durchrauscht den dämmernden Hain, mit dem die Leidenschaft, als wären es Hoffnungskinder, zu scherzen sich vermisst. Aber das verwundete Herz zuckt nicht mehr und ruht in Frieden. Die Todtenglocken tönen, ein Trauermarsch beginnt, so wundersam und eigen, dass man die Thränen fühlt. Die Rührung hat der todten Liebe die letzte Ehre angethan; das Grab hat sie bedeckt. Da ergreift sie die blasse Leidenschaft, und wie gejagt vom Wirbel der Verwaisung braust sie im Presto und lauter Unisono ohne Rast und Ruh unaufhaltsam vorwärts, bis sie den Stein der Erinnerung erblickt, wo sie still steht, sich auf ihn stürzt – und nun erst erklingt in der Höhe die verdoppelte Oktave und im Basse der sehnsüchtige 6/4 Akkord von B-moll zum Schlusse des Ganzen.

Das lmpromptu [op. 36], seinem Wesen nach nichts anderes als eine hingeworfene kurze Fantasie, macht keine grossen Ansprüche; der Einfall muss aber doch des Druckes werth befunden worden sein. Es gibt deren, die so gut ausgearbeitet sind, als irgend ein anderes Tonstück; dann tragen sie ihren Namen mit Unrecht – andere, die zu wichtig sind, weshalb Viele des Glaubens leben, es sei besser, seine eigenen Einfälle als fremde zu spielen. Sind sie aber wirklich schnell hingeworfene Einfälle und im Niederschreiben nicht zu sehr verschönt oder von der Feile zu sehr geglättet, so macht sich in ihnen das eigentliche Grundwesen des Komponisten am Treuesten kund. Chopin ist hier gar nicht zu verkennen. Seine Harmonieverzeichnungen sind ihm zu einer wesentlichen Eigenheit geworden. Durch Vorhalte, Durchgangstöne und Ineinanderschiebung der Akkorde bringt er mit seinem Mehrstimmigkeitsgewebe das gerade Gegentheil von dem hervor, was Andere mit ihren Harmonieverbindungen hervorbringen; ihm ist die Harmonie die wirksamste Schöpferin der Nacht, dass man selten weiss, wo man wandelt. Zieht dies die Liebhaber mystischer Finsterniss bedeutend an, so stösst eben dasselbe die Freunde der Klarheit nicht minder ab, so dass die Stimmen über die meisten seiner Erzeugnisse immer getheilt sein müssen. Analysirt man seine Harmonieverschlingungen, verhüllende Vorhalte und Durchgangstöne u. s. w. wegnehmend, so wird man mit Verwunderung weit eher eine Armuth als einen Reichthum harmonischer Verbindung gewahr. Die Modulazionsübergänge sind nicht selten heftig, gewaltsam, unbestimmt, wovon sich auch hier einige Beispiele finden, die Einige genial, Andere unausstehlich nennen werden. Ist ihm aber die Harmonie ein Hauptmittel der Verdunkelung der dunkeln Sprache der Musik, so ist es konsequent, Auflösungen zu verbergen, unvollkommene statt vollkommener Akkorde ertönen zu lassen und die gewohnte Orthografie in das Gebiet der Willkür oder der Bequemlichkeit zu versetzen. Die Melodieen sind in der Regel am wenigsten eigenthümlich, es wäre denn zuweilen durch vorherrschend pikanten Rhythmus, oft weichlich, was jedoch in Verbindung mit jenen harmonischen Dunkelheiten einen besondern Reiz für nicht Wenige erhält. So ist es auch mit der einfachen Melodie, welche diesem Impromptu zum Grunde liegt. Gegen den Schluss verschmäht es der Komponist nicht, durch Bravourumspielung herrschender Art dem Ganzen so viel Glanz zu geben, als man ihn gern hat. Ueberhaupt wird man Herrn Chopin bei allen seinen Besonderheiten nicht nachsagen können, dass er sich den Moden der Zeit ganz entzöge. So ist es bekanntlich seit einigen Jahren Mode geworden, in recht tüchtigen Kreuz- und Be-Vorzeichnungen zu schreiben. Das thut er hier gleichfalls. Die Sonate geht aus B moll, Es moll und Ges dur; das Impromptu aus Fis dur, wobei der fast stereotyp gewordene Fortschritt in D dur nicht ausser Acht gelassen worden ist. Wenn wir aber den Sonatenschluss auf dem 6/4 - Akkorde dem Karakteristischen höchst angemessen und schön nannten, so müssen wir denselben Schluss in dieser Nummer nur höchst manierirt und unnütz nennen; er hat weiter keinen Grund, als den Grund des Auffallenden, dem freilich Viele huldigen. Uns gefällt das Impromptu wenig. Weit lieber sind uns die Notturnen, am meisten ziehen wir das erste vor.

Gottfried Wilhelm Fink: Rezension der *Valse As-Dur* op. 42, in: Allgemeine Musikalische Zeitung 42/1840, Nr. 40 vom 30. September, Sp. 826

Die eigenthümliche Weise dieses eben so bekannten und in der neuesten Zeit vielfach besprochenen Komponisten herrscht auch in diesem ausführlichen Walzer, der durch freundlich melodische Rhythmen den vielen Freunden des Mannes sich nur noch angenehmer machen wird. Dass man darin das Frappante nicht vermisst, brauchen wir kaum zu erwähnen. Der Walzer empfiehlt sich selbst. Eine eigene Ton-bezeichnung und Mischung des Rhythmischen wollen wir denen, die das Werkchen noch nicht kennen, in Noten hersetzen: [Notenzitat Takte 9–16]

Gottfried Wilhelm Fink: Rezension der *Ballade* op. 38, des *Scherzo* op. 39, der 2 *Polonaisen* op. 40 und der 4 *Mazurken* op. 41, in: Allgemeine Musikalische Zeitung 42/1840, Nr. 51 vom 16. Dezember, Sp. 1043/1044

Wenn über eines Komponisten Eigenthümlichkeiten so oft und so ausführlich gesprochen worden ist, als wir es über Chopins Tondichtungen gethan haben, kann im Allgemeinen nur wenig Neues zu sagen übrig bleiben, am wenigsten, wenn er seine einmal ergriffene Richtung mit solcher Festigkeit verfolgt, wie es dieser Mann in den allermeisten seiner Gaben wirklich thut. Warum sollte er auch wohl eine andere Bahn betreten und seine Individualität dazu zwingen, was anfangs sicher dazu gehörte, da er auf seinem besondern Wege sich so viele Freunde gewonnen hat? Zwar hat er auch seine Gegner. Dieser nicht seltene Fall kann ihm aber in den Augen seiner Verehrer nichts schaden, vielmehr reizt dieser Umstand noch stärkere Opposizion, die noch dazu gar Manches für sich hat. Müssen doch selbst die Gegner dieses Komponisten, sobald sie nur nicht unter die für eine andere Tondichtungsweise völlig eingenommenen gehören, zugestehen, dass er, auch ausser seinen Etüden, deren meiste jetzt ziemlich allgemein als tüchtige Sätze beachtet werden, noch manches Karaktervolle gegeben hat, dem man mit Recht das Ergreifende, wenn auch in seltsamer Art, nicht absprechen kann. Dazu kommt, dass er einen Theil der neuen Spielweise auf dem Pianoforte gefördert hat, die kein junger Klavierspieler, der nicht hinter der Aufgabe seiner Zeit zurückbleiben will, vernachlässigen darf. Es ist also ganz in der Ordnung, dass Chopins neue Werke alsbald Beachtung finden, sobald nur der Titel genannt worden ist. Ob seine Gegner durch seine Beharrlichkeit in seiner Tondichtungsweise in demselben Grade sich von ihm entfernen, als seine Liebhaber sich dadurch angezogen fühlen, ist eine Frage, welche die Zukunft beantworten muss. Vor der Hand kommt jedoch nur wenig darauf an, so wenig als auf irgend eine Rezension, die daher am Zuträglichsten nur kurz zu fassen ist.

Was nun die neue Ballade [op. 38] betrifft, so hat sie einerseits mit der ersten bekannten so viel Aehnliches, dass man sagen muss: Wem die erste gefallen hat, dem wird diese neue sicherlich auch gefallen; andererseits hat sie in Zusammenstellung und Haltung auch wieder so viel Abweichendes, als eine aus anderer Situazion und andern Gefühlsverhältnissen hervorgegangene Wortballade eines und desselben Dichters hat und haben soll. Eigen und seltsam, besonders im Harmonischen der wehmüthig sanfteren Sätze, die mit leidenschaftlichen Bravourpartieen wechseln, ist sie genug. Dass wir selbst nach unserer Persönlichkeit und nach dem, was wir von der Musik verlangen, die Balladen dieses Komponisten nicht unter sein Bestes setzen, das kann und soll keinen Andern abhalten, anderer Meinung zu sein; Jeder hat sich selbst zu vertreten und zu sehen, wie er zum Bessern vorwärts kommt. Viel glücklicher, glauben wir, ist Chopin in seinen Scherzi. Auch dieses Scherzo [op. 39] halten wir für weit gelungener; es ist ganz in seiner Weise, aber in dieser rund und frisch. Wir sind nicht so einseitig, dass wir nur eine oder einige Tondichtungsarten für die allein rechten anerkennen sollten. Mit seiner ersten Polonaise des 40. Werkes steht es noch besser; sie ist prächtig, in Erfindung und Haltung ausgezeichnet, weniger durch eigenthümliche Auffallenheiten als durch folgerechte und tüchtige Entwickelung überaus wirksam, so dass sie allgemein ansprechen muss. Die zweite ist ganz wieder in seiner Weise, wird daher von seinen Freunden für noch origineller, von Manchen aber, besonders einem Theile der neunten und zehnten Seite nach, für zu scharf und hart erkannt werden. Sie enthält Vortreffliches; dennoch ist uns selbst die erste ihrer bestimmten Abrundung wegen lieber. – Und seine Mazurken? Es sind wieder Chopin'sche. Im Grunde gehören sie gar nicht unter das kritische Messer. Es sind volksthümliche Schwärmereien eines Epigonen in Gestalt von Tänzen mit eigenem pikanten Rhythmus. Wird dieser getroffen, so ist auch der Reiz da, den sie allerdings haben. Vorzüglich reizend ist die dritte und vierte.

Robert Schumann: Rezension der *Sonate b-Moll* op. 35,
in: Neue Zeitschrift für Musik 14/1841, Nr. 10 vom 1. Februar, S. 39/40

Neue Sonaten für das Pianoforte.
(Schluß aus Nr. 7.)

– Die ersten Tacte der zuletzt genannten Sonate sich ansehen und noch zweifeln zu können, von wem sie sei, wäre eines guten Kennerauges wenig würdig. So fängt nur C h o p i n an und so schließt nur er: mit Dissonanzen durch Dissonanzen in Dissonanzen. Und doch wie viel Schönes birgt auch dieses Stück. Daß er es „Sonate" nannte, möchte man eher eine Caprice heißen, wenn nicht einen Uebermuth, daß er gerade vier seiner tollsten Kinder zusammenkoppelte, sie unter diesem Namen vielleicht an Orte einzuschwärzen, wohin sie sonst nie gedrungen wären. Man nehme z. B. an, irgend ein Cantor vom Lande kommt in eine Musikstadt, da Kunsteinkäufe zu machen – man legt ihm Neuestes vor – von nichts will er wissen – endlich hält ihm ein Schlaukopf eine „Sonate" entgegen – ja, spricht er entzückt, das ist für mich und noch ein Stück aus der alten guten Zeit – und kauft und hat sie. Zu Hause angekommen, fällt er her über das Stück – aber sehr irren müßt ich mich, wenn er, noch ehe er die erste Seite mühsam abgehaspelt, bei allen heiligen Musikgeistern darauf schwöre, ob das ordentlicher Sonatenstyl und nicht vielmehr wahrhaft gottloser. Aber Chopin hat doch erreicht, was er wollte; er befindet sich im Cantorat, und wer kann denn wissen, ob nicht in derselben Behausung, vielleicht nach Jahren erst, einmal ein romantischerer Enkel geboren wird und aufwächst, die Sonate abstäubt, und spielt und für sich denkt: „der Mann hatte doch so Unrecht nicht."

Mit alle diesem ist schon vorweg ein halbes Urtheil abgegeben. Chopin schreibt schon gar nichts mehr, was man bei Anderen eben so gut haben könnte; er bleibt sich treu und hat Grund dazu.

Es ist zu bedauern, daß die meisten Clavierspielenden, selbst Gebildete darunter, nicht über das hinaussehen und urtheilen können, was sie nicht mit ihren eigenen Fingern bewältigen können. Anstatt so schwierige Stücke erst zu überblicken, krümmen und bohren sie sich tactweise fort; und sind sie dann kaum über die gröbsten förmlichen Verhältnisse im Klaren, legen sie's weg und dann heißt es „bizarr, verworren etc." Gerade Chopin hat (wie etwa Jean Paul) seine Häkelperioden und Parenthesen, bei denen man sich beim ersten Durchlesen eben nicht lange aufhalten darf, um nicht die Spur zu verlieren. Auf solche Stellen stößt man denn auch in der Sonate fast auf jeder Seite, und Chopin's oft willkührliche und wilde Accordschreibung macht das Herausfinden noch schwieriger. Er liebt nemlich nicht zu enharmonisiren, wenn ich mich so ausdrücken darf, und so erhält man oft zehn- und mehrfach bekreuzte Tacte und Tonarten, die wir alle nur in wichtigsten Fällen lieben. Oft hat er darin recht, oft aber verwirrt er auch ohne Grund, und, wie gesagt, entfernt sich dadurch einen guten Theil des Publicums, das (meint es) nicht unaufhörlich gefoppt und in die Enge getrieben sein will. So hat denn auch die Sonate fünf Bee oder B-moll zur Vorzeichnung, eine Tonart, die sich gewiß keiner besondern Popularität rühmen kann. Der Anfang heißt nemlich:

[Notenzitat 1. Satz, Takte 1–4]

Nach diesem hinlänglich Chopin'schen Anfange folgt einer jener stürmischen leidenschaftlichen Sätze, wie wir deren von Chopin schon mehrere kennen. Man muß dies öfter und gut gespielt hören. Aber auch schönen Gesang bringt dieser erste Theil des Werkes; ja es scheint, als verschwände der nationelle polnische Beigeschmack, der den meisten der früheren Chopin'schen Melodieen anhing, mit der

Zeit immer mehr, als neige er sich (über Deutschland hinüber) gar manchmal Italien zu. Man weiß, daß Bellini und Chopin befreundet waren, daß sie, die sich oft ihre Compositionen mittheilten, wohl auch nicht ohne künstlerischen Einfluß auf einander geblieben. Aber, wie gesagt, nur ein leises Hinneigen nach südlicher Weise ist es; sobald der Gesang geendet, blitzt wieder der ganze Sarmate in seiner trotzigen Originalität aus den Klängen heraus. Eine Accordenverflechtung wenigstens, wie wir sie nach Abschluß des ersten Sanges vom zweiten Theil antreffen, hat Bellini nie gewagt, und konnte sie nie wagen. So endigt auch der ganze Satz wenig italienisch – wobei mir Liszt's treffendes Wort einfällt, der einmal sagte: Rossini und Cons.[orten] schlössen immer mit einem „vôtre très humble serviteur"; – anders aber Chopin, dessen Schlüsse eher das Gegentheil ausdrücken. – Der zweite Satz ist nur die Fortsetzung dieser Stimmung, kühn, geistreich, phantastisch, das Trio zart, träumerisch, ganz in Chopin's Weise: Scherzo nur dem Namen nach, wie viele Beethoven's. Es folgt, noch düsterer, ein **Marcia funèbre**, der sogar manches Abstoßende hat; an seine Stelle ein Adagio, etwa in Des, würde ungleich schöner gewirkt haben. Denn was wir im Schlußsatze unter der Aufschrift „Finale" erhalten, gleicht eher einem Spott als irgend Musik. Und doch gestehe man es sich, auch aus diesem melodie- und freudelosen Satze weht uns ein eigener grausiger Geist an, der, was sich gegen ihn auflehnen möchte, mit überlegener Faust niederhält, daß wir wie gebannt und ohne zu murren bis zum Schlusse zuhorchen – aber auch ohne zu loben: denn Musik ist das nicht. So schließt die Sonate, wie sie angefangen, räthselhaft, einer Sphinx gleich mit spöttischem Lächeln.

12.

**Robert Schumann: Rezension der 2 *Nocturnes* op. 37,
der *Ballade* op. 38 und des *Walzers* op. 42,
in: Neue Zeitschrift für Musik 15/1841, Nr. 36 vom 2. November, S. 141/142**

Kürzere Stücke für Pianoforte.
(Schluß.)

Chopin könnte jetzt alles ohne seinen Namen herausgeben, man würde ihn doch gleich erkennen. Darin liegt Lob und Tadel zugleich, jenes für sein Talent, dieser für sein Streben. Denn sicherlich wohnt ihm jene bedeutende Originalkraft inne, die, sobald sie sich zeigt, keinen Zweifel über den Namen des Meisters zuläßt; dabei bringt er auch eine Fülle neuer Formen, die in ihrer Zartheit und Kühnheit zugleich Bewunderung verdienen. Neu und erfinderisch immer im Aeußerlichen, in der Gestaltung seiner Tonstücke, in besonderen Instrumenteffecten, bleibt er sich aber im Innerlichen gleich, daß wir fürchten, er bringe es nicht höher, als er es bis jetzt gebracht. Und ist dies hoch genug, seinen Namen den unvergänglichen in der neueren Kunstgeschichte anzureihen, so beschränkt sich seine Wirksamkeit doch nur auf den kleinern Kreis der Claviermusik, und er hätte mit seinen Kräften doch noch viel Höheres erreichen und Einfluß auf die Fortbildung unserer Kunst im Allgemeinen gewinnen müssen. Begnügen wir uns indeß. Er hat so viel Herrliches geschaffen, giebt uns noch jetzt so viel, daß wir zufrieden sein dürfen und jeden Künstler, der nur die Hälfte geleistet wie er, beglückwünschen müßten. Ein Dichter zu heißen, braucht's ja auch nicht dickleibiger Bände; durch ein, zwei Gedichte kannst du dir den Namen verdienen, und Chopin hat solche geschrieben. Auch die Notturno's [op. 37], die oben erwähnt sind, gehören hierher; sie unterscheiden sich von seinen früheren wesentlich durch einfacheren Schmuck, durch stillere Grazie. Man weiß, wie Chopin sonst sich trug, ganz wie mit Flitter, Goldtand und Perlen übersäet. Er ist schon anders und älter geworden; noch liebt er den Schmuck, aber es ist der sinnigere, hinter dem der Adel der Dichtung um so liebenswürdiger durchschimmert; ja Geschmack, feinsten, muß man ihm lassen, – für Generalbassisten ist das freilich nicht, die suchen nur nach Quinten, und jede fehlende kann sie erbosen. Aber noch manches könnten sie von Chopin lernen, und das Quintenmachen vor Allem. Wir haben noch der B a l l a d e[26] als eines merkwürdigen Stückes zu erwähnen. Chopin hat unter demselben Namen schon eine geschrieben [op. 23], eine seiner wildesten eigenthümlichsten Compositionen; die neue ist anders, als Kunstwerk unter jener ersten stehend, doch nicht weniger phantastisch und geistreich. Die leidenschaftlichen Zwischensätze scheinen erst später hinzugekommen zu sein; ich erinnere mich sehr gut, als Chopin die Ballade hier spielte und in F-Dur schloß; jetzt schließt sie in A-Moll. Er sprach damals auch davon, daß er zu seinen Balladen durch einige Gedichte von Mickiewitz angeregt worden sei. Umgekehrt würde ein Dichter zu seiner Musik wieder sehr leicht Worte finden können; sie rührt das Innerste auf. Der W a l z e r [op. 42] endlich ist wie seine früheren, ein Salonstück der nobelsten Art; sollte er ihn zum Tanz vorspielen, meinte Florestan, so müßten unter den Tänzerinnen die gute Hälfte wenigstens Comtessen sein. Er hat Recht, der Walzer ist aristokratisch durch und durch. –

---

26 Die *Ballade F-Dur* op. 38 ist im deutschen Erstdruck 1840 Robert Schumann gewidmet.

Heinrich Heine: [Über Chopin], in: *Musikalische Saison in Paris,*
in: Lutezia. Berichte über Politik, Kunst und Volksleben. Zweiter Teil, Nr. LVI,
Paris, 26. März 1843 (auch: Burger, S. 256, Mann, S. 148)

[...] Es giebt nur einen den ich ihm [dem Pianisten Sigismund Thalberg, den Heine zuvor außerordentlich gerühmt hatte][27], vorzöge, das ist Chopin, der aber vielmehr Componist als Virtuose ist. Bei Chopin vergesse ich ganz die Meisterschaft des Clavierspiels und versinke in die süßen Abgründe seiner Musik, in die schmerzliche Lieblichkeit seiner ebenso tiefen wie zarten Schöpfungen. Chopin ist der große geniale Tondichter, den man eigentlich nur in Gesellschaft von Mozart und Beethoven oder Rossini oder Meyerbeer nennen sollte. [...]

Robert Schumann: Rezension des *Allegro de Concert* **op. 46, der** *Ballade*
As-Dur **op. 47, der 2** *Nocturnes* **op. 48 und der** *Phantasie f-Moll* **op. 49,**
in: Neue Zeitschrift für Musik 17/1842, Nr. 41 vom 18. November, S. 167/168

Vielem Geistvollen begegnen wir wieder in einigen Compositionen C h o p i n's: sie sind ein Concert-Allegro (Op. 46), eine Ballade (Op. 47), 2 Notturno's (Op. 48), und eine Phantasie (Op. 49)[28], und, wie alle von seiner Hand, im ersten Augenblick als Chopin'sche Compositionen zu erkennen. Das Concert-Allegro hat ganz die Form eines ersten Concertsatzes und ist wohl ursprünglich mit Orchesterbegleitung geschrieben. Wir vermissen in dem Stück einen schönen Mittelgesang, das sonst reich an neuem und glänzendem Passagenwerk ist; wie es dasteht, schweift es zu unruhig vorüber; man fühlt das Bedürfniß nach einem nachfolgenden langsamen Satz, einem Adagio, wie denn die ganze Anlage auf ein vollständiges Concert in drei Sätzen schließen läßt. Das Clavier zur höchsten Selbstständigkeit zu erheben und des Orchesters unbedürftig zu machen, ist eine Lieblingsidee der jüngsten Claviercomponisten und scheint auch Chopin zur Herausgabe seines Allegro's in der jetzigen Gestalt vermocht zu haben; an diesem neuen Versuche sehen wir indeß von neuem ihre Schwierigkeit, ohne deshalb vom wiederholten Angreifen der Sache abzurathen. Bei weitem höher als das Allegro stellen wir die Ballade [op. 47], Chopin's dritte, die sich von seinen früheren in Form und Charak-

---

27 Heine schrieb u.a.: „Dieser Künstler unterscheidet sich vortheilhaft von seinen Claviercollegen, ich möchte fast sagen durch sein musikalisches Betragen. Wie im Leben, so auch in seiner Kunst bekundet Thalberg den angeborenen Tact, sein Vortrag ist so gentlemanlike, so wohlhabend, so anständig, so ganz ohne Grimasse, so ganz ohne forcirtes Genialthun, so ganz ohne jene renommirende Bengelei, welche die innere Verzagniß schlecht verhehlt."

28 Anmerkung unten auf der Seite: Sämmtlich bei Breitkopf & Härtel erschienen.

ter merklich unterscheidet, und, wie jene, seinen eigensten Schöpfungen beizuzählen ist. Der feine geistreiche Pole, der sich in den vornehmsten Kreisen der französischen Hauptstadt zu bewegen gewohnt ist, möchte in ihr vorzugsweise zu erkennen sein; ihr poetischer Duft läßt sich weiter nicht zergliedern. – Die Notturno's [op. 48] reihen sich in ihrem melancholischen Charakter, ihrer graziösen Haltung Chopin's früheren an. Vorzüglich mag das zweite zu Mancher Herzen sprechen. – In der Phantasie [op. 49] begegnen wir dem kühnen stürmenden Tondichter wieder, wie wir ihn schon öfter kennen gelernt; sie ist voll genialer einzelner Züge, wenn auch das Ganze sich einer schönen Form hat nicht unterwerfen wollen. Welche Bilder Chopin vorgeschwebt haben mögen, als er sie schrieb, kann man nur ahnen; freudige sind es nicht. –

13.

Anonymus [August Kahlert]: Rezension der *Tarantelle* op. 43, in: Allgemeine Musikalische Zeitung 44/1842, Nr. 6 vom 9. Februar, Sp. 112

Was uns Chopin gibt, ist uns immer willkommen, und auch Referent zählt sich zu seinen Verehrern, die immer zahlreicher geworden sind. Ist er auch, wie in vorliegender Nummer wieder einmal recht kraus und wirrig in seinen Harmonieen, so ist's doch eine ächte Tarantelle, bei der man am Ende zu Tode gehetzt liegen bleiben kann, wie das auch so sein soll. Auch bei diesem Schuberth'schen Verlagswerke müssen wir bedauern, dass der Korrektor nicht sorgfältiger zu Werke geht. Bei Werken, wo solch ein rascher Harmoniewechsel sich in jedem Takte jagt, muss man die b und # lieber einmal zu viel als zu wenig setzen. Im achten Takte setze man vor g und c im Diskant ein b. – Die zweite Hälfte des siebenzehnten Taktes im Basse muss mit *des* anfangen und die zweite Hälfte des achtzehnten im Basse mit b. Dass wieder grosse Schönheiten und Eigenthümlichkeiten in dieser Tarantelle sind, braucht Referent wohl nicht erst zu erwähnen, und es genügt ihm, dieses Werk des geistreichen Chopin angezeigt zu haben.

Robert Schumann: Rezension der *Tarantelle As-Dur* op. 43, in: Neue Zeitschrift für Musik 19/1843, Nr. 31 vom 16. Oktober, S. 121/122

Kleinere Compositionen für Pianoforte.

(Schluß.)

Ein Stück in Chopin's tollster Manier; man sieht den wirbelnden, vom Wahnsinn besessenen Tänzer vor sich, es wird einem selbst wirblig dabei zu Muthe. Schöne

Musik darf das freilich Niemand nennen, aber dem Meister verzeihen wir wohl auch einmal seine wilden Phantasieen, er darf auch einmal die Nachtseiten seines Innern sehen lassen. Für Recensenten vom rechten Schrot und Korn hat Chopin ohnedies nicht geschrieben. – Das erste Verständniß des Stückes wird leider durch die Druckfehler, von denen es wahrhaft wimmelt, sehr erschwert. –

Notiz in der Allgemeinen Musikalischen Zeitung 44/1842, Nr. 19 vom 11. Mai, Sp. 406

Chopin, welcher sich bekanntlich nur höchst selten öffentlich hören lässt, gab in Paris ein Concert [am 21. Februar in den Salons Pleyel], worin er mehrere neue Kompositionen, namentlich einige Mazurken, vortrug, welche als ausgezeichnete Tonstücke gerühmt werden.

Anonymus [August Kahlert]: Rezension der 3 *Mazurken* op. 50, in: Allgemeine Musikalische Zeitung 44/1842, Nr. 47 vom 23. November, Sp. 937

Ein neues Stück von Chopin ist uns immer eine willkommene Gabe. Besonders in diesen Mazurken steht er wieder so eigenthümlich da. Sie sind vortrefflich und recht eigentlich zum Genuss bestimmt, denn sie sind nicht schwer. Wie reizend ist No. 1! Wie prächtig schreiten die Bässe! wie sinnig und wonnig sind die folgenden Takte:
[Notenzitate: Takte 13–16 und 7–9]
gerade an dem Platze, wo sie stehen! Nicht weniger schön ist No. 2 in As dur. Am genialsten ist aber No. 3, wenn sie gleich nicht eben so ansprechend sein dürfte. Referent freut sich über diese köstliche Gabe und empfiehlt sie dringend.

Anonymus [August Kahlert]: Rezension des *Impromptus* op. 51 (hier unter dem Titel „Allegro Vivace"), in: Allgemeine Musikalische Zeitung 45/1843, Nr. 33 vom 16. August, Sp. 596

Ein ganz reizendes Impromptu in der bekannten und beliebten Manier des Verfassers gehalten, im Anfange etwas zerrissen und unstät umherirrend, aber eigenthümlich und anziehend; die Cantilene Es moll Sostenuto ist sehr schön.

Anonymus [August Kahlert]: Rezensionen der 3 *Mazurken* op. 56 und der 2 *Nocturnes* op. 55,
in: Allgemeine Musikalische Zeitung 46/1844, Nr. 49 vom 4. Dezember, Sp. 820/821

Der Rhythmus nationaler Tänze hat den neueren Componisten bereits reiche Ausbeute gewährt. Die polnischen zumal sind vor anderen durch rhythmische Eigenthümlichkeit ausgezeichnet, und der characteristische Schwung der Mazurka namentlich wurde von Chopin, als er aus seinem Vaterlande sich vor dreizehn Jahren nach Frankreich übersiedelte, in die Salonliteratur des Pianoforte's mit der ihm inwohnenden Poesie eingeführt, ja, er verdrängte die bis dahin von Virtuosen behandelte Polonaise. Er hat jenen scharfen Rhythmus lieb behalten, der ihm für seine weichen, träumerischen Motive einen willkommenen Rahmen bietet, und ist immer wieder zu ihm zurückgekehrt. Die feste Bestimmtheit des Rhythmus gestattet dem Componisten, der nach dieser Seite gebunden ist, nur in harmonischer Hinsicht Freiheit, die Chopin nun auf's Vollständigste benutzt. Die Wendungen sind zuweilen ganz ungewöhnlich, sogar hart, und werden nur durch seine weiche, elastische Spielart so weit gemildert, dass sie dem Ohre nicht verletzend erscheinen. Auf solchen Vortrag, worauf diese Musikstücke hingewiesen sind, kommt Alles an. Die vorliegenden drei Mazurka's liefern abermals für das hier Gesagte an vielen Stellen Beweise. Gleich der erste verhüllt seine Grundtonart H dur zwölf Tacte lang in ein räthselhaftes Gewand. Die Melodie selbst, grösstentheils in eine Mittelstimme gelegt, verlangt in ihren zarten Umrissen sehr viele Pflege, wenn sie nicht verwischt werden soll. Das Alternativ in Es dur (so ist es zur Bequemlichkeit, da Dis dur schwer zu lesen ist, geschrieben), mehr figurirt als melodisch, hebt sich gut von dem ersten Gedanken los. – No. 2 (C dur) wird schnell Freunde finden, weit fasslicher als die anderen beiden, und an die Jugendzeit Chopin's erinnernd. Der liegende Grundton mahnt an die seltsame Instrumentation, die man in einer polnischen Bauernschenke zu hören bekommt. – No. 3 ist originell, doch von harmonischer Unruhe. Es wird mehr hin und her modulirt, als der Gesammtwirkung nützlich ist. Der Character des Mazureks geht in den einer freien Fantasie über. Der Grundgedanke, an sich klein, wird gleichsam zum Spielballe der Laune. Einzelne Wendungen, die bei dieser Gelegenheit vorkommen, sind geistreich und interessant.

Auch die Form des Nocturno's, von Field in der Musikwelt, namentlich in der Claviermusik eingeführt, hat Chopin mit Vorliebe gepflegt, ausgebildet, ihr dauernde Theilnahme gesichert. Man kann hier eigentlich von einer bestimmten

Form gar nicht, sondern nur von der allgemeinen Bezeichnung eines kleinen, elegischen oder doch sanften Tonstückes reden, denn weder in rhythmischer noch harmonischer Hinsicht ist diese Gattung fest bestimmt, vielmehr dem Geschmacke des Erfinders überlassen. Je weniger kühner, muthiger Aufschwung bei Chopin sich findet, desto reicher zeigt gerade seine Schöpfungskraft sich in dem Gebiete milder Trauer, schwärmerischer Wehmuth. Auch seine Heiterkeit ist niemals ungetrübt; der schmerzvolle Ausdruck ist ihr beigemischt. Das erste dieser beiden neuen Nocturno's, worin Jeder, der des Künstlers Styl einmal kennen gelernt hat, ihn leicht wiederfinden wird, ist einfach, sehr edel und gemüthvoll: es verdient Empfehlung, deren es übrigens kaum bedarf. Die Variation in Triolen mit dem Schlusse in Dur – das Stück steht in F moll – geht zuletzt in wenigen gehaltenen Accorden, die einer Frage ähnlich klingen, aus. Das zweite Stück, Es dur, ist schwerer zu verstehen, auch weit schwerer zu spielen. Nicht, als ob hier Bravourpassagen vorlägen, aber das Verhältniss der gleichmässigen Begleitungsfigur zu der Melodie, die sich in lyrischer Freiheit dahinzieht, bedingt die Schwierigkeit; an stricte Eintheilung der Figuren muss man nicht denken, sondern jede der beiden Hände muss durchaus selbständig ihre Aufgabe lösen, sonst erliegt der Reiz dieses zum Studium sehr geeigneten Stückes. Der Werth eines durchaus kunstgebildeten Vortrages kann sich hier sehr geltend machen, da von heftigen, materiellen Effecten nicht die Rede ist.

Anonymus: Rezensionen der *Berceuse Des-Dur* op. 57
und der *Sonate h-Moll* op. 58,
in: Neue Zeitschrift für Musik 23/1845, Nr. 23 vom 16. September, S. 89/90

F r. C h o p i n, **Berceuse**. Op. 57. – Leipzig, Breitkopf u. Härtel. Pr. 15 Ngr.

Die linke Hand beginnt mit einer einfachen, wiegenden, zwischen Tonica und Dominante abwechselnden Begleitungsfigur. Im 3ten Tacte setzt die rechte ein mit einer schwebenden Melodie, wie sie wohl eine Mutter, die, selbst halb wachend, halb träumend, ihren Liebling in den Schlaf lullt, vor sich hinsummen mag. Eine zweite Stimme gesellt sich bald hinzu; und während die Linke wiegend fortfährt, variirt die Rechte das Schlaflied auf mannigfache, träumerisch spielende Weise. Die letzte graziöse und schmiegsame Veränderung zieht sich aus der Höhe mehr nach der Mitte der Claviatur. Allmälig verstummt das zarte Lied. – Wohl selig mag das Kindlein träumen! –

F r. C h o p i n, **Sonate**. Op. **58**. – Leipzig, Breitkopf u. Härtel. Pr. **1** Thlr. **15** Ngr.

Die Gegenwart hat keinen Meister aufzuweisen, dem man ungestört, mit ganzer, ungetheilter Liebe sich hingeben könnte; immer bleiben einige Wenn und Aber im Hintergrunde. Dem Einen fehlt der Contrapunct, dem Andern die Phantasie, dem Dritten wer weiß was? – So geht es Einem auch mit Chopin. Man darf nicht behaupten, daß ihm die Phantasie abgehe oder die musikalische Technik; aber er hat in der Aeußerung beider einige Besonderheiten, die, weil sie vom Herkömmlichen sehr auffallend abweichen, beim ersten Blick bemerkbar sind, und, indem das Auge durch sie von dem, was die Hauptsache ist, abgelenkt wird, von engerer und vertrauterer Bekanntschaft abschrecken. Die Kritik hat dieses Auffallende in Chopin's Compositionen zu wiederholten Malen getadelt und eben durch die Wiederholung des Tadels zu erkennen gegeben, daß diese Abnormitäten in der Schreibweise Chopin's als etwas Zufälliges und zu Aenderndes betrachtet werden müssen. Dem ist indessen nicht so. In allen seinen Compositionen spricht sich die Individualität des Künstlers rein und unverkennbar aus; er m u ß so schreiben, er kann nicht anders. Wer sich durch die barock erscheinenden harmonischen und (seltener) melodischen Wendungen nicht hat abhalten lassen, in das Innere seiner Werke bis zum Kerne vorzudringen, wird mit uns derselben Ansicht sein und eingestehen, daß, wiewohl Manches nicht absolut s c h ö n genannt werden kann, es doch als n o t h w e n d i g bezeichnet werden muß, und keine Stelle geändert werden dürfe, ohne Chopin zu zerstören.

Die vorliegende Sonate will von demselben Gesichtspuncte aus beurtheilt sein. S i e i s t v o n C h o p i n, und somit statuiren wir zugleich alle seine liebenswürdigen Eigen- und Besonderheiten, denen wir hier auf der ersten Seite, beim Anfange des zweiten Theils vom ersten Satze und auf der vorletzten Seite begegnen. Der geehrte Leser weiß nun, daß wir keine blinden Verehrer von Chopin sind; er wird uns um so mehr Glauben schenken, wenn wir ihm versichern, daß trotz allen zugestandenen Schwächen – sind es Schwächen? – die Sonate eine der bedeutendsten Erscheinungen der Gegenwart ist und bleibt. – Wir haben es, betraf es ein Werk, zu dessen Ausführung nur zwei Hände erforderlich waren, nie sonderlich geliebt, Recensionen zu lesen, die da erzählen, der erste Satz sei im C-Tact, der letzte ebenfalls im C-Tacte geschrieben etc. etc., und so wollen wir auch den freundlichen Leser mit einer ähnlichen verschonen und ihm nur verrathen, daß, obgleich allerdings das Interesse mit jedem Satze wächst, das Herz vorzüglich dem Adagio [recte: Largo] zugewendet bleiben und öfter dahin zurückführen wird. Am Schlusse desselben begegnen wir in folgenden zwei Accorden dem eigentlichen Chopin:

Nach mehrmaligem Spielen werden die Finger wie von selbst diese anfangs befremdenden Accorde greifen und somit unsere oben ausgesprochene Behauptung bestätigen.

1716.

August Kahlert: Rezensionen der *Berceuse* op. 57 und der *Sonate*
***h-Moll* op. 58,**
in: Allgemeine Musikalische Zeitung 48/1846, Nr. 5 vom 4. Februar, Sp. 74–76

Eine schaukelnde Bewegung, welche, durch den Bass markirt, während die Melodie zuerst ganz einfach, dann in mehreren Variationen darüber gebaut ist, sich durch das ganze Stück zieht, rechtfertigt den gewählten Titel [„Berceuse"]. Um diesen wiegenden Rhythmus noch mehr hervorzuheben, lässt der Componist fortwährenden consequenten Wechsel im Gebrauche des Pedals bei dem ersten und vierten Achtel anwenden. Der Vortrag des ganzen Stücks ist durch diesen Umstand bedingt. Die Melodie ist nicht so prägnant, sie ist, wo sie als Variation auftritt, so reich figurirt, dass ihre Glieder nur durch jenen Rhythmus des Basses zusammengehalten werden. Wie sich von selbst versteht, erfordern die sehr verschiedenen Figuren der Melodie einen ganz weichen gebundenen Vortrag, die Terzengänge, die gebrochenen Sexten müssen nur wie hingehaucht erscheinen. Wie sich zuletzt Alles wieder zu der ruhigen stillen Weise, womit begonnen wurde, zurückneigt und sich darin verliert, schliesst sich das Ganze sehr wohlgefällig ab, dessen schöne Wirkung nicht ausbleiben kann, wenn jene Feinheiten des Vortrages beachtet werden.

Die Form der Sonate behauptet mitten unter den zahllosen, durch den Modegeschmack hervorgerufenen kleinen Formen der Salonstücke ihre Autorität. Sie bietet, weil sie in ihren drei oder vier Sätzen eine ganze Scala von Empfindungen durchläuft, dem Componisten nicht blos Gelegenheit, seine reichere und ausdauernde Erfindungskraft zu bewähren, sondern sie fördert auch grössere Meisterschaft in Bewältigung ausgedehnterer Formen. Dass Chopin der letzteren Herr ist, sie auf eigenthümliche Weise zu behandeln weiss, hat er längst, am Entschiedensten in der ersten Zeit seines öffentlichen Wirkens, in dem vortrefflichen E moll-Concerte, dargetan. Eben so sehr hat sein Beispiel auch die Menge kleinerer Formen, worin er so vieles Reizende hervorbrachte, in Aufnahme gebracht. Nehmen wir Leistungen, wie diese neue Sonate, daher für einen Wink, dass man in jener Zersplitterung nicht zu weit gehen, dass man die nöthige Sammlung für ausführlichere Schilderung innerer Seelenstimmungen nicht leichtsinnig aufgeben möge. Er weiss selbst sehr wohl, dass der Vortrag eines Dutzend kleiner, eleganter und piquanter Stücke, wovon jedes fünf Minuten spielt, den Zuhörerkreis mehr zerstreut als befriedigt, wenn auch die Mode bei der Einrichtung eines jetzigen musikalischen Salon es also will. Wir heissen Chopin's Sonate aber nicht blos des Beispiels wegen, sondern um ihrer selbständigen Richtung willen willkommen. Die vier Sätze: Allegro, Scherzo, Largo, Presto, sind zwar der Zahl und Gattung nach die üblichen, in der inneren Construction und Durchführung ist aber sein schöpferischer Geist nicht zu verkennen. Der erste Satz ist auf reiches Figurenwerk gebaut, das dem zweiten Gedanken, einem ächt Chopin'schen liedmässigen, von Triolen unterstützten Cantabile, gleichsam zum Rahmen dient. Es ist dieser in den beiden verwandtesten Durtonarten auftretende Gedanke (die Grundtonart des Stückes ist H moll) der Ruhepunct in dem ganzen sehr bewegten Tonbilde. Das Scherzo ist sehr claviermässig, erinnert uns, mit Ausnahme des an vorgehaltenen Noten reichen gesangmässigen Alternativs, an die Gattung der Etude; zur Uebung in der Ausdauer in gebrochenen Figuren sehr empfehlenswerth. Das Largo, worin der eingeschaltete Satz in der Unterdominante uns übrigens am Wenigsten zugesagt hat, ist kurz zusammengedrängt, nach Art der Nocturnen, und ist bei Wiederkehr des Hauptsatzes jede breitere Ausführung vermieden und in der Begleitung eine kleine Variation angebracht. Der Schluss wird manchen Theoretiker stutzig machen, er ist einer der unbestimmtesten, verschwimmendsten, die vielleicht je geschrieben worden sind, nämlich dieser:

da das Ohr das G als übermässige Quinte auffassen und deren Fortschritt nach Gis erwarten muss, während jetzt es gleichsam ohnmächtig in den Dreiklang der Grundtonart zurücksinkt. Wir sind der Meinung, dass, wenn die übrigen Stimmen an einander gebunden liegen bleiben, statt dass der Componist die beiden Accorde von einander abgelöst haben will, die Wirkung noch reizender sein müsste. Die meisten Schwierigkeiten bietet das Finale, und zwar nicht solche, die man mechanische, sondern die man musikalische nennen muss. Die harmonische Vermittelung liegt oft nur in einer einzigen Note; Gründe genug, dass jede einzelne gleich wichtig ist, und doch wird bei dem raschen Tempo leicht manche liegen bleiben und damit sogleich immer dem Ganzen geschadet werden; es ist ein nicht gewöhnlicher Grad von Sauberkeit erforderlich, um das Verständniss aller Intentionen des Componisten zu Wege zu bringen. Dazu tritt noch rhythmische Schwierigkeit, z. B. in der zweiten Behandlung des Thema's, wo die dauernde Begleitung des dreitheiligen Zeitmaasses der Melodie durch Achtel ein sehr feines Gefühl fordert, um eine ungezwungene Verbindung hervorzubringen. So wird denn von den vier Sätzen dieser Sonate das Finale die meiste Sorgfalt seitens des Vortragenden verlangen. Auch ist sie für öffentliche Concerte überhaupt weniger als für kleinere, aufmerksamer Kunstbetrachtung gewidmete Salons geeignet.

Anonymus: Rezensionen der *Barcarolle* op. 60, der *Polonaise-Fantaisie* op. 61 und der 2 *Nocturnes* op. 62,
in: Neue Berliner Musikzeitung, Probenummer vom 16. Dezember 1846, S. 4/5

Fréd. Chopin: Barcarolle pour le Piano. op. 60. Polonaise-Fantaisie. op. 61. Deux Nocturnes. op. 62. Leipzig, bei Breitkopf und Härtel.

Von allen neueren Claviercomponisten hat keiner ein unbestritteneres Recht auf die Prädicate „originell" und „wunderbar" als C h o p i n. Während fast alle übrigen Autoren in einer Art Gütergemeinschaft leben, sich gegenseitig ihre Effecte leihen und in Inhalt und Form sich gleichen wie die Figuren eines Kaleidoskop's, führt C h o p i n uns in eine fremde in sich abgeschlossene Welt, in das Reich seiner innersten unmittelbarsten Empfindungen ein. Was er dem Papiere anvertraut, ist – wie seltsam es auch klingen möge – nie Resultat einer Berechnung oder Coketterie, sondern der wahrhafte, getreue Erguss einer bunten, oft abenteuerlichen Fantasie – momentan gefühlt, momentan wiedergegeben. Aber je subjectiver ein Künstler ist, desto mehr entzieht er sich dem augenblicklichen Verständniss. Wie man sich erst in gewisse Schriftsteller hineinlesen, in ihre Art zu denken und zu combiniren hineindenken muss, um von ihren Schönheiten betroffen zu werden, so muss man sich auch erst in Chopin's Art zu fühlen hineinfühlen, um Genuss aus den Blüthen seiner Fantasie zu saugen. Daher kommt es, dass man nach dem Vortrage einer Chopin'schen Pièce in einem Athemzuge sie „köstlich, unvergleichlich" und „abgeschmackt, gekünstelt, baroque" bezeichnen hören kann, je nachdem Jeder im Stande gewesen ist, seine Gefühle mit denen des Componisten zu parallelisiren.

Chopin wird nie der grossen Menge angehören, aber zum Glücke hat er es auch stolz verschmäht für sie zu dichten, denn von dem Augenblicke an, wo er ihr, oder besser gesagt gewissen Mode gewordenen Effecten huldigen wollte, wäre sein besserer Genius von ihm gewichen, ein Genius, der ihm bis jetzt einen grossen Kreis enthusiastischer Verehrer erhalten hat.

Indem Schreiber dieser Zeilen es vorgezogen hat, statt einer detailirten Besprechung oben bezeichneter drei Piècen im Allgemeinen den Standpunkt anzugeben, von dem aus alle Chopin'schen Werke beurtheilt werden müssen, glaubt er keinen Fehlgriff gethan zu haben; dies wäre der Fall gewesen, wenn diese drei Piècen etwas ganz Abweichendes von des Componisten sonstiger Art gebracht hätten; sie schliessen sich aber gleichmässig seinen früheren Arbeiten an; höchstens könnte man sie, was bei Chopin's Individualität nicht zu verwundern ist, etwas überreizter nennen. Indem wir sie daher seinen Verehrern mit vollem Rechte anempfehlen, namentlich die Fantaisie-Polonaise [op. 61], bleibt uns für „Druck und Ausstattung" nur die Alles sagende Bemerkung übrig, dass sie bei „Breitkopf und Härtel" erschienen sind.

57.

August Kahlert: Rezensionen der *Barcarolle* op. 60, der *Polonaise-Fantaisie* op. 61 und der 2 *Nocturnes* op. 62, in: Allgemeine Musikalische Zeitung 49/1847, Nr. 7 vom 17. Februar, Sp. 115–117

F. Chopin, Barcarole pour le Piano. Op. 60. Pr. 20 Ngr.

Die schaukelnde Bewegung der Barcarole lässt sich zwar nur durch ein zweitheiliges Maass, das den Schlag und Widerschlag der Wellen auszudrücken vermag, repräsentiren, jedoch erhöht es den Charakter, wenn die einzelnen Tactglieder in dreitheiligem Rhythmus, also in Triolen gehalten sind. Am Ruhigsten gleitet das Ganze aber dahin, wenn der Zwölfacheltakt den doppelten Schlag und Widerschlag ausdrückt, und besonders bei grösserer und ausgedehnterer Form des ganzen Musikstückes ist dies ein treffliches Mittel, um die Tactgruppen zu stetigem Flusse zu verbinden. Den Rhythmus, von dem das Gepräge des Ganzen abhängt, lässt *Chopin* zuerst als Begleitungsfigur, wie wir sie in vielen seiner Etuden finden, auftreten, und baut auf dieselbe die zweistimmige Melodie, so dass man sich die Wasserfahrt irgend eines zufriedenen und glücklichen Paares dabei wohl denken kann. In diesem ganz behaglichen Zustande belässt der Componist die Sache nicht, sondern zieht Wendungen, die der Barcarole fern liegen, herein, lässt endlich ein durch Rhythmus und Tonart scharf abstechendes Alternativ Platz greifen. Das Stück steht in Fis dur, dieses nun in A; natürlich leitet sich dies nach Fis und damit auch in die eigentliche Barcarole wieder zurück. Doch hat sie eine neue Gestalt gewonnen. Sie wird durch Verdoppelung der Intervalle, durch mancherlei Passagenwesen ein Salonstück, das seinem ursprünglichen Wesen untreu erscheint, wenn es auch, gut, vor allen Dingen rein gespielt, recht schön klingt. Dieses wirklich und gewissenhafte rein und sauber Spielen wird durch die zahlreichen Vorzeichnungen, die *Chopin*, weil er so gern auf den Obertasten spielt, so häufig anzuwenden genöthigt ist, vielen Dilettanten erschwert. Zugleich aber ist dies eine nicht zu verachtende Uebung.

F. Chopin, Polonaise Fantasie. Op. 61. Leipzig, Breitkopf u. Härtel. Pr. 27½ Ngr.

Ganz frei, rhapsodisch und gleichsam nur präludirend beginnt der Componist, geht dann in vagen Harmonieen in das Maass eines Alla Pollacca über und lässt dann ein Tempo giusto (As dur) eintreten, das einen thematischen Charakter hat. Wir brauchen diesen Ausdruck, um anzudeuten, dass zu einem eigentlichen Polonaisenthema im gewöhnlichen Sinne es doch nicht kommt, so frei und phantastisch ist auch dieses zur w[e]iteren Entwickelung bestimmte Thema beschaffen. Von einer strengeren Durchführung ist auch nicht die Rede. Eine zweite Melodie in der Dominante ist schärfer begränzt, cantabler und um so wohlthätiger, als bis hieher schon sehr viel modulirt worden ist. Nun aber beginnt erst die Fantasie herumzuschweifen, aus Es geht es weiter nach B, nach G moll und H moll und nun in einen selbständigen Satz H dur, der durch ähnliche rhapsodische Figuren als im Anfange sich nach F moll und dann wieder in die Grundtonart As zurückwirft. Diese wird eigentlich erst zuletzt dauernd und planvoll festgehalten. Das ganze Stück schillert in einer gewissen Unbestimmtheit der Tonarten, die freilich bei *Chopin* so oft ihre Reize hat, doch aber diesmal sehr weit geht. Der Name Fantasie ist wohl eben mit Rücksicht auf die Kühnheit dieser Conturen gewählt. Die Theorie fragt hier nach den Gränzen solcher Freiheit, über der sehr leicht die Wirkung des Ganzen verloren gehen kann. Mancher wird nach zwei Seiten diese Polonaise muthlos weglegen. Bei genauerem Verweilen wird manche Einzelheit freilich Genuss verschaffen, indessen können wir nicht umhin, zu bemerken, dass *Chopin*, gerade in seiner blühendsten Kraft, es auch am Meisten verstand, seine Erfindung zu beschränken, zu zügeln. Vermöchte er noch dies über sich zu gewinnen, so würde er durch seine oft so merkwürdigen Combinationen allgemeineren und stärkeren Eindruck erreichen. Der Gedanke, den er hinwirft, ist fast immer glücklich, warum verschmäht er nun so sehr seine feste Gestaltung, besonnene Entwickelung?

F. Chopin, Deux nocturnes pour le Piano. Op. 62. Pr. 22½ Ngr.

Melodisch und ungekünstelt tritt das erste dieser beiden Nocturnes, eine Form, worin uns *Chopin* zum Theil nach *Fields* Vorbilde schon so viel Schönes gegeben hat, auf. Schon nach den ersten acht Tacten aber nimmt der zweite Theil, der sich in Gis moll hält, etwas Geheimnissvolles an, leitet indessen wieder glücklich in das Thema hinein. Unstät modulirt nun der Mittelsatz As dur, welchem dann das Grundthema mit einigen äusserst weich über die gebundenen unteren Stimmen weggleitenden Figuren sich wieder anschliesst. Im Ganzen genommen ist, wenn man sich mit *Chopin's* Spielart ein Mal vertraut gemacht bat, dieses Nocturne von mässiger Schwierigkeit, es enthält manche reizende Wendung. Bedeutend grösser sind die des zweiten, auf den Vortrag eines durchgebildeten Musikers berechnet. Dem Thema: [Notenzitat Takte 1–2], das, wie man sieht, in der Begleitung sogleich grosse Sorgfalt verräth, merkt man noch nicht an, was dahinter steckt, welchen Klippen der Schiffer, der sich in diesen anfangs so friedlichen Strom begibt, begegnen wird. Nach dem Abschlusse des Thema's wird demselben ein Satz in Cis moll mit allerhand künstlichen Figuren im Basse, dann überhaupt lauter figurirten Stimmen entgegengesetzt. Es ist ein Glück, dass das Ganze die Bezeichnung „Lento" an der Stirne trägt, denn sonst möchte von der Reinheit der nicht eben gesparten Modulationen viel verloren gehen. Nach unserer Meinung geschieht des Guten eher zu viel als zu wenig, obgleich sich Alles hier auf einen Plan reduciren lässt. Cis moll, Gis moll , E moll, flüchtige Berührung von G dur, und schnell ist das Mittel gefunden, um die Dominante H dur zu erreichen und damit das Thema wieder einzuführen. Es wird nun auch nicht mehr viel damit vorgenommen, die erwähnte Bassfigur tritt nur noch gegen das Ende hin in die Begleitung. Der Schluss möge noch hier stehen, weil er eigenthümlich genug ist und das frühere Schwanken zwischen E dur und der verwandten Molltonart, woraus bei *Chopin* so oft bemerkenswerthe Wirkungen entstehen, noch ein Mal andeutet: [Notenzitat Takte 79–81, die letzten 3 Takte des Stücks]. Auf der zuletzt eintreten[den] Quinte beruht das Unbestimmte, das Verschwimmende dieses Schlusses, der recht eigentlich der romantischen Schule angehört.

A. K.

Anzeige der 3 *Mazurken* op. 63 und der 3 *Walzer* op. 64,
in: Neue Zeitschrift für Musik 27/1847, Nr. 51 vom 23. Dezember, S. 307
(unter: „Kritischer Anzeiger. Uebersicht der neuesten Erscheinungen
auf dem Gebiete der Musik.")

F. Chopin, Op. 63. 3 Mazourkas. Breitk. u. Härtel. 20 Ngr.
– –, Op. 64. 3 Valses. Ebend. 1 Thlr.
Beide Hefte gehören zu den weniger interessanten Compositionen Chopin's, indem beide nicht sowohl eigenthümlich als vielmehr gesucht erscheinen. Und doch! wie unendlich hoch stehen sie nicht selbst über größeren Werken der gegenwärtigen Modecomponisten!

August Kahlert: Rezensionen der 3 *Walzer* op. 64, der 3 *Mazurken* op. 63
und der *Sonate g-Moll* für Klavier und Violoncello op. 65,
in: Allgemeine Musikalische Zeitung 50/1848, Nr. 13 vom 29. März, Sp. 213–215

F. Chopin, Trois Valses p. le Piano. Op. 64. Leipzig, *Breitkopf & Härtel*. Pr. 1 Thlr.
Wie gern und wie glücklich *Chopin* Tanzrhythmen für Salonmusik ausbeutet, ist allen Dilettanten bekannt, welche kurze Unterhaltungsstücke den grossen Fantasieen oder glänzenden Sonaten vorziehen. Ein eigener feiner Geschmack bewahrt ihn dabei vor Trivialität, durch einzelne kleine Wendungen, die den musikalischen Künstler von dem Tanzcompositeur unterscheiden, würzt er selbst so gleichmässige, wenig pikante Rhythmen als die des deutschen Walzers. Die drei, welche er uns hier vorlegt, Des dur, Cis moll, As dur, bestätigen dies auf's Neue; doch sind sie nicht von gleichem Werthe. Der erste, wenn wir allenfalls das melodische Trio ausnehmen, bewegt sich in allzubekanntem Gleise. Der letzte ist populär gehalten und steht doch eine Stufe höher als Alltagswalzer, die für das praktische Bedürfniss berechnet sind. Am originellsten ist der zweite, mitunter zwar etwas seltsam klingend, doch den bewährten Meister verrathend. Der Charakter ist weich und träumerisch, der Walzerrhythmus tritt übrigens unter dieser bieg- und schmiegsamen Melodie weniger prägnant hervor.

F. Chopin, 3 Mazurka's [op. 63]. Ebendas. Pr. 20 Ngr.
Hier noch mehr als in der Walzerform bewegt sich *Chopin* auf vertrautem heimischen Boden, die Mazurka als Salonstück ist ganz eigentlich seine Schöpfung, und hier ist er auch noch immer erfinderisch. Dass man alte bekannte Wendungen

Chopin's auch diesmal wiederfindet, ist natürlich, er kann seinen Styl nicht verleugnen. So ist die zweite dieser Mazurka's eigenthümlich reizend durch die bei *Chopin* oft angetroffene unbestimmte Mischung der Dur- und Molltonleiter gerade in der Melodie. Er geht am Schlusse so weit: [Notenzitat Takte 55/56, die letzten 2 Takte des Stücks], so dass die kleine Terz erst spät zu ihrem wahren Rechte kommt. Aus solcher Unentschiedenheit, womit die Tonika auftritt, entsteht auch jenes verschwimmende Kolorit, das einen sehnsüchtigen Ausdruck zur Folge hat und das den Nachahmern *Chopin's* unerreichlich geblieben, ja bei ihm selbst schon zur Manier geworden ist.

Chopin, Sonate pour le Piano et Violoncelle. Op. 65. Ebendas. 2 Thlr.

Ein grösseres Werk, auf weitere Ausführung der Formen, auf Verarbeitung ergibiger Motive berechnet, fordert die Kritik mehr als jene hingeworfenen Bluetten heraus, und wenn es einen so berühmten Verfasser hat als diese Sonate, so wird es in doppeltem Maasse der Fall sein. Gegen seine Launen, gegen manches Seltsame seiner harmonischen Kombinationen wollen wir nichts mehr einwenden. Ihm ist längst grössere Freiheit als Anderen zugestanden, auch auf einen kleinen Missbrauch derselben kommt es daher nicht an. Aber was leider immer mehr bei *Chopin* hervortritt, ist ein anderer Mangel, der sich uns in dieser an so vielen jener ihm eigenthümlichen interessanten Züge reichen Sonate aufdrängt. Es ist der Mangel an bestimmt ausgeprägten melodischen Gedanken, an solchen, die sich scharf abschliessen, dass sie thematisches Gewicht gewinnen, dass sie eben, weil sie in jeder Verkleidung schnell wieder erkennbar sind, sich als herrschendes Thema geltend machen. Seine Themata, um ein Gleichniss zu brauchen, waren dereinst (man denke an das Conzert in E moll) mehr lyrisch, jetzt sind sie mehr rhetorisch, ihr melodischer Werth ist jetzt so sehr durch die Harmonie bedingt, dass die Cantabilität darüber verloren geht. Diesmal nun ist er dieser durch ein so günstiges Instrument, als das Cello, wesentlich zu Hilfe gekommen; die diesem gestellte Aufgabe ist schwer, doch sind durch die Verbindung seiner Gesangstellen, denen es an leeren Phrasen auch nicht fehlt, mit dem Klavier gute Effekte bewerkstelligt worden, z. B. im ersten Allegro (G moll) das zweite Thema (B dur), das sich zwischen beiden Instrumenten glücklich vertheilt. Das sehr kurze Largo wird am Unbedingtesten Theilnahme finden. Im Finale zeigt sich die ganze Neigung zur harmonischen Sonderbarkeit. Die Fasslichkeit des Stückes wird nämlich dadurch erschwert, dass dieser G moll Satz bereits im Thema selbst, das eben kein melodisches Gepräge hat, mit der Septime anfängt, und schnell nach D moll, im 12. Takt schon gar nach A moll modulirt. Dieser Quintenzirkel ist im Mittelsatz eines Stückes ganz gut angebracht, so früh angewandt macht er den Hörer irre und lässt kein Interesse an dem Stücke aufkommen. Im Verlaufe wird dies zwar einigermaassen gut gemacht, die Tonika tritt entschiedener auf, doch ist es dann schon zu spät. So ist denn das, was wir an der Sonate zu tadeln haben, dies, dass Alles zu sehr verschwimmt und das Einzelne, das uns lieb werden könnte, nicht zur völligen Geltung kommt.

Flodoard Geyer: Rezension (unter „Neue Werke der Kammermusik")
der *Sonate g-Moll* für Klavier und Violoncello op. 65,
in: Neue Berliner Musikzeitung 2/1848, Nr. 25 vom 21. Juni, S. 188

Unter den g e i s t r e i c h e n Componisten nimmt nun auch Chopin einen der ersten Plätze ein; die h a r m o n i s c h e C o m b i n a t i o n ist bei ihm vorherrschend, die m e l o d i ö s e tritt überwiegend nur in der L i e d f o r m, wie in dem an seine Mazureks erinnernden Menuett und dem kurzen Andante auf, das weiche Element der Mittelstimmen und der hierdurch entstehende sanfte, trübe, klagende Grundton macht ihn zu einem Gemüthsverwandten Spohr's. Seine Cantilene ist zwar gesättigter als bei diesem, seine Thematisirung aber bei Weitem unfasslicher, unpopulärer. Die Stimmen bleiben bei Chopin überwiegend zusammen, sie erdrücken sich fast; ein Reichthum, woraus wie bei Spohr (in dessen Quartetten) nur Nachtheil erwächst, die freie Entwickelung der Stimmen sinkt dadurch herab, und es kann von einem D u o, von einem A l t e r n i r e n der beiden Instrumente kaum die Rede sein. Die Kunst des Contrapuncts, welche durch Auseinandersetzung klar und verständlich macht, scheint Chopin fremd zu sein. Selbst bei dem Reichthum der Harmonie ist er doch durch und durch h o m o p h o n. Die dadurch entstehenden Mängel verdeckt er durch picante Modulationskunst, welche für Manche (wenigstens Deutsche) doch wohl allzugewürzt ist. Dann wieder giebt er mancher Virtuosengrille Spielraum und streut Passagenreihen ein, welche als blosses Fingerwerk nicht am Orte stehen (so zu Anfang und öfter). Chopin führt also eigentlich keinen Gedanken contrapunctisch durch, sondern fügt Note an Note, und die Frage, ob diese sich zu Themen gestalten, möchte verneint werden dürfen. Seine Composition ist überwiegend eine geistreiche Begleitungskunst, der eine eigenthümliche, nicht selten kühne Harmonisirung zu Grunde liegt. Die arbeitenden Mittel sind nicht Resultate gelehrter Studien als vielmehr eine homophone Figurationskunst. Dem Spieler bietet diese ungewöhnlichen Reiz, sie fordert ihm die ganze moderne Technik des Piano's ab. Aber die Grundstimmung seiner Werke ist so voll Wehmuth und Resignation, wenn auch seine Haltung stets ritterlich edel, dass sie weichlich frauenhaft erscheint. Männliche Kraft, Grösse, loderndes Feuer, Entschlossenheit vermissen wir, statt dieser Eigenschaften finden wir Zartheit, Wärme, Wehmuth, Trauer, Ergebenheit, süsses Lächeln unter Thränen. Diese Grundstimmung durchweht alle Arbeiten Chopin's, sie mögen kürzer oder länger sein, und selbst der innigste Verehrer wird eine gewisse Einfarbigkeit derselben nicht ableugnen können. Chopin dürfte nicht unpassend ein musikalischer Einsiedler genannt werden dürfen, der, wenn er in die Welt tritt, fremdartig erscheint, aber desto mehr von dem, welcher ihn aufsucht, geliebt werden möchte. Seine lyrische Natur gehört grösseren Räumen weniger an als der Zurückgezogenheit. Diese Sonate wenigstens dürfte vor einer Zuhörerschaft, welche an das Classische gewöhnt ist, den Erwartungen nicht entsprechen, welche sie vielleicht an den Namen des Componisten anknüpfen

Flodoard Geyer.

Ferdinand Hiller: Nachruf auf Chopin, in: Neue Zeitschrift für Musik 31/1849, Nr. 42 vom 21. November, S. 225–227

(In der Neuen Zeitschrift für Musik 31/1849, Nr. 38 vom 7. November, S. 204 war unter „Tagesgeschichte." zu lesen: „Todesfälle. Am 17sten Oct. starb zu Paris Friedrich Chopin.")

W o r t e
dem Andenken Chopin's geweiht,
durchflochten von Compositionen desselben, vorgetragen in einer
Erinnerungsfeier an den Verstorbenen in Düsseldorf
den 3ten November 1849.[29]

Wohl gleicht das Leben einem flücht'gen Traume
Und schnell entfliehn die Bilder, die es bringt!
Die Jugend braust dahin, die Liebe folgt ihr,

---

29 Dem Hingeschiedenen einen Gruß der Liebe und Verehrung nachzusenden hielt F e r d. H i l l e r in Düsseldorf eine Erinnerungsfeier, an der alle musikalischen Kräfte der Stadt sich betheiligten, und wo das oben mitgetheilte Gedicht gesprochen wurde. Unser geehrter deutscher Meister betrachtet dasselbe als Zeichen seiner Gesinnung gegen den Freund, dem er eine Reihe von Jahren innerlich nahe gestanden. Dem Requiem von Cherubini ging der Trauermarsch aus der eroica voran; ein vierstimmiges, zu diesem Zwecke componirtes Lied („Wie flüchtig ist des Menschen Zeit") folgte; dann schloß sich unmittelbar der Vortrag des Gedichts und der in dasselbe verflochtenen Clavierstücke an, der Chor aus Paulus „Siehe wir preisen selig" beschloß die Feier, die einen allgemein ergreifenden Eindruck zurückließ.

Kaum ist man seiner selber sich bewußt:
Sieht man sich an des Alters eis'ger Schwelle,
Der Strom der Zeit
Reißt schnell uns fort zur Ewigkeit.
Doch ziemt es nicht zu zagen und zu klagen,
Wenn ewigen Gesetzen nur gehorchend
Der Mensch das ihm bestimmte Ziel erreicht
Und hinzieht, woher keine Rückkehr möglich.
Wenn aber Jugend dem Talent sich einet,
Wenn einen Genius die zarte Hülle birgt,
Wenn der, der Tausende erfreut, entzückt,
Auf seiner Laufbahn glänzend stolzer Höhe
Entrissen wird dem lieben trauten Kreise:
Dann mag der Seufzer sich der Brust entwinden,
Die Zähre in dem trüben Auge perlen,
Denn grausam scheint das Schicksal da zu walten,
Spricht unsrer Hoffnung, unsrer Liebe Hohn! – –
Ob wohl das Leben in der Töne Reich
(Dem feenhaften, träumerisch tiefen)
Die, die es leben, schneller leben macht?
Ob wohl das Licht, das ewig flackernde,
Der Lebens-Lampe Oel zu schnell verzehrt?
Ich weiß es nicht, doch fast könnt' es so scheinen.
Wie viele Ihrer sah ich nicht verwelken
Und fallen, eh' des Lebens Herbst erschien!
Und ach, die Besten waren es!
Nicht Alle nenn' ich, – doch gedenkt Bellini's,
Des holden Sängers süßer Melodieen,
Der Malibran, die seine Weisen sang.
An Schubert denkt, der kühn, romantisch, sinnig,
Dem deutschen Liede höchsten Schwung verliehn!
Und Jenes, von euch Allen Vielgekannten,
Und Vielgeliebten, Vielbewunderten,
Des Geist so oft in diesen Räumen waltet! – – [Mendelssohn]
Schon wieder reiht sich ihm ein Neuer an,
Ein Ebenbürt'ger, den er kannt' und liebte,

Und dessen Tönen er oft still gelauscht.
Nur wenige sind hier, die dieses Glück genossen,
Des Glückes, ihn zu kennen, ihn zu hören,
Ihn zu bewundern und – ihn zu lieben!
Wie Vieles war in ihm vereint zu finden,
Was sonst getrennt und fern sich steht!
Des Slaven melancholisch weiches Wesen,
Sorglos verschwendrische Freigebigkeit,
Fränkischer Anmuth leichtgesellige Gabe,
Germanischer Tiefe weiter Bildungskreis,
Die herbe Strenge männlich kräft'gen Fühlens
Und weiblicher Empfindung holde Süße;
Vollendetster Grazie hoher Zauber
Umschwebte all' sein Thun und Lassen,
Umschwebte seine reichen Schöpfungen,
Umgab ihn, wenn er uns damit berauscht.
Seele, Talent und Geist, Persönlichkeit,
So innig waren sie in ihm verbunden,
Mit einer Lilie Blatt und Duft und Blüthe.
Gesänge wunderwürdig, neu und reizend
Schuf er in Klängen, vor ihm unbekannt.
Doch selten hat er Worten sie gesellt,
Denn er auch litt an Polens tiefen Schmerzen,
Er war entfernt, entrückt dem lieben Vaterland,
Deß Laute ihm die einzig Theuern blieben;
Nach Warschau's Fall, nach Polens Unterliegen,
Sah er die traute Heimath niemals wieder,
Jedoch dem Volk, das er das Seine nannte,
Gehörte er auch in der Fremde an,
Und was er auch uns Allen Schönes bot,
Nicht können wir's empfinden wie die Seinen,
Sie rührt, erhebt es mächtiger noch als uns:
Denn es durchwehen seine edlen Lieder
Des Polen Schmerz, des Polen Heldenkraft,
Sein Lieben und sein Hassen und sein Kämpfen,
Des Volkes laute, stürm'sche Freude,

Der ritterliche Muth, des Herzens Sehnen,
Die Höh'n und Tiefen seiner Leidenschaft.
Nicht reizte unsern Freund die laute Masse,
Geschäftig zog er nicht von Stadt zu Stadt
Die Welt mit seines Namens Lärm zu füllen:
Ein kleiner Kreis nur wen'ger Auserwählten,
Die ihn verstanden, ganz ihm hin sich gaben,
Er war es, den am liebsten er beglückt
Mit seiner Phantasieen holdem Strome.
Geliebt wurd' er vom ersten Weib der Gegenwart [George Sand],
Geliebt, und ach – verlassen! – Wie war's möglich,
Daß zu entziehn sich ihm ein Herz vermochte
Das einmal ihm gehört!? – –
                              Genug, genug!
Er ist dahin – zu bessern Regionen
Entflohen ist nun jene Feuerseele,
Der ein zu leichtes Kleid gewoben war!
Die Finger, fühlend gleich der Sensitive,
Vergeist'gen nicht mehr die verwaisten Tasten,
Den Freunden fehlt der Freund, – der Kunst ein Jünger,
Der einzig war und unersetzlich bleibt.
Doch hat er edle Gaben uns gelassen,
Ein köstlich, unvergleichlich, herrlich Erbtheil
(Zu schwer nur, leider! würdiger Benutzung)
In seiner Werke ewig jungem Schatz.
Mehr als dem kalten Wort es je gelingt
(Doch viel zu wenig, um sein würdig Bild zu geben)
Mag jetzt von seines Wesens reicher Fülle
In Tönen Euch ein schwaches Zeugniß werden.
Horcht, wie er, präludirend nur,
Im engsten Raume sich beschränkend
Das Tiefste ausspricht, was das Herz bewegt,
          Praeludium in E-Moll. [op. 28, Nr. 4]
Hört weiter, wie er, gleich dem weisen Arzte,
Der uns den bittern Trank, den heilenden,
Darreicht, gemildert durch des Honigs Süße, –

Die trockne Studie zu verbergen weiß
In Melodieen voller Reiz und Anmuth! –
        Etude in As-Dur [op. 25, Nr. 1]
Ein Liebeslied, ein nächtliches, hört nun –
Mit leisem Flüstern holder Herzens Schmerzen,
Durch wonniges Hoffen, sehnsuchtsvolles Bangen
Erklingt der Sturm der tiefsten Leidenschaft.
        Nocturno in Fis-Dur [op. 15, Nr. 2, Hiller gewidmet!]
Die flücht'ge Laune eines Augenblickes,
Sie nimmt Gestalt und Form – ein Spiel nur scheint es,
Doch oft birgt sich die zärtlichste Empfindung
In solch' ein heiter, muthwillig Gewand.
        Impromptu in As. [op. 29]
Der ächte Pole sei Euch jetzt vorgeführt
In seiner Tänze muthig frischen Klängen,
Bald feierlich, fast wie spanische Grandezza,
Im stolzen Reigen seiner Polonaise;
Dann zierlich schwebend, sporenklingend, jubelnd
In der Mazurka launenhaften Rhythmen.
Doch nur erinnern sollen diese Weisen
An ihren Namen, denn zuviel hat ihnen
Der Künstler mit verschwenderischer Hand
Gegeben, reichster Harmonieen Pracht,
Und neuster, eigenthümlich feinster Führung;
Kaum kann das Ohr, das kunstgewohnte, folgen;
Der Fuß, und wär' er noch so elfenhaft,
Muß ruhn, und nur die Seele darf sich wiegen
Auf dieser Melodieen süßem Spiel.
        Polonaise in Cis-Moll. [op. 26, Nr. 1]
        Masurkas in F-Moll u. B-Dur.
Auch unsres Vaterlandes schlichter Reigen
Hat ihn zu neuem Schaffen angeregt,
Und nie erklang der treue lust'ge Walzer
So anmuthsvoll und edel, wie durch ihn.
Zuweilen möchte man ihn kaum erkennen
In seiner fast zu glänzenden Bekleidung –

Jedoch sie steht ihm gut und lieblich an.

      Walzer in Cis-Moll u. Des-Dur. [op. 64, Nr. 2 und 1]

Der heitern Klänge sei's fortan genug,

Schwer reihn sie sich der heut'gen Feier an,

Und nur, um Euch des lieben Freundes Züge

Zu zeigen, wenn sie lächelnd waren,

Nahm man sie auf in seiner Lieder Folge.

Die Schöpfung einer düstern-grauen Stunde,

Sie sei anjetzo noch von Euch gehört!

Ward sie ihm eingegeben durch Erinnerung

An sein gebrochen Vaterland?

War sie die Ahnung seines frühen Scheidens?

      Trauermarsch in B-Moll. [*Sonate* op. 35, 3. Satz]

Wir müssen enden – Strömt die Quelle auch

In ew'ger Frische reichen Labetrunk,

Man kann und darf nicht zu viel von ihr kosten,

Doch kehrt man gern und oft zu ihr zurück

Wie zu den Melodieen unsres Freundes.

Gedenket sein – weist einen Ehrenplatz ihm an

Im Pantheone liederkund'ger Sänger.

Er war vollendet – hat vollendet,

So ist er doppelt selig denn zu preisen,

Denn ewig leben wird er hier wie dort! –

                Ferd. Hiller.

[Dieser Text erschien unter dem Titel „Chopinfeier (1849)" ohne die Anmerkung auch in: Ferdinand Hiller: *Aus dem Tonleben unserer Zeit. Gelegentliches*, Zweiter Band, Leipzig 1868, S. 264–269.]

Peter Cornelius: Rezension des Buches *F. Chopin* von Franz Liszt,
in: Berliner Musikzeitung Echo 2/1852, Nr. 9 vom 29. Februar, S. 66–68

Beengend und niederdrückend wirken die Abschiedsthränen auf uns, die wir von liebenden Augen an jenen engen, schmalen Reisewagen in's Jenseits, welche man Särge nennt, weinen sehen, und welche mit noch viel mehr Staub belastet werden, als die wirklichen, die da auf der lauten Landstraße des Lebens einherrollen. Und sehen wir gar eine Nation weinen am Grabe ihrer untergegangenen Freiheit, so verzweifeln wir, ihr keinen Trost spenden zu können. Es giebt aber Thränen, welche die Kunst vor dem Auge der leidenden Menschheit wegküßt, und die sich auf dem Hauch ihrer Lippen in ätherischen Wohllaut verwandeln, daß sie versöhnend hineinklingen in ihren Gesang, der uns dann tröstend über den irdischen Schmerz erhebt. So weint die ewigblühende Rebe Mozart im Requiem, solcher Thau unvergänglicher Trauerweiden birgt sich in jener Heldenklage Beethovens, welche *Marcia funebre* geheißen ist, und ihnen gilt dann wohl das Wort des Dichters [Goethe, *Wonne der Wehmut*]: „Trocknet nicht, trocknet nicht, Thränen der ewigen Liebe!"

Nicht ohne ähnliche Stimmung, nicht ohne gleichen Wunsch wird der Musiker das künstlerische Erbauungsbuch aus der Hand legen, welches Franz Liszt dem Andenken Friedrich Chopin's gewidmet hat. Es hieße die edelste Bescheidenheit des Autors verletzen, welche sein Werk in jeder Zeile durchdringt, und welche uns nicht einen Augenblick beim Anschauen der rein dargestellten Persönlichkeit des hingeschiedenen Tondichters einen Seitenblick auf die eigne abzwingt, wollten diese Zeilen mit der gerechten Anerkennung des Dichters beginnen. Wenn wir vor dem lebenathmenden Conterfei von den Händen eines jener alten Maler oft den Meister vergessen und uns in die fremden Züge staunend versenken, die uns noch fest im Herzen stehen bleiben, wenn auch dem Gedächtnisse der Name des Schöpfers entfallen mochte, um wie viel mehr wird der Seelenschilderer, welcher hier in den glühendsten Farben ein herrliches makelloses Künstlerdasein vor uns stellte, seinen höchsten Triumph feiern, wenn wir ihn über sein Werk vergessen. Geht doch die Wirkung des Bildes selbst über den sichtbaren Gegenstand desselben hinaus, und ist der Haupteindruck, den wir von Liszt's Buch empfangen, vor Allem der einer erhöhten Verehrung und Heilighaltung der Kunst selbst; der ewig reinen, lichten Kunst, die durch tausend ungeweihte Hände nicht herabgezogen werden kann aus dem tönenden Aether, in welchem sie schwebt – ein Stern unter den Sternen.

Das also war C h o p i n ! Aus solchem Golde eines stummverblühenden, entsagenden Gemüthslebens waren die Saiten gewebt, die er auf seine Leier spannte. Das waren die Edelsteine seiner Jugenderinnerungen, welche in der Krystallfluth seines Innern versinkend jene wunderbaren Kreise schlugen, welche als Klänge so nahe an unser Herz schweben. Das war seine Vaterlandsliebe, die ihm jene Sirenenstimme lieh, welche schmeichelnd den Ueberwinder selbst in den Abgrund zu locken sucht. Das waren seine Verehrer, seine Mitkämpfer in der romantischen Arena. Das sein

Gutmann, dem er sterbend die Hand küßte, das seine Fürstin Czartoryska, die dem Verscheidenden Stradella's Hymnus an die heilige Jungfrau sang und den Psalm des venetianischen Patriziers [Benedetto Marcello]. Das waren die Blumen, die er liebte und denen er duftklingende Schwestern auf dem Grund seines Herzens erzog. Und jenes *E-moll*-Präludium [op. 28, Nr. 4], in welchem, wie in seinem Leben, die Dissonanzen so schmerzlich klingen und doch ängstlich vor der Auflösung beben, spielte Lefebure Vély [sic!, recte: Lefébure-Wély] zu seinem Requiem in der Magdalenenkirche. Und derselbe Lablache, der zu Beethovens Todesfeier das *Tuba mirum* gesungen hatte, sang es hier, ein Trauerfalter, der von der zersplitterten Eiche zur gebrochnen Lilie flog; und die Viardot und die Castellan, welche auf allen Bühnen des gesanglauschenden Europa seinen wehmuthjauchzenden Masureck ertönen ließen, sangen ihm nun Mozart's Recordare [aus dem *Requiem* KV 626]!

Wenden wir nun den Blick von dem Gemälde einen Augenblick auf den Maler selbst, so sehen wir Franz Liszt mit der reinsten Freude im edelsten Wirken begriffen, von welchem dies Buch ein lebendiges Zeugnis giebt. Aus dem berauschten und weltberauschenden Jünglingsalter des Virtuosenthums heraus und sich reinigend von dessen Schlacken, ist er fest und entschlossen in die Epoche reifen, männlichen Schaffens getreten, welche verborgener, aber desto nachhaltiger und nach allen Seiten hin mächtig anregend wirken wird. Fühlt man es doch aus seinem Streben immer deutlicher heraus, wie wohl er des geweihten Bodens bewußt ist, auf dem er in Weimar steht, und wie er strebt, desselben würdig zu sein. Hier ziehen nicht mehr jubelnde Studenten an seinem Wagen, aber ernste Männer, denen die Kunst Alles gilt, sehen hoffend und vertrauend zu ihm empor. Ein Buch, wie sein Friedrich Chopin, wird keine Lärm- und Lobposaunen erwecken, und für den Plebs hat er sich darin mit einem viel zu aristokratischen Französisch umgeben – aber der denkende und empfindende Künstler wird auf einsamer Kammer Trost und Festigkeit daraus schöpfen, und Manche, die falschen Irrlichtern nachgejagt haben, werden in Liszt's Worten, in denen genug eigne schmerzliche Erfahrung nachklingt, einen milden Leitstern finden, wenn er sagt: „Laßt uns ihm (Chopin) keine künstlichen Blumen streuen! Werfen wir ihm nicht fade und vergängliche Kränze hin! Erheben wir unsre Gefühle Angesichts dieses Sarges! Möchten wir von ihm lernen, Alles zu verwerfen, was nicht den Stempel des edelsten Ehrgeizes trägt; unsre Bemühungen einzig auf Anstrengungen zu richten, welche eine tiefere Spur zurücklassen als die Mode des Tages. Möchten wir auch für uns selbst in der trüben Zeit, in welcher wir leben, Allem entsagen, was der Kunst unwürdig, Allem, was nicht die Bedingungen der Fortdauer in sich schließt, Allem, was nicht einen Abglanz der ewigen, unfaßbaren

Schönheit enthält, welche durch die Kunst und durch welche die Kunst ihre Strahlen entfalten soll. – – Möchten wir, statt so vielen Mühaufwand daran zu setzen, Zuhörer anzuziehen, und ihnen um jeden Preis zu gefallen, uns lieber, wie Chopin es that, bestreben, ein lang hintönendes Echo von dem zurückzulassen, was wir empfunden, was wir geliebt und gelitten haben."

Liszt's Buch wird neben der universellen Sprache, in der es geschrieben, sicher durch deutsche, englische und andre Bearbeitungen die Verbreitung finden, die es verdient, und so den Zweck erfüllen, dem es gewidmet ist. Den Verehrern des tondichtenden Chopin wird es munden wie ein sprudelnder Quell am Wege, auf dem sie ihn ganz und umfassend kennen zu lernen streben. Und so grüße ich scheidend und bewillkommend diese tiefpoetische Sage eines Dichterlebens aus Dichtermunde. Wie jene altdeutsche Heldenschaar den italischen Strom hinrauschen ließ über das Grab ihres geliebten Königs[30], so quille fortan aus diesem Buch ein reicher Born innerster Begeisterung schützend und erhaltend über das immergrüne Grab des unvergeßlichen C h o p i n.

C o r n e l i u s.

[Diese Rezension erschien auch in: *Peter Cornelius: Aufsätze über Musik und Kunst, zum ersten Mal gesammelt und hrsg. von Edgar Istel*, Leipzig 1904, S. 25–28, und in: *Peter Cornelius: Gesammelte Aufsätze. Gedanken über Musik und Theater, Poesie und Bildende Kunst*. Hrsg. und kommentiert von Günter Wagner unter Mitarbeit von James A. Deaville, Mainz u.a. 2004, S. 218–220, auf S. 215–217 der handschriftliche Entwurf zu diesem Essay.]

Eduard Hanslick: Ausschnitt aus einer Konzertkritik zu Chopins *Sonate für Violoncello und Klavier* op. 65, gespielt von Bernhard Coßmann (Violoncello) und Eduard Pirkhert (Klavier),
in: Presse vom 11. Januar 1859 (unter: „Concerte.")

C h o p i n ' s Sonate für Violoncell und Clavier (zum erstenmal) vermochte den Erwartungen der Freunde dieses Tondichters nicht zu entsprechen. Nicht blos zeigt sich darin ein auffallendes Ungeschick, in größeren Formen zu denken und wahrhaft polyphon zu schreiben, auch an der rein melodiösen Erfindung erscheint

---

30 Anspielung auf die Bestattung des Westgotenkönigs Alarich 410 n. Chr. im Busento und das bekannte Gedicht *Das Grab im Busento* von August von Platen.

hier Chopin wie gelähmt durch den bloßen Gedanken, eine S o n a t e schreiben zu sollen. Dieser so hoch und eigenthümlich begabte Componist hat es nie vermocht, die duftigen Blüthen, die er mit vollen Händen ausstreute, zu einem schönen Kranz zu vereinigen. Sein großes Talent bewährte sich nur in kleinen lyrischen Stücken: H e n s e l t und S t e p h e n H e l l e r sind hierin ähnlich organisirt.

Louis Ehlert: [Betrachtungen über Chopin und die Interpretation seiner Musik], in: Louis Ehlert: *Briefe über Musik an eine Freundin*. Zweite Auflage, Berlin 1868, S. 118–125 (XVI.). Erstmals erschienen 1859

Kennen Sie die traurigen Mazurkas von Chopin, diese klagenden Tänze, in denen das tiefste Herzeleid rothe Schnürstiefelchen angelegt hat, um sich todt zu weinen im bachantischen Taumel? Mir liegt ein Stück im Sinne*), Schmerzlicheres können Sie sich gar nicht denken.

O meine müden Füße, ihr müßt tanzen
In bunten Schuhen,
Und möchtet lieber tief
Im Boden ruhen!

Der arme Chopin! War es das Leiden seines Volks, welches ihn bekümmerte, oder war es ein geheimes Weh, ein Liebesschicksal?

An seiner Wiege hatten die Grazien ihren holdesten Zauber gesprochen, wie nicht leicht über einen andern Sterblichen, und die Götter ihm ihr Liebstes mitgegeben, den Adel des Genies. Was der höhere Mensch irgend bedarf, um glücklich zu sein, er hatte es im vollsten Maße: den Lorbeer des Ruhms, das Glück der Liebe, den Schutz der Freundschaft, die Früchte der Arbeit, dies Alles von Jugend und einer unwiderstehlichen Persönlichkeit getragen. Es fehlte ihm nichts, als ein System von Seemannsnerven. Der arme Chopin! seine Seele war mit Aeolsharfensaiten bespannt, auf denen der leiseste Windhauch wunderbar unbekannte Weisen spielte; wie aus heiliger Stille klingen diese seraphischen Legenden an unser Ohr, daß wir aufhorchen, als spräche die Natur selbst mit elementarer Stimme eine räthselhafte Weissagung aus. Ein Poet von so unbeschreiblicher Feinheit der Sprache, von solchem Farbensinn, solch höchster Aristokratie des Gedankens

---

* Op. 17 Nr. 4.

mußte freilich auch sein Nervensystem für sich haben. So zehrte er denn eine Lebenskraft, die kärgere Naturen zu zwei Jubiläen ausgedehnt hätten, schon auf der Höhe seines Sommers auf. Beneidenswerth! Denn nach der Dauer rechnet der Pöbel, wir haben ein anderes Maß. Lassen Sie mich einen einzigen Wonnemonat ein Dichter wie Beethoven sein, und ich würde mich schämen, Ihnen nichts mehr dafür bieten zu können als die Bettelei meines ganzen übrigen Lebens. Vertiefung, Innigkeit ist Alles, und das größte Glück auf Erden, ein unsterbliches Werk schaffen zu können.

Aber daraus, daß wir nichts leisten, stammt all' unsere Unliebenswürdigkeit her; zerbrochen und müde sitzen wir wie Krankenwärter an dem Bette unsrer siechen Hoffnung, der wahnwitzigen Amme, welche uns mit vergifteten Liebesträ.nken großgesäugt hat.

Chopin hat das Unglück gehabt, so populär zu werden, daß es keinen Salon giebt, in welchem er nicht verfälscht oder mißverstanden würde. Der frivole Hang, sich diese geistreichen Weisen auf's willkürlichste auszulegen, in die eigenthümliche Welt des Dichters mit den persönlichsten Gelüsten einzukehren, hat zu jener, die Sinne und das Gemüth beleidigenden Art des Chopinspiels geführt, dessen Charakter sich am Besten durch eine Mischung von Possenhaftigkeit und Unkeuschheit bezeichnen ließe. An die Stelle des Anmuthigen wird das Gefallsüchtige gesetzt, das Freche an die Stelle des Uebermüthigen, das Empfindungsvolle weichlich und das Geniale barock vorgetragen. Nur wer noch die Thräne und das Erröthen kennt, nur wer sein Herz bis in die Fingerspitzen schlagen fühlt, vermag Chopin zu spielen. Scheitern unsere größten Virtuosen an dieser Aufgabe, so können Sie sich vorstellen, was die Dilettanten daraus machen. Unsere musikalischen Gesellschaften, welche die Langeweile und die Eitelkeit auf gemeinschaftliche Tantieme geben, dieser Inbegriff aller Unerträglichkeit und Unbehaglichkeit, welche sich Menschen durch ein ungeschicktes Beieinandersein verursachen, diese Krankenstuben des Vergnügens, in welchen der Verwesungsgeruch tausend im Keim erstickter Gedanken die Luft erfüllt, sind der natürliche Schauplatz für die Charaden und Anagramme, welche unsere Klavierspieler über den Namen Chopin machen. Ich schwöre Ihnen bei Herrmann und Dorothea [Versepos von Goethe] auf mein metrisches Gewissen, daß ich lieber einer Improvisation in Hexametern beiwohnen möchte als diesen widerwärtigen Entstellungen eines Dichters, dessen sonderbare Gluth alle flammenscheuen Finger zurückschrecken sollte. Stellen Sie sich nur das Schicksal einer Composition vor, bei welcher der vorgeschriebene Takt nicht wie eine Kinderruthe hinter dem Spiegel steckt, stellen Sie sich das Durcheinander von Eilungen und Verzögerungen vor, wo die metronomische Pedanterie der Zeiteintheilung aufgehoben ist, und nicht mehr die Pendelschwingungen, sondern die taktfreien Bewegungen des menschlichen Herzens der Dichtung Gewand heben und senken sollen.

Irgend ein geheimer Reiz muß diesen Schöpfungen einwohnen, welcher sich selbst der poesielosen Welt der „höheren Ignoranten" erschließt, wie die Viardot einmal jene Kreise nannte, wo der Klassizität ewige Verbannung geschworen, wo Beyer und Rosellen [zwei minderwertige Komponisten von Salonmusik] mit unbeschreiblichem Verständniß gespielt, und alles für Ambrosia genossen wird, was ungepfeffert und ungesalzen ist. Jener Reiz wirklicher Vornehmheit muß es sein, durch welchen der ächte Adel überall seine Herkunft verräth, der Reiz unnahbarer Anmuth, welcher alle Lebensäußerungen dieser Welt mit Schönheit umkleidet. Weil Chopin ein geborener Aristokrat ist, haben sich ihm selbst diejenigen Salons erschlossen, welche die gute Gesellschaft sonst nicht zu empfangen pflegen. Aber Sie glauben es mir nicht, in welchen abenteuerlichen Verbindungen ich diesen theuren Freund habe begrüßen müssen. Es schaudert einen vor der Popularität. Nicht gespielt werden, oder mißfallen, es sei! Gefallen? Wem? Worauf? Ich habe das H-Moll-Scherzo [op. 20] einmal in einer Gesellschaft so gemeiner Possenreißer gehört, daß es mir war, als begrübe man eine Rose in einem Strauß von Disteln. Denn daß derselbe Geschmack, welcher in einem Chopin'schen Stück doch wenigstens das Poetische ahnt, in einem schlechten Virtuosenstück auch das Gemeine wittern sollte, das wähnen Sie nicht. Die Vorliebe für Chopin ist nur ein Produkt des Instinktes, nicht des Urtheils: was sein Genius Edelstes geschaffen hat, das ist nur Eigenthum einer kleinen Gemeinde. Ich gebe Ihnen meinen Glauben, meine Liebe und meine Hoffnung dafür hin, daß eine Mazurka, wie die angeführte, nur von äußerst Wenigen verstanden wird. Zu fatalistisch ist dieses F, zu düster der schmerzlich fragende Schluß:

O meine armen Augen, ihr müßt blitzen
Im Strahl der Kerzen,
Und schlieft im Dunkel lieber aus
Von euren Schmerzen!

Man hat Chopin krank genannt. Ach, wer unter uns könnte sich der Gesundheit rühmen! Nicht kränker war er wie viele unserer größten Dichter, nicht kränker als Byron, nicht kränker als Schumann, obwohl ich einräumen will, daß

Kalkbrenner gesünder war. Wer aber fragt jetzt nach der robusten Muse des Herrn Kalkbrenner, nach seinen handfesten Passagen und seinen rothbäckigen Melodien? Als ich ein Knabe war, mußte ich eins jener tavernenartigen Stücke spielen, welche damals die deutschen und französischen Pianos überschwemmten. In meiner Einfalt fragte ich einmal meinen Lehrer, ob der Herr Kalkbrenner nicht ein Matrose wäre, wofür ich sehr gescholten wurde. Ich habe nie ein Stück dieses würdigen Mannes spielen können, ohne an gestreifte Beinkleider denken zu müssen. –

Chopin war eine so poetische Natur, daß unter seinen Händen die Etude selbst zum Gedicht wurde. Man spiele die beiden größten derselben, die in Cis- und A-moll [op. 25, Nr. 7 und 11], so augenscheinlich sie für technische Zwecke geschrieben wurden, nur mit völliger Freiheit, und man wird mir einräumen, daß unsere Klavierliteratur nicht viel Leidenschaftlicheres, höher Erregtes geschaffen hat. Und welche bewunderungswürdige Originalität steckt in Ihnen! Da ist auch kein Takt, welcher nicht klavierspielerisch und musikalisch entzückend neu wäre, wie denn Chopin der Erfinder eines ganz neuen Klavierlebens genannt werden muß. Wie schauerlich uninteressant ist vor ihm der Klavierstyl aller Meister, Beethoven ausgenommen; welch eine Litanei abgelebter, todmüder Formen, welch ein erfindungsloses, prosaisches Geklimper! Denn sollte mir Jemand allen Ernstes, ohne den Mund zu verziehen, betheuern, daß er noch heute mit wahrem Vergnügen Klavierstücke von Clementi (ich nehme den „Gradus" allein aus), Dussek, Hummel und Ries spiele, so will ich ihn für einen herzlich guten Mann halten, ja für einen ganz besonders braven, aber meinen Wein tränke ich nicht mit ihm.

Kennen Sie eine Nachtigall, welche so träumerisch helldunkel geschlagen wie die Melodien Chopin'scher Notturnos? Ich will Hafisen nicht wehe thun, aber unsere deutschen Bulbuls scheinen mir liederkrank dagegen.

Hat die Filigranarbeit und die maurische Arabeske etwas so übersinnlich Feines gesponnen wie jene fantastischen Zierrathen, welche aussehen, als wären es blasse Spitzen, von Elfen im Mondlicht geklöppelt? Und nun schlagen Sie eins seiner großen Liebeslieder auf, und blicken Sie dieser himmlischen Leidenschaft in die sommerheißen, gewittertrunkenen Augen!

> Von der ungeheuren Flamme,
> Welche mir im Busen wüthet,
> Ist die Sonne nur ein Funke,
> Der sich in die Luft geschwungen.

Von der „ungeheuren Flamme" ist sein Busen frühzeitig verzehrt worden, er ist den feurigen Tod der Dichter gestorben. Wir aber, die wir sie haben zum Himmel schlagen sehn, die wir uns an dem Nektar berauscht haben, welchen er freigebig kredenzte, lächeln mitleidig über das Küchenfeuer, an welchem der Bürger Dussek und der Biedermann Hummel ihr schmales Göttermahl kochten, und der Nektar des edlen John Field schmeckt uns wie ehrliches Zuckerwasser. Bewahre uns Gott vor historischer Ungerechtigkeit! Sie waren brave, tüchtige Männer, aber bedenkliche Poeten. Getragen von dem Abiturientengefühl eines absolvirten Cursus, spielten sie Klavier nach den frommen Regeln ihrer Vorfahren und komponirten reinliche, gesetzmäßige Stücke mit der philiströsen Behaglichkeit eines durch keine Phantasie beunruhigten Gewissens, unschuldig von den revolutionären Wegen Beethovens auf den Bürgersteig der Convenienz ablenkend, geschützt von der Polizei, beklatscht von den Händen des Kapitals und der Pension, und das Gefühl der Unsterblichkeit sicher mit hinübernehmend, als wäre sie für alle Zeiten durch wohlthätige Legate gesichert. Ich würde mich hüten, über solche Männer bei Lebzeiten ein bitteres Wort zu schreiben. Der Nachwelt sei es erlaubt unparteiisch zu sein, und eine von der Mitwelt zu lebhaft gezollte Bewunderung auf ihr natürliches Maß zurückzuführen.

Für dieses verdrießliche Amt entschädigt sie sich dadurch, daß sie umgestürzte Bildsäulen wieder aufrichtet, und auf verschollene Gräber Kreuze setzt.

Ferdinand Hiller: [Erinnerungen an Chopin], in: *Briefe an eine Ungenannte*, Köln 1877, S. 149–152

Ja, verehrteste Freundin, ich glaube wohl sagen zu dürfen, daß Chopin mich liebte, – aber i c h war in ihn v e r l i e b t. Ich wüßte wenigstens kaum, wie ich die Neigung, die er mir eingeflößt, anders bezeichnen könnte. Seine Gegenwart beglückte mich, – nie wurde ich's müde, ihn sprechen zu hören; hatte ich ihn länger, als es sein mußte, nicht gesehen, so fühlte ich wahrhafte Sehnsucht nach ihm; ich verließ in aller Frühe meine Wohnung, um ihn zu finden, ehe er seine Unterrichtsstunden begann. Etwas Zärtlichkeit mischte sich wohl in die Zuneigung Aller, die ihm nahe standen, – schon sein allzu zarter Körperbau forderte auf, behutsam mit ihm umzugehen. Diese blassen Züge, diese mehr als schlanken Glieder erregten eine Empfindung, wie sie ein enthusiastischer Sammler etwa seinen venezianischen Gläsern oder seinem altsächsischen Porcellan gegenüber im Busen tragen mag. Dabei war er schlangengleich biegsam und anmuthig in seinen Bewegungen.

Sein Organ hatte einen zarten, einschmeichelnden Klang, er muß das Polnische mit geistreicher Gewandtheit beherrscht haben. Französisch und deutsch aber, in welchen Sprachen wir abwechselnd mit einander verkehrten, verstand er zwar bis in ihre feinsten Schattirungen, sprach sie aber nicht fließend, – die Ausdrücke für seine scharfen Beobachtungen und Aperçus öfters suchend als findend. Wenn ich dann, ihn errathend, lächelte, pflegte er auszurufen: „Du verstehst, was ich sagen will! Cela suffit." Und so gab dieser Mangel an Sprachfertigkeit seinem Geplauder einen Reiz, dessen die beredteste Zunge oft ermangelt. Im Allgemeinen erschien er heiter, – ja, er konnte ausgelassen sein, – indeß war der Grundzug seines Empfindens schwerlich ein fröhlicher. Denn er fühlte sich nicht gesund, und der durch die unglückliche polnische Erhebung gebotene Aufenthalt in der Fremde lastete schwer auf ihm, trotz allem, was Paris bietet und was es vollends ihm bot. Ohne Gesellschaft zu sein, liebte er nicht, und es kam wohl auch sehr selten dazu. Morgens mochte er eine Stunde einsam an seinem Flügel zubringen, – aber sogar, wenn er übte, – oder wie soll ich's nennen? – wenn er die Abende Clavier spielend zu Hause blieb, mußte er mindestens einen seiner Freunde in der Nähe haben. Die Tage verlebte er Unterricht gebend, was, wunderbarer Weise, einen großen Reiz für ihn hatte. Freilich waren seine Schüler größtentheils Schülerinnen und gehörten fast ausschließlich den höchsten Kreisen der französischen und polnischen Aristokratie an. In diesen Regionen, in welchen er seit seiner frühesten Knabenzeit verkehrte, fühlte er sich aber durchaus heimisch – vor allen in jenen seiner Landsleute, deren eine große Anzahl, und zwar der Vornehmsten und der Besten damals in Paris eine Zuflucht gefunden hatte. Dazu kam, daß man ihn nicht allein bewundernd verehrte, sondern auch auf das gründlichste verzärtelte.

Von Vornehmthuerei war jedoch keine Spur bei ihm zu finden, – sein einfach freundliches, oft scherzendes und lachendes Benehmen blieb sich den Geringsten gegenüber gleich; wer ihn näher kannte, mochte aber herausfühlen, daß er sich nur Wenigen, und auch dann nur selten hingab. Seines Werthes sich bewußt, fehlte ihm doch die klare Erkenntniß nicht von den Gränzen, die seinem Genie gesetzt waren. Gern mochte er sich als lyrischer Dichter betrachtet wissen, „so etwa wie Euer Uhland", sagte er eines Tages zu mir. Wäre er in seinem Vaterlande geblieben, meinte er, so würde er vielleicht viel für polnische Gesangsmusik gethan haben. Aber in einer andern Sprache als in seinem geliebten Polnisch zu componiren, würde ihm unmöglich gewesen sein. Er ist, ohne Worte, für sein Volk ein Nationaldichter geworden, und es bedurfte keiner Uebersetzungen, um seine Tondichtungen überall zur Anerkennung zu bringen.

Ihnen, verehrteste Freundin, von diesen zu sprechen, hieße Ihnen Dinge sagen, die Sie besser wissen als ich, – wer Chopin spielt wie Sie, der versteht ihn. Aber über sein wunderbares Spiel, das mir bis zum letzten Athemzug vor der Seele bleiben wird, muß ich mich aussprechen. Ich sagte, daß er sich s e l t en hingab, – am Flügel that er es vollständiger, als ich es je bei irgend einem andern Tonkünstler wieder gefunden. Er gab nur sich, – in solcher Abgeschlossenheit, daß jede Erinnerung an irgend etwas Gehörtes wegfiel. So hatte niemand die Tasten eines Flügels berührt, – in so zahllosen Modificationen niemand denselben Tönen zu entlocken gewußt. Rhythmische Bestimmtheit gesellte sich einer Freiheit im Vortrag seiner Melodieen, daß diese im Moment zu erstehen schienen. Was bei Anderen elegante Verzierung, erschien bei ihm wie der Farbenschmuck der Blumen, – was bei Anderen technische Fertigkeit, bei ihm wie der Flug der Schwalbe. Jede Betrachtung einzelner Vorzüge, der Neuheit, der Anmuth, der Vollendung, der Seele, fiel weg, – es war eben Chopin. Sogar den Mangel jener imponirenden Kraft des Klanges, wie sie Liszt, Thalberg und Anderen eigen, empfand man als einen Reiz, – der Energie des Gedankens gesellte sich in dem vergeblichen Kampfe mit der Materie ein Gefühl der Sehnsucht. Selbst das tiefste Verständniß seiner Compositionen, das innigste Sichversenken in dieselben gibt keine Vorstellung von jener Poesie des Vortrages, wie sie ihm eigen war. Jeder Gedanke an Körperlichkeit entschwand, – es war wie das Leuchten eines wunderbaren Meteors, das uns doppelt entzückt in seiner geheimnißvollen Unbegreiflichkeit.

Friedrich Nietzsche: [Über Chopin], in: *Menschliches, Allzumenschliches. Ein Buch für freie Geister*, zweiter Band, Chemnitz/Paris 1880, neue Ausgabe Leipzig 1886

159.

Freiheit in Fesseln – eine fürstliche Freiheit. – Der letzte der neueren Musiker, der die Schönheit geschaut und angebetet hat, gleich Leopardi, der Pole Chopin, der Unnachahmliche – alle vor und nach ihm Gekommenen haben auf dies Beiwort kein Anrecht – Chopin hatte dieselbe fürstliche Vornehmheit der Konvention, welche Raffael im Gebrauche der herkömmlichsten einfachsten Farben zeigt, – aber nicht in bezug auf Farben, sondern auf die melodischen und rhythmischen Herkömmlichkeiten. Diese ließ er gelten, als *geboren in der Etikette*, aber wie der freieste und anmutigste Geist in diesen Fesseln spielend und tanzend – und zwar *ohne* sie zu verhöhnen.

160.

Chopins Barcarole. – Fast alle Zustände und Lebensweisen haben einen *seligen* Moment. *Den* wissen die guten Künstler herauszufischen. So hat einen solchen selbst das Leben am Strande, das so langweilige, schmutzige, ungesunde, in der Nähe des lärmendsten und habgierigsten Gesindels sich abspinnende; – diesen seligen Moment hat Chopin, in der Barcarole, so zum Ertönen gebracht, daß selbst Götter dabei gelüsten könnte, lange Sommerabende in einem Kahne zu liegen.

Eduard Hanslick: Aus der Rezension von Anton Rubinsteins Konzertzyklus von sieben Abenden zur Geschichte der Klaviermusik 1885 in Wien, in: Eduard Hanslick: Aus dem Tagebuch eines Musikers [...] Kritiken und Schilderungen, Berlin 1892, S. 191/92 (unter „Rubinstein.")

Hingegen dünkt es uns nicht motivirt, C h o p i n einen ganzen Abend, also den siebenten Theil der gesammten Musikentwicklung, zu widmen und ihn überdies noch am folgenden Abend mit elf Nummern zu bedenken. Einer der genialsten und eigenartigsten Tondichter, kommt Chopin doch nie auf eine wesentliche Umbildung seines Stils, er erlebt keine Wandlungen, keine einschneidenden Phasen, und bleibt mehr als irgend ein anderer Componist in demselben höchst subjektiven Empfindungskreise verharren. Einen ganzen Abend hindurch ausschließlich diese nervös aufregende Luft zu athmen, dreißig Stücke von Chopin – und wäre jedes für sich das reizendste – rasch nacheinander in sich aufzunehmen, das ist eine starke Zumuthung, die uns weder ästhetisch gefordert, noch praktisch vernünftig erscheint.

Eduard Hanslick: Aus einer Rezension eines Klavierabends von Bernhard Stavenhagen in Wien 1889, in: Eduard Hanslick: Aus dem Tagebuch eines Musikers [...] Kritiken und Schilderungen, Berlin 1892, S. 290/91 (unter „Virtuosen.")

Mit zauberhafter Leichtigkeit, fast zu rasch, läßt er den Chopin'schen Des-dur-Walzer an uns vorüberfliegen. Befremdend fiel es auf, daß Stavenhagen eine Chopinsche Etüde ganz unvermittelt, fast ohne die Hände von der Klaviatur zu heben, an den Trauermarsch anfügte. Mit besondrem Interesse hörten wir Chopins „Fantaisie-Polonaise", op. 61. Sie wird wegen ihrer außerordentlichen technischen Schwierigkeiten wie ob ihres räthselhaften Inhalts selten gespielt. Stavenhagen zügelte die

ersteren vollkommen und erhellte das verwirrende Dunkel des letzteren nach Mög-
lichkeit. Es ist dies eine Phantasie im pathologischen Sinne, das Phantasiren eines
Fieberkranken, dem lockende und wüste Bilder in wirrer Flucht erscheinen. Verge-
bens sucht er sie zu deuten, festzuhalten, zu verbinden: seine Erregung steigert sich
endlich bis zur Tobsucht, aus welcher er in tiefste Ermattung hilflos zurücksinkt.
Ein psychologisch merkwürdiges, aber musikalisch durchaus unerfreuliches Stück.
Wenn L i s z t , der begeisterte Verehrer Chopins, von dieser Composition sagt, sie
stehe als ganz pathologisch außerhalb der Sphäre der Kunst, so ist dem nichts weiter
beizufügen. Es wird erzählt, daß Chopin, als er des Nachts diese eben entstandene
Polonaise sich vorspielte, die Thür seines Zimmers aufgehen sah und ein langer Zug
polnischer Damen und Edelleute in alterthümlicher Tracht an ihm vorbeischritt.
Diese Vision erfüllte ihn mit solchem Schrecken, daß er zur entgegengesetzten Thür
hinausflüchtete und jenes Zimmer des Nachts nicht mehr zu betreten wagte. Ein
polnischer Maler, [Teofil] Kwiatkowski, hat diese Vision „nach Chopins eigenen
Angaben" in einem Bilde dargestellt.

**Hugo Riemann: Artikel „Chopin" in: Musik-Lexikon [...] Fünfte vollständig
umgearbeitete Auflage, Leipzig 1900, S. 193–194**

Chopin (spr. schópäng), F r é d é r i c François, hochbedeutender, Epoche ma-
chender Pianist und feinsinniger, origineller Komponist besonders für Pianoforte,
geboren 1. März 1809 zu Żelazowa Wola bei Warschau (neuere angebliche Rektifi-
kationen des Geburtsdatums widersprechen einander), gest. 17. Okt. 1849 in Paris;
sein Vater war eingewanderter Franzose (Nicolas C. aus Nancy, zuerst Buchhalter in
einer Cigarrenfabrik, dann Privaterzieher, später Lehrer am Gymnasium, zeitweilig
Inhaber einer eigenen Schule mit Pensionat, zuletzt Lehrer an der Ingenieur- und
Artillerieschule zu Warschau), seine Mutter eine Polin, Justine Krzyżanowska. Bereits mit neun Jahren spielte C. öffentlich und wurde als Wunderkind angestaunt.
Seine Lehrer waren ein Böhme, Namens Żywny, und Joseph Elsner, Direktor der
Musikschule zu Warschau. 1830 verließ er als vollendeter Pianofortevirtuose seine
Vaterstadt und wandte sich nach Paris, unterwegs in Wien und München konzertie-
rend. Wie ein Meteor erschien er am Himmel, kurze Zeit in hellem Glanze strahlend
und schnell verlöschend. Er kam fertig nach Paris und hatte einen großen Teil seiner Kompositionen bereits im Portefeuille, darunter seine beiden Klavierkonzerte.
Seine erste Publikation, die Variationen über ein Thema aus „Don Juan" (Op. 2),
entflammte Schumann zu heller Begeisterung, und es war ein hoher Festtag, als C.

eines Tages selbst in Leipzig anlangte. In Paris fand C. schnell einen Freundeskreis, wie er ihn nicht schöner wünschen konnte. Liszt, Berlioz, Heine, Balzac, Ernst, Meyerbeer – Menschen, die ihn verstanden, und an denen er selbst mehr hatte als fade Bewunderer. C. wurde, nachdem er sich als Pianist und Komponist eingeführt hatte, schnell ein überaus gesuchter Lehrer; er ward in den besten Kreisen Mode. Leider zogen bald finstere Schatten über seine zwar sensible, aber von Haus aus nicht melancholische Seele. Symptome eines bedenklichen Brustleidens stellten sich ein, und er mußte 1838 zur Kur nach Majorca. George Sand, die von ihm schwärmerisch verehrte Dichterin, begleitete und pflegte ihn, ließ ihn aber freilich die letzten Jahre seines Lebens im Stich. Das Übel war nicht zu heben und schritt schnell vorwärts. Im Frühjahr 1849 schien eine Besserung einzutreten, und C. führte einen lange gehegten Wunsch aus, indem er nach London reiste und mehrere Konzerte gab; mit Nichtachtung seines körperlichen Befindens machte er verschiedene Gesellschaften mit, besuchte auch noch Schottland und kam völlig erschöpft wieder nach Paris zurück. Im Herbst d.J. starb er; zu seiner Totenfeier wurde auf seinen Wunsch Mozarts Requiem aufgeführt; sein Grab ist zwischen denen von Cherubini und Bellini. C. war eine seltene poetische Natur; wie Heine in Worten, so dichtete er in Tönen völlig frei und unbekümmert um herkömmliche und anerkannte Formen. Aber nicht nur im großen, auch in den Details war er völlig neu und originell; er ist der Begründer eines vorher ganz unbekannten Genres, eines neuen Klavierstils, den Liszt aufgenommen und fortgepflanzt hat, aber ohne ihn eigentlich fortzubilden – er ist nicht fortbildungsfähig, so wenig C. selbst sich nach seinem 20. oder 22. Jahr noch fortentwickelt hat. Schumann hat ihn einige Male in kleinen Stücken kopiert; bekannt ist auch die Anekdote, wie Liszt seine Art zu phantasieren zu völliger Täuschung der Freunde nachahmte – auch in den Nachahmungen ist er sofort kenntlich, aber sie bleiben Nachahmungen. Dabei ist er nicht etwa stereotyp, nicht auf wenige originelle Wendungen und Manieren beschränkt; im Gegenteil, gerade in dem Reichtum derselben liegt vielleicht der Schlüssel zu dem Rätsel seines Wesens. Seine Werke, ausschließlich Klavierwerke oder Werke mit Klavier, sind 2 Konzerte Op. 11 (E moll) und Op. 21 (F moll), Op. 14 Krakowiak (mit Orchester), Don-Juan-Phantasie Op. 2 (mit Orchester), Es dur-Polonäse Op. 22 (mit Orchester), Phantasie über polnische Lieder (mit Orchester), Duo concertant für Klavier und Cello (Thema aus „Robert der Teufel"), Introduktion und Polonäse für Klavier und Cello Op. 3, eine Cellosonate Op. 65, ein Trio (Op. 8 G moll), ein Rondo (C dur Op. 73) für zwei Klaviere, ferner für Klavier allein: 3 Sonaten (C moll, B moll, H moll), 4 Balladen, 1 Phantasie, 12 Polonäsen, 1 Polonäse-Phantasie (Op. 61), 56 Mazurken, 25 Präludien, 19 Nokturnen, 15 Walzer, 4 Impromptus, 3 Ekkossaisen [sic!], Bolero, Tarantella, Barkarole, Berceuse, 3 Rondos, 4 Scherzi, 3 Variationswerke, 1 Trauermarsch, 1 Konzertallegro und 27 Konzertetüden; dazu 17 polnische Lieder, in Summa 74 Opusnummern und 12 nichtnumerierte Werke. Sein Leben wurde beschrieben in phantastischer Weise von Liszt (2. Aufl. des französischen Originals 1879); deutsch von La Mara, 1880, englisch von W. Cooke 1877[31]), ziemlich konfus von M[arceli] A[ntoni] Schulz (Szulc, polnisch 1873), mit kritischer Gewissenhaftigkeit, aber für die Pariser Zeit nicht erschöpfend, von [Maurycy] Karasowski (2. Auflage 1878, 3. Auflage 1881, polnisch 1882) und am besten von Friedrich Niecks „Fr. Chopin as a man and musician" (1888, deutsch von W[ilhelm] Langhans 1889). Vgl. auch Moritz [Karasowski] „Fr. Chopin, sein Leben und seine Briefe" (2. Aufl. 1878), A[rnold] Niggli „Fr. Chopin" (1879), A[gatha] Audley „C., sa vie et ses œuvres" (1880, nach Karasowski), und Ed[uardo] Gariel, „Ch., La tradition de sa musica" (Mexiko 1895). 1880 wurde Ch. in der Heiligengeistkirche zu Warschau eine Votivtafel gesetzt und 1894 zu Żelazowa-Wola ein Denkmal errichtet.

Ferruccio Busoni: [Über Chopin] Notizen zu einem Klavierabend in Zürich, April 1916 (aus: Ferruccio Busoni: Von der Einheit der Musik... Verstreute Aufzeichnungen, Berlin 1922, S. 224/25)

In der Geschichte der Musik nimmt Chopin insofern eine besondere Stellung ein, als er – obwohl er nur für das Pianoforte und für dieses auch nur in kleineren Formen schuf – doch einen entscheidenden Einfluß auf Zeitgenossen und Nachfolger ausübte und allmählich zum populärsten, beliebtesten, jeder Stufe von Musikfreunden zugänglichsten Komponistennamen stieg, einer Stellung, die er noch heute in kaum geschmälertem Maße behauptet. Aber anders erkennen ihn die Musiker (ein Schumann und ein Liszt an der Reihe Spitze), anders erkennt ihn das Publikum. Denn des Publikums Verhältnis zum Künstler beruht seit jeher auf einem w o h l -w o l l e n d e n M i ß v e r s t ä n d n i s, wie es auch nicht anders denkbar ist, noch sein kann. In diesem Fall war es zumeist das Schwärmerische und Empfindsame in Chopins Natur, das einer ungemein großen Zuhörerschaft empfänglichsten Punkt traf,

„Ach, die zärtlichen Herzen!

---

31 Erste englische Übersetzung von Martha Walker Cook wurde 1863 in Philadelphia herausgegeben. Siehe S. 457, Fussnote 50 [Anmerkung von I.P.]

Ein Pfuscher vermag sie zu rühren."

Von autoritativen Musikern darüber vergewissert, daß es hier nicht mit einem Pfuscher zu tun hatte, gab sich das Publikum um so williger jener Seite von Chopins Gemüt hin, die sowohl des Pfuschers als des Publikums nächste Eigenschaft ist. – Aber Chopins tüchtigste Tat besteht in dem nicht mehr verschämten Herauskehren der eigenen Subjektivität, in der Bereicherung der Harmonik und in der Entwicklung des rein Klavieristischen. Sein Subjektivismus fällt zusammen mit dem Drange nach der persönlichen Äußerung jener Zeit; seine Persönlichkeit repräsentiert das Ideal der Balzacschen Romanfigur der 30er Jahre: des blassen, interessanten, mysteriösen, vornehmen Fremden in Paris. Durch das Zusammentreffen dieser Bedingungen erklärt sich die durchschlagende, umfassende Wirkung von Chopins Erscheinung, der eine starke Musikalität das B e s t ä n d i g e verleiht.

Nohant, George Sand's manor house as seen from the gardens, woodcut with an illegible signature in the illustrated weekly magazine *Kłosy*, 1876, vol. VII.

Aspects de la critique des œuvres de Chopin en France

Marie-Paule Rambeau

Lorsqu'il arrive à Paris en octobre 1831, Chopin est totalement inconnu en France. Quelques mois suffisent à le consacrer comme un pianiste hors pair et un créateur original. Il est indiscutable que la France n'a pas marchandé sa sympathie au compositeur polonais, qu'il s'agisse de la presse ou du monde artistique. Il n'a pas eu à affronter l'hostilité ouverte de certains rédacteurs, comme Rellstab en Allemagne ou Davison en Angleterre. L'unanimité de la critique à son propos s'est faite très vite et n'a guère évolué. Ses choix de carrière et la discrétion de sa vie privée l'ont mis à l'abri des impertinences de la presse qui n'ont pas épargné Liszt ou Berlioz, cibles des caricaturistes qui ne se sont jamais attaqué à lui. Après sa disparition, se mettent en place des images forgées par ses contemporains, journalistes, artistes ou écrivains : elles vont susciter par réaction des réserves sur la valeur de son œuvre que le tournant du siècle revisitera en fonction de la querelle qui opposera les partisans de Wagner et ses antagonistes, avant que le culte que Debussy lui vouait n'ouvre de nouvelles perspectives à sa réception. Est-ce à dire que Chopin a été compris, reconnu, apprécié en France plus qu'ailleurs en Europe ? Pour s'en convaincre, il est nécessaire de resituer les critiques dans leur contexte esthétique et socioculturel, sans jamais perdre de vue le poids des modes, des usages linguistiques et des clivages idéologiques qui constituent tout un code à déchiffrer.

Parmi les dispositifs susceptibles d'aider à la promotion d'un artiste, il en est d'essentiels : la critique de la presse qui va orienter l'opinion et le goût du public, et l'édition qui va diffuser ses œuvres. S'agissant d'un compositeur-pianiste, il faut y ajouter la facture instrumentale, véritable faire-valoir des talents. Il se trouve qu'au moment de l'installation de Chopin à Paris, l'essor prodigieux de ces trois secteurs d'activité favorisa le lancement de sa carrière en France.

Après le déclin de Vienne, Paris était devenu, dans les premières années de la Monarchie de juillet la capitale musicale de l'Europe. Elle accueillait toutes les gloires musicales chevronnées aussi bien que les réputations à faire. Elle était le passage obligé, la référence qui consacrait un artiste et décidait de l'avenir de sa carrière. Cela explique l'intensité de la vie musicale dans les lieux les plus divers et l'afflux des artistes étrangers désireux de s'y produire, voire de s'y établir. « Le personnel des pianistes[1] » offrait un éventail chatoyant de virtuoses, chacun insurpassable dans sa spécialité, qui rivalisaient d'excellence pour conquérir la première place dans les suffrages du public mais aussi dans la sanction des spécialistes. L'engouement du public qui constitua certains pianistes en monstres sacrés, dont on guettait les numéros d'adresse, fit fleurir un répertoire de pièces aussi brillantes qu'inconsistantes. Mais un pianiste aussi génial fût-il, n'a pas toujours l'étoffe d'un grand compositeur. Berlioz est le premier à avoir inversé l'ordre traditionnel des termes pour marquer la différence entre un pianiste-compositeur, tel Henri Herz ou Henri Bertini et un compositeur-pianiste comme Chopin. La frontière entre les deux ne paraît pas avoir été toujours nettement repérée par la critique musicale du temps où elle a suscité des controverses, en particulier à propos d'Henri Herz.[2]

Car le bouillonnement du monde pianistique est largement répercuté par les revues musicales dont l'expansion correspond à celle de la presse en général sous la Monarchie de juillet. Stimulée par l'élargissement du public et par l'effervescence du mouvement musical romantique, les journaux musicaux se multiplièrent ; la France rattrapa le retard qu'elle avait pris sur l'Allemagne en la matière. Aux périodiques spécialisés, il faut ajouter les chroniques musicales, sous forme de « feuilletons », annexés à la presse quotidienne à grand tirage, tels *La Presse* ou le *Journal des débats*, ou aux revues littéraires, comme la *Revue des deux mondes*. La critique musicale qui, au début du XIXe siècle, relevait souvent de l'amateurisme, devint affaire de spécialistes, aussi compétents que le musicographe F.J. Fétis, directeur de conservatoire, dont l'autorité n'excluait pas le souci de s'adresser à un lectorat élargi. Les compositeurs eux-mêmes, Liszt et Berlioz en particulier, reven-

---

1 Expression citée par *Le Pianiste* N° du 5 juin 1835

2 Schlesinger le traitait de « nullité musicale » ; la polémique se termina par un duel et une comparution devant le Tribunal correctionnel (Chopin fut cité comme témoin).

diquèrent le droit de participer à un débat où ils étaient engagés prioritairement. La *Gazette musicale* envisagea même que la profession de critique soit sanction-née par un diplôme[3]. Au cours des années, la critique musicale se constitua en genre littéraire, quand le principe romantique de la parenté des arts amena les écrivains à s'en emparer en la vidant de son contenu technique pour l'ouvrir à un langage littéraire et poétique procédant par métaphores et recherchant des équi-valents verbaux à une forme musicale par essence informulable. L'expressivité de la musique de Chopin offrait à cette approche un terrain particulièrement fertile : sous la plume de Gautier, de Janin ou de Legouvé, l'univers musical du Polonais se dessina par touches impressionnistes, en convoquant tout un système de référents poétiques qui allaient fonctionner jusqu'à l'apparition de la musicologie qui, au XXe siècle, le rendrait obsolète.

L'un des artisans les plus actifs de la collaboration entre musiciens et écrivains fut l'éditeur Maurice Schlesinger : il attira à la *Revue et gazette musicale de Paris,* qu'il fonda en 1835 en absorbant la *Revue musicale* de Fétis et sa propre *Gazette mu-sicale,* des écrivains de premier plan, tels Balzac, George Sand et Dumas, conjointe-ment à des journalistes, Henri Blanchard, Maurice Bourges, et à des pédagogues comme François Stoepel. Sa revue fut la plus influente, la diversité et la qualité des articles la plaçaient loin devant ses concurrentes, *La France musicale* des frères Es-cudier et *Le Ménestrel* dirigé par Jacques-Léopold Heugel. En qualité d'éditeur de musique, Schlesinger se reconnaissait le droit d'assurer la publicité des compositeurs qu'il publiait pour que les chefs-d'œuvre ne passent pas inaperçus. Et « les coups de trompette » de la *Revue* accompagnèrent en effet toutes les œuvres de Chopin dont il commença à publier les premiers opus en juillet 1833. Là où les autres périodiques se contentaient d'une recension, la *Gazette musicale* puis la *Revue et gazette musicale de Paris* proposaient une analyse substantielle, bien que rarement technique. Qu'il s'agisse de la publication de ses œuvres ou de ses concerts, Chopin fut constamment encensé dans les journaux de Schlesinger, et cela dès le début de sa carrière parisien-ne. Parmi les rédacteurs de la *Gazette musicale de Paris*, François Stoepel manifesta la compréhension la plus intelligente, la plus sensible aux orientations de l'art de Chopin dont il commenta toutes les publications jusqu'à sa mort en 1836.

Les premières années de la monarchie orléaniste, portée au pouvoir par la bour-geoisie, inauguraient une période d'euphorie économique où la nouvelle classe mon-tante accéda à la culture grâce à l'argent. Elle imposa des goûts en rupture avec la tradi-

---

3 N° du 30 août 1835 p. 194-195

tion culturelle de l'aristocratie d'ancien régime. La musique se démocratisa et pénétra dans la sphère privée des foyers par le truchement d'un instrument moderne, qui allait détrôner le clavecin et devenir emblématique de la culture bourgeoise : le piano. Ce qu'on a appelé « l'âge d'or du piano » correspond exactement aux années parisiennes de Chopin. Si nous sommes aujourd'hui surtout sensibles aux perfectionnements incessants de la facture instrumentale qui ont accompagné le renouvellement de l'écriture pianistique, il faut se souvenir que le piano avait mauvaise presse auprès de certains, qui lui reprochaient son caractère percussif et la sécheresse de sa sonorité, sans parler de son usage prosaïque : Balzac parle de « l'ingrat piano[4] » et le marquis de Custine de « l'instrument le moins fait pour toucher les cœurs[5] ». C'est cet instrument-là pourtant que le toucher miraculeux de Chopin allait faire chanter, en concurrent du *bel canto*. Le coup de cœur qu'il éprouva d'emblée pour les pianos de Pleyel, « non plus ultra[6] », auxquels il demeura fidèle presque exclusivement, lia son nom à la firme en termes d'affinités électives : « Il faut un piano de Pleyel [...] pour caresser une mazourk de Chopin », écrit un rédacteur du *Pianiste* en 1834[7]. Le « salon Pleyel », espace luxueux et assez intime pour être qualifié ironiquement de « boudoir » par un journaliste du *Ménestrel*[8] servit d'écrin à la mise en scène des grands concerts de Chopin, salués comme des événements musicaux très mondains ; leur retentissement favorisait bien entendu la promotion des pianos Pleyel dont son jeu magnifiait les qualités spécifiques.

Dans cette conjoncture propice, le premier concert de Chopin chez Pleyel, le 25 février 1832, créa la surprise. Ce jeune homme inconnu, présenté comme « Monsieur Chopin de Varsovie », se démarquait nettement de la cohorte des pianistes de l'école virtuose parisienne. Fétis ne s'y trompa guère : il consacra à ce concert un compte rendu, très élogieux[9], si l'on considère que son culte pour la musique ancienne ne le rendait pas indulgent à l'égard des jeunes compositeurs de son temps. Il insista sur l'absolue originalité des idées et du style du *Concerto* en *mi* mineur qui apportait le renouvellement qu'on attendait à la musique de piano, ou plutôt (la nuance a son importance) à « la musique des pianistes ». Fétis entendait ainsi situer Chopin dans

---

4   In *Ursule Mirouet*, Paris, Gallimard, Bibliothèque de la Pléiade, 1977, vol. 3, p. 890

5   « Choppin [*sic*], un pianiste dont le talent élégant, poétique et gracieux prête une voix et une âme à l'instrument le moins fait pour toucher les cœurs. » Lettre de Custine à Metternich du 3 janvier 1837. Citée par Jean-René Derré : *Littérature et politique dans l'Europe du XIXe siècle* IIe partie (Presses Universitaires de Lyon, 2006).

6   Lettre de Chopin à T. Woyciechowski 12/12/1831 *Correspondance de F. Chopin*, Paris, Richard-Masse, 1960, vol. 1, p. 48

7   N° du 10 juillet 1834 « Les pianos ».

8   *Le Ménestrel* du 20 février 1848

9   *La Revue musicale* du 3 mars 1832

une sphère où il pouvait lui accorder une place d'excellence ; la référence à « l'orga-nisation puissante » de Beethoven qui, lui, composait de la musique « de piano », imposait une échelle des valeurs indiscutable. Si à Varsovie, les critiques avaient pu comparer le jeune Chopin à Mozart, à Paris Fétis révisait à la baisse la cote du Polo-nais. Par ailleurs le déséquilibre entre la substantielle critique du compositeur et celle de l'exécutant, rapidement esquissée, plaçait Chopin au rang de créateur et non pas seulement de virtuose.

Cet article a certainement, en raison de l'autorité du rédacteur, influencé la réception de Chopin dans la presse musicale au cours des quatre années suivantes (1832-1836), celles où il se fit entendre fréquemment en concerts publics, tous re-censés. On y retrouve en effet les grandes lignes qui définissaient sa personnalité artistique : l'abondance des idées, la nouveauté et la richesse de l'écriture harmoni-que, le génie mélodique et la fantaisie des traits, un jeu privilégiant l'élégance et la grâce au détriment de la puissance sonore. Ce maillage d'appréciations constituera de façon stable la trame des principales critiques qui se diversifient avec la création de nouveaux journaux musicaux : Le Pianiste, fondé par Charles Chaulieu en 1832 et qui cessera de paraître en 1835, se fait le champion du compositeur qui « s'est placé à son début au niveau des grands maîtres[10] » et, malgré son jeune âge, possède « tou-tes les qualités de l'homme fait ». Inconnu en France, Chopin passe en effet pour un débutant, ce qui explique l'enthousiaste recension des Etudes opus 10. En fonction des rédacteurs, tantôt le journal excuse sur la maîtrise du « savant compositeur » les difficultés qui déroutent les pianistes amateurs, tantôt lui recommande une écriture moins « tourmentée » et un usage moins erratique du rubato, « l'effroi des jeunes filles[11] ». Car, faut-il le rappeler, la vocation d'un journal musical était de répondre aux horizons d'attente de ses lecteurs dont dépendait sa survie commerciale. La concurrence était rude et les polémiques entre les journaux très vives, parfois suivies de procès, voire de duels[12] ... Le Pianiste ne manquait pas une occasion de persifler les rédacteurs de la Revue et Gazette musicale de Paris et La France musicale, fondée en 1838, était en guerre ouverte avec ladite revue. Les compositeurs servaient d'enjeu à ces chicanes plus idéologiques que strictement musicales, comme le montreront par la suite les querelles autour de Verdi puis de Wagner. Paul Scudo, dans les co-lonnes de la Revue des deux mondes éreintait Liszt et Berlioz, encensés par la Revue

---

10 N° du 10 novembre 1833

11 N° du 10 mars 1834

12 On peut suivre dans la Gazette musicale de mars 1834 les péripéties du duel entre Schlesinger et Billard, représentant d'Henri Herz.

et Gazette musicale de Paris, tandis que *La France musicale* défendait de tout son poids les pianistes français Bertini et Prudent. On ne sait trop par quel miracle Chopin échappa à ce jeu de massacre. Le consensus de la critique, nonobstant quelques coups de patte bien appliqués, essentiellement dans *Le Ménestrel* et *La Revue des deux mondes*, se fit à son avantage.

Le problème du classement de Chopin dans une école revient comme un leitmotiv dans un grand nombre de critiques. « Les termes de comparaison manquent absolument », constate A. Guémer dans la *Gazette musicale*[13] et Berlioz affirme dès le premier article qu'il lui consacre en 1833 : « Chopin comme exécutant et comme compositeur, est un artiste à part, il n'a pas un point de ressemblance avec aucun autre musicien de ma connaissance [14]». Toutes les métaphores convenues de « la voie nouvelle » tentent de rendre compte à la fois des innovations formelles et harmoniques et de ce que Liszt nommera en 1851 « une nouvelle phase dans le sentiment poétique [15]». Autodidacte, sans lien véritable avec l'évolution musicale contemporaine, Chopin semble s'être révélé comme une apparition. Il faut attendre 1838 pour que *La France musicale* le place au confluent de deux écoles pianistiques, celles de Hummel et celle de Clementi, et, trouvaille moins heureuse, en fasse l'émule de Bertini dans le choix des formes brèves. D'un article à l'autre, les journalistes se renvoient en écho les expressions de « musique bizarre », de « famille excentrique », de « phénomène inexplicable », pour finir par reconnaître que Chopin est le compositeur le plus original que la France possède en ce qui concerne la musique de piano et que, s'il n'est pas le premier, il est unique. Cette originalité, Berlioz en dégage clairement les composantes techniques dans *Le Rénovateur*[16], en listant, sur la base des *Etudes* et des *Mazurkas*, les combinaisons rythmiques, l'invention harmonique, les broderies chromatiques, le traitement très libre de la mesure et le cachet « naïvement sauvage » de ses mélodies. Ces articles datent de l'époque où, autour de Berlioz, s'était formée une « confrérie romantique » dont Chopin était avec Liszt et Hiller l'un des piliers. Il analyse avec pertinence ce qui fait la substance du style de Chopin et formule l'essentiel de ce qu'on retrouve dans l'approche critique ultérieure, y compris la sienne. Dès 1833 Berlioz a compris que l'art de Chopin ne pouvait se communiquer que dans la sphère intime du salon et que sa carrière de concertiste était menacée par la nature délicate et capricieuse de son inspiration. Pour la première fois apparaît dans l'énon-

---

13 N° du 5 janvier 1834
14 *Le Rénovateur* du 15 décembre 1833
15 Liszt : *Chopin,* Paris, Corréa, 1941, p. 251
16 N° du 15 décembre 1833

cé la figure littéraire de la métaphore, chargée d'exprimer la subtilité des nuances et le charme de l'imprévu des *Mazurkas* ; c'est au lutin malicieux de Charles Nodier[17] que Berlioz emprunte sa référence : « Chopin est le Trilby des pianistes ».

Paradoxalement, tout en affirmant que Chopin était exceptionnel, inclassable, les chroniques musicales n'avaient de cesse de le comparer aux grands pianistes de sa génération. Cette confrontation était devenue un jeu auquel les gens d'esprit et le Tout-Paris prenaient plaisir à se livrer. Auréolés de tous les prestiges du talent, de la jeunesse, de la célébrité et de la mode, les pianistes virtuoses des années 1830, dont les portraits ornaient en pleine page les revues musicales, offraient toutes les combinaisons possibles de l'émotion provoquée par la musique, jusqu'à l'envoûtement. Blaze de Bury attribue à Liszt et à Chopin ce qu'il appelle « le règne du pianiste Lovelace et grand seigneur[18] ». Les deux compositeurs émergent en effet nettement par leurs carrures et se retrouvent ipso facto opposés l'un à l'autre dans une confrontation qui devait dominer la réception du phénomène de la virtuosité pianistique parisienne dans la première moitié du XIXe siècle. Placés par la critique à la même hauteur dans la perfection de l'exécution, ils sont représentés, dans un schéma dichotomique, comme deux jumeaux rivaux – « les Dioscures[19] » – ou manichéen, comme l'incarnation de deux principes antagonistes : Liszt est la figure diabolique du musicien possédé, Chopin le visage angélique de l'artiste inspiré. Chez Balzac ce trope fonctionne aussi bien dans les romans que dans les lettres familières : la « perfection raphaélesque » de Chopin est opposée à la « fougue dantesque » de Liszt[20] ; « Le Hongrois est un démon, le Polonais est un ange [21] ». Dans la presse, si friande des exhibitions échevelées de Liszt, les prestations pianistiques de Chopin appellent inévitablement les termes de « distinction » et d' « élégance ». « Il préfère la pensée au tour de force », note *Le Pianiste*[22], et Paul Scudo tranche : « Liszt est un pianiste, Chopin est un poète[23] », la classique hiérarchie entre artiste et poète plaçant Chopin dans l'espace sacré de la transcendance.

Le retrait progressif de Chopin de la scène publique dirigea les feux de l'actualité sur le duel Liszt-Thalberg dont les péripéties s'éternisèrent au point de lasser

---

17 *Trilby ou le lutin d'Argail* est un conte fantastique de Nodier, paru en 1822.
18 *Revue des deux mondes* 1er septembre 1883
19 L'expression est de Wilhelm Von Lenz dans *Les grands virtuoses du piano*, Flammarion, 1995, p.88
20 In *Le Cousin Pons*, Paris, Gallimard, Bibliothèque de la Pléiade, 1977, vol. VII, p. 705
21 Lettre à Mme Hanska du 28 mai 1843. *Lettres à Madame Hanska*, Paris, Editions du Delta, 1968, vol 2, p. 226
22 N° du 5 juin 1835
23 *Critique et littérature musicales*, Lecou, 1852, p.11

l'attention. A cette occasion la discrétion de Chopin apparut comme une sorte d'antidote contre les dérives du spectaculaire. Le célèbre article d'Ernest Legouvé dans *Le Journal de Rouen*, après le triomphal concert de Chopin en mars 1838, traduit l'exaspération de certains mélomanes devant ces joutes pianistiques plus comparables à des numéros d'acrobatie qu'à des célébrations musicales : « Terminez le grand débat qui divise les artistes ; et quand on demandera quel est le premier pianiste de l'Europe, Liszt ou Thalberg, que tout le monde puisse répondre, comme ceux qui vous ont entendu : c'est Chopin. » A la même date, dans la *Revue et gazette musicale de Paris*[24], Heine consacrait un très bel article à Liszt et Chopin, sans toutefois les comparer, pour souligner que Chopin ne mettait pas sa satisfaction à faire applaudir ses mains par d'autres mains, qu'il n'était pas seulement un virtuose, mais un « musicien-poète » dont la patrie véritable était « le pays de poésie ». Constatation ou critique voilée, on ne sait, il situait l'univers d'élection où, à défaut des salles de concerts, il se produisait désormais : les salons de la bonne société dont la distinction répondait à la sienne. « Ses succès sont de nature aristocratique ». La critique allait reprendre à l'envi et commenter diversement ce choix conforme à des options éthiques et esthétiques mûrement réfléchies mais pas toujours comprises : Liszt, dans la *Revue et gazette musicale de Paris* du 2 mai 1841, l'attribue par exemple à la frustration causée par un moyen d'expression trop limité pour le révéler pleinement. L'aversion de Chopin pour la carrière de virtuose est valorisée quand il s'agit de célébrer chez ce compositeur modeste et discret la probité de son engagement artistique. Escudier brosse dans *La France musicale*[25] l'image édifiante d'un artiste-ascète : aucun sacrifice à la mode ni à la publicité, aucune compromission lucrative, mais une existence sans passion, livrée à la méditation et au travail. Chopin est « le pianiste du sentiment par excellence », et ce sentiment a besoin de l'écoute sympathique d'un petit cercle. Mais le revers de cette exigence est l'élitisme esthétique qui a valu à Chopin des critiques acides. La plus nette apparaît chez Liszt qui en son temps avait célébré la haute mission sociale et religieuse de la musique auprès du peuple[26] : Chopin ne s'adresse pas à un public mais à une société. Les plus fielleuses ironisent sur la confidentialité de ces apparitions publiques et sur la délicatesse de la sonorité qu'il tirait de son instrument. Les plus chauds admirateurs de Chopin, sont ceux qui ont la chance d'être assis tout contre son piano, écrit Paul Mérruau dans *Le*

---

24 N° du 4 février 1838

25 N° du 2 mai 1841

26 « Lettre d'un bachelier ès musique II » parue dans la *Revue et gazette musicale de Paris* en juillet 1837.

Courrier français du 10 mai 1841. La *Revue des deux mondes* parle de « révélation » et d' « initiés » et termine par une plaisanterie, qui anticipe sans le savoir l'invention du microphone : « Le jour où l'on inventera un microscope pour les oreilles, ce jour-là M. Chopin sera divinisé [27]». Berlioz lui-même se laisse aller dans le *Journal des débats* à une sévère réprobation du repli hautain de Chopin qui, dans sa tour d'ivoire, s'est coupé du monde des musiciens pour se réserver à une élite sociale : « A moins d'être prince ou ministre ou ambassadeur, il ne faut plus songer au plaisir de l'entendre[28] ». Ce relent d'aristocratisme conduit Maurice Bourges, pourtant très favorable à Chopin, au reproche de sophistication adressé à l'ornementation trop recherchée qui confine au maniérisme : « Trop de recherche fine et minutieuse n'est pas quelquefois sans prétention et sans froideur ». Et il souhaitait que parfois la musique de Chopin se laisse surprendre « en négligé[29] ».

Renoncer à une carrière de virtuose et se produire à l'occasion, c'est aussi rappeler au public la saveur des choses rares et créer l'événement : Berlioz feignit de se demander, à l'occasion du concert chez Pleyel en 1842, si Chopin ne rejouait pas au public la fable de Florian « Le rossignol et le prince »... Il n'est pas le seul à s'étonner que, malgré son silence, la réputation de Chopin soit demeurée inattaquable et toujours aussi rayonnante, comme si, commente Liszt, la postérité était venue avant l'heure. Les trois derniers concerts publics de Chopin en France ont été accompagnés d'une copieuse critique aussi bien dans la presse spécialisée que dans les quotidiens. Ces comptes rendus peuvent être considérés comme des morceaux d'anthologie où le journalisme musical accède à l'écriture littéraire en fusionnant les genres. On y trouve en effet un riche répertoire de tous les *topoï* déclinés du vivant de Chopin, une sorte de métalangue destinée à cerner son esthétique par une approche poétique descriptive ; la terminologie musicale en est à peu près exclue, le langage musical se voit converti synesthésiquement dans l'ordre de l'émotif, du sensoriel. Mélodiste avant tout, Chopin « rêve, pleure, chante[30] », écrit Escudier ; son écriture ornementée, ses arabesques suggèrent à Maurice Bourges le caprice du génie arabe de l'Alhambra ; la limpidité des trilles et des gammes suscite des images de perles, de cristal ou de cloches d'argent. Lorsque cet arsenal est épuisé, on recourt aux sèmes de pureté et d'immatérialité qui empruntent au domaine littéraire des références familières aux lecteurs : Maurice Schlesinger convoque autour de Chopin,

27 N° du 1er avril 1842
28 N° du 13 avril 1842
29 N° du 27 février 1842
30 N° du 2 mai 1841

dans son article de février 1848, tout un univers shakespearien, Ariel, l'esprit ailé, et le char minuscule de la reine Mab, reprenant à son compte le terme dénominatif depuis longtemps consacré, « le Sylphe du piano ». *Le Ménestrel* se livre à la même date à une véritable parodie de cette frénésie métaphorique pour reprocher à Chopin l'absence de carrure de ses compositions et son agogique intempérant : « Rien de terrestre, d'articulé ou de rythmé[31] ». Théophile Gautier, plus tenté par le mythe de l'androgyne, est fidèle dans ses comptes rendus à la créature « éthérée, virginale », à l'ange, qu'avec un mauvais goût consommé, il présente à son dernier concert parisien « assis entre ses deux ailes, pâle comme une ombre, diaphane comme un sylphe[32] ». Il semble d'ailleurs que l'émaciation de Chopin dans la dernière période de sa vie ait impressionné les esprits et accentué ces représentations spectrales, chères au premier romantisme, qui ont contaminé la réception artistique de son œuvre en assimilant abusivement l'homme et le compositeur. La correspondance entre les arts opère par ailleurs des associations plus riches d'implications qui varient en fonction des genres musicaux exploités par Chopin : Young pour les *Nocturnes*, Blondel de Nesle pour les *Ballades*, Lamartine pour les *Etudes* et pour les *Mazurkas* Thomas Moore. Gautier, lui, est sensible à la parenté entre Chopin et l'Allemand Novalis, le poète de la sérénité magique de la nuit. Mais l'artiste le plus fréquemment confronté à Chopin reste Raphaël, archétype à l'époque romantique de la perfection formelle née de l'alliance entre la grâce et la mesure, de l'harmonie entre le dessin et la couleur ; autant de caractères présents dans l'esthétique de Chopin, « Le Raphaël du pianoforte[33] », selon Heine.

Dans la France polonophile qui avait accueilli tant de réfugiés en 1831 et compati à leur drame, la nationalité polonaise de Chopin était de nature à exalter l'image doloriste de l'exilé, gardien de la culture polonaise transplantée en terre étrangère. Contrairement à l'Allemand Heine, qui dépassait par une approche cosmopolite la polonité de Chopin, et mises à part quelques rares tentatives d'annexion à la France de ses origines paternelles, la plupart des musicographes le présentent comme « le barde » de la Pologne vaincue : c'est le cas de Félicien Mallefille, inspiré par la *Ballade* en sol mineur où son imagination « voit » défiler les images désolantes du martyre polonais[34]. Ernest Legouvé souligne à dessein tout ce qu'il y avait d' « hé-

31 *Le Ménestrel* 20 février 1848

32 Article cité par M.H. Girard in *La Fortune de Chopin*, Dijon, 1991, sous la référence erronée : *La Presse* 25 février 1848.

33 Heine : *Lutèce* (20 avril 1841), Paris, Michel Lévy, 1855, p. 187

34 *Revue et gazette musicale de Paris* 9 septembre 1838

roïque » chez ce patriote déguisé en homme du monde[35]. L'enracinement de l'œuvre de Chopin dans l'histoire et la tradition polonaises est diversement interprété. Dans une perspective esthétique, Chopin est présenté comme un compositeur national qui a fait de la Pologne un objet esthétique en élevant la musique populaire au rang de chef-d'œuvre universel et en renouvelant par la saveur particulière du folklore slave un répertoire et des formes périmés, celle du concerto pour piano et orchestre en particulier. Importateur de la musique polonaise en France, Chopin a su apprivoiser, au contact du raffinement de la civilisation française, les rudesses de la « race slave ». L'image du « barbare » Sarmate tente de rendre compte de la violence exaspérée, voire de la brutalité dérangeante de certaines pièces, comme la *Sonate* en *si* bémol mineur ou la *Polonaise-Fantaisie* dont la réception a été plus réservée, même auprès de connaisseurs comme Liszt. Il semble que les Français aient raffolé des Mazurkas que Berlioz classe dans la musique de salon parce que leurs « divines chatteries[36] » plaisent aux belles dames de l'aristocratie. On se demande si la critique n'a pas contribué par ces éloges à suggérer que l'idiome de Chopin procédait de la couleur locale, de l'exotisme policé qui dépaysaient et attendrissaient tout à la fois le public français. Mais la perspective politique de l'engagement artistique de Chopin est assez peu éclairée. Patriote, certes, mais résistant ? On chercherait en vain un critique assez perspicace pour comprendre que Chopin avait renoncé à la carrière de pianiste pour consacrer toute son énergie créatrice à réactiver sans cesse la présence au monde de la Pologne bâillonnée, et qu'il trouvait dans ce don de soi l'accomplissement de toute sa personnalité. Les chroniqueurs lui savent gré surtout de sa générosité à l'égard de ses compatriotes démunis, en recensant régulièrement les concerts privés destinés à leur venir en aide et dont il est la cheville ouvrière et la vedette. On est bien loin en France de la compréhension que Schumann manifeste en Allemagne à la charge politique protestataire des œuvres de Chopin.

Sa disparition prématurée, si elle n'étonna personne, suscita une grande émotion dans son pays d'adoption. Tous les grands journaux lui consacrèrent une chronique nécrologique, unanimement sympathique au génie de l'artiste et à la distinction de l'homme. De ce kaléidoscope de fragments mobiles émerge déjà la carrure du compositeur que désormais il faudrait caser dans l'histoire de la musique. La mort de Chopin coïncida avec la fin de l'âge d'or du romantisme, avec le déclin des icônes du piano

---

35 *Soixante ans de souvenirs*, Paris, Hetzel, 1886, vol 2, p.161
36 *Le Journal des débats* 27 octobre 1849

qui perdit sa primauté en réintégrant le domaine de la musique de chambre ; le recul que donnent les choses achevées simplifia les clivages des catégories esthétiques pour dégager l'essentiel : l'importance historique de Chopin. Nourri des classiques, son style est l'expression de la poésie passionnée qui caractérise l'école romantique, souligne Gautier dans *La Presse*[37] et Bousquet dans *L'Illustration*[38] rappelle que le *Concerto* en mi mineur, jugé si profondément original à sa création, est devenu « classique ». Berlioz, le tirant de sa marginalité, admet que ses compositions pour le piano ont fait école, même s'il demeure inimitable dans l'invention harmonique. Mais cet article du *Journal des débats*[39] n'apporte rien de neuf à la réception de Chopin, pas plus que les autres : l'hommage rendu au mort figeait forcément le vivant dans une représentation typologique sans surprise.

Deux ouvrages, parus d'abord en feuilletons dans la presse, avant d'être publiés en librairie, allaient inaugurer une approche incontestablement innovante du phénomène Chopin. Il s'agit du *Chopin* de Liszt et d'*Histoire de ma vie* de George Sand. *La France musicale* consacra à la biographie de Liszt dix-sept articles entre février et août 1851. Parution soigneusement préparée par des effets d'annonce répétés qui présentaient le livre comme un événement, un « tombeau » de Chopin, écrit par l'un de ses pairs, son ami et son admirateur. C'est la première biographie de Chopin, sans en être une. Car la vie privée tient peu de place, l'information factuelle est lacunaire, souvent fautive. De même la contribution musicologique apparaît décevante ; l'analyse de l'œuvre, si pertinente soit-elle, est esquissée à grands traits, le recours à des exemples précis est occasionnel, et ce dans le but avoué de ne pas rebuter les lecteurs profanes. Le projet de Liszt était ailleurs : faire de Chopin l'archétype de l'artiste romantique, le dépouiller des contingences de l'actualité pour l'élever au rang de héros exemplaire. Tout le discours sur Chopin s'articule autour de cette perspective hagiographique : mal compris, mal applaudi, mal aimé, dévoré par un idéal inaccessible, Chopin a sacrifié à sa vocation artistique une vie promise à la souffrance et à la mort prématurée, « ne se servant plus de l'art que pour se donner à lui-même sa propre tragédie[40] ». L'acte créateur est explicitement comparé à la prière : « Il épancha son âme dans ses compositions comme d'autres l'épanchent dans la prière [41]». La « sainteté » de cette existence implique son apothéose ; la pos-

---

37   N° du 22 octobre 1849
38   N° du 27 octobre 1849
39   N° du 27 octobre 1849
40   Liszt : *Chopin*, Paris, Corréa, 1941, p. 102
41   *Ibidem,* p. 198-199

térité reconnaîtra à sa juste valeur des chefs-d'œuvre auxquels leur temps a accordé une estime trop superficielle.

Cette image de Chopin, George Sand l'exploite dans *Histoire de ma vie,* publiée dans *La Presse* entre octobre 1854 et août 1855, et dont les deux derniers chapitres sont consacrés à sa liaison avec Chopin. Elle aussi le présente comme le « type extrême de l'artiste, dévoré par un rêve d'idéal[42] ». Mais c'est pour regretter que cette attitude esthétique ait nui à la popularité de son œuvre. Plus attachée encore que Liszt au concept de mission civilisatrice de l'art, elle aurait souhaité que ce génie aussi vaste que celui des grands maîtres condescende à se rendre intelligible au plus grand nombre, quitte à censurer sa liberté de créateur, sa modernité trop en avance sur son temps : « Il n'a pas été connu et il ne l'est pas encore de la foule[43] ». C'est pourquoi elle envisage- bien malencontreusement, on le lui a suffisamment reproché – qu'en orchestrant sa musique, on en révèlera la puissance en même temps qu'on la rendra enfin au public qu'elle mérite. Le devenir de l'œuvre de Chopin, elle le prévoit dans la ferveur de la foule mais sans le piano, instrument intimiste du tête-à-tête des happy few. La comparaison qu'elle établit à son avantage entre Chopin et les grands compositeurs classiques, Bach, Mozart, Beethoven, a paru abusivement apologétique ; elle traduisait pourtant le souci de reclasser Chopin dans la continuité d'une tradition que son art précurseur avait élargie : grand dans les petites formes, puissant sans démonstration de force, éloquent dans l'ellipse.

L'autorité de ces deux personnalités artistiques intimement liées à Chopin en ont fait des références indiscutables. Liszt et George Sand ont été compilés, plagiés aussi bien dans la presse musicale que dans les ouvrages encyclopédiques et les monographies qui commencent à paraître dans la décennie 1860. Charles Poisot dans *L'Univers musical* (1857) et Louis Enault dans *Le Papillon* (1861) ne se donnent même pas la peine d'ouvrir les guillemets, ils s'approprient la réflexion et le discours de leurs sources. Fétis, dans la deuxième édition de la *Biographie universelle des musiciens* (1860-68) cite à plusieurs reprises des extraits de l'ouvrage de Liszt, utilisés comme entrées des différentes rubriques qui cernent la personnalité de Chopin. Trente ans après le concert de février 1832, le ton s'est fait plus réservé, toute trace de sympathie a disparu, la personnalité de Chopin est présentée sous un jour peu favorable. Une partie de la célébrité du compositeur est attribuée à « la mode », à ce côté « fashionable » du style que Maurice Bourges pointait en 1842. Le choix des formes

---

42 George Sand : *Histoire de ma vie* V° partie, ch. XIII, Paris, Gallimard, Bibliothèque de la Pléiade, 1971, vol 2, p. 443

43 *Histoire de ma vie* V° partie, ch. XII, *opus cité*, p.421

brèves est analysé non comme un signe de modernité mais comme une déficience créatrice. *Le Dictionnaire Larousse* (1869), mal renseigné sur la partie polonaise de la vie de Chopin, adopte le point de vue de George Sand et fait grief à Chopin de son isolement, en contaminant informations sur la vie privée fournies par la romancière et création musicale. « Son esprit hautain méprisait les masses ; et c'était mal comme homme, mal comme artiste, mal surtout comme Polonais ». La démarche psychocritique sera adoptée par de nombreuses études par la suite qui ne verront pas toujours la différence entre les œuvres autobiographiques de George Sand et ses œuvres de fiction. Il est vrai que Liszt avait donné l'exemple en intercalant dans son *Chopin* des passages du roman *Lucrezia Floriani* où le personnage du prince Karol de Roswald est substitué ex abrupto au vrai Chopin.

La contribution des musicographes contemporains de Chopin, qui l'avaient connu et entendu, procède à partir des années 60, celles de la génération positiviste, d'une perspective exégétique qui se démarque de la paraphrase sur l'œuvre et de la démarche biographique préconisée par Louis Enault, auteur de la première biographie française de Chopin (1856), qui affirmait que, surtout chez lui, l'homme expliquait l'artiste. Antoine Marmontel, qui avait fréquenté le compositeur polonais dans le salon musical de son maître Zimmermann, ouvre son ouvrage critique *Les Pianistes célèbres* (1878) par Chopin. Il avait préparé une édition de ses œuvres publiée en 1867. En pédagogue, il inventorie les fondements techniques de son esthétique (égalité des doigts, emploi de la pédale, qualité du toucher, effets de sonorité) et trouve une heureuse analogie pour suggérer l'art des nuances si particulier au jeu de Chopin : il modulait le son comme les peintres traitent la lumière. Admirateur inconditionnel du virtuose, il pose néanmoins le problème de la valeur musicale de ses productions. Elles lui paraissent manquer de souffle, il n'a été vraiment inégalable, selon lui, que dans la ciselure de l'idée musicale. Blaze de Bury, l'influent critique de la *Revue des deux mondes*, qui n'avait pas toujours été tendre pour Chopin de son vivant, devint l'un de ses plus zélés laudateurs, à proportion de son animosité contre Wagner. Il avait classé Chopin dans un précédent article[44] parmi « les artistes du Nord », en compagnie de Niels Gade et de Jenny Lind, en raison de leur fidélité à leur accent natal. Il afficha clairement son approche critique de surplomb dans un long article « Etudes et souvenirs » (1883) : dégager Chopin des clichés de son époque et, dans un esprit « d'information et de recherche », tenter d'évaluer son héritage. « Le Chopin de 1834 à 1840 est loin d'avoir l'importance de celui que nous pratiquons

---

44 Reproduit dans *Musiciens contemporains*, Paris, Michel Lévy, 1856, p.114-115

maintenant. [...] Il a grandi entre temps[45] ». L'étude est structurée en deux parties qui séparent l'artiste et l'œuvre. La première témoigne de l'acquis de nouvelles sources, d'origine polonaise, et d'une méthode analytique qui s'efforce, sans toujours y parvenir, de dépasser l'anecdote pour démêler les lignes de force d'un tempérament artistique qui se construit en relation avec un contexte. La deuxième partie étudie la part assignée à Chopin entre ses prédécesseurs, en l'occurrence J.S. Bach, et l'école moderne, Massenet, Saint-Saëns et surtout Bizet, tous pianistes à l'origine, imprégnés « par inoculations atomistiques[46] » de ses innovations harmoniques. C'est au sens du rythme que Blaze de Bury mesure l'importance de l'apport de Chopin à la musique française contemporaine à laquelle, dit-il, il faisait totalement défaut. Hippolyte Barbedette, compositeur et musicographe, qui avait eu également le privilège d'entendre jouer Chopin, est l'auteur d'un essai de critique musicale sur Chopin (1861) qui se propose d'expliquer l'œuvre par le tempérament et le milieu de l'artiste, conformément à la méthode de la critique positiviste. Il note lui aussi l'influence décisive de Chopin sur l'école moderne qu'il a libérée de la dictature de la virtuosité creuse, en réintroduisant la sensibilité dans la musique de piano ; pour le dire il recourt spontanément au topos des années 1840 : « il lui donna une âme [47]». Mais il quitte la critique purement esthétique quand il stigmatise, en moraliste, le caractère malsain de certaines œuvres de Chopin qui contiennent des germes morbides contagieux. Ces dérives deviennent caricaturales dans la biographie d'Agathe Audley, parue en 1880, où la musique est réduite à la portion congrue, au profit d'un discours chrétien édifiant sur la pernicieuse influence de George Sand.

Dans le dernier quart du XIXe siècle la présence de Chopin dans le paysage musical français est bien implantée. Les programmes des concerts recensés dans la presse attestent la faveur des interprètes et du public pour un répertoire qui privilégie néanmoins les *Mazurkas*, les *Nocturnes*, les *Valses* et les deux *Concertos*. Les concours des classes de piano du Conservatoire de Paris puisent volontiers dans les œuvres plus difficiles, *Ballades, Sonates, Allegro de concert*. Le *Journal des débats* (26 juillet 1895) se livre à une étude statistique : « Chopin domine dans l'enseignement du piano au Conservatoire. Sur 30 morceaux que les élèves étudient par an, il y en a 3 de Beethoven, 1 ou 2 de Liszt, le reste est de Chopin. » Dans un article de *La Revue latine* (1904), Gustave Amiot recense les manifestations de la « popularité » de Chopin et constate qu'elle est « hors de toute comparaison ». Mais c'est pour déplorer

---

45   *Revue des deux mondes* 1er septembre 1883, p. 851
46   *Ibidem* p. 876
47   Barbedette : *Chopin. Essai de critique musicale*, Paris, Leiber, 1861, p.62

les formes qu'elle prend : évolutions chorégraphiques diverses sur fond d'œuvres orchestrées pour l'occasion, ressassement de pièces de concours, massacres répétés par les pianistes amateurs, biographies anecdotiques, etc. Tombé dans le domaine public, Chopin a été effectivement dépassé par son mythe. Ce mythe s'est nourri de trois stéréotypes : le chantre de la Pologne, le mondain raffiné, l'homme maladif et névrosé, chacun d'eux trouvant son illustration musicale adéquate. A la fin du siècle s'est constitué dans la littérature romanesque tout un réseau de références à la morbidesse décadente des Nocturnes, véritables narcotiques dont abusent les jeunes gens désaxés et les jeunes femmes mal mariées. Parents et éducateurs s'alarment de l'influence débilitante du maître polonais. Niedermeyer interdit à ses élèves de jouer du Chopin, sous prétexte que « ce n'est pas une musique pour jeunes gens[48] » et la puritaine madame Gide refuse que son fils aille écouter Anton Rubinstein dans un programme Chopin. Le mal-être d'une société en crise trouve dans cette musique élégiaque et sensuelle un reflet et un exutoire. Chopin devient le musicien favori d'une classe sociale qui a perdu le goût de l'action. La poésie lyrique se gorge d'images languides ou funèbres inspirées par le génie musical de Chopin. Maurice Rollinat, Anna de Noailles et Proust lui-même sacrifient à cette mode.

Il était inévitable que, par réaction, s'élève une protestation contre une musique si maladivement connotée. S'il fallait n'en retenir qu'une, ce serait celle de l'écrivain Romain Rolland dont la répulsion pour cet aspect de Chopin n'avait d'égal que la fascination qu'exerçait sur lui « l'inventeur magique[49] ». Ce conflit passionnel, qu'il ne parvint jamais à liquider, lui dicta une réserve, pour ne pas dire un mutisme volontaire, à l'égard de l'œuvre de Chopin. Mutisme qu'il rompt en 1894 en consacrant une leçon à Chopin dans le cycle de ses cours au Lycée Henri IV. Il y classe Chopin comme musicien français et reconnaît le poids de son influence non seulement sur ses contemporains comme Schumann, mais sur Wagner dont, avant Debussy, il repère les affinités de *Tristan* avec le chromatisme idiomatique de Chopin. La forme où Chopin lui paraît se rapprocher de Mozart et de Beethoven, c'est la pièce brève, *Prélude ou Etude* où il trouve moins flagrant son manque de souffle.

La popularité de Chopin connut une période d'éclipse relative, dans les années 1885-1900, au moment où la réception des opéras de Wagner divisa la France en deux clans, partisans et détracteurs, et occupa tout l'espace de la critique musicale. L'engouement pour « la musique de l'avenir » dénotait l'appartenance au courant mo-

---

48 Fauré : *Excelsior*, 12 juin 1922
49 *Arlequin*, avril 1910

derniste, la croyance au progrès de l'art ; les salons aristocratiques, comme celui de la comtesse Greffulhe, devinrent les hauts lieux d'un véritable culte pour le dieu Wagner et pour l'art nouveau. L'observateur le plus perspicace de ce phénomène social aussi bien qu'esthétique fut Marcel Proust. Dans *Du côté de chez Swann* (1913), il met en scène dans un salon mondain la jeune Mme de Cambremer, wagnérienne radicale, dont le snobisme intolérant réduit sa belle-mère à cacher sa passion pour Chopin considéré comme un compositeur de salon démodé. Quelques années plus tard *Sodome et Gomorrhe* (1922) allait ajouter une coda à cet affrontement entre générations. Le narrateur révèlera à la jeune femme que Chopin était le compositeur préféré de Debussy, levant par cette seule allusion ses préventions : « Depuis quelques années la musique de Chopin avait retrouvé sa gloire. Même les amateurs dont le goût est difficile pouvaient l'aimer sans honte, les plus grands de nos jeunes musiciens le prisaient. Mais Mme de Cambremer n'en était pas encore informée. Et polonaises et nocturnes avaient encore gardé à ses yeux leur déguisement sordide et suranné [50] ». Dans la réaction des musiciens français au wagnérisme, en particulier dans le cercle de César Franck, Chopin servit de contrepoids à l'influence de la musique étrangère, allemande essentiellement, ainsi que l'envisageait Nietzsche : « Je vénérais en Chopin le privilège qu'il avait eu d'affranchir la musique des influences allemandes, c'est-à-dire de son penchant à la laideur, à l'obscurité, à la mesquinerie, à la précision pédantesque.[51] » Du coup, sa place dans l'histoire de la musique se voyait redéfinie : il faisait le lien entre les clavecinistes français, qui jouissaient alors d'un regain de faveur, grâce aux efforts des sociétés de musique ancienne, et les grands compositeurs- pianistes du XXe siècle, Fauré, Debussy, Ravel. Dans *Le Courrier musical* (1910), Wanda Landowska désignait Chopin comme un « Couperin teinté de romantisme », plus proche de l'esthétique baroque que de l'école romantique.

Dans cet article, Wanda Landowska protestait contre les surinterprétations des pianistes contemporains qui trahissaient de façon outrancière les intentions de Chopin. La critique de la presse se fait l'écho de ces doléances : on accoutre Chopin d'oripeaux qui le défigurent. Dans les premières années du XXe siècle, s'amorce un retour à la tradition pianistique de Chopin, fondé sur des éditions de travail, telle celle de Raoul Pugno, élève de Georges Mathias, parue en deux volumes en 1910 ou d'Isidore Philipp (1897), préfacée par le même Mathias. Par ailleurs la musicologie naissante

---

50 *Sodome et Gomorrhe*, Esquisse XVII, Paris, Gallimard, Bibliothèque de la Pléiade, vol. III, p. 1085. Voir aussi *Sodome et Gomorrhe* II, ii, p. 209-212. Ces Esquisses datent de 1914.

51 Cité par Théodore de Wyzewa « La jeunesse de Nietzsche » *Revue des deux mondes* 1er février 1896, p. 694

s'impose comme une discipline universitaire et fait son entrée à la Sorbonne en 1903. Si l'on ne peut pas dire que la réception de Chopin en a ait radicalement transformée, la critique change de ton, le style en est moins emphatique, moins précieux. Mais aussi plus impertinent, parfois tranchant. Camille Bellaigue, critique musical à la *Revue des deux mondes*, ne se prive pas de répéter que Chopin abuse des fanfreluches et des pompons. Vincent d'Indy, fondateur de la Schola cantorum, obsédé par les lois immuables de la tonalité et de la construction, trouve, en analysant la *Sonate* opus 58 que l'éducation musicale de Chopin a été bien incomplète, et l'accuse d'avoir subordonné la tonalité aux doigtés, au mépris de la logique architecturale : « Tout esprit de construction et de coordination des idées est malheureusement absent[52]. » Camille Saint-Saëns, auquel son maître Stamaty avait interdit d'aller entendre Chopin, explique par la même carence éducative qu'il se soit cantonné au piano. Mais le critique le plus violemment hostile à Chopin est Jules Combarieu, directeur de *La Revue musicale* (*REM*) qui considère avec condescendance son œuvre vieillotte et entreprend d'en dénoncer le caractère foncièrement trivial, dans une analyse au vitriol de l'une de ses Valses qui s'étale sur trois pages de la *Revue* en février 1908.

En contrepartie, on évalue plus clairement la portée de l'œuvre de Chopin et son influence. A l'occasion du centenaire de sa mort, c'est l'un des avantages des commémorations, *Le Courrier musical* fit paraître un numéro spécial dont la qualité des articles et de leurs signataires fait date dans la réception de Chopin en France. Des compositeurs, Maurice Ravel, Déodat de Séverac, des interprètes, Wanda Landowska, Raoul Pugno, Francis Planté, se joignent à des musicologues, Jean Chantavoine, Elie Poirée, pour apporter une contribution solide dont la diversité des éclairages balaye tout le champ des investigations sur l'héritage musical de Chopin. Le point de vue de Camille Mauclair[53] donne la primauté au slavisme de Chopin, le premier importateur de la sensibilité slave dans l'art occidental, avant les compositeurs russes. Il juge Chopin mal compris de son époque qui ignora les solides bases classiques de son œuvre, la maitrise technique des *Préludes* et des *Etudes*, l'inspiration tragique de la *Sonate* en *si* bémol mineur pour se mirer dans le sentimentalisme romantique de ses *Nocturnes*. Chantavoine[54] interroge, à travers le *cantabile* et les formules harmoniques, la parenté de Chopin avec l'art italien dont il a subi les influences indirectement par l'opéra italien et qui, chez lui, « se décompose en nuances

---

52 *Cours de composition*, Livre II, 1ère partie, Paris, Durand, 1909, p. 411
53 « Sur le génie de Chopin » p. 2-5
54 « L'italianisme de Chopin » p.12-15

irisées, troublantes, opalescentes ». Raoul Pugno[55] considère que Chopin a ouvert l'ère de la musique subjective, élargi tous les cadres secondaires de la musique, créé de nouvelles formes comme la Ballade et communiqué à toutes ses productions une unité d'inspiration qui le rend immédiatement reconnaissable ; il assortit ces jugements de citations précises qu'il commente en pianiste. Le plus bel article est incontestablement celui de Maurice Ravel[56] qui reconnaît à Chopin la qualité la plus précieuse : l'inspiration, « l'arrière- pensée » qui transcende la science du métier, qui fait frissonner la matière sonore et en tire des émotions sublimes. Son commentaire de la *Barcarolle,* d'un lyrisme dépouillé, est resté célèbre, tout comme l'invention de la superbe formule : « ce grand slave italien d'éducation ». Tous ces textes ont un souci commun, celui de recontextualiser l'œuvre de Chopin en la plaçant sur le terrain de l'histoire générale de l'art. Et par voie de conséquence, de remettre en question l'idée de sa marginalité géniale, isolée dans son temps et sans postérité artistique, pour souligner au contraire la continuité qui en fait un précurseur des compositeurs français du début du siècle.

La même année, paraît dans *Le Correspondant*[57] un article de fond dû au musicologue Michel-Dimitri Calvocoressi qui constate que la vraie place de Chopin dans l'histoire de l'art musical ne lui a été assignée que de façon récente. Sa gloire, fondée sur un courant de mode, a occultée de son temps l'apport révolutionnaire de son œuvre parce qu'elle « portait l'estampille du bon ton ». Sa musique de piano, banalisée par la faveur du public, a été dépréciée face aux ambitions intellectuelles des courants wagnérien et post-wagnérien. La leçon que les jeunes musiciens de l'école française ont retenu de Chopin, c'est au contraire l'affirmation de l'indépendance de la musique, la liberté de l'inspiration : « Il n'est pas de musicien qui se soit approché plus près de l'idéal qui s'affirme aujourd'hui après bien des hésitations[58] ».

Le problème de l'interprétation de l'identité esthétique de Chopin semble donc ouvert dans la période qui précède la Première Guerre mondiale. On a une meilleure connaissance de sa biographie, grâce à la publication de ses lettres par Mieczysław Karłowicz dans la *Revue musicale (REM)* en 1904 et à la parution de deux monographies de référence, celle d'Elie Poirée (1907) et celle d'Edouard Ganche (1913), fondateur de la première Société Chopin en 1911 ; le recours à la biographie y est organiquement relié à l'œuvre ; les légendes poétisées, véhiculées par les musicographes

---

55 « L'âme de Chopin » p. 20-23
56 « Les Polonaises, les Nocturnes, les Impromptus, la Barcarolle. Impressions » p. 31-32
57 « Frédéric Chopin et son œuvre. A propos de son centenaire ». 10 janvier 1910, p. 585-602
58 *Ibidem*, p. 602

et qui parasitaient la critique musicale sont invalidées par ces travaux. Désormais la ligne de démarcation est tracée entre l'étude méthodique des œuvres de Chopin du point de vue musical et historique, ambition que Fétis n'était pas parvenu à s'imposer véritablement, et l'interprétation à partir d'images préalables, les deux démarches continuant à coexister durant tout le XXe siècle.

La France a eu sur les autres pays européens le privilège d'être choisie par Chopin pour y accomplir sa carrière et son œuvre de créateur. En se fixant à Paris, il a tissé avec les milieux de l'art et de la littérature, des liens qui ont fait de lui une personnalité marquante de la vie culturelle française. A ce titre, sa présence dans la presse, dans la littérature et dans la vie musicale est largement attestée par un matériel documentaire dont la richesse est impossible à restituer dans son ampleur. Tout en reconnaissant ses attaches nationales et son identité d'exilé polonais, la France l'a assimilé peu ou prou à son domaine patrimonial. Il est significatif qu'au moment de sa mort, certains journalistes le désignent comme « notre Chopin ». Cette familiarité a entretenu l'illusion que « la vérité de Chopin » tenait dans quelques images, régulièrement réactivées par la critique, et qui reposaient sur un choix d'œuvres privilégiées, essentiellement pour clavier seul, qui ont assuré sa popularité en France, au premier rang desquelles les *Nocturnes* et les *Mazurkas* diffusées par les concerts et les salons. En ce domaine, l'admiration allait unanimement à la perfection de la forme et à l'homogénéité du style immédiatement identifiable. Mais c'est seulement dans la première décennie du XXe siècle que s'est amorcée une nouvelle lecture de l'œuvre de Chopin qui prenait en compte les œuvres de la dernière période –*Barcarolle, Polonaise-Fantaisie, Sonates* – que leur modernité avait reléguées. La nouvelle compréhension qui se manifesta fut le fait des compositeurs du début du XXe siècle, tel Ravel qui le premier remit en cause l'idée qu'il n'y avait pas d'évolution dans le style de Chopin. L'intérêt du discours produit sur Chopin se recentrait sur les caractères de son écriture, particulièrement la mobilité et la richesse de l'harmonie, qui avaient donné une impulsion nouvelle à la musique contemporaine. Tiré du temple où il régnait en solitaire, Chopin devenait pour la génération symboliste un modèle de liberté créatrice dont elle sut recueillir le message artistique.

Anthologie (1832–1914)

Le temps de Chopin

A – Situation de l'artiste
1 Mais qui est « Monsieur Chopin de Varsovie » ?

« **Revue musicale** », 3 mars 1832, vol. 12, p. 38–39
Concert de M. Chopin de Varsovie.

Dire maintenant d'un pianiste qu'il a beaucoup de talent, ou même si l'on veut un grand talent, c'est indiquer qu'il est l'émule ou le rival de quelques artistes du premier ordre dont le nom se présente aussitôt à la mémoire ; ajouter que sa musique est très bonne, c'est faire supposer que son mérite est analogue à celui des œuvres de Hummel et d'un petit nombre de compositeurs renommés ; mais par ces éloges il est difficile de donner l'idée de la nouveauté, de l'originalité, car, sauf quelques nuances de style et de mérite de facture, la musique des pianistes est en général écrite dans de certaines formes de convention qu'on peut considérer comme radicales, et qui se reproduisent sans cesse depuis plus de trente ans. C'est le défaut du genre, et nos artistes les plus habiles n'ont pu le faire disparaître de leurs ouvrages. Mais voici un jeune homme qui, s'abandonnant à ses impressions naturelles et ne prenant point de modèle, a trouvé, sinon un renouvellement complet de la musique de piano, au moins une partie de ce qu'on cherche en vain depuis longtemps, c'est-à-dire une abondance d'idées originales dont le type ne se trouve nulle part. Ce n'est point à dire que M. Chopin soit doué d'une organisation puissante comme celle de Beethoven, ni qu'il ait dans sa musique de ces fortes conceptions qu'on remarque dans celle de ce grand homme : Beethoven a fait de la musique de piano ; mais je parle ici de la musique des pianistes, et c'est par comparaison avec celle-ci que je trouve dans les inspirations de M. Chopin l'indication d'un renouvellement de formes qui pourra exercer par la suite beaucoup d'influence sur cette partie de l'art.

M. Chopin a fait entendre, au concert qu'il a donné le 26 [25] de ce mois dans les salons de MM. Pleyel et Cie, un concerto qui a causé autant d'étonnement que de plaisir à son auditoire, tant par la nouveauté des idées mélodiques que par les traits, les modulations et la disposition générale des morceaux. Il y a de l'âme dans ses chants, de la fantaisie dans ses traits, et de l'originalité dans tout. Trop de luxe dans les modulations, du désordre dans l'enchaînement des phrases, de telle sorte qu'il semble quelquefois entendre une improvisation plutôt que de la musique écrite, tels sont les défauts qui se mêlent aux qualités que je viens de signaler. Mais ces défauts appartiennent à l'âge de l'artiste ; ils disparaîtront quand l'expérience sera venue. Si la suite des travaux de M. Chopin répond à son début, on ne peut douter qu'il ne se fasse une réputation brillante et méritée.

Comme exécutant, ce jeune artiste mérite aussi des éloges. Son jeu est élégant, facile, gracieux, et a du brillant et de la netteté. Il tire peu de son de l'instrument, et ressemble, sous ce rapport, à la plupart des pianistes allemands ; mais l'étude qu'il fait de cette partie de son art, sous la direction de M. Kalkbrenner, ne peut manquer de lui donner une qualité importante d'où dépend le nerf de l'exécution, et sans laquelle on ne peut modifier les accents de l'instrument. [**François-Joseph Fétis**]

« **La France musicale** », 1er juin 1851, 15ème Année, n° 22, p. 170
Franz Liszt, *Chopin*.

[...] A son arrivée à Paris il donna plusieurs concerts où il fut de suite vivement admiré autant par la société élégante, que par les jeunes artistes. Nous nous souvenons de sa première apparition dans les salons de Pleyel, où les applaudissements les plus redoublés semblaient ne pas suffire à notre enchantement, en face de ce talent qui révélait une nouvelle phase dans le sentiment poétique, et de si heureuses innovations dans la forme de son art.

Hector Berlioz, *Les Soirées de l'orchestre* (1852), Paris : Calmann Lévy 1878, p. 155

– « Qu'est-ce donc que ce nouveau pianiste polonais, dont tous les artistes raffolent et dont la musique est si bizarre ? Je veux le voir, amenez-le moi demain. »
– « Madame, je ferai mon possible pour cela, mais je dois vous avouer que je connais peu l'auteur des mazurkas et qu'il n'est point à mes ordres. »

– « Non, sans doute, il n'est pas à vos ordres, mais il doit être aux miens. Ainsi je compte sur lui. »

Cette singulière invitation n'ayant pas été acceptée, la souveraine annonça à ses sujets que M. Chopin était un petit original jouant passablement du piano, mais dont la musique n'était qu'un logogriphe perpétuel fort ridicule.

« **Le Temps** », 4 septembre 1880, 20ème Année, n° 7076, p. 3
H. Berlioz, *Études et souvenirs de théâtre*.
Cité dans : **Ernest Legouvé, *Soixante ans de souvenirs*,**
Paris : Hetzel 1886, vol. 2, p. 158–159

[...] Je dus [à Berlioz] une autre grande joie musicale.

Un soir, il arrive chez moi : « Venez, me dit-il, je vais vous faire voir quelque chose que vous n'avez jamais vu, et quelqu'un que vous n'oublierez pas ». Nous montons au second étage d'un petit hôtel meublé, et je me trouve vis-à-vis d'un jeune homme pâle, triste, élégant, ayant un léger accent étranger, des yeux bruns d'une douceur limpide incomparable, des cheveux châtains, presque aussi longs que ceux de Berlioz et retombant aussi en gerbe sur son front.

« Mon cher Chopin, je vous présente mon ami Legouvé. » C'était Chopin, en effet, arrivé depuis quelques jours à Paris. Son premier aspect m'avait ému, sa musique me troubla comme quelque chose d'inconnu.

2 Profil d'un compositeur original inclassable

« **Le Pianiste** », 10 novembre 1833, 1ère Année, n° 1, p. 6–7
Études de Fr. Chopin. (Opus 10)

[...] Lorsque vous aurez lu ces *études*, lorsque vous les aurez travaillées, commentées, si vous êtes assez heureuse pour les entendre jouer par l'auteur, il pourra bien vous arriver de les reconnaître à peine. Et prenez garde ! Ne les jugez pas à une première, ni même à une seconde lecture ; agissez comme vous le faites avec les odes de *Lamartine*, que vous aimez tant, – cherchez le vrai sens ; découvrez le chant, toujours gracieux, mais souvent enveloppé de façon à être difficilement trouvé. Ce jeune auteur se place, à son début, au niveau des grands maîtres, – et vous savez qu'il y en a peu –. On a prétendu qu'il méritait l'épithète d'*énigmatique* ; je ne partage pas cet avis [...] Disons, pour être juste, que les compositions de Fr. Chopin sont dans un ordre à part, mais toujours dignes de la peine qu'on se donnera pour les bien rendre. Les gens qui taxaient autrefois Beethoven de bizarrerie, ne le comprenaient pas plus que ne comprennent aujourd'hui Chopin ceux qui le traitent d'énigmatique. [...] Mais je vous affirme que les productions de cette force sont rares, et qu'il est très honorable pour le jeune Chopin de débuter, pour ainsi dire, par un ouvrage où brillent toutes les qualités de l'homme fait.

« **Le Rénovateur** », 15 décembre 1833
Reproduit dans : ***Hector Berlioz. Critique musicale,*** Paris : Buchet-Chastel 1996, vol. 1, p. 119–120

[...] Chopin est un talent d'une tout autre nature. Pour pouvoir l'apprécier complètement, je crois qu'il faut l'entendre de près, au salon plutôt qu'au théâtre, et faire abstraction de toute idée reçue ; on ne pourrait en faire l'application ni à lui, ni à sa musique. Chopin comme exécutant et comme compositeur, est un artiste à part, il n'a pas un point de ressemblance avec aucun autre musicien de ma connaissance. Ses mélodies, toutes imprégnées des formes polonaises, ont quelque chose de naïvement sauvage qui charme et captive par son étrangeté même ; dans ses études on trouve des combinaisons harmoniques d'une étonnante profondeur ; il a imaginé une sorte de broderie chromatique reproduite dans plusieurs de ses compositions, dont l'effet ne peut se décrire tant il est bizarre et piquant. Malheureusement il n'y a guère que Chopin lui-même qui puisse jouer sa musique et lui donner ce tour original, cet imprévu qui est un de ses charmes principaux ; son exécution est marbrée de mille nuances de mouvement dont il a seul le secret et qu'on ne pourrait indiquer. Il y a des détails incroyables dans ses mazurkas ; encore a-t-il trouvé le moyen de les rendre doublement intéressantes en les exécutant avec le dernier degré de douceur, au superlatif du *piano*, les marteaux effleurant les cordes, tellement qu'on est tenté de s'approcher de l'instrument et de prêter l'oreille comme on ferait à un concert de sylphes ou de follets. Chopin est le Trilby des pianistes. [**Hector Berlioz**]

« **Gazette musicale de Paris** », 5 janvier 1834, 1ère Année, n° 1, p. 4–7
Liszt, Ferd. Hiller, Chopin et Bertini.

[...] Si Ferdinand Hiller nous fait connaître la science et la profondeur ornées du goût le plus soutenu ; si Bertini, l'inspiration avec la patience ; si Chopin, la plus exquise sensibilité, rendue par des signes matériels, Liszt, glorieuse pyramide de ce triangle de talents, Liszt sera réellement et particulièrement le génie dans l'exécution. C'est une bonne fortune pour le critique, en devoir d'ériger une bonne renommée, de trouver ainsi une illustration toute prête qui la soulève, et lui tienne pour ainsi dire l'échelle ; mais avec Chopin on n'a pas cette ressource. Les termes de comparaison manquent absolument. Par quelles ressemblances en effet peindre ce jeu tout de sentiment, tout d'expression, cette harmonie parfois brûlante, parfois discrète, obscure, mais toujours sincère. [...] Chez lui pensée, style, conception, tout jusqu'au doigté, tout se montre individuel, mais d'une individualité communicative, expansive, et dont les organisations superficielles méconnaissent seules l'influence magnétique. Ne croyez pas cependant que Chopin soit un de ces esprits turbulents, incommodes aux règles de l'expérience, inhabiles au travail, ou même un de ces talents instinctifs qui jaillissent tout formés des trésors de la nature, comme Minerve du cerveau de Jupiter ; non, chez Chopin, on voit que l'inspiration, quoique maîtresse de la science, n'en néglige point les utiles services; ses harmonieuses Études montrent tant de charme et de savoir, qu'elles paraissent également le secret de l'art et du cœur. [**A. Guémer**]

« **Gazette musicale de Paris** », 15 juin 1834, 1ère Année, n° 24, p. 195
Revue critique. Fantaisie polonaise opus 13

[...] M. Chopin s'est frayé une route nouvelle, et, dès les premiers moments qu'il s'est montré sur la scène, il s'est placé tellement haut, soit par son jeu sur le pianoforte, soit par ses compositions pour cet instrument, qu'il est, pour la grande foule, un phénomène inexplicable qu'elle regarde, en passant, avec étonnement, et que le sot égoïsme, en le considérant, sourit avec un air de pitié, tandis que le petit nombre des connaisseurs seulement, plutôt guidé, du reste, par un vague pressentiment que par un jugement bien arrêté, plutôt par un instinct de progrès que par un sentiment raisonné de jouissance, suit cet artiste dans ses efforts et dans ses créations. Sa musique a un caractère tellement particulier que, dans certains cas, lui seul est à même de se prononcer avec assurance sur l'exactitude d'une note qui paraîtra douteuse. [**François Stoepel**]

« **Le Rénovateur** », 5 janvier 1835
Reproduit dans : *Hector Berlioz. Critique musicale*, Paris : Buchet-Chastel 1998, vol. 2, p. 3

[...] Chopin a eu l'heureuse idée d'exécuter l'adagio de son dernier concerto. Placée entre deux morceaux d'orchestre d'un style violent, cette ravissante composition, où tout ce que la grâce a de plus engageant est réuni aux pensées les plus profondes et les plus religieuses, a plongé l'auditoire dans une sorte de joie calme et extatique, à laquelle on ne l'a guère accoutumé en pareil cas. Tout cela est si différent des adagios traînants et interminables qui alourdissent pour l'ordinaire le milieu d'un concerto de piano ; il y a tant de naïveté unie à une telle fraîcheur d'imagination que, quand la dernière note est tombée comme une perle dans un vase d'or, le public absorbé dans sa contemplation a retenu quelques instants ses applaudissements, il écoutait encore. Ainsi, après avoir suivi l'harmonieuse dégradation des demi-teintes d'un crépuscule du soir, on demeure immobile dans l'obscurité, l'œil toujours fixé sur le point de l'horizon où la lumière vient de disparaître. [**Hector Berlioz**]

« **Revue et gazette musicale de Paris** », 22 mars 1835, 2ème Année, n°12, p. 99
Revue critique. Boléro opus 19. Scherzo opus 20.

Ces deux morceaux sont les œuvres les plus récentes de l'auteur, qui est, sans contredit, le compositeur le plus spirituel et le plus original que nous possédions aujourd'hui, en ce qui touche la musique de piano. Ils ne sont pas très difficiles. Nulle part on n'y trouve de ces passages qui exigent un piano à sept octaves et dont l'effet est déjà tellement usé qu'ils n'offrent plus d'intérêt ; nulle part, de ces séries de triolets alternativement exécutés par la main gauche et par la main droite ; nulle part, enfin, des artifices du même genre, qui, du reste, sont tous sans valeur réelle. Mais, en revanche, ces morceaux offrent, sans interruption, un chant original et caractéristique, réglé par de beaux rythmes et constamment soutenu et accompagné par une harmonie également riche et caractéristique, qui, en raison de la nouveauté des formes employées par l'auteur, présente les véritables difficultés de ces compositions [...].

« **Revue et gazette musicale de Paris** », 17 avril 1842, 9ème Année, n° 16, p. 170–172

[...] J'avoue qu'il y a des talents dont il n'est pas aisé de bien définir la nature. On épuiserait mille fois les trésors de la figure et de la comparaison avant d'avoir pu donner une idée claire et suffisante de certains styles. Celui de M. Chopin, que j'ai tâché plutôt de peindre que d'analyser, appartient à cette famille excentrique. Et peut-être est-ce là le véritable secret du charme répandu dans ses moindres compositions. Il faut renoncer à donner les motifs réels de leur attrait irrésistible pour se contenter de le subir [...].

Ses œuvres [...] ne ravissent pas jusqu'au septième ciel sur les ailes brûlantes de l'enthousiasme ; mais elles inspirent une volupté suave, nuancée de tristesse, le doux sourire parmi les larmes, un plaisir rêveur qui fuit les bruyants éclats et pénètre l'âme d'une vague mélancolie. Après tout, ne suis-je pas un peu hardi d'ériger en principes mes sensations personnelles ? Peut-être les trouvez-vous fort ridicules, et justement contraires aux vôtres. Mais cette disparité d'impressions confirmera bien mieux ce que je vous disais sur la difficulté de préciser le caractère du génie de M. Chopin. Personne du reste ne songe à mettre ce génie en doute ; tous en conviennent, par-ce que tous (j'entends l'aristocratie des intelligences) ne peuvent se défendre d'en éprouver les effets très réels. Les publications assez récentes dont je vous entretien-drai aujourd'hui, portent, comme leurs devancières, ce cachet de personnalité que M. Chopin imprime à tout ce qu'il écrit. On ne saurait s'y méprendre, ses tours de style n'appartiennent qu'à lui, et l'imitation, toute adroite qu'elle soit, n'a pu encore leur dérober cette individualité qui révèle le type original [...].

3 Sur l'échelle des valeurs des « princes du piano »

« Le Pianiste », 20 décembre 1834, 2ème Année, n° 4, p. 31
Chronique. Revue de la quinzaine.

On lit dans le *Constitutionnel* du 5 : « On nous écrit de Caen que MM. Albert de Sowinsky et Robberechts sont venus donner un concert dans cette ville. Leur admi-rable talent a obtenu le succès qu'il méritait. M. Sowinsky est le premier pianiste po-lonais. Son exécution brillante, animée, suave, mélodieuse, a charmé tout l'auditoire. Ses improvisations portent le cachet d'un génie original. Ce concert nous laissera des souvenirs ineffaçables. »

Il résulte de tout ceci que, si Chopin allait à Caen, il ne serait que le second pianiste polonais !!

« Le Pianiste », 20 janvier 1835, 2ème Année, n° 6, p. 45
G. Olivier, *État actuel de la musique en Allemagne et en Italie.*

[...] Sous nos yeux, Liszt, le roi du piano [...], Chopin, F. Hiller et notre Bertini nous apprennent la puissance de cette école nouvelle [...].

<u>Note de la rédaction</u> : Nous sommes entièrement opposés d'avis avec M. G. Olivier : rien de plus clair, de plus saisissable que les belles inspirations de Bertini, et

nous l'en félicitons. Il n'y a nul rapport avec le style des compositions toutes remarquables, d'ailleurs, de Chopin et d'Hiller, et nous croyons que si l'école de ces jeunes compositeurs se propageait, elle reculerait plus qu'elle n'avancerait l'éducation musicale en France. Cette école, qui ne convient qu'aux adeptes, ne peut avoir chez nous rien de populaire et nous ne voudrions pas affirmer que tous ceux qui l'admirent la comprennent. Quant à Liszt, nos lecteurs connaissent parfaitement notre opinion sur son talent. Liszt est une individualité, comme Paganini, Victor Hugo, Berlioz ; il n'y a pas de germe d'école là-dedans ; telle est notre opinion.

« Chronique de Paris », 18 juin 1837
Reproduit dans : *Hector Berlioz. Critique musicale*, Paris : Buchet-Chastel 2001, vol. 3, p. 152–155

[...] Nous étions à la campagne, et notre hôte, M. de C** [Custine], intelligent ami de l'art et littérateur distingué, ne crut pas pouvoir mieux compléter la magnificence du paysage dont il nous faisait si bien les honneurs qu'en demandant au virtuose [Duprez] d'évoquer le génie des temps antiques, au nom de ce grand magicien auquel il est soumis et qu'on appelle Gluck. [...] Dans la même soirée, nous avons eu le plaisir rare et délicat d'entendre Chopin. Heureuse organisation, habileté de mécanisme, richesse d'invention, science acquise, tout concourt à faire de ce compositeur-pianiste un des artistes les plus remarquables de l'époque. Si son nom n'est pas aussi populaire que ceux de Liszt et de Thalberg, c'est, non pas dans la portée, mais dans la nature spéciale de son talent qu'il en faut chercher la raison. Chopin n'aime guère à jouer dans les grandes salles, devant un public turbulent et mélangé ; ses qualités ne sont pas de celles qui imposent, pour ainsi dire, de vive force, l'admiration à la foule ; il aime le calme au contraire, l'attention d'un auditoire, peu nombreux mais sympathique, lui est plus favorable que les plus bruyants applaudissements. Il attache, il émeut, par une sensibilité contenue et une grâce sans afféterie, il étonne souvent par le scintillement capricieux de sa fantaisie ; ce qu'on aime tant en lui, c'est moins le pianiste (bien qu'à ce titre il ait très peu de rivaux) que le compositeur. Sa musique est de la musique de piano, et même des plus compliquées, mais sans aucun alliage de ces traits clinquants, que les doigts des virtuoses introduisent trop souvent dans leurs œuvres. Tout y est intéressant, depuis la première note jusqu'à la dernière. Il n'impose jamais à l'avance une forme à sa pensée, elle revêt d'elle-même celle qui lui est propre. Aussi quelques-uns de ses morceaux sont-ils d'un singulier laconisme ; l'idée complète une fois présentée, avec les développements qu'elle comporte le plus naturellement, la conclusion ne se fait pas attendre, et l'auditeur que tant de réserve étonne et enchante à la fois, en est quitte pour prier l'auteur de recommencer. Son talent d'ailleurs est d'une extrême variété ; études brillantes, mazurkas vives et originales, valses mélancoliques qui réveillent au fond du coeur les premières amours dès longtemps oubliées, ballades aux gothiques contours, fabliaux que le nouveau Blondel semble avoir apportés de la Terre sainte, tant la couleur en est étrange et religieuse, chants de guerre où revivent brûlant d'enthousiasme les malheureux défenseurs de la triste Pologne sa patrie, Chopin excelle également dans ces styles si opposés. Et puis une qualité dont les amateurs subissent l'influence sans la reconnaître, mais dont nous devons tenir fidèlement compte à l'artiste, c'est une richesse d'invention harmonique vraiment extraordinaire, et des combinaisons rythmiques qui lui appartiennent exclusivement. Peut-être l'originalité et la fraîcheur de ces nouvelles formes seraient-elles plus senties, si dans l'exécution, Chopin prodiguait moins les altérations du mouvement, s'il conservait à la mesure un peu plus de régularité. Le nombre des cas où ces altérations sont d'un excellent effet est assez grand, personne ne les saisit avec plus d'à-propos et de bonheur que M. Chopin ; mais il ne faudrait pas que cet affranchissement raisonné de la tyrannie de la mesure pût entraîner le virtuose dans l'excès contraire, et je crois qu'il aurait tort de l'ériger en système et d'en faire une trop fréquente application. [**Hector Berlioz**]

« **Le Journal de Rouen** », 13 mars 1838

[...] M. Chopin est incontestablement l'un des trois ou quatre grands pianistes que possède la France ; il en est qui peuvent l'emporter sur lui dans quelques-unes des possibilités de ce merveilleux clavier, mais dans le genre qu'il cultive et où il excelle, nul ne le surpasse assurément [...].

« **Revue et gazette musicale de Paris** », 25 mars 1838, 5ème Année, n° 12, p. 135

Voici un événement qui n'est pas sans importance dans le monde musical. Chopin qui ne se fait plus entendre au public depuis plusieurs années, Chopin qui emprisonne son charmant génie dans un auditoire de cinq ou six personnes, Chopin qui ressemble à ces îles enchantées où abordent à peine quelques voyageurs et dont ils racontent tant de merveilles qu'on les accuse de mensonge ; Chopin qu'on ne peut plus oublier dès qu'on l'a entendu une fois, Chopin vient de donner, à Rouen, un grand concert, devant cinq cents personnes, au bénéfice d'un professeur polonais. Il ne fallait pas moins qu'une bonne action à faire et que le souvenir de son pays pour vaincre sa répugnance à jouer en public. Eh bien ! Le succès a été immense ! Immense ! Toutes ces ravissantes mélodies, ces ineffables délicatesses d'exécution, ces inspirations mélancoliques et passionnées, toute cette poésie de jeu et de composition qui vous prend à la fois l'imagination et le cœur, ont pénétré, remué, enivré ces cinq cents auditeurs comme les huit ou dix élus qui 1'écoutent religieusement des heures entières ; c'était à tous moments, dans la salle, de ces frémissements électriques, de ces murmures d'extase et d'étonnement, qui sont les bravos de l'âme. Allons, Chopin ! Allons ! Que ce triomphe vous décide ; ne soyez plus égoïste, donnez à tous votre beau talent ; consentez à passer pour ce que vous êtes ; terminez le grand débat qui divise les artistes ; et quand on demandera quel est le premier pianiste de l'Europe, Liszt ou Thalberg, que tout le monde puisse répondre, comme ceux qui vous ont entendu… : C'est Chopin. [**Ernest Legouvé**]

Lettre de Ernest Legouvé à Franz Liszt, février 1840
Reproduite dans : *Correspondance de Liszt*, Paris : J.–C. Lattès 1987, p. 126–127

Dans les arts ce qui me paraît mériter le premier rang, c'est 1'unité, c'est ce qui est complet. Chopin est, je crois, un tout ; exécution et composition, tout chez lui est en accord, et de même valeur ; son jeu et ses œuvres sont deux choses également créées par lui, qui se soutiennent l'une l'autre, qui sont complètes dans leur genre ; Chopin est arrivé enfin à la réalisation de son idéal. Vous au contraire, et je vous l'ai entendu dire, vous n'êtes qu'à mi-route de votre développement ; l'un de vos profils est dégagé, l'autre est encore dans l'ombre ; le pianiste est arrivé ; mais le compositeur est peut-être en retard. [...] Pour moi, je vous le dis sincèrement comme je le pense, le jour où Liszt intérieur sera sorti, le jour où cette admirable puissance d'exécution aura son pendant et son complément dans une force égale de composition [...] ce jour-là, on ne dira pas que vous êtes le premier pianiste de l'Europe, on trouvera un autre mot.

« La France musicale », 1er juillet 1838, 1ère Année, n° 27, p. 1–2
École moderne des pianistes. Adolphe Henselt.

Parmi les pianistes modernes, Chopin peut être considéré à juste titre comme un de ceux qui ont exercé le plus d'influence. Cette école qui étonna d'abord, semble résulter de la fusion des deux grandes écoles dont nous venons de parler [Clementi et Hummel].

Élevé à Varsovie, loin des grands modèles de son art, Chopin fut obligé de le cultiver dans la solitude. Son talent n'est pas sans quelques rapports avec celui de Field ; toutefois sa manière d'attaquer la note est conforme au caractère de ses compositions, riches mais capricieuses et fantasques. Il inventa de nouveaux effets, et l'on trouve dans sa musique une harmonie pleine de charme et d'originalité. Les accords plus larges dont il se sert soutiennent le chant du piano ; ses tournures harmonieuses, ne sont jamais vulgaires ; et l'usage qu'il fait des progressions plagales est ordinairement d'un bel effet. Mendelssohn les a également employées avec succès. En prodiguant ces richesses harmoniques, en ornant ces mélodies de ces mille petites broderies qui leur donnent tant d'élégance, Chopin voulut s'associer à la grande réaction produite par les œuvres d'Henri Bertini. Il contribua, lui aussi, à répandre le goût de ces petits morceaux caractéristiques qui remplacèrent les grands concertos avec accompagnement dont on commençait à se fatiguer. D'ailleurs la poésie sombre, jusqu'à l'excès, qui règne dans sa musique, était d'accord avec le goût dominant du jour ; aussi, quoique jeune encore, il ne s'est jamais surpassé depuis ses premières œuvres, et nous croyons qu'il a épuisé sa verve et sa fécondité.

Il a eu cependant des imitateurs, Hiller, Clara Wieck, Schumann sont au nombre de ces derniers. Thalberg lui-même, qui représente actuellement l'école de Vienne, n'a pu se préserver complètement de cette influence, quoiqu'il ait surpassé celui qu'il a quelquefois imité involontairement ; il n'y a que Mendelssohn qui marche indépendant, et lui-même est devenu un centre influent autour duquel viennent se grouper un grand nombre d'artistes. Il se forme aujourd'hui une école romantique du piano, à la tête de laquelle il faut placer Franz Liszt. Si les œuvres de cet artiste dans lesquelles les règles musicales sont quelquefois méconnues ne lui donnent pas encore le droit d'être mis au nombre des grands compositeurs, la fougue et l'éclat de son jeu le placent très haut comme exécutant. [...] Si l'on compare la musique d'Henselt à celle des autres pianistes, on y reconnaîtra sans doute le style et l'esprit de Chopin ; mais s'il a l'élégance, il n'a pas la monotonie un peu fatigante de ce dernier.

« **Revue des deux mondes** », 14 février 1839, 4ème série, tome 17, p. 545
Revue musicale.

La race des pianistes a singulièrement multiplié depuis quelques années ; ils sont si nombreux maintenant, qu'on ne peut les compter. [...] Dès qu'il s'agit du piano, le talent n'est plus de mise ; il faut absolument parler de génie ; le génie a si bon air lorsqu'il provoque avec ses doigts de flamme la sonorité du clavier ! Et cependant, au fond de cela, combien de tristes imitateurs, combien de médiocrités sonnantes pour deux maîtres vraiment reconnus, Thalberg et Liszt ! Je ne dis pas Chopin, fantôme vaporeux que l'imitation ne peut saisir. [**Henri Blaze de Bury**]

« **La Presse** », 24 avril 1841, p. 3

Le monde musical, tout fatigué qu'il soit de concerts, s'occupe d'une réunion qui aura le pouvoir de ranimer les esprits les plus blasés. Il est un artiste, à Paris, qui a une place tout à fait particulière ; chacun le connaît, chacun l'admire, et presque personne ne l'a entendu. Il ne va pas à Londres, ni à Saint-Pétersbourg, ni à Vienne, et la Russie, l'Angleterre et l'Allemagne le citent et l'attendent. Il ne donne jamais de concerts, et sa réputation reste toujours la même, en dépit de son silence. Les talents les plus éclatants l'honorent et le saluent avec respect ; sa gloire, cachée au fond du cœur, n'éclipse celle de personne, et domine celle de tout le monde : il n'est pas le premier, il est à part. Chacun a déjà deviné que c'est de Chopin qu'il s'agit. Oui, Chopin cédant aux instances de ses admirateurs, c'est-à-dire de ses amis, car l'admirer, c'est l'aimer, consent enfin à donner une soirée chez Pleyel [...].

« **Revue et gazette musicale de Paris** », 12 mars 1843, 10ème Année, n° 11, p. 93
Galerie de la Gazette musicale n° 2. Pianistes célèbres (jeune école).

[...] L'artiste numéroté 4, et qui a nom Chopin, se distingue par d'autres qualités excentriques, et qui lui sont toutes personnelles, toutes particulières : c'est la sévérité dans la grâce ; c'est la fantaisie de la pensée dans l'abstention de la *fantaisie* emprun-tée ; c'est la petite proportion de l'air national, la Mazurka, avec le dédain des petits airs dérangés sous le titre d'arrangement ; c'est Chopin avec sa physionomie et son talent tout exceptionnel ; c'est sa patrie errante enfin qui souffre et chante avec une douce mélancolie. [**Henri Blanchard**]

Henri Heine, *Lutèce*, Paris : Michel Lévy 1855, p. 316–317
Paris, 26 mars 1843.

Il n'y a qu'un pianiste que je lui [Thalberg] préfère, Chopin qui, il est vrai, est plutôt compositeur que virtuose. Près de Chopin j'oublie tout à fait le jeu du pianiste

passé maître, et je m'enfonce dans les doux abîmes de sa musique, dans les douloureux délices de ses créations aussi exquises que profondes. Chopin est le grand poète
musical, l'artiste de génie qu'il ne faudrait nommer qu'en compagnie de Mozart, de
Beethoven, de Rossini ou de Berlioz.

Honoré de Balzac, *Le Cousin Pons* (1847), Paris : Gallimard
– Bibliothèque de la Pléiade 1977, vol. 7, p. 705.

Il trouva des thèmes sublimes sur lesquels il broda des caprices exécutés tantôt
avec la douleur et la perfection raphaélesque de Chopin tantôt avec la fougue et le
grandiose dantesque de Liszt, les deux organisations musicales qui se rapprochent le
plus de celle de Paganini.

Honoré de Balzac, Lettre à Mme Hańska, 5 avril 1843
Reproduit dans : *Lettres à l'étrangère*, Paris : Robert Laffont 1990, vol. 1, p. 663

J'ai appris que vous alliez voir Liszt, homme ridicule, talent sublime ! C'est le
Paganini du piano. Mais Chopin lui est bien supérieur.

Lettre à la même, 28 mai 1843
Ibidem, vol. 1, p. 682

Vous ne jugerez Liszt que quand il vous sera donné d'entendre Chopin. Le
Hongrois est un démon ; le Polonais est un ange.

« La France musicale », 25 novembre 1860, 24ème Année, n° 48, p. 457
La musique, le piano et les pianistes (4ème article)

[...] Alors que cette école [de Thalberg] était souveraine, et que tout était fantaisie sur des thèmes connus, on vit se glisser sur la scène une figure pâle, mélancolique ;
un ange déchu et meurtri : c'était Chopin, le barde ; Chopin le poète de la Pologne.

A peine commencions-nous à goûter le charme de ses mélodies, cris de souffrance de son cœur endolori, qu'il nous a quittés pour retourner dans les régions
éthérées dont il semblait déjà avoir entrevu les douces splendeurs de ses rêves mysti-
ques. Il s'élança dans sa première patrie, laissant derrière lui, comme les traces d'un
brillant météore, les inspirations de son génie divin. Ses *Nocturnes*, ses *Ballades* sont

autant de poèmes pleins de tendresse, imprégnés de larmes, et destinés à murmurer éternellement au cœur de ceux qui l'ont aimé, au cœur de ceux qui possèdent ces deux cordes dont se composait la lyre de ce poète du piano : Mélancolie et Amour [...]. [**Louis-Moreau Gottschalk**]

Hippolyte Barbedette, *Essai de critique musicale*, Paris : Leiber 1861

Quand Chopin parut sur la scène, il n'y avait plus de grands pianistes vraiment originaux. Chopin introduisit dans la musique de piano un élément qui, depuis long-temps, en était absent : la sensibilité. Il transforma le piano et lui donna une âme. Il faut l'avoir entendu pour savoir quelle était, sous ses doigts, la transfiguration de cet instrument. C'était un charme sans pareil, une sorte de magnétisme auquel il était impossible de se soustraire. Chopin a su faire du piano un instrument *solo*.

Sous ce rapport, il a eu une grande influence sur l'école moderne. Quelques unes comprirent qu'un pianiste avait un but plus digne à remplir que celui d'étonner ses auditeurs par les merveilles d'une voltige transcendante.

Paul Scudo, *Critique et littérature musicales*, Paris : Victor Lecou 1862, p. 10–11

Âmes tendres et délicates, esprits élevés, vrais artistes, vous tous pour qui la musique n'est pas un vain bruit, une cohue de sons qui étonnent et enivrent les sens, mais un langage sublime par où se révèlent les joies, les douleurs, les aspirations de notre âme, que ne saurait exprimer la parole ordinaire, laissez là M. Liszt et ses tours de force, et allez entendre M. Chopin, si vous pouvez. M. Liszt n'est qu'un pianiste, et M. Chopin est un poète. (1)

Note 1 : François Chopin, né à Żelazowa Wola, près de Varsovie, est mort à Paris le 17 octobre 1849. Virtuose de premier ordre et compositeur exquis, Chopin appartenait à cette école de musiciens ingénieux et profonds dont Weber et Schubert ont été les fondateurs. Ses compositions diverses pour le piano sont les seules vrai-ment originales qui aient paru en France depuis une trentaine d'années.

« **Revue des deux mondes** », 1ᵉʳ septembre 1883, 3ᵉᵐᵉ Période, 59ᵉᵐᵉ vol, LIIᵒ Année, p. 863
Henri Blaze de Bury, *Études et souvenirs. Frédéric Chopin.*

[...] La légende de Paganini précéda les triomphes non moins fantastiques de Liszt, qui, à son tour, amena l'apothéose de Chopin. Paganini n'avait pour lui que les revenants et les vampires ; Liszt et Chopin fondèrent le règne du pianiste lovelace et grand seigneur. La ligne de démarcation qui jusqu'alors séparait l'artiste du public était levée. La salle de concert devenait un salon où le virtuose recevait en prince ses invités. Si la gloire vient lentement, la renommée a vol d'aigle. Liszt et Chopin eurent bientôt ce qu'ils voulaient ; divers épisodes galants dont s'émut la société rehaussèrent aussi leur prestige.

4 Dans le mouvement romantique

« **Le Rénovateur** », 23 février 1834
Reproduit dans : *Hector Berlioz. Critique musicale*, Paris, Buchet-Chastel 1996, vol. 1, p. 178.

[...] Dans la même soirée, Chopin nous a fait entendre un magnifique concerto de piano étincelant de verve, de grâce, de fraîcheur, de caprices piquants, de traits délicats, de ravissantes arabesques, qu'il a exécuté avec le talent supérieur qu'on lui connaît. J'aurais beaucoup à dire sur Chopin et sa musique ; mais je craindrais le reproche banal de camaraderie. Cependant si je parle quelquefois avec enthousiasme de quelques artistes qui sont mes amis, on aurait tort d'attribuer mes éloges à l'influence des sentiments personnels, car mon amitié pour eux est née au contraire de l'admiration que leurs talents m'ont d'abord inspirée. [**Hector Berlioz**]

« **Revue et gazette musicale de Paris** », 4 février 1838, 5ème Année, n° 5, p. 45–46
Henri Heine, *Lettres confidentielles II.*
Reproduit dans : **Henri Heine, *De tout un peu. Les virtuoses. Berlioz, Liszt, Chopin,*** Paris : Calmann Lévy 1890, p. 306–308

[...] Il serait injuste de négliger, à cette occasion, de parler d'un pianiste qu'on célèbre le plus auprès de Liszt. Chopin peut justement nous servir à prouver qu'à un homme extraordinaire il ne suffit pas de pouvoir rivaliser de perfection technique avec les plus habiles de son art, Chopin ne met point sa satisfaction à ce que ses mains soient applaudies pour leur agile dextérité par d'autres mains. Il aspire à un plus beau succès : ses doigts ne sont que les serviteurs de son âme, et son âme est applaudie par les gens qui n'écoutent pas seulement avec les oreilles, mais avec l'âme. Aussi il est le favori de cette élite qui recherche dans la musique les plus hautes jouissances intellectuelles ; ses succès sont de nature aristocratique ; sa gloire est comme parfumée par les louanges de la bonne société, elle est distinguée comme sa personne.

Chopin est né en Pologne, de parents français, et son éducation a été achevée en Allemagne. Les influences de ces trois nationalités font de lui un ensemble des plus remarquables. Il s'est approprié les meilleures qualités qui distinguent les trois peuples. La Pologne lui a donné son sentiment chevaleresque et sa souffrance historique ; la France, sa facile élégance et sa grâce ; l'Allemagne, sa profondeur rêveuse ; mais la nature lui donna une figure élancée, coquette, un peu maladive, le plus noble cœur et le génie. Il faut certainement accorder à Chopin le génie dans toute l'acception du mot. Il n'est pas seulement virtuose, mais bien poète aussi : il peut nous révéler la poésie qui vit dans son âme ; c'est un musicien poète, et rien n'est comparable à la jouissance qu'il nous procure quand il improvise sur le piano. Il n'est en ce moment ni Polonais, ni Français, ni Allemand, il trahit une plus haute origine : il vient du pays de Mozart, de Raphaël, de Goethe ; sa patrie véritable est le pays de poésie. Il me semble, quand il improvise, que c'est un compatriote qui m'arrive de mon pays et me raconte les choses les plus curieuses qui s'y sont passées pendant mon absence. Il me prend parfois l'envie de l'interrompre pour lui dire : « Et que fait la belle Ondine, qui savait draper avec tant de coquetterie son voile d'argent autour de ses cheveux verts ? Le dieu marin à barbe blanche la poursuit-il toujours de son sot amour suranné ? Les roses ont-elles toujours chez nous ce fier éclat flamboyant ? Les arbres font-ils toujours entendre leurs beaux chants au clair de lune ?… »

« **La France musicale** », 19 février 1851, 15ème Année, n° 3, p. 19
Les Nocturnes de Field.

[...] Sous le nom de Nocturnes, nous avons vu remplacer les timides et sereines tendresses, que Field les chargeait d'interpréter, par des effets étranges et étrangers. Un seul génie s'est emparé de ce genre, pour lui donner le mouvement et l'ardeur dont il était susceptible, tout en lui conservant sa douceur et le vague de ses inspirations. Parcourant tous les tons du sentiment élégiaque, colorant aussi ses rêveries de la profonde tristesse pour laquelle *Young* a trouvé quelques accords vibrants si douloureusement, Chopin dans ses *nocturnes* –poèmes n'a pas seulement chanté les harmonies qui sont la source de nos plus ineffables jouissances, mais aussi les troubles inquiets et agités qu'elles font souvent naître. Son vol est plus haut, quoique son aile soit plus blessée, et la suavité devient navrante, tant elle laisse entrevoir de désolation. [**Franz Liszt**]

« **La France musicale** », 27 avril 1851, 15ème Année, n° 17, p. 130
Franz Liszt, *Chopin.*

[...] Ceux qui voyaient les flammes du talent dévorer insensiblement les vieilles charpentes vermoulues, se rattachaient à l'école musicale dont Berlioz était le représentant le plus doué, le plus vaillant et le plus osé. Chopin s'y rallia complètement et fut l'un de ceux qui mit le plus de persévérance à se libérer des serviles formules du style conventionnel, aussi bien qu'à répudier les charlatanismes, qui n'eussent remplacé de vieux abus que par des abus nouveaux.

Pendant les quelques années que dura cette sorte de campagne du romantisme [...] Chopin resta invariable dans ses prédilections comme dans ses répulsions. Il n'admit pas le moindre atermoiement avec aucun de ceux qui, selon lui, ne représentaient pas suffisamment le progrès. [...] Il donna à nos essais, à nos luttes d'alors [...] l'appui d'une conviction calme et inébranlable, d'une stabilité de caractère également à l'épreuve des lassitudes et des leurres, d'une rare immuabilité de volonté.

Georges Mathias, Préface à : **Isidore Philipp,** *Exercices quotidiens tirés des œuvres de Chopin*, Paris : Hamelle 1897, p. 5

[...] Chopin était classique de sentiment et d'opinion, tout en étant romantique d'imagination.

« **Revue des deux mondes** », 15 mai 1901, 5ème Période, LXXI° Année, vol. 3, p. 462

[...] Aussi le romantisme de Mickiewicz se distingue-t-il de tous les autres par un accent spontané et profond, qui semble résulter moins d'une tendance littéraire que de l'instinctif élan d'un cœur passionné. Il est au romantisme de Schiller et d'Hugo ce qu'est, en musique, le romantisme de Chopin à ceux de Robert Schumann et d'Hector Berlioz. [**T. de Wyzewa**]

B – Le compositeur

1 Polonité : l'accent natal et l'écriture de l'exil

Eugène Sauzay, *Mémoires* Cité par : **Brigitte François-Sappey,** *La vie musicale à travers les Mémoires d'Eugène Sauzay,* « **Revue de musicologie** » LX (1974), nos 1–2

Ma tante Paillet recevait beaucoup, on dansait chez elle tous les dimanches. Un soir, je vis entrer dans le salon un jeune homme blond, de figure délicate et distinguée, qu'une jeune nièce de ma tante, née en Pologne, lui présenta. C'était Chopin. On allait danser ; il se mit au piano et nous joua sa *mazurka* en *si* bémol ; ensuite, il voulut nous apprendre à la danser. Je le sens encore, me prenant les deux mains, et m'entraînant autour du salon, pour me montrer le pas. Revenu au piano, il nous charma par une musique toute nouvelle et une exécution surprenante. Nous ne comprenions pas alors qui nous avions devant nous.

« **Gazette Musicale de Paris** », 29 juin 1834, 1ère Année, n° 26, p. 210
Revue critique. Quatre Mazurkas opus 17

M. Chopin s'est acquis une réputation toute spéciale par la manière spirituelle et profondément artistique avec laquelle il sait traiter la musique nationale de Pologne, genre de musique qui ne nous était encore que fort peu connu. Le mérite de ce jeune compositeur devait surtout trancher remarquablement aujourd'hui où nous déplorons une si triste pénurie dans les formes de l'art, réduits que nous sommes à ce malencontreux galop si commun, si peu gracieux, et qui vient reproduire son rythme trivial jusque dans les ouvertures de nos opéras. La véritable Mazoure polonaise, telle que M. Chopin nous la reproduit, porte un caractère si particulier et s'adapte en même temps avec tant d'avantage à l'expression d'une sombre mélancolie comme à celle d'une joie excentrique ; elle convient si bien aux chants d'amour comme aux chants de guerre, qu'elle nous paraît préférable à bien d'autres formes musicales. [...] Si parfois on a exprimé le désir que M. Chopin voulût bien se résoudre à écrire de la musique un peu moins difficile, nous pouvons affirmer que l'œuvre dont nous nous occupons aujourd'hui répond jusqu'à un certain point aussi à ce vœu. Il faudra cependant pour arriver à une bonne exécution de ces Mazourkas, avoir compris d'une manière intime le caractère du génie de l'auteur, car ici encore il nous apparaît poétique, tendre, fantastique, toujours gracieux, et toujours aimable, même dans les moments où il s'abandonne à l'inspiration la plus passionnée [...]. [**François Stoepel**]

« **Gazette musicale de Paris** », 3 août 1834, 1ère Année, n° 31, p. 251
Revue critique. Rondo à la Krakowiak opus 14

[...] Dans l'œuvre que nous signalons aujourd'hui à l'attention du public, M. Chopin donne un exemple caractéristique de ces deux principaux genres de chants nationaux, ce qui seul donne déjà à sa production un cachet tout particulier, et ne rend que plus intéressante la piquante originalité du spirituel compositeur. [...] L'art du contrepoint, réuni à tant de poésie et à un goût si délicat, est ce que la composition musicale peut offrir de plus élevé : arriver là c'est se montrer le digne émule des plus grands maîtres. [...] Puissent les vrais amis de l'art musical, qui, dans le vain clinquant et le déluge de roulades produits par presque tous les compositeurs modernes, ne trouvent nécessairement pas assez d'occasions de surmonter les difficultés véritables, ne pas se laisser effrayer par l'essor immense que vient de prendre M. Chopin.

Émile Deschamps, *Lettre sur la musique*, **15 février 1835**
Reproduit dans : *Œuvres complètes*, Paris : A. Lemerre 1872–1874, vol. 4, p. 38

[...] Le concert au bénéfice des réfugiés polonais a tourné au bénéfice des auditeurs. Il a été supérieurement ordonné et exécuté. M. Chopin s'est surpassé en jouant un concerto de sa composition qui a électrisé l'assemblée par l'originalité et le coloris du style et par la fraîcheur des mélodies dont lui seul peut rendre sur son piano, la grâce ingénieuse et l'exquise finesse. Vous connaissez M. Chopin, madame ; vos souvenirs feront plus que tous mes éloges. Ce concert était long et il a paru court. C'est une compensation pour tant d'autres qui sont et qui paraissent tout le contraire de cela.

« **Revue et gazette musicale** », 9 septembre 1838, 5ème Année, n° 36, p. 362
Lettre ouverte « A M. F. Chopin sur sa Ballade polonaise ».

Mon cher ami !
Il y a peu de temps, dans une de ces soirées où, entouré de sympathies choisies, vous vous abandonnez sans méfiance à votre inspiration, vous nous avez fait entendre cette ballade polonaise que nous aimons tant. A peine le génie mélancolique

enfermé dans votre instrument, reconnaissant les mains qui ont seules le pouvoir de le faire parler, eut-il commencé à nous raconter ses douleurs mystérieuses que nous tombâmes tous dans une profonde rêverie. Et quand vous eûtes fini, nous restâmes silencieux et pensifs, écoutant encore le chant sublime dont la dernière note s'était depuis longtemps perdue dans l'espace. [...] Pour moi, caché dans le coin le plus sombre de la chambre, je pleurais en suivant de la pensée les images désolantes que vous m'aviez fait apparaître. En rentrant chez moi, j'ai essayé de les rendre à ma manière dans les lignes suivantes. Lisez-les avec indulgence, et quand même j'y aurais mal interprété votre ballade, agréez-en l'offrande comme une preuve de mon affection pour vous et de ma sympathie pour votre héroïque patrie. [**Félicien Mallefille**]

« **Revue et gazette musicale de Paris** », 21 mai 1843, 10ème Année, n° 21, p. 178
Revue critique (musique de piano). Trois Mazurkas par F. Chopin.

[...] Respirant la douceur, la tendresse et l'amour, mais empreint de tristesse et de naïveté. On dirait qu'il y a toujours un souvenir de la patrie absente et opprimée dans les mélodies de ce pianiste-compositeur. Heureuses les nations qui ont des poètes comme Thomas Moore et Chopin ; ils entretiennent par leurs chants les traditions et l'amour du pays où ils sont nés, et le bercent d'un doux et noble espoir d'affranchissement [...]. [**Henri Blanchard**]

« **La France musicale** », 9 mars 1851, 15ème Année, n° 10, p. 73–75
Franz Liszt, *Chopin.*

[...] Chopin a dégagé l'inconnu de poésie, qui n'était qu'indiqué dans les thèmes originaux des Mazoures polonaises. Conservant leur rythme, il en a ennobli la mélodie, agrandi les proportions, et y a intercalé des clairs-obscurs harmoniques aussi nouveaux que les sujets auxquels il les adaptait, pour peindre dans ces productions qu'il aimait à nous entendre appeler des tableaux de chevalet, les innombrables émotions d'ordres si divers qui agitent les cœurs pendant que dure [...] la danse.

[...] Il ne s'affranchissait pourtant jamais d'un sentiment qui formait en quelque sorte le sol de son cœur, et pour lequel il ne trouvait d'expression que dans sa propre langue, aucune autre ne possédant d'équivalent au mot polonais de Żal ! qu'il répétait fréquemment, comme si son oreille eût été avide de ce son, et qui renferme toute l'échelle des sentiments que produit un regret intense, depuis le repentir jusqu'à la haine, fruits bénis ou empoisonnés de cette âcre racine.

« La France musicale », (25 mai 1851) 15ème Année, n° 21, p. 163
Franz Liszt, *Chopin.*

[...] Chopin pourra être rangé au nombre des premiers musiciens qui aient ainsi individualisé en eux le sens poétique d'une nation. [...] Auteur éminemment subjectif, Chopin a donné à toutes ses productions une même vie, et a animé toutes ses créations de sa vie à lui. Toutes ses œuvres sont donc liées par une unité dont il résulte que leurs beautés comme leurs défauts sont toujours les conséquences du même ordre d'émotion, d'un mode exclusif de sentir, condition première du poète pour que ses chants fassent vibrer à l'unisson tous les cœurs de sa patrie [...].

Henri Blaze de Bury, *Musiciens contemporains*, Paris : Michel Lévy 1856, p. 114–115

J'ai dit que c'était un des très grands charmes des artistes du Nord que cet accent natal qui jamais en eux ne se perd ni ne s'altère. Si tant d'autres preuves n'existaient pas de cette vérité, l'exemple de Chopin suffirait. Si vous avez observé en effet cette nature éminente et rare dont le développement s'est accompli presque sous nos yeux, vous aurez vu que des années passées au centre de ce que la civilisation a de plus excessif, n'avaient pu chez lui porter la moindre atteinte à la nationalité. Laquelle de ses compositions, et je parle ici des œuvres de sa seconde manière, de ses nocturnes, qu'il écrivait après dix ans de séjour au milieu des raffinements intellectuels de la société parisienne, laquelle de ses compositions ne respire le génie du Nord ? Où trouverez-vous que l'accent ait fait défaut ? [...] Les Slaves ont dans leur instinct quelque chose de saccadé et de sauvage qui ne se rencontre pas d'ordinaire chez les peuples de la Baltique : quiconque a connu Chopin a pu observer à loisir comment chez lui cette rudesse du sol natal avait été modifiée par des conditions toutes personnelles d'élégance et de distinction. Et pourtant cette physionomie languissante avait ses éclairs d'impatience et de colère ; cette nature douce et fine avait ses emportements, ses brusqueries et ses soubresauts, empreintes originaires, souvenirs du sol barbare dont la trace énergique et profonde se révèle en plus d'une de ces mazourkes si peu comprises de la foule, qui n'en saisit que le côté frivole [...].

Louis Énault, *Chopin*, Paris : E. Thunot 1856, p. 24

Les Slaves se prêtent, ils ne se donnent pas ; et comme si Chopin eût voulu se faire pardonner l'origine française de sa famille, il se montra plus Polonais que la Pologne.

Agathe Audley, *Frédéric Chopin. Sa vie et ses œuvres*, Paris : Plon 1880, p. 2

Tous se rappellent, et non sans émotion, ce pianiste dont la fougue presque sauvage, la grâce élégante, offraient un type d'une originalité exceptionnelle, d'un charme infini, qui plus tard faisait dire de lui avec raison : « Il n'eut ni prédécesseur ni successeur. »

Frédéric Chopin était doué à la fois d'un génie multiple et profond où tous les contrastes se rencontraient sans se heurter : spirituel et vif comme la France à laquelle il appartenait par son père ; fougueux et passionné comme la Pologne qui le revendiquait par sa mère, il devait peut-être une partie du charme et de l'étrangeté de son talent au double caractère de sa double patrie. Toutefois, celle qui prévalut en lui et dont il garda l'ineffaçable empreinte, ce ne fut pas la France, mais la Pologne.

« Le Temps », 4 septembre 1880, 20ème Année, n° 7076, p. 3
Hector Berlioz, Études et souvenirs de théâtre.
Reproduit dans : **Ernest Legouvé, *Soixante ans de souvenirs*,** Paris : Hetzel 1886, vol. 2, p. 160–161

[...] Il y avait un moyen certain de l'arracher au piano, c'était de lui demander la marche funèbre qu'il a composée après les désastres de la Pologne. Jamais il ne se refusait à la jouer ; mais à peine la dernière mesure achevée, il prenait son chapeau et partait. Ce morceau, qui était comme le chant d'agonie de sa patrie, lui faisait trop de mal ; il ne pouvait plus rien dire après l'avoir dit, car ce grand artiste était un grand patriote, et les notes fières qui éclatent dans ses mazurkas comme des cris de clairon, racontent tout ce qui vibrait d'héroïque derrière ce pâle visage qui n'a jamais dépassé la juvénilité.

« La Nouvelle Revue », mars–avril 1897, vol. 105, 19ème Année, p. 546
***Chopin.* Prince de Valori.**

[...] Il est encore un autre préjugé qu'il faut détruire. Chopin n'est pas un génie exclusivement polonais. Les Polonais ont le droit de le revendiquer comme un illustre compatriote ; mais l'art musical le garde comme un de ses plus glorieux enfants.

Que, dans les compositions d'origine polonaise : les *polonaises*, les *mazurkas*, il se soit montré quelquefois saccadé, un peu slave, soit ; mais encore il a élargi et modifié leur cadre. « La rudesse du sol natal avait été modifiée par des conditions toutes personnelles d'élégance et de distinction. » Cependant, cette nature fine et élégante avait des éclairs d'impatience et de colère, des emportements et des soubresauts.

Édouard Ganche, *La Vie de F. Chopin dans son œuvre*, Paris : Société des Auteurs-Éditeurs 1909, p. 18–19

Toujours il songera à sa patrie et toute son œuvre il redira sa douleur patriotique. Persistante, elle influe sur la direction de son talent, sur ses relations, ses préférences ; elle est l'attribut dominant de ses tendances, et son expression se montre encore dans une de ses ultimes compositions, la polonaise-fantaisie (op 61), où il voulait dans son espérance d'un avenir meilleur retracer le martyr de ses compatriotes et leur prochain triomphe.

« Le Courrier musical », n° spécial *Chopin*, 1er janvier 1910, 13ème Année, n° 1, p. 2–5
Sur le génie de Chopin.

[...] Un des traits les plus frappants de son art, c'est qu'il a énormément emprunté au peuple. Avec des mazurkas, des valses et des ballades, issues du génie plébéien d'une race persécutée et misérable, Chopin a immédiatement acquis en France le renom d'un aristocrate raffiné et suprême.

Certes il a fallu pour cela la haute distinction de l'homme, la magie de son jeu, le charme des rythmes slaves apportant dans le romantisme une note insolite et captivante. Mais il a fallu surtout la piété passionnée du musicien à l'égard de sa patrie. Il y a en Chopin le maladif et mélancolique amoureux, et le patriote déterminé à élever le folklore polonais au rang des grands chefs-d'œuvre. Pendant de longues années on n'a voulu songer qu'au Chopin du cénacle Sand, au dandy douloureux. C'est maintenant qu'on aperçoit pleinement l'importance de l'autre Chopin, du Slave exilé.

[...] Et on peut enfin dire que cette société, abusée par quelques concessions pianistiques que la mode arrachait à Chopin, n'a rien compris au vrai sens de son œuvre slave, c'est-à-dire des *Ballades*, des *Mazurkas*, des *Scherzos* et des *Polonaises*. C'étaient pour elle les marques superficielles d'un artiste étranger apportant à son exhibition un peu de couleur locale pour se faire bien venir, et gardant pour ainsi dire la joliesse amusante et voyante du costume national.

Une tout autre pensée hantait Frédéric Chopin. [...] Son idée fixe a été de servir sa patrie selon ses forces et ses aptitudes en faisant accorder droit de cité dans l'Europe occidentale au génie slave que la coalition germanique semblait décidée à étouffer. C'est pourquoi il est allé droit au peuple et a fait du folklore polonais le motif constant de ses inspirations. Il ne s'agit pas du caprice d'un artiste utilisant parfois des thèmes de savoureuse naïveté : l'examen de l'œuvre montre qu'il y a là une volonté préméditée et soutenue.

Comment donc une telle œuvre plébéienne eût-elle pu apparaître dans son vrai sens à un public qui restait fasciné par l'aristocratisme de son auteur ? On peut dire que sur ce point-là Chopin, si fêté, est restait incompris [...].

Le miracle de son art, c'est d'avoir prouvé, avant Schumann, avant Heine, que l'inspiration la plus nettement populaire peut donner la sensation du raffinement suprême, et que l'état d'âme de malheureux paysans peut contenir en puissance les émotions intellectuelles les plus complexes et les plus rares, et devenir la nourriture de l'élite. Cette inspiration fait que la musique de Chopin ne contient aucun élément de dégénérescence et garde sous ses arabesques pianistiques une ligne souple et solide, une « santé harmonique » et une extrême vitalité mélodique, toutes les qualités d'un merveilleux langage émotionnel. [**Camille Mauclair**]

« **Le Courrier musical** », n° spécial *Chopin,* 1er janvier 1910, 13ème Année, n° 1, p. 11–12
Silhouette de Chopin.

[...] Classique ! [...] voilà ce que Chopin est le moins. Mais il est profondément original. Il ne doit rien à l'Italie, aucun art n'étant moins que le sien arrêté, plastique et formel. La France non plus, ni l'Allemagne, ne sauraient le réclamer ou seulement le reconnaître. Il ne fredonne point à la française, il ne chante pas à l'italienne, il pense encore moins à l'allemande. Par le fond et la forme de sa pensée, Chopin diffère de tous les Allemands. [...] C'est que tous les Allemands possèdent, à des degrés inégaux, mais à quelque degré toujours, le génie de la polyphonie et celui de la symphonie. Ils combinent et ils développent. Or ce double génie fait entièrement défaut à Frédéric Chopin [...].

Mais le cœur de sa race battait dans sa poitrine. Je ne sais pas un musicien plus que celui-là patriote et national. Il est polonais plus que tous les autres ne sont français, italiens ou allemands. Il est de son pays, rien que de son pays, et de son pays meurtri et mort sa musique restera comme l'âme immortelle. Âme mélancolique et plaintive, que dans les nocturnes, les ballades, on entendra gémir et regretter éternellement. Âme courtoise et charmante, dans l'intimité des valses et des mazurkas. Âme héroïque, dans les polonaises, dont plus d'une est un chef-d'œuvre épique et triomphal [...].

Et pourtant Chopin n'est pas un des grands parmi les grands. Avec la poésie et la passion, avec la fantaisie, l'emportement chevaleresque et l'enthousiasme, avec tous les dons qui firent le charme, la beauté, la gloire de sa patrie, il porte en lui les mêmes causes de faiblesse et de ruine : des nerfs indomptés et malades, plus d'imagination que de logique, une humeur inégale et le goût du clinquant, du flamboyant, de la fanfreluche et du panache. [...] La maîtrise et la conduite de soi, la discipline, la sagesse, la volonté libre et toute puissante, dans l'art comme dans la vie, voilà les forces essentielles et les souveraines vertus. Chopin n'est pas de ceux qui les ont possédées. [**Camille Bellaigue**]

2 Un langage novateur

« **Gazette musicale de Paris** », 21 septembre 1834, 1ère Année, n° 38, p. 304–306
Revue critique. F. Chopin. « Là ci darem la mano » op. 2 et Concerto op. 11.

[...] Nous devons ranger cet artiste parmi le petit nombre de génies favorisés qui, le but toujours devant les yeux, marchent avec autant de force que de hardiesse, sans s'inquiéter de ce que fait la foule autour d'eux, de ce qu'elle désire, de ce qui est son besoin ou sa mode. Essayons de le suivre dans sa course d'un regard observateur, mais ami ; un homme comme lui ne doit pas plus être blessé par nos scrupules qu'ébloui par notre admiration.

[...] Si nous avons maintenant à émettre notre opinion définitive sur deux œuvres composés à un intervalle de quelques années, nous dirons que, dans le premier, M. Chopin s'était annoncé déjà comme un artiste distingué, qu'il y avait marqué avec précision la nature de son génie, mais qu'il a dépassé de bien loin dans le second toutes les espérances qu'on avait dû raisonnablement concevoir. M. Chopin, soit dans le mécanisme de l'art du piano, soit dans la poésie musicale, s'est élevé au-dessus de tous ses contemporains, grâce à l'instruction qu'il a puisée dans leurs glorieux travaux, mais surtout grâce à la nature qui nous a donné en lui un de ses enfants privilégiés. Puisse-t-il continuer, comme nous le désirons, comme nous le comprenons, et nous sommes certains de l'accompagner de notre attachement jusqu'au faîte le plus élevé de la gloire. [**François Stoepel**]

« **Revue et gazette musicale de Paris** », 2 décembre 1838, 5ème Année, n° 48, p. 493
Revue critique.

[...] Si dans quelques-unes de ces brillantes soirées musicales dont Paris abonde, vous avez entendu de délicieuses mazurkas polonaises, de ces mélodies d'une naïveté et d'une tristesse indéfinissables, vous verrez tout de suite que nous parlons de M. Chopin, de ce pianiste qui se distingue dans la foule des pianistes de premier ordre qu'enfante le XIXe siècle. Afin, sans doute, de se délasser des productions sérieuses qu'il écrit pour le piano, M. Chopin, dans un moment de loisir, a laissé tomber de sa plume un de ces morceaux légers qui font le charme des réunions intimes. C'est une vaporeuse pensée, intitulée *Impromptu*. Au laisser-aller de certaines notes étonnées de se rencontrer et qui forment des dissonances ni préparées ni résolues, on voit tout de suite l'indépendance qui a présidé à ce joli gazouillement de triolets en mesure à quatre temps et dans le ton de *la* bémol majeur. [...] Ce tableau de genre, jeté sur le papier sans prétention aucune, sera goûté par l'élève comme par le pianiste habile. Le premier y verra une étude gracieuse, un exercice pour l'ensemble des deux mains ; le second y reconnaîtra ce faire élégant, distingué, ces licences harmoniques qui décèlent le grand artiste dans la plus légère production. [**Henri Blanchard**]

« **La France musicale** », 9 février 1851, 15ème Année, n° 6, p. 42
Franz Liszt, *Chopin.*

[...] On ne saurait s'appliquer à faire une analyse intelligente des travaux de Chopin sans y trouver des beautés d'un ordre très élevé, d'une expression parfaitement neuve, et d'une contexture harmonique aussi originale que savante. Chez lui la hardiesse se justifie toujours ; la richesse, l'exubérance même, n'excluent pas la clarté ; la singularité ne dégénère pas en bizarrerie baroque ; les ciselures ne sont pas désordonnées, et le luxe de l'ornementation ne surcharge pas l'élégance des lignes principales. Ses meilleurs ouvrages abondent en combinaisons qui, on peut le dire, forment époque dans le maniement du style musical. Osées, brillantes, séduisantes, elles déguisent leur profondeur sous tant de grâce, et leur habileté sous tant de charme, que ce n'est qu'avec peine qu'on peut se soustraire à ce charme entraînant pour les juger à froid sous le point de vue de leur valeur théorique ; valeur qui a déjà été sentie, mais qui se fera de plus en plus reconnaître, lorsque le temps sera venu d'un examen attentif des services rendus à l'art, durant la période que Chopin a traversée.

C'est à lui que nous devons l'extension des accords, soit plaqués, soit en arpèges, soit en batterie ; ces sinuosités chromatiques et enharmoniques, dont ses pages offrent de si frappants exemples ; ces petits groupes de notes surajoutées, tombant comme des gouttelettes d'une rosée diaprée, par-dessus la figure mélodique. [...] Il inventa ces admirables progressions harmoniques, qui ont doté d'un caractère sérieux, même les pages qui par la légèreté de leur sujet ne paraissaient pas devoir prétendre à cette importance.

Franz Liszt, Lettre à Carolyne Wittgenstein, 1ᵉʳ janvier 1876
Reproduit dans : *Correspondance*, éd. Pierre-Antoine Huré, Claude Knepper, Paris : J.-C. Lattès, 1987, p. 516–517

En 1849, je ne comprenais pas encore l'intime beauté des dernières œuvres de Chopin : *Polonaise-Fantaisie, Barcarolle* – et gardais quelque réserve à l'endroit de leur ton maladif. Maintenant je les admire tout à fait [...] Sans prétendre que les dernières œuvres de Chopin équivalent à celles de la 3ème manière de Beethoven, que pendant longtemps on attribuait à sa surdité et à ses aberrations d'esprit, j'affirme et maintiendrai qu'elles sont non seulement très remarquables, mais aussi très harmonieuses, noblement inspirées et artistiquement proportionnées, de tous points à la hauteur du génie enchanteur de Chopin. Nul autre ne doit lui être comparé, il rayonne seul et unique dans le ciel de l'art. Ses attendrissements, ses grâces, ses pleurs, ses énergies et ses emportements ne sont qu'à lui. C'est un divin aristocrate – un archange féminin aux ailes prismatiques ! Pardon de l'expression bizarre qui rend ma pensée.

Antoine Marmontel, *Les Pianistes célèbres*, Paris : Chaix, 1878, p. 9–10

Les compositions de Chopin forment un ensemble important et du plus grand intérêt, car ce maître, qui avait horreur du banal et peu de goût pour le genre populaire, n'a jamais rien écrit en vue des succès faciles. Sa musique, pensée, composée, avec un soin extrême, d'une harmonie toujours élégante, touchant parfois à l'excès de recherche, ses traits ingénieux, admirablement ciselés, sa phrase mélodique, chantante, expressive, d'un sentiment élevé et mélancolique, ne pouvaient plaire qu'à des musiciens d'un goût raffiné, ou à des virtuoses séduits par les contours fins de ses traits nouveaux et ardus. D'année en année, Chopin a donné à son style, si personnel dès le début, plus de force, plus de corps, une individualité encore plus marquée, sans jamais sacrifier aux influences passagères, aux fluctuations de la mode.

« **Revue des deux mondes** », 1er septembre 1883, 3ème Période, LII Année, 59ème vol., p. 851–852

Henri Blaze de Bury, *Études et souvenirs. Frédéric Chopin.*

[...] Le passé s'était contenté d'applaudir dans Chopin l'improvisateur à la mode : c'est du compositeur que les générations actuelles s'occupent, obéissant moins à des curiosités de dilettante qu'à cet esprit d'information et de recherche qui nous passionne. Chopin se rendait-il bien compte de ce qu'il faisait ? Ces trouvailles harmoniques, émerveillement de l'heure présente et dont il a toujours les mains pleines, sont-elles le don gratuit de la bonne fée du piano ou le résultat d'une science acquise ? Ce qu'il y a de certain, c'est que son œuvre demeure un répertoire indispensable à consulter, même pour un musicien de théâtre ; les rythmes surtout y abondent ; les rythmes, cette rareté, cette disette de notre art contemporain, vous les voyez fourmiller, naître les uns des autres par générations spontanées et poudroyer dans un même rayon de soleil. Quelle source de rajeunissement, de vie nouvelle ! Car c'est de ce côté principalement que la difficulté d'être se fait sentir. Nous finissons de manger un vieux fonds appauvri ; si j'excepte Verdi, seul inventif en ce genre, je n'aperçois personne allant aux découvertes. [...] Bizet fut, je crois, le premier chez nous à lire dans la musique de Chopin autre chose que la poésie ondoyante et chatoyante ; il comprit tout le parti qu'une habile rénovation technique pourrait tirer de ce fouillis de richesses : accords étranges, plus qu'étranges, transitions bizarres, incohérences voulues, procédés inopinés d'harmonies contenus dans la *Grande Polonaise* en *fa* dièse mineur et dans la *Polonaise-fantaisie*.

« **Le Courrier musical** », n° spécial *Chopin,* 1er janvier 1910, 13ème Année, n° 1, p. 27

L'œuvre de Chopin. Les Mazurkas, les Valses, les Scherzos.

[...] Les 41 pièces que Chopin a fait paraître en différents recueils sous le titre de *Mazurkas* sont d'une fantaisie, d'une richesse rythmique extraordinaires ; le caractère très particulier des thèmes dont il s'est servi l'a entraîné souvent à des harmonisations des plus curieuses et qui ont dû paraître d'un modernisme outré à l'époque où elles ont été publiées. Bien des critiques auraient crié à la barbarie s'ils avaient regardé de près ces morceaux d'un tour si original et si personnel, mais ils ne leur attribuaient pas assez d'importance pour se donner cette peine ; séduits par le jeu tout de grâce et de charme de l'auteur, ils se contentaient de considérer comme de l'exotisme ce qui était en réalité le début d'un grand mouvement de rénovation harmonique ; celui qui devait aboutir quelque vingt-cinq ans plus tard avec Wagner. Ce dernier, grâce à son intimité avec Liszt, connaissait à fond l'œuvre du Maître polonais et bien souvent dans ces partitions, l'influence de ce dernier est sensible ; certains dessins de violon dans *Tristan et Yseult* ont une curieuse parenté avec quelques traits de piano qui se retrouvent assez fréquemment dans les Etudes et les Préludes ; et bien des procédés de modulations brusques aux tons éloignés (ou soi-disant tels) sont visiblement de même nature que ceux employés par Chopin. Ce dernier fut aussi, en ce sens, un des précurseurs de l'Ecole nationale russe. [**A. Bertelin**]

3 Des audaces techniques et formelles déroutantes

« **Le Pianiste** », 10 mars 1834, 1ère Année, n° 5, p. 78–79
Annonces motivées : 3 Nocturnes opus 15.

Ces nocturnes sont charmants, et ils contiennent les qualités et les défauts de ce jeune et savant compositeur. Pourquoi des idées si fraîches, si gracieuses, sont-elles souvent entravées, gâtées, -nous devons le dire,- par des duretés intolérables, et par une sorte d'affectation à écrire la musique presque comme il faut l'exécuter,- nous disons presque, car tout à fait est impossible) – à écrire ce genre balancé, languissant, tâtonné, ce genre qu'aucun arrangement de valeurs connues ne peut bien exprimer ; le Rubato enfin, ce Rubato l'effroi des jeunes filles, le Croque-Mitaine des mazettes ! [...]

Fr. Chopin aura beau faire, on ne rendra bien sa musique sans l'avoir entendu lui-même l'exécuter ; et nous ne craignons pas d'être démentis en disant qu'on ne l'entend pas assez souvent, et qu'il laisse échapper, par là, un des meilleurs moyens de soutenir ses éditeurs et de faire le succès de ses œuvres. [...] Avec d'aussi grandes qualités que celles dont Chopin est doué, il est à désirer qu'il revienne à une façon d'écrire moins tourmentée et plus à la portée des faibles humains.

« **Le Pianiste** », 10 mai 1834, 1ère Année, n° 7, p. 109–110
Annonces motivées : Rondo opus 16 – 4 Mazurkas opus 17.

Les ouvrages de Chopin, et particulièrement ses nocturnes et ses mazurkas -mazourk- ont une destinée remarquable ; ceux qui les comprennent les trouvent ravissants, et le jugement des autres est tout différent. Nous ne pouvons attribuer ceci qu'aux formes originales et aux harmonies de passage traitées d'une manière toute nouvelle, que l'on y rencontre à chaque instant, et qui choquent l'oreille lorsqu'elles ne sont pas convenablement attaquées ; quant à nous, notre opinion, déjà manifestée dans ce journal, nous place dans la classe des admirateurs ; et quand nous voyons tant d'artistes de talent sans imagination, et d'artistes d'imagination sans talent, nous sommes heureux de rencontrer ces deux qualités dans un très jeune homme qui est entré dans la carrière musicale sous de si heureux auspices.

« **Le Pianiste** », 10 juillet 1834, 1ère Année, n° 9, p. 142–143
Annonces motivées : Fantaisie avec accompagnement d'orchestre, sur des airs nationaux polonais opus 13.

Juger cet ouvrage d'après le piano seul, dépouillé de l'instrumentation qui lui sert de complément, ce serait une injustice, car ici surtout, la partie du piano contient beaucoup d'aridité, de passages quelquefois élégants, toujours difficiles, et le tout sur des motifs d'un caractère étranger dont il faut avoir la tradition. Ce morceau est un de ceux dans lesquels le piano ne peut pas s'isoler. Nous remettons notre analyse jusqu'après l'audition. Chopin est un de ces talents supérieurs qu'il faut étudier jusque dans leurs défauts, et la simple lecture d'un cahier de musique ne suffit pas pour cela.

[...] La musique de Chopin a un caractère tellement particulier que, dans certains cas, lui seul est à même de prononcer avec assurance sur l'exactitude d'une note qui paraîtrait douteuse. Dès lors aussi, la révision des épreuves ne doit être faite que par lui-même ; d'où il résultera qu'il y restera des erreurs que tout autres que l'auteur eût certainement rectifiées [...].

« **Gazette musicale** », 10 août 1834, 1ère Année, n° 32, p. 260
Revue critique. Valse opus 18.

Nous annoncions dernièrement une production de M. Chopin, ses quatre dernières mazourkas, ouvrage qui, malgré toute la richesse des idées, malgré toute la fraîcheur et la nouveauté qu'on y admire, se distingue cependant par une grande simplicité et ne contient que peu ou point de difficultés. Nous devons cette fois encore louer les mêmes propriétés aujourd'hui si rares, dans la valse que nous recommandons à nos lecteurs. Il nous paraît donc suffisamment prouvé que lorsque cet artiste écrit des passages difficiles il n'y est pas poussé par un vain caprice, mais bien par le sens et le caractère du morceau, ainsi que cela devrait toujours avoir lieu dans une création de l'art.[...]

« Revue et gazette musicale de Paris », 4 septembre 1836, 3ème Année, n° 36, p. 312–313
Revue critique. Nocturnes opus 27.

[...] Grétry prétendait que l'accumulation des accidents à la clef dénotait dans le compositeur absence d'idées et mépris des moyens simples. S'il avait lu la musique de M. Chopin, il se serait armé de toute sa prévention contre le jeune et habile pianiste polonais.

Dans les deux nocturnes que nous avons sous les yeux, il y a force dièses, bémols, transitions en harmoniques ; mais il y a aussi ce que nous avons toujours entendu en M. Chopin, mélodie naïve, originale et neuve. Le premier de ces deux nocturnes surtout est d'une grâce enchanteresse et qui rappelle ces mazourkes délicieuses qu'il nous faisait entendre dans les soirées si richement musicales de Zimmermann.

« La France musicale », 5 mars 1848, 11ème Année, n° 9 et 10, p. 68–69
Manuel du pianiste amateur. Auteurs difficiles en dehors de l'école de Thalberg.

M. Frédéric Chopin, né à Varsovie en 1810, est devenu l'hôte de la France depuis la malheureuse révolution polonaise de 1831. Exécutant admirable, improvisateur plein de charme, ses compositions perdent beaucoup à être exécutées par un autre que par lui. L'harmonie en est dure, heurtée, peu naturelle ; les tons bizarres, les modulations d'une extrême fréquence. Cette musique-là a certainement de l'originalité : rendue avec perfection, elle excite la curiosité et commande souvent les applaudissements ; mais ce genre ne convient qu'à bien peu de personnes, et l'on ne doit pas en abuser, car il est plein de périls et d'inconvénients. On comprendra toute notre pensée, si l'on veut ou si l'on peut parcourir jusqu'au bout certaine sonate en trois parties, avec presto final par mouvement semblable. Ce presto final nous paraît quelque chose d'unique en son espèce [...].

« Revue des deux mondes », 1er septembre 1883, 3ème Période, LII Année, 59ème vol., p. 876–877
Henri Blaze de Bury, *Études et souvenirs. Frédéric Chopin.*

[...] Les quakers du contrepoint reprochent à Chopin d'être incorrect ; les quintes, en effet, ne lui causent aucun scrupule, il les emploie allègrement, capable même de s'en montrer prodigue, comme dans la *huitième Etude* (opus 25) et de nous en donner des girandoles. Mais, de ce que son indépendance d'allure exclut certaines formes, on aurait tort d'en conclure qu'il les ignore [...].

Quand Chopin se chamaille avec la règle, c'est presque toujours la règle qui a tort. [...] L'action de Chopin sur le présent ne se discute pas : tous nos maîtres de l'heure actuelle, Bizet, Massenet, Saint-Saëns, sont des pianistes ; à ce titre, tous l'ont fréquenté, et c'est en le jouant, en le respirant qu'ils se sont imprégnés de son génie par inoculations atomistiques. Que de choses, bonnes et mauvaises, semblent nous venir de Wagner et lui doivent leur origine ! Notamment cette altération (moins réelle qu'apparente) du sentiment de la tonalité qui nous fait souvent prendre pour faux ce qui n'est que le résultat voulu d'un *accelerando* plus ou moins pressé de se fondre dans le *ritardando*, ou mieux encore, l'art porté à sa dernière perfection de déguiser, sans en rien ôter, les quantités mathématiques. L'influence de Chopin nous enveloppe en quelque sorte à notre insu ; ses accords, ses enharmonies, ses rythmes surtout nous régénèrent [...].

« Le Correspondant », 10 janvier 1910, 82ème Année, p. 187
Frédéric Chopin et son œuvre. A propos de son centenaire.

[...] Chopin connut le succès ; voilà pourquoi, aussi, tout ce qu'il apportait de nouveau, de hardi, de déconcertant passa inaperçu à la faveur de l'engouement. Alors que d'habitude, les neuf dixièmes au moins de ceux qui se piquent de goût artistique s'accordent pour crier *haro* sur tout novateur, pour protester, au nom des lois de l'art outragées, dès qu'apparaît une création de génie, on accueillit l'apport de Chopin, cet apport si riche en révolutionnaires audaces, et qui aurait dû scandaliser toutes les routines, comme une série de jolis bibelots dont le charme sans danger portait l'estampille du bon ton. Si la critique du temps avait été clairvoyante, si elle avait pris la peine d'examiner même superficiellement ces polonaises, ces mazurkas, ces préludes et ces ballades, elle se serait insurgée comme devant les œuvres de Berlioz ou celles de Wagner, et peut-être plus encore. Mais elle se contenta de souscrire au verdict de la mode, sans même un frémissement. [**Michel-Dimitri Calvocoressi**]

4 « Une âme au bout des doigts »

Honoré de Balzac, *Ursule Mirouet* (1846), Paris : Gallimard – Bibliothèque de la Pléiade 1977, vol. 3, p. 890

Il existe en toute musique, outre la pensée du compositeur, l'âme de l'exécutant, qui, par un privilège acquis seulement à cet art, peut donner du sens et de la poésie à des phrases sans grande valeur. Chopin prouve aujourd'hui pour l'ingrat piano la vérité de ce fait déjà démontrée par Paganini pour le violon. Ce beau génie est moins un musicien qu'une âme qui se rend sensible et qui se communiquerait par toute espèce de musique, même par de simples accords.

« Revue et gazette musicale de Paris », 17 janvier 1847, 14ème Année, n° 3
Bibliographie musicale. Piano. F. Chopin : Deux Nocturnes op. 62.

Entre tous les compositeurs modernes, qui ont écrit pour le piano avec une incontestable supériorité de talent, il n'en est pas de plus fidèle à son individualité que Chopin. Tout ce qui jaillit de sa plume porte l'empreinte d'une originalité constante, et s'acquiert ainsi la haute estime dont jouit son style dans les rangs d'un public d'élite. La forme élégiaque est celle que l'auteur semble rechercher avec le plus de complaisance et de bonheur. Le nocturne particulièrement lui doit une impulsion, une vie nouvelle. Ces deux dernières pages, que l'auteur vient d'ajouter à sa collection, sont dignes en tout de leurs aînées. Toutes deux d'un mouvement lent, toutes deux d'une teinte mélancolique, exhalent de mystérieux parfums de poésie. Ici encore, il faut une exécution fine, délicate, d'une exquise sensibilité. Ces mélodies fiévreuses, cette harmonie inquiète, réclament un toucher sympathique, une âme au bout des doigts [...].

Astolphe de Custine, Lettre à Chopin, février 1848
Reproduit dans : *Correspondance de Chopin*, éd. Bronislaw E. Sydow, Paris : Richard-Masse 1960, vol. 3, p. 325

Vous avez gagné en souffrance, en poésie : la mélancolie de vos compositions pénètre plus avant dans les cœurs : on est seul avec vous-même au milieu de la foule ; ce n'est pas un piano, c'est une âme, et quelle âme ! [...] L'art comme vous le sentez, pourra seul réunir les hommes divisés par le positif de la vie : on s'aime, on s'entend dans Chopin.

« La France musicale », 9 mars 1851, 15ème Année, n° 10, p. 75
Franz Liszt, *Chopin*.

[...] Chopin, dans son exécution, rendait ravissamment cette trépidation, par laquelle il faisait toujours onduler la mélodie, comme un esquif sur le sein de la vague puissante. Dans ses écrits, il indiqua d'abord cette manière, qui donnait un cachet si particulier à son jeu, par le mot de Tempo rubato : temps dérobé, entrecoupé, mesure souple, abrupte et languissante à la fois, vacillante comme la flamme sous le souffle qui l'agite. Il cessa plus tard de l'ajouter dans ses publications, persuadé que, si on en avait l'intelligence, il était impossible de ne pas deviner cette règle d'irrégularité. Aussi toutes ses pièces doivent-elles être jouées avec cette sorte de balancement accentué et prosodié, dont il est difficile de saisir le secret si on ne l'a pas souvent entendu lui-même. Il semblait désireux d'enseigner cette manière à ses nombreux élèves, surtout à ses compatriotes auxquels il voulait, plus qu'à d'autres, communiquer sa méthode d'exécution.

« Le Papillon », 10 mars 1861, 1ère Année, n° 5, p. 105
Louis Énault, *Frédéric Chopin*.

[...] Pour Chopin, la musique était destinée à évoquer les passions, à les rendre sensibles, à en communiquer les frémissements ; il établissait comme un magnétisme invisible entre l'âme de ses auditeurs et les vibrations sonores de l'instrument. Chopin, pour nous servir d'un mot de l'ancienne école, fut un artiste *pathétique*. Cette passion ne prit pas la foule, parce qu'elle se manifesta par des formes et des modes encore inusités, et, dans la musique, ce qui sort de la convention traditionnelle a besoin de l'aide du temps ; il faut le temps et l'accoutumance pour saisir le sens et comprendre la portée des symboles nouveaux. [...] La postérité fera plus pour Chopin que les contemporains, parce qu'elle l'appréciera mieux.

Antoine Marmontel, *Les Pianistes célèbres*, Paris : Chaix 1878, p. 4–5

Comme égalité de doigts, délicatesse, indépendance parfaite des deux mains, Chopin procédait évidemment de l'école de Clementi, maître dont il a toujours recommandé et apprécié les excellentes études. Mais où Chopin était tout à fait lui-même, c'était dans l'art merveilleux de conduire et de moduler le son, dans la manière expressive, mélancolique de le nuancer. Chopin avait une façon toute personnelle d'attaquer le clavier, un toucher souple, moelleux, des effets de sonorité d'une fluidité vaporeuse dont lui seul connaissait le secret.

Nul pianiste avant lui n'a employé les pédales alternativement ou réunies avec autant de tact et d'habileté. Chez la plupart des virtuoses modernes, l'usage immodéré, permanent des pédales est un défaut capital, un effet de sonorité qui produit sur les oreilles délicates la fatigue ou l'énervement. Chopin au contraire, en se servant constamment de la pédale, obtenait des harmonies ravissantes, des bruissements mélodiques qui étonnaient et charmaient. Poète merveilleux du piano, il avait une manière de comprendre, de sentir et d'exprimer sa pensée que, à de rares exceptions près, on a souvent essayé d'imiter sans réaliser autre chose que de maladroits pastiches.

Si nous cherchons un point de comparaison entre les effets de sonorité de Chopin et certains procédés de peinture, nous dirons que ce grand virtuose modulait le son comme les peintres habiles traitent la lumière et l'air ambiant. Envelopper les phrases de chant, les arabesques ingénieuses des traits dans une demi-teinte qui tient du rêve et de la réalité, c'est le comble de l'art, et c'était l'art de Chopin.

« **Revue des deux mondes** », 1er septembre 1883, 3ème Période, LII° Année, 59° vol., p. 870
Henri Blaze de Bury, *Études et souvenirs. Frédéric Chopin.*

[...] Dans cette complète absorption de son âme dans l'âme du clavier se trouve le secret de sa virtuosité sans pareille, de cette coloration technique, de cette vie nouvelle qui caractérise les Etudes et les Préludes. Car il n'y a pas à dire ; un monde inconnu vous est révélé, vous parcourez des régions que ni les Hummel ni les Clementi n'ont explorées ; un pays où l'étude elle-même se fait attrayante pour l'écolier, où c'est la fée Morgane et Titania qui professent, où la difficulté cache ses épines sous des fleurs. Chopin laisse aux pédagogues leurs jardins de racines grecques ; ses exercices, à lui, sont œuvres d'art ; au mécanisme ingrat il marie l'idée, et sa leçon vous promène en plein Parnasse au lieu de vous en indiquer le chemin. A ce compte seul, Chopin eût mérité de survivre. Ses études seront pour le piano moderne ce que représente dans le passé le *Clavecin bien tempéré* de Sébastien Bach, et si jamais le public devait désapprendre ces grâces légères et divinement élégiaques dont Chopin a parlé la langue, il appartiendrait à l'historien de se souvenir du maître virtuose qui sut, par la plus heureuse alliance de la fantaisie poétique et du style dans l'exécution, par l'union étrange des deux sensibilités de l'âme et du toucher, ouvrir une nouvelle voie à la technique du piano.

« Le Correspondant », 10 janvier 1910, 82ème Année, p. 593
Frédéric Chopin et son œuvre. A propos de son centenaire.

[...] Balzac a fait cette remarque, que Chopin « était moins un musicien qu'une âme qui se rend sensible », voulant sans doute exprimer par cette formule que précisément Chopin était avant tout un pur musicien, pour qui tout agencement sonore n'avait de valeur que par sa signification expressive. C'est d'ailleurs ce que Chopin avait lui-même fait ressortir le jour où il déclara qu'il n'y avait « rien de plus haïssable qu'une musique sans arrière-pensée ». Mais non point, comme pourraient le prétendre les partisans du symbolisme philosophique, une arrière-pensée d'ordre intellectuel : au contraire, un sous courant continu de cette vérité expressive, concrète en quelque sorte, qui est le propre de la musique en tant que facteur d'émotion artistique.

C – Le pianiste
1 L'improvisateur

« La Presse », 13 mai 1838, 2ème Année, p. 2

[...] En sortant de ces salons resplendissants, on s'est rendu dans une galerie simplement éclairée par la lumière dirigée sur un grand tableau et une [...] lampe de Sicile ; là, dans une demi-obscurité, M. Chopin a improvisé sur le piano une de ses mélodies harmonieuses dont il a seul le secret. Il a ravi tout le monde, et on venait d'entendre Duprez… Jugez d'après cela du talent de Chopin. [**Sophie Gay**]

Astolphe de Custine, Lettre à Sophie Gay, début juin 1837
Cité par : J.-F. Tarn, *Le Marquis de Custine,* Paris : Fayard 1985, p. 245

Je viens encore d'être enchanté par le magicien, par le sylphe de Saint-Gratien. Je lui avais donné pour thème le ranz des vaches et la Marseillaise. Vous dire le parti qu'il a tiré de cette épopée musicale, c'est impossible. On voyait le peuple de pasteurs fuir devant le peuple conquérant. C'était sublime.

« La France musicale », 5 décembre 1841, 4ᵉᵐᵉ Année, n° 49, p. 434
Nouvelles.

Le concert qui a eu lieu chez Mgr le duc d'Orléans, le 1ᵉʳ décembre, a été magnifique. [...] La partie instrumentale étant représentée par Chopin, le pianiste-poète, dont le génie tout exceptionnel, est resté jusqu'à présent sans rival et sans imitateur. Il a joué une ballade de sa composition, et puis il a improvisé avec une grâce, une élégance, une facilité, qui ont émerveillé son royal auditoire. Après le second morceau, la reine s'est approchée de M. Chopin et lui a adressé les compliments les plus flatteurs [...].

« Almanach du mois », avril 1844
Henri de Latouche, *La journée d'un fou.*
Reproduit dans : **Henri de Latouche, *La Vallée aux loups***, Paris : Michel Lévy 1875, p. 249–251

[...] On revint à la Place d'Orléans, dans le gîte coquettement somptueux du professeur de musique. Ce Polonais, roi du piano, notre fou aurait pu l'entendre dans les splendides concerts où il attire la foule, il le supplia de céder aux instances de ce peu d'admirateurs fervents et recueillis, qui allaient essayer de mettre à s'enivrer de son talent dans la solitude, un peu de cette poésie qui compose si essentiellement sa supériorité sur tous les maîtres. Il céda, le pâle jeune homme qui cache tant de force et d'inspiration sous un aspect valétudinaire, et le premier effet de son mérite fut de faire douter de la nature même de l'instrument où se posaient ses doigts [...] Pour charmer une fille des champs, qui, à la manière d'Apollon chez Admète, a gardé, dit-elle, les brebis aux bords de l'Indre, entre les genêts fleuris de la Vallée Noire, le Polonais trouva sur le plus savant des claviers, les rustiques chansons du Berry, tantôt la phrase finale et plaintive du laboureur sur la colline, tantôt la première partie d'une mélodie que la fileuse emporte avec elle derrière le bois. Voilà la bourrée des noces, voilà la cornemuse des tondailles. Peut-on dessiner un pays tout entier avec plus d'éloquence harmonique ? Mais paix ! Nous sommes sur les champs de bataille d'Ostrolenka. Entendez-vous la prière de l'armée polonaise avant de combattre ? Comment Dieu a-t-il pu refuser la victoire à des soldats qui la demandaient ainsi ! Les larmes gagnaient la noble et pieuse assistance. L'artiste le sentit, et, pour ne pas attrister en finissant cette soirée d'élite, il revint sur la terre, sur la terre espagnole ; car ce talent est universel. Écoutez la guitare des sérénades, imitation qui va jusqu'à reproduire le frôlement sur le manche, au lieu de la corde, du pouce inhabile d'un ménétrier ou des doigts distraits de l'amant.

Elisa Fournier, Lettre à sa mère, 10 juillet 1846
Cité par : **Georges Lubin,** *George Sand en Berry*, Paris : Hachette 1967, p. 28

Quelle soirée nous avons passée, chère mère ! Au milieu de ces impressions délicieuses, je te regrettais plus que jamais, car tu eusses été bien heureuse d'entendre comme nous l'admirable talent de Chopin, il a été d'une complaisance infinie, il était monté à la musique, et il n'a cessé que vers minuit de nous faire passer à son gré par toutes les émotions heureuses ou tristes, gaies ou sérieuses, suivant qu'il les éprouvait lui-même. Je n'ai de ma vie entendu un talent comme celui-là ; c'est prodigieux de simplicité, de douceur, de bonté et d'esprit. Il nous a joué dans ce dernier genre la charge d'un opéra de Bellini, qui nous a fait rire à nous tordre, tant il y avait de finesse d'observation et de spirituelle moquerie du style et des habitudes musicales de Bellini ; puis une prière des Polonais dans la détresse, qui nous arrachait des larmes ; puis une étude sur le bruit du tocsin, qui faisait frissonner ; puis une marche funèbre, si grave, si sombre, si douloureuse, que nos coeurs se gonflaient, que notre poitrine se serrait et qu'on n'entendait, au milieu de notre silence, que le bruit de quelques soupirs mal contenus par une émotion trop profonde pour être dominée. Enfin sortant de cette inspiration douloureuse et rappelé à lui-même après un moment de repos par quelques notes chantées par Mme George, il nous a fait entendre de jolis airs d'une danse appelée la bourrée, qui est tout à fait commune dans le pays et dont les motifs recherchés avec soin par lui, forment un recueil précieux, plein de grâce et de naïveté. Enfin il a terminé cette longue et trop heureuse séance par un tour de force dont je n'avais nulle idée. Il a imité sur le piano les petites musiques qu'on enferme dans des tabatières, des tableaux, etc., et cela avec une vérité telle que si nous n'avions pas été dans le même appartement que lui, nous n'aurions jamais pu croire que ce fût un piano qui résonnait sous ses doigts. Tout ce perlé, cette finesse, cette rapidité des petites touches d'acier qui fait vibrer un cylindre imperceptible était rendu avec une délicatesse sans pareille, puis tout à coup une cadence sans fin et si faible qu'on l'entendait à peine se faisait entendre et était instantanément interrompue par la machine qui probablement avait quelque chose de dérangé. Il nous a joué un de ces airs, la tyrolienne, je crois, dont une note manquait au cylindre et toujours cette note accrochait chaque fois qu'elle eût dû être jouée.

George Sand, *Impressions et souvenirs*, Paris : Michel Lévy 1873, p. 85–87

Chopin n'écoute plus. Il est au piano et il ne s'aperçoit pas qu'on l'écoute. Il improvise comme au hasard. Il s'arrête. Eh bien, eh bien, s'écrie Delacroix, ce n'est pas fini !

– Ce n'est pas commencé, rien ne me vient… Rien que des reflets, des ombres, des reliefs qui ne veulent pas se fixer. Je cherche la couleur, je ne trouve même pas le dessin.

– Vous ne trouverez pas l'un sans l'autre, reprend Delacroix, et vous allez les trouver tous deux.

– Mais, si je ne trouve que le clair de lune ?

– Vous aurez trouvé le reflet d'un reflet, répond Maurice.

L'idée plaît au divin artiste. Il reprend sans avoir l'air de recommencer, tant son dessin est vague et comme incertain. Nos yeux se remplissent peu à peu des teintes douces qui correspondent aux suaves modulations saisies par le sens auditif. Et puis la note bleue résonne et nous voilà dans l'azur de la nuit transparente. Des nuages légers prennent toutes les formes de la fantaisie ; ils remplissent le ciel ; ils viennent se presser autour de la lune qui leur jette de grands disques d'opale et réveille la couleur endormie. Nous rêvons d'une nuit d'été. Nous attendons le rossignol. Un chant sublime s'élève.

George Sand, *Dernières Pages. Le Théâtre des marionnettes de Nohant*, Paris : Calmann Lévy, 1877, p. 124

Le tout avait commencé par la pantomime, et ceci avait été de l'invention de Chopin ; il tenait le piano et improvisait, tandis que les jeunes gens mimaient des scènes et dansaient des ballets comiques. Je vous laisse à penser si ces improvisations admirables ou charmantes montaient la tête et déliaient les jambes de nos exécutants. Il les conduisait à sa guise et les faisait passer, selon sa fantaisie, du plaisant au sévère, du burlesque au solennel, du gracieux au passionné. On improvisait des costumes afin de jouer successivement plusieurs rôles. Dès que l'artiste les voyait paraître, il adaptait merveilleusement son thème et son accent à leur caractère. Ceci se renouvela durant trois soirées, et puis, le maître partant pour Paris, nous laissa tout excités, tout exaltés, et décidés à ne pas laisser perdre l'étincelle qui nous avait électrisés.

2 Inspiration et travail : une dialectique problématique

George Sand, *Histoire de ma vie* (1854–1855), V° partie, ch. XIII, éd. Georges Lubin, Paris : Gallimard – Bibliothèque de la Pléiade 1971, vol. 2, p. 446–447.

Sa création était spontanée, miraculeuse. Il la trouvait sans la chercher, sans la prévoir. Elle venait sur son piano soudaine, complète, sublime, ou elle se chantait dans sa tête pendant une promenade, et il avait hâte de se la faire entendre à lui-même en la jetant sur l'instrument. Mais alors commençait le labeur le plus navrant auquel j'aie jamais assisté. C'était une suite d'efforts, d'irrésolutions et d'impatiences pour ressaisir certains détails du thème de son audition : ce qu'il avait conçu tout d'une pièce, il l'analysait trop en voulant l'écrire, et son regret de ne pas le retrouver net, selon lui, le jetait dans une sorte de désespoir. Il s'enfermait dans sa chambre des journées entières, pleurant, marchant, brisant ses plumes, répétant et changeant cent fois une mesure, l'écrivant et l'effaçant autant de fois, et recommençant le lendemain avec une persévérance minutieuse et désespérée. Il passait six semaines sur une page pour en revenir à l'écrire telle qu'il l'avait tracée du premier jet.

J'avais eu longtemps l'influence de le faire consentir à se fier à ce premier jet de l'inspiration. Mais quand il n'était plus disposé à me croire, il me reprochait doucement de l'avoir gâté et de n'être pas assez sévère pour lui. J'essayais de le distraire, de le promener. Quelquefois emmenant toute ma couvée dans un char à bancs de campagne, je l'arrachais malgré lui à cette agonie ; je le menais aux bords de la Creuse, et pendant deux ou trois jours, perdus au soleil et à la pluie dans des chemins affreux, nous arrivions, riants et affamés, à quelque site magnifique où il semblait renaître. Ces fatigues le brisaient le premier jour, mais il dormait ! Le dernier jour, il était tout ranimé, tout rajeuni en revenant à Nohant et il trouvait la solution de son travail sans trop d'efforts ; mais il n'était pas toujours possible de le déterminer à quitter ce piano qui était bien plus souvent son tourment que sa joie, et peu à peu il témoigna de l'humeur quand je le dérangeais.

Eugène Delacroix, *Journal*, mercredi 7 avril 1849, éd. André Joubin, Paris : Plon 1932, vol. 1, p. 283–284

Dans la journée, il m'a parlé de musique et cela l'a ranimé. Je lui demandais ce qui établissait la logique en musique. Il m'a fait sentir ce que c'est qu'harmonie et contrepoint ; comme quoi la fugue est comme la logique pure en musique, et qu'être savant dans la fugue, c'est connaître l'élément de toute raison et de toute conséquence en musique. J'ai pensé combien j'aurais été heureux de m'instruire en tout cela qui désole les musiciens vulgaires. Ce sentiment m'a donné une idée du plaisir que les savants, dignes de l'être, trouvent dans la science. C'est que la vraie science n'est pas ce que l'on entend ordinairement par ce mot, c'est à dire une partie de la connaissance différente de l'art. Non, la science envisagée ainsi, démontrée par un homme comme Chopin, est l'art lui-même, et par contre l'art n'est plus alors ce que croit le vulgaire, c'est à dire une sorte d'inspiration qui vient de je ne sais où, qui marche au hasard et ne présente que l'extérieur pittoresque des choses. C'est la raison elle-même ornée par le génie, mais suivant une marche nécessaire et contenue par des lois supérieures.

Eugène Delacroix, *Journal*, mercredi 20 avril 1853, *Ibidem*, vol. 2, p. 22–23

En revenant avec Grzymała, nous avons parlé de Chopin. Il me contait que ses improvisations étaient beaucoup plus hardies que ses compositions achevées. Il en était pour cela sans doute, comme de l'esquisse du tableau comparée au tableau fini. Non, on ne gâte pas le tableau en le finissant ! [...] en renonçant au vague de l'esquisse, [l'artiste] se montre davantage dans sa personnalité, en dévoilant ainsi toute la portée, mais aussi les bornes de son talent.

3 Un univers de prédilection : les salons

Camille Pleyel, Lettre à Victor Schoelcher, sans date
Cité par : **J.-J. Eigeldinger, *L'Univers musical de Chopin*, Paris : Fayard 2000, p. 337**

J'ai été prendre Chopin pour le mener chez Mme Gangler [...] ; je trouvai le pauvre garçon si souffreteux, que je me fesais (sic) un cas de conscience de lui faire quitter le coin de son feu ; [...] nous trouvons dans le petit salon que vous connaissez M. et Mme Legouvé, Mme d'Arlu, Mlle Spitz [...] ; Mme Gangler chante deux admirables airs de Haendel, puis notre petit homme si pâle, si étique, si souffrant, s'assied devant le piano [...], essaye quelques notes, fait résonner quelques cordes, touche quelques accords et le voilà électrisé et bientôt les mélodies les plus suaves, les plus touchantes jaillissent comme par enchantement de ce clavier auquel, semblable à Prométhée, il vient de communiquer l'âme et la vie.

« **La Presse** », 7 mars 1847, 11ème Année, n° 3857, p. 2
Reproduit dans : **Delphine de Girardin,** *Lettres parisiennes*, Paris : Librairie
nouvelle 1856, vol. 3, p. 264–266.

[...] Mademoiselle Méara est élève de Chopin. Il était là, il assistait au triomphe de son élève, et l'auditoire inquiet se demandait : L'entendrons-nous ? Le fait est que, pour des admirateurs passionnés, voir Chopin dans un salon se promener toute la soirée autour d'un piano et ne pas l'entendre jouer, c'était le supplice de Tantale. La maîtresse de maison eut pitié de nous ; elle fut indiscrète, et Chopin a joué, a chanté ses chants les plus délicieux ; nous mettions sur ces airs, joyeux ou tristes, les paroles qui nous venaient à l'esprit ; nous suivions avec nos pensées ses caprices mélodieux. Nous étions là une vingtaine d'amateurs sincères, de vrais croyants et pas une note n'était perdue, pas une intention n'était méconnue ; ce n'était pas un concert, c'était de la musique intime, sérieuse, comme nous l'aimons ; ce n'était pas un virtuose qui vient jouer l'air convenu et qui disparaît ; c'était un beau talent, accaparé, harcelé, tourmenté sans égards et sans scrupules, à qui l'on osait redemander les airs chéris, et qui, plein de grâce et de charité, vous redisait la phrase favorite, pour que vous puissiez l'emporter correcte et pure dans votre mémoire, et vous laisser longtemps bercer encore par elle en souvenir. Madame une telle disait : « De grâce, jouez ce joli nocturne dédié à mademoiselle Sterling [sic]. – Celui que nous avons nommé le dangereux. » – Il souriait et jouait le fatal nocturne. – « Moi, reprenait une autre femme, je voudrais entendre une seul fois, jouée par vous, cette mazurka si triste et si charmante. » Il souriait encore, et il jouait la délicieuse mazurka. Les plus profondément rusées cherchaient des biais pour arriver au but : – « J'étudie la grande sonate qui commence par cette belle marche funèbre, et je voudrais savoir dans quel mouvement doit se jouer le finale. » Il souriait un peu de la malice et il jouait le finale de la grande sonate, un des plus magnifiques morceaux qu'il ait composés. Le piano que fait résonner Chopin se métamorphose : ce sont des accords inconnus, des sons qu'on a rêvés peut-être, mais qu'on n'a jamais entendus nulle part [...]. [**Delphine de Girardin**]

« **La France musicale** », 16 mars1851, 15ème Année, n° 11, p. 82
Franz Liszt, *Chopin.*

[...] Toutefois, s'il nous est permis de le dire, nous croyons que ces concerts fatiguaient moins sa constitution physique que son irritabilité d'artiste. Sa volontaire abnégation des bruyants succès cachait, ce nous semble, un froissement intérieur. Il avait un sentiment très distinct de sa haute supériorité ; mais peut-être n'en recevait-il pas du dehors assez d'écho et de réverbération, pour gagner la tranquille certitude d'être parfaitement apprécié. L'acclamation populaire lui manquait, et il se demandait sans doute jusqu'à quel point les salons d'élite remplaçaient par l'enthousiasme de leurs applaudissements, le grand public qu'il évitait ? Peu le comprenaient ; mais ce peu le comprenaient-ils suffisamment ? Un mécontentement assez indéfini peut-être pour lui-même, du moins quant à sa véritable source, le minait sourdement. On le voyait choqué presque par les éloges. [...] A travers les phrases polies par lesquelles il les secouait souvent, comme une poussière importune, on pouvait avec un peu de pénétration s'apercevoir qu'il se jugeait non seulement peu applaudi, mais mal applaudi, et qu'alors il préférait n'être pas troublé dans sa placide solitude et son sentiment.

George Sand, *Histoire de ma vie* (1854–1855), V° partie, chapitre XIII, éd. Georges Lubin, Paris : Gallimard – Bibliothèque de la Pléiade 1971, vol. 2, p. 441–442

Il était l'homme du monde par excellence, non pas du monde trop officiel et trop nombreux, mais du monde intime, des salons de vingt personnes, de l'heure où la foule s'en va et où les habitués se pressent autour de l'artiste pour lui arracher par d'aimables importunités le plus pur de son inspiration. C'est alors seulement qu'il donnait tout son génie et tout son talent. C'est alors aussi qu'après avoir plongé son auditoire dans un recueillement profond ou dans une tristesse douloureuse, car sa musique vous mettait parfois dans l'âme des découragements atroces, surtout quand il improvisait, tout à coup, comme pour enlever l'impression et le souvenir de sa douleur aux autres et à lui-même, il se tournait vers une glace, à la dérobée, arrangeait ses cheveux et sa cravate, et se montrait subitement transformé en Anglais flegmatique, en vieillard impertinent, en Anglaise sentimentale et ridicule, en juif sordide. C'étaient toujours des types tristes, quelque comiques qu'ils fussent, mais parfaitement compris et si délicatement traduits qu'on ne pouvait se lasser de les admirer.

Franz Liszt, Lettre à Wilhelm Von Lenz, 1872
Cité par : **S. Sitwell, *Liszt*,** Paris : Buchet-Chastel 1961, p. 53

Vous exagérez, je pense, l'influence que les salons parisiens exercèrent sur Chopin. Son âme n'en était nullement affectée, et son œuvre d'artiste demeure transparente, merveilleuse éthérée, et celle d'un incomparable génie – totalement étrangère aux erreurs d'une école et aux petites futilités d'un salon. C'est un être angélique et féerique ; plus encore, il sait faire vibrer la corde héroïque qui n'a jamais vibré avec autant de grandeur, de passion et de vigueur que dans ses *Polonaises*.

4 Les trois concerts chez Pleyel : des événements exceptionnels

George Sand, Lettre à Pauline Viardot, 18 avril 1841
Reproduit dans : *Correspondance de G. Sand*, éd. Georges Lubin, Paris : Garnier, vol. 5, p. 282–283.

Une grande, grandissime nouvelle c'est que le petit Chip Chip va donner un grrrrrand concert. Ses amis le lui ont tant fourré dans la tête qu'il s'est laissé persuader. Cependant il se flattait toujours que cela serait si difficile à arranger qu'on y renoncerait. Les choses ont été plus vite qu'il ne croyait. A peine avait-il lâché le oui fatal, que tout s'est trouvé fait comme par miracle, et que les 3/4 de ses billets étaient pris, avant qu'on eût même annoncé, alors il s'est réveillé comme d'un songe, et l'on ne peut rien voir de plus drôle, que le méticuleux et irrésolu Chip Chip obligé de ne plus changer d'avis. Il espérait que vous viendriez et que vous chanteriez pour lui, accompagnée par lui. Quand j'ai reçu votre lettre et qu'il a perdu cet espoir, il voulait défaire son concert. Il n'y avait plus moyen ; il s'était trop engagé. Il a été se jeter dans les bras non, je veux dire, aux pieds de Mme Damoreau. Mr Ernst lui raclera de son beau violon, et voilà. Ce cauchemar chopinesque se passera dans les salons de Pleyel, le 26. Il ne veut pas d'affiches, il ne veut pas de programme, il ne veut pas de nombreux public, il ne veut pas qu'on en parle. Il est effrayé de tant de choses que je lui propose de jouer sans chandelles, et sans auditeurs sur un piano muet.

« La France musicale », 25 avril 1841, 4ème Année, n° 17, p. 147
Concert de M. Chopin.

Les nombreux admirateurs du talent hors ligne de M. Chopin sont enfin parvenus à décider le célèbre artiste à se faire entendre en public. Ainsi une occasion solennelle va se présenter où l'on pourra mettre en parallèle le génie, oui, le génie modeste d'un pianiste-compositeur, qui n'a jamais eu recours à des moyens excentriques pour attirer sur lui l'attention du public, avec les prétentions exagérées d'autres pianistes-compositeurs dont tout le talent consiste à se faire encenser dans les journaux par des amis maladroits. Chopin est un de ces artistes qui vivent de rêverie, qui ne recherchent pas le bruit de la foule pour y mêler leurs voix criardes et sans harmonie : Chopin est le poète du cœur, le pianiste inspiré qui vous émeut toujours par une forme d'exécution pleine de grâce et de suavité ; rien en lui n'est tourmenté, n'est exagéré ; c'est l'artiste tel que nous le voulons, tel que nous le comprenons, mélodiste avant tout, simple, naturel, plein de goût, de tendresse, d'élévation, de douceur et de passion tout à la fois.

« **La France musicale** », 2 mai 1841, 4ème Année, n° 18, p. 156–157

[...] Nous avons parlé de Schubert parce qu'il n'est pas une autre nature qui ait avec Chopin une analogie plus complète. L'un a fait pour le piano ce que l'autre a fait pour la voix. [...] Ecoutez Chopin et vous comprendrez bien vite qu'il n'a fait aucun sacrifice à la mode, qu'il ne s'est pas prosterné devant les caprices du mauvais goût pour arriver à la fortune et à la renommée. Cet artiste, ce poète, a marché au rebours de tous les talents excentriques qui, depuis quinze ou vingt ans, font tous les efforts imaginables pour devenir populaires ; il a fui le grand air ; il a mieux aimé une existence fragile, sans éclat, sans lutte, sans passion. Pendant que tant d'autres artistes livraient leurs noms au vent de la publicité, lui rêvait en silence, demandant à son cœur des pensées de jeunesse et d'amour, des formes belles et caressantes. La poésie est une si noble compagne dans l'isolement !

Chopin avait peur du bruit ; il n'osait pas se montrer devant une assemblée nombreuse dont il n'était pas sûr d'être compris, comme il craignait l'effet des applaudissements. Que d'efforts, que de luttes il a dû s'engager entre sa tête et son cœur avant de se résoudre à affronter les regards de ses juges, non... de ses admirateurs. L'artiste, le poète plutôt, a cédé enfin ; il s'est montré, on l'a entendu et on l'a applaudi, tant applaudi que depuis près de huit jours il ne sait plus ce qu'il a fait, ce qu'il a vu, ce qu'il a entendu.

Chopin est un pianiste de conviction. Il compose pour lui, il exécute pour lui ; ce qu'il exécute et ce qu'il compose, tout le monde l'écoute avec un intérêt, un charme, un plaisir infini. Ne cherchez pas sous ses doigts de ces grands effets qui vous étonnent, de ces tours de force qui ébranlent votre tête. Chopin ne veut pas de ce genre bruyant dont tout le mérite consiste à surpasser, sur le piano, les cris les plus aigus de l'orchestre. Mais écoutez comme il rêve, comme il pleure, comme il chante avec douceur, tendresse et mélancolie ; comme il exprime parfaitement tous les sentiments les plus tendres et les plus élevés. Chopin est le pianiste du sentiment par excellence.

On peut dire que Chopin est le créateur d'une école de piano et d'une école de composition. Rien en vérité n'égale la légèreté, la douceur avec laquelle l'artiste prélude sur le piano ; rien encore ne peut être mis en parallèle avec ses œuvres pleines d'originalité, de distinction et de grâce. Chopin est un pianiste à part qui ne doit et ne peut être comparé à personne. [**Léon Escudier**)

« **Revue et gazette musicale de Paris** », 2 mai 1841, 8ème Année, n° 31, p. 245–246

Lundi dernier, à huit heures du soir, les salons de M. Pleyel étaient splendidement éclairés ; de nombreux équipages amenaient incessamment au bas d'un escalier couvert de tapis et parfumé de fleurs, les femmes les plus élégantes, les jeunes gens les plus à la mode, les artistes les plus célèbres, les financiers les plus riches, les grands seigneurs les plus illustres, toute une élite de société, toute une aristocratie de naissance, de fortune, de talent et de beauté.

Un grand piano à queue était ouvert sur une estrade ; on se pressait autour ; on ambitionnait les places les plus voisines, on se disait qu'il ne fallait pas perdre un accord, une note, une intention, une pensée de celui qui allait venir s'asseoir là. Et l'on avait raison d'être ainsi avide, attentif, religieusement ému, car celui que l'on attendait, que l'on voulait voir, entendre, admirer, applaudir, ce n'était pas seulement un virtuose habile, un pianiste expert dans l'art de faire des notes ; ce n'était pas seulement un artiste de grand renom, c'était tout cela et plus que tout cela, c'était Chopin.

Venu en France il y a dix ans environ, Chopin, dans la foule des pianistes qui à cette époque surgissait de toutes parts, ne combattit point pour obtenir la première ni la seconde place. Il se fit très peu entendre en public ; la nature éminemment poétique de son talent ne l'y portait pas. [...] La musique c'était sa langue ; langue divine dans laquelle il exprimait tout un ordre de sentiments que le petit nombre seul pouvait comprendre. Ainsi qu'à cet autre grand poète, Mickiewicz, son compatriote et son ami, la muse de la patrie lui dictait ses chants, et les plaintes de la Pologne empruntaient à ses accents, je ne sais quelle poésie mystérieuse qui, pour tous ceux qui l'ont véritablement sentie, ne saurait être comparée à rien Si moins d'éclat s'est attaché à son nom, si une auréole moins lumineuse a ceint sa tête, ce n'est pas qu'il eût en lui peut-être la même énergie de pensée, la même profondeur de sentiment que l'illustre auteur de *Konrad Wallenrod* et des *Pèlerins* ; mais ses moyens d'expression étaient trop bornés, son instrument trop imparfait ; il ne pouvait à l'aide d'un piano se révéler tout entier. De là, si nous ne nous trompons, une souffrance sourde et continue, une certaine répugnance à se communiquer au dehors, une mélancolie qui se dérobe sous des apparences de gaieté, toute une individualité enfin remarquable et attachante au plus haut degré.

Ainsi que nous l'avons dit, ce ne fut que rarement, à de très distants intervalles, que Chopin se fit entendre en public ; mais ce qui eût été pour tout autre une cause presque certaine d'oubli et d'obscurité, fut précisément ce qui lui assura une réputation supérieure aux caprices de la mode, et ce qui le mit à l'abri des rivalités, des jalousies et des injustices. Chopin, demeuré en dehors du mouvement excessif qui, depuis quelques années, pousse l'un sur l'autre, et l'un contre l'autre, les artistes exécutants de tous les points de l'univers, est resté constamment entouré d'adeptes fidèles, d'élèves enthousiastes, de chaleureux amis qui, tout en le garantissant des luttes fâcheuses et des froissements pénibles, n'ont cessé de répandre ses œuvres, et avec elles l'admiration pour son génie et le respect pour son nom. Aussi cette célébrité exquise, toute en haut lieu, excellemment aristocratique, est-elle restée pure de toute attaque. Un silence complet de la critique se fait déjà autour d'elle, comme si la postérité était venue [...].

Nous n'entreprendrons pas ici une analyse détaillée des compositions de Chopin. Sans fausse recherche de l'originalité il a été *lui*, aussi bien dans le style que dans la conception. A des pensées nouvelles il a su donner une forme nouvelle. Ce quelque chose de sauvage et d'abrupt qui tenait à sa patrie, a trouvé son expression dans des hardiesses de dissonance, dans des harmonies étranges, tandis que la délicatesse et la grâce qui tenaient à sa personne se révélaient en mille contours, en mille ornements d'une inimitable fantaisie.

Dans le concert de lundi, Chopin avait choisi de préférence celles de ses œuvres qui s'éloignent davantage des formes classiques. Il n'a joué ni concerto, ni sonate, ni fantaisie, ni variations, mais des Préludes, des Études, des Nocturnes et des Mazurkes. S'adressant à une société plutôt qu'à un public, il pouvait impunément se montrer ce qu'il est, poète élégiaque, profond, chaste et rêveur. Il n'avait besoin ni d'étonner ni de saisir ; il cherchait des sympathies délicates plutôt que de bruyants enthousiasmes. Disons bien vite que ces sympathies ne lui ont pas fait défaut. Dès les premiers accords il s'est établi entre lui et son auditoire une communication étroite. Deux *Études* et une *Ballade* ont été redemandées, et sans la crainte d'ajouter un surcroît de fatigue à la fatigue déjà grande qui se trahissait sur son visage pâli, on eût redemandé un à un tous les morceaux du programme.

[...] Son succès, quoique très grand, est resté en deçà de ce qu'il devait prétendre. Toutefois, nous le disons de conviction, Chopin n'a rien à envier à personne. La
plus noble et la plus légitime satisfaction que puisse éprouver l'artiste n'est-elle pas
de se sentir au-dessus de sa renommée, supérieur même à son succès, plus grand
encore que sa gloire ? [**Franz Liszt**]

« **Le Ménestrel** », 2 mai 1841, 8ème Année, n° 22, p. 3

Voilà bientôt quelques années que nous n'avions entendu ce sentimental pianiste ; a-t-il progressé ? non, car Chopin tient peu de souci des secrets mécaniques
du piano ; chez lui point de charlatanisme ; le cœur et le génie seuls parlent, et à ces
titres, son organisation privilégiée n'a rien à gagner. Pour bien apprécier Chopin, il
faut aimer les impressions douces, il faut avoir le sentiment de la poésie : entendre
Chopin, c'est lire une strophe de Lamartine.

Les compositions de Chopin vous frappent encore bien plus que les nuances
délicates de son jeu ; Schubert n'a jamais été mieux inspiré ; et l'on peut assurer
que les œuvres de Chopin sont autant de délicieuses perfections d'harmonie et
de mélodie ; c'est surtout sous ce rapport que nous le préférons à Liszt, bien que
celui-ci, en abandonnant les compositions originales, nous donne aujourd'hui
l'idée de ce que peut son talent dans l'arrangement des œuvres de nos célèbres
compositeurs. Mais tout admirable que soit son morceau sur *Robert le Diable*
même, Meyerbeer peut en revendiquer quelques honneurs, tandis que dans Chopin tout est imagination et création. Ce n'est pas que nous prétendions voir en
Chopin le plus grand des pianistes ; non, il a son individualité, tout comme Liszt
dont la chaleur et la foudroyante exécution sont certainement hors de toute ri-
valité [...].

« **Journal des débats** », 16 mai 1841, p. 1
Concert de Liszt au Conservatoire.
Reproduit dans : ***Hector Berlioz. Critique musicale***, Paris : Buchet-Chastel 2003,
vol. 4, p. 505

[...] Le concert de Chopin a eu lieu peu de jours après celui de Liszt. Son talent
de pianiste est d'une supériorité et d'une originalité incontestables ; mais ses productions, par leur caractère naïvement étrange, par la hardiesse des rythmes et des
harmonies, par un style mélodique capricieux, fugitif, insaisissable, sont bien plus

remarquables encore. Malheureusement il faut joindre à une organisation musicale exquise, développée d'ailleurs par l'étude, une attention extrême pour saisir au vol cette multitude de pensées délicates et fines dont l'ensemble constitue le style de Chopin, et dont plusieurs doivent nécessairement passer inaperçus dans les grandes salles et devant le grand public. C'est pourquoi, sans doute, l'occasion d'entendre cet admirable virtuose se présente si rarement. Il redoute les assemblées tumultueuses et mélangées ; ne se sentant pas appelé à les dominer, à leur tenir tête, le silence et le recueillement d'un auditoire choisi lui sont indispensables [...].
[**Hector Berlioz**]

« **Revue et gazette musicale de Paris** », 27 février 1842, 9ème Année, n° 9, p. 82–83
Soirée musicale de M. Chopin.

Si la musique est réellement une architecture de sons, comme l'a dit ingénieusement une femme célèbre, convenez que M. Chopin, le pianiste-compositeur, est un bien élégant architecte. Vous savez quelles formes originales revêt sa gracieuse fantaisie. En parcourant avec un intérêt toujours plus vif ces petits chefs-d'œuvre si curieusement, si délicatement travaillés, on en vient malgré soi à rêver de l'Allambrah, du Généralife, de tous ces délicieux caprices du génie arabe réalisés dans les monuments de Grenade la merveilleuse. La pensée se complaît dans le spectacle de cette opulence de bon goût. L'ordre fait toujours si bien, associé à la richesse ! Et c'est là surtout le caractère distinctif des créations de M. Chopin. Sa féconde imagination sait se diriger au milieu des plus brillants écarts ; elle n'abandonne jamais un certain fil conducteur qui rattache l'une à l'autre, avec une précieuse habileté, les diverses parcelles de son œuvre.

Le style de M. Chopin est encore éminemment aristocratique. Il s'en exhale comme un parfum de bon ton ; c'est quelque chose d'exquis, de fashionable, passez-moi le mot un peu usé. Aussi point de banalité dans le caractère général ; point de lieux communs dans les détails. Le défaut contraire serait peut-être celui qu'une critique rigoureuse pourrait relever. Trop de recherche fine et minutieuse n'est pas quelquefois sans prétention et sans froideur. La musique ressemble à une belle personne qu'on aime sans doute à rencontrer divinement parée, mais qu'on ne serait pas fâché de surprendre de temps en temps en négligé.

Du reste, loin de nous la pensée de faire une mauvaise querelle à M. Chopin. Il a, lui aussi, beaucoup de ce naturel charmant quand il le veut, c'est-à-dire lorsqu'il n'abuse pas de son étonnante facilité à trouver des formes d'ornementation neuves, mais parfois un peu maniérées. Et puis ne sait-on pas que les imperfections naissent toujours de l'exagération des qualités ? Après tout, ces quelques taches disparaissent dans l'ombre quand on envisage un talent par son côté lumineux. Chez M. Chopin le génie mélodique a un caractère si expressif, si tendre, si distingué, son style harmonique est si richement doté, que l'impression première, toujours irrésistible, désarçonne la critique qui se tenait prête à fournir la carrière, la visière baissée, la plume en arrêt.

Voyez aussi quel est le succès de M. Chopin aux rares apparitions qu'il fait en public. Songez à tout ce que dit l'empressement avec lequel on recherche les moyens de l'entendre ; artistes et amateurs font foule autour de lui. Ah ! C'est qu'il y a là plus d'un sujet d'admiration. Le compositeur n'est pas seulement tout ce que l'on vient applaudir ; c'est aussi le virtuose, le séduisant pianiste qui sait faire parler à ses doigts un prestigieux langage, qui épanche toute son âme brûlante dans cette exécution vraiment complète ; c'est qu'il y a dans ce jeu exceptionnel une personnalité dont nul autre n'a le secret ; c'est que le clavier se transforme en quelque sorte et devient presque un organe nouveau, quand il obéit à la fiévreuse impulsion d'un génie tendre et passionné. Liszt, Thalberg excitent, comme on sait, de violents transports. Chopin aussi en fait naître, mais d'une nature moins énergique, moins bruyante, précisément parce qu'il fait vibrer dans le coeur des cordes plus intimes, des émotions plus douces. Les premiers soulèvent une exaltation qui déborde impérieusement par les éclats de la voix et du geste. L'autre pénètre plus au fond peut-être ; les sensations qu'il excite ont quelque chose de plus concentré, de plus voilé, de moins expansif ; mais elles n'en sont pas moins délicieuses. [**Maurice Bourges**]

« **La France musicale** », 27 février 1842, 5ème Année, n° 9, p 82–83
Concert de M. Chopin.

[...] Ainsi donc, Chopin a donné, dans la salle de M. Pleyel, une soirée charmante, une fête toute peuplée d'adorables sourires, de minois tendres et rosés, de petites mains blanches et modelées, une fête magnifique où la simplicité se mariait à la grâce et à l'élégance, et où le bon goût servait de piédestal à la richesse. [...] Le premier succès de la soirée a été pour Mme George Sand. Dès qu'elle a paru avec ses deux charmantes filles, tous les regards se sont portés vers elle. D'autres auraient été ébranlés par tous ces yeux braqués comme autant d'étoiles ; mais George Sand se contentait de baisser la tête et de sourire. Pourquoi donc aussi s'aviser d'avoir une telle célébrité littéraire ?

Chopin a joué huit morceaux. Les compositions de cet artiste ont toutes entre elles une ressemblance parfaite de formes ; la pensée seule varie, et ce n'est pas une de leurs moins brillantes qualités. Poète et poète tendre avant tout, Chopin s'attache à faire dominer la poésie. Il fait de prodigieuses difficultés d'exécution, mais jamais au détriment de sa mélodie, qui est toujours simple et originale. Suivez les mains du pianiste, et voyez avec quelle merveilleuse facilité il exécute les traits les plus gracieux, rapproche les distances du clavier, il passe du piano au forte et successivement du forte au piano ! Les magnifiques instruments de M. Pleyel se prêtent admirablement à ces diverses modifications. En écoutant tous ces sons, toutes ces nuances, qui se suivent, s'enchevêtrent, se séparent, se réunissent pour arriver à un même but, la mélodie, ne croyez-vous pas entendre de petites voix de fées qui soupirent sous des cloches d'argent, ou une pluie de perles qui tombent sur des tables de cristal ? Les doigts du pianiste semblent se multiplier à l'infini ; il ne paraît pas possible que deux mains seulement puissent produire des effets de rapidité aussi précis et aussi naturels. Ne demandez pas à Chopin de simuler avec le piano les grands effets d'orchestre. Ce genre d'exécution ne convient ni à son organisation ni à ses idées. Il veut nous étonner par sa rapidité légère, par ses mazurkes aux formes nouvelles, et non vous donner des attaques de nerfs et vous faire tomber en syncope. Son inspiration est toute de poésie tendre et naïve ; ne lui demandez pas de grands coups de doigts, des variations diaboliques ; il veut parler au cœur et non pas aux yeux ; il veut vous aimer et non vous dévorer. Voyez : le public est tombé en extase ; l'enthousiasme est à son comble : Chopin a atteint son but. [**Léon Escudier**]

« **La Presse** », 1ᵉʳ mars 1842, p. 3
Théâtres – fêtes et concerts.

Le concert de Chopin a été tel que nous l'avions prévu, tout à la fois éclatant et charmant. Ces divines délicatesses de son et de pensée, ces grâces exquises, ont été applaudies par ces quatre cents auditeurs comme les plus brillants morceaux. C'est que sous ses formes vaporeuses et insaisissables, il y a une originalité puissante. L'amour, la mélancolie, la douleur, tout se reflète dans ces petits chefs-d'œuvre, et puis, derrière ces gracieuses et tendres mélodies, passent et résonnent des traits de combat, de marches guerrières et funestes… souvenir lointain de sa patrie héroïque, écho douloureux des sanglots de Varsovie… c'est qu'il y a deux hommes en Chopin, le patriote et l'artiste, et l'âme de l'un nourrit le génie de l'autre. [**Ernest Legouvé**]

« **Revue des deux mondes** », 1er avril 1842, 4ème série, tome 30, p. 159
Revue musicale.

[...] Parlerai-je de M. Chopin ? Avec lui, les choses ont un vernis de plus haute élégance. Le talent de M. Chopin ne se produit qu'à de longs intervalles, et s'entoure alors de toute sorte de soins minutieux et de ménagements. M. Chopin n'admet à ses révélations annuelles qu'un public d'initiés, qu'un monde tout d'élite; il faut à son talent exquis, délicat, merveilleux, mais fragile et d'une ténuité qui se dérobe à l'analyse, un auditoire expressément composé d'organisations nerveuses, de natures presque éthérées; il y a dans le jeu de M. Chopin quelque chose de perlé, de rare, d'éolien, que de simples mortels ne pourraient saisir. Le jour où l'on inventera un microscope pour les oreilles, ce jour-là M. Chopin sera divinisé. (Article non signé)

« **Journal des débats** », 13 avril 1842, p. 2

[...] Chopin se tient toujours à l'écart ; on ne le voit ni aux théâtres ni dans les concerts. On dirait qu'il a peur de la musique et des musiciens. Tous les ans une fois il sort de son nuage, et se fait entendre quelques instants dans le salon de Pleyel. Alors seulement le public et les artistes sont admis à admirer son magnifique talent. Pour tout le reste de l'année, à moins d'être prince, ou ministre, ou ambassadeur, il ne faut plus songer au plaisir de l'entendre. Tant d'autres joueraient sur les places publiques, si l'on voulait le leur permettre !! Est-ce timidité de la part de Chopin, ou bien est-ce pour faire songer ses admirateurs à la fable de Florian, "Le Rossignol et les moineaux" ? Le succès de son dernier concert a été tel, qu'un artiste doit être bien philosophe pour ne pas succomber à la tentation d'en obtenir plus souvent de pareil, quand il ne dépend que de lui. Son jeu est toujours le type de la grâce capricieuse, de la finesse et de l'originalité, et ses nouvelles compositions ne le cèdent point à leurs aînées pour la hardiesse harmonique et la suavité de ses mélodies. [**Hector Berlioz**]

« **La Presse** », 31 janvier 1848, p. 1

Une bonne nouvelle circule : on dit que Chopin se déciderait à donner un concert public, Chopin, ce mystérieux artiste que les rares privilégiés ont seuls le bonheur d'entendre. S'il se résout à cet effort, nul doute qu'il n'obtienne un immense succès : après Liszt, Thalberg et Doehler, Chopin paraîtra neuf sans aucun effort pour atteindre à l'originalité. Chopin c'est l'élégance mélancolique, la grâce rêveuse, la sensibilité virginale, tout ce que l'âme a de délicat, de tendre, d'éthéré. Il module, il soupire sur cet instrument rebelle et, sous ses doigts, le clavier semble effleuré par une aile d'ange. Nous attendons impatiemment ce concert et nous ferions un crime à Chopin de ne pas le donner. On n'a pas le droit d'être un grand artiste seulement pour quelques uns. Talent oblige autant que noblesse. [**Théophile Gautier**]

« **Le Ménestrel** », 20 février 1848, 15ème Année

[...] Si du Palais des Champs Élysées vous voulez passer au boudoir Pleyel, rue Rochechouart, vous y trouverez Chopin, le sylphe du piano, l'artiste insaisissable ne tenant que d'un doigt à ce bas monde et n'existant que des rêveries d'en haut. Entendez jouer Chopin, c'est le soupir de la fleur, la brise des nuages ou le murmure des étoiles : rien de terrestre, d'articulé ou de rythmé ; impossible de suivre ou de démêler la mesure et la carrure de sa musique. Si fait, parfois Chopin daigne descendre à la musique des mortels, il s'attache un instant à Mozart, par exemple, dont il a si noblement exécuté le *Trio* avec Alard et Franchomme, et alors il joue en mesure et d'une façon admirable. Mais si de semblables excès lui arrivaient souvent, Chopin perdrait toute sa poésie, la terre briserait ses ailes et nous n'aurions plus qu'un pianiste !

« **Revue et gazette musicale de Paris** », 20 février 1848, 15ème Année, N° 8, p. 58

Un concert de l'Ariel des pianistes est chose trop rare pour qu'on le donne, comme tous les autres concerts, en ouvrant à deux battants les portes à quiconque veut entrer. Pour celui-ci, une liste avait été dressée : chacun y inscrivait son nom ; mais chacun n'était pas sûr d'obtenir le précieux billet : il fallait des protections pour être admis dans le saint des saints, pour obtenir la faveur de déposer son offrande, et pourtant cette offrande était d'un louis ; mais qui n'a pas un louis de trop dans sa bourse, lorsqu'il s'agit d'entendre Chopin ?

De tout cela, il est résulté naturellement que la fine fleur de l'aristocratie des femmes les plus distinguées, des toilettes les plus élégantes, remplissaient mercredi les salons de Pleyel. Il y avait aussi l'aristocratie des artistes et des amateurs, heureux de saisir à la volée ce sylphe musical, qui avait promis de se laisser approcher, voir et entendre, une fois par hasard, et quelques heures durant.

Le Sylphe a tenu sa parole, et avec quel succès, quel enthousiasme ! Il est plus facile de vous dire l'accueil qu'il a reçu, les transports qu'il a excités, que de décrire, d'analyser, de divulguer les mystères d'une exécution qui n'a pas d'analogue dans notre région terrestre. Quand nous aurions en notre pouvoir la plume qui a tracé les délicates merveilles de la reine Mab, pas plus grosse que l'agate qui brille au doigt d'un alderman, de son char si menu, de son attelage si diaphane, c'est tout au plus si nous arriverions à vous donner l'idée d'un talent purement idéal, et dans lequel la matière n'entre à peu près pour rien. Pour faire comprendre Chopin, nous ne connaissions que Chopin lui-même : tous ceux qui assistaient à la séance de mercredi en sont convaincus autant que nous.

[...] Ne nous demandez pas comment tous ces chefs-d'œuvre petits ou grands, ont été rendus. Nous l'avons déclaré d'avance, nous renonçons à reproduire ces mille et mille nuances d'un génie exceptionnel, ayant à son service une organisation de même espèce. Nous dirons seulement que le charme n'a pas cessé un seul instant d'agir sur l'auditoire, et qu'il durait encore après que le concert était fini. [**Maurice Schlesinger**]

L'après-Chopin

A – Célébrations posthumes
1 Chronique nécrologique

« **Le Ménestrel** », 21 octobre 1849, 16ème Année
Frédéric Chopin.

L'art du piano vient d'éprouver une grande perte. Notre célèbre pianiste Chopin a succombé cette semaine, mercredi 17, à deux heures du matin, à la maladie de poitrine dont il était affecté depuis longtemps. Cet automne de 1849 nous aura donc ravi l'une de nos plus grandes gloires artistiques. On peut qualifier ainsi Chopin, qui cultivait son art avec religion, avec poésie, et qui fuyait avec une sorte d'affectation le contact public ou les applaudissements de la foule. Son genre de talent procédait, du reste, du style rêveur et romantique qui exclut le bruit et les grands auditoires. On peut dire qu'à l'inverse des pianistes modernes, pour Chopin, le piano avait toujours trop de son, et qu'il ne se préoccupait absolument que d'en « sentimentaliser » le timbre. Chopin évitait donc avec soin tout ce qui pouvait le rapprocher du fracas pianistique de l'époque ; sa musique ainsi que sa manière de jouer s'individualisaient ; aussi les doigtés de Chopin sur le clavier étaient-ils en dehors des traditions habituelles, révélant un cachet spécial, et comme la personnification de son talent.

« **Revue et gazette musicale de Paris** », 21 octobre 1849, 16ème Année, N° 42, p. 334
Nécrologie. Frédéric Chopin.

Il a cessé de vivre [...] cet artiste éminent, qui, dès son entrée dans la carrière, s'était placé au premier rang parmi les célébrités contemporaines, et s'y distinguait par une physionomie de talent plus individuelle que tout autre [...].

Jamais peut-être aucun artiste n'eut plus que lui le physique de son talent. Autant il était frêle de corps, autant il était délicat de style : un peu plus, il s'évaporait en impalpable et en imperceptible. Sa manière de toucher le piano ne ressemblait à celle de personne : elle perdait nécessairement dans une vaste salle ; à la portée d'une confidence, c'était quelque chose de délicieux. On surnommait Chopin l'Ariel du piano. Si la reine Mab eût voulu se donner un pianiste, c'est à coup sûr Chopin qu'elle aurait choisi, et la plume divine qui a décrit le fantastique attelage de la Fée aux songes, pourrait seule analyser les enchevêtrements compliqués, infinis, de cette phrase chargée de notes, et pourtant légère comme la dentelle, dans les plis de laquelle le compositeur enveloppait son idée.

« La Musique. Gazette de La France musicale », 21 octobre 1849, N° 42, p. 1

Encore une gloire musicale qui vient de s'éteindre. Chopin, que la maladie avait brisé depuis quelques années, au point de rendre méconnaissables la figure et le corps de cet artiste, Chopin est mort le 17 de ce mois. C'est une perte, une grande perte pour les arts. Les pianistes regretteront ce compositeur d'élite, dont le cœur débordait de poésie, et les salons pleureront cet esprit distingué, qui avait trouvé dans les classes élevées de la société les relations les plus honorables. Pauvre Chopin ! Il faisait peur à voir dans les derniers temps ; triste, affaissé, pâle, amaigri, les yeux accablés. La mort, la cruelle mort opérait ses ravages dans le sang de l'artiste ; et un beau jour, tout s'est glacé, et de cet aimable poète, de ce musicien tant aimé, il n'est resté que le souvenir de son talent et de son esprit.

Ceux qui ont vu Chopin dans l'intimité et qui ont pu apprécier les qualités de son âme généreuse, ceux qui lui ont entendu jouer avec l'expression la plus touchante de l'amour ou de la douleur ses plaintives mélodies, ah ! ceux-là seuls savent ce que valait ce noble caractère, et ce que renfermaient sa tête et son cœur, d'inspiration, de tendresse, de suave passion. Rêve féerique que celui de ce musicien, qui a traversé la vie au milieu des fleurs et des battements de mains, qui vient de partir pour le pays des divines harmonies, suivi des prières et des larmes de ses amis et de ses admirateurs. Tenez, il me semble le voir encore, faible, le souffle lui manquant, tendre ses mains vers le piano, et là, soupirer avec son sang les rêveries amoureuses, les plaintes de la vie, les joies célestes.

On était ému, on se sentait aller à la tristesse ; on suivait avec avidité l'aimable pianiste qui rendait avec une surprenante vérité l'effet des passions ; Oh ! oui, nous le pleurons, parce que nous l'avons aimé et que nous avions pour lui une affection de frère, et que nous aurons toujours présente à la pensée la figure mélancolique de cet ami infortuné qui laisse derrière lui une renommée inattaquable.

« **La Presse** », 22 octobre 1849, p. 1

Le Novalis du piano, Frédéric Chopin est mort après une agonie qui n'a guère duré moins de vingt ans.

Le public musical de l'Europe regrettera en lui non pas seulement un des trois ou quatre plus illustres pianistes de son époque, mais surtout un compositeur d'un génie vraiment individuel. La grâce élégante, la mélancolique rêverie, le style soutenu, nourri de l'étude des anciens et empreint au plus haut degré de la poésie passionnée qui caractérise l'école moderne, toutes ces qualités réunies faisaient de la moindre production de Chopin une chose exquise et précieuse comme le croquis d'un grand maître.

Sa santé débile lui avait interdit depuis longtemps la faculté de se faire entendre en public où son talent si délicat, si exquis brillait peut-être moins que dans les réunions intimes où il pouvait à l'aise se livrer à de capricieuses inventions. Tous ceux qui ont eu le bonheur de le voir et de l'entendre dans cette précieuse intimité pleurent en lui un éminent artiste, d'un cœur noble et d'un esprit distingué. [**Théophile Gautier**]

« **Le Journal des débats** », 22 octobre 1849, p. 2

Nous ne voulons pas que le grand artiste Chopin soit mort cette semaine, sans que son nom soit prononcé par nous avec tous les sentiments d'un respect sincère et d'une profonde pitié. Un plus habile que moi dira sans doute ici-même, à cette place, quel fut ce jeune homme à peine connu par la foule, qui était entouré d'une si profonde admiration, d'un culte sincère par les amis passionnés de son génie. Il était la musique même et l'inspiration même ; il touchait à peine à la terre que nous foulons, son talent ressemblait à un rêve ! Ceux-là seulement qui l'ont entendu peuvent se faire une idée de ce talent si fin, si délicat, si varié, qui s'adressait à ce que l'âme humaine a de plus honnête et de plus charmant. Il évitait, comme d'autres les recherchent, le bruit, la fanfare et même la renommée. On l'appelait l'*Ariel du piano*, et la comparaison était juste. Il avait grandi dans l'exil, il y est mort, entouré d'exilés comme lui à qui il rappelait la patrie absente. O l'infortuné ! comme il a souffert ! quelle lutte acharnée contre la mort !

Il a vécu 10 ans de miracle, d'un souffle prêt à s'envoler ; mais la mélodie et l'harmonie, ses deux sœurs, le retenaient ici-bas, et il ne pouvait pas s'en séparer ! A la fin, il est mort, dans tout le calme et toute la sérénité d'une jeunesse honnête, chrétienne, solitaire, cachée, consacrée à l'étude, au travail, à la méditation !

De tous les artistes de nos jours, c'est Chopin qui s'est le plus emparé de l'âme et de l'esprit des femmes. Ses élèves, et il a fait des élèves dignes de lui, l'aimaient d'une tendresse quasi maternelle ; elles l'entouraient d'un enthousiasme mêlé de vénération, tant sa musique leur parlait un honnête et chaste langage. [**Jules Janin**)

« **Le Journal des débats** », 27 octobre 1849, p. 2

Après une longue et terrible agonie, Chopin vient de mourir. Nous n'emploierons pas à son sujet la formule ordinaire en disant que sa mort est une perte pour l'art. Hélas ! Chopin était perdu pour la musique depuis assez longtemps. Sa faiblesse et ses douleurs étaient devenues telles qu'il ne pouvait plus ni se faire entendre sur un piano ni composer ; la moindre conversation même le fatiguait d'une manière alarmante. Il cherchait en général à se faire comprendre autant que possible par signes. De là l'espèce d'isolement dans lequel il a voulu passer les derniers mois de sa vie, isolement que beaucoup de gens ont mal interprété et attribué les uns à une fierté dédaigneuse, les autres à une humeur noire, aussi loin l'une que l'autre du caractère de ce charmant et excellent artiste. Loin d'être morose, Chopin, au temps où ses souffrances étaient encore tolérables, se montrait d'une bonhomie malicieuse qui donnait un irrésistible attrait aux relations que ses amis avaient avec lui. Il apportait dans la conversation cet humour qui fit le charme principal et le caractère essentiel de son rare talent.

Ses compositions pour le piano ont fait école. La grâce la plus originale, l'imprévu du tour mélodique, la hardiesse des harmonies s'y trouvent réunis à un système entier d'ornementation dont il fut l'inventeur et qui est resté inimitable. Ses Études pour le piano sont des chefs-d'œuvre où se retrouvent concentrées les qualités éminentes de sa manière et ses plus rayonnantes inspirations. Nous les placerons même au-dessus de ses célèbres Mazurkas qui, dès leur apparition, valurent à Chopin un succès passionné auprès des femmes surtout et le rendirent le favori de tous les salons aristocratiques de l'Europe. Ce luxe de mélodies exquises, leur allure à la fois fière et souriante, leur dédain de tout entourage vulgaire, leur passion contenue ou concentrée, leurs divines chatteries, leur retentissement pompeux ont en effet une sorte d'affinité avec les mœurs du monde élégant pour lequel elles semblent faites.

Aussi Chopin, malgré son magnifique talent d'exécution n'était-il pas l'homme de la foule, le virtuose des grandes salles et des grands concerts. Il avait renoncé à ces tumultes depuis longtemps. Un petit cercle d'auditeurs choisis, chez lesquels il pouvait croire à un réel désir de l'entendre, pouvait seul le déterminer à s'approcher du piano. Que d'émotions alors il savait faire naître ! En quelles ardentes et mélancoliques rêveries il aimait à répandre son âme ! C'était vers minuit d'ordinaire qu'il se livrait avec le plus d'abandon ; quand les gros papillons du salon étaient partis, quand la question politique à l'ordre du jour avait été longuement traitée, quand tous les médisants étaient à bout de leurs anecdotes, quand tous les pièges étaient tendus, toutes les perfidies consommées, quand on était bien las de la prose, alors, obéissant à la prière muette de quelques beaux yeux intelligents, il devenait poète et chantait les amours ossianiques des héros de ses rêves, leurs joies chevaleresques et les douleurs de la patrie absente, sa chère Pologne toujours prête à vaincre et toujours abattue. Mais, hors de ces conditions que tout artiste doit lui savoir gré d'avoir exigées pour se produire, il était inutile de le solliciter. La curiosité excitée par sa renommée semblait même l'irriter et il se dérobait le plus tôt possible à un monde non sympathique quand le hasard l'y avait fait s'égarer. Je me rappelle un mot sanglant qu'il décocha un soir au maître d'une maison où il avait dîné. A peine avait-on pris le café, l'amphitryon, s'approchant de Chopin, vint lui dire que ses convives, qui ne l'avaient jamais entendu, espéraient qu'il voudrait bien se mettre au piano et jouer quelque petite chose. Chopin s'en défendit dès l'abord, de manière à ne pas laisser le moindre doute sur ses dispositions. Mais l'autre insistant d'une façon presque blessante en homme qui sait la valeur et le but du dîner qu'il vient de donner, l'artiste coupa court à la discussion en lui disant de sa voix faible et interrompue par un accès de toux : « Ah ! Monsieur… j'ai… si peu mangé ! » Malgré le produit considérable de ses œuvres et des leçons qu'il donnait, Chopin ne laisse pas de fortune ; les malheureux Polonais que l'exil a tant de fois amenés à sa porte savent où cette fortune a passé. Au dernier moment la constante admiration de Chopin pour Mozart lui a fait désirer que l'immortel *Requiem* fût exécuté à ses funérailles. Son digne élève, M. Gutmann, a recueilli ce vœu avec son dernier soupir. [**Hector Berlioz**]

« **Revue et gazette musicale de Paris** », 4 novembre 1849, 16ème Année, N°44, p. 348–349

[…] Ce talent fut surtout compris, profondément senti par les femmes, non par ces jolies petites serinettes humaines qui n'aspirent qu'à faire entendre dans un salon une brillante fantaisie afin d'inspirer celle de les épouser, et dire bientôt après en parlant de musique et de piano : « Depuis mon mariage, j'ai négligé tout ça », mais par les dames, sinon de la haute, du moins de la bonne société, où l'on reconnaît toujours une aristocratie, celle du talent. Mmes de Belgiojoso, de Peruzzi, etc. étaient les disciples, les admiratrices, les amies du pauvre artiste mélancolique, aux inspirations vaporeuses, fines, délicates. Elles aimaient à le suivre alors qu'il berçait son auditoire intime de ses capricieuses arabesques mélodiques sur une harmonie inattendue, étrange, mais distinguée, classique, pure et pourtant souffreteuse, qui semblait un chant de cygne, un hymne de mort. [**Henri Blanchard**]

2 La perspective de la postérité

« **La France musicale** », 9 février 1851, 15ème Année, n° 6, p. 42
Franz Liszt, *Chopin*.

[...] Quelle que soit donc la popularité d'une partie des productions de celui que les souffrances avaient brisé longtemps avant sa fin, il est néanmoins à présumer que la postérité aura pour ses ouvrages une estime moins frivole et moins légère que celle qui leur est encore accordée. Ceux qui, dans la suite, s'occuperont de l'histoire de la musique feront sa part, et elle sera grande, à celui qui y marqua par un si rare génie mélodique, par de si heureux et si remarquables agrandissements du tissu harmonique, que ses conquêtes seront préférées avec raison à mainte œuvre de surface plus étendue, jouée et rejouée par de grands orchestres, chantée et rechantée par la foule des *prime donne*.

En se renfermant dans le cadre exclusif du piano, Chopin, à notre sens, a fait preuve d'une des qualités les plus essentielles à un écrivain : la juste appréciation de la forme dans laquelle il lui est donné d'exceller ; et néanmoins ce fait, dont nous lui faisons un sérieux mérite, nuit à l'importance de sa renommée.

« **La France musicale** », (16 février 1851, 15° Année, n° 7, p. 49–50
Franz Liszt, *Chopin*.

[...] Il a écrit de beaux *concertos* et de belles *sonates* ; toutefois il n'est pas difficile de distinguer dans ces productions plus de volonté que d'inspiration. La sienne était impérieuse, fantasque, irréfléchie. Ses allures ne pouvaient être que libres, et nous croyons qu'il a violenté son génie, chaque fois qu'il a cherché à l'astreindre aux règles, aux classifications, à une ordonnance qui n'était pas les siennes, et ne pouvaient concorder avec les exigences de son esprit, un de ceux dont la grâce se déploie surtout lorsqu'ils semblent aller à la dérive.

[...] De sourdes colères, des rages étouffées, se rencontrent dans maints passages de ses œuvres, et plusieurs de ses *Études*, aussi bien que ses *Scherzos*, dépeignent une exaspération concentrée, et dominée par un désespoir tantôt ironique, tantôt hautain. Ces sombres apostrophes de sa muse ont passé plus inaperçues et moins comprises que ses poèmes d'un plus tendre coloris. Le caractère personnel de Chopin a pu y contribuer. Bienveillant, affable, facile dans ses rapports, d'une humeur égale et enjouée, il laissait peu soupçonner les secrètes convulsions qui l'agitaient.

George Sand, *Histoire de ma vie* (1854–1855), V° partie, chapitre XII, éd. Georges Lubin, Paris : Gallimard – Bibliothèque de la Pléiade 1971, vol. 2, p. 420–422

C'est là [à Majorque] qu'il a composé les plus belles de ces courtes pages qu'il intitulait modestement des préludes. Ce sont des chefs-d'œuvre. Plusieurs présentent à la pensée des visions de moines trépassés et l'audition des chants funèbres qui l'assiégeaient ; d'autres sont mélancoliques et suaves ; ils lui venaient aux heures de soleil et de santé, au bruit du rire des enfants sous la fenêtre, au son lointain des guitares, au chant des oiseaux sous la feuillée humide, à la vue des petites roses pâles épanouies sur la neige.

D'autres encore sont d'une tristesse morne et, en vous charmant l'oreille, vous navrent le cœur. Il y en a un qui lui vint par une soirée de pluie lugubre et qui jette dans l'âme un abattement effroyable. [...]

Le génie de Chopin est le plus profond et le plus plein de sentiments et d'émotions qui ait existé. Il a fait parler à un seul instrument la langue de l'infini ; il a pu souvent résumer en dix lignes qu'un enfant pourrait jouer des poèmes d'une élévation immense, des drames d'une énergie sans égale. Il n'a jamais eu besoin de grands moyens matériels pour donner le mot de son génie. Il ne lui a fallu ni saxophones ni ophicléides pour remplir l'âme de terreur ; ni orgues d'église ni voix humaines pour la remplir de foi et d'enthousiasme. Il n'a pas été connu et il ne l'est pas encore de la foule. Il faut de grands progrès dans le goût et l'intelligence de l'art pour que ses œuvres deviennent populaires. Un jour viendra où l'on orchestrera sa musique sans rien changer à sa partition de piano, et où tout le monde saura que ce génie aussi vaste, aussi complet, aussi savant que celui des grands maîtres qu'il s'était assimilés, a gardé une individualité encore plus exquise que celle de Sébastien Bach, encore plus puissante que celle de Beethoven, encore plus dramatique que celle de Weber. Il est tous les trois ensemble, et il est encore lui-même, c'est-à-dire plus délié dans le goût, plus austère dans le grand, plus déchirant dans la douleur. Mozart seul lui est supérieur, parce que Mozart a en plus le calme de la santé, par conséquent la plénitude de la vie. Chopin sentait sa puissance et sa faiblesse. Sa faiblesse était dans l'excès même de cette puissance qu'il ne pouvait régler. Il ne pouvait pas faire, comme Mozart (au reste Mozart seul a pu le faire), un chef-d'œuvre avec une teinte plate. Sa musique était pleine de nuances et d'imprévu. Quelquefois, rarement, elle était bizarre, mystérieuse et tourmentée. Quoiqu'il eût horreur de ce que l'on ne comprend pas, ses émotions excessives l'emportaient à son insu dans des régions connues de lui seul. [...]

Il avait eu quelquefois des idées riantes et toutes rondes dans sa jeunesse. Il a fait des chansons polonaises et des romances inédites d'une charmante bonhomie et d'une adorable douceur. Quelques unes de ses compositions ultérieures sont encore comme des sources de cristal où se mire un clair soleil. Mais qu'elles sont rares et courtes, ces tranquilles extases de sa contemplation !

Eugène Delacroix, *Journal*, 29 juin 1853, éd. André Joubin, Paris : Plon 1932, vol. 2, p. 72

Que Chopin est un autre homme que cela ! Voyez, leur ai-je dit, combien il est de son temps, comme il se sert des progrès que les autres ont fait faire à son art ! Comme il adore Mozart, et comme il lui ressemble peu ! Son ami Kwiatkowski lui reprochait souvent quelques réminiscences italiennes qui sentent, malgré lui, les productions modernes des Bellini, etc. C'est une chose aussi qui me déplaît un peu. Mais quel charme ! Quelle nouveauté d'ailleurs !

« Le Temps », 7 septembre 1861, 1ère Année, n° 135, p. 3
Critique musicale.

Les compositions de Chopin n'obtiennent point de popularité et ne sauraient en obtenir dans un temps où le succès de la musique de piano est le plus souvent en raison inverse de sa valeur réelle. Elles ne furent appréciées que par un public d'élite. « Chopin, dit M. Énault, fut le pianiste des duchesses ». Heureuses les duchesses qui ont compris Chopin !

La grande foule des gens qui se persuadent jouer du piano ne jouent guère un morceau de Chopin que comme une sonate de Mozart ou de Beethoven pour se donner l'air de savoir jouer la musique « classique » ; mais ils ont hâte de retourner à cette légion de platitudes qui ne sont qu'une mosaïque de petits airs et de traits insignifiants, d'une exécution plus brillante que difficile.

Bien jouer la musique de Chopin est un éloge presque aussi grand et aussi difficile à mériter que de bien jouer la musique de Beethoven. [**Johannes Weber**]

Antoine Marmontel, *Les Pianistes célèbres*, Paris : Chaix 1878, p. 13

Nous avons souvent, entre artistes, agité la délicate question du classement de l'œuvre de Chopin, comme compositeur de musique de chambre. L'importance et la réelle influence de son style échappaient à toute contestation ; mais, unanimes dans notre admiration pour le virtuose, nous étions très divisés sur la valeur musicale de ses productions. Compositeur expressif, original pour beaucoup, – élégant, gracieux, « charmeur » pour plusieurs, – excentrique, incompréhensible pour les pauvres d'esprit, – Chopin restera un des maîtres les plus discutés de notre époque, et cependant maître de génie, dans la sérieuse acception du mot.

Je n'entends pas établir de comparaison entre Chopin et les aigles au vol puissant que leurs premiers coups d'aile ont portés aux cimes les plus hautes. Il n'a jamais eu ni ces sublimes audaces, ni ces témérités heureuses. La tendresse, l'émotion, le charme intime ou poignant de ses compositions ne remplacent pas le grand souffle, absent ou intermittent ; l'inspiration de Chopin s'élève parfois, mais pour retomber brisée sur le sol, elle n'a pas le vol égal, libre, dégagé qui seul peut soutenir dans les régions éthérées. Mais le génie ne consiste pas seulement à trouver des formes encore inconnues dans le domaine de l'art ; il consiste aussi à raffiner ce métal précieux, le minerai introuvable pour le vulgaire, l'idée, l'inspiration avec leur enveloppe rugueuse ou diaphane.

C'est dans ce sens que Chopin restera un compositeur de génie, – grand poète en de courtes strophes, – grand peintre en de petits cadres.

« La Nouvelle Revue », novembre–décembre 1886, 8ème Année, vol. 43, p. 441–442
Bulletin bibliographique.

Parmi les maîtres contemporains, il n'en est point dont la figure soit demeurée entourée d'une auréole plus poétique que celle de F. Chopin, cet artiste incomparable dont la fougue presque sauvage, la grâce élégante, offraient un type d'une originalité exceptionnelle et d'un charme infini. Mais à côté du compositeur génial et du prodigieux exécutant, il y avait chez Chopin un homme d'un caractère aimable, de goûts délicats, d'aspirations élevées et d'un cœur affectueux. Ajoutez à cela le prestige d'une mort prématurée, et vous ne vous étonnerez plus du souvenir ineffaçable que conservent encore aujourd'hui au jeune maître tous ceux qui l'ont connu. [**Ad. Badin**]

« **Le Courrier musical** », **n° spécial** *Chopin,* 1ᵉʳ janvier 1910, 13ᵉᵐᵉ Année, n° 1, p. 20–23
L'Âme de Chopin.

[...] On ne peut éprouver qu'une grande reconnaissance pour ce novateur audacieux dans sa simplicité qui a su atteindre son noble but d'ouvrir une ère nouvelle à la musique. Car il n'y a pas à se le dissimuler, il l'a ouverte et largement ouverte cette ère de musicalité subjective et signifiante dans laquelle nous sommes aujourd'hui.

Il faut se répéter qu'avant lui on ne connaissait dans la forme classique que la Sonate, le Concerto et les Variations ; et bien entendu ces pièces légères des XVIIe et XVIIIe siècles [...] dont leurs appellations mêmes de Chacone, Musette, Tambourin, Passe-pied, Rigodon, Courante, Gavotte, Menuet, etc., disent assez qu'elles ne constituaient généralement pas autre chose que d'élégants prétextes à danses.

Chopin rompit délibérément avec cette production charmante mais superficielle. Il était trop indépendant d'autre part pour se plier aux formes fixes et si dans sa *Sonate* en *si* bémol mineur la première partie reste d'une belle tenue classique, tout de suite après il lâche les rênes à son génie et nous donne avec le Final ces quatre pages sublimes de bourrasque poétique où se déchaîne le vent du grand lyrisme par quoi Chopin se soulève vraiment cette fois à la hauteur des cimes beethovéniennes.

Chaque fois d'ailleurs qu'il s'est essayé à remplir les vieux cadres, il y a médiocrement réussi. Sa *Sonate* pour piano et violoncelle, son trio, sont beaucoup moins représentatifs de son tempérament que le reste de son œuvre. On le sent plus à l'aise dans des pièces d'une structure moins nettement délimitée, telles que les Études, les Préludes, etc.

Les Études n'étaient guère jusqu'à lui que de fastidieux devoirs de mécanisme. Chopin leur a bien conservé leur incontestable utilité technique, mais il leur a communiqué un tel souffle de musique qu'elles sont devenues de magnifiques poèmes musicaux d'une variété énorme passant par toute la gamme des passions humaines.

Quant aux Préludes, on ne possédait avant les siens que ceux de Bach. [...] Tout ce que la musique peut donner en grâce, en passion, en lyrisme, en drame, en béatitude, en fraîcheur, passe dans ces pages qui comportent en même temps une technique extrêmement nombreuse, fournie, souple et toujours admirablement pianistique [...].

Mais c'est ailleurs que Chopin se montre plus novateur encore et plus original. Cette fois il ne renouvelle plus : il crée. Il crée le *Nocturne* et il crée la *Ballade*. Ces deux formes lui appartiennent en propre et elles sont peut-être les plus immortelles filles de son esprit [...].

Mais quels que soient le cadre qu'il donne à ses œuvres, le titre dont il les désigne, ou le caractère qu'il leur imprime, sa musique est toujours d'une unité d'inspiration qui la rend reconnaissable entre toutes. On sent que tout ce rayonnement part d'un même centre, cette chaleur d'un même foyer, qui est son âme d'amant, de patriote et de poète.

Elle a beau être, cette musique, parfois quintessenciée, un peu morbide même, elle reste continûment de l'admirable musique. [...] Mais ce qu'elle est par-dessus tout, c'est individuelle, c'est intime, c'est prenante, avec une intention perpétuelle de dire, de révéler quelque chose d'une âme et de se confier à vous comme à un ami, comme un héros ou comme une amoureuse.

La conséquence de ce parti pris d'intimité fut un développement intense de l'art et de la composition pianistiques. Avant Chopin, le piano semblait avoir atteint l'apogée de sa puissance et de son expressivité. Le prodigieux artiste et l'exécutant colossal qu'était Liszt avait établi une technique fulgurante dont l'épanouissement avait en quelque sorte contraint le piano à déborder de sa formule ordinaire pour se prêter aux luxuriances des combinaisons nouvelles et aux vertigineuses vélocités des traits.

Chopin, concurremment avec Schumann d'ailleurs, alla plus loin, bénéficia de ce mécanisme, mais l'asservit en quelque manière aux besoins de son inspiration ; et parvint à faire du piano un instrument multiple, coloré, dont il apparut bien alors qu'on n'avait pas épuisé toutes les ressources. Ce fut comme un réveil des puissances endormies dans ses flancs.

On ne peut pas vraiment dire qu'il y eut là la variété d'un timbre orchestral. Tout au contraire, c'est bien toujours et seulement de la musique de piano, inspirée par le piano, écrite pour le piano, mais combien plus variée, d'une palette combien plus riche que tout ce qu'on avait fait jusqu'alors (si l'on en excepte cependant les sonates de Beethoven).

Lorsqu'on joue Chopin, les différences de *sonorité* deviennent plus que nécessaires : le son doit être pesé, ménagé, étouffé avec les inflexions d'une voix ; on est conduit à demander au piano un grand nombre d'effets qu'on n'en tirait pas auparavant, qu'on ne songeait pas à en tirer et qui répondent aux exigences de cette nouvelle matière musicale.

L'originalité de ses traits, la grâce, la préciosité un peu maladive parfois de ses groupes de petites notes et de ses appoggiatures appelle un toucher très différent. En un mot c'est toute une école pianistique nouvelle qui s'ouvre avec Chopin, et qui par sa douceur, sa souplesse, sa variété, ses combinaisons rythmiques et l'indépendance nécessaire des doigts se distingue franchement de l'école de Liszt, plus encombrée de notes superflues et d'un fracas polyphonique souvent inutile. [**Raoul Pugno**]

« **Le Courrier musical** », n° spécial *Chopin*, 1ᵉʳ janvier 1910, 13ᵉᵐᵉ Année, n° 1, p. 35
Les Sonates, les Concertos, le Trio, les Fantaisies, les Variations.

[...] Les génies de cette sorte ne peuvent être l'objet de comparaisons ; il les faut accepter tout entiers tels qu'ils sont ou s'éloigner d'eux. Irons-nous reprocher à Chopin ses sonates mal bâties ? Non, certes ; il faut écarter de nous la tentation d'une telle critique, ici vaine et stérile. Chopin ne pouvait faire que ce qu'il a fait. Cela est bien ainsi. [...] Ce dandy aux gants blancs réalise le type idéal du rhapsode, du chanteur ambulant qui va semant aux quatre vents du ciel sa joie et sa douleur. A ceux que la musique de Chopin remue toujours profondément ; à ceux qui estiment qu'en raison même de son lyrisme subjectif, elle est entre toutes les musiques du passé, une de celles qui restent les plus proches de la sensibilité contemporaine, une seule attitude s'impose : oublier toute autre considération pour rechercher avec un zèle pieux, jusque dans les œuvres moins parfaites que la mode dédaigne ou que l'oubli menace, les moindres témoignages de cet art patricien, fruit délectable d'un égoïsme providentiel. [**Albert Groz**]

« **Le Courrier musical** », n° spécial *Chopin*, 1ᵉʳ janvier 1910, 13ᵉᵐᵉ Année, n° 1, p. 12–15
L'italianisme de Chopin.

[...] Sur Frédéric Chopin, l'action de la musique italienne n'est donc pas seulement très forte : elle est prépondérante [...].

Chopin aime, comme un Rossini ou un Bellini, ces ardents *cantabile*, dont le pathos s'épanche avec une chaleur langoureuse, qui portent jusqu'à une note culminante l'effort de leur passion offerte et retombent ensuite en une suppliante pâmoison [...].

414

Chopin n'aime pas seulement la mélodie des Italiens, il aime leur harmonie, ces suites de tierces ou de sixtes, flatteuses à l'oreille, à la fois faciles et riches de sonorités, et qui accouplent deux lignes mélodiques comme les duos du répertoire. [...] Et puis ces tierces ou ces sixtes, lorsque les reflets du mineur viennent les assombrir, ne chantent-elles pas, d'une voix toujours séduisante, l'infini de la tristesse et de la mélancolie ? Ces formules se rencontrent, dans l'œuvre de Chopin, presque à chaque page [...].

Les ornements mêmes dont Chopin use si volontiers ressemblent moins aux cadences des classiques et aux fioritures des pianistes allemands – les Moscheles, les Hummel – qu'aux fusées vocales qu'égrènent sur de complaisants « points d'orgue » ou seulement selon leur caprice, les virtuoses du *bel canto*. Et le *tempo rubato* enfin, si caractéristique de Chopin, où donc en prend-il l'exemple, sinon dans le modèle des ténors ou des soprani du théâtre italien, qui imposent au chef d'orchestre le respect de leurs bonnes notes, de leurs beaux cris, [...] de tous ces artifices qui rendent la voix plus touchante, l'accent plus pathétique, la sensualité plus frémissante, avec ses alternatives d'évanouissements et de sursauts.

Cette parenté de Chopin avec l'art italien de son époque semble donc évidente et assignable par plus d'un trait. [...]. Toutefois l'influence qu'il en ressent n'est qu'une influence d'importation. Sa sensibilité est du reste trop originale pour qu'aussitôt elle ne modifie pas profondément les sucs dont elle se nourrit et qu'elle assimile. Le tour italien prend, dans la musique de Chopin, une morbidesse indécise qu'il n'a point chez les Italiens autochtones ; cet art rutilant se décompose chez lui en nuances irisées, troublantes, opalines ; ce n'est plus qu'un parfum lointain, quelque chose d'affecté parfois, ailleurs de naïvement nostalgique. Et pour le définir il faut ce mot, lui-même dégradé : « *italianisant* ». [**Jean Chantavoine**]

« Le Courrier musical », n° spécial *Chopin,* 1er janvier 1910, 13ème Année, n° 1, p. 26
L'interprétation de Chopin.

[...] Et on a fait de ce Couperin teinté de romantisme, le romantique le plus outré, le plus criard ; on lui a suggéré l'âme de la rue, la sentimentalité des vieilles filles et tous les gros sentiments du cinématographe. [...] Ses amis ne cessaient pas de lui reprocher son caractère trop renfermé, sa grande réserve et sa tenue hautaine. Et ses interprètes modernes lui font faire des aveux d'une importunité indécente. [**Wanda Landowska**]

B – Le « Mythe Chopin »

1 La légende en marche

« Journal des débats », 4 novembre 1849, p. 4
Allocution de Charles Blanc, directeur des Beaux-arts à la distribution des prix au Conservatoire national de musique de Paris.

[...] Maintenant me pardonnerez-vous de consacrer encore quelques mots pieux à la mémoire de Chopin, du barde polonais qui fit aimer les chants de son pays à toutes les femmes du nôtre, et dont les funérailles ont été conduites... par Mozart ! Poète rêveur, frêle et gracieux, nous l'avons vu passer comme une vivante élégie ; vous l'avez endormi doucement aux sons d'une musique sublime.

« Le Temps », 4 septembre 1880, 20ème Année, n° 7076, p. 3
Hector Berlioz, *Études et souvenirs de théâtre.*
Reproduit dans : **Ernest Legouvé, *Soixante ans de souvenirs*,** Paris : Hetzel 1886, vol. 2, p. 159

Je ne puis mieux définir Chopin, qu'en disant que c'était une *trinité charmante*. Il y avait entre sa personne, son jeu et ses ouvrages un tel accord qu'on ne peut pas plus les séparer, ce me semble, que les divers traits d'un même visage. Le son si particulier qu'il tirait du piano ressemblait au regard qui partait de ses yeux ; la délicatesse un peu maladive de sa figure s'alliait à la poétique mélancolie de ses Nocturnes ; et le soin et la recherche de sa toilette faisaient comprendre l'élégance toute mondaine de certaines parties de ses œuvres ; il me faisait l'effet d'un fils naturel de Weber et d'une duchesse ; ce que j'appelais ses trois lui n'en formaient qu'un.

Son génie ne s'éveillait guère qu'à une heure du matin. Jusque là, il n'était qu'un pianiste charmant. La nuit venue, il entrait dans le groupe des esprits aériens, des êtres ailés, de tout ce qui vole et brille au sein des demi-ténèbres d'une nuit d'été. Il lui fallait alors un auditoire très restreint et très choisi. La moindre figure un peu déplaisante suffisait pour le déconcerter. Je l'entends encore, un jour où son jeu me semblait un peu agacé, me dire tout bas en me désignant du regard une dame assise en face de lui : « C'est la plume de cette dame ! Si cette plume-là ne s'en va pas, je ne pourrai pas continuer ! » Une fois au piano, il jouait jusqu'à épuisement. Atteint d'une maladie qui ne pardonne pas, ses yeux se cerclaient de noir, ses regard s'animaient d'un éclat fébrile, ses lèvres s'empourpraient d'un rouge sanglant, son souffle devenait plus court ! Il sentait, nous sentions que quelque chose de sa vie s'écoulait avec les sons, et il ne voulait pas s'arrêter, et nous n'avions pas la force de l'arrêter ! La fièvre qui le brûlait nous envahissait tous !

Maurice Rollinat, *Névroses. Chopin,* Paris : Charpentier, 1885, p. 53–55

Chopin, frère du gouffre, amant des nuits tragiques
Âme qui fus si grande en un si frêle corps,
Le piano muet songe à tes doigts magiques
Et la musique en deuil pleure tes noirs accords.

L'harmonie a perdu son Edgar Poe farouche
Et la mer mélodique un de ses plus grands flots.
C'est fini ! le soleil des sons tristes se couche,
Le Monde pour gémir n'aura plus de sanglots !

Ta musique est toujours – douloureuse ou macabre –
L'hymne de la révolte et de la liberté,
Et le hennissement du cheval qui se cabre
Est moins fier que le cri de ton cœur indompté..

La morbide lourdeur des blancs soleils d'automne ;
Le froid humide et gras funèbres caveaux ;
Les bizarres frissons dont la vierge s'étonne
Quand l'été fait flamber les cœurs et les cerveaux ;

Tout cela, torsions de l'esprit, mal physique,
Ces peintures, ces bruits, cette immense terreur,
Tout cela, je le trouve au fond de ta musique
Qui ruisselle d'amour, de souffrance et d'horreur.

Réponse de George Sand à l'envoi des *Névroses*, 21 janvier 1873
Reproduit dans : *Correspondance de George Sand*, éd. Georges Lubin, Paris :
Garnier 1989, vol. 23, p. 410

Tu n'as pas compris Chopin si tu n'y as vu que le côté déchirant. Il avait aussi le côté naïf, sincère, enthousiaste, et tendre. Ce n'était pas un génie incomplet.

Camille Mauclair, *Une causerie sur Chopin*, Conférence donnée le 11 juin 1909 salle Pleyel avec le concours de Raoul Pugno.
Reproduit dans : *La Religion de la musique*, Paris : Fischacher 1928, p. 222

C'était une figure représentative pour les poètes autant que pour les musiciens : et cette figure était celle d'un souverain, d'un jeune Hamlet traversant le romantisme. Elle réunissait tous les dons qui méritent un culte dans une chapelle spéciale : le prestige d'un charme personnel qui a enthousiasmé les contemporains, l'attrait d'un jeu qui semble bien avoir été inimitable, l'auréole de la plus intellectuelle des maladies et d'une mort prématurée, la révélation d'une musique exceptionnelle qui portait d'un seul coup à son plus haut degré l'art intimiste, l'art du subjectivisme le plus intense, et enfin la concentration de cet art sur un instrument auquel rien de semblable n'avait jamais été demandé. La figure ainsi constituée se présentait avec une originalité tellement insolite et apparaissait si parfaitement cohérente qu'elle dépassait la réalité et se classait d'emblée parmi les plus attirantes figures du roman. Elle en avait le style, le mystère et la séduction. En elle plus peut-être qu'en tout autre l'homme et le musicien s'identifiaient indissolublement et le tout formait un rêve vivant, une entité, à tel point qu'on ne recherche pas sérieusement les rapports de Chopin avec l'évolution musicale de son siècle. Il semblait logique et il était plus agréable de l'envisager comme un être inclassable. Et c'est de cette idée que devaient naître à la fois l'adoration fidèle et l'admiration maladroite dont sa mémoire et son œuvre ont été et sont encore l'objet.

2 Le rejet des mythes

« La Renaissance musicale », 19 juin 1881, 1ère Année, n° 16, p. 3–5
Livres (Kleczynski-Barbedette).

[...] Il faut se féliciter en tout cas de voir l'une des plus sympathiques figures que présente l'histoire de l'Art moderne, se fixer peu à peu et se montrer de face et non de profil ; il faut particulièrement savoir gré à M. Kleczynski d'avoir remis en lumière, en relief, ce qu'il appelle si justement le côté viril de cette figure, le côté sur lequel une auréole complaisamment élargie, de rêveuse sentimentalité, laissait à peine tomber quelques rayons.

Cette manière, nous allions dire cette manie, de se prononcer sur le caractère, sur la valeur du compositeur polonais, dans un sens borné, sinon exclusif, tenait surtout à deux raisons.

D'une part, il avait porté au dernier degré de perfection un genre dans lequel Field, son précurseur, n'avait laissé en comparaison que de pâles ébauches : celui du *Nocturne*. Or qui dit nocturne dit nécessairement mélancolie et tout ce qui s'ensuit. Et de là vient que, en dépit de l'énergie inusitée que parfois Chopin a su introduire jusque dans ce domaine réservé, sa physionomie en a gardé, aux yeux du grand nombre, un nuage fait d'ombre et de langueur.

En outre, ses airs de danse, si variés, si originaux, et dont la plupart sont restés justement célèbres, étaient le plus souvent empreints de ce qui caractérise les chants d'origine slave : tonalités indécises, vague rêverie, arrière-pensées mystérieuses, dérobées, sous l'expression de la gaieté [...].

Ce qui, par exemple, est tout à fait imprévu et vraiment étrange, c'est la conclusion de M. Barbedette, lorsque, arrivé au terme de ses analyses consciencieuses et presque toujours remarquables par leur finesse, il demande la mise en quarantaine des œuvres du compositeur polonais comme suspectes de contenir des germes morbides et des principes contagieux. En effet, comment croire qu'à une sensibilité exquise, tantôt exaltée jusqu'à pousser les cris les plus éloquents, tantôt profondément repliée jusqu'à ne trouver, pour s'épancher, que le murmure le plus discret, le plus mystérieux, mais toujours pure, toujours sincère, il appartienne d'exercer de si perfides influences ? Non, il n'y a rien à redouter de ce côté pour le goût musical. [**Léonce Mesnard**]

Romain Rolland, *Printemps romain. Choix de lettres à sa mère (1889-1890)*, Cahier 6, Paris : Albin Michel 1954

On ne me fera jamais croire que Schumann et Chopin soient des classiques ; ce sont des femmes nerveuses, ou des virtuoses malsains ; le peu que j'ai voulu d'eux, autrefois, je n'en veux plus. [20 mai 1890, p. 283]

[La meilleure élève de Sgambati] joue Chopin, comme si elle l'avait composé : elle le rend presque simple. Malheureusement, elle ne sort pas de cette musique qui est mon ennemie née : Chopin, Liszt, Schumann, Sgambati, etc., la musique des âmes vagues, et des doigts de virtuose. [2 juin 1890, p. 300]

« **Arlequin** », avril 1910, N° 4, p. 166–167
Romain Rolland, *Le centenaire de Chopin.*

Cité par : Zbigniew Naliwajek, *Chopin vu par Romain Rolland*, dans : *Frédéric Chopin et les lettres. Actes du Colloque franco-polonais organisé par le Centre de Civilisation Française à l'Université de Varsovie avec la collaboration de la Société Frédéric Chopin (Varsovie, décembre 6–7.12.1988*, éd. Joanna Żurowska, Varsovie : Éditions de l'Université de Varsovie 1991, p. 115

J'évite de parler de Chopin. Vous ne trouverez son nom dans aucun de mes livres.

Vous savez si j'hésite à dire quand j'aime ou quand je hais ! – Mais tous les deux ensemble !… *Odi et amo.* L'amour que j'ai pour Chopin m'empêche de dire le mal que je pense de lui. Je le regarde comme un des plus beaux poètes de la musique, un inventeur magique d'harmonies, de formes musicales (plus grand compositeur que Schumann), un créateur non seulement de rêves admirables, mais de l'étoffe des rêves de créateurs plus puissants que lui – (Wagner lui-même). Et, en même temps, il y a toute une partie de son être que je déteste, – le bellâtre, le dandy, le virtuose : – le Mozart de la *Foire sur la place.*

Je l'aime, je l'admire, je le plains, je ne puis le souffrir, je lui en veux, il m'émeut, il m'irrite… C'est une femme qu'on aime et qui vous trompe : on ne peut pas en parler de sang-froid. Plus tard… quand je serai très vieux, et que je ne l'aimerai plus…

« **La Revue latine** », 25 octobre 1904, 3ème Année n° 10, p. 629–640
Variétés. Chopin et la légende.

On m'excusera (pour une fois) de ne pas comparer Chopin à Jérémie. […] Je n'ai voulu, ce qui a quelque chance de nouveauté, que présenter ici les déformations et caricatures qu'inflige une certaine célébrité à un artiste naturel et discret. Il me semble qu'à dégonfler seulement ces vessies multicolores, qui ne sont pas des lanternes, j'aurai aidé à discerner Chopin qu'elles offusquent et dissimulent. […]

Beaucoup d'honnêtes gens sont ainsi exaspérés contre ce musicien par la qualité de ses admiratrices et les intolérables grimaces de leur admiration. Par elles il est lamentable, par elles il est tortillé, par elles il est féminin jusqu'à devenir asexué.

Aucun artiste n'a été aussi frénétiquement adopté par les filles de M. Prud-homme, de M. Poirier et de M. Homais. La popularité actuelle de Chopin est hors de toute comparaison ; Schumann se défend et se réserve encore un peu. Grieg n'est pas encore banal, il est vivant. Mais il n'est concert de piano, il n'est audition intime, où Chopin ne figure ; récemment, une Américaine le mimait et le dansait devant un public fashionable sur une de nos grandes scènes. Ce qu'il y a de plus contestable dans quelques-unes de ses dernières inspirations sert tous les ans de prétexte à des acrobaties au concours final du Conservatoire. [...] Il n'est personne qui ne soit ex-posé, après un dîner en ville, pour peu qu'il y ait un ou une pianiste parmi les convi-ves, à entendre non pas massacrer, mais distiller, perler, effilocher un nocturne, une mazurka ou une polonaise de Chopin [...]. [**Gustave Amiot**]

« Le Courrier musical », n° spécial *Chopin*, 1ᵉʳ janvier 1910, 13ᵉᵐᵉ Année, n° 1, p. 23
L'Âme de Chopin.

[...] Chopin a été longtemps prisonnier d'une réputation injustifiée de composi-teur décadent, efféminé et il a passé aux yeux de bien des générations pour le chantre exclusif des langueurs maladives et des morbidesses romantiques. Il a été accaparé par un public spécial de bas-bleus et de poitrinaires contre lequel il est bienséant de le défendre.

Non, Chopin n'est pas un névrosé ni un malade ; c'est un tendre, mais pas un faible ; un raffiné, mais pas un mièvre ; un complexe, mais pas un alambiqué : c'est un éloquent, ce n'est pas un rhéteur ; et ses pages les plus dolentes gardent encore une distinction qui les préserve de la décadence. Il y a toujours au fond de sa musique, une souvenance plus ou moins vive de sa bonne humeur première et il est beaucoup plus en force qu'en plainte, en rythme qu'en abandon. On a cru l'honorer en affadis-sant ce que telles de ses inspirations pouvaient contenir déjà d'un peu bizarre ; en fai-sant un sort à chaque note ; en soupirant de pâmoison à ses moindres modulations ; et en associant aux émotions qu'il faisait naître le souvenir des peintres déliquescents et des écrivains faisandés de littérature [...].

Certaines interprétations l'ont mutilé, défiguré, ont supprimé toute clarté, toute simplicité, toute énergie, toute pureté, toute mesure. Chopin avait le jeu tendre et enveloppant, cela est certain ; et il jouait de préférence devant les dames. [...] Mais il jouait sain, fervent, passionné. Berlioz lui reprochait son trop d'indépendance rythmique ; cela ne revenait pas à dire qu'il fût mou ; et c'est plutôt par un sens trop exalté de l'accentuation de la phrase qu'il finissait par en altérer le rythme qui devenait ainsi plus sensible, moins métronomique, plus profondément musical.

Il faut donc se garder de considérer Chopin comme un artiste imbu de maniérisme et de préciosité ; mais il importe au contraire d'admirer en lui un musicien de fière race qui a su interpréter avec une noblesse rare, ou séduisante ou robuste, les plus profondes passions et les plus doux sentiments de l'âme humaine. [**Raoul Pugno**]

« Le Courrier musical », n° spécial *Chopin,* 1er janvier 1910, 13ème Année, n° 1, p. 36–37
Lettres sur Chopin.

[...] Ne pas aimer Chopin ! Autant dire ne pas aimer la musique ; tout au moins, à l'envers de ce que s'imagine ce groupe austère – c'est l'aimer superficiellement ; c'est aussi faire preuve de quelque rudesse : car Chopin est profond et raffiné [...].

Et quelle richesse d'invention, quelle étonnante diversité d'idées ; que toutes ses audaces (tout est nouveau, « avancé » dans Chopin) paraissent naturellement, sincèrement senties ! Et quelle puissance aussi ! Car son inspiration dont on a trop indiqué le côté féminin, atteint [...] une puissance, une grandeur qui soutiennent dans notre art très peu de comparaisons. Évitons donc, de peur de nous amoindrir nous-mêmes, de parler légèrement de Chopin. [...] Honorons aussi en lui notre race, car, on l'oublie trop souvent, son père était français, né à Nancy. Et ce n'est pas seulement le hasard de sa vie française qui lui inspira cette beauté de forme, cette concision de pensée, cette mesure, le dessin si parfait de ce modèle d'écriture musicale ; c'est le cerveau latin qui s'alliait à l'âme slave pour, harmonieusement, en préciser le rêve. [**Édouard Risler**]

3 Notes discordantes

« **Revue des deux mondes** », 1er décembre 1842, vol. 32, p. 860
Revue musicale.

[...] Que Mme Pauline Viardot n'interroge-t-elle les grands modèles qui [...] vaudraient mieux pour elle que toutes ces inspirations plus ou moins psychologiques puisées dans les romans du jour, et qui finiraient par devenir aussi insaisissables que le sont au piano les vaporeuses nuances du jeu microscopique de M. Chopin. [**H. W. = Henri Blaze de Bury**]

« **La France musicale** », 23 février 1851, 15ème Année, n° 8, p. 58
Franz Liszt, *Chopin.*

[...] Dans la *Polonaise-fantaisie*, qui appartient déjà à la dernière période des œuvres de Chopin, à celles qui sont surplombées d'une anxiété fiévreuse, on ne trouve aucune trace de tableaux hardis et lumineux ; [...] Une élégiaque tristesse y prédomine, entrecoupée par des mouvements effarés, de mélancoliques sourires, des soubresauts inopinés, des repos pleins de tressaillements. [...] Peintures peu favorables à l'art, comme celles de tous les moments extrêmes [...] où les nerfs, en cessant d'être des organes de la volonté, réduisent l'homme à ne plus devenir que la proie passive de la douleur ! Aspects déplorables que l'artiste n'a avantage d'admettre dans son domaine qu'avec une extrême circonspection !

Anaïs Lebrun de Bassanville, *Les Salons d'autrefois*, 3ème série, Paris :
J. Victorion 18[65], p. 283

[Émile] Prudent était moins élogieux pour les trois plus grands pianistes de l'école moderne qu'on ne le fut pour lui, il disait de Chopin [...] : « Chopin est un illuminé, un Swedenborg musical, une organisation élégiaque qui mène beaucoup trop souvent sa rêverie en partie de plaisir dans un cimetière. »

« **Le Figaro** », *Supplément littéraire du dimanche*, 28 avril 1888, 14° Année, n° 17, p. 67
L'ennui dans la musique. I - Les morts.

[...] Voici un musicien, non plus du troisième mais au moins du second, quelques hommes et toutes les dames disent même de premier ordre : Chopin. Il a été le musicien par excellence du piano ; c'est là son originalité, et son infériorité. On n'écrit pas impunément pour un instrument, surtout pour un instrument comme le piano, sans tomber dans la musique de mécanisme et d'exécution. Chopin est un rêveur mélancolique, un merveilleux improvisateur, le plus sentimental des compositeurs Il a donné de la poésie aux sèches sonorités du clavier ; du moelleux à la phrase classique. Il a trouvé quelques mélodies admirables, il en a trouvé beaucoup de charmantes. Écoutez pourtant certaines de ses œuvres, notamment le concerto en *mi* mineur, si finement joué le Vendredi Saint par M. Planté : c'est à pleurer d'ennui. Ne parlons pas de l'orchestre, avec lequel Chopin n'a jamais compté. Mais le piano lui-même ! Pour une phrase élégante ou touchante, et autour de cette phrase même, quel déluge de notes, quel bavardage inutile, quel enguirlandement insupportable de toute mélodie avec des trilles, des *gruppetti*, des gammes, des ornements de toute espèce. Chopin ne peut rien dire comme tout le monde. Il fait précéder ou suivre chaque phrase, chaque note d'une fanfreluche ou d'une fioriture ; sa musique bronche et bégaye à chaque mesure. Ce Slave élégiaque aurait mis des pompons à la Vénus de Milo. [**Camille Bellaigue**]

« **La Revue musicale** », 15 février 1908, 7ème Année, n° 4, p. 97–100

[...] Je me rappelle que, dans mon enfance (il y a une trentaine d'années !), le nom de Chopin était prononcé comme une sorte de nom cabalistique. Chopin, c'était le compositeur rare, sélect, en dehors de ceux dont les œuvres sont accessibles aux intelligences et aux talents moyens ; le premier venu ne pouvait pas comprendre toute la poésie de Chopin ; il fallait être initié. Chopin était réservé aux connaisseurs et aux grands virtuoses. Dire qu'on jouait du Chopin, surtout en suivant « la tradition », c'était se décerner une sorte de brevet de distinction, et se classer à part, bien au-dessus du vulgaire.

Aujourd'hui, je trouve que cette musique (sauf une dizaine d'œuvres peut-être sur quatre-vingts environ) a singulièrement vieilli,- beaucoup plus vieilli que celle de Beethoven (qui elle-même, çà et là, ne laisse pas d'avoir des rides). Oui, pour être sincère avec moi-même, je suis obligé de dire que plusieurs de ces prouesses pianistiques, jugées autrefois de qualité si brillamment originales et romantiques, me paraissent franchement *communes*, précisément dépourvues de distinction.

[...] Chez ce compositeur « nerveux et enfiévré », quelle carrure et quelle santé ! quelles couleurs rubicondes et quel geste gaillard de villageois en goguette ! Non, tout cela ne vient pas de l'âme ; je ne sens pas, comme dit Schumann, l' « intériorité ». C'est du fracas, de la bouffissure, de la poudre aux yeux, de l'expansion facile, du n'importe quoi de premier jet, tout ce qu'on voudra d'extérieur et de gros qui tire l'œil et l'oreille, – sauf le langage secret du cœur ou le rêve de musicien-poète qui se fait mélodie et rythme. [...]

[...] Où est né Chopin ? est-ce en Pologne ou à Marseille ? Était-il plutôt de *Toulouse même* ?... Pauvre Chopin devant qui s'est pâmée toute une génération !

Comme nous sommes loin de lui ! L'expérience nous a rendus difficiles, et nos exigences ne me paraissent pas illégitimes [...].

Ce qu'il y a de fâcheux dans la musique de Chopin (et particulièrement dans le recueil des 43 Mazurkas, dont plusieurs sont fort belles), c'est, avec un certain goût du poncif, l'abus des papillotes et des mouches, des fausses gentillesses pianistiques et des notes inutiles. Il fait un terrible abus des effets de manchettes. [**Jules Combarieu**]

C – L'accueil de l'Histoire
1 Les premières monographies de référence

Élie Poirée, *Chopin*, Paris : Laurens 1907

Cette extraordinaire popularité, que pourrait justifier, sans l'expliquer complètement, la valeur de l'artiste que fut Chopin et de son œuvre, provient de ce que Chopin, comme pianiste, réalisa un type jusqu'ici unique et que, compositeur, il créa une forme typique très reconnaissable et très frappante. Il y a une mélodie à la Chopin comme il y a des figures à la Raphaël, à la Rubens, à la Rembrandt. Mais cette phrase mélodique qui incarne, pour le public, le génie d'un artiste dont la réputation de son vivant alla peut-être plus au virtuose qu'au compositeur, cette phrase n'est pas seulement un document intéressant pour l'histoire de l'évolution musicale, elle fait partie d'une œuvre encore très vivante, elle inaugure une écriture, une technique qui représentent les tendances et les procédés de l'art moderne. On aime ou on n'aime pas la musique de Chopin, mais on ne peut rester indifférent devant une telle éclosion d'art, si peu préparée par le passé, apparaissant tout d'un coup et spontanément. [p. 5–6]

[...] Dans son ensemble l'œuvre du compositeur semble devoir être regardée comme une œuvre de transition. Ses types mélodiques ont l'eurythmie de l'ancienne école, ils conservent le balancement régulier et continu, les courbes et les sinuosités gracieuses de la danse, – dont les classiques se sont inspirés si abondamment dans la symphonie ; mais ils offrent aussi des éléments nouveaux et féconds, ils sont exprimés en une belle langue, riche, variée, infiniment et délicatement nuancée. L'œuvre de Chopin marque donc une étape dans l'histoire de la musique pure qui, après lui, cherchera une expression de plus en plus précise, ira de plus en plus vers le théâtre par des routes diverses, par la suite d'orchestre, le poème symphonique, la musique à programme, et qui, de même que la poésie, évoluera à son tour vers l'épopée, vers le symbolisme dont Wagner réalisera le type avec une magnificence incomparable [...]. [p. 12]

Chopin, comme Wagner, usa fréquemment [...] de l'écriture chromatique. Le chromatisme chez Wagner, représente presque toujours la difficulté de l'effort, l'arrêt devant l'obstacle à vaincre et qui reste insurmontable, il est un élément dramatique, comme dans *Tristan* ; l'écriture chromatique, dans la musique de Chopin, a surtout un but pianistique, c'est le conduit qui relie deux groupes mélodiques, un trait de virtuosité pure, le moyen de donner à une mélodie plus d'élan, plus de légèreté et de mobilité. C'est aussi un artifice élégant, un geste se faisant plus raffiné, saisi dans de plus petites nuances ; ce pourra être également l'écho d'une plainte douce et résignée, d'un accent douloureux.

Nous sommes donc en présence de conceptions d'art distinctes, si elles ne sont pas opposées ; alors que la conception wagnérienne est d'un réalisme poétique très saisissant, celle de Chopin se plaît au vague, elle flotte entre le rêve et la passion, elle va volontiers vers les souvenirs du passé un instant ranimés pour retomber bientôt dans le néant décevant des choses. Elle associera donc aux formes rêveuses de l'Allemagne les formes passionnées de l'Italie, où l'effort momentané donne l'illusion de la force, de l'acte volontaire. Extrêmement féminine, elle ne dédaigne pas les supercheries de la femme, elle en a les petites roueries innocentes. Quand la mélodie de Chopin pleure, quand elle se lamente, sa tristesse, pareille à celle d'une jeune veuve, ne lui fait pas oublier qu'elle est jolie. Les couleurs sombres lui siéent infiniment et son deuil aime à s'entourer de broderies, de dentelles et de bijoux. Nous aimons mieux la douleur plus simple, plus crue, moins habillée ou moins parée. Chopin lui-même nous donnera cette impression dans certaines parties de son œuvre dans les études, les scherzos, dans les ébauches, quand il ne *fignole* pas le morceau, quand il n'écrit pas pour le public distingué, pour les belles dames qui sont son auditoire préféré, en un mot, pour le dire crûment, quand il n'a pas mis ses gants blancs et sa cravate de cérémonie. En ces esquisses d'une valeur plus haute que les longs morceaux, Chopin fait véritablement du grand art, il se rapproche des maîtres, si même il ne les égale pas [...]. [p. 76–77]

Par la connaissance parfaite qu'il a des ressources harmoniques, par sa compréhension instinctive des éléments dissonants et de leur rôle, Chopin inaugura un nouveau système d'écriture. Wagner viendra bientôt, qui donnera à ce système toute son ampleur, en faisant de ces combinaisons dissonantes le principe courant du discours musical, où la mobilité est ainsi plus accentuée, la sonorité plus riche, plus pleine, et plus égale. Chopin, en cela, est donc un précurseur, – si l'on en doutait, il suffirait de lire ce qui se jouait et se publiait de son temps. Ces nouveautés, ces licences contre la règle ne furent pas admises du premier coup. [...] Plus tard aussi presque tous les musiciens s'engageront dans la voie que le maître a ouverte, et qui sera continuée, agrandie. Mais où personne ne l'a dépassé, là où il semble inimitable, c'est dans les adaptations qu'il a réalisées de cette écriture pour le piano [...]. [p. 80–83]

Les contemporains de Chopin, excepté sans doute en Allemagne, ignorèrent presque complètement cette belle composition [la *Sonate* en *si* bémol mineur], ils ne connurent pas beaucoup mieux les Études, les Préludes et les Scherzos. Ces œuvres maîtresses n'ont été vraiment mises en lumière que de nos jours, faisant apparaître tout le génie de l'artiste, révélant au grand public un maître insoupçonné, et Chopin est considéré aujourd'hui, à juste titre, comme le véritable fondateur de la musique de piano. Sans lui il manquerait non seulement à l'histoire générale de l'art musical un chapitre important, mais l'histoire du piano n'existerait pas, et, à supposer l'œuvre entière de Chopin anéantie, on peut affirmer, même Schumann subsistant, qu'il serait presque impossible de comprendre comment la musique de piano a passé sans transition des formes classiques anciennes aux formes actuelles. [p. 119]

Édouard Ganche, *Frédéric Chopin. Sa vie et ses œuvres* (1913), Paris : Le Mercure de France 1919, p. 313–315

La musique de Chopin est une explosion de sensibilité humaine ; elle est l'expression absolue de son émotivité et de ses idées. Elle est inspirée par deux éléments fondamentaux : l'amour et le patriotisme. Chopin est un patriote ardent et un poète hypersensible. Il introduit dans son œuvre tout ce qui peut exalter sa patrie. Il la chante dans ses *Scherzos* et ses *Ballades*, il la défend par le rythme guerrier de ses *Polonaises*, il la fait aimer par les thèmes populaires utilisés dans ses *Mazurkas*. Sa poésie, sa sensibilité de slave sont répandues sur tout son œuvre.

Des sujets d'inspiration aussi vastes ont permis à Chopin de donner à ses compositions des aspects infiniment variés. S'il est un élégiaque, il est aussi un lyrique et son œuvre garde un parfait équilibre de vitalité et de force. Dans ses premières œuvres le virtuose transparaît, mais peu à peu il s'efface devant le poète et le vrai musicien. Il est classique d'idées et romantique d'inspirations ; il subit l'influence du romantisme sans se soumettre à ses règles ; il garde, en réalité, une parfaite indépendance.

Son merveilleux instinct d'harmoniste le jette sur une voie nouvelle. Il inaugure un nouveau système d'écriture par l'utilisation des éléments dissonants et prépare ainsi les procédés de l'école moderne. Il cherche les combinaisons d'accords les plus rares, il évite les alternances vulgaires, il emploie l'écriture chromatique pour relier les groupes mélodiques, ou, par élégance, et il adapte cette écriture au piano avec un art inimitable.

Nouvelle aussi est la mélodie de Chopin ; elle possède une grâce et une délicatesse dont les classiques ont ignoré l'expression. La phrase mélodique de Chopin est longue, sinueuse, parfois ornée de gruppetti, coupée de fioritures ou de traits rapides. [...] Liszt employa dans ses œuvres les mêmes procédés que Chopin, mais postérieurement, comme la date des compositions des deux artistes le prouve. Chopin fut donc bien le novateur et Liszt l'imitateur.

2 Du côté des encyclopédies

Dictionnaire de la conversation et de la lecture, éd. William Duckett, Paris : Firmin Didot 1853–1860, vol. 5, p. 530

[...] Chopin était un des trois ou quatre musiciens de notre siècle qui avaient véritablement ce qu'on appelle *un style à eux*. Jamais artiste n'a réuni à un aussi haut degré de ses inspirations le culte des traditions classiques aux innovations les plus hardies. Quels que soient les progrès que le piano ait fait en dernier lieu entre les mains de Listz [sic], de Thalberg, de Doehler, jamais on ne ravira à F. Chopin la place à part qu'il occupe dans l'art. C'est un de ces génies tellement individuels qu'ils se dérobent à l'imitation.

François-Joseph Fétis, *Biographie universelle des musiciens* Paris : Firmin-Didot, 1866–1868, vol. 2, p. 284–285

[...] Chopin était âgé de vingt-deux ans lorsqu'il se fit entendre à Paris pour la première fois chez Pleyel, devant une réunion d'artistes : il y produisit une vive sensation en jouant son premier concerto et quelques-uns de ses premières pièces détachées. L'opinion de cet auditoire d'élite assigna tout d'abord à son talent la place exceptionnelle qu'il occupa jusqu'à son dernier jour. Toutefois quelques critiques se mêlaient aux éloges. Kalkbrenner trouvait mille incorrections dans le doigter de Chopin : il est vrai que le pianiste polonais avait un système singulier d'enjambement du troisième doigt de chaque main, par lequel il suppléait souvent au passage du pouce. Un tel système était aux yeux du classique disciple de Clementi l'abomination de la désolation. Field, qui entendit Chopin vers le même temps, le jugea aussi peu favorablement, et déclara que c'était *un talent de chambre de malade*. [...] Son patriotisme qui le rapprochait incessamment de ses compatriotes, exerça aussi une puissante influence sur son talent : la direction que prit son génie dans ses ouvrages en fut évidemment le résultat. Sans cesse il était ramené comme à son insu aux airs de danses caractéristiques de son pays et en faisait le sujet des œuvres dans lesquelles l'originalité de son talent se manifeste de la manière la plus remarquable. On a de lui deux concertos et d'autres pièces avec orchestre, un trio pour piano, violon et violoncelle, de grandes études et des sonates où l'on remarque un talent distingué ; mais son génie ne déploya toute son originalité que dans ses polonaises, mazoureks, nocturnes, ballades et autres pièces de peu d'étendue. Il est grand dans les petites choses ; mais les larges proportions ne vont pas à sa frêle organisation. [...]

Dès son arrivée à Paris, Chopin s'était livré à l'enseignement : la distinction remarquable de sa personne, non moins que la supériorité de son talent, le faisait rechercher comme professeur par les femmes des plus hautes classes de la société. Il forma parmi elles beaucoup de bons élèves qui imitaient son style et sa manière : la plupart ne jouaient que sa musique, pour laquelle il y a eu dans certains salons une prédilection qui allait jusqu'au fanatisme. Loin d'éprouver le dégoût qu'ont eu beaucoup d'artistes célèbres pour les leçons, Chopin semblait s'y plaire lorsqu'il rencontrait dans un élève le sentiment uni à l'intelligence. [...] Près de ses élèves, son penchant à la rêverie mélancolique disparaissait entièrement, du moins en apparence. La sérénité se peignait sur ses traits : il était souriant comme si l'ennui et la fatigue se fussent transformés en plaisirs [...].

Le génie de Chopin était élégiaque. Parfois ses compositions ont le style élégant et gracieux ; mais plus souvent le sombre, le mélancolique, le fantasque y dominent. Il eut aussi çà et là de l'énergie dans sa musique : mais elle sembla toujours l'épuiser, et sa nature délicate le ramena incessamment au petit cadre fait pour elle. C'est là surtout qu'il a le mérite suprême de l'originalité. Sa mélodie a des allures qui ne sont celles d'aucun autre compositeur ; elle n'est pas exempte d'affectation, mais elle est toujours distinguée. Il n'est pas rare de rencontrer dans son harmonie des successions d'accords qui trahissent le sentiment tonal ; mais parfois il est assez heureux pour que l'inattendu ne soit pas sans charme. En somme Chopin fut un artiste de grande valeur : si l'on a exagéré le mérite de ses œuvres, et si la mode a exercé son empire dans leur succès, il n'en est pas moins vrai que ces œuvres occupent dans l'art une place qu'aucun autre compositeur n'avait prise, et où il n'aura pas de successeur.

Pierre Larousse, *Grand dictionnaire universel du XIXe siècle*, Paris 1869, vol. 4, p. 185–186

Chopin (Frédéric-François), célèbre pianiste et compositeur, né à Żelazowa-Wola, près de Varsovie, le 8 février 1810, mort à Paris le 17 octobre 1849. Sa famille, d'origine française, jouissait d'une médiocre fortune ; de là peut-être, certains froissements dans l'organisation nerveuse et la vive sensibilité de l'enfant qui devaient plus tard se refléter dans ses œuvres, empreintes généralement d'une profonde mélancolie. La constitution de Chopin était frêle et maladive. Son enfance fut quasi végétative ; il vivait en dedans, et rien, dans les premières années de son existence, ne faisait pressentir le futur génie. A l'âge de neuf ans, il commença l'étude du piano sous la direction de Zywny, musicien d'origine bohême, fervent sectateur de Bach. Les leçons durèrent sept années. Pendant ce temps, le prince Antoine Radziwill, dilettante distingué, frappé de l'exécution délicate et pleine de sentiment de Chopin, se chargea généreusement de faire donner au jeune virtuose une éducation complète que rendait impossible la position précaire de sa famille. Il fit entrer Chopin dans un des meilleurs collèges de Varsovie et paya sa pension jusqu'à l'achèvement de ses études. Ses progrès en musique furent si rapides qu'au bout d'une année il paraissait en public et interprétait avec succès un concerto de Girowetz. Le jeune pianiste prenait en même temps des leçons de composition sous Joseph Elsner. Peu de mois avant la révolution de 1830, Chopin dont le talent était déjà apprécié en Pologne et en Russie, quitta sa patrie avec le dessein d'entreprendre des excursions à l'étranger. [...] Une fois dans la capitale française, Chopin oublia Londres et nous resta. Le jeune virtuose, avec sa physionomie languissante d'enfant du Nord, sa nature douce et fine, mais surtout par la nouveauté de ses compositions et son jeu admirable, produisit une vive sensation. C'est en 1832 que Chopin se fit entendre pour la première fois en public à Paris, dans la salle Pleyel, devant une imposante réunion d'artistes. Cet auditoire d'élite lui assigna immédiatement la place tout à fait à part qu'il devait occuper jusqu'à son dernier jour. Les plus grandes familles polonaises alors en résidence à Paris s'empressèrent de patronner leur jeune et brillant compatriote, et, dans les premières années de son séjour à Paris, Chopin vécut dans les salons des princes [...], où se développaient, dans une atmosphère essentiellement aristocratique, la finesse et la grâce nerveuse de ses poésies musicales, fleurs de serre chaude, disait avec quelque raison un critique de l'époque. [...] Sa vie d'artiste se concentra presque tout entière dans le monde d'élite et dans l'intimité.

[...] Malgré notre profonde admiration, nous pourrions dire notre vénération pour le grand artiste que le monde a perdu, nous devons dire toute la vérité sur son caractère ; et les faits vrais que nous empruntons aux *Mémoires* de Mme Sand, quelque pénible qu'il soit pour nous de les révéler, aideront à la compréhension des côtés bizarres, tourmentés et pour ainsi dire *meurtris* de ses compositions. [...] Son esprit hautain méprisait les masses ; et c'était mal comme homme, mal comme artiste, mal surtout comme Polonais ; ajoutons à cela qu'un vieux levain d'amertume lui restait de la tentative infructueuse qu'il avait faite au théâtre des Italiens [...].

Ce grand artiste occupe dans l'art une place à part que nul n'a pu lui dérober ; tout son génie est individuel et inimitable. Outre les mazurkas, genre qu'il a popularisé en Occident, Chopin a composé deux concertos de piano, un grand nombre d'études, de nocturnes, etc. Quelque prodigieuse que fût l'exécution chez lui, c'est surtout par l'inspiration que son individualité se recommande. Quelle fantaisie et quelle grâce dans les mille improvisations échappées à sa plume ! Délicatesse et force, tout y est. Les motifs se déroulent comme à travers les mélancoliques vapeurs d'une nuit du nord ; les notes s'éparpillent en folles cascades, et, dans le charme où vous plonge cette musique, tout sentiment de la difficulté se perd. Tandis que le collier de perles s'égrène sur les touches d'ivoire, la mélodie vous emporte au pays slave et le cœur fait écho à ces voix profondes qui lui parlent si intimement d'amour et d'espérance, de patrie peut-être !

Ce qui frappe tout d'abord dans les compositions de Chopin, c'est l'accent natal, c'est cette espèce de nostalgie que semble produire chez certaines natures vibrantes le souffle de la muse du nord. Cet accent à part, on le trouve surtout dans ses mazurkas, dans ses nocturnes, dans ses ballades. [...] Toutes les qualités qui constituent l'originalité créatrice se trouvent à l'envi chez Chopin. Et qu'on ne croie pas qu'il n'existe dans son œuvre que des motifs vaporeux, que des mélodies aériennes, que la grâce rêveuse. Son inspiration savait trouver aussi des accents pleins de force, de puissance et d'éclat [...].

La Grande encyclopédie, éd. MM. Berthelot, Derenbourg, Dreyfus, Paris : H Lamirault 1885–1902, p. 353
Allemagne.

[...] A côté de lui [Schubert], moins varié peut-être, mais non moins poète, Chopin, français par son père, slave par sa mère, Allemand par son éducation musicale et assez italien par goût, enrichit la musique de mélodies nouvelles, d'harmonies délicates et tendres. Chopin est moins génial que les grands maîtres dont nous avons parlé ; mais il est de leur famille, il est avec eux, plus qu'eux peut-être, le chantre délicat de la mélancolie et de la douleur. Il annonce en quelque sorte un maître moderne par excellence, Schumann, dont le génie exerce en ce moment sur l'Allemagne une influence prépondérante.

Albert Lavignac, *La Musique et les musiciens*, Paris : Delagrave 1898, p. 490

Chopin : Grand virtuose et célèbre compositeur ; n'a écrit que pour le piano, sauf un *Trio* et une Polonaise pour piano et violoncelle, dont la partie de violoncelle fut arrangée par Franchomme.

Ses œuvres possèdent un charme mélancolique et une exquise poésie qu'on chercherait vainement chez tout autre auteur. [...] Bien que la France fût sa patrie d'adoption, bien que sa famille fût d'origine française, je n'hésite pas à le classer, en raison de ses affinités, dans l'école romantique allemande.

3 Présence de Chopin dans la littérature

Charles Baudelaire, *L'œuvre et la vie de Delacroix*, **dans :** *Œuvres complètes,* Paris : Gallimard – Bibliothèque de la Pléiade 1976, vol. 2, p. 761

[...] Dans sa délicieuse étude sur Chopin, Liszt met Delacroix au nombre des plus assidus visiteurs du musicien-poète, et dit qu'il aimait à tomber en profonde rêverie aux sons de cette musique légère et passionnée qui ressemble à un brillant oiseau voltigeant sur les horreurs d'un gouffre.

André Gide, *Journal. Feuillets 1913*, Paris : Gallimard – Bibliothèque de la Pléiade 1955, p. 395

Chopin.
Pour Beethoven, assurément la *quantité* de son importe ; pour Chopin seulement la qualité (pianissimo dans la *Barcarolle*).
Pas de diamant plus limpide.
Pas de perle de plus belle eau.

André Gide, *Si le grain ne meurt*, Paris : Gallimard – Bibliothèque de la Pléiade 1955, p. 465

En 1883, Rubinstein vint donner une suite de concerts, à la salle Érard. [...] Il y en eut un consacré à Chopin auquel j'aurais bien voulu également assister, mais ma mère tenait la musique de Chopin pour « malsaine » et refusa de m'y mener.

Robert de Montesquiou, *Roseaux pensants*, Paris : Fasquelle 1897, p. 259–260

J'ai tenté dans un poème de mes *Chauves-souris*, une transposition d'un peu de l'art de Chopin, le plus absolu des maîtres du piano, le spécialiste ravissant, dont l'âme toute de musique s'est entière, et pour toujours infiltrée en cet instrument qui la distille à jamais en sonorités cristallines. Dieu des jeunes hommes et des femmes, Chopin nous apparaît un peu tyrannisé par celles-ci. La légende et la peinture nous transmettent sur ses derniers moments des récits toujours excessifs, de comtesses et de princesses usurpant l'heure du prêtre à lui chanter préventivement ses œuvres posthumes. Et c'est un type qui méritera d'être buriné par le roman contemporain, que ces dernières élèves de Chopin qu'on se montre dans les concerts, celles qui détiennent la tradition directe du véritable trait, la fioriture authentique du maître.

Je pense parfois avec admiration et non sans terreur aux chiffres que fournirait en une année et en un siècle, un compteur nombrant, jour à jour, le jeu de telle mazurka, ou de certaines des études du troublant Slave. Et pourtant le rabâchage, bien au-delà de la satiété, n'a pu dévelouter ces œuvres de leur prestigieux mystère [...].

Marcel Proust, *Les Plaisirs et les jours. Portraits de musiciens* (1896), Paris : Gallimard – Le Livre de poche 1971, p. 156

Chopin
Chopin, mer de soupirs, de larmes, de sanglots
Q'un vol de papillons sans se poser traverse
Jouant sur la tristesse ou dansant sur les flots.
Rêve, aime, souffre, crie, apaise, charme ou berce,
Toujours tu fais courir entre chaque douleur
L'oubli vertigineux et doux de ton caprice
Comme les papillons volent de fleur en fleur ;
De ton chagrin alors ta joie est la complice :

L'ardeur du tourbillon accroît la soif des pleurs.
De la lune et des eaux pâle et doux camarade,
Prince du désespoir ou grand seigneur trahi,
Tu t'exaltes encore, plus beau d'être pâli,
Du soleil inondant ta chambre de malade
Qui pleure à lui sourire et souffre de le voir…
Sourire du regret et larmes de l'Espoir !

Marcel Proust, *Contre Sainte-Beuve* (1908–1909), Paris : Gallimard – Bibliothèque de la Pléiade 1971, p. 281

Chopin, ce grand artiste maladif, sensible, égoïste et dandy qui déploie pendant un instant doucement dans sa musique les aspects successifs et contrastés d'une disposition intime qui change sans cesse et n'est pendant plus d'un moment doucement progressive sans que vienne l'arrêter, se heurtant à elle et s'y juxtaposant, une toute différente, mais toujours avec un accent intime maladif, et replié sur soi-même dans ses frénésies d'action, avec toujours de la sensibilité et jamais de cœur, souvent de furieux élans, jamais de détente, la douceur, la fusion à quelque chose d'autre que soi, qu'a Schumann.

Marcel Proust, *Du côté de chez Swann* (1913), 2ème partie : **Un Amour de Swann,** Paris : Gallimard – Bibliothèque de la Pléiade 1987, vol. 1, p. 326

Le pianiste ayant terminé le morceau de Liszt et ayant commencé un prélude de Chopin, Mme de Cambremer lança à Mme de Franquetot un sourire attendri de satisfaction compétente et d'allusion au passé. Elle avait appris dans sa jeunesse à caresser les phrases, au long col sinueux et démesuré, de Chopin, si libres, si flexibles, si tactiles, qui commencent par chercher et essayer leur place en dehors et bien loin de la direction de leur départ, bien loin du point où l'on avait pu espérer qu'atteindrait leur attouchement, et qui ne se jouent dans cet écart de fantaisie que pour revenir plus délibérément – d'un retour plus prémédité, avec plus de précision, comme sur un cristal qui résonnerait jusqu'à faire crier – vous frapper au cœur.

[…] Elle s'était grisée dans la solitude de son manoir, à ralentir, à précipiter la danse de tous ces couples imaginaires, à les égrener comme des fleurs, à quitter un moment le bal pour entendre le vent souffler dans les sapins, au bord du lac, et à y voir tout d'un coup s'avancer, plus différent de tout ce qu'on a jamais rêvé que ne sont les amants de la terre, un mince jeune homme à la voix un peu chantante, étrangère et fausse, en gants blancs. Mais aujourd'hui la beauté démodée de cette musique semblait défraîchie. Privée depuis quelques années de l'estime des connaisseurs, elle avait perdu son honneur et son charme, et ceux mêmes dont le goût est mauvais n'y trouvaient plus qu'un plaisir inavoué et médiocre. Mme de Cambremer jeta un regard furtif derrière elle. Elle savait que sa jeune bru [...] méprisait Chopin et souffrait quand elle en entendait jouer. Mais loin de la surveillance de cette wagnérienne, [...] Mme de Cambremer se laissait aller à des impressions délicieuses.

Romain Rolland, Cours sur la musique française, donné au Lycée Henri IV (1894)
Cité par : **Zbigniew Naliwajek, *Une leçon inédite de Roman Rolland sur la musique française*,** dans : ***La Fortune de Frédéric Chopin 2. Actes d'un colloque, Dijon, 18 mars 1994*,** éd. Joanna Żurowska, Hanna Wróblewska-Straus, Zbigniew Naliwajek, Varsovie : TiFC 1995, p. 56–57.

Une influence non moins grande, non seulement sur l'art français, mais sur la musique de toute l'Europe, appartient à un autre romantique, un simple pianiste, que je classe tout entier parmi les Français, bien qu'il ne le soit qu'à demi, *Chopin* [...].

Chopin a une supériorité marquée sur les 2 autres romantiques, c'est qu'il n'a aucune intention littéraire. C'est un parmi les plus musiciens parmi les compositeurs. Point de titre, de livret, de programme. Ce sont des scherzos, des ballades, des mazurkas, des sonates, – les titres les plus généraux : rien que du sentiment et de la musique. En cela il est très différent de Schumann, dont chaque petite œuvre s'appuie sur une idée intellectuelle précise.

On le rapproche avec raison de Musset. C'est la même sincérité, le même lyrisme pur ; et parfois aussi les mêmes défauts dans la déclamation, – quelque chose d'un peu trop en dehors, de trop complaisamment bercé dans leur tristesse. C'est aussi le même dandysme, le même amour des finesses, des élégances, des mondanités. Dans les pièces les plus belles, on trouve de petites mièvreries, que Chopin polit et repolit avec un soin infini ; tandis que les grandes phrases mélodiques lui viennent toutes seules.

Rêveur, malheureux, féminin, enfant gâté, charmant, nerveux et malade, – il l'est toujours dans tout ce qu'il écrit, et n'est que cela. – Aucun effort pour sortir de lui-même ; et avec raison, – il n'a que cela à dire, que ses heures de spleen, et ses instants d'humour ; c'est le plus subjectif des hommes.

Très romantique quant au fond, il est toujours extrêmement soucieux de la forme, mais avec quelque recherche voisine de mignardise. Il y a trop de gentillesse dans ses nocturnes dont le sentiment dominant est en général douloureux. Mais il faut faire la part du temps et des imitateurs médiocres, qui ont rendu banal et insignifiant, ce qui était alors original et plein de charme.

Ce qui maintenant nous plaît le plus en lui, ce sont les pièces à forme plus rigoureuse, comme les Préludes et les Études. Quelques-unes sont d'une simple et grande beauté. Je ne crains pas de dire que rien ne rappelle davantage Beethoven, Mozart et les grands classiques ; mais le souffle est trop court, et s'arrête en chemin. Le sentiment dominant est une mélancolie énervée, devenant tantôt violente et tantôt câline. Dans toutes ces œuvres, une grande richesse d'harmonies, dont beaucoup étaient absolument nouvelles alors, et furent une révélation. Très grande richesse et ingéniosité d'invention dans les dessins d'ornement et d'accompagnement. Il fut un des premiers à user de cette forme, depuis devenue commune : la main gauche dessinant les arabesques de dentelles uniformément légères, tandis que la main droite chante une plainte plus ou moins tragique. – Chopin avait une connaissance admirable des ressources du piano ; c'était le compositeur-pianiste par excellence ; c'était là quelquefois un écueil. Dans ses morceaux de concert, il sacrifie parfois à la virtuosité [...].

Chopin n'a jamais pu écrire pour l'orchestre, les cordes, ni le théâtre (une seule sonate piano et violoncelle), et les concertos sont très mal orchestrés et perdent à être entendus avec accompagnement.

Il eut une très forte influence sur la musique contemporaine, – influence dont vous vous faites difficilement une idée, – et non pas seulement sur les pianistes, mais sur tout l'art, qu'il avait enrichi d'harmonies nouvelles. Non seulement les romantiques comme Schumann en ont profité, mais Wagner lui-même, très fortement s'en est inspiré dans *Tristan et Ysolde* même.

4 La réception des compositeurs au tournant du XXe siècle

Claude Debussy, *La Revue blanche*, 1er juillet 1901
Reproduit dans : **Claude Debussy, *Monsieur Croche*, L'Imaginaire**, Paris : Gallimard 1971, p. 50–51

[...] Ne devrions-nous pas connaître la *Tétralogie* en entier, et depuis longtemps ? D'abord, ça nous en aurait débarrassé, et les pèlerins de Bayreuth ne nous agaceraient plus avec leurs récits… Jouer Les *Maîtres chanteurs*, c'est bien ; *Tristan et Isolde*, c'est mieux (l'âme charmante de Chopin y apparaît à des tournants de musique et en commande la passion).

[…] M. Pierre Lalo, dans un feuilleton du journal *Le Temps* exclusivement consacré à cette sonate [de Dukas], lui sacrifiait du même coup celles qu'écrivirent Schumann et Chopin. Certes la nervosité de Chopin sut mal se plier à la patience qu'exige la confection d'une sonate ; il en fit plutôt des « esquisses » très poussées. On peut tout de même affirmer qu'il inaugura une manière personnelle de traiter cette forme, sans parler de la délicieuse musicalité qu'il inventait à cette occasion. C'était un homme à idées généreuses, il en changeait souvent sans en exiger un placement à cent pour cent qui est la gloire la plus claire de quelques-uns de nos maîtres.

Claude Debussy, *Préface à : **Édition Durand des œuvres de Chopin*** (1915)

La musique de Chopin est une des plus belles que l'on ait jamais écrites. L'affirmer en 1915 n'est qu'un hommage facile par lequel on ne saurait se débarrasser de son importance et de l'influence qu'elle n'a cessé d'avoir sur la musique contemporaine. Par la nature de son génie, Chopin échappe au jeu des classifications : l'influence de Field, purement d'époque, fut légère ; son italianisme, son chromatisme, diversement critiqués, ne sont que les formes d'une sensibilité aiguë, qui lui resteront particulières.

Chopin était un délicieux conteur de légendes amoureuses ou guerrières, qui souvent s'échappe vers cette forêt de *Comme il vous plaira* où les fées sont seulement les maîtresses de l'esprit. Si la liberté de sa forme a pu tromper les commentateurs, comme l'abondance des traits, faire croire à un souci de virtuosité, il faut pourtant en comprendre la valeur de mise en place et la sûre ordonnance.

Alexandre Déodat de Séverac, *Les Préludes, les Études, les Ballades, la Berceuse.*
Souvenirs. **« Le Courrier musical », n° spécial** *Chopin,*
1er janvier 1910, 13ème Année, n° 1, p. 30–31

[…] Mais l'on dirait que Chopin (avec ce sens de la mesure qu'il tenait peut-être un peu de son origine à demi française), lorsqu'il abordait cette forme du Prélude, prenait plaisir à faire œuvre d'orfèvre, et à dire en peu de mots des choses parfaites. Ses dons de trouveur sont tellement grands qu'il n'essaye même pas de faire jaillir de cette merveilleuse matière tous les développements qu'elle contient en germes. Il invente, il invente toujours et c'est toujours expressif et passionné, et c'est toujours beau ! La variété de ces *Préludes* et des *Études* est surprenante. Ce sont des exemples de la beauté condensée si je puis dire [...].

Si l'on voulait analyser la beauté de ces pièces, il faudrait les citer toutes, l'une après l'autre, tellement chacune d'elles contient une valeur, une grâce, une grandeur ou un charme particuliers. Elles sont remplies de tant de nouveautés harmoniques et mélodiques qu'un examen minutieux ne pourrait intéresser que des techniciens.

Il vaut mieux les écouter et se livrer à elles ! Mais il n'est pas défendu de réfléchir ensuite et de constater que c'est de cette œuvre-là que date l'art de l'écriture actuelle du piano. Sans doute la jeune école française doit beaucoup à Liszt et à Franck, mais je crois que les *Études* sont le point de départ (déjà parfait) de ce que l'on essaie de faire aujourd'hui.

Vincent d'Indy, *Cours de composition musicale*, vol. 2, Paris : Durand 1909

[...] Avec l'œuvre de Chopin, nous voyons apparaître ce que l'on a appelé depuis le style pianistique, style dont les effets ont été et sont encore déplorables à bien des points de vue. Toutes les compositions de piano examinées par nous jusqu'ici demeuraient exclusivement *musicales*, qu'elles fussent signées Bach, Rameau, Haydn, Beethoven ou même Schubert, c'est-à-dire que le souci légitime de l'effet instrumental y était toujours subordonné aux droits et aux exigences de la musique. A l'époque romantique, cependant, s'introduisirent, dans la musique, deux erreurs fort graves, dont Chopin exagéra les effets en raison même de son insuffisance d'instruction véritablement musicale : les tonalités choisies pour les doigtés avantageux et non pour la logique architecturale de l'œuvre, les passages entiers écrits uniquement pour la virtuosité et n'ayant aucun rôle utile dans l'équilibre de la composition.

Paul Dukas, *Chronique musicale. A propos du monument de Chopin.*
« La Revue hebdomadaire », 1er décembre 1900, 10ème Année, vol. 1, p. 130–134

[...] Assez de temps s'est écoulé, à l'heure où nous sommes, pour qu'on puisse juger l'importance de l'œuvre de Chopin, non seulement au point de vue de la musique de piano, mais par rapport à l'évolution musicale de notre temps. Il nous est permis, maintenant, de mesurer l'influence qu'elle a exercée sur la production artistique de la seconde moitié du siècle : cette influence a été considérable. Elle s'est même manifestée, d'une manière très indirecte, il est vrai, sur des maîtres dont le génie semble tout opposé à celui de Chopin. Aussi me paraît-il intéressant, puisque l'actualité m'en fournit le prétexte, de tenter de déterminer la part qui doit revenir à l'auteur des *Nocturnes* et des *Ballades* dans l'histoire des transformations que le langage musical a subies depuis l'époque classique.

Ce qui distingue plus particulièrement la musique contemporaine de celle de la période précédente, c'est avant tout sa grande mobilité harmonique ; cette mobilité est inhérente au style des instruments à clavier, moins favorisés que les voix ou les instruments à cordes sous le rapport des modifications de sonorité qui tendent à varier l'expression. [...] Les qualités de sonorité des meilleures créations d'Érard ou de Pleyel réagirent sur la technique des œuvres de piano, de façon à développer à l'infini les possibilités de cet ordre, reléguant peu à peu au second plan la manière d'écrire en harmonies figurées qui convenait aux vénérables mécaniques dont le son avait une durée presque nulle. De la sorte Chopin vint à l'heure où ce souple organisme s'accommodait le mieux au langage harmonique tout neuf et d'une richesse merveilleuse que, dès l'abord, il lui fit parler. Sous ce rapport, on peut dire que sa musique apparaît comme la résonance même de l'âme de l'instrument et qu'elle n'eût pas été possible avec l'aide d'aucun autre. Mais il porta ce verbe à un si haut point d'éloquence et de perfection qu'il devait retentir plus loin que le cercle intime où Chopin le reléguait. Les groupements de notes imprévus, les transitions chromatiques notamment, et les rapprochements de tonalités hardis qu'il prodiguait sur le clavier comme en se jouant, devaient peu à peu pénétrer dans le domaine plus vaste de la musique d'orchestre et jusque dans le drame, comme nous l'allons voir. C'est cette liberté et cette complexité de la trame harmonique, jointes à une dextérité d'écriture tout à fait digne d'admiration, qui assurent à bien des pages de Chopin, basées sur des idées quelconques ou entachées de maniérisme italien, un intérêt durable. C'est par elles aussi qu'il participe au mouvement qui, par degrés, nous conduit à la complète émancipation des règles étroites de ce qu'on nommait autrefois la *basse fondamentale*.

Cependant il n'apparaît pas que l'importance des découvertes de Chopin dans cet ordre d'idées ait été saisie par les musiciens qui détenaient alors l'admiration publique. On rencontre bien parmi les contemporains immédiats du maître un nombre notable de fades imitateurs. On n'en trouve point qui, s'inspirant de ses principes de mobilité et de richesse harmoniques, aient su les appliquer à des créations douées d'une vie indépendante [...].

Quant aux musiciens qui vivaient aux côtés de Chopin, pas un ne semble avoir aperçu ce qu'il y avait de fécond dans sa manière de traiter l'harmonie. Tout au moins aucun d'eux n'a-t-il tenté de se l'approprier. Il est vrai que, pour la plupart, ils ne s'occupaient que de théâtre et que le théâtre n'avait alors avec la musique que des rapports assez relâchés. Ce n'est ni chez Meyerbeer ni chez Auber, ni comme on pense chez Adolphe Adam, qu'il faut chercher un écho des raffinements de Chopin. Berlioz, le seul compositeur d'alors qui ne fût pas un théâtral, était absolument réfractaire aux innovations du genre de celles qu'apportait Chopin. Il détestait l'harmonie chromatique, l'enharmonie et les modulations rapides [...].

Ce n'est guère qu'une dizaine d'années après la mort de Chopin que le principe dont la musique de piano lui avait fourni matière à de si riches applications commença à entrer dans la pratique de la musique d'orchestre ; cela, grâce à un admirateur et à un interprète dont l'énorme influence sur la musique de notre époque [...] n'a peut-être pas été encore comprise. J'ai nommé Franz Liszt. [...] C'est dans les œuvres d'orchestre de Liszt, notamment dans les premières, que le maniement de l'harmonie, tel que Chopin l'avait conçu, apparaît, pour la première fois, sous forme non d'une copie servile, mais comme principe d'un mode d'expression plus libre et d'une émancipation progressive des us et coutumes de la tradition d'école. [...] Il n'est pas sans intérêt de remarquer que l'influence de Chopin s'est étendue, par Liszt, jusqu'à Wagner lui-même. Certaines pages du second acte de *Tristan et Yseult* semblent directement issues des *Nocturnes* ou des *Préludes* de Chopin. De même on peut remarquer que les musiciens qui se rattachent le plus directement à Liszt, comme, par exemple, la majorité des compositeurs de la nouvelle école russe, sont aussi ceux dont la tournure d'idée et le sentiment harmonique rappellent davantage Chopin. Parmi les musiciens français, Emmanuel Chabrier est également de ceux-là.

Il est évident qu'un maître dont le rôle, quoique caché peut-être aux yeux de la foule, a été si considérable, doit être compté parmi les plus grands de son époque. [...] Il sied d'autant mieux de lui rendre hommage que cette manifestation prend, en raison des circonstances, le caractère d'un témoignage d'admiration rétrospectif. En effet, l'évolution musicale que Chopin annonçait est aujourd'hui accomplie et devait s'accomplir avec une rapidité semblable à celle qui l'a distinguée. Les ressources du chromatisme, le culte de la surprise harmonique perpétuelle sont choses éminemment fragiles ; il n'est guère de genre d'effet sur lequel la sensation se blase plus vite. Le plus récent mouvement de l'art contemporain accuse un retour à une conception musicale toute différente, et beaucoup plus ancienne que l'harmonie, qu'elle est appelée sans doute à émanciper complètement. L'art des Primitifs, celui de J.S. Bach, celui des dernières œuvres de Beethoven, l'art contrapontique, en un mot, semble appelé à fournir plus d'éléments à la période qui s'ouvre que cet art harmonique dont Chopin fut un des plus heureux adeptes. Néanmoins la gloire de Chopin n'est pas diminuée par l'achèvement de l'évolution dont son œuvre marque un des points d'accomplissement les plus importants.

« **Excelsior** », 12 juin 1922, p. 2
Gabriel Fauré Entretiens avec.

Ma première éducation musicale a été d'une rigueur excessive. Nous ne pouvions pas jouer du Schumann ou du Chopin. Niedermeyer estimait que ce n'était pas de la musique pour jeunes gens.

César Franck, *Mémoires d'Emmanuel Fauré*
Cité par : **Joël-Marie Fauquet, *César Franck*,** Paris : Fayard 1999, p. 688–689.

J'ai entendu plusieurs fois César Franck entre 1880 et 1890 jouer du piano [...] dans ces réceptions amicales du boulevard saint-Germain, il exécuta de Chopin *Préludes* et *Études*, notamment les Préludes 4, 9, 10, 13, 15, 17, 21, 25. (On retrouve un écho de cette dernière pièce, aux premières mesures du piano, dans le quintette.) Il traduisait avec une ampleur magnifique, due non seulement à l'ouverture de sa main, mais à la passion qu'il y mettait, les *Études* 9 et 11, où les écarts, formidables, étaient pour lui un jeu. Et il ne manquait jamais de dire qu'il aimait les ouvrages de Chopin « moins en pianiste qu'en musicien.

Maurice Ravel, *Impressions*. « **Le Courrier musical** », n° spécial *Chopin*,
1er janvier 1910, 13ème Année, n° 1, p. 32

« Rien de plus haïssable qu'une musique sans arrière pensée. » Frédéric Chopin.

La musique aux *musiciens*. Véritable interprétation de l'idée de Chopin. Pas aux professionnels, diable ! *Musicien* : créateur ou dilettante ; être sensible au rythme, à la mélodie, à l'harmonie, à l'atmosphère qui créent les sons. Frissonner à l'enchaînement de deux accords, comme au rapport de deux couleurs. La matière : cela importe d'abord, dans tous les arts. Le reste en découle.

Des exemples : la danse avant lui : grâce, gaîté, un peu de sentiment parfois. Tout cela un peu en dehors. Même les *Laendler* de Schubert, pourtant délicieuses de musique.

L'apport est flagrant dans les *Polonaises* ; avant lui : marche de fête, solennelle, brillante, toute extérieure. Voir Weber, Moniuszko, etc. De Chopin, une seule (*la* maj. Op. 40) dans ce style traditionnel. Mais combien supérieure, par l'inspiration, la richesse harmonique, à toutes celles de ses contemporains. Déjà, la *Grande Polonaise en ré* bémol est d'une autre portée, avec sa véhémence héroïque, et la chevauchée splendide du milieu. Souvent, il introduit dans ces danses un élément douloureux, poignant, jusqu'alors inconnu (*ut* mineur. op. 26).

Parfois, ce sentiment tragique s'élève jusqu'au sublime (*Polonaise-Fantaisie la* bémol, op. 61). A tel point qu'on a pu y découvrir toute une épopée. La sincérité des impressions, douleur ou héroïsme, évite l'emphase… [...].

Chopin ne se satisfait pas de bouleverser la technique pianistique. Les *traits* sont inspirés. A travers ces successions brillantes, d'adorables, de profondes harmonies se perçoivent. Toujours l'arrière-pensée qui se traduit souvent par un poème intense de désespoir.

La matière est encore plus condensée dans les Nocturnes. La sensibilité de l'auditeur est au point ; souvent satisfaite… Tant mieux : que faire entendre après cela ? Indication pour un artiste de génie : pièces à exécuter après les œuvres de Chopin. Reproche fréquent : Chopin n'a pas évolué. Soit. Sinon évolution, il y a chez lui un épanouissement splendide : *Polonaise-Fantaisie*, *Prélude posthume* (op. 46), *Barcarolle* (op. 60).

La *Barcarolle* synthétise l'art expressif et somptueux de ce grand slave, italien d'éducation. Cette charmante école latine, joyeusement vivante, à peine mélancolique, sensuelle, mais d'une lamentable facilité, abandonne volontiers, sinon l'âme, à l'instar de Molina, du moins l'inspiration, dans ses pires lieux, pour rejoindre plus vite la divinité. Chopin a réalisé tout ce que ses maîtres, par négligence, n'exprimèrent qu'imparfaitement

Dans la *Barcarolle*, ce thème en tierces, souple et délicat est constamment vêtu d'harmonies éblouissantes. La ligne mélodique est continue. Un moment, une mélopée s'échappe, reste suspendue, et retombe mollement attirée par des accords magiques. L'intensité augmente. Un nouveau thème éclate, d'un lyrisme magnifique, tout italien. Tout s'apaise. Du grave s'élève un trait rapide, frissonnant, qui plane sur des harmonies précieuses et tendres. On songe à une mystérieuse apothéose…

Camille Saint-Saëns, *Préface à l'ouvrage d'Édouard Ganche* : *Frédéric Chopin.*
Sa vie. Ses œuvres (1913), Paris : Le Mercure de France 1919, p. 9–10

« Chopin ! » il fallait entendre, sous le règne du bon roi Louis-Philippe, de quel air précieux et gourmet les femmes prononçaient les deux syllabes de ce nom, en pinçant délicatement les lèvres. Ce nom facile à prononcer, l'élégance des manières de l'artiste, ont certainement contribué beaucoup à son prodigieux succès. Par surcroît, il était poitrinaire dans un temps où la bonne santé n'était pas à la mode ; [...] Ce « jeune malade à pas lents », étranger avec un nom français, fils d'un pays malheureux dont tout le monde en France plaignait le sort et espérait la résurrection, avait tout ce qu'il fallait pour plaire au public d'alors, et tout cela le servait mieux encore que son talent parfaitement incompris de ce même public.

Cette incompréhension, on en voit la preuve dans la popularité d'une certaine grande *Valse* en mi bémol, oubliée maintenant et qui résonnait alors sur tous les pianos, à l'exclusion des œuvres de Chopin caractéristiques de son talent. Il n'avait que de rares admirateurs dignes de ce nom [...].

Les temps ont changé. Après de trop longues années stériles. [...] La « Valse en *mi* bémol » est reléguée pour jamais au magasin des accessoires, et toutes les fleurs de rêve écloses dans le jardin de l'artiste merveilleux que se disputent la France et la Pologne, s'épanouissent en liberté, répandant leur parfum. On les admire et on les aime. Les comprend-on bien ?

Les études musicales de Chopin avaient été incomplètes, si bien que les grandes compositions vocales et orchestrales lui étaient interdites et qu'il a dû se borner au piano, dans lequel il a su découvrir un monde. Mais sa spécialité égare le jugement. On pense trop au « piano », à l'instrument considéré comme but, quand on interprète ses œuvres ; on oublie le musicien et le poète ; car Chopin est surtout un poète, que l'on peut comparer à Musset ; comme celui-ci, il est le poète de la femme et de l'amour. [...] Sauf dans quelques *Polonaises* où le patriotisme fait seul entendre sa voix, la femme est toujours présente ; tout se rapporte à elle, et c'est à ce point de vue qu'il faut se placer si l'on veut donner à ses œuvres leur vrai caractère. La passion, tantôt débordante, tantôt contenue ou latente, vibre toujours dans ses œuvres, leur donne cette chaleur intérieure qui les fait vivre d'une vie si intense, et que l'on remplace trop souvent par une exécution maniérée, disloquée par des contorsions qui sont tout le contraire de son style, fait d'émotion et de simplicité. Ce dernier mot peut étonner, quand on parle d'une musique hérissée d'*accidents*, aux harmonies et aux arabesques si compliqués ; mais il ne faut pas, comme on le fait d'ordinaire, s'accrocher à ces détails ; c'est le fond qui est simple ; c'est de la simplicité du cœur qu'il s'agit et c'est elle qu'il faut mettre au jour, sous peine de trahir complètement les intentions de l'auteur.

Chopin, qui n'était pas resté suffisamment sur les bancs de l'École où il avait été le condisciple de Schumann, se défiait de lui-même ; il demandait et parfois suivait de pernicieux conseils, ignorant qu'il voyait plus clair, guidé par son instinct génial, que tous les savants sans génie.

The Scott Monument in Edinburgh against the backdrop of Castle Rock
Autograph letter written by Fryderyk Chopin to Marie de Rozières: 'Je Vous remercie bien de Vos bonnes lettres…', Keir, Perthshire, 2 October 1848, addressed envelope, two sheets, writing on all four pages, 270 x 230 mm. Collection: Muzeum Fryderyka Chopina, Warsaw [M/211].

Chopin in music criticism
in nineteenth-century England

Rosalba Agresta

During the Victorian era, the English press experienced a considerable expansion: the total number of Victorian titles exceeds 50,000, of which 200 had a substantial portion of writings about music.[1] It was not only the specialized musical press that saw this spectacular development from the 1830s, but also the general press (daily and weekly newspapers), which carried regular columns on music.[2] The following selection contains mostly articles printed in the major music journals of the day, such as *The Musical World* and *The Musical Times*, but it also contains extracts from the general press (*The Atheneaum*, *The Times*, *The Morning Post*), since during the Victorian era professional music journalists worked, often anonymously, for more than one periodical and not necessarily for specialized music journals. Musical writings in the general press were often of a critical value comparable to those in specialized music journals.

The critiques on Chopin during his lifetime.[3]

Chopin's reputation in England was not based on his concerts. Unlike Herz, Thalberg, and the other virtuosos, who made several *tournées* in London and in the provinces, Chopin did not step onto the English public stage until 1848. Accordingly, in a period when composers' reputations were much influenced by performances of their own music, Chopin's case is quite particular. During his lifetime, the critical reception of his work in England refers more or less exclusively to the editions published by Wessel and hardly ever contains accounts of his own legendary gifts as a performer.

1   See J. Don Vann and Rosemary T. VanArsdel, eds. *Victorian Periodicals: A Guide to Research*, New York, 1978, pp. 3-4.

2   See Leanne Langley, "The Musical Press in Nineteenth-Century England", *Notes*, 46 (March 1990), p. 585.

3   The English reception of Chopin's music during the composer's lifetime is more widely analyzed in my PhD dissertation *La reception de Chopin au Royaume Uni (1830-1860)*, which is in preparation at the Ecole Pratique des Hautes Etudes (Paris), under the direction of Madame Catherine Massip.

Chopin visited England twice. It is a well-known fact that his first journey was not for professional reasons,[4] so only a few details are known to Chopin's scholars. After his engagement with Maria Wodzińska had broken up, he made a few days' trip to London with his friend and publisher Camille Pleyel in July 1837. His compatriot Stanisław Koźmian, who had settled in London after the November Uprising, showed them the city's monuments and curiosities. Chopin wished to remain incognito and did not give a concert. When Pleyel was invited by the piano manufacturer James Broadwood to dine at his house, he introduced Chopin under the name of Mr. Fritz. The incognito, however, could only be preserved as long as Chopin kept his hands off the piano.[5] An anonymous article published in *The Musical World* on 23 February 1838 did not fail to record the event: "During his short visit to the metropolis, last season, but few had the high gratification of hearing his extemporaneous performance. [...] He is, perhaps, par eminence, *the most delightful of pianists for the drawing room*."[6]

This is one of the rare occasions on which the English press presented Chopin as a salon composer during his lifetime. He was generally considered first and foremost a virtuoso, even after 1835, when he progressively gave up the public stage.[7] The English critics described his music as the starting point for the development of the so-called "Romantic school". Chopin's etudes in particular exemplify all the elements of the new musical language and allow pianists to familiarize themselves with the style of a Liszt or a Thalberg.[8] In this respect, it must be added that the meaning of the expression "Romantic school", as referred to the piano, was largely pejorative. Although there was no definition of the word "Romantic" in the English press, the critics employed it as a synonym for "popular", in order to indicate the virtuoso compositions of Thalberg, Herz, Döhler, Liszt and Dreyschock. Therefore, the "Romantic

---

4 However, Jeffrey Kallberg has demonstrated that Chopin's first journey to London had important consequences for his editorial practices in England: from 1837 he started to provide manuscripts to his English publisher. (See J. Kallberg, "Chopin in the Marketplace: Aspects of International music publishing industry in the first half of the Nineteenth Century", in *Chopin at the Boundaries: Sex, History and Musical Genre*, Cambridge Mass. 1996, pp. 203-207.)

5 See Frederick Niecks, *Frederick Chopin as a Man and Musician*, 2 vols. London, Novello, 1888, i, p. 312.

6 *The Musical World* (hereafter *MW*), 102 (23 February 1838), p. 120. Emphasis added. NB issue numbers refer to the "first" series; the volume and issue numbers of the "new" series, which were used only for the period 1838-1841, are omitted to avoid confusion. "First" series numbering runs consecutively up to no. 301 (30 December 1841); thereafter, each successive volume begins with its own issue no. 1..

7 The reasons that led Chopin to give up the virtuoso career are examined in Jean-Jacques Eigeldinger, "Les premiers concerts publics de Chopin à Paris (1832-1838)", in *L'univers musical de Chopin*, Paris, 2000, pp. 191-227.

8 See *MW*, 113 (10 May 1838), pp. 34-35, *MW*, 128 (23 August 1838), pp. 275-8.

school" was a "new" school – opposed to the "classical" one – that had forgotten the lessons of the great composers such as Mozart and Beethoven and only aimed at public acclaim. As an unidentified critic stressed in the pages of *The Musical World*, "Romantic" compositions have "beginnings and ends, but for the most part [they contain] nothing between their extremes save scraps of themes uncouthly intermingled, and long streams of passages of which the difficulty is pretty generally understood to be the chief recommendation".[9] The same criticism was made of Chopin by the editor of *The Musical World*, George Macfarren,[10] in the article that opened the famous polemic about Chopin's works in 1841: "Chopin does not want for ideas, but they never extend beyond eight or sixteen bars at the utmost, and then he is invariably *in nubibus*".[11] Macfarren's charges against Chopin were heavy both on account of his style and language: he claimed that Chopin was incapable of organizing his thematic material in a formal structure owing to his "ignorance" of classical forms and that the "strain after originality" rendered both Chopin's melodies and harmonies "intolerable, tiresome, and ridiculous". Although he recognized Chopin as an "expert doer of little things",[12] Macfarren maintained that "even those little things are sullied by extravagant affectation", which bears the most palpable "errors and ugliness". On the other hand, Macfarren considered Chopin as the summit of the Parisian school of "hyperbole and nonsense", namely the "romantic" school; his criticism clearly leans on the opposition between the classical and virtuoso schools. One must stress that this opposition acquired in Macfarren's words a nationalist flavour, opposing Chopin, the composer of "absurd and hyperbolical extravagances", to the English composers William Sterndale Bennett and George Alexander Macfarren, representatives of the great German school of composition, from Beethoven to Mendelssohn.

Macfarren's criticism provoked responses in defence of Chopin, none of which was effective. Christian Rudolph Wessel, the publisher of Chopin's music in England, sent a letter to the editor of *The Musical World*, in which he stressed the immense celebrity of the composer on the Continent, making a list of musical and literary figures who had celebrated the art of Chopin. "A Professor of Music", whose letter is not reproduced in the following selection, repeated the arguments of Wessel and maintained that the comparison between Chopin, Bennett and Macfarren was pointless.

---

9 *MW*, 225 (16 July 1840), p. 45.

10 Although this article has long been attributed to Davison, the review was written by the editor of *The Musical World*, at that time George Macfarren; see herein p. 471.

11 *MW*, 292 (28 October 1841), p. 276.

12 *MW*, 294 (11 November 1841), p. 309.

"An Amateur" declared that Chopin should not be criticized for his faults, because they derive from the example of certain works of Beethoven, namely the posthumous quartets. It is obvious that these assertions criticizing Beethoven, whose works were already part of the English canon, would arouse harsh criticism from the detractors of Chopin's style.[13]

Although not directly involved in the polemics of 1841, *An Essay on the Works of Frederic Chopin* by James William Davison can be considered the best response to Macfarren's criticism of Chopin. This book, published by Wessel and known as the "yellow-book" for the colour of its cover, presents Chopin as an eminent poetical composer, whose music is imbued with a philosophical essence which renders it inaccessible to all but the few. According to Davison, the failure to appreciate Chopin's works was essentially due to an incapacity to comprehend the composer's intentions; his music requires not only a finished pianist to overcome the technical difficulties that it contains, but also a "philosophical thinker" to interpret its depth of thought.[14] With a rich, sometimes inflated and visionary language, full of literary, philosophical and biblical quotations, Davison described the heavenly character of Chopin's music, whose originality of language and structures makes it difficult to understand on first acquaintance and which requires true *faith* for a full comprehension.[15] Thus Davison created a new and original trope in Chopin reception: the imagery of the prophet, which linked Chopin to another of Davison's idols, Mendelssohn. In fact, at this time, Davison placed Chopin alongside Mendelssohn and Sterndale Bennett as specimens of those modern composers whose works did not share the degenerate character of virtuoso music.

This kind of criticism is repeated in articles published in *The Musical Examiner*, the short-lived journal edited by Davison and published by Wessel (1842-1844). Nevertheless, after succeeding to Macfarren as editor of *The Musical World* in May 1843, Davison devoted only three articles to Chopin up to 1847,[16] when he defined him as "A Polish piano-forte player who has composed some rondos and dance-tunes

---

13 See *MW*, 294 (11 November 1841), p. 309. Besides the editor of *The Musical World*, "Inquirer" wrote a particularly harsh response to the letter of "An Amateur". (See *MW*, 295 (18 November 1841), pp. 323-324).

14 See J. W. Davison, *An Essay on the Works of Frederic Chopin*, London, Wessel, [1842-43], pp. 3 and 6.

15 Ibid., p. 6.

16 The three articles, reproduced in the following selection, are *MW*, 18/31 (3 August 1843), pp. 262-63, *MW*, 18/32 (10 August 1843), p. 271, *MW*, 18/33 (17 August 1843), pp. 275-276.

(*mazurkas*) for the instrument".[17] The apparent reason for this drastic change was Chopin's refusal to sign the letter of condolence sent by the German musicians living in Paris to Mendelssohn's widow for, in the words of Davison, "the musician who does not merely respect, but revere, worship, idolize the name of Mendelssohn, I do not, I *cannot* consider a worthy follower of his art, and therefore, owing him no respect, I pay him none".[18] Thus, the critic who, between 1842 and 1844, had celebrated Chopin as one of the best of living composers, dismissed him in 1847 as a waltz "compounder", whose name is not worth being quoted amongst the names of German musicians, the only representatives of true art.

Much has been said about Davison's amazing volte-face. His biographer, Charles Reid, claimed that Davison's writings from 1842 to 1844 were only moved by self-interest, since the *Essay* as well as *The Musical Examiner* were published by Chopin's editor, Wessel.[19] In order to reinforce his thesis, Reid reminded his readers of the frequent accusations of bribery made to Davison by his contemporaries.[20] It is true that Wessel could have had some interest in promoting Chopin's music and that he published many of Davison's works, and it is equally true that Davison's review of the Impromptu Op. 29, published in *The Musical World* on 3 February 1842, does not display the most laudatory terms; nevertheless, one should be cautious about Reid's assertions, for Davison did not hesitate to pay a last homage to Chopin after his death, affirming that "the death of M. Chopin cannot but be lamented by all the lovers and followers of the art".[21] Although in the obituary notice, Davison left the merit of Chopin's music to the judgment of posterity, he recognized him as one of the most gifted composers who have contributed to the repertoire of the piano.[22]

As we have seen, between 1843 and 1847 there are only a few articles on Chopin in *The Musical World* and none at all in *The Musical Times*.[23] This gap in the press is

---

17 *MW*, 22/49 (4 December 1847), p. 767.

18 *MW*, 22/50 (11 December 1847), p. 786.

19 See Charles Reid, *The Music Monster, A Biography of James William Davison, Music Critic of The Times of London, 1846-78*, London, 1984, pp. 26-28.

20 Ibid., pp. 39-41 and 61-64.

21 *MW*, 24/45 (10 November 1849), p. 706.

22 Ibid. p. 706.

23 The silence of *The Musical Times* is not surprising, since Novello, editor and proprietor of the journal, utilized it to advertise and popularize the edition of sacred and choral music published by his firm, and in particular the oratorios of Mendelssohn, Spohr and Handel. (For the editorial philosophy of Novello's firm, see Victoria Cooper, *The House of Novello, Practice and Policy of a Victorian Music Publisher, 1829-1866*, Aldershot 2003; for the editorial policies of *The Musical Times*, see also Meirion Hughes, *The English Musical Renaissance and the Press: 1850-1914: Watchmen of Music*, Aldershot 2002, pp.85-88). Chopin's music, and piano music in general, was not part of Novello's interests, so *The*

only filled by some items by Henry Fothergill Chorley, the music critic of *The Athenaeum*. Chorley had become acquainted with Chopin during his frequent journeys to Paris and this influenced his perception of Chopin's works. In fact, he considered Chopin the "most graceful and fantastic of all the pianists", [24] "one of the most individual modern composers", [25] whose originality can only be expressed through his own performances. According to Chorley, Chopin's frail physique affected not only his interpretations but also his compositions; as he stressed in his reviews of Chopin's London concerts in 1848, the composer and the interpreter are inseparable in Chopin's works, so he is the only one who can properly interpret the poetry of his own music.[26] Chorley found many "eccentricities" in the music of Chopin (the overturning of the third on the fourth finger, the "twelfths, and other such troublesome extensions",[27] "his peculiar system of harmony"),[28] which are nevertheless redeemed by the elegance, the grandeur, and the "speaking expressiveness different from that of any other composer"[29].

Yet Chorley's criticism was not without reservations; in his view, the Polish composer was incapable of continuous effort, as his extended works demonstrate with their lack of the essential requisites of form. "It is not by his great concert pieces, or by his one instrumental trio, or by his sonata (a sonata in name only), that he will be remembered; but by his studies, his preludes, his romances, his mazurkas".[30] This was a kind of criticism that would perdure until the twentieth century. But those remarks are not intirely negative, as Chorley explained: "Chopin, however, is not, as the foregoing remarks might seem to imply, incapable of grand, as well as graceful inventions. One or two of his studies and preludes have a largeness and dignity of outline which more muscular composers might envy".[31] Unlike many later critics, Chorley recognized the dignity of Chopin's miniatures, and his reservations concerning Chopin's language and style did not prevent him from considering Chopin a great composer.

Musical Times did not devote any article to Chopin before the 1860s, except a little paragraph announcing Chopin's death (*The Musical Times*, 66 (1 November 1849), p. 230).

24 *The Athenaeum*, 704 (24 April 1841), p. 324.
25 *The Athenaeum*, 740 (1 January 1842), p. 18.
26 See *The Athenaeum*, 1079 (1 July 1848), p. 660 and *The Athenaeum*, 1081 (15 July 1848), p. 708.
27 See *The Athenaeum*, 791 (24 December 1842), p. 1115.
28 Ibid., p. 1115.
29 *The Athenaeum*, 996 (28 November 1846), p. 1224.
30 *The Athenaeum*, 740 (1 January 1842), p. 18.
31 Ibid. p. 18.

The reception of Chopin after his death

In the years following Chopin's death, English critics devoted comparatively few articles to his music. Several of these are translations of foreign texts, such as Heine's "About Music and Musicians"[32] or his comparison between Chopin and Liszt,[33] Joseph d'Ortigue's note about the letters of Barbedette on Chopin's music,[34] and Schumann's criticism of Chopin's work[35]. Besides these translations, which are not included in the following selection, some lengthy articles by English critics are devoted to new editions of Chopin's works, such as the *Deux Valses Mélancoliques*, first published by Ewer in 1854,[36] and Boosey's new edition of the mazurkas, published in 1860[37]. In the former review, the unsigned critic did not express any opinion on the works, since they were "pure Chopin". The latter embodied a certain shift in Chopin reception towards a more widely nationalistic reading of his music, which was not restricted to the mazurkas alone, but also embraced larger works, such as the concertos and sonatas. It is important to point out that the mazurkas were published with a critical introduction by Davison, whose point of view was far from that of the *Essay*, but, as one might expect, was also somewhat different to that in his articles of 1847. For commercial reasons, he could not have expressed entirely negative views of Chopin's music. Along with a detailed biographical sketch, which is extensively borrowed from the biography of Chopin by Liszt,[38] Davison presented Chopin as a composer who had the right "to be styled *inventor*",[39] since "he has enriched the means of *effect* by such a varied store of graceful and brilliant devices, that he must be accorded a place among those who have materially aided in the progress of the art of pianoforte playing"[40]. Such a statement is quite amazing, since a few pages later we read that "Chopin's genius was not of that high order, his talent was not of that exclusive stamp, his acquirements were not of that remarkable depth, to influence the real progress of art, for good or for

---

32 See *MW*, 36/34 (21 August 1858), pp. 541-542.

33 See *MW*, 37/34 (20 August 1859), pp. 535-536.

34 See *MW*, 39/31 (3 August 1861), pp. 485-486.

35 See *MW*, 45/7 (16 February 1867), pp. 102-104; *MW*, 45/15 (13 April 1867), pp. 230-231; *MW*, 45/16 (20 April 1867), pp. 244-245; *MW*, 45/17 (27 April 1867), pp. 262-264; *MW*, 46/41 (10 October 1868), p. 700.

36 See *MW*, 32/29 (22 July 1854), p. 492.

37 See *MW*, 38/13 (31 March 1860), pp. 199-201.

38 Liszt's *F. Chopin* was published in Paris by Escudier in 1852.

39 *The Mazurkas and Valses of Frederick Chopin, with Memoir by J. W. Davison*, London, Boosey, 1860, p. i.

40 Ibid.

bad".[41] Once again, Davison's criticism of Chopin is dual. While continually defining Chopin as a "poet", he also finds his music corrupted by physical and mental illness, which renders his talent one-sided and his compositions "constantly somber and monotonous".[42]

Writing in *Contemporary Review* shortly after the publication of the mazurkas, the Reverend Hugh Reginald Haweis defined Chopin as "essentially a national musician",[43] whose works were deeply marked with the love of his country. According to Haweis, the national aspect of the music of Chopin was not limited to the polonaises and the mazurkas, but also concerned the scherzos, ballades and waltzes, works in which Chopin revealed himself as the most accomplished of piano composers. Haweis's article is highly laudatory and inverts the criticisms addressed to Chopin during his lifetime; he depicts Chopin as an original composer, whose works are marked by a complete absence of the commonplace. These assertions, however, only refer to Chopin's smaller compositions, whereas his concertos are considered more ambitious than successful. "He was great in small things, but small in great ones",[44] wrote Haweis, signifying that the old idea of a composer who could not master higher musical forms was still alive and well.

After 1850, besides articles reviewing new editions, Chopin's name could also be found in sections devoted to concert reviews. Actually, the press reflected the development of concert life in the second half of the nineteenth century through the greater attention paid to the description of programmes. If, previously, the critics had written only about works they considered of capital importance, namely the symphonic repertoire, in the second half of the century, reviews were more comprehensive and described all the music performed in concerts. This change in the critics' attitude is of major importance for the study of Chopin reception, since it allows us to trace the presence of his music in concert life. The analysis of concert programmes reveals that, from the 1850s, Chopin's works were performed in concerts of "high" pretention, such as the Musical Union matinées.[45] However, in the aesthetic hierarchy of the day,

---

41 Ibid., p. v.

42 Ibid.

43 Hugh Reginald Haweis, "Schubert and Chopin", *Contemporary Review*, 2 (May-August 1866), p. 101.

44 Ibid., p. 102.

45 For the history of the Musical Union, see Christina Bashford, "John Ella and the Making of The Musical Union", in Christina Bashford and Leanne Langley, eds, *Music and the British Culture, 1785-1914, Essays in Honour of Cyril Ehrlich*, Oxford 2000, pp. 194-214, and *The Pursuit of High Culture: John Ella, Chamber Music, and Victorian London*, Woodbridge, Rochester, 2007.

solo piano music was still considered as belonging to an "inferior" order in comparison to symphonic repertoire, and the critics dispensed with solo piano works in a few words, such as "elegant trifles for the pianoforte",[46] "languid and love-sick Nocturne (in D flat)",[47] "noisy polonaise",[48] "very dull Scherzo (Op. 31),[49] and so forth. Interesting as they are for the study of Chopin reception in England, such remarks cannot be fully understood if removed from their context, and they require thorough study grounded on analysis of concert programmes. This is why they have not been included in the following selection, except for some items relating to the concerts of Charles Hallé and Clara Schumann, which are given as examples.

Towards the end of the century, there was a renewal of interest in Chopin in the English press. In 1877 the Londoner publisher William Reeves issued Martha Walker Cook's translation of Liszt's biography of Chopin.[50] As we have seen, Liszt's monograph was not unknown to Davison, who had read it in the original French edition published in 1852, but the publication of an English translation attracted much wider interest and gave rise to many critiques. Reviewing Liszt's book in *The Musical Times*, an unidentified critic hailed it as a "rhapsody", the lack of biographical details compensated for by the "masterly analysis of the inner meaning of his [Chopin's] pianoforte works".[51] The critic especially welcomed Liszt's assertions of Chopin's incapacity to write in Classical forms, a subject that, as we have seen, was recurrent during Chopin's lifetime. Once again, under the authority of Liszt's words, an English critic recognized Chopin's talent for smaller compositions but denied him the mastery of the "higher" class of music.

Joseph Bennett's reception of Liszt's work was quite different. Writing in *The Musical Times* in 1882, Bennett criticized Liszt's book as "rhapsodical, not to say hysterical", since it "puts Chopin before us as a psychological phenomenon, invests him with strange attributes provocative of awe and mystery, and surrounds him with the halo of a very peculiar heroism".[52] In Bennett's view, Liszt was the person best qualified to write a book about Chopin owing to their friendship and their "mutual feeling" in artistic matters, but, on the other hand, Liszt's impulsive personality made

---

46   *MW*, 31/51 (17 December 1853), p. 798.
47   *MW*, 32/20 (20 May 1854), p. 343.
48   *MW*, 29/50 (13 December 1851), p. 789
49   *MW*, 34/26 (28 June 1856), p. 407.
50   Martha Walker Cook's English translation of Liszt's book was first published in 1863 in Philadelphia by F. Leypoldt. William Reeves published a second translation, by John Broadhouse, in 1900.
51   *The Musical Times* (hereafter *MT*), 410 (1 April 1877), p. 184.
52   *MT*, 467 (1 January 1882), p. 12.

him ill-suited to the work of a biographer. Thus, through a series of seven articles, Bennett traced a biographical sketch of Chopin, in order to demonstrate the inaccuracy of Liszt's *Life of Chopin*.[53] He reproached Liszt for his lack of precision, for example in the details describing Konstancja Gładkowska or in the false assertion that Prince Radziwiłł had funded Chopin's education. But the main reproach concerned the characterization of the composer as a man constantly affected by illness, which, according to Liszt, was reflected in his music and rendered him unable to express himself fully as a musician. Liszt's reading of Chopin's dislike for public concerts as a "voluntary abnegation" which "veiled an internal wound" was, according to Bennett, derived from Liszt's own "inner consciousness";[54] the prince of virtuosos, applauded by the masses, could not grasp Chopin's satisfaction with the limited audience of a salon and believed that his apparent satisfaction concealed the uneasiness of a misunderstood genius.

Bennett's portrait of the Polish composer is mostly based on the biographies of Liszt and Karasowski,[55] and on George Sand's recollections *Histoire de ma vie*, but it also gives an accurate description of Chopin's stay in Great Britain, which relies on the notes of Broadwood's associate, A. J. Hipkins[56]. The most interesting article in Bennett's series on Chopin is the last, in which the critic expresses his own views on the composer's music. Bennett recognized the distinctive and peculiar nature of Chopin's genius, which rendered his art misunderstood during his lifetime. According to Bennett, Chopin could not stand comparison with Beethoven; but, on the other hand, certain characteristics of his art made him worthy of acceptance among the great composers. In fact, Chopin was "the high priest of a sweet and subtle art-mystery".[57] His greatness lay not in the depth or the high ideals of a Beethoven but in the infinite loveliness and charm which characterize the "minute things of art" that Chopin produced.

The last word on Chopin's biography was uttered by Frederick Niecks in *Frederick Chopin as a Man and a Musician*,[58] a book considered by contemporaries as *the* biography of the Polish master, written "once for all" by the Edinburgh University pro-

---

53 The seven articles by Bennett treat respectively of Chopin's Polish origins, youth, first concerts, residence in Paris, love affairs, concerts in England, and death. Subsequently, in 1884, Bennett wrote a biography of Chopin, published in the series "Novello's Primers of Musical Biography".

54 *MT*, 467 (1 January 1882), p. 13.

55 Maurycy Karasowski, *Friedrich Chopin: sein Leben, seine Werke und Briefe*, Dresden, Ries, 1877.

56 See *MT*, 472 (1 June 1882), pp. 314-317.

57 *MT*, 473 (1 July 1882), p. 374.

58 Niecks, *Frederick Chopin* (see above, n. 5).

fessor.[59] In order to sketch a life of Chopin against its historical, artistical and social background, Niecks not only assembled information from previous biographies, chiefly those of Liszt and Karasowski, but also supplemented them with reports from the press and with many reminiscences by Chopin's friends, pupils and acquaintances. The result of Niecks's efforts was a more comprehensive and balanced biography, giving a picture of Chopin's life freed of the poetic accessories and exaggerations which had characterized earlier biographies. Furthermore, Niecks was the first to provide readers with "an anatomy of the composer's style".[60] From the first pages of his biography, Niecks stressed the close relationship between Poland and the music of Chopin, arguing that this national dimension rendered it too original to be fully understood at once. Niecks summed up: "A subtle poet, be he ever so national, has thoughts and corresponding language beyond the ken of the vulgar [...]. Chopin, imbued as he was with the national spirit, did nevertheless not manifest it in a popularly intelligible form, for in passing through his mind it underwent a process of idealisation and individualisation".[61]

One can wonder what Niecks thought about the widespread idea of "Chopin's incapacity to write in large forms". The biographer recognized Chopin's lack of qualities for the successful composition of sonatas and concertos, but he stressed that, in an epoch when concerto form was often modified, Chopin always adhered to the standard form, unmistakably using Hummel as his model. According to Niecks, the concerto was better suited to Chopin's talent than the sonata, since piano concertos were governed not just by the rules of sonata form but also by the need for virtuoso display. It was this element that could have allowed Chopin to master the sonata, a form that his talent did not apprehend. But, on the other hand, concertos demand skills in writing for the orchestra, and "Chopin lacked such aptitude entirely".[62] Once again, we can see the "old" criticism returning, but, unlike other critics, Niecks placed the emphasis on Chopin's ineptitude both in writing for the orchestra and in conceiving large-scale forms.

To sum up: in examining Chopin reception in nineteenth-century England one finds two leitmotifs that are linked: the poet who expresses his own individuality in

---

59 Niecks's book was published on 1888 and was reprinted twice with additions, in 1890 and 1902. Numerous subsequent biographies of Chopin were based on Niecks's work, such as James Huneker, *Chopin: The Man and His Music*, New York 1900.

60 Jim Samson, *The Music of Chopin*, Oxford 1994, p. 1.

61 Niecks, *Frederick Chopin*, i, p. 133.

62 Ibid., i, p. 206.

his music (which in the second half of the century echoes Chopin's nationality), and the composer who is not fitted for the "higher" musical forms. With respect to this subject, A. Redgrave Cripps was the sole critic to strongly oppose the common view of Chopin's weakness in conception and design, declaring him a master of form. For Cripps, abstract or theoretical notions of form should be forgotten and Chopin's own standpoint adopted. Only then can one perceive that "it is in the wealth of resources exhibited within the limits of that form [that] his mastery is shown".[63] Since the supremacy of Chopin in smaller forms was widely recognized, Cripps's main concern was to demonstrate that the composer also had a talent for larger forms. Thus, he stated that the perfection of Chopin's smaller and larger works derived from his "exquisitely delicate sense of design" and that he made use of the same principles of construction in nocturnes, preludes, and concertos. As long as the perfection of the smaller composition was attributed to a "felicitous phraseology" and not to the mastery of form, the perfection of the larger composition would not be understood.

Cripps admitted that sonata form was not congenial to Chopin, since his music was too subtle, flexible and individual, and he argued that this fact had prevented Chopin from being recognized by theorists. However, as Beethoven's sonatas hardly correspond to the theorist's idea of sonata form, Cripps equally hoped that "in some years Chopin's works will be similarly recognised, and we shall have students casting their first attempts at composition in forms suggested by him".[64]

Cripps's articles were written in 1914: the close of the "long nineteenth century" planted the seeds of a new appreciation of Chopin's music in England.

Textual note

The articles are arranged chronologically. The original orthography has been respected (for example "pianiste" instead of "pianist" and "for ever" instead of "forever"). The orthography of names has been modernised (Döhler instead of Doehler), but the orthography of Chopin's first name has been respected (Frédéric, Frederic and Frederick). Evident misprints have been corrected.

Capitalisation has been modernised and punctuation respected, including the often used dashes (–). Original footnotes are marked with asterisk, dagger, etc.;

---

63 *MT*, 858 (1st August 1914), p. 519.
64 *MT*, 860 (1st October 1914), p. 614.

the present editor's footnotes are numbered. Editorial additions are shown in square brackets [ ].

The authors of signed articles are given in bold type, with the article's title. For articles signed with initials, the author's name has been given in square brackets. The authors of unsigned articles are identified, where possible, in footnotes. All the articles in *The Athenaeum* have been attributed, without explanations in footnotes, to Henry Fothergill Chorley, that journal's music critic.

Musical works have been identified in footnotes, except for unique works in the composer's output, for example Chopin's Barcarolle. Individuals not generally familiar are identified in footnotes.

Anthology

Chopin's playing
The pale wizard's fingers,
With magical skill,
Make a music that lingers
In memory still.[65]

Anonymous, "New Music", *The Court Magazine and Belle Assemblée,* 4 (February 1834), p. 89.[66]

[...] The *Album des Pianistes de Première Force* is a collection of the most difficult pieces of music, intended only for those players who have obtained the greatest facility of execution. Let such pianists sit down to the *Fantasie* [sic] *Militaire,*[67] and *Les Clochettes*[68] by Pixis; when they have mastered these difficulties, let them attempt *Hommage à Mozart,*[69] by Frederick Chopin; and when they can play the latter, nothing ought to intimidate them. Chopin is the most ingenious composer that ever wrote, but with his compositions he ought to send us hands with which to play them, for we have met many passages we could not execute with our own. His *Trois Nocturnes,*[70]

---

65 *Fraser's Magazine for Town and Country,* 224 (August 1848), p. 232.

66 This article is a review of the fourteenth book of Wessel's series *Album des pianistes de première force.*

67 *Fantaisie Militaire,* Op. 121, published also by Hofmeister in Leipzig as *Fantaisie militaire pour le piano avec accompagnement de grande orchestre et musique militaire.*

68 *Les Trois Clochettes, Grand Rondeau brillant,* Op. 120.

69 The Variations on "Là ci darem", Op. 2 were published by Wessel in 1833 under the title *Homage* [sic] *à Mozart.*

70 Nocturnes, Op. 15, published by Wessel in the series *L'Amateur Pianiste* under the title *Les Zephirs.* Both the catalogues of Kobylańska and Chomiński/Turło and also Chopin's First Editions Online

written in imitation of the *Murmurs of the Seine*,[71] and his *Variations Brillantes*, on the air *"Je vends des Scapulaires"*,[72] are a trifle easier. Yet even these require considerable application for their performance. [...]

Anonymous, "*Album des pianistes de première force. No. 35*[sic].[73] *Grande Polonaise Brillante, précédée d'un Andante Spianato pour le Piano forte; dédiée à Mad. D'Est, par Frederick Chopin (De Varsovie)*. Wessel", *The Musical World*, 49 (17 February 1837), p. 138.

It will require a *player* of the *"première force"* to scramble through this piece. To such, therefore, and the fagger of nine hours a day, and the solitary prisoner – if any there be, indulged with a piano – we recommend it for practice; and when their task is accomplished, they will be in a condition to play an uncommon number of notes is a short time.

Anonymous, "*Il Lamento e la Consolazione, Deux Nocturnes*,[74] *pour le pianoforte, par Frederic Chopin*. Wessel. *La Méditation, Scherzo*,[75] *pour le pianoforte, Par Frederic Chopin*. Wessel", *The Musical World*, 102 (23 February 1838), p. 120.[76]

Frederic Chopin is a pianiste of the highest order of merit. The enquiring student cannot exercise his energies more profitably than in obtaining an insight into the peculiarities of his style, evincing as it does, a perfect knowledge of the powers of his instrument; the amateur will not fail to be delighted in listening to his delicate melodies, the elegance and appropriateness of their detail, the graceful variety of his harmonies, the beautiful system he adopts in their disposition, and the striking finish

---

(CFEO) give May 1834 as the date of publication. Since there is no entry in the Stationers' Hall registers for the Nocturnes, Op. 15, this review is the sole source allowing us to date the edition to January 1834.

71   Nocturnes, Op. 9, published by Wessel in June 1833 in the series *L'Amateur Pianiste* under the title *Les Murmures de la Seine*.

72   The Variations on "Je vends des Scapulaires", Op. 12, were published by Cramer, Addison & Beale in January 1834 (see CFEO).

73   The Polonaise, Op. 22 was published as no. 34 in the series *Album des Pianistes de Première Force*.

74   Nocturnes, Op. 32.

75   Scherzo, Op. 31.

76   According to Niecks, the author of this unsigned article was James William Davison (see Niecks, *Frederick Chopin* i, p. 312) but there is no evidence of Davison's journalistic activity for *The Musical World* at that time.

displayed in the execution of the whole. If M. Chopin was not, perhaps, the most retiring and unambitious of all living musicians, he would, before this time, have been celebrated as the inventor of a new style, or school of pianoforte composition. During his short visit to the metropolis, last season, but few had the high gratification of hearing his extemporaneous performance.[77] Those who experienced this pleasure will not readily lose its remembrance. He is, perhaps, *par eminence*, the most delightful of pianistes for the drawing room. The animation of his style is so subdued, its tenderness so refined, its melancholy so gentle, its niceties so studied and systematic, the *tout ensemble* so perfect, and evidently the result of an accurate judgment and most finished taste, that when exhibited in the large concert room, or the thronged saloon, it fails to impress itself on the mass. The *fuoco e forza* is assuredly not his *forte*; for although his *passagio* [sic] requires vigour and considerable mechanical precision, yet is it ever combined with the simple and graceful, the delicate and pathetic. We may remark, that his nomenclature, although distinguished for accuracy, frequently, *a prima vista*, suggests the notion of much difficulty, which, however, subsides on a better acquaintance with his works. [...]

Anonymous, "Metropolitan Concerts. Mr. Wessel's soirées", *The Musical World*, 117 (7 June 1838), p. 97.

[Review of Wessel's concert (2 June 1838)]
[...] The first movement of the Concerto in E minor by Chopin, [...] although very difficult, is too small in feature, and indistinct in outline, to prove very attractive. [...]

Anonymous, "*Douze Grand* [sic] *Études, en Deux Livraisons pour le Pianoforte dediées* [sic] *à ses amis J.* [sic] *Liszt et Fred.* [sic] *Hiller, par Fred. Chopin. Edited with additional fingering by his pupil J. Fontana. Book I.* Wessel & Co",[78] *The Musical World*, 113 (10 May 1838), pp. 34-35.

In witnessing the prodigious execution of a Liszt or Thalberg, often do we hear the wonder-struck spectator ask how was it possible to acquire such an amazing

---

77 Chopin visited London in July 1837. He did not give any public concert, but he played at the house of the piano manufacturer James Broadwood (see Niecks, *Frederick Chopin* i, p. 312).

78 The Études, Opp. 10 and 25 were published by Wessel in two sets each. The first series has an unauthorized dedication to Hiller.

mastery of the instrument? The answer to this inquiry is easy, when it is recollected that harmonical combinations are limited, that the scales are limited, that the natural extent of the human hand (to a certain degree) [is] limited, and hence that the mere *mechanism* of pianoforte playing is confined within the compass of a few rules. We believe that about seven or eight rules embrace the whole art of fingering, and the balance of the hand over the instrument; and that having once acquired a mastery over these positions, all those productions which are written for the display of mere execution, are comparatively easy to execute. Thus to the practised formalist, the caprices of Thalberg, – the mysticism of Liszt, – the ever-varied *romanza* of Henselt[79] present no difficulties, because the passages are no other than exemplifications of defined and certain rules in mechanism, which if departed from in these extraordinary flights of execution, would become altogether impracticable. The really difficult music is that of your original thinker; he who is writing from the genial glow of his own pure and vivid thoughts. Thus Beethoven and Mendelssohn in their pianoforte compositions, here and there exhibit passages which, although not of themselves difficult, become so from their introduction, and peculiarity of situation across the instrument.

Composers of "studies for the pianoforte", have, in many instances, thought too much of themselves, and too little of their patrons – the rising artists. Thus one has contented himself with writing fine music, another difficult music, and a third that which is showy and brilliant. Still there was wanted one which should commence on *a system of mechanism*, which proceeding by degrees through the various difficulties of execution – the extension of the common chord in arpeggios – the diatonic and chromatic scales – the three forms of the chord of the ninth, &c. &c. – should at its termination disclose every possible combination of passage in execution. No set of studies, in our minds, meets this view of the essential objects of a *studio* so perfectly as the "*Études pour le pianoforte par Frederic Chopin*". There is nothing ephemeral in their character, or construction as compositions – the harmony is solid and excellent, the superstructure elegant and novel in passage, and rich and melodious in its cantilena; but notwithstanding these valuable and important features in the work – the development of a mechanism, a *systematic* mechanism is always the primary consideration with the composer. M. Czerny has, we understand, said of this work

---

79 Adolph von Henselt (1814-1889) was a German composer and pianist. He began concert tours across Germany at 1836 and 1837 and played in St. Petersburg in 1838. There he became court pianist and inspector of musical studies at the Imperial Institute of Female Education. Though Henselt performed rarely in public, he was considered one of the greatest virtuosos of his time. His compositions were mainly for piano, including a piano concerto, two sets of studies, and a number of salon pieces.

that it forms a new era in the history of pianoforte performance. We can unhesitatingly declare, that the student who masters its details, having an observant eye to its principles, will forget the meaning of the word "difficult", at least as connected with composition for the pianoforte. [...] Henselt has, in his *etudes caracteristiques* [sic],[80] invented one or two new positions, or rather a *grouping together* of several known and commonly used extensions, all of which are to be found in the studies of M. Chopin. [...] As the attention of our artists is now so turned towards the improvement of the genius of the pianoforte, and the creation of a school of composition peculiarly its own, in no wise dependent on the orchestra or the organ, experience discovers shorter methods to the attainment of skill and ability, which although minute in detail, claim from their clear and well digested arrangement, the preference of both professor and pupil. The command of the "*Ne* [sic] *plus ultra*" of mechanical excellence, is placed within the reach of study and perseverance, but to whom ought to be ascribed the honour of the invention we are not prepared to declare. The *school* is seen in the works of Liszt, Thalberg and Henselt; and the *system* is partially developed in the studies of M. Rhein,[81] and altogether so in those of M. Chopin.

Anonymous, "*Douze Grand* [sic] *Études pour le Piano, par F. Chopin, Op. 25, Book III* – Wessell [sic] *& Co.", The Musical World*, 128 (23 August 1838), pp. 275-8.

In a former notice of M. Chopin's compositions, we observed that this composer had made prodigious advances in extending the genius or capabilities of the pianoforte; and in "the creation of a school of composition peculiarly adapted to the instrument, and in no wise dependent on the orchestra or organ". The continuation of the Studies has been executed in a manner corresponding to the high opinion we have entertained of the author's abilities. The votaries of less modern schools of composition will probably, on a first introduction to M. Chopin, pronounce him a grievous innovator on established modes of thought and expression – one factiously disposed to disturb the calm of previous mannerism, and to shake the venerable foundations of authority. No doubt innovation is a terrible charge amongst those "who judge of

---

80 Henselt's *Douze Études Caractéristiques*, Op. 2, were published in Leipzig in 1837.

81 Charles Laurent Rhein (1798- 1864) won the Premier Prix de piano at the Paris Conservatoire in 1818. According to Fétis, Rhein was one of the best piano teachers in Paris between 1818 and 1832. He composed two sets of studies (Opp. 42 and 44).

men's heads as they do of their perukes, by the fashion";[82] but we think few of our readers belong to this class of philosophers, although they may not have followed the example of our composer, who appears to have divested himself of old opinions and faded discoveries, and to have "turned himself out stark naked in search of new inventions".[83] But if our readers are unbiassed and free to examine the "inventions" of the Warsaw pianist, there still remain those from whom he will probably encounter opposition and dislike. Nor is this more than may be rationally expected. The introduction of entirely new methods often changes the relative position of men engaged in professional pursuits, and obliges many to descend from stations which they have long occupied to those much lower in the scale of intellectual advancement. [...]

M. Chopin, in extending the field of possibilities as regards manual dexterity, has invented a vocabulary of sounds, a musical dialect or phraseology with which we have hitherto to be unacquainted. This is the natural result of an increase of physical power in the musical artist when combined with even an average portion of the intellectual faculty. [...] Thalberg and Döhler,[84] although evidently formed in the school of Chopin, have rendered particular features more prominent, and in one or two instances increased its capabilities. [...]

This work, as exemplifying the elements of the modern school of pianoforte playing, as revealing the mode by which the young pianists of Germany have acquired an European celebrity, and as affording an opportunity for English artists to arrive at the same degree of popularity, is an object of high interest to our students and professors. Whoever wishes to become a Thalberg or a Döhler, a Henselt or a Rosenhain,[85] must familiarize himself with the new thoughts and expressions of M. Chopin. The arena is unoccupied; we have no native artist who is an adept in the new school [...] But should the season of next year bring out an English Thalberg, it will be only effected by the writings of a Chopin. [...] A new school has arisen which has attracted as much attention in the world of pianoforte playing, as did the writings of Rossini on their

---

82 John Locke, *An Essay Concerning Human Understanding*, Hayes Barton Press, 1768, p. 3.

83 Ibid. p. 638 (original: "turned himself out stark naked, in quest afresh of new notions?").

84 Theodor von Döhler (1814-1856) was an Austrian pianist and composer. He studied in Naples with Benedict and in Vienna with Czerny. From 1836, he began a series of international tours as a virtuoso in Leipzig, Berlin, Paris, London, Holland, Belgium, and Saint Petersburg, where he married the Russian Princess Cheremetev in 1846. Afterwards, he gave no more public performances and settled in Florence in 1848. French critics described Döhler as a Thalberg imitator (see Dana Gooley, *The Virtuoso Liszt*, Cambridge 2004, p. 55).

85 The German virtuoso and composer Jacob Rosenhain (1813-1894) made his London debut in a Philharmonic concert (17 April 1837). In the autumn of the same year, he settled in Paris and became a prominent figure through his chamber-music evenings given with Alard and Ernst.

first appearance in the operatic hemisphere. Startling as these compositions may be from their novelty and elaboration – however they may affect systems previously in beneficial operation, and deemed impregnable by universal consent and approbation – we are convinced they are the result of ascertained truth, and that, as they deserve, so they will receive a patient and unremitting investigation on the part of the aspiring and diligent student. [...]

Anonymous, "*Impromptu*[86] *pour le Pianoforte, composé par Frederic Chopin*", *The Musical World,* 225 (16 July 1840), p. 45.

This composition has rather more interest for the musician than the usual run of productions by the disciples of the school to which M. Chopin belongs. An essential point in this, which may be termed the *exhibitive*, class of pianoforte writing, seems to be the purposed avoidance of the sonata, concerto, or other regular forms of composition, and the adoption of the fantasia, impromptu, or some other vagrant affair of a similar kind in which lack of the attributes of scholarship is excused by the undefined nature of the work. Regularity of structure is easily dispensed with in an undertaking which has no recognized form; and thus are produced, with incredible rapidity, compositions for the pianoforte, intended merely as tests of manual dexterity, and which may be described as having beginnings and ends, but for the most part containing nothing between their extremes save scraps of themes uncouthly intermingled, and long streams of passages of which the difficulty is pretty generally understood to be the chief recommendation. Although belonging to the same class of writing, M. Chopin's Impromptu is neither so outrageously difficult nor so deficient of musician-like treatment as most things of its kind. The principal subject is an elegant strain of melody, slightly pastoral in character, and sustained by an accompaniment, in two parts, very tastefully contrived. The repetition of this, an episode of a widely different character, and a kind of *coda* in which the theme may be detected amid a brilliant shower of demi-semiquavers assigned to the right hand, form the substance of a piece which, though it cannot be considered classical, has, at least, many points of imaginative beauty to recommend it.

---

86 Impromptu, Op. 36.

Anonymous, "*Trois Grandes Valses brillantes,*[87] *pour le pianoforte, par Frederic Chopin*", *The Musical World*, 230 (20 August 1840), p. 126.

The second of these waltzes is now before us. It is a production very moderate both as to the merit and difficulty; – it opens in A minor with what may be called a violoncello solo on the pianoforte, and proceeds without discovering anything especially worthy of notice until we arrive at the first sixteen bars in A major, wherein, at the top of the fifth page, we find a passage of singular ugliness, and which is subsequently aggravated by repetition in the minor mode. After a kind of *trio* in A major, the original subject recurs, and the waltz terminates.

Great names often sanctify very questionable doings, and we take this to be a case in point. M. Chopin's waltz is very well in its way, but were any English writer of one half the reputation of M. Chopin to publish any affair of the like kind, it would unquestionably have at least twice the amount of merit to recommend it.

Anonymous [George Macfarren],[88] "*Souvenir de la Pologne. Seventh set of Mazurkas.*[89] *Frederic Chopin*. Wessel and Stapleton", *The Musical World*, 292 (28 October 1841), pp. 276-277.

Monsieur Frederic Chopin has, by some means or other which we cannot divine, obtained an enormous reputation, a reputation but too often refused to composers of ten times his genius. M. Chopin is by no means a putter down of commonplaces; but he is, what by many would be esteemed worse, a dealer in the most absurd and hyperbolical extravagances. It is a striking satire on the capability for thought possessed by the musical profession, that so very crude and limited a writer should be esteemed, as he is very generally, a profound and classical musician. M. Chopin does not want for ideas, but they never extend beyond eight or sixteen bars at the utmost,

---

87 Waltzes, Op. 34.

88 This article has often been attributed to J. W. Davison, but there is no evidence that Davison is the author (see Niecks, *Frederick Chopin* ii, p. 279; Reid, *The Music Monster* (see above, n. 19), pp. 26-27). In fact, though the article is not signed, one can assert that it was written by the editor of *The Musical World*, since the replies to the letters of Wessel and "An Amateur" are explicitly signed "Ed. M. W." Now, Davison became the editor of the journal in 1843 (see Richard Kitson, introduction in *The Musical World 1836-1891*, Ann Arbor, 1996, vol. i, p. xiii; Richard Kitson, "James William Davison, Critic, Crank and Chronicler: A Re-evaluation", in Bennett Zon, ed., *Nineteenth-Century British Music Studies*, Aldershot 1999, p. 301). Therefore the author of this article is not Davison but George Macfarren, who was the editor of the *The Musical World* in 1841.

89 Mazurkas, Op. 41.

and then he is invariably *in nubibus*. The greatest art in musical composition is that which is employed in prolonging or developing any thought that may arrive – the thought may be the result of natural ability, but the faculty of using it happily – of making it give character to an extended work – of working out of it all of which it is capable – of causing it to be not only the original feature, but the prevailing sentiment – this enviable faculty belongs only to the *practised* as well as *gifted* composer; and this faculty is utterly unexhibited by M. Chopin – indeed, the works of this author invariably give us the idea of an enthusiastic schoolboy, whose parts are by no means on a par with his enthusiasm, who *will be* original whether he *can* or not. There is a clumsiness about his harmonies in the midst of their affected strangeness, a sickliness about his melodies despite their evidently *forced* unlikeness to familiar phrases, an utter ignorance of design everywhere apparent in his lengthened works, a striving and straining after an originality which, when obtained, only appears knotty, crude, and ill-digested, which wholly forbid the possibility of M. Chopin being a skilled or even a moderately proficient artist. It is all very well for a feverish enthusiast, like M. Liszt, to talk poetical nothings in *La France Musicale*, about the philosophical tendency of M. Chopin's music;[90] but, for our parts, we cannot by any manner of means see the connexion between philosophy and affectation, between poetry and rhodomontade, and we venture to call the ears and the judgment of any unprejudiced persons to witness that the entire works of M. Chopin present a motley surface of ranting hyperbole and excruciating cacophony. When he is not *thus* singular, he is no better than Strauss[91] or any other waltz compounder; and being thus singular, he is by many degrees more intolerable, more tiresome, and ridiculous. M. Liszt is reported to have said that there was "an aristocracy of *mediocrity* in England, at the head of which was William Sterndale Bennett";[92] he might, with a vast deal more of

---

90 There are no articles by Liszt on Chopin in *La France Musicale* in 1841.

91 Johann Strauss I (1804-1849). This identification is supported by the fact that Strauss I made a 33-week British tour with his orchestra in 1838, with enormous success. Moreover, Johann Strauss II did not make his public début as a composer and conductor until 1844.

92 William Sterndale Bennett (1816-1875) was one of the leading British composers of the nineteenth century. In 1826 he was admitted to the Royal Academy of Music, where he studied piano under W. H. Holmes and Cipriani Potter, and composition under W. Crotch. In 1832 Bennett wrote his first piano concerto, arousing the admiration of Mendelssohn, who invited him to Germany not as a pupil but as a friend. During his sojourns in Leipzig (1836; 1838-9; 1841-42) Bennett performed in the Gewandhaus concerts, and his compositions and piano playing were praised by both Mendelssohn and Robert Schumann. Bennett's reputation in Germany was so great that he was even offered the conductorship of the Gewandhaus Orchestra, a position he ultimately turned down. On his return to England, Bennett had a successful career in London as a pianist, conductor and teacher. As a composer, he was most productive from 1832 to 1842; his later years were not creatively fertile and he was preoccupied mostly with

truth, have asserted, that there is an aristocracy of hyperbole and nonsense in Paris, of which himself and his friend, the *philosophic* Chopin, are at the summit. If Messrs. Sterndale Bennett and George [Alexander] Macfarren[93] be *mediocre*, most true is it that Messrs. Frederic Chopin and Franz Liszt are super-magnificent; not two things can bear a more superlative difference to each other than the opposite schools thus eminently represented; if one be *good* the other must perforce be *bad* – allow this, and we are content – let posterity award to each its real desert. There is an excuse at present for poor Chopin's delinquencies, he is entrammelled in the enthralling bonds of that arch-enchantress, Georges [sic] Sand, celebrated equally for the number *and excellence* of her romances and her lovers; not less we wonder how she who once swayed the heart of the sublime and terrible religious democrat, Lamennais, can be content to wanton away her dream-like existence with an artistical nonentity like Chopin. We have said so much of the man, that we have neither space nor inclination to say much of the music; suffice it – such as admire Chopin, and they are legion, will admire these Mazurkas, which are super-eminently Chopin-ical; that do *not* we.

Wessel and Stapleton, "Correspondence. M. Frederic Chopin. To the Editor of Musical World", *The Musical World*, 293 (4 November 1841), pp. 293-294.

SIR, – with all respect for the superior judgment almost invariably displayed in your "Review" department, we feel it a duty to ourselves, and also to the public we serve, to say a word in reply to your wholesale denunciations of the works of M. Chopin, in the last Number of *The Musical World*. As we are the sole proprietors of his numerous compositions, perhaps you will not condemn our intrusion, on this occasion, for a moment, on your invaluable time. We were led to purchase the copyright of these works – firstly, from our own opinion of their merits; secondly, from their immense popularity abroad; and lastly, from the unanimous praises accorded to them by some of the highest authorities of the present day; among whom we need only mention the

---

his teaching duties (see Nicholas Temperley, "William Sterndale Bennett" in *The New Grove Dictionary of Music and Musicians*, ed. Stanley Sadie, London 1980).

93 George Alexander Macfarren (1813-1887) was the son of the critic George Macfarren (1788-1943). He learnt music from his father before entering the Royal Academy of Music in 1829, where he eventually became professor. Macfarren was one of the most prolific English composers of the nineteenth century. His compositions include several operas, oratorios and cantatas, nine symphonies, three piano sonatas, and several pieces for concertina. Macfarren was a passionate musical nationalist: he took an active role in the founding of the Society of British Musicians (1834) and sought to restore old English musical characteristics in many operatic works. He also delivered many lectures and wrote theoretical works, such as *The Rudiments of Harmony* (1860) and *Counterpoint: a Practical Course of Study* (1879).

names of Hector Berlioz, Ferdinand Hiller, Henri Herz, Robert Schumann, Sigismund Thalberg, Ignace Moscheles, François Liszt [...] George Sand [...] H. de Balzac, Jules Benedict,[94] Madame de Belleville Oury,[95] Theodore Döhler, Frederic Kalkbrenner, John [Johann Baptist] Cramer, Jacques Rosenhain, Charles Czerny [...] Mendelssohn Bartholdy, Clara Wieck, Alexander Dreyschock,[96] Adolphe Henselt [...] and other eminent pianists and composers. With such authority to back our private opinion, we did not hesitate to arrange with M. Chopin for the copyright of *all* his compositions,[97] and their reception by the musical public generally has borne us out in our anticipations of a successful result to our undertaking. In our admiration of Chopin, we by no means wish to depreciate the undisputedly high claims to distinction of Messrs. Sterndale Bennett and G. Alexander Macfarren, with whom we do not *wish* to compare him [...] With regard to Chopin being entangled in the trammels of the celebrated Georges [sic] Sand, we imagine it rather an incentive to great performances than a drawback on his mental exercise, to endeavour, by his writings, to please the fancy and emulate the praise of one of the most brilliant writers of Europe – acknowledged as much for her critical acumen on subjects of art as for the unrivalled beauty of her literary productions. Depend upon it, Mr. Editor, Madame Georges [sic] Sand considers Chopin anything rather than a NONENTITY, or she would hardly, as you eloquently remark, "trifle

---

94 Sir Julius Benedict (1804-1885) was a British composer and conductor of German birth. Benedict studied with Hummel and then with Weber, who treated him as a member of his family. In 1825 the impresario Barbaja took him to Naples, where he remained for nine years as conductor at the San Carlo and Fondo theatres. In 1834 Benedict went to Paris, where he met Chopin. In 1835 he settled in London, where he was appointed conductor of the Opera Buffa at the Lyceum Theatre, musical director at Drury Lane (1838-48) and conductor at Her Majesty's Theatre (from 1852). Benedict's musical engagements were not limited to the opera: he conducted the Norwich Festival from 1845 to 1878, the Liverpool Philharmonic Society from 1876 to 1880 and accompanied for many years at the Monday Popular Concerts. Furthermore, Benedict devoted himself to teaching and editing piano music: he published an edition of Beethoven's piano works and major works by Dussek, Mendelssohn and Weber.

95 Anna Caroline de Belleville (1808-1880) was a German pianist of French descent. Between 1816 and 1820 she studied with Carl Czerny in Vienna and in 1830 she toured to Warsaw, where she met Chopin and aroused his admiration (see *Correspondance de Frédéric Chopin, I, L'Aube, 1816-1831*, ed. and tr. Bronislas Edouard Sydow with Suzanne Chainaye, Denise Chainaye and Irène Sydow, Paris 1981, p. 172). In July 1831 she made her London début in a concert at Her Majesty's Theatre with Niccolò Paganini; in October of the same year she married the English violinist Antonio James Oury and settled in England.

96 Alexander Dreyschock (1818-1869) was a Czech pianist and one of the most astonishing virtuosos of his time. Owing to the exceptional agility of his left hand, he was said to have two right hands. Although Dreyschock principally played his own pieces, his repertoire also included many classic works, which he rendered with faultless precision, but in a manner cold and essentially prosaic.

97 Though Wessel emphasizes that he was the only proprietor of the copyright of Chopin's work, it must be noted that Cramer actually held the rights to the Variations, Op. 12.

away her dream-like existence" in his society. Trusting to your invariable liberality and fair dealing for inserting this at your earliest convenience, and once more apologizing for our intrusion, we beg leave to remain,

Your very obedient servants and constant readers,
WESSEL AND STAPLETON.
67, Frith Street, Soho, Nov. 1, 1841.

We trust always to maintain the character for "liberality" and "fair dealing" which Messrs. W. and S. accord to our journal. Respecting M. Chopin, though somewhat startled at the formidable array of testimony brought against us, we can but re-assert our opinion [...] We cannot recognise M. Chopin in the rank where fashion has stilted him; but we readily grant him the merit of doing clever eccentric trifles; and whatever the long list of counsellors the spirited publishers have consulted may have *said* to the contrary, we are persuaded they must *think* with us, that such a species of ingenuity has no more to do with high art, than the contriver of a Dutch toy is entitled to a place beside the inventor of the steam engine, or the fabricator of a Paris caricature to be lauded as a second Raphael. This is, unhappily, an age for trifling, and the duty of a critic seems to us to be the most fitly exercised when it tends to the correction of a debility in the public taste – to shew [sic] that adroitness is not genius – that fashion is not intrinsic value – that extravagant attempt is not poetical achievement – that there is a wide distance between the genuine virtue of those who scatter ingots in our path, and those who throw glittering sand in our eyes – and that eminence belongs, of right, only to the truly great, and to the age that fosters greatness. We think Messrs. Wessel and Stapleton have misinterpreted their counsellors, and have mistaken their author's popularity for his artistical value. If M. Mendelssohn, Dr. Schumann, or M. Potter[98] will assert that M. Chopin is entitled to be considered a great musician, we will endeavour to believe them, and succumb accordingly. If the redoubtable knot of "distinguished critics", *par excellence*, above mentioned, have been unable to discover anything undeserving of "unanimous praise" in M. Chopin's

---

98 Philip Cipriani Hambley Potter (1792-1871) was a central figure in London musical life as a pianist, conductor and teacher. He studied with many distinguished masters, such as Thomas Attwood, William Crotch, John Callcott, and Joseph Woelfl. In 1817 he went to Vienna, where he received encouragement from Beethoven. From 1819 to 1836, Potter appeared often as a soloist, giving the English premieres of many Mozart concertos. In 1822 he began teaching at the Royal Academy of Music, where his students included W. S. Bennett and G. A. Macfarren. Potter focused more and more on his educational work and prepared editions of keyboard music by Mozart and Beethoven.

works, we venture to assure them and the publishers that there will be no difficulty in pointing out a hundred palpable faults, and an infinitude of meretricious uglinesses, such as, to real taste and judgment, are intolerable. [...] Ed. M. W.

An Amateur, "Correspondence. M. Frederic Chopin. To the Editor of the Musical World", *The Musical World*, 294 (11 November 1841), p. 309.

SIR, [...] I certainly disagree with you entirely in your opinion of the merits of M. Chopin's music. To me he appears an eminently poetical thinker, and, what is more, fully capable of developing his ideas in the happiest, if not in the profoundest manner. [...]

You accuse him of being affected, – granted; he may be so occasionally; but the same blemish may frequently, without injustice, be laid to the charge of Beethoven, – witness his Sonata in C minor, Op. 111, so greatly extolled by his admirers – the first movement of which I allow to be sublime; but the last, with submission, is surely downright nonsense; witness his Sonata, Op. 78, in A major,[99] the first movement of which gave rise to that peculiar mode of thought since so exuberantly developed in the works of two of the greatest writers of the present day – Mendelssohn Bartholdy, and Sterndale Bennett, – while the March, the Canone, and the Finale,[100] are little better than the sporting of an extravagant and unrestrained fancy; witness the concluding movement of the eighth Symphony in F; the abrupt finish of the *Intermezzo alla Turca*, in B flat, in the same symphony,[101] – the repeated climax after climax to the magnificent finale of the C minor Symphony – literally tiresome, from the constant recurrence of the full cadence – the *Razoumoffsky quartett* in E minor,[102] and lastly, *all* the posthumous quartetts without exception. Why, then, should M. Chopin, who is assuredly not comparable to Beethoven, be vituperated and condemned for occasionally following the example set him by such high authority? I willingly concede his failings on this point; but I cannot be induced to believe that he could have written his superb Concerto in E minor, or his unrivalled pianoforte Preludes and Studies, without possessing a most elaborate knowledge of the mysteries of his art, joined to an exhaustless flow of beautiful and original thought. He is, moreover, as happy

---

99 This is an error. It must be the Sonata, Op. 101. The Sonata, Op. 78 is in F major.

100 The Sonata, Op. 78 has only two movements: Adagio cantabile/Allegro ma non troppo and Allegro vivace.

101 "An amateur" calls *Intermezzo alla Turca* the *Allegretto scherzando* in B flat major.

102 Quartet, Op. 59 No. 2.

in small things as in great, which his melancholy Waltz in A minor, Op. 34,[103] his brilliant and joyous *Invitation pour la danse*,[104] and his never-enough-to-be-admired Mazurkas [...] can amply testify. I am, Sir, with apologies for thus troubling you, your obedient servant,

An Amateur.

We have said our say upon this subject, and we feel no disposition to gainsay it – indeed, our correspondent virtually confesses the weakness of the defense he has undertaken, when he is reduced to the extremity of corroborating his client's virtues by comparing them with what he presumes to be the defects of Beethoven. We still maintain our original assertion to be true – that M. Chopin is an expert doer of little things, his concerto and other lengthy works affording no proofs to the contrary; and that even those little things are sullied by extravagant affectation, and a straining after originality, which, uncontrolled by sound knowledge or judgment, leads him into the commission of the most palpable errors and uglinesses, any one of which we take to be incompatible with the characteristics of a "great musician". [...] ED. M. W.

Anonymous [Henry Fothergill Chorley], "Contemporary Musical Composers. Frederic Chopin", *The Athenaeum*, 740, (1 January 1842), pp. 18-19.

[...] We have styled M. Chopin one of the most individual modern composers: and, indeed, the man and his music are one. The former, frail as a shadow, pale, gentle, gracious in demeanour, and as unworldly in all his incomings and outgoings, as if he pursued his imaginative career in a wood rather than in that most worldly of cities, Paris, – offers one of the many examples furnished by contemporary annals of Music, studied and wrought out poetically; that is, in harmony and conjunction with other liberal tastes and accomplishments. The extreme delicacy of M. Chopin's physical conformation, which makes his appearances in public very rare, and, comparatively speaking, ineffective, has also had its influences in determining the character of his works. It is at once to be perceived, that the latter have been written by one endowed with a man's strength, but a woman's *sensitiveness* of finger: and that, in their execution, force can be better dispensed with than flexibility. Were not M. Chopin's hand, indeed, less vigorously knit than the hands of the Clementis and Hummels of the

---

103 Waltz, Op. 34 No. 2.
104 Waltz, Op. 18.

regular and solid school, it would have been impossible for him to project, far more to carry out, that peculiar mode of execution inculcated in his Studies, and without some knowledge of which his music becomes a dead letter. We need but instance his favourite treatment of the third and fourth fingers, whether they be called upon to enact extensions hitherto undreamed of, or in defiance of all established formulas, to pass over or under each other, by way of maintaining undisturbed a particular position of the hand, or of imparting a peculiar emphasis to an accompanied melody. So uncouth and unattainable will both these feats be found by many students, – the stiff, the short, and the heavy handed, that here, together with a characteristic, we come upon a bar betwixt our author and that general popularity which other writers for the pianoforte have commanded.

[...] A certain fragility and delicacy, akin to those of form and feature, are discernible in M. Chopin's compositions. He seems incapable of continuous effort. It is not by his great concert pieces, or by his one instrumental Trio,[105] or by his Sonata[106] (a sonata in name only), that he will be remembered; but by his studies, his preludes, his romances, his mazurkas – musical gems every one of them, to which a single idea or form suffices, or where a prescribed nationality of character supplies that filling-up, which one of more vigorous fibre will draw from his own stores of resource and science. Chopin, however, is not, as the foregoing remarks might seem to imply, incapable of grand, as well as graceful inventions. One or two of his studies and preludes have a largeness and dignity of outline which more muscular composers might envy [...]

We have not half exhausted Chopin's characteristics; but some of them are as difficult to catch as the tints of mother-of-pearl, and to commit to paper, as the irregular but limited music of birds. His peculiar harmonies, for instance, which render his works, at first acquaintance, so crude and ungracious in perusal, are things that must be felt, but which it is hard to describe. At first, his constant use of the passing note in chords and combinations, will importune the ear, almost as an annoyance. It is one cause, in addition to his predilection for extreme keys, of the general pensiveness of colour which pervades M. Chopin's writings. He may be often spirited, but he his rarely, if ever, brilliant. By degrees, however, the listener will find, that constant uncertainty (to venture a seeming paradox) produces very nearly as much unity and completeness of effect as a general certainty. The ear, again and again disappointed, will begin to regard the natural answer it used to seek as the unreal and episodical

---

105 Trio, Op. 8.
106 Sonata, Op. 35.

thing. As to the artistic soundness of such a principle of musical colouring, much might be objected. We are, however, rather attempting to define a manner, than to apportion its specific value. But it must not be concealed, that such an art of clothing frequently enables old thoughts to pass muster as new ones; that, – apart from the ethereal sweetness and fancy of many of M. Chopin's *motivi*, – a fair proportion of his notions belong to other owners, so "rhymed, twirled" and decked out in a rainbow dress of delicate hues and imperceptible shadings, that neither pilferer nor pilfered is cognizant of the deed; and it is but the analyst, who, penetrating beneath the surface, can detect coincidences and similarities too strong to be other than the offspring of Memory. [...]

[James William] D[avison], "*Impromptu for the Piano-forte. Frederic Chopin. Op. 29*. Wessel & Stapleton", *The Musical World*, 17/5 (3 February 1842), p. 35.

One of our correspondents has spoken most enthusiastically of this work, and with some degree of reason. It is the best thing we have hitherto seen from the fantastic pen of Chopin, and might (a few oddities excepted) have been written by a much more eminent composer. The first two pages, in which the very striking and original opening phrase is admirably and fully developed, are perfect; the next two (episodic) we like not at all, having no relation what ever, either in character or management with the rest; and the last two are the first two repeated, with a short coda. Every Chopinist should make himself master of this Impromptu, since, in addition to its being superlatively Chopinical, it has much abstract merit of its own, and is, moreover, excellent as a study for extensions. If Chopin would always write like some parts of this, we should be glad to welcome him oftener. He has decided ability; and were it not for the injudicious rhodomontade of his Parisian admirers, enough to overturn any composers' equilibrium, we should have some hopes of him.

Anonymous [H. F. Chorley], "New Publications", *The Athenaeum*, 791, (24 December 1842), p. 1115.

[...] In noticing three of Chopin's recent compositions – a Thirteenth and Fourteenth Nocturne,[107] and a Third Ballad,[108] – we shall not point out the general

---

107 Nocturnes, Op. 48.
108 Ballade, Op. 47.

characteristics of this interesting master, but only the peculiarities which mark the new works. The Thirteenth Nocturne is a happy specimen of Chopin's style, for those who can execute it. The sighing, interrupted, pathetic, leading subject is full of languid grace and delicate pathos: while the more pompous strain in the major key, subsequently introduced, is effective, both from the flow of its melody and the rich variety of its harmonies: the amplification of this *corale*, too, on repetition, has a brilliancy most inviting to all such as care for the effect to be produced by climax. But the short-fingered pianist need not ask for this Nocturne, however tempted by our description – twelfths, and other such troublesome extensions being constantly demanded to the executant. Let him take comfort, however, that the modern propensity to stretch the hand can go no further! The Fourteenth Nocturne is less engaging, though its central movement is impressive and melodious. The Ballad is full of beauty, full of eccentricity. [...] Chopin has hardly ever carried further his peculiar system of harmony than in this ballad; and the tenth and three subsequent pages will tax severely the faith and the patience of his admirers. Nothing but the nicest possible execution can reconcile the ear to the crudeness of some of the modulations. These, we presume, are too essentially part and parcel of the man, ever to be changed; but it is their recurrence, as much as the torture to which he exposes the poor eight fingers, which will hinder him from ever taking a place among the composers who are at once great and popular.

J. W. Davison, *An Essay on the Works of Frederic Chopin*, London, Wessel, [1842-43], pp. 1-12.

[...] Frederic Chopin [is] an illustrious instance of pure and unworldly genius, of true and artistic intelligence – unbending to the polyhedric wand of motley fashion – despising the hollow popularity awarded by an ill-judging and unreflecting mob   laughing at the sneers of shallow critics, who, unable to comprehend "the subtle-souled pschychologisms"[109] [sic] of real genius, lay bare to the public their plenary ignorance, and, ill fitted to appreciate the unvitiated motives of exalted merit, expose the dullness of their feeble capacity to the contempt of the illnatured, and the pity of the wise. On surveying the entire works of Frederic Chopin, we find their grand characteristic to be – a profoundly poetic feeling, which

---

109 Davison employs the definition of Coleridge given by Shelley: "a mighty poet and a subtle-souled psychologist" (Percy Bysshe Shelley, *Peter Bell the Third*, Part Fifth (Grace), 378-379).

involves a large degree of the transcendental and mystic – is essentially and invariably of passionate tendency, of melancholy impression, and metaphysical colouring. Chopin does not carry off your feelings by storm, and leave you in a mingled maze of wonder and dismay; he lulls your senses in the most delicious repose, intoxicates them with bewitching and unceasing melody, clad in the richest and most exquisite harmony – a harmony which abounds in striking and original features, in new and unexpected combinations. The first works which Chopin presented to the world, though, of course, not endowed with the decisive and individual character of his now perfected style, clearly pronounced themselves the offspring of a vigorous intellect – of energetic originative genius, untrammeled by conventionalities, unfettered by pedantry. As he has progressed, his style has grown up and expanded like some goodly tree, which casts the shadow of exuberant foliage over a labyrinth of untrodden paths; a refuge for all beautiful and fantastic shapes – children of his etherial [sic] fancy, of his plastic and glowing imagination. [...] One thing is certain, viz. – to play with proper feeling and correct execution, the preludes and studies of Chopin, is to be, neither more nor less, than a *finished pianist* – and, moreover – to comprehend them thoroughly, to give a life and a tongue to their infinite and most eloquent subtleties of expression – involves the necessity of being in no less degree *a poet* than a pianist – a philosophical *thinker* than a musician. Common-place is instinctively avoided in all the works of Chopin – a stale cadence, or a trite progression – a hum-drum subject, or a worn-out passage – a vulgar twist of the melody, or a hackneyed sequence – a meagre harmony, or an unskilful counterpoint – may in vain be looked to throughout the entire range of his compositions – the prevailing characteristics of which, are – a feeling, as uncommon as beautiful – a treatment, as original as felicitous – a melody, and a harmony, as new, fresh, vigorous, and striking as they are utterly unexpected, and out of the ordinary track. In taking up one of the works of Chopin, you are entering, as it were, a fairy-land, untrodden by human footsteps – a path, hitherto unfrequented, but by the great composer himself; and a faith and a devotion – *a desire to appreciate, and a determination to understand* – are absolutely necessary, to do it any thing like adequate justice. [...]

He who enters upon the study of Chopin's poetical music with the heartlessness of an infidel, or the indifference of a sceptic, will be at a discount for his trouble; let him cease his endeavours to attain, what, to him, FROM LACK OF FAITH, is unattainable; let him descend from the loftiest clouds of ideal sublimity, and grovel amid the mire of the mindless mummery of the *popular* composers, and the unmythical in art – Chopin is beyond him. He, on the other hand, who approaches him with a veneration, and a faith, and a love, pre-created by the coupling of anticipation and desire, will find, to his delight, his most extravagant preconceptions realized, and will at once declare, that Chopin is by far the most poetical, by many degrees the most purely intellectual of modern piano-forte writers. [...]

If the *intellectual* be the highest order of music – if the *poetical* be an essential in art – then it must be allowed, by all who know enough of the works of Chopin, that, among modern writers of piano-forte music, he reigns pre-eminently without a rival. [...] Chopin is a vigorous and original thinker, and to write like Chopin involves the necessity of being endowed with the invention and impulses of Chopin, without which, a mere effigy – a mere plaster-of-Paris imitation of his life is the result. In fine, Chopin is a composer of decided and individual genius, and cannot be mimicked by the children of mediocrity. [...]

Anonymous,[110] **"Chopin", *The Musical Examiner*, 14 (4 February 1843), pp. 93-94.**

Though it is undoubtedly true that Frederic Chopin stands at the head of the modern Romantic school, and equally true that every member of the school, from Adolph Henselt down to Theodore Döhler, is his servile imitator, yet there exists in the music of Chopin a poetical *vis*, and an intellectual bias, which raise it far above that of his compeers, and create, in all imaginative hearers, a love that endures for ever – unlike the evanescent passion we feel for music which has merely a licentious prettiness, a ribald effrontery, or a fascinating coquettishness to recommend it. The acute Spinosa, in his "Ethics", tell us, that, no love but intellectual love can be eternal: "*hinc sequitur*" (this is the corollary to a proposition he has just been demonstrating), "*nullum Amorem præter* AMOREM INTELLECTUALEM *esse æternum*".[111] From which splendid truth we may gather, that, whereas the writings of the large majority of modern composers, may, and often undoubtedly do excite intense momentary admiration – yet, from the absence of *the intellectual power*, they are utterly incapable of giving birth to a *durable* affection; while, on the other hand, the deeper motives of the Chopinical writings, though frequently rendering them harder of immediate access to the intelligences of such, as are not trained in transcendental subtleties – yet, in the end, having broken down the barrier, which fatuity, or perverseness, or incapacity of

---

110 Stylistic evidence indicates that this article was written by Davison, who inserted it, as a postscript, in a reprint of *An Essay on the Works of Frederic Chopin*.

111 Spinoza, 'De potentia intellectus seu de liberate humana', Prop. XXXIV, in *Ethica*.

any sort, may have erected in front of the comprehensive and appreciative faculties, they triumph over all less stoutly resistant obstacles, and march right up to the gates of the citadel of THE HEART, which they enter, and inhabit forever. But we must be in some degree, pre-educated, to arrive at a full comprehension of the mystic beauty of Chopin's music. [...]

Chopin is, in himself, modest, unassuming, simple, as a child. Though a prophet in his art, he is unconscious of his mission – though a legislator in music, he wots not of his law-making. He is *instinctively* the great musician. He creates fine music, simply *because he cannot help it*; he could no more prick down a common-place idea, than could Milton a platitude, or Bacon a paradox; in his least conceptions there is the artist seen through the attire in which he clothes them; to write like himself is all he aims at – to imitate a contemporary would be out of his nature; though, unrivalled, he is without an enemy – though beyond all, in his own peculiar sphere, *he is acknowledged by all*; if a young composer go to him with a manuscript, he receives him with open arms and if the young composer possess *any* merit, he retires with the knowledge of how to make use of it. Chopin will not compose to order – his ideas come to him at certain intervals, and *must* then be put in shape, or they torment his existence; should even his publishers, on any special occasion, pay a visit to Chopin, for the purpose of demanding a new manuscript composition – so there be such an one as they require, in the musician's portfolio – good – they may have it; but if not, there is not the sum of money that could induce Chopin to undertake *an order* for any kind of composition whatever – from the highest to the lowest – from the concerto to the mazurka. The piano playing of Chopin is beyond all praise – it is undoubtedly one of the most finished things on record – it has all the excellencies of the most famous classical pianists, from Steibelt and Dussek, down to Mendelssohn and Bennett, and all the executive powers of the more flashy performers, of whom no model existed of yore, but who in Thalberg and Liszt have their principal representatives. To sit by Chopin, and hear him extemporize for half an hour, is, of all conceivable things, the most delightful. His very touch alone is ravishing; and when he brings out the tone of the instrument, and makes it sing as a forlorn maiden, weep as a rejected lover, mourn as an unappreciated poet, shout as a reeling bacchanal, sport as a young lion, stalk as a fierce giant, gambol as an innocent child, howl as a famished wolf, declaim as an inspired orator, – all this, and more than all this, and all in infinite diversity, and yet in exquisitely symmetrical form – you are ready to fall at his feet, and worship him as a spirit of some other sphere, in whose presence you have no right to be, and to whom you pray that he may not destroy you; but a glance at his mild expressive countenance, as he turns his head, pleased that he should have given such unfeigned delight – and your awe for his genius is melted into love for his humility, and you are tempted to exclaim HERE INDEED IS A POET AND A MAN!

Anonymous, "Philharmonic Society", *The Times*, 18261 (4 April 1843), p. 4.

[...] The novelty of the evening was Chopin's Concerto.[112] The celebrity of his lighter compositions had raised the expectations of the audience, but the result was rather disappointing. It is the first work on a large scale which Chopin has attempted, and while it bears the mark of a clever composer, it is as that of one who has ventured into a new region and aims at eccentricities without producing any great effect. The slow movement was the most agreeable portion of the concerto; but on the whole it was dry and unattractive. To Madame Dulcken's[113] playing it would be almost impossible to give too high praise, the brilliancy of the player compensating in a great measure for the comparative inefficiency of the composition, and the applause that was bestowed being certainly awarded to the pianiste rather than to the composer. [...]

Anonymous, *The Musical Examiner*, 23 (8 April 1843), p. 157-59.[114]

[...] The great event of the evening was the first appearance of Chopin's name in the Philharmonic programmes. It is difficult to account for the singular fact that the works of the creator of the Thalberg-Liszt-Döhler school should be so little known in this country, unless it be true, as asserted on the Continent, that British musicians are greater bigots than the artists of any other nation, and are dogmatically opposed to any innovations on what they designate as the standard class in composition. [...] There is endless variety in Chopin's writings, from the profoundly philosophical theme to the light, cheerful and brilliant subject. With all his enormous talent Chopin is one of the most modest and retiring of men. It is with the utmost persuasion than he can be induced to give, once

---

112 The Concerto, Op. 21 was first played at the Philharmonic Society on 3 April 1843 by Louise Dulcken.

113 Louise Dulcken (1811-1850) was the younger sister of the violinist Ferdinand David. In 1828 she settled in London where she met with considerable success both as soloist and teacher (Queen Victoria was among her pupils). She made several appearances as soloist at the Philharmonic Society and gave a series of *soirées* each season.

114 Article reprinted from *The Morning Post*.

during a season, a *matinée musicale*. He prefers to play amongst a few friends and brother artists. The latter, whatever may be their country, receive from him a warm welcome, and he is delighted to encourage the efforts of young aspirant for fame. Of late years he has been in very indifferent health, and to look upon the pallid visage with consumptive hue – to watch those small, and cramped hands, it would be little supposed that in a few moments he could transport his auditors to other worlds – create a dreamy future – inspire the remembrance of the past – and make them alternately weep, as he breathes forth a soul-inspired melody, or smile at some animated and gay theme his playful fancy may suggest. Of all pianists, M. Chopin may be ranked the greatest in the power of creating emotions. Liszt, Thalberg, Henselt, Döhler, John Cramer, Rosenhain, Kalkbrenner [...] all acknowledge the supremacy of Chopin's genius. [...]

The endless diversity of the subjects, and their luxuriant artistic treatment, render this concerto a most extraordinary production. It is a rich, glowing, and prolific conception, carried out with boldness, and the highest finish withal. Chopin's flexible imagination is developed with a *verve*, which, like an impetuous torrent, sweeps everything before it. [...]

Anonymous [H. F. Chorley], "Concerts of the week", *The Athenaeum*, 814, (3 June 1843), p. 534.

[...] There may not be nerve enough in the romance, studies, fantasias, *notturnos* [of Chopin], however rendered, to sustain them in competition against the healthier and more massive music of the great pianoforte composers, but they have an exquisite charm wholly their own and the number is increasing of those who will be grateful to all administering it so skillfully, as the prodigy [Carl Filtsch[115]] and the artist [Charles Hallé[116]] here mentioned.

---

115   Carl Filtsch (1830-1844) was the most gifted student of Chopin. A child prodigy, he gave several concerts in Paris, London and Vienna between 1843 and 1844. In London he won the admiration of Davison, who hailed him as an accomplished musician and as the most worthy interpreter of Chopin's music (see *The Musical Examiner*, 33 (17 June 1843), pp. 237-238). Davison's opinion was shared by several critics and composers, including Chopin and Liszt (see Jean-Jacques Eigeldinger, *Chopin vu par ses élèves*, Paris 2007, pp. 185-187, and Eigeldinger, "Carl Filtsch, miroir de Chopin", in *L'univers musical de Chopin*, Paris 2000, p. 265-284).

116   Charles Hallé (1819-1895) was an English pianist and conductor of German birth. Hallé studied in Darmstadt and Paris, where he became friendly with Chopin, Liszt and Berlioz. In 1848, Hallé moved to England, and in 1849 he settled in Manchester, where he started a series of classical chamber concerts and founded the Halle Orchestra.

Anonymous, "S. James's Theatre", *The Times*, 18324 (16 June 1843), p. 5.

[Review of Carl Filtsch's concert, 14 June 1843]

On Wednesday night, [...] a young pianist, whose name is Filtsch, and who is a pupil of Chopin, played for the first time before a London audience, and met with a very favourable reception. [...] The specimens given of Chopin's music were of a very agreeable kind,[117] being of that lighter sort of composition in which he is so well known to excel, that it is a subject of regret among musicians to find him wasting his time on works of a larger and mere elaborate character. [...]

Anonymous, "Second *Scherzo* in B flat minor. Frederic Chopin. Wessel and Stapleton", *The Musical World*, 18/31 (3 August 1843), pp. 262-63.

We have long since pronounced this Scherzo, one of the most remarkable things in modern pianoforte music. The admirable performance of Charles Filtsch, who has recently executed it with such eminent success, in public and private,[118] has confirmed our opinion of its exalted and manifold beauties. The music of Chopin, and the present scherzo especially, addresses itself to the heart rather than to the brain. Its wild and melancholy nature – its sweet and fresh turns of melody – its strange and unearthly harmonies – its novel and frequently rhapsodical form – one and all bespeak it the music of a poet, which appeals to affectionate and sensitive natures, rather than to the cold worldling for appreciation. Its popularity is however rapidly advancing. The second Scherzo, thanks to little Filtsch, in a great measure, thanks also to that excellent pianist Hallé,[119] in no small measure, has led the way – and one by one, we prophecy, its companions will win their way into the hearts of all musicians who have a higher feeling than the common for their art. We sincerely and gladly recommend this scherzo as a good specimen of the thoughtful and original conceptions of its highly gifted author.

---

117 Filtsch played the Nocturne, Op. 32 No. 1, the Impromptu, Op. 29 and the Waltz, Op. 18.

118 Filtsch played the Scherzo, Op. 31 at the Hanover Square Rooms on 4 July 1843 (see *The Musical Examiner*, 36, (8 July 1843), pp. 261-263).

119 Charles Hallé played the Scherzo, Op. 31 at the Hanover Square Rooms on 7 July 1843 (see *The Musical Examiner*, 36 (8 July 1843), p. 266).

The Musical World, 18/33 (17 August 1843), pp. 275-276.[120]

[...] Chopin has been injured in two ways – he has been over-rated and under-rated. He has been over-rated by the enthusiasts of the romantic school, with Dr. Liszt and Dr. Schumann at their head, who have elevated him into a position which he has surely never intended to occupy – and what of really good and great was in him, has been sadly endangered by the conceit begotten of extravagant applause. He has been underrated by the followers of the classical school, represented by Mendelssohn and Spohr, who, with a very superficial knowledge of his writings, have set him down as a charlatan, only differing from the crowd in superior and hyper-daring eccentricity. The injustice of both sides is manifest to the calm observer. To place Chopin by the side of Beethoven or Mendelssohn is not more or less absurd than to depreciate him to the level of Thalberg or Döhler. He cannot be a thoroughly great composer, because he lacks the first requisite of greatness – viz., the *power of continuity*. He cannot, moreover, be classed among the common herd, since he is eminently an original thinker and is blessed with an inexhaustible invention, and a deep well of new and touching melody. Chopin is incapable of producing a symphony or an overture – that is to say, a good symphony or overture – because, though he has fancy enough to supply admirable materials, he has not a sufficient development of the organ consistency – the bump of epicism, it may be called – to enable him to demonstrate, carry out, amplify, and complete, his original notions. His concertos, *par exemple*, his longest published works, are remarkable for this deficiency. Brilliant and effective as they are, they stop short of greatness in their lack of continuous feeling. The subjects are all excellent, but they fail to give a colouring to the whole. The entire work is not a consequence of his first idea, as in the concertos of Beethoven and Mendelssohn, but wholly independent of it – so much so, indeed, that the *motivi* of either of Chopin's concertos would serve as well for the other as for that to which they appertain. Therefore is Chopin incapable of a large and profound work of art. But, on the other hand, in compositions of less important aim – in fantasias of all kinds, where the fancy may sport, unrestrained by the shackles of form – in short movements, *pot pourris*, and *capriccios*, Chopin's rich fund of ideas, his pleasant fancy, his melancholy humour, his fresh and fluent melody, his elegant graces, his piquant remplissage, his poetical and passionate colouring, are displayed to consummate advantage; and place him apart from the herd of composers of this or

---

120 This article, published on the front page, has no title. Moreover, since the main editorial page was traditionally allotted to the editorial article, the position of this article indicates that it was probably written by the editor of the journal, Davison.

any other age. Let this, then, be borne in mind – Chopin cannot produce a lengthened work; – (his sonata, for instance, is a decided failure – it is neither more nor less than a formless, capricious, vague and disconnected fantasy) – he cannot produce a lengthened work; – but, as a general writer of pianoforte music, such as the judgment of the present era has sanctified by its approval, we say boldly, *he has no superior* – and if we except, among living authors, Mendelssohn and Sterndale Bennett, *no equal*. This is saying much, we allow, but certainly no more than is due to the merits of the man.

Our young English composers have been unwarrantably and even ridiculously prejudiced against the writings of Chopin. Their very slight acquaintance with them places their opposition in a manifestly absurd light. It is sheer bigotry – in many cases, ignorant coxcombry, and nothing better. We have no patience with this utter condemnation of the efforts of a musician of striking and original genius, with nothing but obstinacy and the most ungenerous and narrow-sighted prejudice for its base. [...]

Chopin is a distinguished musician, if not a Beethoven. Let us give real merit its due; which will be a surer method of acquiring our own deserts than the method we have hitherto so rashly and stupidly adopted. Let us pluck the mote from our own eye, and then look into that of our brother. [...]

Anonymous, "Frederic Chopin's Complete Works for the Pianoforte" (published by Wessel and Stapleton), *The Musical Examiner*, 112 (21 December 1844), pp. 87-89.[121]

The modern school of pianoforte composition may be classed under three heads, the classical, the brilliant, and the romantic. At the head of the first section, which has its origin in Mozart and Beethoven, and of which Dussek, Steibelt, Woelfi [sic], and Carl von Weber were brilliant disciples, [stand] Felix Mendelssohn Bartholdy, Ignace Moscheles, and our countryman Sterndale Bennett. At the head of the second section, which took root in the lighter effusions of those twin stars of piano music, Dussek and Steibelt, [...] may be placed Henry Herz and Sigismund Thalberg. At the head of the third section, which can be traced to some of the most fantastic effusions of Beethoven and Weber, undoubtedly reigns preeminent Frederic Chopin. We may just mention another school, that of Sebastian Bach and his endless progeny, Handel, Paradies, and the Scarlattis [...], which is not properly a school of pianoforte music, the character of that instrument having so entirely changed. It might appropriately be called the Clavier school [...]. Our business is,

---

121 Article reprinted from *The Morning Post.*

however, with the romantic school, of which Frederic Chopin is the most brilliant ornament. Among his satellites we may reckon Liszt, Schumann, Taubert,[122] and, perhaps, Stephen Heller. Lest we should be placed among the zealous upholders of Chopin's supremacy over all modern composers for the piano, we will at once state what we conceive to be his faults. First, and foremost in consequence, he has not studied the resources of his art with sufficient ardour to develop that which is within him, so that his deeper works seem rather indications of something that ought to be great, than real efforts of genius. Secondly, he is morbid and affected, the result of which is a frequent want of nature in his works, and a manifest indifference to unique plan and truth of colour. Thirdly, he avoids the primal requisite of the highest order of music, fellowship of his brother artists, thinks lightly of their compositions, and thus loses the opportunity of learning many useful and essential things, which undoubtedly he would learn and profit by, but for his moody love of solitude and capricious waywardness. Chopin himself receives quite another sort of treatment at the hands of his compatriots, for never yet did artist boast a more obstinate knot of enthusiasts than his disciples and imitators. With them Chopin and music are synonymous terms. They esteem him the greatest pianist that ever lived, and the profoundest composer for his instrument. This opinion, however, is not entertained by the first living authorities, though none dispute the original genius and deep poesy of the man, and all allow his consummate knowledge of the character of the pianoforte. At all events, it is an undeniable fact that Chopin's pianoforte studies are more in vogue now than those of any other master, and that a thorough acquaintance with his works is considered a *sine quâ* [sic] *non* in the education of all pianistes who aspire to public display. [...]

The writings of Chopin may be divided into three sections. In the first section we would place his Concertos and other compositions, in which are combined the pianoforte and orchestra. The First Concerto, [...] though long and occasionally rambling, is full of interest. [...] The second section into which we would divide the works of Chopin, includes his three wild Scherzos,[123] his wilder Sonata,[124] and his Fantasia in A flat.[125] [...] In this second section we may reckon a host of minor works, for piano

---

122 Wilhelm Taubert (1811-1891) was a German conductor, composer and pianist. In 1831 he became assistant conductor and accompanist for Berlin court concerts. Between 1845 and 1848 he was music director of the Berlin Royal Opera, and was also court conductor in Berlin from 1845 to 1869. His compositions include six operas, four symphonies, piano works, and more than 300 songs.

123 Scherzos, Opp. 20, 31 and 39.

124 Sonata, Op. 35.

125 The Fantasy, Op. 49 is in F minor. It is not possible that the author means the Polonaise-

solo, in the bravura style, amongst which the most worthy of notice are three charming *Ballades* (a kind of song without words) in G minor, F major and A flat. (Ops. 23, 38, and 47). There is a melancholy beauty about the first of these which has a charm almost indefinable but quite irresistible. We may also place under this section the *Notturni*, of which there are fourteen. These are short expressive compositions, remarkable for that graceful employment of the *tempo rubato*, in which Chopin excels all known pianists. Some of them are perfect gems of melody and refinement. [...] The Impromptus, too, belong to the same section. The first of these, in A flat major, Op. 29, is one of the most sparkling of his brighter works. The *motivo*, in triplets, is light as a fairy footfall, and its development replete with delicate touches and masterly treatment. It is in such impulsive movements that Chopin most excels. Carried away by his first thought, he has not time to become elaborate, or to obscure his meaning by excessive modulations and forced progressions. And this brings us to the mazurkas, those delightful inspirations, whose wild and plaintive beauty has served most to secure for Chopin the reputation of original thought. These, with some other light effusions, such as Waltzes, Boleros, Tarantellas, &c., form the third and last section into which his compositions may be divided. Liszt happily designates the Mazurkas "cabinet pictures". They are, indeed, "exquisite embodiments of fugitive thoughts",[126] involving in their short career much of quaint loveliness, and more of deep passion. Dance music of so high an order was never before conceived. The Waltzes of Mozart, Beethoven, and Weber, graceful as they are, must yield the palm, without contestation, to the *mazurkas* of Chopin. [...] We have not included the twenty-four Preludes, Op. 28, and the twenty-four grand Studies, Ops. 10, 24 [sic], 25, in any of the above sections, since they form of themselves a complete *studio* for the pianoforte, combining examples in all styles, and attacking every kind of difficulty, ancient or modern, likely to obtrude itself to the student's path. A better and more comprehensive course of practice for the instrument is no where to be met with. As music these studies have an advantage possessed by few things of the kind. Of all Chopin's productions, they are undoubtedly the most ingenious and beautiful. Chopin's career has been slow. For a long time he remained unknown in Paris, until his celebrity in this country brought him into repute abroad, and now he can demand his own price for whatever he composes, in every region where music is cultivated. [...] The life of Chopin at present is anything but one of emulation or industry, he composes three or four

---

Fantasy, which was published in 1846.

126 J. W. Davison, *An Essay on the Works of Frederic Chopin*, London, Wessel [1842-3], p. 4.

pieces in a year, which he either throws aside, or sends to his publishers in Germany, France, Italy, Spain, Belgium, Russia, and England[127] – for his FUTURE has been "bought up" at all these places. He teaches very rarely, his extreme delicacy of health precluding the possibility, and his easy circumstances doing away with the necessity of such exertion; when he does teach, his terms are *two guineas for a short lesson*. But the influence of the celebrated Madame Georges [sic] Sand has been anything but beneficial to Chopin, and we much doubt whether he will ever be more than he is now; of course what he has written will gradually be better known.

Anonymous [H. F. Chorley], "Concerts of the week", *The Athenaeum*, 968 (16 May 1846), p. 507.

[...] How long will artists consent to move forward like sheep who follow one another? There is a library of graceful, delicate, and original compositions, – difficult enough, to boot, to satisfy the most ambitious person – in the writings of Chopin; totally unknown to the English public. Surely, some of his grand polonaises, mazurkas, studies, and *notturni* would be far more welcome than this [Leopold de Mayer's[128]] miniature copying of that which is essentially colossal, and the charm of which merely lies in its execution. Let us hope that our hint will not be thrown out in vain. [...]

Anonymous [H. F. Chorley], "New Publications", *The Athenaeum*, 996 (28 November 1846), pp. 1224-1225.

Three new compositions, by M. Chopin, have reached us: A Barcarolle[129] – A Polonaise Fantasie[130] [sic] – and his 17th and 18th Nocturnes[131]. None of these must

---

127 Owing to copyright reasons, Chopin's works were published simultaneously in France, England and German-speaking states. Chopin did not deal directly with Italian, Russian or Spanish publishers, but he sold to the firm Breitkopf & Härtel the rights for Germany and all European countries, with the exception of France and England. Chopin's methods of publication and the role of Breitkopf as distributor of Chopin's works throughout Europe are analyzed in Jeffrey Kallberg, "The Chopin Sources: Variants and Versions in later Manuscripts and Printed Editions", PhD diss. University of Chicago 1982, and "Chopin in the Marketplace", in *Chopin at the Boundaries: Sex, History and Musical Genre*, Cambridge, Mass. 1996, pp. 161-214.

128 Leopold de Mayer (1816-1883) was an Austrian virtuoso. He began studying with Czerny and Schubert in 1833. After two years of intensive study, he made long concert tours in Russia, England, France and America, obtaining enormous success.

129 Barcarolle, Op. 60.

130 Polonaise-Fantasy, Op. 61.

131 Nocturnes, Op. 62.

be approached by such pianists as would "run and read". Not only does M. Chopin delight in extreme keys to an almost morbid excess, but his peculiarities of notation are very puzzling: while the perpetual extensions he demands from the hands, the fragmentary nature of his phrases, the eccentricity of his passages, and the perpetual *hesitation* of his harmonies, must severely test the surest and more experienced musician. Were there M. Chopin's sole claims on consideration, we should warn our "clients" from trafficking in his wares; since the utmost familiarity with their style could be of no general service to the student. But there is an elegance in M. Chopin's music – an occasional grandeur – a sort of speaking expressiveness different from that of any other composer – and a touch of nationality, which redeem his singularities, and warrant the impression that the latter are part and parcel of his nature, not merely assumed to astonish or conceal defects. [...]

Anonymous [H. F. Chorley], "New Publications", *The Athenaeum*, 1014 (April 1847), p. 369.

[Review of *Le Rêve, Chant des Pélerins, Deux Romances, Trois Nocturnes, La Gondola, Chant d'Amour* by Wallace[132]]

[...] In short, after the *Lieder* of Mendelssohn and the earlier Impromptus of Chopin – for Chopin's genius has seemed, of late, losing itself in mysticism – we know not a more attractive collection of modern *bagatelles* than this.

[J. W.] D[avison], "Letters from Paris, No. 11, To Desmond Ryan,[133] Esq.", *The Musical World*, 22/49 (4 December 1847), p. 767.

Wednesday, Dec. 1. – MY DEAR RYAN, – In my apostrophe to the sentiment and good taste of the French musicians, I reckoned, it appears, without my host. The address to Dr. Mendelssohn's widow proceeds solely from the German musicians

---

132 The Irish composer Vincent Wallace (1812-1865) made his early reputation in Dublin as a pianist and violinist. In 1836 he moved to Sydney, where the Australian press hailed him as the "Australian Paganini". He gave concerts in Chile, New Orleans, Philadelphia, Boston and New York. In 1845 he returned to London, where he appeared at a concert in the Hanover Square Rooms (8 May 1845). The production of his opera *Maritana* at Drury Lane (November 1845) established his position as an opera composer for the London stage.

133 Desmond Ryan (1816-1868) worked as music and drama critic for *The Morning Post*, *The Morning Herald* and *The Standard*. He was sub-editor of *The Musical World* from 1846 to 1868. He composed verse for three of Davison's songs ("Sweet Village Bells", "The Lover to His Mistress", "I Have Mine Eyes Tearless").

resident in Paris; the "natives" have nothing to do with it. [...] Meanwhile the following is an English version of the memorial addressed to Madame Mendelssohn by the German musicians [...]:

To the widow of Felix Mendelssohn Bartholdy.

"The death of Felix Mendelssohn Bartholdy is an irreparable loss to the musical art, of which he was the most worthy representative; for its younger followers, of whom he was the safest guide; for Germany, of which he was one of the most illustrious children; and for humanity itself, which he honored, by his worth as by his genius. All his actions, in private life as in artistic endeavour, were stamped with a rare purity, a lofty aim, worthy of is admirable genius, worthy of the sublime models which he found in his beloved country generally, and in his own family in particular. As his youth was nourished in a pious veneration for the sanctity of art, so all his life was consecrated to the worship of that which to him was the most dear, and all his efforts, all his creations were dedicated to its glory.

It is for this that the tears which fall upon his tomb are not only the tears of a family in desolation, of friends in despair! His memory lives and will live in all hearts that beat, with holy rapture, for the beautiful, the noble, and the true.

It is for this that the cry of mourning for his loss, so immense, so irretrievable, is uttered with as much anguish, with as much sincerity, from the Thames to the Danube, from the Seine to the Volga, in every part of civilized Europe, as in the little town of Leipsic which he so often and so long honored and made happy by his immediate presence.

May it, then, be permitted to us, German artists, far from our own country, to offer to the much-beloved master the last acknowledgments of our gratitude and our grief, and to place respectfully in your hands, Madame, the expression of our sentiments for the illustrious defunct.

Paris, 28th Nov. 1847. In the name of the German musicians resident in Paris:

J. Rosenhaim

G. [sic] Kalkbrenner

H. Panofka

S. Heller

C. Halle

F. P. Pixis

E. Wolff

The above are the worthy representatives of the German musicians in Paris. The number of signatures was proposed to have been *eight* but you will perceive there are here but *seven*. This was the result of an error. A Polish piano-forte player, M. Frederic Chopin, who has, I believe, composed some rondos and dance-tunes (*mazurkas*) for the instrument, was applied to, by mistake, I presume, on the part of the German musicians, for his signature. M. Chopin, however, declined to give it. The following was his reply: "*La lettre venant des Allemands, comment voulez-vous, que je m'arroge le droit de la signer?*".

It is true that the signature of M. Chopin, affixed to a manifesto from the German musicians, might strictly have been considered an *arrogation* of a right not invested in his specialty; yet the Germans are very clever in composing waltzes, and here would have been a sympathy of talent if not of blood between M. Chopin and the representatives of Germany; but then, on the other hand, Mendelssohn never wrote either waltzes or mazurkas, which, doubtless, acted as a stimulus to M. Chopin in refusing to affix his signature – for he might reasonably say to the departed musician : "Si MOI, je suis musicien, qu'est ce que tu es, TOI?". The resolution of the question would be as difficult as Euclid's most abstruse problem – its consideration as perplexing as the *pons asinorum*.[134] Salomon said: "Even this also is vanity!".[135]

However, the want of M. Chopin's signature has not yet decided the German musicians upon withdrawing the memorial to Madame Mendelssohn. I question, indeed, whether the question of withdrawal will be raised. What a pity that Musard is not German; he would consent to affix his signature without difficulty; for, in his way, he is *an artist*. There is M. Alkan[136] too, a German pianist, – why was *he* not applied to?

[J. W.] D[avison], "Letters from Paris, No. 12, To Desmond Ryan, Esq.", *The Musical World*, 22/50 (11 December 1847), pp. 785-786.

[...] I have been reproached by some persons for the *bitterness* which dictated my observations, last week, *apropos* of M. Chopin and the late Felix Mendelssohn

---

134 *Pons Asinorum* (The Bridge of Asses) is the name given to Euclid's fifth proposition in Book 1 of his *Elements* of geometry, which states that the angles at the base of an isosceles triangle are equal to one another. According to Brewer's *Dictionary of Phrase and Fable,* the reason it came to be known as the *pons asinorum* is that this was the first theorem that gave boys trouble understanding.

135 Book of Ecclesiastes, 2:1.

136 Charles Valentin Alkan (1813-1888) was a French composer and one of the greatest virtuoso pianists of his day. Early in his life he was socially active and good friends with prominent musicians and artists including Chopin, Liszt and Delacroix. After 1848 he gradually withdrew from the concert platform, and he lived a reclusive life in Paris until his death.

Bartholdy. The reproach is unjust; no bitterness gave birth to those remarks, but re-spect to the departed master, in whose single person was the concentrated essence of all music, and whose death is as though from now to a century forward were to be a blank in the progress of the art. The musician who fails in respect where re-spect is so manifestly due – nay, I will go further, the musician who does not merely respect, but revere, worship, idolize the name of Mendelssohn, I do not, I *cannot* consider a worthy follower of his art, and therefore, owing him no respect, I pay him none. Understand well, that I only speak of M. Chopin, *the musician*; of M. Chopin, *the man*, I know nothing, not enjoying the advantage of his acquaintance. If not to admire the music of M. Chopin be proof of bitter spirit, let me for ever called "bitter"; I like it not, nor can I like it – it sins against all my notions of the properties of art, and presents no *ideal* attraction to my fancy. If to think that M. Chopin forgets him-self in not readily paying homage to Mendelssohn – who in comparison to the Polish pianist is as the sun to a spark flickering in a tinder box – and entitles me to charge of bitterness, once more I am content to be styled "bitter", and strong in faith, exult in my bitterness. But, gravely, the accusation is absurd; what I have said, was not bitter, but sweet to all rightly constituted minds; – in confirmation whereof I appeal to MM. Rosenhaim, Hallé, Heller, Panofka, Kalkbrenner (Kalkbrenner was not too arrogant to give his name), Pixis, Wolff, and the German musicians in Paris whom they have the honor to represent on so worthy and melancholy an occasion.

Anonymous [H. F. Chorley], "New Publications. *Deux Valses pour la* [sic] *Piano, par* F. Chopin",[137] *The Athenaeum*, 1071 (6 May 1848), p. 467.

Whereas other more robust pianists announce a concert or see company at Erard's or Broadwood's, by way of acquainting the "Monster London" with the ar-rival of "themselves and suite", – M. Chopin, whose extreme fragility of health is, un-happily, historical as the cause of his few and uncertain public appearances, quietly publishes Two Waltzes – his sixty-fourth work. Nor must the offering be counted as a frivolous one because of its title. These Waltzes, it is true, are less developed than

---

137 Review of the first two Waltzes from Op. 64, published by Cramer, Beale & Co. on 29 April 1848 and by Wessel on September 1848 (see CFEO). The third waltz was published late in the year (for the publication history of the Waltzes, Op. 64 see Christophe Grabowski, "Publication des *Valses* op. 64 dans un contexte historique et documentaire", in Jean-Jacques Eigeldinger, ed., *Interprétations*, Geneva 2005, pp. 53-68).

the three in A minor, D flat major, and F major (Op. 34);[138] but they have, still, more originality and style than many a heap of notes calling itself sonata or concerto by contemporary composer, thinking to claim honours as a classical writer. It is true that one, in D flat major,[139] is dreamy; that the other, in C sharp minor,[140] though more vigorous, is wild and quaint, – both totally unlike the buoyant and piquant tunes by which [Johann] Strauss [I], Lanner, Labitzsky,[141] and Gung'l[142] set the world dancing in a *four-in-a-bar* step (so absurd is Fashion!). It is true that M. Chopin's notation is, by fits, needlessly teazing, – that his harmonies from time to time are such as require his own sliding, smooth, delicate finger to "carry off". It is true that old-fashioned steady pianoforte players who have no touch of waywardness, or gipsy wildness, or *insanity*, in their treatment of the instrument, will point to single bars with Mr. Burchell's monosyllable[143] – utterly unable, moreover, to make anything of the whole. But there is a world of real – as well as of *affected* – romance in Art; and though no wise man could confine himself exclusively to this, no liberal one will refuse to enter it in turn. And seeing that nothing stands still, nor is exactly repro-duced, – and believing that *romantic* music appears so simultaneously just now in all the countries of Europe as to indicate a desire which *will have* satisfaction, – such individual *reveries*, such delicately-tinted sketches, such melodies near akin to the Æolian harp's caprices, as M. Chopin gives us, must be allowed to possess the gen-eral value of artistic significance and consistency, as well as an exquisite charm for particular listeners when in a particular mood. He is distinctly, gracefully, poetically natural; and, therefore, as we long ago said, when there was small idea of his ever coming to England,[144] well worth studying in his writings. Those are fortunate who

---

138 The keys given here are wrong: the first waltz of Op. 34 is in A flat major, the second in A minor and the third in F major.

139 Waltz, Op. 64 No. 1.

140 Waltz, Op. 64 No. 2.

141 Joseph Labitzky (1802-1881) was a Bohemian violinist, conductor and composer. In 1825 he founded his own orchestra and he gave several concerts in Vienna, Prague, Warsaw and London. La-bitzky composed over 300 dances, but in the latter part of his career, he was unable to challenge the supremacy of Gung'l and Johann Strauss as a waltz composer.

142 Joseph Gung'l (1809-1889) was a Hungarian composer, bandmaster and violinist. Known as the "Graz Strauss", and the "Berlin Strauss", Gung'l composed over 436 dance melodies and several marches, which found their way into the German military music repertory.

143 Mr. Burchell is a character in *The Vicar of Wakefield*, a novel published by Oliver Goldsmith in 1766. Chorley refers here to Mr. Burchell's habit of ejaculating "fudge" (nonsense) to everything his neighbours affected to believe (see Oliver Goldsmith, *The Vicar of Wakefield*, Courier Dover Publica-tions, 2004, pp. 34-35).

144 See *The Athenaeum*, 740 (1 January 1842), pp. 18-19.

have means of gaining a further insight into the matter, by hearing the composer perform his own compositions.

Anonymous [H. F. Chorley], "M. Chopin's Matinée",[145] *The Athenaeum*, 1079 (1 July 1848), p. 660.

It is not too much to say that, at a period when so many sources of pleasure appeared to be exhausted, – when mechanical skill, too, has been carried to a point precluding the hope of much further discovery – M. Chopin gave his audience yesterday week an hour and a half of such musical enjoyment as only great beauty combined with great novelty can command. We have had by turns this great player and the other great composer, – we have been treated to the smooth, the splendid, the sentimental, the severe in style, upon the pianoforte, one after the other: M. Chopin has proved to us that the instrument is capable of yet another "mode" – one in which delicacy, picturesqueness, elegance, humour may be blended so as to produce that rare thing, a new delight. His treatment of the pianoforte is peculiar: and though we know that a system is not to be "explained in one word", we will mention a point or two so entirely novel that even the distant amateur may in part conceive how from such motions an original style of performance, and thence of composition, must inevitably result. Whereas other pianists have proceeded on the intention of equalizing the power of the fingers, M. Chopin's plans are arranged so as to utilize their natural inequality of power, – and if carried out, provide varieties of expression not to be attained by those with whom evenness is the first excellence. Allied with this fancy are M. Chopin's peculiar mode of treating the scale and the shake, and his manner of sliding with one and the same finger from note to note, by way of producing a peculiar *legato*, and of passing the third over the fourth finger. All of these innovations are "art and part" of his music as properly rendered; and as enacted by himself, they charm by an ease and grace which, though superfine, are totally distinct from affectation. After the "hammer and tongs" work on the pianoforte to which we have of late years been accustomed, the delicacy of M. Chopin's tone and the elasticity of his passages are delicious to the ear. He makes a free use of *tempo rubato*; leaning about within his bars more than any player we recollect, but still subject to a presiding sentiment of measure such as presently habituates the ear to the liberties taken. In music

---

145 Chopin's first semi-public concert in London took place on 23 June 1848, at 99 Easton Place, the residence of Adelaide Kemble Sartoris.

not his own we happen to know that he can be as staid as a metronome; while his Mazurkas, &c. lose half their characteristic wildness if played without a certain freak and licence, – impossible to imitate, but irresistible if the player at all feel the music. This we have always fancied while reading M. Chopin's works: – we are now sure of it after *hearing* him perform them himself.

The pieces which M. Chopin gave at his *Matinée* were *Notturni*, Studies, *La Berceuse* (a delicate and lulling dream with that most matter-of-fact substratum, a ground bass) – two Mazurkas – and the two new Waltzes.[146] Most of these might be called "gems" without misuse of the well-worn symbol. Yet if fantasy be allowed to characterize what is essentially fantastic, they are not so much gems as pearls – pearls in the changeful delicacy of their colour, – in occasional irregularities of form, not destructive, however, of symmetry – pearls in their *not* being the products of health and strength. They will not displace and supersede other of our musical treasures, being different in tone and quality to any possessions we already enjoy; but inasmuch as Art is not final, nor Invention to be narrowed within the limits of experience, no musician, be he ever so straight-laced or severe – or vowed to his own school – can be indifferent to their exquisite and peculiar charm. It is to be hoped that M. Chopin will play again; and the next time some of his more developed compositions, – such as Ballads, *Scherzi*, &c., if not his Sonatas and *Concerti*. Few of his audience will be at all contented by a single hearing.

Anonymous, "Miscellaneous", *The Musical World*, 23/28 (8 July 1848), p. 444.

M. Chopin has lately given two performances of his own pianoforte music, at the residence of Mrs. Sartoris (late Miss Adelaide Kemble),[147] which seem to have given much pleasure to his admirers; among whom Mdlle. Lind, who was present at the first, seems to be the most enthusiastic. We were not present at either, and, therefore, have nothing to say on the subject. – *Vivat Regina!*

---

146 Waltzes, Op. 64 Nos. 1 and 2.

147 The English soprano Adelaide Kemble Sartoris (1814-1879) was the younger daughter of the actor Charles Kemble. She studied in Paris (where she met Chopin), Germany and Italy. In 1841 she returned to England and on 2 November appeared with great success in an English version of *Norma* at Covent Garden. In 1843 she married Edward John Sartoris and retired after a brief but brilliant career.

Anonymous [H. F. Chorley], "M. Chopin's Second Matinée",[148] *The Athenaeum*, 1081 (15 July 1848), p. 708.

Little is to be added to the general character of this charming and individual artist which we gave on a former occasion.[149] But M. Chopin played better at his second than at his first *Matinée* – not with more delicacy (that could hardly be), but with more force and *brio*. Two among what may be called M. Chopin's more serious compositions were especially welcome to us – his Scherzo in B flat minor[150] and his Study in C sharp minor.[151] The former we have long admired for its quaintness, grace and remarkable variety, – though it is not guiltless of a needlessly crude and hazardous modulation or two; – the latter, again, is a masterpiece – original, expressive and grand. No individual genius, we are inclined to theorize, is one-sided – however fondly the public is apt to fasten upon one characteristic and disproportionately to foster its development: and if this crotchet be based on a sound harmony, M. Chopin could hardly be so intimately and exquisitely graceful as he is if he could not on occasion be also grandiose. At all events, the remark is eminently illustrated by certain among his Polonoises (let us instance those in A[152] and A flat major[153]), and by several of his Studies – that in C minor[154] not forgotten, as well as the one which has here tempted us to generalize. [...]

**Anonymous, "Music in Manchester. (From our Correspondent)",
The Musical World, 23/37 (9 September 1848), pp. 577-578.**

The concert given on Monday evening (Aug. 28) by the directors attracted a very elegant and numerous assemblage of visitors. The causes of attraction were many. First there were the vocalists, of whom the chiefest was Mademoiselle Alboni, decidedly the greatest contralto that ever appeared in this country, and one of the greatest artists of the day; Signor Salvi, the celebrated tenor, who yields to none but Mario in celebrity; the Signora Corbari, an engaging and delightful singer, who has

---

148 Chopin's second *matinée* took place at the house of Lord Falmouth, 2 St. James's Square, on 7 July 1848.
149 See *The Athenaeum*, 1079 (1 July 1848), p. 660.
150 Scherzo, Op. 31.
151 Etude, Op. 10 No. 4 or Op. 25 No. 7.
152 Polonaise, Op. 40 No. 1.
153 Polonaise, Op. 53.
154 Etude, Op. 10 No. 12 or Op. 25 No. 12.

won no small degree of repute by her performances at the Royal Italian Opera in two seasons; and lastly, M. Chopin, the French-celebrated pianist and composer, who is a novelty in these parts. [...] You must pardon me if I venture to say very little of Mons. Chopin's pianoforte playing. He neither surprised me, nor pleased mc entirely. He certainly played with great finish – too much so, perhaps, and might have deserved the name of *finesse* rather – and his delicacy and expression are unmistakable; but I missed the astonishing power of Leopold the Mayer, the vigour of Thalberg, the dash of Herz, or the grace of Sterndale Bennett. Notwithstanding, Mons. Chopin is assuredly a great pianist, and no one can hear him without receiving some amount of delectation. [...]

M., "Chopin at Edinburgh", *The Musical World*, 23/42 (14 October 1848), pp. 668-669.

Frederic Chopin, the eminent pianist and composer, who has been staying for a short time in Scotland, gave the musical public of Edinburgh an opportunity of hearing him play a selection of his own compositions at the Hopetoun Rooms on Wednesday evening. The attention and delight with which M. Chopin's performance was listened to by a brilliant and judicious audience may be taken as a proof that his talent is properly appreciated here. [...] So much has been written about the peculiar beauty of Chopin's playing, that any additional praise from this part of the world can hardly be necessary. It may be sufficient to say, that the exquisite delicacy of his touch, and the consequent beauty of tone, and the perfectly finished manner in which every passage is played can scarcely be surpassed. [...]

Anonymous,[155] "Music in Paris. (From our Correspondent)", *The Musical World*, 24/42 (20 October 1849), p. 657.

I regret much to announce to you the death of Frederick Chopin, the celebrated pianist and composer. [...] Although he had for some time ceased to take any active part in musical matters, and had almost entirely abandoned both playing and composing, the death of M. Chopin cannot but be lamented by all the lovers and followers of the art. He was certainly one of the most eminent and one of the most original

---

155 The author of this article is James William Davison, who was in Paris and subsequently gave a detailed description of Chopin's funeral (see article of 10 November 1849).

men in his particular sphere, and his influence on his contemporaries has been very considerable. Should I learn any more particulars of his death I will let you have them next week. [...]

[J. W.] D[avison], "Chopin. (From our own Correspondent)", *The Musical World*, 24/45 (10 November 1849), pp. 705-706.

Paris, November, 1849.

Frederic Chopin was born at Zelazowavola [sic], near Warsaw, in 1810, and died in Paris on the 17th of last month, before he had completed his 40th year. [...] Chopin, who was a Catholic, having always expressed a wish that the *Requiem* of Mozart should be performed at his funeral, it was determined that his desire should be accomplished. [...]

The ceremony, which took place on Tuesday (the 30th ult.,) at noon, in the Church of the Madeleine, was one of the most imposing we ever remember to have witnessed. The great door of the church was hung with black curtains, with the initials of the deceased, "F. C.", emblazoned in silver. On our entry we found the vast area of the modern Parthenon entirely crowded. The nave and aisles, the choir, the galleries above the magnificent porticos that adorn the walls, the interstices behind and between the columns of the porticos, the organ gallery, and the gallery that runs round the choir, immediately under the windows, were alive with human beings, who had come to see the last of Frederic Chopin. Many, perhaps, had never heard of him before – for Chopin's was neither a popular talent nor a popular name – many more were doubtless indifferent both to the man and to his influence; some few were there who felt a deep and sincere interest in the proceedings; but the pomp and pageantry had an equal attraction for all. There could not have been less than 4000 persons present. In the space that separates the nave from the choir, a lofty mausoleum had been erected, hung with black and silver drapery, with the initials "F. C." emblazoned on the pall. At noon the service began. The orchestra and chorus (both from the Conservatoire, with M. Girard as conductor), and the principal singers (Madame Viardot-Garcia, Madame Castellan, Signor Lablache, and M. Alexis Dupont), were placed at the extreme end of the church, a black drapery concealing them from view. [...] A solemn march was then struck up by the band, during the performance of which the coffin containing the body of the deceased was slowly carried up the middle of the nave. Meyerbeer, Camille Pleyel, the Prince Czartoryski, Eugene [sic] Delacroix (the painter), and other well-known individuals, officiated as chief mourners, each holding a *cordon* of the pall. As soon as the coffin was placed in the mausoleum, Mozart's *Requiem* was begun. The imposing effect of this mighty inspiration, with such executants, and on such occasion, needs not to be told. The march that accompanied the body to the mausoleum was Chopin's own composition, from his first pianoforte sonata, instrumented for the orchestra by M. Henri Reber.[156] During the ceremony M. Lefébure Wély,[157] organist of the Madeleine, performed two of Chopin's preludes upon the organ, one of the finest in Paris. The solos in the *Requiem* were sung by the four artists we have named above. After the service, M. Wély played a voluntary, introducing themes from Chopin's compositions, while the crowd dispersed with decorous gravity. The coffin was then carried from the church, all along the Boulevards, to the cemetery of Père la Chaise [sic] – a distance of three miles at least – Meyerbeer and the other chief mourners, who held the *cordons*, walking on foot, bare-headed. A vast number of carriages followed, and the procession was beset and incommoded by crowds of curious people. At Père la Chaise [sic], in one of the most secluded spots, near the tombs of Habeneck and Marie Milanollo,[158] the coffin was deposited, in a newly-made grave. The friends and admirers took a last look, ladies in deep mourning threw garlands and flowers upon the coffin, and then the gravedigger resumed his work, and began filling up the pit which he had dug for the last home of poor Chopin. The ceremony was performed in silence. Much to the disappointment of many persons, but in consonance, we are disposed to believe, with the wishes of the deceased, no discourse was pronounced over the body.

This is not the place to criticise the merits of Chopin as a pianist and composer. Time will show, when the influence of his presence amongst us has faded away, whether the high reputation he enjoyed as a composer (of his peculiar merits as a pianist there cannot be a question) was wholly or partially merited, or whether, as some insist, his genius and influence have been greatly overrated by his immediate circle of admirers, and only tacitly admitted by the mass, who, knowing little or

---

156 Henri Napoléon Reber (1807-1880) was a French composer. He became professor of harmony at the Conservatoire in 1851 and succeeded Fromental Halévy as professor of composition in 1862.

157 Louis Lefébure-Wély (1817-1869) was organist at the Madeleine from 1847 to 1858 and then at St. Sulpice from 1863 to his death. His exceptional pedal technique led Franck to dedicate his *Final* to him, and Alkan his *Douze études pour les pieds seulement*. As a composer, Lefébure-Wély wrote works for organ, piano, chamber ensemble and orchestra.

158 Maria Milanollo (1832-1848) was an Italian violinist. She studied with her older sister, Teresa, before both completed their violin training with De Bériot. From 1842 the Milanollo sisters began a series of extended European concert tours which took them to England, Belgium, France, Germany, Bohemia, Switzerland and northern Italy, rivalling Paganini in artistic and financial success. Maria's career broke off in 1848, when she suddenly died of tuberculosis.

nothing of his writings, were too apathetic, or too indifferent, to examine them on their own account. At any rate, it must be acknowledged that Chopin, by some means or other, was able to acquire the name of a musician at once profound and inventive, and, whatever may be our own opinion, we are not at present inclined to dispute his claims to be considered one of the most original, if not the most gifted and accomplished, composers who have contributed to the *repertoire* of the pianoforte. [...]

Anonymous, "Musical Traits and Memorials, by Tartini's Familiar. Frederic Chopin", *Bentley's Miscellany*, 27 (January 1850), pp. 185-191.

[...] While the subject is fresh in my mind I wish to speak a little concerning one of the most graceful, delicate, and original artists who ever added treasure to the stores of instrumental music, I mean Frederic Chopin. Those who knew him during his many years' residence in Paris, or who *divined* him (for acquaintance under such circumstances becomes almost impossible) during the hurries and confusions of the London season of 1848, will bear me out in stating that he well merited his memorial. Perhaps it may serve the purpose of drawing a stranger or two more within the enchanted circle of his music.

For enchantment there is in Chopin's works: which implies that their beauty has something fantastic, capricious, delicate, not altogether natural. [...] I have known amateurs in no respect stupid or ill-educated who could not bear a particular rhythm, or particular key; and the jealousy betwixt vocal and instrumental players is "old as time and clear as day". But apart from all these barriers which Bigotry and Self-conceit delight in throwing up betwixt good Christians and their pleasures, I have often remarked that in some persons of taste a relish for what is fantastic, elvish, delicate, humorous, is totally wanting. [...] On such amateurs (and probably they might be devout Handelians, or severely dramatic Gluckists, or implicit believers in Mozart as the one idol), the music of Chopin would be wasted; and the name be thought hardly worthy of admission within their Pantheon of half-a-dozen divinities, whereof self is not the smallest. [...]

I will not indulge in any long-drawn or technical analysis of the peculiarities of Chopin's compositions. Never has so long a series of works more intensely individual been produced – his Mazourkas, how rationally pensively, quantly freakish! – his Ballads, *Notturni* and Preludies [sic], how tenderly and melodiously poetical: – his Polonoises, how pompous and stately! There is one in A major,[159] of grandeur

---

159 Polonaise, Op. 40 No. 1.

as yet unequalled, which I never hear without its calling up some coronation-festival, so gorgeously regal is its step. His Studies, again, are of the highest order: and this not solely as finger-exercices, but also as compositions – in spite of the peculiar notation adopted, which renders them sometimes needlessly difficult to decipher. Two remarks, however, must be offered – since they will supply *a key* to Chopin's peculiar manner to those whom Chopin's music in any respect attracts. The left hand of the player is never to be out of *tempo*: the right hand may almost always (save in the case of some distinctly formal instrumental figure) indulge in *tempo rubato*. Again, whereas other pianoforte masters insist on the equality of the fingers – in spite of the anatomical lock and key put by Nature on the motion of the third digit, – Chopin provided for their inequality: wishing, as he once told me, so far as was possible, to develope [sic], not to destroy, the individuality of each member of the hand. Hence a system of fingering, which might possibly have made the Clementis and Hummels as irate as such gentlemen are apt to become when anything in the least new is broached and the wisdom of which is open to controversy, – but which is still a system.

Those, however, who knew and who loved the man (for the two things were one), will best taste and render the peculiar humour of Chopin's music – will best understand how it will bear a certain dash of private judgment on the part of the player – but not the slightest touch of exaggeration. Pianists of the *hammer-and-tongs* school – or who can do nothing without a *métronome*, are warned off Chopin's fairy-land. His interpreters ought to have hands as long as Perugino's angels, and as delicately firm as though they were framed on adamant. The uttermost precision and the most sensitive ease are all too little to play Chopin's music as he played it himself. For, though anything but foolish – anything but weak (there is iron in the rose) – he was a curious compound of fantasy, feeling, and strength – one of the most wayward, tender, *spirituel* persons I have ever conversed with. Alike remarkable for his simplicity and for his self-consciousness – he could be as eagerly irritable as a child about some little mistake in a concert-*programme*, as eagerly entertained over the toys of art or luxury, with which his *appartement* was filled by his friends and pupils. He could divert himself with trifling courtesies and mysteries – making genial sport, to those who were in his confidence, of his own interest in such things. Yet never did artist more quietly trust in his own genius as sufficient for his own success, nor more worthily hold himself remote from the intrigues, and the littlenesses, and the fevers, with which the intercourse betwixt performer and public, the connexion betwixt art and letters, are now spoiled and mixed up in France – than Chopin. There was in his nature a mixture of delicacy and pride, which cleared him of any possible participation in the practices of Parisian journalism. Traffic he could not – directly or indirectly. He was loved and admired as a *bon camarade*, but it was said of him truly, that into the shop he would not, could not, go. Hence arose his extreme aversion to playing in public, and not altogether, as some have stated it from his physical weakness. It was further his fancy that the best artists are unequal, and that it is only perfect mediocrity which can be perfect always – and when the clock strikes. And he knew, too, that the wayward, quaint, mournful playfulness of his mazurkas and ballads, and *notturni*, ought always to have not only the air, but, in some degree, the reality of improvisation, which few men can control. I have never been thoroughly satisfied in the playing of Chopin's more poetical music by any performer, save by Liszt; when Liszt is in his gentler mood, and sits dreaming away at the piano, – calling upon his supernatural memory to give up its treasures for the delight of one or two intimates and of himself. But as the best written account of playing is about as unsatisfactory as the lessons for dancing printed in a book, the solemn perusal of which (with illustrative diagrams) once surprised me into a hearty laugh, greatly to the offence of its author – let us "come away from the piano". [...] A monument to his [Chopin's] memory is projected; but do what sculptor or epitaphmonger will they will not better the old adage that Chopin's best monument is in his music. His death leaves us almost without a composer for his instrument meriting the name.

Anonymous, "The Musical Union", *The Musical World*, 25/17 (27 April 1850), p. 254.

[Review of Charles Hallé's concert at the Musical Union, 23 April 1850]

[...] After the Sonata[160] Mr. Hallé trifled away a quarter of an hour with two nocturnes and a polonaise of Chopin, the merits of which we confess our inability to perceive. We are bound, however, to add that the general feeling differed from our own, and that M. Hallé's performance, vague and dreary as the music itself, was unanimously applauded. Still we cannot think Mr. Ella[161] might have chosen some more intelligible, if not more favourable, example's [sic] of Chopin's style from the large catalogue of works at his disposal. [...]

---

160 Mendelssohn's Cello Sonata, Op. 58.

161 John Ella (1802-1888) was an English violinist, concert manager and critic. Besides his teaching activity, he wrote music criticism for *The Morning Post* (1826–42) and *The Athenaeum* (1830–34), and contributed to the *Musical World* and the *Court Journal*. In 1845 he founded the Musical Union, a socially élite concert society devoted to the high-quality performance and serious contemplation of Chamber music. See Christina Bashford, "John Ella and the Making of the Musical Union" and *The Pursuit of High Culture: John Ella, Chamber Music, and Victorian London* (see above, n. 45).

Anonymous *The Athenaeum*, 1234 (21 June 1851), p. 668.

[...] We have always felt a strong persuasion that the individuality of Chopin as a composer was sure to bring his pianoforte music one day into request, – no writer since Beethoven having appeared in style so unique, and so innocent of the slightest reference to model, ancient or modern. Now, we perceive that the Notturnos, Balades [sic], &c. of the Polish poet – for a poet Chopin was – are creeping into our chamber *programmes*; and two of the newest arrivals – a Mdlle. Meara[162] and a M. Teleffsen [sic][163] (the latter, we believe, a Dane or a Norwegian) are expressly commended as "having the tradition" of the most exquisite and fanciful of modern pianists. [...]

Anonymous, "Reviews of Music", *The Musical World*, 29/30 (26 July 1851), pp. 471-472.

[...] In his mazurkas, [Jacob Blumenthal[164]] has shown himself capable of imitating Chopin without caricaturing the eccentricities of the great Polish pianist, out of whose ashes Franz Liszt, with the powerful aid of M. Escudier of the *France Musicale*, is convulsively endeavouring to raise a Phœnix.[165] We wish him joy of the task. If Franz Liszt fail in persuading the world that Chopin was a Phœnix, he may perhaps succeed in convincing posterity that he himself was a Goose.

In his imitations of Chopin (Mazurkas, books 3 and 11[166] – which we can recommend as really pretty and sparkling pieces), M. Jacques Blumenthal has successfully

---

162   Camille Dubois-O'Meara (1828-1907) studied with Chopin between 1843 and 1848. She made her first appearance as a professional pianist in Paris in 1847, when she played the Concerto, Op. 11 with Chopin. After the death of her master, she was regarded as the truest representative of Chopin's tradition. For further details see J. J. Eigeldinger, *Chopin vu par ses élèves* (see above, n. 115), pp. 212-214.

163   The Norwegian pianist Thomas Dyke Acland Tellefsen (1823-1874) studied in Paris with Chopin from 1844 to 1847. He became a close friend of the Polish composer and accompanied him on his journey to Britain in 1848. Tellefsen gave his first concerts in England in the first half of 1849; by 1851 he was regarded as one of the outstanding pianists of his time and was especially admired as an interpreter of Chopin's music. In 1860 he published a twenty-volume *Collection des Œuvres pour le piano par Frédéric Chopin* (Richault). For further details see Eigeldinger, *Chopin vu par ses élèves*, pp. 236-238.

164   Jacob Blumenthal (1828-1908) was a German composer and pianist. He studied at the Paris Conservatoire under Halévy from 1846 and he settled in London in 1848 as a pianist and piano teacher. He wrote several salon pieces, comprising nocturnes, mazurkas and ballades.

165   Liszt's book *F. Chopin* was published in 1852 by Escudier. It was first issued as a series of seventeen lengthy articles, in *La France Musicale* (5 February – 17 August 1851).

166   Mazurkas, Opp. 7 and 21 by Blumenthal.

avoided the forced originality, the harmonic oddities, the intervallic crudities, and the moony melancholy of his model. [...]

Anonymous, "Music at Manchester (From our own correspondent",
The Musical World, 31/49 (3 December 1853), pp. 766-767.

[Review of Hallé's concert at the Town Hall, Manchester, 24 November 1853]

[...] Last, not least, Charles Hallé himself appeared in a triple selection from Chopin. We preferred the Prelude in A flat[167] to either of the studies[168]; the last one in F strongly reminded us of the Highland Fling. The great merit in the selection of all these solo pieces is that none were *too long* – a secret worth knowing – but which Hallé seems to understand fully. After listening for two hours at a stretch (with only ten minutes' interval), to classical chamber music of the highest order, it cannot be expected that long solo displays could be patiently endured, however great the talent.

Anonymous, *"Deux Valses mélancoliques* for the pianoforte. By Frédéric Chopin.
J. J. Ewer and Co.; Wessel and Co.", The Musical World, 32/29 (22 July 1854), p. 492.

These Waltzes, which were written in the album of a certain Countess P. – (Chopin was a great man for the ladies, and especially for countesses, duchesses, princesses, and so forth) – in 1844, three or four years before the death of the composer, having never been published in his lifetime, will be a *bonne bouche* for the admirers of the romantic and Polish composer. They are full of that tender languor for which all his music is characterised, and, moreover, are charming examples of his style. The first is in F minor, the second in B minor. Both are very short, and, for Chopin, uncommonly easy. As the mere announcement of their publication, will make all pianists – amateur or professional – anxious to possess them, we shall not attempt to describe them. And, indeed, there is no further description required, when we have said that they are pure Chopin – Chopin in his simplest and least affected mood, though as plaintive and sentimental as ever, if not as "swoony" – as the author of *Modern German Music, Recollections, and Criticism* would say.[169] In the one in F minor we find

---

167 Prelude, Op. 28 No. 17.

168 The programme printed in the review indicates that the studies played were in C sharp minor (Op. 25 No. 7) and in F major (Op. 10 No. 8 or Op. 25 No. 3).

169 The author of *Modern German Music, Recollections, and Criticism* was the English critic Henry Fothergill Chorley.

our old friend which is always welcome – as Chopin – often as it occurs.

Anonymous, "Mad. Clara Schumann's Recital", *The Musical World*, 34/22 (31 May 1856), p. 343.

[Review of Clara Schumann's recital at Hanover Square Rooms on 27 May 1856]

[...] The Nocturne and Polonaise[170] by Chopin are eminent among the strangely unfinished rhapsodies of that composer. Enormously taxing to the player, the labour bestowed on them can never be repaid by the result, even when they are executed by an imaginative pianist like Mad. Schumann, or one of unfailing mechanism, like M. Hallé. [...]

Anonymous, "Reviews. *The Classical Pianist* (used at the Royal Academy of Music), a selection of movements from the works of the great masters, edited by Brinley Richards[171] (Honorary Member, Associate, and Professor of the Royal Academy of Music)", *The Musical World*, 36/3 (16 January 1858), p. 35.

Vol. II of Mr. Brinley Richards' "selection of *movements*" begins with the *whole of* the late Chopin's lengthy, incoherent, plotless, shapeless and inconceivably dreary Sonata in C minor (Op. 4). What such a work can possibly have to do with the "classics", we are at a loss to guess. This sonata shows clearly that even a man of original talent is unable to achieve anything of importance without the technical experience acquired through well-directed study in early life. Here Chopin was lamentably deficient, and thus only his smaller compositions are acceptable to those who regard music from a serious point of view. A clearer proof of his want of fluency, and insensibility to form – the results of imperfect education – could not be adduced than the Sonata in C minor (C *minor* by courtesy), which drags the weary reader through twenty-eight closely printed pages, made up of passages without brilliancy and modulations without interest, based upon themes without melody or rhythm. Mozart himself could

---

170 The programme printed in the review indicates that the Nocturne was in C minor (Op. 48 No. 1) and the Polonaise in A flat Major (Op. 53 or Op. 61).

171 The Welsh pianist Henry Brinley Richards (1817-1885) studied at the Royal Academy of Music, where he later became a professor and a director. According to Niecks, Richards studied in Paris with Chopin, who also assisted him in the publication, by Troupenas, of his first composition. Richards was a prolific composer of vocal and piano music, almost all of which is now largely forgotten. He is best remembered for his song "God Bless the Prince of Wales" (1862), which has been adopted as an English national anthem.

have done little or nothing with such a subject as that of the *allegro maestoso*. [...] The *finale* – a *presto* – is about as badly off for a theme, and the *menuetto* not much better. [...] Let not such unmusical devices be mistaken for the aberration of genius. They are merely the tricks and artifices of self-satisfied incompetency.

Anonymous, "Chopin a poet and a Pole", *The Musical World*, 36/35 (28 August 1858), pp. 550-551.[172]

We do not think that there are many instances in the history of any art, where an author of decided talent, and even genius, leaves no trace of his style but that which is to be found in his own works. In the musical world, it is Frederic Chopin who furnishes one of these very rare instances. Although he has ploughed a new path in the field of musical literature, as applied to the pianoforte; although he has produced a series of compositions which contain all the elements for the foundation of a new school, yet no such school has ever been formed. There have been a few attempts to imitate his style, but of these attempts nothing is felt, and in our days nobody would think of composing as did Chopin, although the character and the treatment of his works are just as modern as they were twenty years ago. We have had successful Beethovenites, Schummanites, Mendelssohnites, &c., but we have not one disciple of Chopin who can lay claim to distinction. And yet this very man was a teacher almost all his life. A score of amateurs and artists whom he taught are still living, but the musical world at large knows little or nothing of them.

And why? Because that which formed the originality of Chopin was such a mixture of rare gifts, circumstances, and especially nationality, that a reproduction will still depend upon the fate of the latter, even if all the former conditions should be complied with. Moreover, Chopin's art was based entirely upon his individuality; it was his own art; tradition and school had very little to do with it. His melodies were his own, and his harmonising them was certainly such as it would be difficult to find again in the works of any other master. But perhaps it is with regard to Chopin more incorrect than in reference to any other modern composer of distinction, to speak separately of his melody and his harmony. Both are with him one and the same thing; they emanated at the same moment from his inspired soul; and to play them separately would produce, in a great many instances, nothing but a mass of unmeaning,

---

172 Article reprinted from the *New York Musical Review*, 9/16 (7 August 1858), pp. 243-244. The title of the original article is "Frederic Chopin".

mostly discordant sounds. The proof of this latter opinion may be found in the fact that generally his compositions are only a weak echo of his more perfect improvisations. Those who heard his earliest efforts in this respect tell us that it was impossible to detect anything in them which, with regard to ideas and treatment, reminded in any way whatever of the pianoforte music which preceded his.

If we come now to analyse, as far as is possible, the character of his music, we must first recognise the tone of Polish nationality which prevails in every one of his compositions. Chopin was before all things a Pole; and although he lived the greater part of his life away from his fatherland, yet he constantly kept up his relations with it. [...] The Polish character of his music is, however, to be looked for not only in those of his compositions which belong to the nation of themselves, such as Mazourkas, Polonaises &c., but also in his Concertos, Sonatas, in short, in every one of his inspirations. It is that mourning, that doleful resignation, suddenly bursting forth into a momentary wild passion; that constant melancholy; that smiling amid tears; that constant hoping and trusting for a change, which characterises the nation as well as the music of Chopin. When a Pole heard the beautiful adagio of his Sonata, known under the name of *Funeral March*, and published in a separate form,[173] he exclaimed: "Only a Pole could have written that!". And he was right; only a Pole could have mourned like that; could have given himself up to such dark, gloomy views as are expressed in the first and last part of the march, relieved by the beautiful beam of hope and resignation in the middle. But let us add, at the same time: "Only a poet could have found such sounds of sadness, love, and resignation". Chopin was not only a Pole, but also a lyrical poet, full of imagination and the loftiest aspirations. His muse was not the epic, as revealed by Beethoven in his Sonatas, but the ballad, the tale of the heart, with all its varied emotions of love and sorrow. His powers were not sufficient for a concerto or sonata (as can be easily ascertained by looking at those of his compositions which he has published under these titles); but he not only had the finest appreciation of form for the smaller poems, such as mazourkas, polonaises, ballads, etc., but he knew also how to fill them with the loftiest ideas, and to treat them accordingly. The greatest delicacy of touch, the greatest refinement, reign throughout. Nothing is common or careless; you feel that the author shrunk from anything which was not thoroughly noble and refined. He was like the "Sensitive Plant", which Shelley has immortalized; and what the English poet did for his favourite plant, Chopin's music did for himself.

---

173 Wessel published the *Marche funèbre* in a separate form after Chopin's death (see MW 24/46 (17 November 1849), p. 733).

Like all modern composers, Chopin could not make large steps; but the small ones he did make had the charm of poetry and novelty. His breathing was short in music as well as physically; for, for more than twenty years he was a victim to consumption. No doubt this dreadful disease had a great influence upon the development of his talent, although, perhaps, the reflex of this constant struggle with life in his music formed, and forms still, for a great many, its greatest attraction. Especially do women seem attracted by the wand of his muse – women of refined feeling, education, and social standing. No doubt that these women are his greatest admirers and his best pupils. A Countess in Paris plays his music better than we ever heard it rendered by any other professional or non-professional performer, not even Liszt excepted. It seems that it requires the fine and insinuating feeling of a refined and intelligent woman, to enter into all the secresies [sic] of this wonderful talent, just as it requires her physical strength to play this music effectively, perhaps a few of his polonaises excepted. Chopin himself, for instance, was too weak to play on an Erard piano; his usual companion was one of Pleyel's semi-grands. And he was also too weak to perform often in public. [...] Chopin died a meteor on the zenith of the world of art, just as his own countrymen vanished from the world of nations. As long as there is no hope for the regeneration of the latter, there will be no hope for the reappearance of a genius like Frederick Chopin.

Anonymous, "Reviews. *Chopin's Mazurkas, in eleven books, complete, with a Biographical and Critical Introduction* – edited by J. W. Davison (Boosey and Sons)", *The Musical World*, 38/13 (31 March 1860), pp. 199-201.

"Chopin for the many" will, perhaps, appear an anomaly to those who look upon the individual Chopin as a spirit, dwelling away from the mass of artistic workers, and devouring his own heart in defiance of the oracle of Pythagoras – "*Cor non edite*" (which will be disregarded by secret mourners, so long as the world lasts). Equally anomalous will it sound to all who have read (and can understand) the rhapsody published by Messrs. Wessel and Stapleton, some twenty years ago, under the name and title of *An Essay on the Works of Frederic Chopin*, in which Shelley's definition of Coleridge
"He was a mighty poet,
And a subtle-souled psychologist"[174]

---

174   P. B. Shelley, *Peter Bell the Third*, Part Fifth (Grace), 378-379.

is placed to the account of Chopin himself [...]. But the real fact is, that what is intrinsically good and true, however at the outset confined to a narrow circle of appreciation, *must* in the end find its way to "the many", from whom it will receive the stamp of immortality. That which never can by any chance become popular is somewhere intrinsically wrong. "Popular" is one thing – "vulgar" is another; and we must beg our readers to admit a wide difference in the signification of the two epithets. The popularity of *The Ratcatcher's Daughter*[175] is a very dissimilar matter from the popularity of Mendelssohn's *Lieder ohne Worte*, and springs from wholly dissimilar sources. The first finds its way speedily to the barrel-organ; the last must not aspire to such distinction, for it would never be likely, under any circumstances, to obtain it; and indeed it would be a pity if the contrary were true. The Mazurkas of Chopin stand much in the same predicament, notwithstanding that they proceed directly, in the majority of instances, from the fountain of National Tune, in which Chopin's country (Poland) is so individual and so rich. The poet-musician has endowed them with a new physiognomy, and in effecting this has separated them for ever from those vulgar sympathies with which art has nothing whatever in common. Probably among the numerous productions of Chopin, the mazurkas are the most genial and characteristic. The natural offspring of his peculiar idiosyncracy [sic], they breath his spirit, reflect his sentimentality, and are the truest *media* of communication between his inner self and the outside world, which he, like all men specially gifted – men of genius, in short – was born to delight. We verily believe that there is more of the genuine spirit of Chopin in one of these brief Mazurkas, than in the whole of his concertos, sonatas, and larger compositions put together. Whereas, in his elaborate compositions, he was stilted, mannered, and catachrestical, in his mazurkas (and the minor effusions) he is nearly always spontaneous, natural, and therefore, *sympathetic*. With this conviction, we can endorse, without reservation, the words with which the editor, whose labours are now before us, sums up the paragraph in which he briefly glances at the entire production of Chopin:

"That Chopin, however, excelled less in works of '*longue haleine*' than in those of smaller pretensions, will hardly be denied. His *études*, his preludes, his *valses*, his nocturnes, and above all his mazurkas, are quite enough to save him from oblivion, whatever may eventually become of his concertos and sonatas. The variety with which in the mazurkas he has said the same thing some fifty times over, will go fur-

---

175 The popular song "The Ratcatcher's Daughter" was written by the Music Hall singer Samuel Cowell in the 1850s.

ther than anything else to prove that Chopin's genius, whatever its eccentricities and failings, was decidedly *inventive*. The best of the mazurkas are without question those that smell the least strongly of the lamp, those which, harmonised in the least affected manner, are easiest to play, and bear the closest affinity to (in some cases are almost echoes of) the national dance tunes of his country. Some of them are gems, as faultless as they are attractive, from whatever point of view regarded: others, more evidently labored, are less happy; but not one of them is wholly destitute of points that appeal to the feelings, surprise by their unexpectedness, fascinate by their plaintive character, or charm by their ingenuity".[176]

The distinction between Chopin's more ambitious efforts and those which (like the mazurkas) came most directly from his natural genius may be likened to the distinction between the formalities of high-bred society and those in the humbler spheres of life in Poland. The Polish gentleman preserves, in his vocabulary of polite intercourse a strong imprint of the hyperbolical features of oriental phraseology. The expressions, "*Very powerful*" and "*Very enlightened, Sir*", are still indispensable. That of "*Benefactor*" ("*Dobrodzi*") is frequently employed in conversation; while the customary salutation between gentlemen, or from gentlemen to ladies, is, "*I throw myself at your feet*" ("*Padam do Nog*"). The people's salutation, on the other hand, is "*Glory to God*" ("*Slawa Bohu*"[177]). The works of Chopin might, without any great impropriety, be classed under the two heads of *Padam do Nog* (including concertos &c.), and *Slawa Bohu* (including mazurkas &c.).

Mr. Davison's general view of Chopin, as a man and as an artist, will, probably, be regarded by some as scarcely favourable, if not indeed somewhat prejudiced. It certainly differs *in toto* from that inculcated in the *Essay* – or "Yellow Book", as it was nick-named – on Chopin, which at the time of his appearance was (truly or erroneously), attributed to his pen. We have shown how he speaks of the mazurkas in Messrs. Boosey's new edition; see how he raved about the same exquisite trifles in the "Yellow Book".

"Among the lesser compositions of Chopin, the MAZURKAS – those "cabinet pictures", as Liszt has happily designated them – those green spots in the desert – those quaint snatches of melancholy song – those outpourings of an unworldly and tristful soul – those musical floods of tears, and gushes of pure joyfulness – those exquisite embodiments of fugitive thoughts – those sweet complaints of unacknowledged

---

176 *The Mazurkas and Valses of Frederick Chopin, with Memoir by J. W. Davison*, London, Boosey, 1860, p. vi.

177 Correctly in polish: "*Dobrodziej*", "*Padam do nóg*", "*Chwała Bogu*" [editor's note].

genius – stand alone and unrivalled. These are wholly and individually creations of Chopin, which none have dared to imitate, (for who, indeed, could aspire to imitate that which is inimitable?) portraying in vivid colours the patriotism and home-feeling of the great Polish composer, (we need hardly remind our readers that Poland boasts the honor of having given birth to Chopin) affording vent in passionate eloquences, to the beautiful and secret thoughts of his guileless heart. Of these there are eight sets, all of the rarest loveliness – sparkling with genius – redolent with fragrant thought – very nosegays of sweet and balmy melody. If we have a preference, where *all* is beauty unsurpassed, it is for the first and sixth sets, which for quaint and happy melody, rich and delicious harmony, ingenious and novel treatment, are unrivalled since music was an art."[178]

We have not quoted more than a third of this rhapsody, at the end of which, on throwing down his pen, the writer might appropriately have addressed Chopin in the Polish formula, after the *Grand Seigneur* has entertained his guests with a magnificent feast – "*Czym bohat, tym rad*"[179] (which, paraphrased in English, would be "Deign to pardon what is unworthy of you, but it is all my poor wealth that I place at yout feet"); for surely such a banquet of literary adulation was never served up to king or hero, even by the historiographers who recounted the virtues and exploits of the Cæsars. However, "Let by-gones be by-gones"; the modern opinion is probably the sounder of the two, and we have no wish to quarrel with it. [...]

Hugh Reginald Haweis,[180] "Schubert and Chopin", *Contemporary Review*, 2 (May-August 1866), pp. 80-102.

In passing from the great gods of music, like MOZART and BEETHOVEN, to those delightful tone-poets and singers with which Germany has of late abounded, we could scarcely find any names more dear to the heart of the true musician than those of FRANZ SCHUBERT and FREDERIC CHOPIN.

Schubert, the prince of lyrists – Chopin, the most romantic of pianoforte writers, Schubert rich with an inexhaustible fancy – Chopin perfect with an exquisite finish,

---

178 J. W. Davison, *An Essay on the Works of Frederic Chopin*, London, Wessel [1842-3], pp. 3-4.

179 Correctly in polish: "*Czym chata bogata tym rada*" [editor's note].

180 The Reverend Hugh Reginald Haweis was an amateur violinist and a writer on music. Born in Egham, in 1838, he obtained a master's degree from Cambridge University in 1864. Haweis contributed to many periodicals and lectured on musical topics at the London Institution and in many provincial towns. He is the author of two volumes on music: *Music and Morals* (W. H. Allen, 1873) and *My Musical Life* (W. H. Allen, 1884).

each reaching a supreme excellence in his own department, whilst one narrowly escaped being greatest in all – both occupied intensely with their own meditations, and admitting into them little of the outer world – both too indifferent to the public taste to become immediately popular, but too remarkable to remain long unknown – both exhibiting in their lives and in their music striking resemblances and still more forcible contrasts – both now so widely admired and beloved in this country – so advanced and novel, that although Schubert has been in his grave for thirty-eight years and Chopin for seventeen, yet to us they seem to have died but yesterday – these men, partners in the common sufferings of genius, and together crowned with immortality in death, may well claim from us the tribute of memory to their lives, and of homage to their inspiration. [...] What Schubert was to the songs of Germany, Chopin was to its pianoforte music; but whilst the genius of Schubert ranged freely over every field of musical composition, that of Chopin was confined within certain narrow limits. Born into the mid-current of that great wave of Romanticism first set in motion by Schubert, he was destined, with the aid of Liszt and Berlioz, to establish its influence permanently in Paris. [...].

Chopin was essentially a national musician. Although he lived much in France, his music is never French. "He sings to one clear harp, in divers tones",[181] the swan-song of his people's nationality. His genius was elegiac. He is more often tender than strong, and even his occasional bursts of vigour soon give way to the prevailing undertone of a deep melancholy. His country is ever uppermost in his thoughts. His polonaises reflect the national ardour of a noble but unhappy patriotism. His mazourkas and scherzos are full of the subtle coquetry and passionate sensibility of his gifted countrywomen, whilst his ballads* are nothing but the free, wild songs of his native land, transcribed for the first time by himself.

He, first of all musicians, understood the dignity of manners and the language of deportment, and with varied utterance he seems to be continually reminding us that

"Manners are not idle, but the fruit
Of noble nature and of loyal mind".[182]

His dance music has added a strange and fascinating solemnity to the graces of the ball-room, – elevating a mere pastime into what may almost be called a philosophy.

---

181 Lord Alfred Tennyson, *In Memoriam*, verse I.
182 Tennyson, *Guinevere*.

As a romance writer for the pianoforte, he had no models, and will have no rivals. He was original without extravagance, and polished without affectation. It is to him we owe the extension of chords struck together in *arpeggio*, the little groups of superadded notes, "falling like light drops of pearly dew upon the melodic figure", he also invented those admirable harmonic progressions which lend importance to many a slender subject, and redeem his slightest efforts from triviality. Of Schubert he once remarked, that "the sublime is desecrated when followed by the trivial or commonplace".[183] A certain rollicking fun, and vulgar though powerful energy, that frequently peeps out in Schubert's marches, was abhorrent to him. Perhaps he hardly appreciated the enormous range of men like Beethoven or even Schubert. His own range was limited, but within it he has probably never been equalled in absolute perfection of finish. His works are marked by a complete absence of commonplace, and you will search throughout them in vain for a slovenly chord or an unskillful combination. His boldness is always justified by success, and his repetition by a certain weird and singular pathos.

He was great in small things, but small in great ones. His two concertos with orchestral accompaniments are more ambitious than successful. The other instruments, like the general public, seem to stifle and embarrass him, and we long to have Chopin alone again at the pianoforte. [...]

* There are sixteen published. They are very little known. No. 12, "My Joy", and 10, "Riding Home from the Fight", are quite remarkable.[184]

Anonymous, "Cristal Palace Concerts", *The Musical World*, 44/50 (15 December 1866), p. 791.

[...] Chopin's *Krakoviak, grand rondeau de concert*, for pianoforte, with orchestral accompaniments.[185] This composition is anything but "grand"; and we very much doubt whether Schumann-Eusebius, Schumann-Florestan, or Schumann under any other *nom de plume*, would have taken off his hat to it as he describes himself as having done to the *Variations on "Là ci darem"*,[186] by this same (through many people, and by none more remarkably than through Schumann) somewhat over-

---

183 F. Liszt, *Life of Chopin*, tr. Martha Walker Cook, 4th edn, Boston, Ditson 1863, p. 154.

184 Haweis alludes here to the Songs, Op. 74.

185 The *Rondo à la krakowiak*, Op. 14, was played at the Crystal Palace by Edward Dannreuther (1844-1905).

186 Schuman's article is reproduced here, pp. 234-239.

estimated Chopin. Although the leading theme has an unmistakable Cracovian turn, the whole character of the piece is rather "nigger" than Polish; and we doubt whether Mr. Sutherland Edwards,[187] or any other authority on Polish music, &c., would have recognized it as genuine. The orchestral accompaniments to this rondo are trivial at the best. The pianoforte part, however, is difficult, if neither showy nor brilliant [...]

Anonymous, "Reviews. *Mazurkas, pour piano*, par F. Chopin. (Novello, Ewer and Co.)", *The Musical Times*, 319 (1 September 1869), p. 212.

The genius of Chopin was perhaps more decisively shown in his Mazurkas than in any other compositions which he has bequeathed to us. These characteristic dances of his native country seemed to inspire him with the deepest feeling; and, although in these, as in most of his works, we generally find that tinge of melancholy which formed part of his nature, they are so full of life and healthful vigour as to render them always acceptable to an audience. But Chopin's compositions stand so thoroughly apart from the conventional music of the day, that mere plodding pianists can neither play them nor comprehend them: the phrases are so quaint and peculiar, and the various touches (although carefully indicated by the punctuation of the composer) require to be so thoroughly under the command of the performer, that even his simplest Mazurkas demand earnest study before they can be rendered as the composer intended. "Passage players" (as Beethoven used contemptuously to designate mere mechanical executants) need not therefore trouble themselves with works requiring an intellectual perception of phrasing which they have never cultivated; but pianists who have learned to regard music as a language in which to express poetical feeling, will find in the little volume before us a mine of treasure, all the more welcome because so thoroughly unlike any with which they have previously become acquainted. [...]

---

187 Henry Sutherland Edwards (1828-1906) was an English writer and journalist. He was correspondent of *The Times* at the coronation of Alexander II of Russia (1856), in the camp of the insurgents at Warsaw (1862-63), and he wrote reports on the Franco-Prussian War in 1870. Edwards's later journalism was often on musical subjects, and by the 1860s he was part of the circle of critics associated with J. W. Davison. Besides farces, pantomimes and novels, Edwards wrote *Rossini and His School* (1881), *Famous first Representations* (1886), *The Prima Donna: Her History and Surroundings from the Seventeenth to the Nineteenth Century* (two volumes, 1888).

Anonymous, "Notes on Music", *The Academy*, 2 (1 May 1871), pp. 240-241.

[...] Chopin's Concerto[188] is very seldom heard in public, owing no doubt to the great difficulties of execution which it contains. [...] The work itself is not representative of Chopin's real power, the orchestra being treated simply as a foil to the pianoforte, without any characteristic features of its own; besides which, the principal motives, founded in part on national dance-rhythms – though they would be of extreme beauty in little *pièces de salon* – have hardly enough importance to fill up the larger forms of a concerto.

Anonymous, "Reviews. *Life of Chopin*, by Franz Liszt. Translated from the French by M. Walker Cook (William Reeves)", *The Musical Times*, 410 (1 April 1877), pp. 184-185.

As a rhapsodical criticism upon the genius and writings of Chopin this volume will be welcomed by all who believe that one who can so eloquently interpret the most abstruse compositions of the great Polish composer with his fingers is fully justified in also using his pen to spread still more widely a knowledge of his works in the great world of art. Considering that the book contains only eight chapters, and that the birth and early career of Chopin are not treated of until chapter vi, it is certainly a misnomer to call it a "Life" of the artist; but the masterly analysis of the inner meaning of his pianoforte works amply compensates us for any shortcoming in other respects. We are glad to find that so ardent an admirer of Chopin as the author of this treatise agrees with us that the composer was not at his best when he attempted to write in classical form. [...] There can be no possible reason why this [Chopin's] "wild will" should not have free play in the production of such exquisitely coloured sketches as Chopin has left us; but let us not run into the danger of believing that form should be set aside because such an erratic nature could not bend to its conditions. Not the least interesting part of this book is the graphic sketch of Poland; the remarks upon the polonaise and mazourka showing us how truly national are the specimens of these dances, which rank amongst the best of Chopin's smaller pianoforte works. [...] No one knew better than Liszt the sensitive nature of Chopin; and it is impossible to avoid feeling a deep sense of gratitude to his biographer for so delicately touching those peculiarities of his character which

---

188 Concerto, Op. 21.

might otherwise have been misinterpreted by the word. [...]. We have already said that the book before us is a rhapsody; but it must be remembered that its author is no *dilettante* admirer of Chopin, but an earnest fellow-worker in the art which he ennobled. Let us therefore contribute our good word to help it forward, as we would tend a flower which springs up spontaneously over the grave of one we loved.

Joseph Bennett,[189] "The Great Composers, n. XI. Chopin", *The Musical Times*, 467 (1 January 1882), pp. 12-15.

In the rhapsodical, not to say hysterical, book known as the "Life of Chopin", by Franz Liszt, the great virtuoso of the pianoforte gives the remarkable composer with whom we are now concerned a very curious character. He tries to put Chopin before us as a psychological phenomenon, invests him with strange attributes provocative of awe and mystery, and surrounds him with the halo of a very peculiar heroism. Noting this, we should also remember that Liszt does not speak without authority. He is generally credited with keen discernment; he had abundant opportunities of studying Chopin's character – even that innermost side which a man shows but to very few; and between the two musicians a bond of sympathy existed stronger than any arising from their common art – the bond of, on many points, a mutual feeling. Yet, we shall, by-and-by, find reason to doubt the accuracy of Liszt's sketch. It will appear to us probably that the biographer, if so we may call him, regarded his subject through a false medium, which distorted its outline and changed its colour. The fact is that men, in trying to reproduce another, very often unconsciously reproduce themselves, or, at any rate, create an ideal formed out of a reflection of their own individuality. This may have been the case with Liszt, who, of all persons, is about the least fitted for the higher work of a biographer. Such work demands self-abnegation, judicial calmness, the repression of all partisanship, and the faculty of weighing evidence with care before accepting its proof without reserve. Whereas the eminent man of whom they speak is picturesque and impulsive, of irrepressible personality,

---

189 Joseph Bennett (1831-1911) was one of the most prolific music critics of the second half of the nineteenth century. He was the music critic of *The Sunday Times* and, by 1870, of *The Daily Telegraph*. In addition he wrote many articles for the *Pall Mall Gazette, The Graphic, The Pictorial Times, The Musical World* and *The Musical Times,* and he was the editor of Novello's *Concordia.* Bennett was highly influenced by his friend J. W. Davison. He strongly supported the work of the English composers Parry, Cowen, Stanford, Mackenzie, Goring Thomas and Sullivan, whose music marks, in Bennett's view, the beginning of the English Musical Renaissance. See Meirion Hughes, *The English Musical Renaissance and the Press 1850-1914: Watchmen of Music,* Aldershot 2002, pp. 44-61.

intensely sentimental, and, if his affections be concerned, generous to the last degree. A writer thus characterized would, when engaged upon the life of his hero, naturally exaggerate points possessed by the two in common, and incline to make of him that which he has conceived as an ideal self. [...]

Without attempting to understand the secretiveness of a musician [Chopin] who reveals all his feelings in the language which best expresses them, it must be confessed that we have here a singular character, and one that excites our curiosity as well as our interest. A man, outwardly gentle and amiable, is distracted within by a tempest of feeling to which a frail body denies expression. [...] Observe what a striking figure the picturesque Liszt makes of his fellow. The canvas has about it the wildness and gloom of Salvator Rosa; the awfulness of one of Turner's thunder-skies. Chopin is Prometheus chained to his rock, and "subtilising" the passionate thoughts that rise in him against the inflexible deities. Shaking off the enthralment under which Liszt's fancy places us, we are naturally tempted to ask, in a matter-of-fact way, what it was that so cruelly tortured the Polish master. The answer is inadequate, even though Liszt represents him as well-nigh continuously at death's door. [...]

The Polish musician never courted popular applause, and his voluntary abnegation, we are told, "veiled an internal wound". [...] We shall find after a while that there is not sufficient evidence to establish this argument, and we can even now see that Liszt may have evolved it from his own "inner consciousness". The artist always before the public, always living, moving, and having his being in public applause, would naturally be startled at seeing another artist clinging to the privacy of his immediate circle, and turning aside from every path leading to praise. He would be unable to understand such a phenomenon, and seeking a reason for it in himself would fix upon the, to him, greatest possible calamity – lack of appreciation. Liszt further accounts for Chopin's dark fate and lurid surroundings by the contrast between an ardent imagination, allied to violent feelings, and his physical organization. [...] But waiving further reference to the Chopin whom Liszt shows to us, we may say, without questioning every detail, that the picture is overdrawn, overcoloured, and so far false that it has led to serious misconception. The Chopin best known in our time is, without question, that of Liszt, which the Prince Carol of George Sand resembles sufficiently to serve for a confirmation. This is why we have drawn attention to the portrait at the outset. The ideal of the sentimental and picturesque pianist, with its double in that of the impressionable lady novelist, should be kept at hand for frequent inspection in the light of fact. [...]

Joseph Bennett, "The Great Composers, n. XI. Chopin", *The Musical Times*, 473 (1 July 1882), pp. 372-375.

[...] Chopin's death seems to have made but little impression in England. The leading musical journal of the day had not an editorial word to say about it, and was content to insert fifteen lines from a Paris correspondent [...] The flowers that covered the remains of Chopin were in themselves tributes of affection, but they foreshadowed the homage of admiration which his works were destined to command when better known. It was not in the nature of things that the master should hear with living ears the shouts of an applauding world. His art was too distinctive and peculiar for that. His ideas as well as his utterance were strange, and the spirit that animated his music was in itself *sui generis*. He had, therefore, to die only half understood; but, let us hope, with a consciousness that Time, the great revealer, would do for him what remained to be done. Be that as it may, time has accomplished the task, and now Chopin suffers from excess of favour. His music, so difficult in spirit, and by no means easy as regards the letter, is in everybody's hands, and sounds from every concert platform, but how grievously abused! [...] To the few, however, Chopin is something more than a fashion blindly followed. He is the high priest of a sweet and subtle art-mystery; the delineator of ideas which are "caviare to the general", the revealer of a world, in little no doubt, but with a complex and elaborate beauty discernible by all who with patience look at it in the true light. This is Chopin's peculiar distinction and glory. He was no Beethoven, to scale the highest height and sound the deepest depth of music. He laboured within a small field, but he showed what infinite loveliness and charm may be found in the minute things of art as well as of nature.

**Anonymous, "Reviews. *Novello's Primers of Musical Biography.*
– *Frederic Chopin – Hector Berlioz*. By Joseph Bennett (Novello, Ewer and Co.)",
The Musical Times, 498 (1 August 1884), pp. 472-473.**

The idea of including biographies of eminent musical composers amongst the "Primers"[190] issued by Messrs. Novello is an exceedingly happy one; for, as it tells us in the Prospectus of the Series, "Knowledge of what a man is, helps the understanding of what he does". It is also good that the execution of this task has

---

190 The series *Novello's Primers of Musical Biography* includes the biographies of Chopin, Berlioz, Rossini, Cherubini and Meyerbeer. All the biographies were written by Bennett.

been entrusted to Mr. Joseph Bennett, not only because he is eminently fitted for it, both in a literary and artistic sense, but because he is not likely to allow the biographies, even of his favourite composers, to degenerate into mere specimens of rhapsodical hero-worship. Perhaps no man has been more subject to this treatment than Frederic Chopin, his "Life" by Liszt being, as Mr. Bennett truly observes, an attempt to put the composer before us "as a psychological phenomenon". There was certainly very much in the poetical and sensitive temperament of Chopin to favour this idea; but facts are stubborn things, and unfortunately many of Liszt's assertions in support of his theory are directly contradicted by Karasowski in his well-known Biography of this artist,[191] a book frequently quoted from in the work before us. No music ever more perfectly reflected the individuality of its composer than that of Chopin, and we can imagine that all real lovers of his works will like to become acquainted with his inner character. Mr. Bennett's book effectually supplies this want. [...]

Walter Macfarren,[192] *Memoires. An Autobiography*, **London 1905, pp. 58-59.**

[...] The advent of the Polish composer and pianist here exercised a very potent influence on musical taste. [...] It was not so much the perfection of his technique as the great variety of his touch, embodying every shade of tone, and his exquisite management of what is known as *tempo rubato* that impressed me. Some people entertain the notion that Chopin's music must be always played out of time, whereas nothing is farther from the truth, for in his interpretation of his own music, the subtle distinctions between *rallentando* and *accelerando* were so delicately managed that you never lost the sense of time and rhythm. [...]

Life and Letters of Sir Charles Hallé, Being an Autobiography (1819-1860)
with Correspondence and Diaries, **ed. C. E. et Marie Hallé, London, Smith Elder, 1896, pp. 31-33.**

---

191 William Reeves published an English translation by Emily Hill of Karasowski's *Friedrich Chopin: sein Leben, seine Werke und Briefe* in 1879, as *Chopin. His Life and Letters.*

192 Walter Macfarren (1826-1905) was the youngest son of George Macfarren and the brother of George Alexander Macfarren. In 1842 he entered the Royal Academy of Music, where he studied piano with Holmes and composition with his brother and Potter. He was highly esteemed as a pianist and from 1846 to 1903 was professor of piano at the Royal Academy of Music. Macfarren's compositions had no lasting impact, but made a contribution to the musical life of his time.

[...] I found myself sitting beside Chopin. The same evening I heard him play, and was fascinated beyond expression. It seemed to me as if I had got into another world. [...] I sat entranced, filled with wonderment, and if the room had suddenly been peopled with fairies, I should not have been astonished. The marvellous charm, the poetry and originality, the perfect freedom and absolute lucidity of Chopin's playing at that time cannot be described. It was perfection in every sense. He seemed to be pleased with the evident impression he had produced, for I could only stammer a few broken words of admiration, and he played again and again, each time revealing new beauties, until I could have dropped on my knees to worship him. I returned home in a state of complete bewilderment. [...] With greater familiarity my admiration increased, for I learned to appreciate what before had principally dazzled me. [...]

Frederick Niecks, *Frederick Chopin as a Man and Musician*, London, Novello, 1888, i: pp. 205-206.

[...] With Chopin writing a concerto or a sonata was an effort, and the effort was always inadequate for the attainment of the object – a perfect work of its kind. He lacked the peculiar qualities, natural and acquired, requisite for a successful cultivation of the larger forms. He could not grasp and hold the threads of thought which he found flitting in his mind, and weave them into a strong, complex web; he snatched them up one by one, tied them together, and either knit them into light fabrics or merely wound them into skeins. In short, Chopin was not a thinker, not a logician – his propositions are generally good, but his arguments are poor and the conclusions often wanting. [...] Notwithstanding their many shortcomings, the concertos may be said to be the most satisfactory of Chopin's works in the larger forms, or at least those that afford the greatest amount of enjoyment. In some respects the concerto-form was more favourable than the sonata-form for the exercise of Chopin's peculiar talent, in other respects it was less so. The concerto-form admits of a far greater and freer display of the virtuosic capabilities of the pianoforte than the sonata-form, and does not necessitate the same strictness of logical structure, the same thorough working-out of the subject-matter. But, on the other hand, it demands aptitude in writing for the orchestra and appropriately solid material. Now, Chopin lacked such aptitude entirely, and the nature of his material accorded little with the size of the structure and the orchestral frame. And, then, are not these confessions of intimate experiences, these moonlight sentimentalities, these listless dreams, &c., out of place in the gaslight glare of concert-rooms, crowded with audiences brought together to a great extent rather by *ennui*, vanity, and idle curiosity than by love of art? [...]

Since Beethoven the form has been often modified [...] Chopin, however, adhered to the orthodox form, taking unmistakably Hummel for his model. Indeed, Hummel's concertos were Chopin's model not only as regards structure, but also to a certain extent as regards the character of the several movements. In the *tutti*'s of the first movement, and in the general complexion of the second (the slow) and the third (rondo) movement, this discipleship is most apparent. But while noting the resemblance, let us not overlook the difference. If the bones are Hummel's (which no doubt is an exaggeration of the fact), the flesh, blood, and soul are Chopin's. In his case adherence to the orthodox concerto-form was so much the more regrettable as writing for the orchestra was one of his weakest points. Indeed, Chopin's originality is gone as soon as he writes for another instrument than the pianoforte. [...]

Frederick Niecks, *Frederick Chopin as a Man and Musician*, London, Novello, 1888, ii: pp. 212-220.

[...] In Chopin's works there are clearly distinguishable two styles – the early virtuosic and the later poetic style. The latter is in a certain sense also virtuosic, but with this difference, that its virtuosity is not virtuosity for virtuosity's sake. The poetic style which has thrown off the tinsel showiness of its predecessor does not, however, remain unchanged, for its texture becomes more and more close, and affords conclusive evidence of the increasing influence of Johann Sebastian Bach. Of course, the grand master of fugue does not appear here, as it were, full life-size, in peruke, knee-breeches, and shoe-buckles, but his presence in spite of transformation and attenuation is unmistakable. It is, however, not only in the closeness and complexity of texture that we notice Chopin's style changing: a striving after greater breadth and fulness of form are likewise apparent, and, alas! also an increase in sombreness, the result of deteriorating health. [...]

Another prejudice, wide-spread, almost universal, is that Chopin's music is all languor and melancholy, and, consequently, wanting in variety. Now, there can be no greater error than this belief. As to variety, we should be obliged to wonder at its infiniteness if he had composed nothing but the pieces to which are really applicable the epithets dreamy, pensive, mournful, and despondent. But what vigour, what more than manly vigour, manifests itself in many of his creations! Think only of the Polonaises in A major (Op. 40, No. 1) and in A flat major (Op. 53), of many of his studies, the first three of his ballades, the scherzos, and much besides! [...]

The opinion that every peculiarity which distinguishes his music from that of other masters is to be put to the account of his nationality, and may be traced in Polish folk-music, is erroneous. But, on the other hand, it is emphatically true that this same folk-music was to him a potent inspirer and trainer. Generally speaking, however, Chopin has more of the spirit than of the form of Polish folk-music. The only two classes of his compositions where we find also something of the form are his mazurkas and polonaises; and, what is noteworthy, more in the former, the dance of the people, than in the latter, the dance of the aristocracy. In Chopin's mazurkas we meet not only with many of the most characteristic rhythms, but also with many equally characteristic melodic and harmonic traits of this chief of all the Polish dances.

Polish national music conforms in part to the tonality prevailing in modern art-music, that is, to our major and minor modes; in part, however, it reminds one of other tonalities – for instance, of that of the mediaeval church modes, and of that or those prevalent in the music of the Hungarians, Wallachians, and other peoples of that quarter.[193]* [...] Chopin, while piquantly and daringly varying the tonality prevailing in art-music, hardly ever departs from it altogether – he keeps at least in contact with it, however light that contact may be now and then in the mazurkas.[194] Further, he adopted only some of the striking peculiarities of the national music, and added to them others which were individual. These individual characteristics – those audacities of rhythm, melody, and harmony (in progressions and modulations, as well as in single chords) – may, however, be said to have been fathered by the national ones. [...]

George Sand tells us that Chopin's works were the mysterious and vague expression of his inner life. That they were the expression of his inner life is indeed

---

193 The strictly diatonic church modes (not to be confounded with the ancient Greek modes bearing the same names) differ from each other by the position of the two semitones: the Ionian is like our C major; the Dorian, Phrygian, Lydian, Mixolydian, Aeolian. &c., are like the series of natural notes starting respectively from D, C, F, G, A, &c. The characteristic interval of the Hungarian scale is the augmented second (A, B, C, D#, E, F, G#, A) [original footnote].

194 One of the most decided exceptions is the Mazurka Op. 24, No. 2, of which only the A flat major part adheres frankly to our tonality. The portion beginning with the twenty-first bar and extending over that and the next fifteen bars displays, on the other hand, the purest Lydian, while the other portions, although less definite as regards tonality, keep in closer touch with the mediaeval church mode than with our major and minor [original footnote].

a fact which no attentive hearer can fail to discover without the aid of external evidence. For the composer has hardly written a bar in which, so to speak, the beating of his heart may not be felt. Chopin revealed himself only in his music, but there he revealed himself fully. And was this expression of his inner life really "mysterious and vague"? I think not! At least, no effusion of words could have made clearer and more distinct what he expressed. For the communications of dreams and visions such as he dreamt and saw, of the fluctuating emotional actualities such as his sensitive heart experienced, musical forms are, no doubt, less clumsy than verbal and pictorial ones. And if we know something of his history and that of his nation, we cannot be at a loss to give names and local habitations to the impalpable, but emotionally and intellectually-perceptible contents of his music. We have to distinguish in Chopin the personal and the national tone-poet, the singer of his own joys and sorrows and that of his country's. But, while distinguishing these two aspects, we must take care not to regard them as two separate things. They were a duality the constitutive forces of which alternately assumed supremacy. The national poet at no time absorbed the personal, the personal poet at no time disowned the national. His imagination was always ready to conjure up his native atmosphere, nay, we may even say that, wherever he might be, he lived in it. The scene of his dreams and visions lay oftenest in the land of his birth. And what did the national poet dream and see in these dreams and visions? A past, present, and future which never existed and never will exist, a Poland and a Polish people glorified. Reality passed through the refining fires of his love and genius and reappeared in his music sublimated as beauty and poetry. No other poet has like Chopin embodied in art the romance of the land and people of Poland. And, also, no other poet has like him embodied in art the romance of his own existence. [...]

Anonymous, "Niecks's « Chopin »", *The Musical Times*, 552 (1 February 1889), pp. 73-75.[195]

This new and valuable biography of Chopin has been compiled with characteristic Teutonic patience and exhaustiveness. The author tells us that the work of gathering together his materials, sifting them, and placing them in order, occupied all the available hours of ten years. We can well believe it, but not a moment of that time has been wasted. The result is a two-fold satisfaction. In the first place,

---

195 Review of Niecks, *Frederick Chopin as a Man and Musician*, London, Novello, 1888.

we now know all there is to know about the Polish musician, and next, the author has done that which loudly called for doing. We have no desire to disparage unduly other works on the same subject. Liszt's rhapsodical production is of value to a certain extent, beyond the revelation it makes of the writer's own individuality, and Karasowski's "Life", with all its faults and shortcomings, will ever be entitled to a place in the bibliography of its theme. But both Liszt and Karasowski lived too near their hero, and lacked the comprehensiveness of view which takes in all, and sees things in their true proportion. Mr. Niecks has had the advantage of writing from a better standpoint, while not so distant as that he was unable to search for facts in a clear and favourable light. The author gives us particulars of the sources whence his information has been gathered. These are not limited to books, pamphlets, and newspapers, but extend to Chopin's pupils, friends, and acquaintances, many of whom are mentioned by name. [...] Mr. Niecks obviously entered upon his task in an impartial spirit. He does not shrink from giving his opinion, or from expressing it with emphasis; but we cannot fail to see that the conclusions stated are the result of a judicial inquiry, and transparently honest in their origin and object. We have here, in fact, a standard work entitled to the respect which an authority commands. [...]

Frederick J. Krowest,[196] *Musical Groundwork: being A First Manual of Musical Form and History for Students and Readers,* **London, Warne, 1890, p. 233.**

CHOPIN (F.), though a Pole, is intimately associated with the history of French music. He, through the medium of the pianoforte alone, has left an undying name in music. For the cultivated amateur as well as for the professional his mazourkas, nocturnes, polonaises, and studies possess a peculiar charm – notably in their grace and melodic figure. His style was one of dreamy, delicate pathos, with a sentiment and colouring caught by no other composer.

---

196 Frederick J. Krowest was an English writer, musician and critic. Born in London in 1850, Krowest held several appointments in London and in country churches as organist and choirmaster. He composed some church music and songs. For some years he was favourably known as a tenor singer, under the name of Arthur Vitton. Furthermore, he wrote several articles in the *National Review* and was for many years the London critic of the American journal *Church's Musical Visitor*. Besides his journalistic activity, Krowest was the author of *Phases of Musical England* (1881), *Musical History and Biography, in the Form of Question and Answer* (1883), *Musical Groundwork* (1890), *Dictionary of British Musicians* (1895), and *The Story of British Music,* 1895.

William Henry Hadow, *Studies in modern music, Second series, Frederick Chopin, Antonin Dvořàk, Johannes Brahms*, London, Seeley, 1895, pp. 153-169.

[...] Chopin was to some extent affected by the tonality of his native music. A large number of the Polish folk-songs are written, not in our modern scale, but in one or the other of the ecclesiastical modes: notably the Lydian, which has its fourth note a semitone sharper, and the Dorian, which has its third and seventh notes a semitone flatter than the major scale of Western Europe. [...] Of this tonal system, some positive traces may be found in the Mazurkas, the cadences of the thirteenth, seventeenth and twenty-fifth, the frequent use of a sharpened subdominant, and the like; while on the negative side it may perhaps account for Chopin's indifference to the requirements of key-relationship. [...] As a Pole, he approached our western key system from the outside, and although he learned its language with wonderful skill and facility, he never wholly assimilated himself to the method of thought which it implies.

It is quite possible that, in any case, Chopin would have found himself incapable of dealing with large masses. The want of virility, which has already been noted in his character, appears beyond question in his music; leaving untouched all the grace and tenderness, all the rare and precious qualities of workmanship, but relaxing into an almost inevitable weakness at any crisis which demands sustained force or tenacity. When he is at his strongest, we miss that sense of reserve power, that quiet irresistible force, "too full for sound or foam", which characterizes the dignity of the noblest art. He can be passionate, vehement, impetuous, but he expands himself in the effort. He can express agitation, challenge, defiance, but he lacks the royal magnanimity that will never stoop to defy. Even his melody is never sublime, never at the highest level. Its more serious mood stands to the great tunes of Beethoven as Leopardi stands to Dante, rising for a moment on a few perfect lines to follow the master's flight, and then sinking back to earth under some load of weariness or impatience. [...]

To sum up, Chopin can claim no place among the few greatest masters of the world. He lacks the dignity, the breadth, the high seriousness of Palestrina and Bach and Beethoven: he no more ranks beside them than Shelley beside Shakespear [sic], or Andrea beside Micheal Angelo. But to say this is not to disparage the value of the work that he has done. If he be not of the "di majorum gentium", he is nonetheless of the Immortals, filled with a supreme sense of beauty, animated by an emotional impulse as keen as it was varied, and upholding an ideal of technical perfection at a time when it was in danger of being lost by the poets or degradeted by the *virtuosi*. In certain definite directions he has enlarged the possibilities of the art, and though he has, fortunately, founded no school – for the charm of his music is wholly personal – yet in a thousand indirect ways he has influenced the work of his successors. At the same time, it is not as a pioneer that he elicits our fullest admiration. We hardly think of him as marking a stage in the general course and progress of artistic History, but, rather, as standing aside from it, unconscious of his relation to the world, preoccupied with the fairyland of his own creations. [...]

James Gibbons Huneker, *Chopin: The Man and His Music*, London, Reeves, 1901, pp. 122-135 and 212.[197]

[...] Born in the very upheaval of the Romantic revolution – a revolution evoked by the intensity of its emotion, rather than by the power of its ideas – Chopin was not altogether one of the insurgents of art. Just when his individual soul germinated, who may tell? In his early music are discovered the roots and fibres of Hummel and Field. His growth, involuntary, inevitable, put forth strange sprouts, and he saw in the piano, an instrument of two dimensions, a third, and so his music deepened and took on stranger colors. The keyboard had never sung so before; he forged its formula. A new apocalyptic seal of melody and harmony was let fall upon it. [...] The literary quality is absent and so is the ethical – Chopin may prophesy but he never flames into the divers tongues of the upper heaven. [...] His name was as the stroke of a bell to the Romancists; he remained aloof from them though in a sympathetic attitude. The classic is but the Romantic dead, said an acute critic. Chopin was a classic without knowing it; he compassed for the dances of his land what Bach did for the older forms. With Heine he led the spirit of revolt, but enclosed his note of agitation in a frame beautiful. [...]

Chopin, like Flaubert, was the last of the idealists, the first of the realists. The newness of his form, his linear counterpoint, misled the critics, who accused him of the lack of it. Schumann's formal deficiency detracts from much of his music, and because of their formal genius Wagner and Chopin will live. [...]

Chopin is the open door in music. Besides having been a poet and giving vibratory expression to the concrete, he was something else – he was a pioneer. Pioneer

---

197 Huneker's book was first published in New York by Scribner's Sons in 1900.

because in youth he had bowed to the tyranny of the diatonic scale and savored the illicit joys of the chromatic. It is briefly curious that Chopin is regarded purely as a poet among musicians and not as a practical musician. They will swear him a phenomenal virtuoso, but your musician, orchestral and theoretical, raises the eyebrow of the supercilious if Chopin is called creative. A cunning finger-smith, a moulder of decorative patterns, a master at making new figures, all this is granted, but speak of Chopin as path-breaker in the harmonic forest – that true "forest of numbers" – as the forger of a melodic metal, the sweetest, purest in temper, and lo! you are regarded as one mentally askew. Chopin invented many new harmonic devices, he untied the chord that was restrained within the octave, leading it into the dangerous but delectable land of extended harmonies. And how he chromaticized the prudish, rigid garden of German harmony, how he moistened it with flashing changeful waters until it grew bold and brilliant with promise! [...]

Chopin is the musical soul of Poland; he incarnates its political passion. First a Slav, by adoption a Parisian, he is the open door because he admitted into the West, Eastern musical ideas, Eastern tonalities, rhythms, in fine the Slavic, all that is objectionable, decadent and dangerous. He inducted Europe into the mysteries and seductions of the Orient. His music lies wavering between the East and the West. [...]

Chopin's music is the aesthetic symbol of a personality nurtured on patriotism, pride and love; that it is better expressed by the piano is because of that instrument's idiosyncrasies of evanescent tone, sensitive touch and wide range in dynamics. It was Chopin's lyre, the "orchestra of his heart", from it he extorted music the most intimate since Sappho. Among lyric moderns Heine closely resembles the Pole. Both sang because they suffered, sang ineffable and ironic melodies; both will endure because of their brave sincerity, their surpassing art. [...]

Astounding, canorous, enchanting, alembicated and dramatic, the Chopin studies are exemplary essays in emotion and manner. In them is mirrored all of Chopin, the planetary as well as the secular Chopin. When most of his piano music has gone the way of all things fashioned by mortal hands, these Studies will endure, will stand for the nineteenth century as Beethoven crystallized the eighteenth, Bach the seventeenth centuries in piano music. Chopin is a classic. [...]

Anonymous, "Frederick Chopin", *The Musical Times*, 805 (1 March 1910), pp. 145-150.

[...] In this year [1828, Chopin] wrote the Sonata in C minor, known as Op. 4, but not published until 1851,[198] two years after his death. This work exhibited weakness rather than strength, and therefore cannot be regarded as representative of his peculiar ability. He soon realised that the true bent of his genius found freer vent when it was unfettered by forms and anything savouring of pedantry. [...] With all the aural experience he enjoyed of the best music of the period, he assimilated little or nothing that did not fit in with his own idiom. His compositions now developed in boldness and originality, and he began to stir the critics. [...] It is remarkable that, save for about a dozen songs,[199] most of which are of little musical value, Chopin composed only for the pianoforte. It seemed that his musical conceptions were dominated by the pianoforte keyboard, and the possibilities of its manipulation by ten fingers assisted by the pedal. A good deal of his music demands a subtle kind of *rubato* inexpressible in notation. [...]

Many able writers have expended their eloquence and ability in expounding the distinctive characteristics of Chopin's style. The influence of Chopin over the pianoforte technique and composition are admitted by all to have been very great.

On these points the following authoritative opinions, which we are fortunately enabled to place before our readers, will be read with interest. [...]

PROFESSOR FREDERICK NIECKS

Chopin is undoubtedly one of the most exquisitely poetical musicians the world has seen, and if the stress is laid on "exquisitely", and the qualification "romantic" added, it may be unhesitatingly said that he was not only one of the most, but indeed *the* most poetical musician the world has seen. His superiority among the post-classical composers for the pianoforte as to originality and beauty of style and matter is universally recognised. The influence exercised by him on the development of music generally is, on the other hand, too much overlooked. He was a creative and inspiring power not merely in pianism, but also in music at large. To be convinced of this we have only to realise the difference between Chopin's harmonic resources and kind and degree of expressiveness, and those of his predecessors. Original as Schumann was, he was greatly influenced by Chopin. On Liszt the latter's influence was,

---

198 Cocks published the Sonata, Op. 4 in 1851 in the series *The Classical Pianist*, edited by Henry Brinley Richards.
199 The Songs, Op. 74 were first published in England by Stanley Lucas, Weber & Co. in 1874.

of course, much more powerful, for Liszt's originality as a composer was less, and his familiarity with his fellow-pianist's compositions greater. But Wagner, too, must have been strongly influenced by the Polish master, whether directly or indirectly does not matter. No doubt the chromatic texture and the psychological and intimately subjective may be said to have been in the air at that time; but Chopin was indisputably the first to give a strong impulse in that direction. Chopin owed much to Poland – to the country, the people, and the folk-songs and folk-dances; but Poland owes infinitely more to him. Although a patriotic Pole, he was neither an average nor a typical Pole. Nations imagine that they produce geniuses. That, however, is mere foolish self-complacency and vaingloriousness. Geniuses are gifts. Poland had as little to do with the making of Chopin as Italy, England, and Germany with the making of Dante, Shakespeare, and Goethe. Genius is the result of a felicitous but fortuitous concurrence of circumstances. Chopin's pianoforte style is as such an ideal style – the nature of the instrument and the nature of the style are co-extensive. This could not be said of Liszt's pianoforte style, which is more many-sided but less pure. Chopin's pianoforte style is also a virtuosic style. Virtuosity, however, is there as a means to a higher end, not for its own sake. No pianist-composer's music is so much played as Chopin's, and no composer's music is so rarely well played. In fact, if the present state of matters prevails much longer, the public must lose its belief in Chopin as the most poetic of pianist-composers.

MR. TOBIAS MATTHAY[200]

I am asked to say a few words as to Chopin's influence on pianoforte technique. It would, of course, require a volume to answer fully the question. Chopin's beneficent influence on pianoforte playing and pianoforte writing is indeed incalculably great; and although it is true that that influence is immensely strong as regards technical novelty and improvement, it is still greater from a purely musical point of view, for no one has used the instrument to express feeling so intimately as he has done. As regards technique, his strength lies in the fact that he has more accurately gauged the potentialities of the instrument than anyone has done before or since – we must put him even above Liszt himself in this respect, in spite of all the marvels that giant wrought.

---

200 Tobias Augustus Matthay (1858-1945) was an English teacher, pianist and composer. He studied at the Royal Academy of Music with Sterndale Bennett, Macfarren and Sullivan and also taught there from 1876 to 1925 as professor of piano. In 1900 he founded his own school (Tobias Matthay Piano School) to propagate his theories of piano technique, which were based on a detailed analysis of arm movements and on muscular relaxation.

Chopin's success in thus making his musical and poetic invention synchronise so perfectly with the acoustical and mechanical possibilities of his instrument must be attributed, in the first place, to his infinitely fine musical ear, which forbade his writing the inappropriate.

It is difficult to determine exactly how far his own particular ways of key-treatment (touch or technique) influenced his invention, or how far his poetic feeling compelled him to gain his particular playing-technique, but the results are clear enough. The more salient features of the pianistic progress he wrought are found in the enormously greater delicacy and variety of tone he demanded in his cantabiles, the musicality and often the extreme lightness of his passage-work, and the laying-out of this in note-groups beyond the octave limit, and his extensive use of chromatic passing-notes; and perhaps more notable still than these points, his revelation of the immense possibilities of the *Rubato* element, and his constant but subtle use of the damper-pedal.

With regard to his cantabile no doubt his invention was here greatly influenced by his own technical habits. From the internal evidence of his music, the remarks of his pupils and the shape of his hand, it is conclusively proved that he well knew the use of what we now term "flat finger" weight-touch, a singing tone produced by a perfectly elastically used finger in conjunction with release of the whole arm,[201] thus admitting far greater beauty and variety of singing-tone than that of the earlier touch methods. Again, his own playing clearly influenced his passage invention, a passage-technique quite original as regards a lightness and swiftness before undreamt of, as for instance in so many of his wonderful filigree cadenzas – a lightness obviously to be attributed to his having thoroughly mastered those problems of key and muscle which we now sum up under the heading of "Agility touch". We may admit that these improvements in pianoforte treatment had been in a measure led up to by earlier composers, yet Chopin leapt leagues ahead of them.

But what we have to thank him most for is the deep poetic feeling underlying all his music. Except in his very earliest works we never find him writing a passage for the mere sound of it, or the mere playing of it. However brilliant the rush of sounds, they are always written as a direct and inevitable expression of his mood or feeling. It is because he never swerved from this, his ever-present purpose to express feeling

---

201 For further details on the "flat finger" touch and its application in the execution of Chopin's music see Tobias Matthay, *The Art of Touch in All its Diversity*, London 1903 (repr. 1905), p. 176 and 225.

through the musically beautiful, that he became and has remained the greatest piano-forte writer, and that his music will for ever glorify our instrument.

Mr. Frederick Corder.[202]

It has always seemed to me that Chopin has not yet received adequate recognition as harmonist. Until about a generation ago he was looked upon with something like contempt by those fine crusted old musicians like my teachers Hiller and Macfarren, both of whom openly declared that music had said its last word with Mendelssohn. Even the broad-minded Prout only ventured to give two insignificant illustrations from Chopin in his harmony book.[203] Theorists regarded him as a writer of elegant drawing-room music on the same plane as Henselt, but addicted to a sad misuse of those hateful chromatic chords. The people who could only play his easiest nocturnes and the A minor *Valse*[204] used to cry fie! upon him for being so sentimental, forgetting that these pieces were just the "pot-boilers" by which he won the affections of the pianists. Now I come to think of it, when I played the F minor Fantasia at my examination for the Mendelssohn Scolarship in 1875, there was only one English musician – Arthur Sullivan – out of a committee of fifteen who knew anything of the work.

Chopin arrived at a fortunate time. The romantic tendency in music, initiated by Spohr and Weber in opera, was beginning to make itself felt in abstract music. In an incredibly short space of time the diatonic track of Mozart and Beethoven was obliterated by the chromatic experiments of Schumann, Liszt, and Wagner. Incited by their example, Chopin distanced all his contemporaries in the ease with which he manipulated the new progressions, and especially in the marvellous grace with which he crowned them with melody. However intricate the harmonic web, Chopin's melody never lacks charm – charm of a tender and always refined kind. Austerity was a mood he never knew. From the marvellous mazurkas to the great ballades you can find no page that is not absolutely attractive. [...]

Towards the end of his life Chopin recognised more clearly the power which a real mastery of counterpoint bestows. The result of his studies may be noted in the

---

202 Frederick Corder (1852-1932) was an English composer, teacher and translator. He studied at the Royal Academy of Music, where he earned a Mendelssohn Scholarship, which enabled him to study for four years abroad. He went to Cologne, where he studied with Hiller, and then moved to Milan. On his return to England he became conductor at the Brighton Aquarium (1880–82) and professor of composition at the Royal Academy of Music (from 1888). Corder wrote three operas, but he is best remembered for his translations of Wagner's operas.

203 See Ebenezer Prout, *Harmony: Its Theory and Practice*, London, Augener, 1889, pp. 172 and 184.

204 Waltz, Op. 34 No. 2. The two examples are from the Nocturne, Op. 32 No. 2 and the Waltz, Op. 34 No. 2.

growing polyphonic character of the last works, the Barcarolle, the *Polonaise Fantaisie* and the last two nocturnes. Had he attained to his "third period", it is pretty certain that he would have bequeathed us a wealth of wonders; it is even possible that he might have experimented with the orchestra, which up till then he had hardly thought about. But this is not very likely, since he found the best setting for his ideas in the most limited of forms. That a man could exhibit such endless variety of invention in such unpromising ground as the mazurka and polonaise afford, is to my mind the highest evidence of his greatness. I could discourse for pages on his codas and concluding cadences alone; but it is needless when their beauties are at everyone's reach. It is a very superficial remark to say that Chopin is sentimental: all chromatic progressions convey a greasy, sickly impression; but can the writer of the A flat Polonaise,[205] the first and third Scherzos, the *Allegro de Concert*, and many such dashing compositions be adequately described by such an epithet? Surely not. [...]

Alfred Redgrave Cripps,[206] "Chopin as a Master of Form", *The Musical Times*, 858 (1 August 1914), pp. 517-519.

There is probably no musician who has been at once so fortunate and so unfortunate in his posthumous fame as Frederic Chopin. Fortunate, in that he has attracted the attention of many to whom, as a rule, music makes but little appeal; unfortunate, because, largely through that very circumstance, a somewhat false picture of him has little by little been built up. His name has served as a peg on which to hang much empty rhetoric. Thus, we have Chopin the sentimentalist, Chopin the "tone-poet", Chopin the lover, Chopin the (supposed) patriot; but Chopin the musician – for him, indeed, we have very far to look.

It must be admitted, however, that more serious writers who have professedly treated Chopin from a purely musical point of view have not been altogether unaffected by the "literary" or "popular" view just spoken of. Indeed, far from correcting it, they have, if anything, rather confirmed it. [...] Unfortunately this general view of what may be called the spiritual quality of Chopin's music finds very naturally its reflection in a similar estimate of his position as a musician pure and simple, and especially as a master of form. [...] We may quote the following passage from Sir Hubert Parry (whose authority is beyond question), in which precisely the same opinion is

205 Polonaise, Op. 53.
206 Alfred Redgrave Cripps (1882-1950) was active as a composer and critic between the 1910s and 1930s. As a critic he wrote some articles in *The Musical Times* and *The Musical Quarterly*.

somewhat more crisply put: "His [Chopin's] work is not often great in conception or noteworthy in design, but it is the spontaneous expression of a poetical, refined, and sensitive temperament".[207]

Now, as to Chopin's position in Art in regard to the actual intrinsic or spiritual value of his work it is of course impossible to argue. What means much to one man means little or nothing to another, and there simply is an end of the matter. But with regard to Chopin as a musician, as a master of design, the case is different. Here we have something palpable, something we can weigh, and measure, and discuss, and come to a definite decision about. It may be said, however, that after all a man's "form" – the mould in which he casts his thoughts – may generally be taken as the measure of the worth of the thoughts themselves. At least is this so in music, where the two are inseparably connected. Should it appear, therefore, that Chopin, far from being the mere wayward and individual genius, the mere artificer of dainty trifles that he is generally supposed to be, is as a matter of fact a master of form second to none, – should this appear, we shall have already gone a great way towards showing that the general estimate of his ultimate or spiritual quality is correspondingly mistaken. [...]

Of the perfection of Chopin's writing for the instrument there is indeed no need to speak: it is sufficiently recognised, in words at least (though perhaps it is only those who have actually *played* his works who can have any conception of how very perfect that perfection is), by all who have written on him. But what needs to be pointed out is that it is precisely because Chopin was not a pianoforte writer at all, in any special sense, that his writing is so perfect. Chopin, that is to say, was not *primarily* a writer for the pianoforte. We cannot imagine him scheming out special effects for the instrument, as Liszt, or even Schumann (in rather a blundering way) did, and then incorporating them in music. In the whole of his music – in the whole, that is, of his mature writing – there is hardly an instance of a passage dragged in merely for the sake of display, or to fill up, or for the sake of some special effect; every passage exists only for the sake of its relation to the whole, and apart from that whole would have no meaning. The perfection of his pianoforte writing, in short, lies in this – that it is only part of a greater perfection: and it is only when this is recognised that we can appreciate in any true sense even the perfection of his pianoforte writing itself. [...] We must not hope to find in Chopin examples of what theorists are pleased to regard as "form" in the abstract, – or if we do we shall be disappointed.

---

207   C. Hubert H. Parry, *Summary of the History and Development of Mediaeval and Modern European Music*, London, Novello, 1892, p. 84.

Theoretical writers are fond of dividing form into different categories, – the "sonata form", "rondo form", the "dance form", and the like. For Chopin – as a composer – such divisions simply did not exist. Indeed, if we would do justice to him we shall do best to start by forgetting that there is such a thing as form, in the abstract, at all. Only then shall we be in a position to view the matter from Chopin's own stand-point; and only then, therefore, can we realise what he aimed at, and how perfectly he achieved his aim. [...]

It is, however – and this fact cannot be too strongly emphasised – *not* the mere fact that most of Chopin's compositions can be reduced to a certain form, or for-mula (satisfying to the eye), that makes him a master of form; otherwise any duffer who can compose in accordance with some predetermined scheme (and what duffer, alas! cannot?) would be a master of form. *It is in the wealth of resource exhibited with-in the limits of that form that his mastery is shown.* [...] Tonality, or key-relationship, as a factor of form, is of course most important, and Chopin's attitude in regard to this is particularly worthy of notice. It is often supposed that here he is wildly revolutionary; but a very little consideration of his works will show that this is quite a mistake. It is true that he often, even in the smaller pieces (though by no means always), eschews the well-worn contrasts of tonic and dominant; but where he does so it is obviously from no mere eccentricity or waywardness, but from an artistic de-sire to obtain greater variety through a wider or more subtle contrast. Where he thus avoids what are called the "nearly related" keys it is noticeable that he very often, in fact nearly always, chooses some key (either major or minor) *at the distance of a third (major or minor) above or below his tonic.* Examples of this are so numerous that it can hardly be necessary to quote any. But it is in the larger pieces [...] that this use of the distance of the third as the basis of the principle of tonal contrast is most clearly displayed [...]

A. Redgrave Cripps, "Chopin as a Master of Form (Continued)", *The Musical Times*, 859 (1 September 1914), pp. 576-567.

[...] It is part of the orthodox view that Chopin's supposed helplessness in the larger forms is thrown into the stronger relief by contrast with his absolute perfection in the smaller. Thus, Dr. Hadow [...] writes: "His limitations are plain and unmistak-able. For the larger types of art, for the broad architectonic laws of structure on which they are based, he exhibits almost total disregard. His works in "sonata form", and the forms cognate to the sonata, are, with no exception, the failure of a genius which has already overstepped its bounds".[208] And again (dealing there, however, more particularly with the question of Chopin's nationality as shown in his choice of keys), he says: "not only in his efforts at sonata-form does he show himself unable to hold together a complex scheme of keys, but in works of a more loose structure his choice seems to be regulated rather by hazard that by any preconceived plans [...] He allows his modulations to wander where they will, and is so intent of perfecting each phrase and each melody, that he has no regard left to bestow on the general principles of construction".[209] [...] It may be remarked that so long as Chopin's perfection in the smaller forms is attributed merely to a "felicitous phraseology", instead of an exquisitely delicate sense of design, this contrast may be said to be almost inevitable. As a matter of fact, however, Chopin's works cannot thus be divided into two classes, – the smaller pieces in which he succeeded and the larger in which he failed. Precisely the same principles of construction which he makes use of in his smaller pieces are exhibited also in the larger; with the only difference that it is in the larger pieces that they find their fullest application, and that absolute mastery, therefore, is the most triumphantly displayed. [...]

---

208   W. H. Hadow, *Studies in modern music, Second series, Frederick Chopin, Antonin Dvořák, Johannes Brahms*, London, Seeley, 1895, p. 151. It is worth noting that in the sequences following this quotation Hadow recognises the originality of Chopin: "Of choral compositions, of symphony, of opera, he has not left us a single example. But when all this has been admitted, it still remains true that he is a great master, great in his exquisite sense of beauty, in his almost unerring skill, and in the deliberate and reasoned audacity with which he has extended the range of musical expression".

209   Ibid., p. 154.

Index of names

Bassanville, Anaïs Lebrun de *see* Lebrun de Bassanville

Báthory, Stephen, King of Poland 137

Batory, Stefan *see* Báthory

Baudelaire, Charles 432

Bäuerle, Adolf 226, 230, 231

Bayer, Aloys 234

Beale *see* Cramer, Addison & Beale; Cramer, Beale & Co., publishers

Beda *see* Schumann, Clara

Beethoven, Ludwig van 11, 18, 24, 30, 49, 50, 61, 63, 68, 82, 89, 90, 111, 118, 123, 124, 130, 131-133, 138, 148, 149, 153, 160, 162, 164, 165, 167, 171, 172, 176, 181, 184, 188-190, 194, 196, 197, 204, 209, 218, 222, 227, 235, 244, 247, 252-254, 260-262, 280, 288, 290, 311, 312, 315, 317, 318, 333, 341, 343, 344, 349, 352, 361, 375, 410, 411, 413, 424, 432, 436, 438, 441, 451, 452, 456, 458, 460, 465, 472-475, 485, 486, 488, 504, 508, 512, 514, 515, 519, 522, 526, 528, 532

Belgiojoso, Princesse Cristina Trivulzio 408

Bell, Sigismund 102

Bellaigue, Camille 134, 346, 373, 424

Belleville, Anna Caroline de *see* Oury

Bellini, Vincenzo 53, 117, 288, 306, 323, 386, 410, 414

Benedict, Sir Julius 467, 472

Bennett, Joseph 19, 457, 458, 517, 519, 520

Bennett, Sir William Sterndale 451, 452, 470-474, 481, 486, 498, 530

Bériot, Charles-Auguste de 500

Berlioz, Hector 28, 40, 71, 123, 124, 129, 152, 168, 182, 183, 194, 196, 208-211, 216, 323, 329, 330, 333, 334, 335, 337, 339, 340, 350-354, 356, 357, 361, 363, 365, 370, 380, 396, 397, 400, 407, 416, 421, 440, 472, 483, 513, 519

Bertelin, A. 377

Berthelot, Marcellin 431

Bertini, Henri(-Jérôme) 330, 334, 352, 355, 359

Beyer, Ferdinand 316

Billard, Mr 333

Bizet, Georges 343, 376, 380

Blahetka, Joseph L. 11

Blanc, Charles 416

Blanchard, Henri-Louis 331, 360, 368, 374, 408

Blaze de Bury, Henri 335, 342, 343, 360, 362, 369, 376, 379, 383, 423

Blondel de Nesle *see* Nesle, Blondel de

Blumenthal, Jacob [Jacques] 506

Böcklin, Arnold 40, 133

Bogusławski, Władysław 35, 45, 90, 91, 104

Bohdanowa *see* Zaleska

Boosey & Sons; Boosey & Co., publishers 455, 509, 511

Borodin, Aleksandr Porfir'yevich 152, 168

Botkin, Vasily [Vasiliy] Petrovich 148, 155, 158

Bourgault-Ducoudray, Louis (Albert) 186

Bourges, Maurice 331, 337, 341, 398

Bousquet, Georges 340

Brahms, Johannes 90, 109, 166, 219, 222, 224, 526, 536

Breitkopf & Härtel, publishers 16, 45, 90, 215, 216, 218, 225, 259, 263, 266, 268, 273, 278, 290, 294, 295, 298-300, 302, 489

Brenning, Mary Krebs *see* Krebs-Brenning

Brewer, Ebenezer Cobham 492

Broadwood, company 493

Broadwood, James 450, 464

Brockmann, Monika 225

Brodziński, Kazimierz 23

Brzowski, Józef 24, 27, 31, 44, 53, 59, 274

Brzowsky, Józef *see* Brzowski

Buchet-Chastel, publishers 352, 353, 356, 363, 391, 396
Bülow, Hans von 90
Burger, Ernst 221, 233, 276, 290
Bürger, Gottfried August 30, 75, 318
Bury, Henri Blaze de *see* Blaze de Bury
Busoni, Ferruccio 10, 150, 219, 221, 324
Byron, Lord [George Gordon (Noel)] 49, 128, 149, 159, 316

C., Princess M. *see* Czartoryska
Callcott, John Wall 473
Calvocoressi, Michel-Dimitri 347, 380
Cambremer, Mrs de 345, 434, 435
Castellan, Jeanne Anaïs 312, 499
Chabrier, (Alexis-)Emmanuel 440
Chainaye, Denise 472
Chainaye, Suzanne 472
Chantavoine, Jean (François Henri) 346, 415
Chaulieu, Charles 53, 333
Chechlińska, Zofia 14
Cherubini, Luigi 115, 305, 323, 519
Chlebowski, Bronisław 94
Chłopicka, Zofia *see* Klimańska
Chodecki, Aleksander 69
Chodkiewicz, Jan Karol 137
Chomiński, Józef Michał 462
Chopin, Emilia 67
Chopin, Fryderyk Franciszek *passim*
Chopin, Izabela *see* Barcińska
Chopin, (Tekla) Justyna *née* Krzyżanowska 115, 322
Chopin, Ludwika *see* Jędrzejewicz
Chopin, Nicolas [Mikołaj] 13
Chorley, Henry Fothergill 454, 461, 475, 477, 483, 489, 490, 493-495, 497, 505
Cichocki, Józef 24
Cichowska, Ludwika *née* Dupont 86
Cichowski, Adolf 86

Clementi, Muzio 49, 317, 334, 358, 382, 383, 428, 475, 502
Cocks, Robert 529
Coleridge, Samuel Taylor 478, 509
Combarieu, Jules (Léon Jean) 346, 425
Comte, Auguste 28, 34
Cook, Martha Walker 114, 199, 201, 324, 457, 514, 516
Cooper, Victoria 453
Copernicus, Nicolaus 43, 53
Corbari, Mrs 497
Corder, Frederick 532
Corneille, Pierre 59
Cornelius, Peter 310, 313
Corot, Jean-Baptiste 128
Correggio, Antonio Allegri da 208
Cortot, Alfred 10
Coßmann, Bernhard 313
Couperin, François 345, 415
Cowell, Samuel 510
Cowen, Sir Frederic [Frederick] Hymen 517
Cramer, Addison & Beale, publishers 463
Cramer, Beale & Co., publishers 493
Cramer, Johann [John] Baptist 49, 472, 483
Cripps, Alfred Redgrave 19, 460, 533, 535
Croce, Benedetto 8, 9
Crotch, William 470, 473
Cui, César 152, 162-165, 168
Custine, Astolphe de 332, 356, 381, 384
Czarniecki, Stefan 137
Czartoryska, Marcelina *née* Radziwiłł 45, 74, 100, 101, 117, 312
Czartoryski, family 101
Czartoryski, Prince Adam 499
Czerny, Carl 50, 53, 465, 467, 472, 489
Czerny, Zygmunt 8

Damoreau-Cinti, Laure 392
Dannreuther, Edward (George) 514
Dante Alighieri 40, 95, 526, 530

541

Habeneck, François-Antoine 72, 500
Hadow, William Henry 526, 535, 536
Haendel *see* Handel
Halévy, Jacques-Fromental 171, 268, 500, 504
Hallé, C. E. 520
Hallé, Marie 520
Hallé, Sir Charles [Halle, Carl] 457, 483, 484, 491, 493, 503, 505, 506, 520
Handel [Händel, Hendel], George Frideric [Georg Friederich] 176, 203, 215, 280, 389, 453, 486
Hańska, Ewa 335, 361
Hanska, Ewa *see* Hańska
Hanslick, Eduard 173, 219, 222, 313, 321
Hardenberg, Friedrich von *see* Novalis
Härtel *see* Breitkopf & Härtel
Haslinger, publishers 215, 236
Haslinger, Tobias, publisher 225, 230, 237
Hausegger, Zygmunt 42
Haweis, Hugh Reginald 19, 456, 512, 514
Haydn, Joseph 49, 61, 82, 102, 131, 258, 438
Hegel, Georg Wilhelm Friedrich 25
Heine, Heinrich 24, 73, 134, 148, 180, 219, 221, 222, 268, 276, 290, 323, 336, 338, 360, 363, 372, 455, 527, 528
Heinemann, Michael 222
Heller, Stephen 274, 314, 487, 491, 493
Helman, Zofia 11
Henri IV, King of France 344, 435
Henselt, Adolf (von) 69, 147, 156, 158, 170, 212, 223, 314, 358, 359, 465-467, 472, 480, 483, 532
Herder, Johann Gottfried 23
Hérold, (Louis Joseph) Ferdinand 171, 268
Herrmann, Joachim 221, 315
Herz, Henri [Heinrich] 50, 52, 53, 115, 236, 241, 258, 272, 330, 333, 449, 450, 472, 486, 489
Hetzel, Jules, publisher 339, 351, 370, 416

Heugel, Jacques-Léopold 331
Heymann, Carl 163
Hill, Emily 178, 520
Hiller, Ferdinand (von) 12, 16, 53, 157, 215, 216, 222, 224, 305, 309, 310, 318, 334, 352, 355, 356, 359, 464, 472, 532
Hipkins, Alfred (James) 458
Hippius, Adelaida 150
Hirsch, Rudolf 217, 271
Hoesick, Ferdynand 31, 32, 37, 38, 43, 74, 122, 178, 179
Hofmann, Josef [Józef] 151, 163, 164, 196, 197
Hofmeister, Friedrich, publisher 462
Holmes, William Henry 470, 520
Homais, Mr 421
Homer 16
Homma, Martina 225
Horace 250, 251
Horaz *see* Horace
Hordyński, Władysław 58
Hryszczyńska, Helena 222
Hughes, Meirion 453, 517
Hugo, Victor 356, 365
Humboldt, Alexander von 215
Hummel, Johann Nepomuk 11, 27, 49, 52, 71, 115, 176, 183, 190, 194, 203, 215, 227, 246, 254, 261, 317, 318, 334, 349, 358, 383, 415, 458, 472, 475, 502, 522, 527
Huneker, James Gibbons 38, 127, 130, 133, 450, 527
Hünten, Franz 50, 53, 236, 272
Huré, Pierre-Antoine 375
Hüschen, Heinrich 222

Igumnov, Konstantin (Nikolayevich) 198
Indy, Vincent d' 345, 438
Istel, Edgar 313
Ivanov, Mikhail Mikhailovich 153, 177-180

Marcello, Benedetto 312

Marmontel, Antoine-François 342, 375, 382, 411

Massenet, Jules 130, 343, 380

Massip, Catherine 449

Maszewski, Mr 188

Maszyński, Piotr 117

Matejko, Jan 43, 134, 135, 137, 139

Mathias, Georges 345, 365

Matthay, Tobias (Augustus) 530, 531

Mattis, D. 231

Mauclair, Camille 346, 372, 418

Maupassant, Guy de 112

Maurin, Nicolas-Eustache 212

Mayer, Leopold de 489, 498

Meara [Méara] see Dubois, Camille

Meck, Nadezhda von 189

Melcer-Szczawiński, Henryk 131

Mendel, Hermann 79, 88

Mendelssohn-Bartholdy, Felix 18, 50, 90-92, 124, 125, 143, 166, 168, 175, 176, 180, 181, 194, 196, 215, 216, 219, 222, 234, 270, 272, 306, 359, 451-453, 465, 470, 472-474, 481, 485, 486, 490-493, 503, 507, 510, 532

Menter, Sophie 163

Mercadante, Saverio 255

Merk, Josef 76

Mérruau, Paul 337

Metternich, Klemens von 332

Meyerbeer, Giacomo 64, 91, 125, 180, 215, 216, 234, 272, 290, 323, 396, 440, 499, 500, 519

Michałowski, Aleksander 44, 46, 90, 104, 117, 185

Michel, Albin, publisher 419

Michelangelo 40, 131, 526

Mickiewicz, Adam 15, 25, 29, 30, 32, 33, 43, 49, 55, 56, 75, 80, 95, 105, 108, 111, 128, 134, 138, 141, 178, 180, 365, 394

Mickiewitz see Mickiewicz

Miculi, Carl [Carol] see Mikuli

Mikhaiłov, N. N. 200

Mikuli, Karol 199

Milanollo, Maria 500

Milanollo, Teresa 500

Milstein, Yakov 198

Milton, John 481

Mochnacki, Maurycy 11, 23, 24, 48

Moke see Pleyel, (Camille) Marie (Denise)

Molière 149, 159

Moniuszko, Stanisław 14, 26, 27, 34, 41, 64, 78, 89, 123, 125, 126, 165, 202, 442

Montesquiou, Robert de 433

Moore, Thomas 338, 368

Morhange, Charles-Valentin see Alkan

Moscheles, Ignaz 50, 115, 175, 179, 215, 223, 241, 246, 254, 258, 268, 415, 472, 486

Mozart, Wolfgang Amadeus 11, 12, 49, 61, 102, 117, 118, 123-125, 131, 148, 162, 168, 189, 190, 194, 203, 205, 209, 210, 216, 227, 229, 231, 235, 237, 244, 254, 258, 261, 263, 277, 280, 290, 311, 312, 323, 333, 341, 344, 361, 364, 401, 407, 410, 416, 420, 436, 451, 462, 473, 486, 488, 499, 501, 500, 506, 512, 532

Mukhanov [Muchanov], Maria see Kalergis-Mukhanov

Müller von Asow, Erich Hermann 223

Müller, brothers 270

Müller, Friederike née Streicher 216, 217

Münchheimer, Adam 27, 96, 125

Musard, Philippe 492

Musorgsky, Modest see Mussorgsky

Musset, Alfred de 39, 128, 196, 435, 443

Mussorgsky, Modest 152, 168

Naliwajek, Zbigniew 420, 435

Napoleon I Bonaparte 137, 141, 182

Napoleon III Bonaparte 182

147, 149, 150-152, 164, 165, 168-171, 173-175, 321, 344, 433

Rubinstein [Rubinshteyn], Nikolay (Grigor'yevich) 194

Rückert, Friedrich 273

Rudziński, Witold 26

Rupprecht, Mr 232

Ryan, Desmond 490, 492

Rymarowicz, Caesar 221

Sabała 112

Sadie, Stanley 471

Saint John *see* John, Saint

Saint-Saëns, Camille 130, 343, 346, 380, 443

Salvi, Lorenzo 497

Samson, Jim 9, 14, 16, 459

Sand, George 13, 73, 74, 82, 84, 91, 105, 116, 130, 180, 196, 197, 200, 201, 205, 206, 211, 308, 323, 326, 331, 340-343, 371, 386-388, 391, 392, 398, 409, 418, 431, 458, 471, 472, 489, 518, 523

Sartoris, Adelaide Kemble 495, 496

Sartoris, Edward John 496

Sauzay, Eugène 366

Sayn, Princess Caroline *see* Wittgenstein

Scarlatti, Alessandro *and* Domenico 486

Scharlitt, Bernhard 221

Scheffer, Ary 150

Schenker, Heinrich 129

Schiller, Friedrich 249, 365

Schlechta, Karl 224

Schlesinger, Maurice, publisher 13, 75, 330, 331, 333, 337, 402

Schlesinger, Stanislav 154, 191

Schmidt *see* Gubrynowicz & Schmidt, publishers

Schoelcher, Victor 389

Schreyer, Johannes 41, 129

Schubert, Franz 159, 176, 181, 196, 216, 218, 222, 234, 235, 262, 268, 306, 362, 393, 396, 431, 438, 442, 456, 490, 513-515

Schucht, Johann 33, 79, 80

Schulz, Marceli Antoni *see* Szulc

Schultze, Walther Siegmund 224

Schumann, Clara *née* Wieck, Clara 53, 157, 169, 216, 223, 270, 274-276, 359, 457, 472, 506

Schumann, Robert 12, 14, 16, 18, 24, 27, 51, 53, 75, 77, 79, 80, 85, 87, 88, 90, 91, 111, 123, 124, 128, 131, 138, 143, 149, 150, 157, 159, 160, 164, 165, 167-169, 173, 176, 180, 181, 184, 188, 189, 191, 194, 196, 197, 205, 215-219, 221-224, 234, 235, 240, 257, 260, 263, 264, 268, 270, 273, 274, 276, 278, 279, 281, 286, 288-291, 316, 322-324, 339, 344, 359, 365, 372, 413, 419-421, 424, 427, 432, 434-437, 441, 444, 455, 470, 472, 473, 485, 487, 514, 527, 529, 532, 534

Schuncke, Charles 268

Schuncke, Ludwig 268

Scriabin [Skryabin], Aleksandr Nikolayevich 15, 16, 130, 152, 154, 196, 201

Scribner, publisher 527

Scudo, Paul [Pierre, Pietro, Paulo] 333, 335, 362

Seeley, publisher 526, 536

Segantini, Giovanni 128

Senkovsky *see* Senkowsky

Senkowsky, Osip Ivanovich 157

Serov, Aleksandr Nikolayevich 147-149, 152, 160-162

Sévérac, (Alexandre) Déodat de, Baron de Beauville 346, 437

Sgambati, Giovanni 419, 420

Shakespear *see* Shakespeare

Shakespeare, William 49, 526, 530

Shelley, Percy Bysshe 478, 508, 509, 526

Index of works by Fryderyk Chopin

Nocturne in B major, Op. 62 No. 1, The Newberry Library, Chicago
Source Commentary by Jeffrey Kallberg

from the series **WORKS BY CHOPIN. FACSIMILE EDITION**

WORKS BY CHOPIN. FACSIMILE EDITION
The world's first complete edition of Chopin's musical manuscripts. Each volume comprises two books: the facsimile and a source commentary in six languages.

For further details, please visit our website: *www.chopin.nifc.pl/facsimile*

Layout and typesetting
Pracownia DTP Aneta Osipiak-Wypiór

Music typesetting
Piotr Kołodziej, Studio Orfeo

Printed by
LEGRA Sp. z o.o.

Printed in Poland